WHO'S WHO
in
AFRICA

Leaders for the 1990s

by
ALAN RAKE

The Scarecrow Press, Inc.
Metuchen, N.J., & London
1992

British Library Cataloguing-in-Publication data available

Library of Congress Cataloging-in-Publication Data

Rake, Alan.
  Who's Who in Africa : leaders for the 1990s / by Alan Rake.
    p.   cm.
  Includes index.
  ISBN 0-8108-2557-0 (acid-free paper)
  1. Statesmen--Africa, Sub-Saharan--Biography. 2. Africa, Sub-
Saharan--Politics and government--1960- I. Title.
DT18.R35 1992
920.067--dc20   92-8166

CONTENTS

PREFACE

Who's Who in Africa is an attempt to provide pen portraits of the most prominent political figures in Africa, south of the Sahara. It concentrates on those in power, those recently in office, and those most likely to succeed, whether from the ranks of the opposition or from relatively minor positions in the ruling structure. It tries to spot the up and coming figures who might take a future leadership role in their countries, as well as those already well established.

In content it is similar to the book, "Who's Who in Africa" produced by John Dickie and myself as long ago as 1973, but not revised since. It is similar in scope and concept, but so much in Africa has happened in the 18 years that have passed, that the cast of characters has dramatically changed. Only about a quarter of those in the old book reappear in the new and they need total reassessment.

Who's Who in Africa has been conceived as a unique work of reference with in depth personalities of Africa's leaders, giving their entire life history from the date of birth to the present, with particular reference to their political achievements. The profiles are presented on a country by country basis. The countries are in alphabetical order, with a brief introduction giving essential country facts, such as the nature of the constitution and the political parties. There is also an index listing all the personalities covered, with cross referencing to countries.

Each profile has a short assessment of the character and career of the person concerned, followed by the entire life history in strict chronological order so that rapid reference can be made to key dates and times.

To keep the book to a manageable length, only the top personalities have been included. This is sufficient to cover the top leadership, but not the ranks of junior ministers, the military or civil service, unless the personality concerned has political potential. Nor does it attempt to cover prominent personalities in cultural, artistic, religious or business fields unless the person concerned is also in politics.

Emphasis has also been given to the most important or populous African countries. Thus Nigeria, South Africa, Kenya, Ghana, Tanzania, Uganda, Zimbabwe and the Cote d'Ivoire have comparatively high coverage compared with minor Sahelian states, or the smaller offshore islands.

Covering Africa's multitude of countries at a time of sweeping change has often been difficult, but I have had the help of friends cultivated over nearly 35 years of consistent work on magazines for Africa. The correspondents of *New African* and *African Business*, have been indefatigable in filling in the gaps left by copious documentary research. In many cases we have built profiles of entirely undocumented figures, not covered by any other published work, or even official biographies put out by information ministries. Some of the former marxist countries are particularly shy of publishing any personal information about their leadership, but I have managed to cover the top leadership of such countries as Angola, Mozambique, Ethiopia and Somalia where there is very little existing material.

All the facts are presented as fairly and accurately as exhaustive research can make possible, the assessments however are subjective. An attempt has been made to go much further than the dry list of facts appearing in conventional Who's Whos. I have tried to produce a book which includes insight, anecdote and comment and a general assessment as well as a list of dates and events. Every effort has been made to be fair and accurate, yet interesting.

Naturally a work of this kind could not have been completed without the help and advice of many people, particularly those who provided me with the basic facts from Africa.

I would especially like to thank William Onyango and Barrack Otieno from Kenya, Epajjar Ojulu and Crispus Mundua (Uganda). Others who gave me their unstinting help were, Setorwu Gagakuma (Ghana), Mike Pitso and Thulo Hoeane (Lesotho), Teklall Gunesh (Mauritius), Josiah Uguru (Nigeria), Francois Misser (Burundi and Rwanda), Moyiga Korokoto Nduru (Sudan), Norman Sowerby (Swaziland), Sylvester Chiposa (Zambia), Tanjong Lucas (Cameroon), Nianduillet Nicholas (Niger), Prince Ebow Godwin (Togo) and Joel Sebonego (Botswana).

Sadly three correspondents, Brown Lenga (Tanzania), Eben Davies (Sierra Leone) and Salif Bargery (Côte d'Ivoire) died in the years when the book was under production. I would like to pay a particular tribute to them.

Though all these friends supplied me with basic facts and often checked my copy for accuracy, the comment on the personalities concerned is entirely my own.

In London I received great help from Patrick Gilkes, particularly on Ethiopia, from Bob Astles (Uganda), Dot Keet (Mozambique Information office), Professor Richard Greenfield (Somalia), Ahmed Rajab (Comoros) and Guy Arnold who brought back material from Namibia for me.

I would not have been able to complete the setting of the book without the help of Helen Moroney, Linda Van Buren and particularly, Baffour Ankomah in London, who slaved over the final proofs for weeks.

I also derived much help from the excellent new volumes that have appeared in southern Africa since I did my last book, *Who's Who in South African politics* by Shelagh Gastrow and published by the Ravan Press, PO Box 31134, Braamfontein 2017, South Africa was invaluable, as was the *Political Who's Who of Namibia* by Joe Putz, Heidi Von Egidy and Perri Kaplan, published by Magus Company, PO Box 20178, Windhoek 9000, Namibia. I also made frequent references to the excellent *Historical Dictionaries of Africa* published by the Scarecrow Press Inc, Metuchen, New Jersey, USA.

Finally I would like to thank those like Sean Moroney, Dick Hall, Derek Ingram and Albert Daub, without whose constant encouragement I would never have summoned the effort to re-embark on such a time consuming and complex task. But like many authors, once the work was underway, I found it fascinating, particularly chasing those important, but faceless figures who seem to have spent a lifetime trying to ensure that no systematic biographical material was ever written about them.

November 1991
Alan Rake
Managing Editor
New African
London

ANGOLA

Population: 10.0m (1990 estimate)
Independence: 11 November 1975
Head of State: José Eduardo dos Santos
Government: President Dos Santos on 20 March 1991 promised that the government would introduce a new legal and constitutional framework that would bring multi-party democracy to Angola. As part of the peace agreement with UNITA, it was agreed that multi-party elections would be held in September 1991.
Parties: Former ruling party - *Movimento Popular de Libertacao de Angola* (MPLA). Main armed opposition party - *Unaio Nacional para Independencia Total de Angola* (UNITA), plus many newly emerging parties, in the era of political liberalisation.

DOS SANTOS, Jose Eduardo

Angolan politician. President 21 September 1979 -

Young, pragmatic and moderate and until 1990 tramelled by the strict disciplines of the marxist party system and by economic problems, he had little alternative but to follow in the footsteps of his predecessor Agostinho Neto. Only gradually did he assert himself and gain confidence so that he was in a position to negotiate an acceptable peace agreement with the US and South Africa, trading the phased withdrawal of Cuban troops from Angola for long term peace and security. Gradually, as the 1980s proceeded, he showed that he was emerging as a leader in his own right. He finally made a compromise with UNITA and put Angola on the road to democratisation.

Born 28 August 1942 in Luanda. Educated locally and grew up in the shanty town of the capital city. He became an active member of the youth wing of the Popular Movement for the Liberation of Angola (MPLA) at the age of 19. Enlisted in the MPLA guerrilla army in 1961, the year of the launch of the armed struggle against the Portuguese. Went to Leopoldville, capital of the Congo as a youth leader and then became the representative for the party in Congo-Brazzaville in 1963. Went to the Soviet Union for further studies, marrying a Russian wife and graduating in petrochemical engineering and oil at the University of Baku, in 1969 and in military telecommunications in 1969-70.

He returned to Angola and resumed the guerrilla war against Portugal 1970-73 becoming second in command of the MPLA Telecommunication Services in the second political region of Cabinda. He fought in the northern front in 1974. In September of the same year he was elected to the Central Committee and Politbureau where he ranked fifth. He became Minister of Foreign Affairs in the first government formed after independence on 11 November 1975 and later First Deputy Prime Minister 1975-78. As Foreign Minister he swung Zambia away from its support for UNITA on a visit in March 1976. He later explained to foreign investors that it was not Angola's policy to nationalise foreign firms unless they had been abandoned by their owners.

On 9 December 1978 the posts of Prime and deputy Prime Ministers were abolished by the politbureau, but he was immediately appointed Minister of Planning and head of the National Planning Commission. Before Agostinho Neto died of cancer while under treatment in the Soviet Union on 10 September 1979, he had already made Dos Santos his deputy and it was generally understood that he would be Neto's sucessor. This was confirmed by a unanimous vote of the Central Committee and he was sworn in, at the age of 37, on 21 September 1979. In a brief inaugural address he pledged to continue the policies pursued by President Neto and to honour all Angola's international comittments.

Though Neto had consolidated the power of the MPLA, he left his successor with many problems. The shattered economy had still not recovered from the departure of the Portuguese and was short of both financial and human resources. The war against UNITA and South Africa continued and created a huge drain on finances and heavy dependence on the Soviet bloc and on Cuban troops and technical advisers for support.

Dos Santos' strategy was to gradually improve diplomatic and commercial relations with the West while trying to break US support for UNITA. He was successful in gaining world sympathy and recognition, but South Africa and the US continued to support UNITA.

The solution only came in terms of a general settlement for southern Africa first mooted in the Lusaka accord of January 1984, in which South Africa pledged to withdraw its troops from Angola and to grant independence for Namibia, while Angola agreed to drop its support for the South West Africa People's Organisation (SWAPO). Though this agreement did not stick, continuing US pressure for a settlement eventually paid off, but not before the principle of "linkage" had been accepted in which phased withdrawal of Cuban troops in return for the withdrawal of South African forces, was accepted by Angola as part of the price for peace.

Dos Santos first had to strengthen his own position before he could make the necessary concessions towards the peace initiative. In October 1984 he dismissed his foreign minister and assumed control of foreign affairs personally. At the second congress of the MPLA in December 1985 he dropped Lucio Lara, the party ideologue and two other guerrilla veterans considered by the US to be obstacles to regional peace. He also strengthened his authority in the 13-man politbureau and prepared the way for the gradual democratisation of his regime.

These internal power shifts allowed him to test the real intentions of South Africa and the US and by 1988 he found them amenable to a real agreement. After a flurry of meetings a peace formula was finally secured. South African troops withdrew from Angolan soil by 1 September 1988 and an agreement was signed in New York on 22 December, to start the independence process in Namibia. Dos Santos also agreed to a phased withdrawal of Cuban troops from Angolan soil. These diplomatic achievements left him in a stronger position than at any time since he had first assumed power.

On 23 June 1989 he attended a meeting called by President Mobutu at his palace at Gbadolite, Zaire and under the approving eyes of 18 African Heads of State, shook hands with the UNITA leader, Jonas Savimbi for the first time since independence. This historic meeting agreed to a ceasefire and though it did not secure immediate results set in train a series of peace talks between UNITA and the Angolan government, which continued into 1991.

On 20 March 1991 Dos Santos promised to introduce multi-party democracy as one of the preconditions of a peace agreement with UNITA. After much diplomatic activity and several false dawns, an agreement was finally signed in Lisbon on 31 May 1991 which brought to an end the 17-year-old civil war.

His main task was to disarm and integrate the rival armed forces and get a liberalised economy moving again. Meanwhile he allowed political activity to resume through the formation of new parties, pending elections due in September 1992.

LARA, Lucio Barreti de

Angolan politician. First secretary People's Assembly.

The mestico, eminence grise and party theoretician of the MPLA from the early days when he was a co-founder of the party. A left-wing ideologue and one of the pro-Soviet, Netist faction who were originally followers of President Agostinho Neto. He remained in a position of considerable power in policy-making and party organisation under Neto, until he was dropped from the politburo in September 1985.

Born 9 April 1929 at Huambo (Nova Lisboa) in central Angola, the son of a wealthy mestico sugar planter. Educated at secondary schools in Huambo and Lubango. He went on to the universities of Lisbon and Coimbra in Portugal. His burning interest in politics led him to participate in a number of student and worker organisations.

In December 1956 he was one of the co-founders of the Popular Movement for the Liberation of Angola (MPLA). While working as professor of physics and chemistry (1954-61) he became one of the MPLA leaders in exile, representing the movement at international meetings and pan-African conferences. He also travelled widely in the Soviet Union and Eastern Europe.

In 1960 he opened the first MPLA headquarters abroad in Conakry, Guinea. At the first party conference in Leopoldville in 1962, when Agostinho Neto became leader of the party, he was elected to the executive committee and became responsible for the political education and training of cadres.

The MPLA opened the armed struggle in December 1961 with an attempt to release political prisoners from prisons in Luanda. Lara was later given various active responsibilities in the field when fronts were opened in Cabinda and eastern Angola. In September 1974 he was elected to the politburo and the central committee. The ceasefire in the guerrilla war with Portugal led to his return to Angola where he helped open the first MPLA office in Luanda. He became secretary-general of the MPLA and the party theoretician and chief ideologue. He had a key role in policy-making and a specific role in the Central Committee Secretariat in charge of the organisation of the party. At that period he could be described as Agostinho Neto's chief lieutenant.

But his leftist ideological views did not wear so well with the new leader José dos Santos who took over on Neto's death in September 1979. Dos Santos wanted to improve relations with the United States while Lara wanted to remain loyal to his old Soviet allies. At the second congress of the party at Luanda on 2 December 1985 dos Santos dropped Lara from the politburo though he remained first secretary of the People's Assembly.

NASCIMENTO, Lopo Fortunato Ferreira do

Angolan politician. Territorial Administrative Minister, 5 March 1991-

A Mbundu from Luanda, his political pedigree is beyond reproach, with an almost lifelong membership of the MPLA and two terms of imprisonment under the Portuguese. He was appointed Prime Minister immediately after independence, but he found it difficult to sustain his position as President Neto gradually took more power to himself, though he is still generally categorised as being in the Netist group. He also has the ideological disadvantage of being considered pragmatic and pro-Western, frequently negotiating with investors and international oil companies. He appeared to be 'banished' when posted to be governor of the 5th region but confounded his rivals by taking the opportunity to make the region a model for development. He was rewarded by being appointed Territorial Administrative Minister on 5 March 1991. He remains a charismatic and enigmatic politician who is destined to be one of the pillars of the future government.

Born 10 June 1942, a Mbundu from Luanda. Educated in Luanda, finishing his studies in the Vincente Ferreira Commercial School. Took an early interest in nationalist politics and was twice arrested by the Portuguese secret police, PIDE, in 1959 and 1963. He worked as a trade union organiser after his release in 1968.

An early member of the MPLA, he was appointed to the central committee and the politburo at the Moxico conference in September 1974. He then became the MPLA representative on the Presidential Council in the three-party transitional government from January to November 1975, in the run-up to independence. He became chairman of the council and escaped an assassination attempt by the FLNA.

Independence came on 11 November 1975, but was followed almost immediately by the civil war with the FLNA and UNITA. The MPLA President Dr Agostinho Neto appointed him Prime Minister. In December 1975 he travelled to Nigeria and Ghana to explain the stand of his party and government. He said that Angola would remain totally independent and non-aligned, but by 1976 his government had been forced to bring in Cuban troops to meet the South African threat.

On 27 November 1976 he gave up his role as Head of Government to President Neto but remained a " direct associate of the President". His role was more precisely defined as to "co-ordinate Government activity and supervise activities of provincial commissars."

The sixth plenary meeting of the Central Committee of the party gave President Neto new powers to appoint or dismiss members of government, thus weakening Nascimento's postion, but he remained as Premier while taking on additional responsibility as Minister of Internal Trade on 31 August 1977. At the first congress of the MPLA on 4 December 1977 he was re-elected to the Central Committee and the Politburo.

On 9 December 1978 he was suddenly dismissed from the Premiership following a clean sweep by Neto, who abolished the posts of Prime Minister and Deputy Prime Minister so that he could "maintain direct contact with ministers without going through an intermediary". There was also criticism from the ideologues in the party about the "need to intensify the struggle against the petit bourgeoisie."

President Jose Eduardo dos Santos came to power in September 1979 and reappointed Nascimento Minister of External Trade in 1980 and added Planning to his portfolio on 20 March 1981, with trade removed on 14 August 1982. His position as Planning Minister was confirmed in April 1983. At the second MPLA Congress in Luanda, in December 1985 he was moved to become Chairman of the war-torn fifth military region, headquartered in Lubango.

There he followed a reformist reconstruction programme for the region, supported by the UN Development Programme and by an increasing number of aid donors. His approach became a model for the economy as a whole and the introduction of the *Saneamento economico e Financeiro* (SEF) being implemented at national level with IMF support. Later he became Commissioner for Huila province. His reward came on 5 March 1991 when Dos Santos brought him into the cabinet as Territorial Administrative Minister.

RODRIGUES, Alexandre Manuel Duarte Kito

Angolan politician. Minister of Interior 9 July 1980-28 March 1989.

Something of a maverick in the strictly structured system of the Marxist government. During nine years as Minister of Interior, he became best known for his persistent negotiations with the treacherous South Africans in an attempt to gain a lasting peace for his country. Just as these negotiations seemed to have borne fruit with the Brazzaville agreement of December 1988, he was dismissed as minister, though he continued his role as a bridge between various factions in government and as a fixer of business deals on behalf of the state.

Famed as a guerrilla fighter against the Portuguese under his guerrilla nickname 'Kito', with the rank of Lieutenant-Colonel. He came to prominence when President José dos Santos gained power in September 1979 and appointed him Deputy Minister of Internal Order. Then on 9 July 1980 he was promoted to Minister of Interior. He held this position for nine years and served the government in many other ways than those directly related to his ministry. Thus he became involved in the early efforts to secure a lasting peace with South Africa at the beginning of the 1980s. He led the Angolan delegation, met the South African Foreign Minister Pik Botha, and negotiated an early agreement in Lusaka on 21 May 1984. He repeated the exercise at Cape Verde in April 1985 and had further meetings in Lusaka in November 1985.

On 10 December 1986, when the rank of general was introduced into the Angolan army for the first time, he was promoted to Lieutenant-General. His role as a negotiator continued at Brazzaville in April 1987. Suddenly, on 28 March 1989, he was dismissed from the post that he had held unchallenged for nine years. Diplomats claimed that it was part of the "process of renewal" following the signing of peace accords with South Africa and Cuba in Brazzaville in December 1988, but after years of peaceful negotiations on these precise issues, it seems unlikely that he would have been removed unless there had been some fundamental disagreements with the President.

During the negotiations in 1989 over a peace agreement with Unita Kito gave support to the mediation of President Mobutu of Zaire. This created divisions in the politburo and considerable criticism of his stance.

SAVIMBI Jonas Malheiro
Angolan guerrilla. Leader of Unita.

A pioneer nationalist who has spent most of his adult life in the bush at the head of his guerrilla army. A man of great charisma and charm who argues consistently that he would like a democratic solution to Angola's problems. But he was totally rejected by the Marxist government in Luanda which was not prepared to share power with a strong and determined opponent who did not share their ideology. This confined him to his guerrilla role which he sustained in the south-east of the country for 14 years. It also forced him into dependence on support from South Africa and the USA.

Born 3 August 1934, son of a stationmaster at Munhango on the Benguela railway line. Educated at the protestant school at his father's village of Chilesso near Andulo before going to the Dondi Mission School,

Silva Porto Secondary school and Sa da Bandeira.

In September 1958 he was awarded a scholarship by the United Church of Christ to study medicine at Lisbon university, but he left Portugal early in 1960 for Switzerland, studying political science first at Fribourg University then at Lausanne.

After a meeting with Kenya's Tom Mboya at a student's conference in Kampala, Uganda in July 1961, he joined Holden Roberto's Unaio das Populacoes de Angola (UPA) and was appointed secretary-general. With Roberto he played a key role in negotiations with the Partido Democratico de Angola (PDA) for the creation of the Frente Nacional de Libertacao de Angola (FLNA) on 27 March 1962. As Foreign Minister for its government in exile, he went to the UN in November 1962 with a petition for Angola's right to self-determination.

In July long simmering differences with Roberto resulted in a split. *1964* At an OAU meeting in Cairo he anounced his resignation from the FLNA, accusing Roberto of 'flagrant tribalism'. He moved to Brazzaville and set out his aims for a liberated Angola through the group, Amis du Manifeste Angolais, (AMANGOLA).

On 23 March 1966 he founded the Unaio Nacional para Independencia Total de Angola (UNITA) with a solid base of support in southern Angola and the nucleus of a guerrilla force, the Forcas Armadas de Libertacao de Angola (FALA). He was ordered out of Zambia following an attack on the Benguela railway on 25 December 1966 and obliged to transfer his headquarters from Lusaka to Cairo in October 1967.

After eight months in Egypt he decided to take command of UNITA from inside Angola and slipped into the country in July 1968. Although not recognised by the OAU, he built up huge support in the east and south of the country. In June 1974 he finally agreed a ceasefire with the Portuguese and mobilised support for his party in the south of the country.

He signed the Alvor agreement with the other nationalist parties in January 1975, giving UNITA equal representation with the other Angolan nationalist movements. But the three groups were at loggerheads from the start and fighting broke out between them in the race to power. Though Savimbi tried on at least three occasions to bring the groups together, he did not have the support in Luanda enjoyed by the Movemento Popular de Libertacao de Angola (MPLA) and his attempted alliance with Roberto was always tenuous.

Finally, as the MPLA began to receive Soviet and Cuban reinforcements he was forced to take to the bush and cultivate an alliance with the South Africans. In November 1975 a South African column took a string of southern cities and came within striking distance of Luanda, but the thrust was abandoned in the face of the Cuban military build-up.

Savimbi was forced back into the bush in south-eastern Angola where he remained permanently despite all attempts to dislodge him. Savimbi's support came from the Ovimbundu people, the most populous group in Angola. He had overwhelming support in the south of the country and was able to extend permanent control to a large area around his capital, Jamba. His guerrillas made frequent strikes in other parts of the country not under his command.

Successive campaigns against him were mounted by the MPLA and the Cubans but he proved remarkably resilient and was frequently reinforced by South Africans in times of major crisis. The US government also continued to give Savimbi support, either overtly or covertly through the CIA.

Savimbi travelled frequently internationally, particularly in the USA, drumming up support for his cause and international journalists were frequent visitors to his headquarters at Jamba. He continued to campaign for a settlement and a share of power after democratic elections. But he began to lose the diplomatic battle in 1988, when the major powers and the Angolan and South African governments all wanted to achieve an end to the war. South Africa agreed to withdraw its troops permanently from Angola in return for a phased withdrawal of the Cubans. In the process there was a settlement in Namibia removing the Namibian guerrillas from Angolan soil.

The peace agreement worked out at the end of 1988 and signed in New York in December left Savimbi in the cold, as the South Africans pledged not to give him further military assistance. His only major backer was the USA as he sought a political solution. In a series of interviews at the beginning of 1989 he said he was only asking for direct negotiations with the MPLA, leading to a government of national unity, followed by democratic elections. He remained exposed to renewed military assault by government forces and those Cubans who remained in Angola. But UNITA, well supported by the USA through Zaire, did unexpectedly well in a prolonged battle for the strategic southern town of Mavinga early in 1990 and made progress in the north. By April new peace talks were being held under Portuguese auspices, with Savimbi showing genuine interest in a political settlement.

An agreement was finally signed in Lisbon on 31 May 1991 which brought to an end the 17-year-old civil war. Savimbi declared his intention to take up the democratic, electoral challenge.

TONA, Pedro Maria "Pedale" (Colonel-General)
Angolan politician. Minister of Defence, 9 July 1980–

One of the most senior members of the central committee and politbureau of the party since Agostinho Neto's time; put in charge of the defence portfolio by President José dos Santos, where he was in charge of the national strategy in the continuing war with South Africa. Considered to be one of the pro-Cuban members of the party worried by the withdrawal of the Cubans and suspicious of making a deal with UNITA.

Distinguished during the liberation struggle under his guerrilla nickname 'Pedale'. He rose fast in the Popular Movement for the Liberation of Angola (MPLA) and became a member of the politbureau with the rank of colonel. In October 1978 he addressed the first MPLA/Party of Labour youth conference in Luanda. Immediately after President José dos Santos assumed power, he made Pedale his Deputy Minister of Defence, in his first cabinet, on 11 November 1979.

On 9 July 1980 he became full minister at a time Angola was involved in a series of border skirmishes with South Africa. He not only planned Angolan strategy but kept the press informed on the campaigns of the FAPLA forces. On 10 December 1986 when the rank of general was established in the Angolan army for the first time and was assumed by the President, Pedale was made Colonel-General. In February 1986 he took on the additional portfolio of Minister of State.

His forces were involved in a pitched battle with UNITA for control of Mavinga in April 1990. By May he admitted that Mavinga had fallen, but said his opponent's victory was "meaningless in view of its scarce population and lack of political and administrative structures."

VAN DUNEM, Pedro de Castro Dos Santos 'Loy'
Angolan politician, Foreign Minister 23 Jan 1989–

A school mate of President José dos Santos in Luanda. He made his mark in the liberation struggle, rising to the rank of Lieutenant-Colonel and was given junior posts by President Neto, but really rapid advancement only came when dos Santos took over in September 1979. He is considered to be the 'president's man' in the cabinet and politbureau. Best known for nearly a decade as Minister of Petroleum and Energy. Became Foreign Minister in January 1989.

A Moscow trained MPLA leader who made his mark in the independence struggle under the guerrilla name 'Loy'. On 26 November 1976 President Agostinho Neto appointed him third deputy Prime Minister under Lopo de Nascimento. His task was to supervise the ministries of industry, energy, transport, agriculture, construction, housing and fisheries.

On 9 December 1978 he was dismissed when the posts of Prime Minister and Deputy Prime Minister were abolished by the Political Committee, a move justified by President Neto on the grounds that he needed to have direct contact with his ministers without operating through intermediaries. On 17 January 1979 Neto made him Minister for Provincial Co-ordination, but it was after José dos Santos became President in September 1979 that he was appointed to the important Ministry of Oil and Natural Resources, where he made wide contact with the international oil industry, particularly among those Americans working offshore at Cabinda with the Gulf oil company.

Dos Santos also had him promoted to the Politbureau in 1983 in face of considerable opposition from Agostinho Neto's old comrades. On 3 July 1987 he took on the additional portfolio of Minister of State for Production which put him in effective charge of the ministries of oil, agriculture, industry, transport, public works and fisheries. On the dismissal of Afonso Van Dunem "Mbinda", he took on the important ministry of Foreign Affairs on 23 January 1989, just as Angola was trying to negotiate a peace agreement in Southern Africa and a lasting solution with UNITA.

The difficulties involved in these negotiations caused considerable divisions in the Politburo, with much criticism heaped on him by his fellow members over the way he approached the problem of Jonas Savimbi. But agreements with South Africa were reached in December 1988 and by 1 March 1990 he was able to receive Pik Botha, the South African Foreign Minister, for the first time in Luanda, in order to pave the way for a heads of state meeting between the two former enemies. He was fully involved in further peace negotiations with UNITA which took place under Portuguese auspices, starting in April 1990.

VAN DUNEM, Afonso 'Mbinda'
Angolan politician. Foreign minister, April 1985–January 1989.

One of the pro-Cuban group in the party alarmed at the Cuban withdrawal from Angola and very suspicious of UNITA. His dismissal as foreign minister came at a time when President José dos Santos was trying to work out an agreement with UNITA, but he remains the member of the politbureau responsible for external relations.

He made his name in the independence struggle under the guerrilla name 'Mbinda'. He rose fast in the Popular Movement for the Liberation of Angola, (MPLA) and became a member of the central committee and secretary for information. On 14 March 1978 he was appointed director-general of the Angolan News Agency, ANGOP. After President José dos Santos came to power in September 1979 he was not given any immediate portfolio but in 1982 was put in charge of foreign relations on the central committee secretariat.

He was formally appointed Foreign Minister by Presidential decree on 15 April 1985, but it was significant that as Foreign Minister, he did not always play as great a part in obtaining a peace agreement in Southern Africa and negotiating with the UNITA rebels as some of his colleagues in other ministries. On 23 January 1989 he was relieved of his foreign portfolio though he remains the member of the Politbureau responsible for Foreign Affairs.

BENIN

Population: 4.68m (1990, World Bank)
Independence: 1 August 1960
Head of State: Nicephore Soglo
Government: Multi-party system ushered in by parliamentary elections of February 1991 and the presidential elections of March 1991, which ousted Kerekou and established Nicephore Soglo as President. It was the first time in Africa that a sitting president had been overturned in democratic elections.
Parties: Majority party following the elections - the Union for the Triumph of Democratic Renewal (UTR), composed of three parties which support Soglo.

ALLADAYE, Michel

Benin army officer, former minister and politician.

A clever, cool soldier turned politician who took power as one of the 'three musketeers', close colleagues of Mathieu Kerekou who carried out the coup of 26 October 1972. Always one of the top men in Dahomey (later Benin) and one of the few people with real influence over Kerekou. He outlasted the other musketeers, until he was dismissed, many would say unfairly, as Minister of Education following the university and school riots of mid-1985.

Born 1940 at Abomey. Educated at the Lycée Victor Ballot, the French military academy at St Cyr and the Ecole Supérieure for Engineering, Versailles, France. Returned to command the 1st Engineers Corps at Kandi 1963-67. Promoted Captain 1967. Worked in engineering unit and Army General Staff Command and rose to Commander of the Directorate of Military Engineers.

He was one of Mathieu Kerekou's closest collaborators when he took power in the military coup of 26 October 1972. He was brought into the first military government as Minister of Foreign Affairs. One of his first acts was to overcome traditional Francophone suspicion and speak out on behalf of Benin joining the Economic Community of West African States (ECOWAS), which was dominated by powerful Nigeria rather than the Francophone rival, CEAO.

Elected to a six-man Politbureau by the Benin People's Revolutionary Party (PRPB) on 17 May 1976. Switched to Minister of Justice under the new civilian constitution in February 1980. Minister of Interior and Public Security, 1 January 1983. Moved to Secondary and Higher Education August 1984, to tackle the rising discontent of the university and student population. Dismissed and suspended from all activity within the PRPB on 11 June 1985. The official line was that Alladaye was guilty of negligence in applying Presidential directives aimed at averting student disturbances, but independent commentators claim that he was simply following alternative policies to Kerekou as very real student grievances were ventilated.

KEREKOU, Mathieu Ahmed
President 27 October 1972 - 25 March 1991.

Known as Django to his close family and friends, Mathieu Kerekou became President of his country after he took power in the military coup of 27 October 1972. He survived more coup attempts than most other African leaders and preserved his position only by using the full apparatus of the single party and his extensive security system. He survived strikes by teachers, students and civil servants as his country headed for bankruptcy in 1988/89; then in 1990 he promised to democratise the system. This brought his downfall in the presidential elections of March 1991.

Born 2 September 1933 at Koufra, Natitingou, in the Atakora province of northern Dahomey (as Benin was then called). He is a Bariba. After schooling in Mali and Senegal he went to the Officers School at Frejus in France.

He served in the French army until 1961 when he joined his national army in Dahomey. Aide de Camp to President Hubert Maga 1961-63. He first came to public notice when, as the commander of the paratroop unit at Ouidah, he played a vital role in the coup which overthrew General Soglo on 17 December 1967. Although he was the key man on the military committee that set up the coup and became chairman of the Revolutionary Military Council 1967-68, he was not given a position in the government that was subsequently set up under President Alley and Prime Minister Kouandété. He preferred to exercise influence behind the scenes and was the key man in the army.

After the army handed over power in the summer of 1968 to Dr Emile Zinsou he went back to barracks and then to France on a year's course, where he missed Kouandété's second coup in December 1969.

There were further attempted coups and leadership struggles, in which he emerged as the army strong-man in the early 1970s. The civilian politicians were jostling for power, with three Presidents actually agreeing to take the presidency in rotation, when Kerekou finally decided to put an end to the bickering, extravagance and corruption at the top and staged his coup on 27 October 1972.

He appointed himself President, Prime Minister and Minister of Defence, then detained all members of previous governments and set up a commission of inquiry into their activities. He formed an entirely military government made up of army officers under 40 years old.

After the commission reported, he announced a "programme for the revolution" which stressed national independence and called for a revision of the traditional co-operation agreements with France. His first major act was to assert that Marxism-Leninism would be the national ideology. He embarked on a programme of nationalisation in which many leading French firms were affected.

Schools were also nationalised and the legal system reorganised, with local committees encouraged to play an important part in regional government. On 18 October 1985 he foiled a full-scale mercenary invasion by troops of the former President Emile Zinzou. Decrying the coup as an imperialist plot, he took the opportunity on 30 November 1975, to change the historical name of Dahomey to the Popular Republic of Benin.

In 1979 Kerekou held the first elections since he came to power, to set up a National Revolutionary Assembly (ANR) which was designated as the supreme authority of the state.The old military Revolutionary Council (CNR) was disbanded and in this way Kerekou converted his regime into a civilian one. But he ensured that the Party of the Popular Revolution of Benin (PRPB) remained the sole party and that he was the sole candidate for the Presidency in the elections of December 1979.

But theoretical Marxist structures were not popular with many Beninois and there were a number of unsuccessful attempted coups. From the beginning of the 1980s Kerekou began to move towards more pragmatic policies behind the screen of revolutionary rhetoric.

He began to encourage private investment and reform corrupt and inefficient state-owned companies. Under pressure from the IMF, he even embarked on a programme of privatisation and the encouragement of private enterprise. At the same time he removed many of his more leftist supporters and reduced the size of the national assembly and the number of ministers. All these moves enhanced his personal power.

He showed his confidence in 1984 by releasing three former presidents and granting amnesty to other political prisoners. At the same time relations with France improved while political ties were still maintained with Eastern bloc countries.

But the economy suffered endemically from border problems with neighbours, mounting debt commitments and budgetary imbalances. This led to the adoption of IMF-sponsored financial measures and painful economic readjustments, achieved at the cost of considerable internal dissension. Teachers, students and civil servants went on strike for several months in mid-1989 over the non-payment of salaries. There were several attempted coups including one serious one in March 1989 in which many of Kerekou's long-time associates and members of the Presidential Guard were involved. Kerekou survived despite the internal and external pressures against him.

On 2 August 1989 he was re-elected as President for another five-year term. He was the only candidate put forward by the National Assembly, which voted for him by 198 votes out of 200 votes cast. But discontent among workers, students and members of the armed forces continued. Finally, he caved in to growing demands for a pluralist multi-party system.

In March 1990 he called a national conference and set up the High

Council of the Republic as a transitional body to prepare for the inauguration of democratic institutions.

In the Presidential elections of March 1991 he found himself challenged for the first time. Among the challengers were Nicephore Soglo (the interim Prime Minister) and Albert Tevoedjre (who led an alliance of smaller parties). Four aspirants were defeated in the first round. This left a straight contest between Kerekou and Soglo. On 25 March 1991 Kerekou was soundly defeated winning only 32.4% of the votes. It was the first time on mainland Africa that an incumbent President had been defeated at the polls, relinquishing his presidency. In an extraordinary statement during the election contest, Kerekou asked "forgiveness from the victims of the deplorable and regrettable incidents" that had taken place during his 17-year military regime. He proclaimed his "deep, sincere and irreversible desire to change." From 4 April 1991 he retired to his house in the Cotonu business quarter and stayed indoors, conducting his social and business life late at night. But he was planning to retire to a house he was building in Atacora, his home region in the north west.

SOGLO, Nicephore
Benin economist and politician, President 25 March 1991 -

One of the new wave of technocratic leaders taking over from the old guard that ruled Africa from the time of independence three decades ago. He was the non-political technician par excellence, having spent most of his career in a cosmopolitan international environment particularly at the IMF and the World Bank, where he was Director for Africa. As Prime Minister, then as President, he inherited a bankrupt economy and a politically volatile nation, but he was clearly the choice of the people, who did not consider that he would be too influenced by his Washington associations.

Born 1934 in Togo. He studied at the Sorbonne and continued with an Albert Camus scholarship in 1962, at the prestigious School of National Administration (ENA) in Paris, graduating in the same year as the man who became French Minister of Interior Pierre Joxe. He returned to Benin and began his career as an inspector of finance. At that time he was put in charge of an investigation into a financial scandal concerning some associates of Mathieu Kerekou. His report cleared Kerekou himself.

He rose to become Minister of Finance (1965-67) in the military government of Colonel Christophe Soglo who overthrew President Sourou Apithy, in a military coup on 29 November 1965.

His international career took off when he became a governor at the IMF and then, from 1979-86 the Director for Africa at the World Bank. He tried hard, with the backing of the Kerekou government to be elected to the presidency of the African Development Bank in 1985, but failed in his attempt.

On 27 February 1990 the national conference called to usher in democracy, appointed him interim Prime Minister with "full governmental powers" to administer the country in the transition to multi-party government. President Mathieu Kerekou confirmed this appointment on 12 March. His task was to restore a bankrupt economy - easier said than done; government workers were still waiting for up to two years pay arrears. He said that he had, "only eleven months" to get the economy right. In addition he had to preside over an orderly transition to civilian rule.

In January 1991 he registered his candidacy for the Presidential elections along with 14 other candidates. He was sponsored by the Union for Liberty and Development (ULD). The incumbent President Mathieu Kerekou was his main rival.

The strains of office and electoral pressure had a serious effect on Soglo's health. When he went to vote for himself on 10 March at the Cocotier primary school, he had to be helped out of his car by security men and supported into the polling station. At his next public appearance in the run off elections of 24 March, he was worse. To the dismay of the enthusiastic crowd which had gathered, he needed the support of two people, one on either side to get to the polling station and back to his car. He had to be carried in a chair which his son had brought. Rumours burgeoned in Cotonu that he was suffering from a juju spell put on him by political enemies. He took this sufficiently seriously to put out a statement that he was not dead, nor suffering from a mysterious illness. He had been diagnosed as having typhoid fever and a kidney problem.

On 25 March 1991 he became the first person on mainland Africa to defeat a sitting president in democratic elections since independence three decades earlier. He won 67.8% of the votes against 32.2% for Mathieu Kerekou who had ruled the country since 1972, when he seized power in a coup.

But he was still ill and the juju rumours continued, so he went to France for treatment on 13 April. He was treated for two months at the military hospital Val-de-Grace and then went to convalesce at a special centre in the south of France. He returned home to be greeted by a crowd of thousands on 8 June.

BOTSWANA

Population: 1.27m (1990, World Bank)
Independence: 30 September 1966
Head of State: Quett Masire
Government: Presidential democracy in a multi-party system, with free elections every five years.
Parties: Majority party Botswana Democratic Party. Opposition - Botswana National Front, Botswana People's party.

CHIEPE, Gaositwe Keagakwa Tibe

Botswana diplomat and politician. Minister of External Affairs, 14 September 1984 –

A kindly, maternal figure with a dedication to hard work. She was Botswana's first woman high commissioner in London and first woman minister. She had wide experience in the Botswana cabinet in other important ministries before President Quett Masire recognised her genuine and friendly diplomatic talent and assigned her the sensitive post of Minister of External Affairs.

Born 1922 in Serowe and educated at Serowe Primary School then at Tigerkloof Secondary in South Africa and at the University of Fort Hare in South Africa and Bristol in England, where she took an LLD.

She returned home to become an education officer in Botswana over 1948-62. She became Senior Education Officer in 1962 and Deputy Director of Education in 1965 and Director in 1968. In 1970 she was selected by Sir Seretse Khama as Botswana's first woman High Commissioner to Britain. The government, counting its costs, also expected her to cover Sweden, Norway, Denmark, West Germany, France, Belgium, Nigeria and the EC. After four successful years in London she returned home to become the first woman in the cabinet from 1974 as Minister of Commerce and Industry. In January 1977 she was reshuffled to Mineral Resources and Water Affairs.

On 14 September 1984 President Quett Masire appointed her to one of the most difficult and sensitive posts in the government as Minister of External Affairs. South Africa was putting pressure on Botswana to sign a non-aggression pact and was threatening economic sanctions. While not agreeing to sign a pact of this kind, she agreed to " some effective and practical arrangement between the security forces of our two countries, to ensure the territory of neither is used for the planning of sabotage or terrorism against the other." Her great fear was that South Africa would mount armed raids and reprisals on the pretext of chasing African National Congress guerrillas. In June 1985 a raid took place and at least 15 people were killed. Chiepe immediately claimed compensation from the South Africans, but was refused. A further raid took place in

March 1988.

Mrs Chiepe frequently talked to the South Africans on security matters. She had one round of talks in Pretoria early in December 1989 with the South African Foreign Minister, Pik Botha. A few days later South African armed forces cynically mounted another raid on a border village. Under her guidance relations with South Africa improved, when it dropped armed hostility in 1990 and ended apartheid in 1991.

KGABO, Englishman M.K.

Botswana politician. Minister of Home Affairs, September 1984–October 1989.

A veteran politician who worked his way up through the civil service and figured in all the post-independence governments until he was dropped by Sir Seretse Khama in 1974. A strong personality with abundant energy, he bounced back as Minister of Home Affairs a decade later in September 1984, before retiring in October 1989.

Born 1925 at Kwaneng and educated at Kanye, going to the local teachers' training college. He joined the Bakwena administration as secretary of the school committee and later became treasurer, councillor and member of the licensing board. In November 1964 he became a Justice of the Peace.

At the elections of March 1965 he won the Molepolole East constituency and was made Parliamentary Secretary to the Ministry of Agriculture on 5 March. He undertook a study tour on development financing that took him to Britain, USA, the Soviet Union, France and Switzerland. In October 1966 he was made Minister of Local Government and Lands. After re-election for his constituency in October 1969 he was confirmed in his cabinet post. In 1973 he was reshuffled to Minister of Information and Broadcasting, but was dropped on 30 October 1974, without explanation by Sir Seretse Khama. A long period followed when he was out of the cabinet, but on 14 September 1984, following the first elections after the death of Sir Seretse Khama, he was appointed to the important post of Minister of Home Affairs by Dr Quett Masire. He was dropped from the cabinet and retired from politics in the reshuffle of 13 October 1989.

MASIRE, Quett Ketumile Joni (Dr)

Botswana politician. President 17 October 1980–

Though he comes from the minority Bangwaketse tribe, his election as successor to Sir Seretse Khama in 1980 was almost a formality. A founder-member of the Botswana Democratic Party and life-long colleague of Sir Seretse, he was popular among his colleagues and had gained a reputation for being an able administrator. For more than a decade he had played a vital role in the economic development of his country. After his accession to power he continued the tradition that had established Botswana as a democratic, moderate, rational country whose main problem was its relationship with its powerful neighbour, South Africa.

Born 23 July 1925 at Kanye. A Bangwaketse. Educated locally and at Tigerkloof, South Africa. He became a journalist and joined the *African Echo* as a reporter and rose to become director of the paper. In 1958 he went into politics, becoming a member of the Bangwaketse Tribal Council and the African Council in the days of the British administration. In 1961 he stood for the Legislative Council as the member for Kanye South, won the seat and was appointed to the Executive Council. He and Seretse Khama launched the Botswana Democratic Party on 29 January 1962. It was a moderate party which enjoyed the support of the traditional chiefs and the whites. He was appointed secretary-general of the BDP and became editor of the party newspaper *Therisanyo.*

He triumphed again in the Kanye South elections on 2 March 1965 and was appointed Deputy Prime Minister on 3 March. He was a leading negotiator at the pre-independence constitutional conference in February 1966. When Botswana became independent on 30 September 1966 under Seretse Khama, he was appointed Vice-President and Minister of Finance.

Always eager to take on new challenges, he was given the additional responsibilities of Development Planning when the ministry was first created on 1 September 1967. A month later he was awarded an honorary Doctorate of Law at the St. John's University, New York. He became so engrossed with his governmental responsibilities that he lost touch with his constituency. He paid the price by being beaten at Kanye by ex-Chief Bathoen of the Botswana National Front in the 1969 general elections.

He was returned to the National Assembly as one of the four specially elected members chosen by the Assembly itself. He was reappointed Vice-President and Minister of Finance and Development Planning.

On 13 July 1980 Sir Seretse Khama died at the age of 59. A secret ballot of the National Assembly was held and Quett Masire was elected on 18 July and then unanimously endorsed by the legislature on 21 July.

His Presidency received a vote of confidence in the general elections of September 1984 when the BDP won 29 out of 34 seats, though it was contested by six political parties with 78% of the electorate voting.

Botswana was under continual pressure from South Africa, which mounted armed raids and indulged in various other destabilisation tactics. Though Masire protested that there were no ANC bases in Botswana, in March 1986 he was virtually compelled to expel the ANC representatives from the country. But further South African attacks and reprisals followed. In June 1988 Masire announced the capture of two members of a group of South African troops who had attacked Botswana forces south of Gaborone.

In August 1989 he was singled out as the third African head of state to get the annual Africa Prize for Leadership for the sustainable end of hunger. This was largely in recognition of the importance he has always attached to sustaining agriculture despite the dominance of mining in the Botswana economy and despite the devastating droughts that have afflicted his country.

In the elections of October 1989 he led his party to a landslide victory by winning 31 out of the 34 seats contested. He took the opportunity to thoroughly reshuffle his cabinet.

MMUSI, Peter Simako
Vice President 22 January 1983 -

A solid, reliable politician who has been close to the top in the political hierarchy since he plunged into politics in 1974. A keen sports lover, and a self-made economist and international civil servant, he has been Vice President and Minister of Finance and Development for most of his career. His one episode of uncertainty was in 1984 when he twice lost a controversial electoral contest against the leader of the opposition, but he has since re-established himself as an MP and resumed the vice presidency.

Born: 16 May 1929 at Mmankgodi village, Kwaneng district. His father was a migrant mineworker working on the South African Rand, so he spent most of his early years there, doing his primary education in Krugersdorp and Randfontein. He returned to Botswana to do his secondary education at St Joseph's College, Kgale, about 10km from the capital, Gaborone, 1945-48. He decided to become a teacher and went back to South Africa for training at Mariazelle, Cape Province.

Back in Botswana he started teaching at his old school, St Joseph's, 1951-56. He continued teaching at Lobatse 1956-61.

Always seeking new opportunities, he became an assistant clerk to the Legislative Council 1961-63. He then moved to an area which fascinated him as Labour officer, 1963-65, before being promoted Commissioner of Labour, 1965-74. He then resigned to take up politics on behalf of the ruling Botswana Democratic Party.

In 1974 he was elected member of parliament for Kweneng South and appointed Assistant Minister of Finance and Development on 30 October. In the same year he got the presidential order of meritorious service from President Seretse Khama.

In January 1977 he was appointed Minister of Commerce and Industry and was moved to the important ministry of Home Affairs in July of the same year.

In the October 1979 elections he switched constituencies and stood for Gaborone South, where he narrowly defeated the sitting MP, opposition leader Dr Kenneth Koma, who also failed when he challenged Khama for the presidency. Mmusi was rewarded on 23 October 1979 when Khama appointed him Minister of Works and Communications.

On the death of Seretse Khama the new President Quett Masire, appointed Mmusi to his old ministry that of Finance and Development, on 13 July 1980.

On the death of Vice President Lenyeletse Seretse, President Masire promoted Mmusi to that post, the number two spot in the Botswana hierarchy, on 22 January 1983.

At the peak of his career, he was in for a shock in the fiercely contested general elections of September 1984. He narrowly defeated the persistent challenge of Dr Kenneth Koma who claimed that there had been electoral irregularities and that he had been cheated. At the same time a ballot box full of uncounted votes was discovered. The courts declared the election for the Gaborone south seat null and void. A new election was then called for November and in that contest Mmusi was defeated by 742 votes.

President Masire responded by making him a specially elected member of parliament and keeping him in the post of Minister of Finance. Though his future had hung in the balance he gradually restored himself and was reappointed Vice President. The Botswana Democratic Party also showed a vote of confidence by re-electing him chairman of the party for the third successive term on 15 July 1985. He held the party chairmanship from 1981.

In the October 1989 elections he went back to his old Kweneng South constituency, which includes his home village of Mmankgodi, and won comfortably. After the elections, President Masire shifted him to Minister of Local Government and Lands, on 13 October 1989.

He was the first chairman of the Southern African Development Co-ordination Conference (SADCC) on its formation in 1980 and has been consistently re-elected to that post. He is also chairman of the African caucus of the IMF and World Bank.

MOGWE, Archibald Mooketa

Botswana politician. Minister of Mineral Resources and Water, 14 September 1984–

One of the more senior ministers in the Botswana cabinet but as a career civil servant and an appointed member in the National Assembly, he lacked a political base. He held the difficult foreign ministry for a decade and since 1984 has been Minister of Mineral Resources and Water Affairs.

Born 29 August 1921 at Kanye, the son of Reverend M.T. Kanye. Educated locally, then went for teacher training in South Africa and university at Reading and Oxford in Britain.

He returned home to become an education officer over 1957-64. He entered the foreign service, becoming a Permanent Secretary in the Foreign Office in 1966 and the Senior Permanent Secretary to the Cabinet and the Head of Public Service over 1968-74.

On 30 October 1974 President Seretse Khama rewarded him for his loyal service in the ranks by nominating him to the National Assembly and appointing him Minister of State for External Affairs. When Quett Masire succeeded to the Presidency, he confirmed Mogwe as Minister of

Foreign Affairs on 22 July 1980.

He contested the Gaborone North seat in the first elections since Seretse Khama died in September 1984, but was defeated. The vote against him was considered to be part of a general urban protest against high unemployment and housing problems, rather than anything personal. President Masire took advantage of the constitution and brought him back on 14 September 1984, as one of the four specially nominated members, but he did lose the Foreign Ministry to Mrs Gaositwe Chiepe and was reshuffled to become Minister of Mineral Resources and Water Affairs. It was felt that new blood was needed in the Foreign Ministry, where South Africa was pressing Botswana to sign a non-aggression pact. After the elections of October 1989 in which the BDP won a fifth landslide victory, he retained the post of Minister of Mineral Resources.

MORAKE, Kebathlamang Pitseyosi
Botswana politician, Minister of Health, 13 October 1989 –

Born 21 November 1930 at Tonota. Educated at Tonota School 1939-47, followed by a teacher's training course at Kanye until 1950. Went to Tigerkloof, South Africa, where he obtained a junior certificate.

He began teaching at Tonota in 1953 and spent 11 years there, rising to head teacher. In 1965 he was sent to England on an advanced teaching course at the Institute of Education in Newcastle. In preparation for a political career after independence on 30 September 1966, he was sent on a political training course in Britain, West Germany, Zambia, Tanzania and Kenya. On his return he became executive secretary of the Botswana Democratic Party and editor of the party newspaper, *"Yherisanyo"*.

In October 1969 he became a specially elected MP to the National Assembly and Assistant Minister at the President's Office with special responsibility for information services. He undertook assignments for Sir Seretse Khama, sometimes representing him at meetings. In 1970 he studied broadcasting on a study tour in Britain. He became Assistant Minister of Local Government and Lands in April 1972. He was promoted to full minister in charge of education on 30 October 1974. It was a post he held unchanged for 15 years, setting a sound educational base for his rapidly developing country. He was switched to Minister for Health by President Masire on 13 October 1989.

NWAKO, Moatlagola P.K.
Botswana politician and minister.

One of the most senior members of the cabinet from the time he first became Minister of Agriculture in 1965. He held ministerial appointments continuously until 1989, both under Sir Seretse Khama and Dr Quett Masire. Studious looking in his spectacles, he is a lively outdoor speaker, skilled in getting his views across to ordinary people. A keen sports fan, he was responsible for promoting soccer on a national league basis. As Minister of Commerce and Industry since 1977, he presided over much of Africa's fastest growing economy.

Born September 1932 in the Ngwato area. Educated locally then at South Africa's Tigerkloof Secondary School, where he obtained his senior certificate in 1948. He returned home and joined the Bakwena and Bamangwato Tribal Authorities and rose to become treasurer. In 1954 he became secretary and treasurer of Moeng college, 1954-64. During this period he also served on the African Advisory Council and became deputy chairman of the Wages Board at the national abbatoirs.

His political career took off on 1 March 1965 when he won a seat for Tswapong North to the Legislative Council, later to become the National Assembly. On 5 March 1965 Seretse Khama brought him into government as Minister of Agriculture. A year later he became Minister of State for External Affairs and spent much of his time over the next three years representing his country abroad at conferences.

Re-elected for Tswapong North in October 1969, he was appointed Minister of Health, a portfolio he held simultaneously with Labour and Home Affairs until 1974, when he continued with Health alone until 1977 when he became Minister of Commerce and Industry. When Dr Quett Masire took over on the death of Sir Seretse in July 1980, he maintained full confidence in Nwako and asked him to continue as Minister of Commerce, a post he held until 13 October 1989.

BURKINA FASO

Population: 9.04m (1990, World Bank)
Independence: 5 August 1960
Head of State: Blaise Compaoré
Government: New constittution approved by referendum in June 1991 allows for the division of powers between the President and parliament. Other parties can organise freely. They were recognised officially in January 1991. Presidential elections scheduled for November 1991 and democratic parliamentary elections scheduled for December 1991.
Parties: Majority party in transitional government, ODP/MT. Other parties tolerated in run up to elections.

COMPAORÉ, Blaise

Burkina politician. President 15 October 1987–

The dear, close, childhood friend of Thomas Sankara, who rose to the number two spot in the power hierarchy under him, but then suddenly engineered the coup which killed him. A cunning, silent, retiring man, far more conservative and pragmatic than his charismatic predecessor, he has since consolidated his rule and has executed other colleagues who were said to be planning another coup plot. More respected than loved and well supported by conservative forces externally, particularly by his father-in-law, President Houphouët Boigny of Côte d'Ivoire.

Born 1950, in Ziniaré near Ouagadougou. He did his military training at the officers school in Yaoundé, the capital of Cameroon. He returned home as a second lieutenant in 1975. Three years later on a para-commando course in Morocco in 1978, he met Thomas Sankara and fell under his spell. Sankara explained his political philosophy: "One day we must do something". Sankara was soon appointed commandant of the para-commando school at Po and Compaoré was appointed his deputy. In 1981 when Sankara was made Secretary of State for Information in 1981 by President Saye Zerbo, Compaoré was promoted commander at Po.

This placed him in a good position to benefit from the coup of 7 November 1982, carried out by non-commissioned officers. They handed over power to Jean Baptiste Ouedraogo, an army doctor, who immediately brought Compaoré onto his People's Provisional Salvation Council (CPSP). But he and Sankara soon fell out with Ouedraogo who, at one stage, threatened to put them on trial before an ad hoc committee of CPSP members.

Sankara was detained by the Ouedraogo government, causing the mutiny of the commando unit at Po. Ouedraogo released him from detention in June 1983, and sent him together with Compaoré, to negotiate with the rebellious men. But on his return Sankara was re-arrested. Compaoré then brought the commandos out in rebellion once more, again seizing control of Po.

It was the mutiny of Compaoré's commandos which gave Sankara the opportunity to carry out his own coup on 4 August 1983. He rewarded Compaoré by making him a member of the National Revolutionary Council (CNR) on 24 August 1983 and immediately appointed him Minister of State to the Presidency, virtually the number two spot in the new regime.

Later Compaoré commented, "We were not political virgins. We had known for a long time which among us should be president, minister of this or that. We did not know who could oppose us fundamentally... Thomas, Lingani, Zongo and me."

Compaoré fully endorsed the revolutionary populist policies of the new government and personally ordered the house arrest of 15 politicians of the old order including former Presidents Maurice Yameogo and Saye Zerbo in December. He claimed that the security of the state had been at risk.

During the Sankara regime Compaoré appeared to endorse the quirky radical policies of his colleague, but his importance was demonstrated when he was one of the few ministers not dismissed nor sent to work on building sites to sample the life of ordinary people. While the group held together ideologically, personality differences soon began to develop. Compaoré relied heavily on a semi-official political organisation called the Burkina Communist Union (UCB) and other leaders of the CNR had their own supportive factions.

In mid-1987 came the first reports that Sankara had been out-voted on various issues and rivalry and suspicion set in among the top leaders. Compaoré began to suspect that steps were being taken to remove him. On 15 October 1987 he seized power in a pre-emptive strike. It turned into a bloody coup in which Compaoré's commandos opened fire on Sankara, killing him and 13 of his associates. While Compaoré probably did not himself order Sankara's execution, the death of such a popular leader raised an international outcry and demonstrations internally. Compaoré took to his bed for three days, saying later that he "deeply regretted" his friend's death. He has remained highly sensitive over the issue ever since. An attempted rebellion at the Koudougou garrison was rapidly quelled. Many of Sankara's family and friends were arrested and detained.

Compaoré declared himself President and, appearing for the first time in public on 18 October 1987, said that he had been forced to carry out a pre-emptive coup. He initially ruled through existing structures, but early in 1988 Sankara's CDRs were replaced with Revolutionary Committees (RCs) who were no longer allowed to carry arms, a move that was widely acclaimed.

He soon revealed himself to be more conservative and pragmatic than his predecessor. He introduced a "rectification process" which entailed "more hard work and less talk". He appealed to private investors to build a revolutionary state. He cracked own on the opposition, detaining many prominent political and union leaders. He abolished the more extreme revolutionary measures of the Sankara government and dropped some unpopular taxes.

In September 1989, while Compaoré was on a two-week trip to China (he was one of the few African Heads of State to support China's repression of its students), two senior lieutenants were accused of attempting a coup. The Minister of Defence, Commander Jean Baptiste Lingani, and the Minister of Economic Promotion, Captain Henri Zongo were executed by firing squad after being accused of trying to blow up the plane bringing Compaoré back from his Asian tour. "Now the Burkina people know that they have only one chief," he commented shortly afterwards.

In response to demands for more democracy and a multi-party form of government, he set up a commission to draft a new constitution in May 1990, "to formalise the legal existence of other political formations in the anti-imperialist struggle." This showed he was prepared to legalise exisiting left-wing parties and follow the general African trend towards democratisation.

His party formally abandoned Marxism-Leninism in March 1991. He endorsed the new constitution, adopted by referendum in June, which provided for the separation of Presidential powers and election of the President for a seven-year term, by universal suffrage.

On 16 June he named a new transitional government to lead the country to multi-party rule following elections due in November.

DIENDERE, Gilbert (Captain)
Burkina soldier, Executive Secretary of the Politbureau. Secretary for Defence, 4 March 1990–

A young soldier whose rise to the number two spot in the Burkina regime is almost entirely due to his allegiance to President Blaise Compaoré. As head of security he has carried out most of the tasks which Compaoré cannot carry out publicly. He was responsible for the arrest and execution of Jean Baptiste Lingani and Henri Zongo for plotting against Compaoré when he was away on a tour of Asia in September 1989.

Born 1959. Joined the army and rose fast under Thomas Sankara and even faster under Blaise Compaoré, who made him adjutant of his renowned para-commando regiment at Po before appointing him captain in charge of presidential security and director of military intelligence.

The official version of what happened is that Diendere got wind of the coup which Jean Baptiste Lignani and Henri Zongo planned to carry out while Compaoré was away on an Asian tour in September 1989. Diendere ordered the arrest and execution of the coup plotters. But there were press reports that he had actually acted as an agent provocateur in telling Lingani and Zongo that a coup was already brewing, inviting them to join it.

He was rewarded on 21 September by being appointed Secretary General of the Executive Committee and in charge of security in the political bureau of the new ruling party that Compaoré was setting up, the *Organisation démocratique et populaire - mouvement du travail (ODT - MP)* generally known as the Popular Front. This placed him in the position generally acknowledged as the number two spot in the Compaoré regime. On 4 March 1990 he was made Secretary for Defence and Security on the Executive Committee.

ZERBO, Saye (Colonel)

Burkina soldier and politician. President 25 November 1980 – 7 November 1982.

An old style soldier who served with the French in Indo China and Algiers. He tried to bring peace and stability under a tough military government to his poor country, torn by strikes and political intrigues. He came to power in a bloodless coup and tried to cure national problems by orthodox military methods but little in the way of political creativity. He was ousted two years later by junior ranks. He was then put under house arrest only to be accused of fomenting a counter-coup against Thomas Sankara.

Born 1932 at Tougan, in the Samo tribe. He joined the French army in 1950 and trained as a paratrooper, serving in Indo-China and Algeria. He transferred to the Upper Volta army in 1961. He did further studies at the Military Academy Frejus and courses at the Artillery School and Staff college. He graduated from the Ecole Supérieure de Guerre in 1973.

On 11 February 1974 when the Head of State, General Sangoulé Lamizana, suspended the constitution and dissolved the national assembly to reassert military rule, he appointed Major Saye Zerbo as his Minister of Foreign Affairs. He held this post until 1976 when he took command of the combined regiment at Ouagadougou and the Directorate of the Bureau of Studies of the Armed Forces.

But serious shortages of essential foods, wrangling between politicians and continual unrest among the trade unions gave Zerbo the excuse for a military coup which he carried out bloodlessly on 25 November 1980. There was considerable evidence that Gen Lamizana, who came from the same Samo tribe, even the same village, as Zerbo may have agreed to his own removal. A 31-man Military Committee of Recovery for National Progress (CMRPN) was established, staffed mainly by younger officers. It suspended the constitution, dissolved the national assembly and banned all political activity. Colonel Zerbo assumed the presidency and took on the role of Prime Minister and Chief of Staff.

But conflict between the government and trade unions continued. The unions, chafing under the restrictions of political freedoms and economic austerity measures, mounted wildcat strikes, while Zerbo's own officers became dissatisfied with his leadership. On 7 November 1982 a group of non-commissioned officers seized power and attacked Zerbo for corruption, the suppression of individual liberties and the arrests of workers and students. They passed power on to Major Jean Baptiste Ouedraogo. Zerbo was put under house arrest and not allowed to receive more than three visitors at a time.

On 9 September 1983 he was arrested after being accused of planning a counter coup against the regime of Thomas Sankara, just five weeks after he had assumed control. In December, he and the former President Maurice Yaméogo and 13 other old politicians were placed under full arrest, rather than house arrest after being accused of "associating with foreign enemies of the revolution."

On 22 April 1984 he was put on trial before a people's tribunal on corruption charges. He was asked to account for £28m missing from state funds. He was found guilty and sentenced to 15 years' imprisonment– (seven suspended) and ordered to refund 61m CFA francs of "embezzled public funds." In September 1985 he had his prison term reduced by one year. On 3 January 1986 he had his sentence further commuted to house arrest.

BURUNDI

Population: 5.49m (1990, World Bank)
Independence: 1 July 1962
Head of State: Pierre Buyoya
Government: Military, with the President determining and executing policy through the Military Committee for National Salvation, but pluralism now accepted and a constitutional commission has been established to examine the modalities of change. Multi-party debate tolerated.
Parties: Single party: *Union pour le Progres National (UPRONA).* Other parties being formed.

BAGAZA, Jean Baptiste

Burundi soldier. President November 1976-September 1987.

Former President of Burundi who was deposed by his colleagues in the military coup of September 1987. A strong Tutsi soldier, with a commanding presence, he himself came to power in a military coup in November 1976 and started his regime with a number of much needed reforms, but as his rule progressed he became increasingly autocratic and dictatorial and unpopular with many of his closest colleagues. He also became involved in a prolonged dispute with the Catholic Church. This gave cause for the successful coup against him, forcing him into exile in Belgium.

Born 29 August 1946, at Murambi in the south. A Tutsi-Hima. Educated locally, then joining the army at the Officer School, Brussels and the Belgian Military School, Arlon.
He returned home in September 1971 to become Assistant to the Chief of Staff, General Thomas Ndabemeye. In May 1972 he was placed in charge of G-4 Logistics in the General Staff. In November 1972 he jumped the ranks of commandant and major, was promoted Lieutenant Colonel and became Chief of Staff in the armed forces, second in command in the army.
On 1 November 1976 he led a bloodless coup which toppled Michel Micombero. He justified his actions by saying that the former President had created a new monarchy, debased the Union for National Progress, UPRONA and had violated the constitution. He said, "The Burundi people have been pushed into this not by any material interest but through their faith in the Burundi nation."
Once in control he made a major effort to encourage national reconciliation and integration. He abolished the old system of land tenure and introduced agrarian reforms in which Tutsi overlords were compelled to hand over land to the Hutu peasants. He vested more power in the UPRONA party and introduced a new constitution in 1981 with

an elected national assembly where first elections were held in October 1982.

In July 1984 he was elected as Head of State on the basis of direct suffrage winning 99.63% of the vote as the sole candidate. As his regime consolidated he became more autocratic brushing aside those who disagreed with him. In the mid-1980s a conflict developed with the Catholic Church. Priests were deported and detained. In September 1986 he announced the nationalisation of Catholic seminaries and placed further restrictions on the Church in 1987.

His conflict with the Church, in a highly religious country, and his increasingly autocratic methods, led to considerable unpopularity and his human rights record was criticised internationally by Amnesty International and others.

On 3 September 1987 while he was away attending a conference of Francophone Heads of State in Canada, his army colleague Pierre Buyoya carried out a successful military coup and deposed him. Buyoya accused him of many of the same charges that he had laid against Micombero when he took power in 1976 – corruption, violation of the constitution and an incoherent economic policy which favoured a class of civil servants and private individuals.

He said that the coup had been carried out by "young boys without a great deal of political experience", and vowed to return home. But in November when he attempted to fly home unannounced, the government discovered what was afoot and refused the plane permission to land at Bujumbura. After being denied political asylum in Uganda, he eventually took up exile in Belgium.

BUYOYA, Pierre
Burundi President, 2 October 1987–

A soldier of courage and inner strength with a strong charisma. Never content with being a simple soldier, he became a keen member of the party and served under two Presidents as member of the Central Committee. But he and the younger officers became estranged from his former colleague Jean Baptiste Bagaza. Basically a quiet and peace loving man who likes to consult and listen, he finally summoned up the courage to seize power and set about repairing relations with the Catholic Church and democratising the regime. His efforts stumbled on the massacres and racial violence between the Tutsi and the Bahutu of August 1988. Though he is a member of the Tutsi tribe, he felt the time had come to take positive action to secure permanent national reconciliation.

Born 24 November 1949 into a modest Tutsi family, at Rutovu in Bururi province. Did primary education locally. In 1967 he went to Belgium for secondary and university studies in social science. He then did military training, finishing at the tank training school at Arlon, in 1975. He returned home to become commander of a local armoured squadron. He went for further training in the tank training school at

Cavalrie, France from August 1976 to January 1977.

On his return home he was again made commander of an armoured battalion and became the chief training officer for the Chief-of-Staff in the armed forces. He also pursued his political interests, being a keen member of the single party UPRONA, the Union for National Progress. In 1979 he was elected to the central committee of the party and re-elected in 1984. Meanwhile, he found time to do further military training at the West German War School, 1980-82.

As the regime of Jean Baptiste Bagaza got itself into difficulties, clashing with the Catholic Church and losing support both at home and abroad, Major Pierre Buyoya began to distance himself from his former colleague and became openly critical. On 3 September 1987 he led a successful coup supported by most of the army while Bagaza was out of the country attending a summit of French speaking leaders in Canada. Buyoya accused the former President of corruption, violations of the constitution and an incoherent economic policy which particularly favoured a class of civil servants and private individuals.

Buyoya suspended the 1981 constitution and all organs of UPRONA and dissolved the national assembly. He set up a Military Committee of National Salvation (CMSN). On 2 October 1987 he was sworn in as President and promptly announced the release of some 600 political detainees. He lifted restrictions imposed earlier on the Catholic Church and allowed many churches closed by the Bagaza government to reopen. He toured the country to find out the wishes and objectives of the people.

But he did not give relations between the ruling Tutsi and the Bahutu priority attention, and tensions between the different tribes continued, only to explode in another tribal massacre in August 1988. The incident provoked by a clash between the majority Tutsi army and Bahutu civilians, resulted in thousands of deaths on both sides and an international outcry recalling the genocide of 1972. Buyoya blamed the violence on Burundi refugees who had come from abroad to inflame the Bahutu population. "When the people began to kill, to pillage and to burn, the army intervened ... there were losses, there were deaths."

The national shame over the massacres bit deep and Buyoya resolved to try and achieve a permanent solution. He appointed a new cabinet in October 1988 in which the Tutsi and Bahutu had equal representation. He also set up a Committee of National Unity which was instructed not only to find out the causes of the troubles, but to formulate permanent policies to reconcile the two groups. When the committee reported in May 1989, Buyoya instructed it to draft a Charter of National Unity that would be a precursor to a constitution and the eventual return to elections and parliamentary government.

He worked hard to eliminate tribalism and ensure systematic political reform. In December 1990 the Hutus gained a majority in the Central Committee of the UPRONA party for the first time and provided its Secretary General. Many prominent Hutus returned from exile. In February 1991 Buyoya gave them a majority in a new cabinet.

On 1 May 1991, Buyoya declared that he was in favour of pluralism and looked forward to the report of the constitutional commission which was due to report in July.

KADOYI, Aloys (Lt-Col)
Burundi soldier and politician, Interior Minister 1 October 1987 - 13 February 1991.

A Tutsi in a key role in the drive for national reconciliation launched by President Pierre Buyoya after the racial incidents of August 1988. He saw Kadoyi as a firm but fair colleague who would make an excellent Minister of the Interior and added this responsiblity to his post on the Executive of the Military Committee for National Salvation.

Born 1945, a Tutsi at Nyabiraba. Primary education at Rutovu 1953-59, before going to the Mugera Seminary, the Burasira Seminary and the College of Saint Esprit, Bujumbura finishing in 1966.

He attended the University of Burundi in 1966 before going for military training in Egypt in 1967. He did his officer training there, followed by frequent courses at the Inter-army school of Frounzd in the Soviet Union. He was promoted fast becoming a platoon commander in 1970, company commander in 1973 and unit commander 1976-77. He became head of the Logistics Office in 1981 before being promoted to Director General of Instruction and Operations at the Ministry of Defence. In 1984 he became commander of the Higher Institute for Military Officers.

After the military coup of September 1987, President Buyoya spotted his talents and he became a member of the Military Committee for National Salvation, CMSN. He was appointed Minister of the Interior on 1 October 1987. He held this post until 13 February 1991 when President Buyoya wanted to demilitarise his cabinet in preparation for pluralist government.

MBONIMPA, Cyprien
Burundi politician. Minister of Foreign Affairs, 1 October 1987–

A suave Tutsi diplomat who has always been with the foreign service. He made his name as ambassador to Brussels in the first half of the 1980s, before being appointed Foreign Minister in President Buyoya's new government.

Born 26 December 1946, a Tutsi at Batwemba, Bururi. Educated at the Ecole Normale de L'Etat, Bujumbura, 1960-65. He went on to do law studies at the National School of Public Administration 1968-70 gaining diplomas in law and diplomatic relations from the International Institute of Public Administration in Paris, 1970.

He joined the civil service in the immigration department in 1971 and went on to become the first secretary at the embassy in Brussels 1973-75, then charge d'affaires, Moscow 1975-76 . He became a counsellor to President Jean Baptiste Bagaza, 1976-78, then Director-General of the Written Press in the Ministry of Information, 1978-80.

In 1980 he was appointed ambassador to Brussels and chief of the Burundi mission to the European Community. He remained in the prestigious posting until 1985. During this period he took a major part in negotiations over the third convention between the ACP and EC.

After the coup of 3 September 1987 which ousted Bagaza from power, Pierre Buyoya, the new leader, made him Minister of Foreign Affairs and Co-operation, an appointment that was reconfirmed in the reshuffle of 19 October 1988. He retained his ministry in February 1991 in the run up to democratic government.

NIYIBIGIRA, Gerard

Burundi civil servant. Minister of Finance, 19 October 1988-

A long-standing academic and civil servant with wide international experience in research institutions and development organisations. He was singled out for ministerial promotion by President Pierre Buyoya when he came to power following the coup of September 1987.

Born in 1946, a Hutu, at Ntega. He went to local schools at Sasa and Kanyinya before going to the Small Seminary at Mureke, then the Middle Seminary at Burasira where he finished his studies in 1966.

He did two years' studies in humanities at Bujumbura University before going to Prague University, Czechoslovakia, where he obtained a degree in economic and social science. He became a research assistant at the university, 1970-74, while studying for his doctorate in economic and social science. He then worked in the research centre for the pottery and glass industry of Walbrzych, Poland, as head of the department for scientific, technical and economic education, 1974-76.

He returned home and became Financial Director at Burundi University and then counsellor, first to the Prime Minister and Minister of Planning and then to President Jean Baptiste Bagaza.

In 1979 he was appointed Director of Economic Development Programmes at the permanent executive secretariat of the Economic Community of the Great Lake Countries– Zaire, Burundi and Rwanda. After the coup of September 1987 which toppled Bagaza the new President Pierre Buyoya brought him into his cabinet as Minister of Planning. On 19 October 1988 when more Bahutu were brought into the cabinet following the massacres of September, he was promoted to Minister of Finance.

RUSUKU, Simon (Major)

Burundi soldier. Minister of Transport 1 October 1987–

The most qualified military engineer in Burundi, with a long period of training in France and the Soviet Union behind him. Since the coup of

September 1987, he enjoys the dual role as minister and member of the ruling Military Committee for National Salvation.

Born 19 May 1948. Primary education at Kibumbu, 1955-61. He went on to the college of Saint Esprit, studying Latin and science.

He went on to the University of Burundi before deciding on a military career. He entered the Officers School of the Armed Forces, 1969-71. He then became an instructor at the school for three years. He continued at the School of Applied Engineering at Angers, France and qualified as an engineer officer.

He returned to take command of the engineers at Kamenge camp for four years. He went for further training at the War School for Engineering Units at Moscow, 1981-85, where he gained a diploma as master of military science and engineering construction.

In 1986 he became Director of Engineering for the armed forces. After the coup which toppled Jean Baptiste Bagaza in September 1987, he was appointed to the Military Committee for National Salvation. In President Pierre Buyoya's first cabinet he was appointed Minister of Transport, Posts and Telecommunications, on 1 October 1987.

SIBOMANA, Adrien
Burundi politician. Prime Minister, 19 October 1988-

A young Bahutu professor of physics and mathematics, who worked quietly as Vice-President of the National Assembly over 1982-87. His big chance came after the inter-tribal violence of August 1988, when President Buyoya identified him as the man who could play a leading part in the Commission for National Unity and in drawing up a charter for national reconciliation. He also became the first Bahutu to be made Prime Minister since 1965.

Born 1953 at Bukeye into a Bahutu family. After primary education at Bukeye he went on in 1966 to the Bujumbura Small Seminary, completing a diploma in humanities in 1972. He then taught for a year at Muyinga school before going to Bujumbura university to read for a mathematics and physics degree, which he gained in 1977.

Almost immediately he started teaching as a professor of mathematics and physics at the college of Notre Dame of Gitega, 1977-79. He then became director of Kamenga Technical School 1979-82.

A keen member of the Union for National Progress Party (UPRONA) he was elected to and became Vice-President of the National Assembly, 1982-87, and Governor of the Province of Muramvya, 1987-88.

After the inter-tribal violence of August 1988 President Buyoya brought a majority of young Hutu into his government in a new initiative for national reconciliation. On 5 October 1988 he appointed Sibomana as Vice-President of the Commission of National Unity set up to find out the reasons for tribal violence and formulate a permanent solution through a Charter of National Unity. On 19 October he promoted him still further, making him his Prime Minister and Minister of Planning; 12 out of the 22 ministries were given to Hutus. He was the first Hutu to hold the Premiership since the ill-fated Pierre Ngendandumwe, who was assassinated after a few months in office in 1985.

In March 1989 he blamed the Libyans for involvement in a coup plot and for trying to destabilise Burundi; 70 Libyans including the charge d'affaires were expelled from Burundi.

CAMEROON

Population: 11.98m (1990, World Bank)
Independence: 1 January 1960
Head of State: Paul Biya
Government: Opposition agitation led to the government adopting a new law on 6 December 1990 allowing for a multi-party form of government. New post of Prime Minister created May 1991. Elections due by end of 1991.
Parties: Government party, *Rassemblement Démocratique du Peuple Camerounais* (RDPC). Early in 1991 a host of opposition parties were registered including the Social Democratic Front (SDF) and the Union of Cameroonian People (UPC).

BIYA, Paul
President of Cameroon from 6 November 6 1982.

A civilised and highly educated man, with vast experience of government at the highest level. He is taking time to achieve the reforms that he first intended. He finds himself blocked by the entrenched Cameroonian bureaucracy and by the attitudes and policies of those in power during the Ahidjo era.

When he first took over from Ahmadou Ahidjo he promised to bring a new style of government and "more authentic democracy and an open society". At first there were some signs of relaxation of control and a freer press, but two coup attempts and the ingrained bureaucratic autocracy of the Cameroon system of government delayed real change. In 1990 Biya hesitated over the introduction of a multi-party system and resisted it, though an opposition party established itself under the provisions of the constitution.

Born 13 February 1933 in the southern village of Mvomeoka. Second son of a Catholic catechist, Etienne Assam of the Boulou tribe, a sub-division of the Fang.

Sent at the age of seven to the Catholic mission at Ndem. One of his French tutors thought him so promising that he set him on a religious career. At 17 he was sent to a Catholic seminary run by the Saint Esprit fathers at Akono. At 21 he went to the General Leclerc Lycee in Yaounde to study Latin, Greek and philosophy. He won a bursary to the University of Paris where he developed a taste for classical music, tennis and cycling.

Returned to Cameroon in 1962 and was appointed to President Ahidjo's office as head of the Department of Foreign Development Aid. Director of the Cabinet 1962-63. Head of the cabinet of Education

Minister William Mboumoua, who later became Secretary-General of the OAU. Back in the President's office 1967-68. Minister of State and Secretary-General to the President 1968-75. Further promoted by Ahidjo, he became Prime Minister in June 1975.

He also rose fast in the single party system, becoming a member of the Political Bureau of the Cameroon National Union (UNC) in 1980. When President Ahidjo resigned on 6 November 1982, worried by doctors' reports concerning his health, he handed over, in accordance with the Cameroonian constitution, to Paul Biya.

At first he had Ahidjo's blessing but Biya set about ridding himself of some of the former president's closest lieutenants and favourite ministers, many of whom were northeners, replacing them with his own men (often southerners).

On 22 August 1983 Biya announced the discovery of an attempted coup, which was largely interpreted as an attempt by Ahidjo to regain power if not for himself then for his northern comrades.

Biya called a special party congress in September 1983 and forced the resignation of Ahidjo from the party chairmanship and ensured his departure for exile in France. Biya then reshuffled his cabinet for the fourth time since his accession to power and declared his intention to redraw the provincial boundaries to give himself greater control. He did not appoint a new Prime Minister and concentrated more power in his own hands.

A much more serious coup attempt followed on 6 April 1983, when rebel elements from the presidential guard, formerly recruited by Ahidjo, attempted to seize the palace. Fighting raged for three days and the streets were littered with the bodies of fallen soldiers, though the government admitted only 73 dead.

He was overwhelmingly re-elected President on 14 January 1984. At the quinquennial congress of March 1985 he promised more democracy within the party, but said there was no question of permitting any opposition. He also had the party renamed as the *Rassemblement Democratique du Peuple Camerounais* (RPDC).

In August 1985 he carried out a wide-ranging reshuffle, dropping many of the more conservative ministers. Subsequent elections showed that he was allowing more choice of candidates within the party. In August 1986 Cameroon became the fourth black African state to restore diplomatic relations with Israel (first severed in 1973).

In the municipal elections of October 1987 multiple lists of candidates, approved by the party, were allowed for the first time. A similar system was used in the general elections of April 1988. In the Presidential election Biya was the sole candidate and obtained 98.75% of the votes cast.

In the first half of 1990 Cameroon was caught up in the continent-wide rush towards multi-party democracy. The dissidents noted that under the constitution the formation of other political parties was legal and proceeded to set up the Social Democratic Front, with much popular support.

At first Biya tried to suppress the growing movement and came down firmly in favour of the maintenance of a one-party state, saying his opponents based their case on foreign ideologies. But in mid-1990 he weakened in the face of determined opposition by politicians, students and sections of the press.

A wave of political agitation made him promise multi-party elections first by 1993, then by the end of 1991. He authorised the formation of opposition parties and passed some of his powers to a Prime Minister in April 1991.

BOOH BOOH, Jacques Roger

Cameroonian politician. Minister of External Relations, May 1988–

A highly qualified foreign affairs specialist who has spent his lifetime's career in the foreign ministry culminating in the prestigious ambassadorships to Moscow then France. He was called up as Minister of External affairs in May 1988 after President Biya had dismissed the former minister for making decisions without consulting him.

Born 5 February 1938 at Makak, in the Nyong and Kelle division of Centre Province. Educated locally and then at the University of Paris (Pantheon-Sorbonne) where he did a doctorate degree in law. His doctoral thesis was on the dynamics of the last battles of the liberation struggle in southern Africa. He also has a bachelor's degree in public law and diplomas from the French Institut des Hautes Etudes Internationales and Institut des Hautes Etudes d'Outre Mer, where he emerged as top of his class.

He returned to join the foreign ministry where he has been successively the Director of Africa/Asian affairs, Minister Counsellor, deputy permanent representative at the United Nations Minister Counsellor in Brussels. He then became the ambassador to Moscow 1981-83, and to France 1983-88.

When President Biya dismissed his former foreign minister William Eteki Mboumoua, over the recognition of Hungary, he called for the services of M. Booh Booh and made him Minister of External Relations in May 1988.

FONCHA, John Ngu

Cameroon politician. Former Vice-President, 1961-68.

A tireless advocate of union between British-ruled southern Cameroon and the French Cameroons, he devoted his political life into achieving this rather than unity with Nigeria. He had changed his country's destiny and was rewarded with the Vice-Presidency of the new Federal state set up in October 1961. But disappointment was to follow, he was not able to resist the pressures for total absorption into Eastern Cameroon. He left public life before President Ahidjo forced the country into a unitary state in June

1972. In May 1990 he resigned from the party and advocated multi-party democracy, becoming one of the most prominent national leaders to join the opposition movement.

Born 21 June 1916 at Bamenda in North-West Province. He went to the Bamenda Government School, St Michael's School Bunguma, Nigeria and the St.Charles Teacher Training College, Onitsha.

He taught at various Catholic schools in the Bamenda area from 1942. He spent his spare time in political organisation, first with the Cameroon Youth League, founded in 1943, then the Kamerun National Federation, (KNF) in 1949.

In December 1951 he was elected to Nigeria's Eastern House of Assembly. As parties formed and reformed, he remained faithful to the objective of eventual unification between Southern and Eastern Cameroon. He worked towards this goal first through the Kamerun United National Congress in 1951, then the Cameroon National Congress in 1953. When his colleagues again let him down in that party, he broke away to found the Kamerun National Democratic Party in 1955.

The KNDP became the official opposition in the Eastern House of Assembly and in the January 1959 elections won a 14-12 majority. He was sworn in as the Prime Minister of the quasi-federal territory of Southern Cameroon. He then refused to participate in the Nigerian Federal elections and demanded a plebiscite over the question of unification with Eastern Cameroon.

A referendum was called in February 1961 and he scored a resounding victory for unification. In July he met President Ahidjo who agreed to a Federation between the two Cameroons. On 1 October 1961 the Southern Cameroon joined the Republic of Cameroon, which had achieved its independence a year earlier. He became Vice-President of the new Federal Republic and at the same time Prime Minister of West Cameroon (formerly Southern Cameroon) which had its own House of Assembly.

In March 1965 he was re-elected Federal Vice-President but his KNDP party was absorbed into Ahidjo's Union Nationale Camerounaise (UNC) in 1966. Then in 1968 he was forced to resign and was replaced by Salomon Muna who was prepared to go along with Ahidjo in total unification of the Cameroon. Foncha left active politics in May 1970, before Cameroon became a unitary state in June 1972.

But he remained vice-president of the government party, the Rassemblement Democratique du Peuple Camerounais (RDPC) until May 1990, when a determined attempt was being made to establish an official opposition party. Suddenly he resigned his RDPC vice-presidency and declared himself in favour of a return to the Federal system and for the establishment of multi-party democracy. He was the most important political figure to make such a move and gave a major boost to the opposition movement.

HAYATOU, Sadou

Cameroonian politician. Prime Minister, 25 April 1991 -

A young and upwardly mobile technocrat who was thoroughly grounded in banking and commodity control before his rapid promotion to the ministries of Agriculture, Planning and then Finance. Much appreciated in international business circles, he is an able negotiator.

Born 1942 in Garoua. Educated locally then he went to France for secondary education at Vic-en-Bigorre and then at Toulouse university. He took a degree in Economics and a diploma from the Institut de Hautes Etudes d'Outre Mer in Paris.

On his return to Cameroon in 1968 he became assistant, later director in charge of basic commodities. He also came to international attention as vice-president of the Alliance of Cocoa Producing Countries (1969-70) and President of the Inter-African Coffee Organisation (1970-71).

In 1976 he became Directeur General of International Bank for Commerce and Industry in Cameroon (BICIC) and in 1979 Administrator DG. He was also promoted fast politically, becoming secretary for press, information and propaganda in the Central Committee of the *Rassemblement democratique du peuple Camerounais* (RDPC).

In July 1984 he was appointed Minister of Agriculture by President Paul Biya. On 24 August 1985 he was reshuffled to Planning and Territorial Administration. On 4 December 1987 he was promoted to Minister of Finance in order to tackle some of the problems left by his predecessor concerning non-payment of deals agreed between investors and the state and to effectively supervise the tightening of tax and customs controls. He has been given the specific task of organising the better collection of state revenue.

On 25 April 1991 Biya appointed him Prime Minister. It heralded a significant division of powers between the President and Hayatou who would be responsible for day to day government, and the appointment of the cabinet. His job was also to supervise the transition to pluralism and the holding of general elections.

MBELLA MBAPPE, Robert (Professor)

Cameroonian civil servant and politician. Director of President's Cabinet, November 1986.

A brilliant, protestant, law student turned ambitious politician holding the ministerial portfolios of Posts and Telecommunications and National Education before being given the key role as the Director of President Biya's own office (cabinet).

Born 21 October 1937 at Ebone. Primary eduction at the Protestant Mission school and at the regional school Douala Akwa before going on to the Lycee General Leclerc. Read law in France at the Ecole Nationale de la France d'Outre Mer, then at the Law and Science Faculty of

Bordeaux University. He continued highly successful law studies ending with a doctorate in Bordeaux in 1969.

Meanwhile, he returned to Cameroon and became a public prosecutor starting in Yaounde in 1966 and at the court of appeal in Garoua, 1967-70, rising to become principal secretary to the Attorney General in 1973 when he was made Chancellor of Yaounde university. Over 1980-83 he was the Attorney General at the Supreme Court.

On 18 June 1983 came his first full ministerial appointment when President Paul Biya made him Minister of Posts and Telecommunications. He was reshuffled on 7 July 1984 to National Education.

In 1985 he was elected to the Central Committee of the *Rassemblement Democratique du Peuple Camerounais* (RPDC) and secretary for organisation in the party. On 21 November 1986 President Biya spotted him as the right man to take control of his own office and made him director of his cabinet.

NGANGO, Georges

Cameroonian politician. Minister of Education November 1986 – April 1989.

Professor at Yaounde after more than a decade in France doing advanced studies in theology, law, economics and sociology. Paul Biya spotted his talent and made him Minister of Information in 1983 then Education in 1986. His downfall came when he tried to 'harmonise' the French and English systems of education, causing great resentment among the English speakers. This led to his dismissal in May 1989.

Born 17 June 1932 at Elongango, in Sanga Maritime. Educated locally before going to France 1959-62 to study theology at Strasbourg university, then Bordeaux 1962-64 and Lyon 1964-65 to do a four-year degree in economics. He did further doctoral studies in economics and sociology in France.

He returned to Cameroon and was put in charge of the faculty of Law and Economic Sciences at Yaounde university from 1971-73, becoming a professor at the University in 1974. He is the author of many economic and political publications including *Paul Biya or the incarnation of discipline*, which appeared in May 1983.

Paul Biya made him Minister in charge of Missions at the presidency, where he worked as a close presidential aide, before promoting him to Minister of Information and Culture on 18 June 1983 and then reshuffling him to Minister of National Education on 21 November 1986.

His sudden dismissal came in May 1989 following attempts to introduce radical reforms into the educational system. He tried to assimilate the General Certificate of Education used by English-speaking Cameroonians into the French Baccalaureat system. There has been a long tradition of resistance to attempts to tamper with the English-based educational system, so Ngango's new moves caused an outcry among English speakers. Rather than provoke a serious confrontation, President Biya decided to dismiss Ngango out of hand.

NGU, Niba John

Cameroonian businessman. Minister of Agriculture, May 1988–

Until 1988 he was known as the general manager of the Cameroon Development Corporation (CDC). Paul Biya brought him in as Minister of Agriculture at a critical time for the Cameroon economy.

Born 1932 at Baforchu, Mezam division in North West province. Educated locally and then at the prestigious St Joseph's College, Sasse near Buea, graduating in the early 1950s. He went to the University of Science and Technology in Kumasi, Ghana, then Britain to qualify as an accountant in 1959.

He returned to become secretary and chief accountant of the West Cameroon Development Agency 1960-65. In 1965 went to the *Banque des Etats de l'Afrique Centrale* (BEAC) in Paris to study French banking systems.

He returned in 1960 and was appointed State Controller in the Presidency before being seconded to the CDC in March 1968 as assistant financial controller. He was promoted to financial controller in 1970 and general manager in December 1974. After being returned for a second term as President, Paul Biya carried out a major reshuffle in May 1988 and appointed Ngu to his first ministry as Minister of Agriculture. There his task was to increase agricultural production and exports to help counter the deteriorating economic situation.

TESSA, Paul

Cameroonian politician. Minister of Works and Transport May 1989–

The ultimate technocrat. Paul Tessa has worked in a whole host of Cameroonian ministries and in two Presidents' offices as a top adviser. He briefly held the post of Secretary -General to the Presidency, in Paul Biya's cabinet, a post which replaced that of the Prime Minister in 1964.

Born 10 August 1938 at Fomopea in Dschang. Educated locally, entering the junior seminary at Melong and later the Lycee Leclerc. He then left for France where he studied public law and political science.

He returned home in 1965 and worked at the General State Inspectorate 1965-69. He then became Charge de Mission and technical adviser at the Presidency under President Ahmadou Ahidjo, 1969-73. His first full ministerial appointment came in 1972 when he was made Minister of Equipment, Housing and Lands. In 1976 he was named technical adviser to the Ministry of Economic Affairs and Planning and later Chief of the Judicial Affairs department in the Ministry of Trade and Industry. He became Secretary General to the President on 16 May 1988 and Minister of Works and Transport on 13 May 1989.

CAPE VERDE

Population: 371,000 (1990, World Bank)
Independence: 5 July 1975
Head of State: Antonio Monteiro
Government: Free multi-party elections held on 13 January 1991 for the first time since independence. This led to the defeat of the government by the Movement for Democracy (MPD). On 17 February Aristides Pereira was defeated by Antonio Monteiro who took 73.5% of the vote. He then became President.
Parties: Majority party Movement for Democracy (MPD). Former ruling party - *Partido Africano da Independencia de Cabo Verde* (PAICV).

MONTEIRO, Antonio Manuel Mascarenhas Gomes
Cape Verde President, 17 February 1991 –

After giving his early support to the liberation cause he soon became disillusioned with the marxist policies of the PAIGC and concentrated on his academic and legal calling. He returned home to pursue a brilliant career as president of the national assembly and later the supreme court, before challenging President Pereira in the first democratic presidential elections in February 1991 when he triumphed handsomely.

Born 16 February 1944 at Santa Caterina, on the island of Santiago. He did his primary education at Assomada and secondary studies at the Liceu de Praia, in the capital. He decided to study law and went first to Lisbon University and then Coimbra, both in Portugal, where he took his masters degree in law. In 1967 he left hurriedly for Belgium in order to avoid being conscripted into the Portuguese colonial army. There he completed his doctorate degree at the Catholic University of Louvain, before taking up a job at the inter-university law centre.

There he joined the *Partido Africano da Independencia do Guine e Cabo Verde (PAIGC)* and took part in the liberation struggle (1969-71) before breaking with the party over its marxist ideology.

In 1977, two years after independence, he returned home and became secretary general of the National Assembly, then judge in the Supreme Court and finally president of the Supreme Court (1980-90). During this period he led a number of Cape Verdian delegations abroad and helped the OAU draw up a new charter on human and people's rights.

As the winds of democratisation swept Cape Verde at the end of 1990, he decided to challenge the sitting President Aristidies Pereira in the Presidential elections. He was given the backing of the new opposition party *Movimento Para Democracia*(MPD). In the assembly elections of January, the MPD swept the poll and its candidate Carlos Veiga became Prime Minister. The first contested presidential elections since independence, followed in February. The MPD was flush with its earlier successes and swept Montieiro to victory taking 73.5% of the total vote. He triumphed in all the individual islands as well as in the overall poll. He was formally sworn in on 22 March 1991.

PEREIRA, Aristides Maria

Former Cape Verde President, 5 July 1975 – 17 February 1991.

A pragmatic, intellectual, founder-member of the PAIGC and a veteran of the liberation struggle in Guinea-Bissau against the Portuguese. He tried to hold the two diverse territories together after independence in his capacity as leader of the party, but after the Bissau coup in September 1980, he accepted the situation and concentrated his energies as President of Cape Verde. He was challenged in the first multi-party elections in February 1991 and heavily defeated.

Born 1924 on Boa Vista island, Cape Verde, where he was educated before being trained as a telecommunications engineer. He became increasingly involved in nationalist politics against the Portuguese. He was one of the founder members of the African Party for the Independence of Guinea and Cape Verde, (PAIGC) in 1956. In 1959 he led a strike. His political activities increasingly irritated the authorities as he was chief of telecommunications until he decided to leave and join the PAIGC in exile in Conakry, the capital of the Republic of Guinea, in 1960. There he became a member of the Political Bureau and the Central Committee. When the liberation struggle got underway in 1961, he left for Guinea Bissau and organised the party clandestinely in Bissau and other urban areas.

In 1964 he became joint secretary-general of the PAIGC, in effect second-in-command to Amilcar Cabral. He became a member of the War Council in 1965 and in 1970 a member of the Executive Committee for the War with specific responsibility for security and foreign affairs. On Cabral's assassination in Conakry on 20 January 1973, he assumed the leadership of the party. He retained this position after Guinea Bissau's independence was formally recognised by Portugal on 10 September 1974, but when Cape Verde also became independent on 5 July 1975 he returned home to Cape Verde, stood for elections and won a decisive victory. The assembly then elected him as President.

He established a one-party state that was comparatively tolerant. Those arrested for an attempted coup in 1977 were released under amnesty in 1979. Attempts to forge union with Guinea Bissau finally floundered with the coup of November 1980. Pereira was still technically leader of the PAIGC in both countries, but after the coup all links were deleted from the constitution and the Cape Verde branch of the party, renamed itself the African Party for the Independence of Cape Verde (PAICV). Pereira remained its President.

Pereira was re-elected President in February 1981 and relations with

Bissau were restored in June 1982, with a mutual co-operation agreement following in February 1988. He paid a visit to Bissau in April 1989.

Pereira's main problem as President was sheer economic survival with a huge increase in population, no room for agricultural expansion and recurring drought. The economy has teetered on the brink of disaster through the 1980s.

In 1990 Cape Verde was caught up in the continent-wide rush towards multi-party democracy. In February 1990 the National Council of the party met under Pereira and decided to revise the constitution to allow other parties to participate. It also decided that the Presidential elections of December 1990 would be held under direct universal suffrage for the first time, rather than by the chamber of deputies. Pereira welcomed and encouraged this transition to democracy.

On 26 July 1990 he said that he was standing down as party leader because the President had to be above party politics. It was also a first step towards democratisation.

His party was defeated in the January 1991 assembly elections and the omens for the first presidential elections to be held under a pluralist system, were bad. He was heavily defeated everywhere except in the remotest islands and gained less than 30% of the poll. His opponent Antonio Monteiro was duly elected. He accepted his defeat with dignity. He said the people had chosen "by democratic means without social upheaval," showing they were masters of their own destiny.

PIRES, Pedro Verona Rodrigues
Cape Verde politician. Prime Minister July 1975 – 14 January 1991

It is unusual for presidential deputies to survive long in African politics, but Pedro Pires is an exception. He has remained the friend and loyal deputy of President Aristides Pereira since the death of Amilcar Cabral in January 1973, before independence. He was responsible for negotiating independence in 1974 both for Cape Verde and Guinea Bissau with the Portuguese and has been Prime Minister of Cape Verde ever since.

Born 29 April 1934 at the Ilha do Togo. Educated at Licee Gil Eanes de Sao Vincente and at Lisbon University where he read science. He left Portugal to return home in 1961 and join the African Party for the Independence of Guinea and Cape Verde (PAIGC) in the liberation struggle. He became a member of the party's central committee in 1965 and a member of the Permanent Committee of the War Council (CEL).

Operating from the liberated areas of Guinea Bissau, he was the commander for the southern frontier region. He was involved in the administration of the large parts of Guinea Bissau that had been liberated by the PAIGC over 1971–74. He rose to the rank of Major. He became Pesident of the National Committee for the Liberation of Cape Verde in 1973, assistant state commissioner in the first Government of Guinea Bissau, 1973–74. In 1974 he led the negotiations for independence with the government of Gen Antonio de Spinola, which had taken over from Salazar, and signed the agreement on 10 September 1974 which formally brought independence.

He became the director of PAIGC policies during the transitional government prior to independence at the beginning of 1975. He stood for elections and was elected a deputy to the national assembly in Praia in June. At independence on 5 July 1975, he became Prime Minister and made his maiden speech in Mindelo, capital of northern Cape Verde on 7 July, calling for hard work, austerity, and non-alignment. He became a member of the permanent committee of CEL in 1977.

After the coup of November 1980 in which Guinea Bissau broke from the union with Cape Verde, he became Deputy Secretary General (still under Aristides Pereira) of the renamed African Party for the Independence of Cape Verde (PAICV).

On 27 July 1990 when Pereira stepped down from party leadership at an extraordinary congress of the PAICV Pires was unanimously elected to take over.

In the first multi-party elections of January 1991 the PAICV party was heavily defeated by the new Democratic Movement (MPD) party, losing two thirds of its assembly seats. Carlos Viega became the new Prime Minister and Pires tendered his resignation on 14 January 1991.

VEIGA, Carlos Alberto Wahnon de Carvalho
Prime Minister, 26 January 1991 -

Unlike his rivals in the former ruling party he was neither a freedom fighter, nor a marxist ideologue. Always an individualist, he first came to politics as an independent member of parliament, then as the coordinator of the opposition. He was the right man at the right time. His rise to power coincided with popular rejection of the one party system and the wave of democratisation and political reform that was sweeping the African continent.

Born: 1950 in Mindelo, Sao Vincente to Alfredo Jose, the eldest of five children. After doing studies locally he went to the University of Lisbon in 1971 to take a law degree.

Following a brief tour in Angola, another Portuguese colony, he returned to Cape Verde after independence, on 5 July 1975. He soon became involved in nationalist politics, joining the *Partido Africano da Independencia do Guine e Cabo Verde* (PAIGC). He became a judge in the Ministry of Public Administration (1975-80), then Director General for Internal Administration and finally Attorney General.

In 1979 he left the party, then renamed the PAICV, after the break with Guinea. He had been accused, along with Education Minister Manuel Faustino, of leading a Trotskyist faction. He claimed that he left in protest against the party's rigidity and illiberalism.

He became president of the Cape Verdean bar association (1982-86). He also ran a thriving law practice in the capital, Praia, where he acted as legal consultant to various state companies and buisinesses.

In 1985 he stood as an independent candidate for the National Assembly. He won a seat despite the near monopoly of the party and became deputy vice president of the Special Permanent Commission on constitutional and legal issues (1985-90).

He was soon identified as an independent thinking liberal, concerned about human rights and economic decentralisation. His timing was right as the Cape Verde became caught up in the drive towards democratisation and multi-party government that was sweeping Africa. In 1990 he was elected president of an opposition coalition, the *Movimento Para Democracia* (MPD) an association of about 600 technocrats and intellectuals who were calling for democratic reform. In April it issued a manifesto in Paris demanding a multi-party system. He found the PAICV party in a receptive mood having already accepted *de facto* multi-partyism at its third party congress in November 1988.

On 3 June 1990 the MPD called a meeting of about 800 people at Praia. Veiga told the government that his party was willing to discuss the transition to democracy with them or any other political force. It also called for revocation of article four of the constitution which enshrined the PAICV as the sole party.

The two parties met at a round table conference on 22 September and agreed a date for democratic elections. In November the MPD became a political party and declared itself in favour of flexible bureaucracy and true and effective administrative decentralisation. Carlos Veiga was formally installed as President-founder.

In the elections of January 1991, the MPD which had only been in existence for 10 months, scored a heavy defeat over the PAICV which had dominated Cape Verde from the time of independence. It took more than two thirds of the parliamentary seats, winning 56 to the PAICV's 23. The defeated premier and PAICV leader promptly resigned on 14 January and Veiga was called upon to form a government. He commented, " We won because we were able to articulate and respond to popular dissatisfaction simmering for many years which the PAICV failed to perceive...Our biggest virtue was to voice the discontent of the people and the need for change."

He appointed a cabinet full of young technocrats like himself, "a government of individuals with proven competence who will assume responsibility for their performance."

He promised to dissolve the political police and eliminate the "left-overs of the one party state." But he said that he would not change foreign policy radically.

The Presidential elections remained to be fought. Here Antonio Mascarenhas Monteiro, for the MPD, challenged President Aristides Pereira a man who had fought for independence against Portuguese colonialism. But Monteiro won gaining 73.5% of the vote and assumed the Presidency. Veiga remained Prime Minister and is responsible for day to day government. His challenge is to revive the poor, drought stricken economy and to encourage tourism.

CENTRAL AFRICAN REPUBLIC

Population: 2.92m (1990, World Bank)
Independence: 13 August 1960
Head of State: General André Kolingba
Government: Presidential government under a single party system, ruling through a mainly civilian council of ministers, but a national commission charged with revising the constitution and laying the groundwork for pluralism was set up on 7 June 1991.
Parties: Sole official party - *Rassemblement Démocratique Centrafricain* (RDC). There are a number of active opposition parties, based overseas, grouped under the *Parti Revolutionnaire Centrafricain* (PRC).

BOKASSA, Jean Bedel

Central African Republic, President 1 January 1966 - 20 September 1979

Once "Emperor" of the Central African Empire (Republic), he is now living out the remainder of his life in prison after being found guilty for murder and embezzlement during his regime. A diminutive and ageing figure, but once one of the most feared dictators on the African continent.

Born 22 February 1921, the son of a village chief. When he was only six years old his father was assassinated and his mother committed suicide, leaving a family of 12. This unstable background may go some of the way to explain his strange character.

His uncle Barthelemy Boganda, hailed as the first politician and father of the Central African Republic, died in an air crash four months after he had led his country to self-government.

Jean Bedel was educated at mission schools in different parts of the country, but he had a minimum formal education when he joined the Free French army at the age of 18. He fought with the Free French forces which liberated the neighbouring city of Brazzaville. Later he went to Indo-China and won 12 medals in the field, an experience which made him a great medal collector throughout his life. He was commissioned in 1949 and left the French army in 1961 as a captain.

With independence in August 1960, President David Dacko asked him to establish a Central African army and he rose to become Commander-in-Chief in January 1963 and Chief of General Staff in 1964. When Dacko got into trouble trying to prune his corrupt, overpaid, civil service, it gave Bokassa the chance to intervene which he did on New Year's Eve, 1966. He arrested Dacko, abrogated the constitution and promoted himself President.

He then concentrated on keeping himself in power and as he bent the state and the army to his will, he became increasingly autocratic and demanding.

He made himself life President and later in December 1977 had himself crowned as Emperor of his tiny country. In one of the poorest countries in Africa, he lavished £14 million on his own personal glorification and on the imperial trappings that he considered appropriate.

He became increasingly unpopular and extreme, participating personally in acts of savage barbarism. He personally led his police in beating up vagrants in front of his palace and took part in the beating of schoolchildren who had refused to buy and wear uniforms provided by his wife's clothing factory. Many school children died.

Eventually his sadism and paranoia lost him most of his friends and France connived at his replacement on 20 September 1979, by David Dacko, the man he had earlier toppled. He then went into exile in the Ivory Coast but he proved to be a difficult guest who would not respect the niceties of Ivorian hospitality and eventually took refuge in France.

But he was never happy there, and became so short of money that he could not pay his heating bills in the European winter. He began a campaign to be allowed to return home, but his compatriots refused to accept him. After seven years in a cold and foreign land he simply got on a plane and risking all returned home on 23 October 1986. Instead of the welcoming crowds that he expected, he was immediately put in prison and eventually tried on charges of murder and embezzlement.

The trial lasted for many months and though he tried to defend himself and blame others, he was eventually convicted and sentenced to death by firing squad, in June 1987. He had been found guilty of a series of gruesome crimes and he had even been accused of cannibalism by some witnesses, though this was not proven. All appeals in the Higher courts were rejected. However, General André Kolingba, the current ruler, after consulting his Higher Justice Commission commuted the sentence to forced labour for life. He spends most of his time in a four feet by six feet cell in the De Roux military camp swatting flies with a well thumbed bible and telling stories of the girls he used to chase in Paris during the World War.

GBEZERA-BRIA, Michel

Central African Republic politician. Minister of Foreign Affairs, 5 July 1988 - 5 July 1990.

A man whose whole career has been in the foreign service, under Bokassa and the Presidents who followed. After distinguished service through the early 1980s as his country's Permanent Representative to the United Nations, he returned home to have his career crowned with his appointment as Foreign Minister in July 1988. He was sacked, in a general purge of ministers by Kolingba, in July 1990.

Born 1946 at Boussougoa. Educated locally and at Brazzaville Law School. He went to France to the Caen school of economics and the Institute of Public Administration. He returned home and joined the civil service in 1973, earning his first ministerial appointment under Bokassa as vice-minister in charge of diplomatic missions in 1975. In 1976 he became Deputy Minister of Foreign Affairs and on 18 July 1978 Minister of Public Works, Labour and Social Security.

He was shuffled to State Comptroller over 1979-80, until the new President David Dacko appointed him as his country's Permanent Representative to the United Nations in Geneva, 1980-83 and then to the United Nations in New York, 1983-88. He was brought home for a short spell as Minister of Justice before being appointed Foreign Minister on 5 July 1988.

KOLINGBA, André (General)
Central African Republic President, 1 September 1981-

Very much a soldier's soldier. A man of style, always fashionably dressed with a strong belief in traditional values, strong personal leadership and friendship with France and the West. He claimed that he took power in September 1981 to prevent a breakdown of law and order. He imposed firm but comparatively humane military rule. Gradually he has civilianised government, bringing in civilians as ministers and through the party, while maintaining firm personal control as Head of State. But he has never had anyone executed during his tenure of office, no matter what the offence.

Born 1935 in the Yakoma tribe. After a general education, he joined the French army and became a career officer, winning rapid promotion, 1954-62. He transferred to the nascent Central African army on independence and rose fast to become a general in 1973. He was appointed ambassador to Canada in 1975 and subsequently to West Germany. He was promoted Chief of Staff of the armed forces in July 1981 by President David Dacko, a weak, indecisive and sickly leader who had been restored to power by the French two years previously. The regime was unstable, plagued by strikes and demonstrations. A bomb attack by an opposition group on a Bangui cinema revealed the underlying discontent.

This gave Kolingba his chance to intervene in a bloodless coup on 1 September 1981. He said that he had "demanded and obtained" Dacko's resignation and that he had taken "full presidential powers." He said the country had experienced a "sterile and violent six months in which there had been violations of democracy and intolerable challenges to reason, honour and rights."

He suspended the constitution and banned all activities by political parties until further notice. He called for a privileged relationship to continue with France. He wanted France to pay the salaries of the civil service for at least a year. He said that this would "leave his hands free to reorganise the country and lay the foundations for economic recovery."

He set up a full military regime under a Committee for National Recovery consisting entirely of soldiers. He said, "Of course the new ministers may not be qualified, but they are leaders and we already have the technicians. Above all we need leaders and law and order. When we have order everything else will follow."

Though he first talked about returning the country to civilian rule, the military held on to power for four years. By 1985 he felt able to democratise government, appointing civilians to the majority of posts. Opposition, manifest in a number of minor coup attempts and student protest, was handled firmly, but with certain compassion. Unlike Bokassa, Kolingba never executed anyone no matter what the offence.

He imposed a classical African-style military government, firm but fair, heavily dependent on France and struggling with an economy that has few natural resources except some diamonds and coffee. Lack of finance forced him to accept IMF reforms and conditionalities.

In May 1986 he announced the creation of a single party, the Rassemblement Democratique Centrafricain (RDC). In November 1986 a referendum was held in which he asked for a further six-year mandate as Head of State, a consolidation of his powers and a legislature with largely advisory functions. He secured approval from 91% of the electorate. In December he reshuffled his ministers and strengthened his own position still further by taking personal responsibility for the defence portfolio. In July 1987 he authorised the first legislative elections for 20 years.

Jean Bedel Bokassa caused considerable embarrassment when he returned unexpectedly from exile on 23 October 1986. Kolingba immediately put him under arrest and later on trial on charges of murder and embezzlement. The trial lasted many months and he was eventually convicted and sentenced to death by firing squad in June 1987, but Kolingba commuted the sentence to life imprisonment.

He came under pressure in early 1990 from a large group of civil servants, intellectuals and former ministers to reform the single party system. His response was to call an extraordinary meeting of the executive committee of the party and to reject multi-partyism, warning of the dangers of accepting "political systems which seemed to work in other countries."

As a first step towards democratisation he agreed to sharing his powers with a Prime Minister, by appointing Edouard Frank to that post on 16 March 1991. He promised democracy and multi-party rule on 22 April and set up a national commission to revise the constitution and lay the groundwork for pluralism on 7 June 1991.

CHAD

Population: 5.72m (1990, World Bank)
Independence: 11 August 1960
Head of State: Idriss Déby
Government: Presidential rule through a Council of Ministers under
a single party, but following a national conference in May 1991
commissions have been established to introduce pluralism,
fundamental rights and freedoms and hold elections in May 1992.
Parties: The government coalition party is the *Mouvement
Patriotique du Salut* (MPS), the party of Idriss Déby.

ACHIEK Ibn Oumar, Sayyid

Chad politician and guerrilla leader. Special adviser to the President, 18
December 1990 –

*One of the original warriors of the Chadian civil war who started with
the pro-Libyan Democratic Revolutionary Council, (CDR) under its boss
Ahmat Acyl. Since handing in his guns he has devoted more time to
another passion, that of writing prolifically for pamphlets and magazines.
He was a decade younger than the other principal Chadian leaders. When
Ahmat died in July 1982, he took over the leadership when still only 31
years old. Goukouni Oueddi, the other key opposition figure, wanted him
to join his Transitional Government of National Unity, (GUNT) but
Achiek was his own man, briefly ousting Oueddi from the GUNT
leadership in 1986. But when Libya grew tired of war he began
negotiations with the Habré government, finally returning home, in
November 1988, and taking on the Ministry of Foreign Affairs in March
1989. He survived the December 1990 coup by Idriss Déby and became his
presidential adviser.*

Born 1951 at Batha of Arab descent. He came into political prominence
as a member of Ahmat Acyl's Democratic Revolutionary Council (CDR),
the pro-Libyan group. After the first Kano peace conference in March
1979 he was given a minor post in the first Transitional Government of
National Unity (GUNT) and was then promoted to Minister of Labour
and Minister of Education on 12 July 1981. When Hissene Habré took
Ndjamena in June 1982, Acyl Ahmat and Achiek joined with Wadelkader
Kamougué's forces to resist his advance southwards.

Ahmat Acyl was killed in a bizarre accident when he walked into the
propeller of an aeroplane and Achiek assumed the leadership of the CDR
on 19 July 1982. Habré triumphed in the south and Achiek withrew to
Salamat and Biltine in the east, where he was near the Sudanese border.
He also served as Minister of Defence in the GUNT government in exile.
But he was never entirely happy in his alliance with Goukouni Oueddi,
whose GUNT was suffering from a series of splits and defections. Achiek

was dismissed as minister in August and he concentrated on the leadership of his own CDR party.

But in November 1984 he was detained by GUNT forces in northern Chad for almost a year until he was prepared to sign the Cotonou agreement of August 1985, setting up a coalition of opposition parties. Goukouni said that he would only release him if he would sign the agreement, so Achiek had little alternative. But Goukouni's hold over him did not last; by 11 August 1986 Achiek pulled the CDR out of the new alliance and fighting broke out between the forces of the two men in the Ennedi mountains. Habré then made overtures to bring him over to the government side, though Achiek protested that both sides were equally responsible for the sorry situation in Chad.

In yet another bizarre change of course, in November 1986, Goukouni boycotted a meeting called by most factions of GUNT in Cotonou and Achiek was elected as the new leader. He then set out on a tour of sympathetic African countries explaining why he had assumed command. But by July 1987 he was removed from the leadership of his own CDR, because, in the words of the new leaders, he had been incapable of leading the CDR and preventing the split in GUNT which had led to the loss of northern Chad to Habré.

As the opposition leaders defected and divided, some going over to Habré, Gadaffi decided to accept defeat in northern Chad and recognise the Habré government. Achiek was arrested briefly in mid-June 1988 in Libya, but Gadaffi continued his negotiations with Habré. It was then that Achiek decided to turn the page once and for all and wipe out the aftermath of the civil war by working for peace, saying that he was in favour of, direct, immediate and unconditional talks with the current regime. Though the Chadian government at first queried his sincerity, on 19 November 1988 he signed a reconciliation agreement with Habré in Iraq, returned to Ndjamena on 20 November and attended Habré's party Congress. In mid-December 1,000 of Achiek's CDR also returned from the Sudan and were integrated in the government forces. Achiek was rewarded by being made minister of Foreign Affairs on 3 March 1989. When Idriss Deby took power he retained Achiek as his presidential adviser.

DEBY, Idriss
Head of State, 4 December 1990 –

A former Chief of Staff and loyal supporter of the Chad President Hissene Habré who became involved in a coup plot against his former leader in April 1989 and fled the country. He then became Habré's most formidable opponent, heading a small army based in Sudan's Darfur region supported by Colonel Gadaffi and by the Sudanese government. After a brilliant campaign, lasting just a few weeks, he seized power in December 1990.

Born 1956. A Zaghawa (Bidayet or Beri) in the remote Fada oasis in
Ennedi, eastern Chad. He joined the army in the early 1970s, passing
out at the officer cadet school in Ndjamena in 1975. In 1976 he went to
France to qualify as a pilot at the Aeronautic Institute at
Amaury-le-Grange at Hazebrouck. He rallied to Hissene Habré in 1978,
forging the alliance between his own Zaghawa and Habré's Daza people.
As Chief-of-Staff of Habré's Forces Armes du Nord (FAN), he was a hero
of the campaign that restored his leader to power, leading his troops into
Ndjamena on 2 June 1982 and immediately afterwards into southern
Chad. As Chief-of-Staff of the government forces and close colleague of
Habré in the Ndjamena government, he repulsed Goukouni Oueddi in
the campaign of mid-1983. But Habré became suspicious and sent him
to a do a higher officer training course in Paris, in 1985, where he
developed excellent contacts with the French top brass. On his return
Habré made him his military adviser.

But as Habré consolidated his position in 1988 and began to share
power with other returning refugees, he became less dependent on his
Zaghawa supporters, like Déby, and they found their efforts to build a
power base in the Ndjamena government were frustrated. On 1 April
1989 Déby and two other close colleagues were accused of plotting a coup
in which the new Foreign Minister, Achiek Ibn Oumar came near to
assassination. Déby and his troops fought their way to the Sudanese
border and after several skirmishes, escaped into exile, but his colleague
Hassan Djamous, the former army commander, was captured and killed.
Déby escaped to Darfur, then proceeded to Lagos. On 8 April he issued
a press statement in Lagos accusing the government of tribalism,
extortion and injustice.

He later went to Libya where he briefed Colonel Gadaffi on what he
knew of Habré's plans and troop dispositions. Gadaffi then encouraged
him to set up in opposition in Libya and raise fresh troops while liaising
with dissident elements inside Chad. He responded by establishing his
own political movement, the *Mouvement Patriotique du Salut* (MPS),
allied to the National Salvation Front and taking the battle to Habré in
Sudan's Darfur province in October 1989. His troops were involved in
fierce fighting inside Chad in March 1990, where there were heavy
casualties on both sides.

With Libyan financial and material support Déby led his MPS
guerrillas across the Sudanese border in November 1990. He fought a
series of pitched battles with government forces. Despite Habré's
personal intervention, he met little resistance from government troops.
His guerrillas crossed the breadth of the country in just over two weeks
and seized Ndjamena at the beginning of December 1990, putting Habré
to flight.

He was appointed Head of State on 4 December 1990 and set up a
Council of State, with an Executive Committee dominated by his own
MPS party. Other parties provided ministers.

Though his story is complex, he got rid of the Libyans and gradually convinced his rivals to abandon opposition and return home to join the government.

DJIDINGAR, Dono-Ngardoum (Michel)
Chadian politician and minister.

A veteran politician and southern traditional leader who has served with most regimes from the days he was one of the first members of the pre-independence legislative assemblies and Chad's representative to the French Community, to the present time. Self-educated, he is a good mixer, easy-going and affable. This has led him to many important board jobs with African and international organisations which he has held with great tenacity while surviving Chad's bewildering changes of fortune.

Born 1928 at Dono-Manga. A traditional farmer with little schooling, the son of a *chef du canton*. Over his lifetime he has had ten wives and more than 30 children. His keen interest in politics led him to victory in the Territorial Assembly in 1957 and the Legislative Assembly as member for Logone on 31 May 1959. He also became a senator to the French Community. President Francois Tombalbaye made him Minister of Finance, Posts and Telecommunications in 1961, ministries he held, with small variations to his portfolios, throughout the 1960s at a time Tombalbaye carried out frequent purges. He became a member of the political bureau of the ruling Chad Progressive Party, (PPT) and later of the executive committee of the National Movement for the Cultural and Social Revolution (MNCRS).

On 23 May 1971 he became Minister of Agriculture and Rural Development, and in 1973, Minister of Stockbreeding. He remained in the cabinet until the coup of April 1975 when he retired to become mayor of his hometown, Logone.

Goukouni Oueddi brought him back to serve in his *Gouvernement d'union nationale de transition* (GUNT) as his Prime Minister from 16 May 1982 until Hissene Habré seized power on 19 June 1982. He was retained as Minister of Agriculture and Rural Development. He founded the *Rassemblement d'Unité et Démocratie Tchadienne* which urged national reconciliation. Habré appreciated its value as he tried to get his opponents to defect and return to Ndjamena. He was made Minister without portfolio in March 1986 and then Minister for State in the President's office in September 1987.

DJOGO, Djibril Négué (General)
Chadian soldier. Minister of Transport and Civil Aviation, 3 March 1989 – 4 December 1990.

A popular and able soldier without strong political feelings except loyalty to his own southern people, he tried tirelessly to find a constant role in Chad's turbulent politics. He was the loyal servant of successive regimes and became best known as Goukouni Oueddi's number two and chief of staff. But when Hissené Habré finally established himself in June 1982, he became disillusioned with the quarrelling politicians in exile and was one of the first to rejoin the Ndjamena government in December 1985.

Born 1932 into a Catholic family in the southern Sara region. He joined the French colonial forces and was sent for training to the Ecole General Leclerc in Congo-Brazzaville. He went to France for officers training at Frejus and St Maxient and won his paratroop wings. He fought in the Algerian civil war and served later in Ouagadougou, Upper Volta (Burkina Faso). On his return to Chad in 1964, he was made deputy chief of staff of the armed forces and commander of the first infantry battalion. After a quarrel with his superior officer he was sent to be military prefect in the far north, Bourkou-Ennedi-Tibesti, and army commander of the northern sector.

President Francois Tombalbaye suddenly recalled him in 1967 to be commander of the gendarmerie. He earned a reputation as an efficient soldier and was promoted fast, becoming a general and head of Tombalbaye's military cabinet in July 1972. But on 2 April 1972 he was arrested following clashes between his gendarmerie and Tombalbaye's presidential guard. The real coup came two weeks later on 13 April, organised by General Odingar. Djogo was released, promoted to the Supreme Military Council (CSM) and made Minister of Finance.

On 13 April 1976 his wife was injured during a grenade attack on General Malloum. On 28 May Malloum reorganised the army, establishing a National Defence Commission with Djogo as its secretary-general. When Goukouni Oueddi took power in February 1979, Djogo found himself as the representative of the south in the various Governments of National Unity and Transition (GUNT) which followed. He was briefly Vice-President and Deputy Premier before retiring with the remnants of the Chadian forces to Sarh, the capital of the south.

Hissené Habré took Ndjamena in June 1982 and Djogo, still a GUNT man, eventually joined Goukouni Oueddi in the north, who made him chief-of-staff of his *Armée du Liberation National*. He led the attacks on Faya Largeau and Abéché in June and July 1983. It was only French intervention and defence of the 15th parallel that prevented a final assault on Ndjamena.

But as Goukouni's offensive ground to a halt, Djogo became increasingly disenchanted with his leadership and on 21 March 1985 set up a new opposition group the Chad Democratic Front (FTD) comprising various smaller opposition parties in exile. As Goukouni's hold became weaker, Djogo found that his *codos* (commandos) in Southern Chad had gone over to Habré, so he too decided to throw in his lot with the established government in December 1975 and returned to Ndjamena. He told a news conference that he had come to the conclusion that there was no armed solution to the civil war and urged other exiles to follow his example and return home. On 23 March 1986 Habré appointed him Minister of Justice. He then played a major part in encouraging other exiles to return home. He was reshuffled to Minister of Transport and

Civil Aviation on 3 March 1989. He retained that ministry until the coup of Idriss Déby in December 1990.

HABRÉ, Hissené
Chadian guerrilla leader. President 21 October 1982 - 1 December 1990.

Of all Chad's war lords Hissené Habré was the most aggressive, determined and consistent. Tall, handsome and a brilliant student he built up a network of contacts in France. Though still comparatively young, his whole career was devoted to achieving and holding power in his country. His ruthless determination and organisational skill brought him victory for a time, but the battle was long and ferocious against a host of rivals, particularly Goukouni Oueddi backed by his powerful Libyan allies. When Habré took power in Ndjamena for the second time in June 1982, he convinced France and the USA that the survival of Chad depended on him alone and he won their grudging support. It was when he lost the support of France, in December 1990 that he was pushed from power by Idriss Déby.

Born 1936 in Faya Largeau, the son of a Dadza (Toubou) shepherd. Educated locally, he obtained employment as a clerk in the Pioneer corps of the French army. He went into government service and was rapidly promoted both by the French and President Francois Tombalbaye. He was made deputy prefect of Moussoro in 1963. He was sent to Paris for higher education at the *Ecole des Sciences Politiques* and went on to read law, returning to Ndjamena in 1971.

He returned to government service and soon President Tombalbaye sent him to negotiate with Abba Siddik, the leader of the *Front de Liberation Nationale*, FROLINAT. Siddik promptly converted him to the FROLINAT cause but he was unhappy with Siddik's cautious leadership and the two soon fell out. Siddik, in his turn, accused him of being a CIA spy and stooge of the French. Habré then teamed up with Goukouni Oueddi and became the joint leader of the *Forces Armées Nationales* (FAN) in the Tibesti mountains, in the north of the country.

On 21 April 1974 his forces, estimated at less than 500, attacked Bardai and attracted international attention when he captured several Europeans including Christophe Staewen, a cousin of the West German President, and Françoise Claustre, a French lady archaeologist. West Germany paid a ransom for Staewen but France refused and Claustre remained his prisoner until January 1977. He fell out with Goukouni over the Claustre affair and Habré tried to go it alone with a small army of a few hundred men. But he found this isolation difficult to sustain and made his peace with President Malloum and joined a government of national union as Prime Minister on 29 August 1978. But lack of trust between him and Malloum led to a struggle for power, Goukouni took advantage of this and within a few months captured Ndjamena at the end of the year.

After a series of peace meetings and realignments Habré was made Minister of Defence in the weak and disorganised *Gouvernement d'Union Nationale de Transition*, (GUNT) but he was determined not to play second fiddle to Goukouni for long and on 22 March 1980 fighting broke out between his FAN forces and those of FAT. The fighting continued for nine months, much of the capital was destroyed and Habré hung on until he was finally expelled by the intervention of Libyan troops. By 14 December 1980 Habré's troops were defeated and he was forced to flee into exile, first to the Cameroon and later to Sudan where he rebuilt his army with the help of the CIA. While the OAU called for a ceasefire and organised a peacekeeping force, Habré proceeded to invade the north and after a series of spectacular successes in the field, taking one town after another in May, he finally captured Ndjamena on 7 June 1982.

On 19 June 1982 he declared himself interim Head of State, established a Council of State and pursued the war against Abdelkader Kamougué's forces in the south, finally forcing him into exile in August. On 21 October 1982 Habré was sworn in as President and boasted that for the first time in 17 years the 14 Chadian administrative regions were under a single authority.

But Goukouni was not finished. He forged a Libyan alliance and reconquered the north in 1983 taking the pivotal town of Faya Largeau in June. Habré was being bombed by Libyan planes and attacked by superior forces on the ground which eventually brought intervention on his behalf by the US sending its AWACS spy planes, Zaire which dispatched 2,000 troops and ultimately France which flew in its paratroops in Operation Manta, to prevent Goukouni crossing the 15th (later the 16th) parallel.

Trouble continued in the south where the people felt that they had been ignored by Habré's government, but he gradually restored power over the rebellious commandos in the south, while complaining to his Western allies about Libyan ambitions in the north. In March 1986 he reshuffled his cabinet to broaden its political base and accommodate erstwhile allies of Goukouni who were now coming over to the government side. These included former GUNT supporters General Djogo and later, Colonel Kamougué.

Habré went on the offensive against the Libyans at the beginning of 1987. His forces, not supported by the French beyond the 16th parallel, took Fada, Zouar and Ouadi Doum. By April 1987 he had liberated the whole of the north except the Aouzou strip.

Habré was better established than ever and he took advantage of a volte-face in Libyan policy when on 25 May 1988 Colonel Gadaffi, speaking in a major speech to celebrate the 25th anniversary of the OAU, said that he was willing to recognise the Chad government. Habré accepted the offer and relations were restored for the first time since 1982.

Goukouni Oueddi refused reconciliation despite Libyan pressure, but Habré skilfully divided the opposition and encouraged more leaders to cross over to him. Achiek Ibn Oumar, the most significant of the external leaders returned to Ndjamena in November 1988 bringing most of his troops with him. Habré rewarded him with the Ministry of Foreign affairs. On 10 December 1989 Habré was returned with 99 percent of the vote, as President for the next seven years.

His forces were involved in fierce fighting with those of his former lieutenant Idriss Déby operating from Darfur, in March 1990. Habré appeared to have won a breathing space by victory over his Libyan backed opponents in April. But Habré consistently underestimated Déby's determination. His rival gradually built up his own guerrilla force in Sudan, before launching a series of attacks into Chad.

Habré theoretically had an army of 30,000 men but they were discontented and demoralised and began to desert in large numbers after Déby invaded in November 1990. This time France refused to extend him any protection. He flew west to take personal command of his troops, but was heavily defeated, suffering heavy casualties. He was himself almost killed but made it back to Ndjamena, then hurriedly fled by helicopter on 1 December, to the Cameroon, leaving behind his seals of office. He eventually received political asylum in Senegal and moved there.

LASSOU, Gouara

Chadian politician. Minister of Agriculture, 3 March 1989 - 1 December 1990.

A young, ambitious and energetic soldier turned politician who survived successive changes of government since the military coup of 1975. Throughout he remained constant to the established government in Ndjamena. A nominal leftist and Habré loyalist despite his southern origins, he matured into a highly articulate foreign minister and Chad's international voice from July 1984 until he lost the ministry on the return of Achiek Ibn Oumar in March 1989.

Born 1948 in Torrola in the south-west, a Moundang, one of the principal tribes related to the Sara. Educated at the Ecole General Leclerc, Brazzaville (1961-65) and at the Bouar Military Academy. He went straight into active military service in Bardai against the FROLINAT guerillas and later in Sarh, in the south. He was promoted fast.

After the coup of April 1975, which toppled President Francois Tombalbaye, he was appointed to the Supreme Military Council and was made Minister of Agriculture by General Felix Malloum. He continued as a minister in the joint Malloum-Habré government of 1978 and then under Goukouni Oueddi's *Gouvernement d'union nationale de transition*, (GUNT) as Minister of the Civil Service, Minister of Defence and Minister of Education.

On 28 June 1984 he was elected executive secretary of the executive bureau of the newly formed National Union for Independence and Revolution (UNIR). This was virtually the number two spot in the Habré regime. Further promotion followed when he was promoted to Foreign Minister on 25 July 1984 to replace the long-standing incumbent, Idriss Miskine, who died of complications arising from malaria in January.

From that point onwards he became increasingly well known as Chad's principal international spokesman. His objectives were to maintain the French alliance, express the Chad government viewpoint at the various international peace initiatives and to encourage defections amongst the opposition. In January 1985, in front of the UN Security Council, he accused the Libyans of attempting to assassinate President Habré by means of a remote-controlled bomb. In October 1985 he addressed the 40th General Assembly of the UN complaining that despite the peace agreement of September 1984, Libyan troops had "not retreated even one inch." But by April 1986 he was internationally trumpeting Chad's sensational victory over Libya in the north.

Gadaffi suddenly changed his policy and said that he was willing to recognise the Chad government at a speech to the Organisation of African Unity on the occasion of its 25th anniversary. Lassou had the task of turning promises into reality. He failed at a meeting in Libreville in July 1988, but on 3 October diplomatic links were formally restored. He was reshuffled to the Ministry of Agriculture on 3 March 1989, following the return of the opposition leader Achiek Ibn Oumar. This was not seen as a demotion as he remained close to Habré and executive secretary of UNIR, until Idriss Déby's coup of December 1990.

OUEDDI, Goukouni
Chad guerrilla leader. President August 1979 to June 1982.

A tall, handsome warrior-chief from the Toubou tribe whose lifetime has been dedicated to winning and holding power in his divided country. He did briefly hold the Presidency at the beginning of the 1980s but power was wrested from him by his great rival, Hissène Habré, in July 1982 and he has been unable to win military victory since.

Born 1944 at Zouar. He is the only remaining son of the Derde, selected by the council of notables as a super-chief and recognised as the spiritual head of the Toubou. His four brothers all perished in the early years of the Chad civil war in the late 1960s, in the rebellion against the southern government under President Francois Tombalbaye.

Goukouni formed the second army of the National Liberation Front of Chad (FROLINAT) in 1972. For some time he served as second in command to Hissène Habré, but he had wider support among his Toubou people and took the opportunity to break with Habré over the kidnapping of the French archaeologist Madame Claustre.

While Habré kept Madame Claustre hostage, trying to secure a huge ransom, Goukouni emerged as leader of the Northern Armed Forces Command Council in 1977. In March 1978 he became chairman of the Revolutionary Committee of FROLINAT, a post he held until 1984.

FROLINAT's objective was to defeat the central government in the capital Ndjamena and to secure a fair share of power for the Moslem people of the north. The French did a deal with Habré bringing him into central government as Prime Minister, while Goukouni, leading his own *Forces Armées Populaires* (FAP), continued to fight in the north with Libyan support. His forces captured the central town of Bardai in July 1977 and after defeating the national army in some pitched battles, occupied a large part of the north of the country. Meanwhile fighting broke out in Ndjamena itself between forces of Habré and the Prime Minister Felix Malloum.

Nigeria brought all parties together at two major reconciliation meetings. Goukouni and Habré were asked to form a provisional government in April 1979. Goukouni became a minister of state under the leadership of Col. Mohammed Shawa. A further meeting of all parties was held on 14 August 1979 in Lagos. This time Goukouni was allowed to assume the Presidency of the Government of National Unity and Transition (GUNT) with Nigerian backing.

But arguments over the agreements and personality differences with Habré, then his Minister of Defence, soon surfaced and fighting erupted again in March. This time it became a physical battle for the control of Ndjamena. Goukouni called in Libyan support and Habré was eventually defeated in December 1980.

Goukouni then decided to strengthen his position by signing an agreement, on 6 January 1981, for the eventual political union between Chad and Libya, and authorising permanent Libyan intervention in certain aspects of Chadian affairs. This move was immensely unpopular even among Goukouni's supporters and it angered both Nigeria, which had set up the Lagos accord, and France, which still had forces stationed in Chad. Most of the other factions were opposed to the continued Libyan occupation of the north of the country and eventually agreement was reached for a phased Libyan withdrawal supervised by an OAU peace-keeping force.

But Habré stepped up his offensive from the Sudanese border to the east and soon filled the vacuum in the north left by the Libyan departure. His forces gradually gained ground and finally entered Ndjamena unopposed on 7 June 1982. Totally defeated and without effective allies, Goukouni fled to Cameroon and from there to Algeria. His forces retreated south complaining of lack of arms and ammunition and of Goukouni's disastrous eighteenth months of leadership in which he failed to achieve unity or set up a proper administration. Many of Goukouni's former ministers changed sides and were given jobs in Habré's government.

But Goukouni regrouped and with Libyan help pushed back into the north at the beginning of 1983. His forces captured the key northern town of Faya Largeau in June and reached Abéché on 8 July. Habré appealed for help and the French and Americans responded. The French set up Operation Manta to prevent Goukouni's forces crossing the 15th, later the 16th parallel of latitude.

Goukouni could make no further progress against the combined Franco-Chadian forces. He tried to rally the disparate opposition groups at a conference in August 1985, in which a Supreme Revolutionary Council of GUNT was set up with himself as president. But GUNT gradually disintegrated and Goukouni refused to attend OAU reconciliation talks in March 1986. Goukouni also fell out with his Libyan masters and by October 1986 was claiming to be under house arrest in Tripoli. He then declared himself willing to negotiate with Habré, who was still firmly entrenched in Chad and gradually winning over the opposition groups to his side.

Goukouni was mysteriously wounded in a fracas with Libyan troops in Tripoli, while his opposition allies deserted en masse to form a reconstituted GUNT. Goukouni quit Libya to live in Algiers while Habré and the Libyans finally settled their own differences with a peace agreement. Goukouni also patched up his quarrel with Libya and returned to Tripoli but he could never bring himself to negotiate with Habré, so he and the rump of the GUNT remained the principal opposition in Libya, though with declining influence.

On 23 September 1989 a clash occurred between two factions in FAP in which three men were killed. Adoum Togoi, leader of one faction, then declared that he wanted to call a special congress and assume the FAP leadership. Goukouni arrived in Libya from Algiers to successfully resist his claim.

Goukouni continued to live in Algiers. As Chad began to democratise, he formed a coordinating group of opposition organisations. He returned home on a short trip on 18 May 1991 and met President Déby. He said that his intention was to "take the pulse of the political situation in the country".

COMORO

Population: 465,000 (1990, World Bank)
Independence: 6 July 1975 (France renounced sovereignty 3 January 1976)
Head of State: Said Mohammed Djohar
Government: Presidential rule under a single party, but a pluralist system was discussed at round table talks in March and July 1991 to establish a government that would separate the powers of President and Prime Minister.
Parties: The former ruling party is the *Union Comorienne pour le Progrès* (UCP) but the presidential elections of 1990 brought out a plethora of parties. There are a number of unofficial opposition groups based overseas.

DJOHAR, Said Mohammed

President of the Comoro islands, 12 March 1990-

'Papa Djo', as he is fondly known on the islands, is a devout Muslim who never misses his prayers. He has two wives and eight children. He is a believer in a "peaceable, tolerant Islam". A relaxed man who loves reading, and watching documentary and political films. He likes playing dominoes and the local game 'Uboo'. He speaks French and Malagache fluently, but confesses that he has had "no business experience." Largely regarded as a diplomat and conciliator, heavily dependent on his connections with the assassinated President Ahmed Abdallah, he turned out to be a determined and tough fighter when it came to wresting the Presidency from seven other potential candidates. After months of confusion, following Abdallah's assassination, he finally emerged as President in March 1990 and immediately set about establishing his own team.

Born 1918 in Madagascar. He studied to be a teacher and completed his schooling and teacher training on the island. He was already 22 when he left and settled in the Comoro island of Anjouan as a secondary school teacher. He did not go into politics until the late 1940s. In 1947 he was named by the French colonial government, as a general Counsellor for Anjouan.

Over 1957-70 he held a number of ministerial portfolios, first under Dr Said Mohammed Cheikh, the Head of Government when the Comoros became self-governing in December 1961. When Dr Cheikh died in March 1970, he continued office under his successor, Prince Said Ibrahim.

In 1972 he was elected speaker of the national assembly. In the turbulent years that followed, the Comorian politicians were vying amongst themselves for power and fighting France for full independence. Djohar became the personal secretary of the emerging leader Ahmed

Abdallah who unilaterally declared independence on 6 July 1975 and became president of the new state.

Djohar was sent to Madagascar as the Comoros ambassador. He was there when his half brother Ali Solih seized power in the coup of 3 August 1975. Ali Solih established an extreme, militant Maoist regime in which he offended one power group after another. But despite the family connection (Djohar and Solih had the same mother) Djohar disagreed with the coup attempt and quit politics altogether, until Solih was overthrown in May 1978.

Ahmed Abdallah was restored to power by a group of white mercenaries led by the Frenchman, Colonel Bob Denard. Djohar was then called back out of retirement and appointed president of the chamber of commerce. In 1987 he was named President of the Supreme Court, the position which brought him to power following the assassination of Abdallah, in November 1989, by Denard's mercenaries who had remained on the island and built a position of power for themselves.

Djohar automatically became interim President under the constitution in a situation of confusion, rivalry and power squabbling that was exceptional even by Comoro standards. A struggle for power ensued between the mercenaries implicated in the coup and French troops who had been sent in to take control. The French emerged supreme, the mercenaries were expelled, and arrangements were made for new Presidential elections.

Registration for candidates began on 10 January 1990 with seven contenders, besides Djohar, representing a variety of parties and alliances. There was a query over Djohar's candidacy as a law had been passed stating that the interim president should not be allowed to compete for the presidency, but by a quirk of fate Abdallah had not signed this decree.

The elections on 18 February were postponed after only a few hours, amid widespread allegations of fraud. They were finally held on 11 March by which time two main contenders had emerged – Dhojar supported by the Udzima (Unity party) and his chief rival M. Mohammed Taki, who had returned from exile in Paris to great fanfare. The elections were very close and the results, giving Djohar a slender victory, were bitterly contested by Taki, who immediately filed a suit for fraud.

But Djohar assumed office and in a major interview with Agence France Presse described himself as "an eclectic president" whose measures would be characterised by moderation. " I want to be above party politics... the arbiter, the paternal figure." He said that he favoured a multi-party system.

On 22 March 1990 he formed his first government, taking the opportunity to make a complete break from the cabinet team of Ahmed Abdallah. He brought back many ministers who had been dropped by Abdallah during his incumbency. A prominent figure Prince Said Ali Kemal, who had been the Comorian ambassador in France, was given the senior ministry – Economy and Trade.

In 1991 Djohar warmly espoused the democratisation process. He called a round table conference in March and a referendum in May. But soon constitutional progress fell behind schedule. A deadlock was reached at a second round of constitutional talks in July. Djohar went to the limits to satisfy other parties, but divisions remained over federalism, the power of the islands and the question of leadership. Djohar proved politically inept and did not have the charisma need to run a feudal society like the Comoros. He also showed that he lacked a power base when confronted by powerful rivals.

On 3 August 1991, the President of the Supreme Court tried to oust him on the grounds that he was mentally "unfit" to run the country. Djohar, himself a former Supreme Court President, got full support from France and resisted this challenge. He put his rival under house arrest.

CONGO

Population: 2.22m (1990, World Bank)
Independence: 15 August 1960
Head of State: General Denis Sassou–Nguesso
Government: Transitional government established on 8 June 1991 with a 153 member Higher Council of the Republic headed by Prime Minister Andre Milongo. Pluralist general elections due March 1992, presidential elections May 1992, independence flag and national anthem replaced marxist flag in June 1991.
Parties: Former ruling party - *Parti Congolais du Travail* (PCT) challenged by a plethora of new parties including the *Mouvement Patriotique du Congo (MPC)* and the Congolese Movement for Democracy and Unified Development (MCDDI).

GOMA, Louis Sylvain

Congolese soldier and politician. Prime Minister 2 December 1975 – 11 August 1984. Also 14 January – 8 June 1991.

A very young soldier who enjoyed a meteoric rise under President Marien Ngouabi after playing a part in bringing down the government of Massamba Debat. He was promoted fast in the army, rising to Chief of Staff and Commander-in-chief, then embarked on a political career, becoming a minister and then Prime Minister at the age of 34, a post he held for nearly ten years. He was suddenly dropped as PM in August 1984, but became President of the newly created Constitutional Council. He headed the first transitional government which led Congo to multi-party democracy.

Born 28 June 1941 at Pointe Noire. Educated locally then went for military education in France at Versailles and St Cyr. He returned home and became assistant director of the military engineers (army engineer corps) 1966. In 1968 he was promoted captain and became Chief of Staff of the Congolese People's Army in the same year, as a reward for the part he played in bringing down the government of Alphonse Massamba Debat.

In 1969 he took up politics, joining the *Parti Congolais du Travail* (PCT). President Marien Ngouabi appointed him Commander-in-Chief of the army in February 1960, a post he relinquished in April when he became Secretary of State for Defence, then Minister of Public Works and Transport, 1970-74. He was elected to the Central Committee in 1970. In December 1971 he had the ministry of civil aviation added to his transport portfolio.

He supported Ngouabi through the attempted coups of February and May 1972 and was sent to deliver a personal message to the Presidents of Chad and the Central African Republic.

In January 1973 he was promoted from captain to major. He was elected to the politburo in January 1975 and on 2 December 1975 Ngouabi appointed him Prime Minister and chairman of the planning commission. Ngouabi was assassinated in March 1977, but Goma remained prime minister and became second vice president of the new military committee in April.

Colonel Joachim Yhombi Opango took over as President, but he was forced to hand over his powers to the central committee (of which Goma was a member) in February 1979. Goma continued as Premier and was ranked number three in the regime after the new President Denis Sassou Nguesso and Thystere Tchicaya. He was twice reconfirmed as Prime Minister in April 1979 and December 1980.

Suddenly Sassou Nguesso dropped him from his cabinet in August 1984 but clearly there were no doubts on the score of loyalty because he immediately bounced back in September as President of the Constitutional Council, a new body set up to scrutinise new legislation before it is adopted by the national assembly.

Nguesso turned to him again when he needed a new prime minister to head the interim government in the run up to multi-party democracy. On 14 January 1991 he was brought back as Prime Minister. But he found his power cut from under him by the national conference in March and by the dominance of the opposition in the government which followed. He was again voted out of office on 8 June 1991.

POUNGUI, Ange-Edouard
Congolese politician, Prime Minister, 11 August 1984 – 6 August 1989

A youthful marxist who became a respectable banker and Prime Minister of his country. A leading politician since the late 1960s. Played an important role in the government of Marien Ngouabi before carving out a career in banking. He was then brought back by Denis Sassou Nguesso who wanted a man of experience as his Prime Minister. He was demoted to become the head of the Economic and Social Council in August 1989, before leaving the PCT and forming a party of his own in February 1991.

Born: 1942. Educated locally. Graduated in economics. Active in school and student unions. His political career started in the late 1960s when he was an active member of the executive committee of the youth wing of the National Revolution Movement, JMNR, where he was one of the leading Marxists. He was also the President of the Congolese pupils and students union, UGEEC, whose congress in July 1968 roundly condemned the government of President Massamba-Débat. This contributed to Débat's downfall in the coup of August 1968.

The new President, Marien Ngouabi, made him a member of the National Council of the Revolution, CNR, and in 1969, Secretary of State for Foreign Affairs and later the President of the economic and social commission of the CNR.

When the Congolese Workers Party, PCT, was formed in December 1969, he became a member of the Politbureau. In June 1971 Ngouabi named him Minister of Finance and in August 1972, Vice President and Minister of Planning. On 30 August 1973 he was dropped from the government in the wake of the appointment of Henri Lopes as Prime Minister, but he remained a member of the Politbureau of the PCT and of the State Council. He became Assistant Director General of the Bank of Central African States, BEAC, 1976-79.

In 1980 he became President of the *Banque Commerciale Congolaise* and in 1983 its Director General. President Denis Sassou Nguesso took power in August 1979 and on 11 August 1984 brought in Poungui as his Prime Minister. In November 1985 he confronted demonstrating students who were ransacking cars and shops and explained to them the needs for government austerity. He remained Prime Minister during various reshuffles in the 1986-89 period.

After almost exactly five years as Prime Minister the Central Committee of the party demoted him on 6 August 1989 to head the economic and social council, making way for Alphonse Poaty-Souchlaty in the premiership.

He resigned from the PCT as Congo prepared for multi-party government in December 1990. By February 1991 he announced the formation of his own party, the Union of Social Democracy (UPSD) which supported private enterprise and individual freedom.

SASSOU-NGUESSO, Denis (Gen.)
Congo politician. President 8 February 1979–

Possibly the best dressed Head of State in Africa, he wears immaculate tailored suits and facial make up. He is a setter of fashion and style. But for all that, he is a consummate politician, carefully balancing the interests of his own northern Mbochi tribe with those in other parts of the country and in foreign policy playing along with East and West. His rhetoric has always been radical, in accordance with the tone set by the Congolese Labour Party, (PCT) but his actions in government show him to be a hard-headed realist, prepared to compromise with the IMF and secure financial assistance mainly from the West.

Born 1943 at Edou in the Owando district in the Mobochi tribe. Educated locally and at Loubomo Secondary School. He joined the army and did much of his military training in France. A thoroughly politicised soldier, he combined his professional vocation with membership of the Congolese Labour Party (PCT) from 1968 onwards, being elected to the Central Committee of the party. After the assassination of President Marien Ngouabi on 18 March 1977, the Congo passed into a period of extreme political turbulence.

Nguesso was appointed First Vice-President of the Military Committee of the PCT, which virtually ruled the country, while Colonel Joachim Yombi Opango emerged as Head of State. But the two men, though colleagues, were long-time opponents and rivalry continued. Opango, faced with a rapidly deteriorating economy and social discontent manifested in workers' strikes, began to lose ground both in the party and government and was eventually obliged to hand over power.

On 8 February 1979 Nguesso was designated Chief of State by the PCT Central Committee, while Opango was thrown out. On 31 March, at the Third Extraordinary Congress of the PCT, Nguesso was named as president of the party and head of state and government. In July 1979 a new socialist constitution was approved by referendum. On 14 August 1979 he was sworn in before the National Assembly as President for a term of five years.

After taking full power, Nguesso's style was to pose as an extreme left wing Marxist pledged to follow the tradition of Ngouabi socialism, while in practice following a pragmatic, pro-Western policy which allowed a considerable degree of economic liberalism.

He survived by maintaining a balance between the pro-Soviet upholders of socialist orthodoxy – a group to which he originally belonged – and the pro-Western pragmatists who formed a majority among the middle class. But in May 1981 he visited the Soviet Union and signed a treaty of friendship and co-operation, becoming one of the few Francophone African states to sign a fully-fledged treaty. He also made sure to maintain close relations with France by giving preferential treatment to visiting French ministers.

On 30 July 1984 he was unanimously re-elected as President for a further five–year term by the central committee of the PCT. The party congress also strengthened his personal powers. He took advantage by strengthening the pro-Western faction in his next cabinet reshuffle. He also personally assumed the post of Minister of Defence and National security. He then announced the release from detention of Yohmbi Opango though he remained under house arrest.

But tribal discontent continued and after a number of bomb explosions in 1982 a number of promient southerners were brought to trial, among them one of the founder members of the PCT. Then in July 1987, 20 army officers were arrested, many of them from a rival northern tribe, the Kouyou. The opposition leader Pierre Anga was killed in September while trying to organise an armed uprising.

On 30 July 1989, at the fourth congress of the PCT, Sassou Nguesso was unanimously re-elected chairman of the party Central Committee, thereby securing another five–year mandate as Head of State. During the Congress the moderates triumphed over the hardliners, further strengthening his hand.

In October 1989, he began his third mandate as President of the PCT and announced that deputies that were not members of the party would be allowed in the national assembly. Though they represented special interests, Nguesso claimed that it was all part of the process of gradual Perestroika and liberalisation. During the course of 1989 he was promoted from Colonel to full General.

In his 1991 New Year's day speech, he enthusiastically endorsed moves towards democratisation calling for a national conference to plan the "future of the country".

The conference opened on 25 February with his call to "end all sectorianism and petty political intrigues," but disagreement broke out the next day when opposition parties rejected government proposals for the running of the conference. The meeting was delayed. When it resumed two weeks later, the opposition had established the conference's sovereignty.

From then onwards Nguesso found himself outmanoeuvred and humiliated as the congress proceedings were broadcast to the world. As more than 30 opposition parties pressed home their advantage, he found his Presidential powers gradually being whittled away. He was even subjected to a personal attack by the man he ousted, General Joachim Yhombi-Opango who demanded a further inquiry into the circumstances of the assassination of President Ngouabi in 1988.

The conference finally agreed that there would be general elections in March 1992 and a presidential election in May 1992.

TCHICAYA-THYSTERE, Jean Pierre
Congolese politician.

A southerner and the former guardian of the Marxist purity of the governing party, he became the second most important figure in the regime when he helped President Denis Sassou Nguesso to power after the collapse of the Yhombi Opango regime. But the fact that he was a southerner and ideological Marxist was turned against him. He was ousted from the party then brought to trial on flimsy charges which did not stick in court. He was finally amnestied in August 1988, but remained in the political wilderness.

Born 7 January 1936. A Vili and former member of the royal family of Loango. Educated locally, then in France. He returned to become the director of the Lycée Chaminade (1965-67) and the Ecole Normale Supérieure until 1971.

In December 1971 President Marien Ngouabi appointed him Minister of Technical and Higher Education. He retained the portfolio in the cabinet of the first Premier Henri Lopez in August 1973. In January 1974 he paid an official visit to Great Britain and in December replaced Jean Ganga Zandzou as president of the central committee of the ruling Parti Congolais du Travail.

He went to France with Denis Sassou Nguesso as the guest of the French Communist Party in June 1975. On 12 December President Ngouabi set up a new "revolutionary executive machine" or "high command" in the PCT, with Tchicaya in charge of party headquarters, organisation and administration. Further promotion came when he became a member of the State Council formed on 6 January 1976. In March he was instrumental in putting down the general strike called by the union confederation and telling the workers to return to their jobs.

President Ngouabi was assassinated in March 1977 and Colonel Joachim Yhombi Opango took over but he was forced to hand over his powers to the central committee (of which Tchicaya was a member) in February 1979. At the PCT extraordinary congress in March he emerged as one of the most important members of the committee, which passed power over to Colonel Denis Sassou Nguesso.

At that time he reached the peak of his power as the leading party ideologue in the politburo and guardian of its Marxist purity, but Sassou Nguesso clearly felt he was a threat and proceeded to ease him out. First he appointed one of his main rivals, Daniel Abibi, as Minister of Information then, at the third party congress of July 1984 he ousted Tchicaya from the central committee.

In August 1986 he was among ten people brought to trial charged with having caused bomb explosions in 1982. One was in a Brazzaville cinema, in which nine people were killed and almost 100 injured. This was a time when Tchicaya was a fully-fledged member of the central committee and politburo of the party, so the charges were largely put down to tribal considerations. Tchicaya's French lawyer called for the acquittal of all defendants, saying that the trial was scandalous because of the total absence of proof. Tchicaya was given a five year suspended sentence.

On the occasion of the 25th anniversary of the revolution, in August 1988, he was granted an amnesty along with all other political prisoners.

CÔTE D'IVOIRE

Population: 12.34m (1990, World Bank)
Independence: 7 August 1960
Head of State: Felix Houphouet Boigny
Government: Powers of President and Prime Minister separated following the democratic elections of November 1990. Houphouet Boigny comfortably won the presidential election. A Prime Minister now runs day to day government and selects the Council of Ministers in the national Assembly.
Parties: The *Parti democratique de la Côte d'Ivoire* (PDCI) is the majority party. The main opposition parties are the *Front Populaire Ivoirien* (FPI) and the *Parti Republicain de la Côte D'Ivorie* (PRDCI).

AKE, Simeon
Ivorian politician. Foreign Minister, July 1977 – November 1990.

One of the new generation of ministers introduced by President Houphouet Boigny when he made a clean sweep in 1977. His career has been confined almost entirely to diplomacy and foreign affairs. After spending more than a decade as his country's permanent representative to the UN, he spent the next decade as Foreign Minister. A firm believer in dialogue with South Africa as a means of ensuring change in the south of the continent.

Born 4 January 1932 at Bingerville. Educated locally and at the Universities of Dakar, Senegal and Grenoble, France, where he read law. He returned home to begin his career in government. He became Chef du Cabinet to the Minister of Public Service in 1959, before being transferred to the United Nations as first Counsellor to the Côte d'Ivoire mission in 1961.

He returned home to become Director of Protocol in the Foreign Ministry (1963-64), then ambassador to Britain, Sweden, Denmark and Norway (1964-66). He served as permanent representative of the Côte d'Ivoire to the United Nations for more than a decade (1966-77) returning home to become Minister of Foreign Affairs on 30 July 1977 when President Houphouet Boigny made a major sweep of top ministers in his government.

He remained in the Foreign Ministry for more than a decade. There he shared the views of his President over dialogue with South Africa, welcoming two South African Presidents to the Côte d'Ivoire for discussions. He was also behind the recognition of Israel in December 1985 and the restoration of proper diplomatic relations for the first time since they were broken in 1973 over the Arab-Israeli war. Though Houphouet Boigny dismissed many of his top ministers in a major reshuffle on 16 October 1989, Ake was retained in the ministry he had already held for more than 12 years.

ALLIALI, Camille

Côte d'Ivoire politician. Minister of State 1983 - October 1989.

The mayor of Toumoudi who has considerable support from the Baoulé chiefs; always in the running as a possible successor to Houphouet Boigny. A skilled diplomat who made his mark as ambassador to France. His loyalty and solid dependability was demonstrated by holding the ministry of Justice over 1966-83, a total of 16 years. After that he became Minister of State without portfolio.

Born 23 November 1926 at Zahakro, Toumoudi. A Baoulé. Educated at Dakar High School and later at the Champollion High School and the Faculty of Law, Grenoble, where he took an LLB degree. Practised for a year in Grenoble then admitted to the Abidjan bar. Elected territorial councillor in 1959 and became Deputy and first Vice-President of the National Assembly. Over 1959-60 a senator of the French Community.

Sent to Paris in May 1961 as ambassador to France and permanent representative at the United Nations Educational, Scientific and Cultural Organisation (UNESCO). Still remembered as one of the most polished of African diplomats.

Recalled to Abidjan in 1963, he became on 15 February Minister Delegate for Foreign Affairs, taking over from President Houphouet Boigny. Minister of Justice and Seals from 1966-83. On 18 November 1983 he was switched to Minister of State without portfolio in which capacity he can help the President with any special assignments. He also has particular responsibility for party affairs as director of the *Parti Democratique de la Côte d'Ivoire* (PDCI). In a major cabinet reconstruction on 16 October 1989, Houphouet Boigny reduced the cabinet from 39 to 29 members and ministers of state from eight to four. Alliali was one of the casualties, being dropped as Minister of State.

BANNY, Jean Konan

Côte d'Ivoire politician. Minister of Defence, February 1981 – November 1990.

One of the more senior ministers with long spells as Minister of Defence but curiously he was once convicted of plotting and condemned to death. He has since worked his way back up the party hierarchy and was given his old ministry back in February 1981. He held this office until the major reshuffle in November 1990.

Born 14 July 1929 at Divo. Studied law and was called to the bar in Côte d'Ivoire. He became Minister of Defence but was arrested during the coup plot of 1963. He was tried and condemned to death but later freed under an amnesty.

He was re-elected a deputy on 16 November 1975 and won the seat in President Houphouet Boigny's home town, Yamoussoukro, in November 1980. By then he was established in the ruling PDCI as a member of the executive committee of the Political Bureau. He was reappointed

Minister of Defence on 2 February 1981 and has held that position since that date. Houphouet Boigny carried out a major reshuffle in October 1989 in which many of the top ministers were dismissed, but Banny's experience as Minister of Defence was such that he retained his post.

BÉDIE, Konan

Côte d'Ivoire politician, President of National Assembly 22 November 1980 –

A pratical economist with strong academic background, has had a distinguished career as Minister of Finance and Governor and adviser to the IMF and World Bank. Over the last decade he has been the most likely choice to succeed Houphouet Boigny and for the decade before that he was among the top two or three in the Ivorian hierarchy. In the event of anything happening to the President, the constitution lays down that he should take over in the interim and organise elections for a new President. This would give him a head start over his rivals.

Born: 5 May 1934 at Dadiekro, a Baoulé. Educated at the primary school Daoukro, Bingerville. Higher Primary School and Dabou Teachers College before taking an LLB in France, followed by a doctorate at the University of Poitiers. Worked as a civil servant in France then Abidjan 1959–60. Diplomatic Counsellor at the French Embassy, Washington March–August 1960. Founded the Côte d'Ivoire mission to the UN, 1960, Côte d'Ivoire's Charge d'Affaires to the US. August–December 1960. He was then appointed ambassador to the US, when only 26 and remained in that prestigious post for six years until 1966.

On 21 January 1966 he returned to Abidjan to take up the appointment of Minister–Delegate for Financial affairs. Promoted Minister of Economy and Finance 3 September 1968. During his ministry he found time to take a doctorate in economic science at Poitiers, presenting a thesis entitled "Trade conditions between developed and underdeveloped countries". He held this important ministry for eleven years, but was then dismissed with three other prominent ministers in a major reshuffle in July 1977.

President Houphouet Boigny said that he was separating with some of his ministers who had served him for up to 14 years with "great pain" but that he had to take into account "internal realities". It was generally thought that he was referring to the hitherto buoyant economy which was beginning to run out of steam and into debt. Bédié had also presided over the too rapid expansion of sugar refineries leading to a major misallocation of resources and mounting debt. But Bédié who had been an IMF Governor and World Bank administrator concurrently with his ministry (chairing the World Bank and IMF assemblies in 1974) landed the post of special adviser for African affairs to the President of the International Finance Corporation, part of the World Bank group, which put him in a position to rally international support for his home country in the difficult years which followed.

Bédié returned home in triumph when he was elected President of the new National Assembly on 22 December 1980. In that capacity, if anything happened to the President, he would take over under the constitution. As acting President he would be in charge of organising new presidential elections. The promotion was particularly significant as he succeeded Philippe Yacé, hitherto considered to be the most likely successor to the ageing President. Yacé had earlier, in September been removed as Secretary General of the *Parti democratique de la Cote d'Ivoire* (PDCI).

It was at this stage that Bédié became the favourite for succession though Houphouet was reluctant to commit himself to an heir. He created a new post of Vice President but left it vacant so that none of his rival candidates could assume the succession would fall on them. On 3 January 1986 Bédié was re-elected President of the Assembly.

He was one of the first Ivorians to mention the idea of introducing a multi-party system, early in 1990 – an idea which blossomed into full democratic government after the November elections.

BRA KANON, Denis

Côte d'Ivoire politician. Minister of Agriculture 1977 - October 1989.

Once one of the most powerful and established of all the Ivorian leaders, he was Minister of Agriculture for 12 years over 1977-89 and Mayor of Daola since 1980. He represents the Bété people in government and the party, where he has been a member of the politbureau since 1985.

Born 4 January 1936, a Bété. His main diploma was in agricultural engineering. He was appointed general director of SATMACI, the Technical Assistance Company for the Agricultural Modernisation of the Cote D'Ivoire (1966-77). Vice-president of the Economic and Social Council (1971-77). A lifelong member of the PDCI, he was elected to the Politbureau in 1975.

His first ministerial appointment came on 30 July 1977 when Houphouet Boigny made him Minister for Agriculture, a crucial ministry in a country almost wholly dependent on its agricultural export earnings. He became mayor of Daola in 1980. On 18 November 1983 he had the ministries of Water Resources and Forestry added to his agricultural portfolio.

He was dismissed as a minister in a major reshuffle on 16 October 1989. Commentators thought the move reflected Houphouet Boigny's disappointment over agricultural production and pricing policies and the lack of replanting of the major export crops such as coffee, cocoa and palm oil. Others thought he was taking the blame for the enforced slashing of the producer price of cocoa and the discontent among farmers that ensued.

DONA-FOLOGO, Laurent
Ivorian politician. Minister of Information, July 1974 - October 1989.

Dapper, smooth and cultivated, he controlled the Information, Sport and Culture portfolios virtually the whole time since he first became a minister in 1974. His sporting connections earned him the nickname "Adidas". Once he described President Houphouet Boigny as "plugged into eternity". He always cultivated his leader's adulation, turning many sporting events into demonstrations in his support. Long regarded as one of the younger, rising stars in the ruling party hierarchy, he was unexpectedly dismissed in a major cabinet reshuffle on 16 October 1989. He was elected General Secretary of the Parti democratique de la Cote d'Ivoire (PDCI) at an extraordinary congress on 14 April.

Born 12 December 1939. A Senufo from the north. Educated locally and at the Ecole Superieure de Journalisme de Lille. Took up journalism as a career and became editor-in-chief of the national daily, *Fraternité Matin* (1964-67). This was an ideal training for his promotion to Minister of Information on 24 July 1974. He also became a member of the executive committee and politburo of the PDCI from 1970. He was reshuffled to become Minister of Mass Education, Youth and Sports from 1978-83. In July 1986 in a major reshuffle the Information and Culture portfolios were added to those he already held "in recognition of his tireless eloquence in promoting the party and government."

As Information Minister in 1975, he promoted dialogue with South Africa and arranged for the visit of South Africa's President John Vorster to his country. He also campaigned tirelessly to get a Nobel Peace prize for Houphouet Boigny. He has written a book in his praise and has introduced a Houphouet Boigny award. Commentators were surprised when, despite his close connections to the leader, he was suddenly dismissed as a minister on 16 October 1989. He went into private business and started to organise the publication of a bilingual magazine for Africa. He made a comeback in April 1991 at the PDCI congress when he was appointed Secretary General. As the party had soundly defeated the opposition in the November 1990 elections, this was a significant appointment.

GNOLEBA, Maurice Seri
Ivorian politician. Minister of State, November 1983-October 1989.

A banker, accountant and economist and one of the Kru-Bété leaders in the party. President Houphouet Boginy became particularly dependent on him as a Minister of State after 1983 when his chief responsibility was the management of the mounting Ivorian foreign debt and the constant reschedulings with foreign creditors that became necessary. He earned the nickname 'Minister for Debt' but was sacked in October 1989 for failing to persuade creditors to adopt more generous attitudes.

Born 11 June 1935 at Behouo in Daloa. Read economics and accountancy, qualifying for a diploma from the Treasury School. Started work in the Treasury, becoming director-general of the public accounts department. Going on to the Central Bank of West African States (BCEAO) as an administrator. In 1974, he became a member of the politbureau of the Democratic Party of the Ivory Coast (PDCI) and on 24 July 1974 was brought into the cabinet by President Houphouet Boigny as Minister of Trade.

On 2 February 1981 he was reshuffled to become Minister of Planning and Industry and on 18 November 1983 Minister of State without portfolio. Houphouet Boigny had a handful of senior ministers around him in this capacity who served as an inner cabinet and carried out special assignments.

Gnoleba's special responsibility was to supervise the management of the growing mountain of foreign debt and the frequent reschedulings with international creditors, which became necessary. He was sacked by Houphouet Boigny on 16 October 1989 for what commentators described as 'failing to obtain sufficient creditor flexibility'. In other words, he had not been sufficiently successful in getting Ivorian debt renegotiated.

HOUPHOUET–BOIGNY, Felix
Ivorian politician. President since November 1960.

Ruling longer than any other African Head of State, he has been President of his country since 1960 but the acknowledged leader much longer, since the birth of Ivorian nationalism in the 1940s. He has the sophisticated self-assurance of a man who has been in command for the whole of his political life. He was a French cabinet minister for 13 years and is saturated in French culture and as much at ease in Paris as Abidjan or his birthplace turned capital, Yamoussoukro.

Always tactful, pragmatic and tolerant, he is conservative, intensely cautious and unwilling to risk national interests for any great pan-African design. From the time he turned his back on the communists in the 1950s, he has been 'un homme sage', the best African friend of France, outliving de Gaulle and the French leaders who were his early colleagues.

Short, stocky, with an amiable gnome-like face masking the cunning and instinct of his land-loving Baoulé people, his greatest contribution is in home affairs, where he delivered the economic miracle of the 1960s and 1970s, though he faltered when trying to adjust the economy in the 1980s.

In politics he is subtle, devious and always prepared to reform and absorb the opposition. He adopted 'dialogue' as one of his key words and his universal solution to major crises. In the Cote d'Ivoire these have been few and far between while his gentle, but firm hand, has been on the tiller.

Born 18 October 1905 in a chief's family at Yamoussoukro, a rich coffee growing area which became capital of the country. Educated at Bingerville Higher Primary School, before entering Dakar School of Medicine and Pharmacy where he graduated in 1925.

A well-off planter and bush doctor for almost 20 years, he gained a reputation as a famous *guerrisseur* (healer). In 1944 he formed the African Agricultural Union to combat colonialism and the prevalent practice of forced labour. It soon gained 20,000 members. In 1945 he converted the Agricultural Union into the Parti Democratique de la Cote d'Ivoire (PDCI). In November he was elected as a deputy to the French National Assembly and added 'Houphouet' to his name, meaning 'battering ram'.

In October 1946 he helped found the *Rassemblement démocratique Africain* (RDA), a pan-African movement for all the Francophone territories, and the PDCI became the local branch for the Cote d'Ivoire. The PDCI, prompted by the French Communist Party, became involved in a series of strikes, boycotts and demonstrations, reaching a climax on 24 January 1950, when a warrant was issued for his arrest. If he had not been a privileged member of the French Assembly, he would have been imprisoned.

The French colonial authorities took severe repressive measures. He decided that there was no future with the Communists and he transferred his allegiance to the French Socialists under François Mitterrand. The change did not come soon enough for the PDCI to escape bad defeat in the 1951 elections.

The French sent a new, sympathetic Governor-General to Abidjan and Houphouet took advantage to rebuild the party, turning his back on Communism for ever. The PDCI-RDA won seven seats in the January 1956 elections and he was made a French cabinet minister.

As Minister-Delegate to Guy Mollet, the French Prime Minister, he played a leading part in drawing up the *loi cadre* for the French colonies, a blueprint for internal autonomy. In the 1957 elections under the new constitution, the PDCI took 95% of the votes. He continued as a minister in Paris. He was Minister-Delegate to Prime Minister Guy Mollet (February 1956-June 1957); Minister of State under PM Bourges Manoury (June-November 1957); Minister of Public Health and Population under PM Felix Gaillard (November 1957-April 1958); Minister of State under PM Pierre Pfimlin (May 1958); Minister of State under Charles de Gaulle (June 1958-January 1959) and under Michel Debré until 23 May 1959.

The French colonies were given the choice of federation between themselves or autonomy and association with France. Houphouet was strongly anti-federal. He and De Gaulle designed a scheme for holding a referendum giving a choice between total independence or autonomy within the French community. The two men toured Africa campaigning for a 'Yes' vote for association with the French community. All countries voted in favour except Guinea.

In April 1959 he became Prime Minister of the Côte d'Ivoire, while still retaining his French ministry and when Mali persuaded De Gaulle to allow 'independence within the French Community', he followed suit and led his country to independence on 7 August 1960.

On 27 November 1960 he was elected President by 98% of the votes cast. Over 1961-70 he was his own Minister of Foreign Affairs and also headed for a time the Ministries of Interior, Defence, Agriculture and Education. In January 1963 there were serious plots, with over 100 arrested, including prominent ministers. Many were condemned, but he commuted the death sentences. Another plot was discovered in 1964 but by the end of the year the opposition had been thoroughly suppressed and he was able to embark on his liberal economic policies - stimulating foreign investment and encouraging farmers with good prices and the best marketing system in West Africa.

In 1965 he was elected President for another five years. In August 1966 he released three former ministers and nearly a hundred political detainees and pardoned a group of exiles who had been sent back from Ghana after Nkrumah's overthrow in 1966.

On 24 May 1969 he ordered the closure of Abidjan University following an outbreak of student unrest. He dealt with the crisis with a technique he developed over the years of holding 'dialogues' in public with the students.

In 1970 he celebrated the tenth anniversary of independence with a massive vote of confidence as he was re-elected President. In November 1970 he announced a summit conference to discuss a dialogue with South Africa. Pan-African opinion was unprepared for this initiative, but he stuck with his dialogue policies and sent a delegation to South Africa in 1971 and received South African Premiers on several visits to Côte d'Ivoire in the years that followed.

In 1975 he was re-elected President for a fourth five-year term and he had a constitutional amendment passed that would allow for the President of the National Assembly to succeed him in the event of his death. In July 1977 he carried out an extensive purge of his senior ministers as they faced new economic challenges. Throughout the 1970s Houphouet had presided over a near miracle economy with staggering rates of growth and soaring exports. But misdirected investment, falling commodity prices and growing debts caused the economy to collapse in the 1980s.

In September 1980, following a coup plot earlier in the year, the seventh congress of the PDCI was called and Houphouet announced democratisation in which the single party list system would be abolished. He was re-elected for another term in October and in February 1981 carried out a complete cabinet reshuffle, bringing some new, younger technocrats into his ministerial team. He also promised that he would appoint a Vice-President who would take over from him in the event of his death. But, fearing a succession struggle, he never filled this post.

Worsening economic conditions almost provoked a general strike in February 1981. A year later unrest spread to the students who did go on strike. Houphouet closed the university and suspended grants. Further strikes by teachers in May 1983 were followed by more action from doctors and pharmacists. Houphouet responded by sacking his education minister and ordering the teachers back to work.

On 27 October 1985 he was re-elected as President for a sixth five year mandate. Elections to the National Assembly followed. All candidates were PDCI members but only 64 of the original 114 were returned to the national assembly.

On 18 December 1985 Houphouet restored diplomatic relations with Israel which had reluctantly been broken off in 1973. It was a mark of his increasing pragmatic conservatism, but to prove his impartiality he also re-established diplomatic links with the Soviet Union. In April 1986 he announced that the country should be officially called Côte d'Ivoire and not by its translated name of the Ivory Coast.

In 1988 he began construction of a huge basilica at his home town Yamoussoukro. It was a cathedral standing taller than St Peter's in Rome and occupying a larger area than the Holy See. Its official cost was 40bn CFA ($115m). Unofficial estimates were more than twice that sum. Houphouet insisted that the finance was coming entirely from himself and his family. There were 8,000 square metres of stained glass windows, one of them depicting a picture of Houphouet himself kneeling at the feet of a blond Christ.

Houphouet's opponents put this down as the fantasy of an old man determined to make his name immortal. Already well into his eighties, he was also trying hard to secure nomination for a Nobel Peace Prize on the grounds that he had played a major part in arranging peace talks between conflicting parties in Southern Africa. But as he became more frail he made more frequent trips to Paris to have medical check-ups. He also spent more time in private and his public appearances became less frequent, while his lieutenants jockeyed for position in the succession stakes.

Three months of strikes and demonstrations, culminating in an army mutiny among junior ranks in May 1990, provoked an unprecedented crisis. Houphouet responded by suppressing the immediate trouble and by confirming the move that he had already made in April, to allow opposition parties to register, thus creating the foundations for a multi-party democracy.

In the presidential elections of 28 October 1990 Houphouet soundly beat his rival Professor Laurent Gbagbo, taking 82% of the vote. This triumph was repeated when the PDCI won the parliamentary elections with 163 out of the 175 seats, leaving the opposition disunited and without an effective voice.

Under the new constitution a prime minister was appointed for the first time. The new PM, Allasane Ouattara selected a new cabinet and presented it to Houphouet for approval. He assumes the day to day running of the government while the President, though still Head of State, adopted a more neutral, symbolic role.

KOFFI, Aoussou
Ivorian businessman and politician.

A well connected and affable businessman and diplomat turned politician, related to president Houphouet Boigny. He is known mainly for his years with the inter-African airline, Air Afrique, which he struggled to run from its Abidjan base for more than a deccade. After that he became Minister of Public Works and Transport until he was dropped in October 1989.

Born: 1924 at Yamoussoukro, a cousin of President Houphouet Boigny. Educated locally and at the *Ecole Speciale des Travaux Publics* in Paris. He began his career in the ministry of public works where he rose to become *Chef du Cabinet* to the minister. He was appointed Minister of State for Industry and Planning before being appointed ambassador to Italy, then to Belgium, Netherlands and the EC.

In 1969 he was made president of the authority for the improvement of the Bandama Valley, one of the major state rural development projects launched in the days of Ivorian economic prosperity. In 1973 he became chairman of the inter-African airline *Air Afrique*, with its multiple financial problems. After more than a decade struggling to make the airline solvent he surrendered the chairmanship in June 1985.

On 9 July 1986 he was made Minister of Public Works and Transport. On 16 August 1987 he was kidnapped in a bizarre incident by two former business associates whose motive was allegedly either money or revenge. Earlier Aoussou had fired them from the management of a jointly-owned hotel complex. A massive police hunt was launched as there were worries because he was suffering from hypertension. However, he was released within a week and resumed his duties as a minister. The incident came as some embarrassment to President Houphouet Boigny but Koffi was allowed to maintain his ministry until his sudden dismissal in a major reshuffle on 16 October 1989.

KONE, Abdoulaye
Ivorian financial administrator and politician.

A financial specialist who has been involved with the leading economic ministries since the early 1970s - from the days in which the Ivorian economy was a showpiece for all Africa, to recent times when restructuring and retrenchment has become the order of the day. He controlled the main economic ministries from the late 1970s until he resigned for health reasons from the Ministry of Economy and Finance in October 1989. He has also found time to be president of the Société Nationale de Financement, SONAFI and to be on the board of governors of the African Development Bank.

Born 13 April 1933 at Seguela. Educated locally and at the *Ecole Nationale du Tresor* (Treasury) in Paris. He returned home in the days when the economy and French planning methods were flourishing and became the Director of the Special Investment Budget (BSIE) until 1971, then Secretary of State for the Budget (1971-76). On 4 March 1976 he was promoted to full Minister, first for the Budget (1976-77) and then of Economy, Finance and Planning (1977-86).

He had to face the problems of the economy in the 1980s as commodity prices declined and the debt burden rose to unsustainable levels. This involved a programme of economic retrenchment and negotiations with the International Monetary Fund for support. In July 1986, faced with further restructuring and a mounting burden of work, his ministry was divided into three. He maintained control of Economy and Finance, but Planning and the Budget were hived off to two other ministers. As problems became increasingly acute at the end of the 1980s, Houphouet Boigny carried out a major reshuffle on 16 October 1989. Koné, who had already asked to go for health reasons, was allowed to depart.

OUATTARA, Alassane Dramane

Banker, economist. Prime Minister of Cote d'Ivoire, 7 November 1990 –

One of the new wave of young technocrats thrust into power by the political changes sweeping Africa in the 1990s. Long respected as a brilliant economist (the writer of numerous books and papers about West African economies and banking), he also made his mark as an international civil servant, working for many years with the IMF and with the Central Bank of West African States (BCEAO). He was plucked out of the comfy life of West African banking and given the mission of sorting out the Ivorian economy in the newly created post of Prime Minister, in November 1990.

Born: January 1943 in Dimboroko, he did his higher studies in the USA, getting a doctorate in economics. He was appointed deputy governor of the Central Bank of West African States (BCEAO) from January 1983 - October 1984. He then joined the International Monetary Fund, where he was director of the Africa department and advisor to the director general, 1984-88.

In October 1988 he became governor of his old bank, the BCEAO. He was appointed President of the Inter-ministerial Coordination Committee for stabilisation and the economic recovery programme in April 1990. It was a time of economic and political crisis with mounting debt, unbalanced budgets, growing political opposition and the people taking to the streets.

Ouattara launched his new recovery programme in June, aiming at extensive privatisation, reducing government expenditure and at staving off international creditors. He set himself 100 days to stabilise the economy and 1,000 days to get the economy growing again.

Houphouet Boigny who had paraded Ouattara in the public limelight on a number of occasions, suddenly brought him in over the heads of the establishment politicians as his economic genie. Then on 7 November he appointed him to the newly created post of Prime Minister, where he was responsible for recommending a new government to the President and for leading the new team to restore the economy and national stability.

After one year as economic supremo he announced himself to be on target. In an interview with *Jeune Afrique* magazine he admitted that his main problem had not been dealing with the aid donors and international institutions, but the difficult decisions he had to make at home. He gave notice to 7,000 government workers who were the main breadwinners with extended African families dependent on them. He set up new teams in the ministries, changing not only the ministers but many of the senior personnel. He sold off 3,500 government vehicles used by privileged bureaucrats.

He also began tough negotiations throughout 1991 with the IMF over a structural adjustment programme that would take into account the requirements of a newly democratic system.

By the second half of 1991 he had locked horns with the students and teachers. On 20 June he ordered the dissolution of the student federation following the killing of a student in a campus riot. This spurred further strikes and demonstrations amid calls from opposition leaders that he should resign.

USHER, Assouan Arsene

Ivorian politician and former minister.

Somewhat eclipsed in Ivorian politics since his dismissal as Foreign Minister in 1977. He established his reputation in this post and earlier as the Ivorian representative to the UN. He fell on hard times financially when he lost his official posts but was soon doing special assignments for the President where he could use his belief in dialogue with South Africa and put his moderate diplomacy into effect. He helped arrange the peace initiatives in Southern Africa at the end of 1988.

Born 24 October 1930, at Grand Lahou. A Nzima. Educated locally then at St Augustin seminary at Bingerville, the Professional Training School and the Lycée in Abidjan. He went on to the Lycée Renard, Vendome in France and graduated at the Bordeaux Faculty of Law and Political Studies. He was attached to Houphouet Boigny's cabinet when he was Minister Delegate to the French government, then Minister of Special Affairs in the government of Guy Mollet (1954-56).

He returned home in 1957 to become a lawyer in the Abidjan Court of Appeals. Over 1957–58 he was director of the Caisse d'Allocation Familiales. Elected to the Legislative Assembly in March 1958, he was its vice-president until November 1960, when he was sent to New York as the first representative of the Ivory Coast to the UN. He held the post until 21 January 1966, when he became Minister of Foreign Affairs. During this period he represented his country on the UN Security Council.

He returned to become a member of the Politbureau of the Ivory Coast

Democratic Party (PDCI). On 30 July 1977 he was dismissed as Foreign Minister in a massive reshuffle which seemed motivated mainly by the President's disappointment over economic performance. Usher was sacrificed along with other major economic ministers. Though not reappointed as a minister, he remained a strong man in the party and after being rescued from near bankruptcy emerged as driving force in foreign policy. He was sent to strengthen links with the Arab countries and to help promote peace talks between Angola, South Africa and Cuba, in 1988.

YACE, Philippe

Côte d'Ivoire politician. President of Economic and Social Council

Tough, authoritarian and not very popular among his rivals, he reached the position towards the end of the 1970s when he was considered to be the heir apparent to President Houphouet Boigny who was 15 years older. As secretary-general of the party and President of the National Assembly, he wielded great power but suddenly he appeared to lose the confidence of Houphouet. He faded from the scene for some years, but bounced back on 3 February 1986 when he was made President of the Economic and Social Council, the number three spot in the hierarchy.

Born January 23 1920 at Jacqueville, 40 miles from Abidjan. A member of the small Alladjan tribe. Educated at Bingerville Higher Primary School and later at the William Ponty School, Senegal.

A school teacher for two years before enlisting with the Free French forces. Highly decorated in the World War he went back to teaching in 1946 at the same time that he became active in regional politics. In 1949 he was elected secretary-general of the Cote d'Ivoire Teachers' Trade Union and four years later he took on the country's top political job as secretary-general to the ruling PDCI.

In March 1952 he was elected to the Territorial Assembly. He was re-elected in November 1960, 1965 and 1970. He was also appointed Great Councillor of French West Africa in 1952 and a Senator of the French Community from 1959 to 1961. As President of the National Assembly in 1960 he reached a prestige post in the Ivorian system. In 1961 Houphouet Boigny made him President of the Supreme Court.

But he was heavily identified with the functioning and success of the regime and he began to lose favour with the President as economic austerity threatened at the end of the 1970s. He gradually lost popularity as he had to carry out unpleasant tasks on behalf of the President. Then suddenly in September 1980 he was removed from the prestigious job of secretary-general of the PDCI by the abolition of his party job, under the pretext of general 'democratisation'. At first he hung on to his post as President of the National Assembly, but in December 1980 he lost that post too to Henri Konan Bédié. Nor was he appointed to the vacant post of vice-president though this was thought to be a distinct possibility at the time.

But maybe Houphouet was simply telling him that he could not assume that he was the 'constitutional dauphin' as some commentators would have it. On 3 February 1986 he bounced back by being elected President of the Economic and Social Council, sometimes regarded as the number three spot in the Ivorian hierarchy.

DJIBOUTI

Population: 404,000 (1990, World Bank)
Independence: 26 June 1977
Head of State: Hassan Gouled Aptidon
Government: Presidential rule through a Council of Ministers.
National Assembly: The President and the Deputies are elected by the ruling party on a single list.
Parties: The sole official party since 1981 is the *Rassemblement Populaire pour le Progrès* (RPP). A number of banned parties exist both inside Djibouti and abroad.

BARKAT, Gourad Hamadou

Djibouti Prime Minister, September 1978–, first vice-president of *Rassemblement Populaire pour le Progrès* (RPP).

An almost wholly self educated man who rose from rags to the pinnacle of political power. Starting as a labourer and mechanic in Djibouti port and from the minority Afar tribe, he found himself in the thick of Djibouti's factional politics of the 1950s and 1960s. He changed leadership allegiance many times, but eventually emerged as Prime Minister in September 1978. Since then he has been the constant and reliable number two to President Gouled Aptidon.

Born officially in 1930, though the true date is probably about 1925. An Adarassoul Afar from Tewao in Dikhil district, he had no formal schooling and worked for several years as a mechanic in the port of Djibouti and on the Addis Ababa-Djibouti railway.

His early interest in politics caused him to follow Mahmoud Harbi who was demanding independence from France in 1958, but he decided instead to join Hassan Gouled and actually voted for association with France in the referendum of the same year. But his way forward was through Afar politics. He joined the *Regroupement démocratique Afar* (RDA) led by Ali Aref who appointed him Minister of Education in his government in 1960.

He stood for Djibouti in the 1962 elections to the French National Assembly, and won very few votes, but he was re-elected in 1963 to the territorial assembly and was appointed Minister of Health in the new government of Ali Aref. In September 1965 Aref backed him in his election as a senator.

When a parliamentary assembly was formed in 1968, he won the Dikhil seat on the RDA list and was re-elected in 1973. In 1974 he was re-elected senator. When Ali Aref formed a new party, *Union nationale pour l'indépendance*, UNI in December 1975, Barkat followed him, but in June 1976 when France withdrew its support for Aref, Barkat broke away and formed the *Fronde parliamentaire*. He was returned for Dikhil in May 1977, but received no ministerial appointments in the governments of Abdullah Mohammed Kamil.

After independence in June 1977, came a period of great tension between the Afars and the Issas, when there were many resignations at the top. Hassan Gouled Aptidon became President and, following the resignation of another Afar leader, Ahmed Dini, Barkat suddenly found himself appointed Prime Minister in September 1978. Gouled thought that he would be more co-operative than his Afar predecessor and so it proved. Barkat declared that his government would follow a policy of rapid detribalisation in an effort to strengthen national unity. A long period of stability followed. It was consolidated by the formation of the *Rassemblement Populaire pour le Progres* (RPP) in March 1979, which Barkat joined. He was elected first vice-president of the politbureau.

In February 1981 Gouled was directly elected President and Barkat continued as Prime Minister, consolidating his number two ranking in the regime. On 2 October 1986, in a major cabinet reshuffle he was reconfirmed as Prime Minister with responsibility for port affairs.

When President Gouled dissolved his government on 17 November 1987, Barkat was again re-appointed Prime Minister though he was asked to concentrate ministerially on planning and land development rather than the port. On 20 November 1988 he was reconfirmed as first vice-president of a restructured polibureau.

GOULED APTIDON, Hassan
Djibouti politician. President June 1977–

An experienced politician now in his seventies and active in nationalist politics since the early 1950s, he has been President of his country since June 1977. A heavy smoker and coffee drinker, he is often difficult to approach but he combines political tact with a strong, forceful personality. Despite the dire predictions for the future of his tiny country, sandwiched between more powerful neighbours, he has managed to maintain full independence while strengthening his own position. He has gradually consolidated his presidency with comparatively little organised opposition either inside or outside Djibouti. His main relaxation is poker; he likes to play a game every evening if he has time.

Born October 1916 at Garissa near the port of Zeila, French Somaliland. There is some dispute about his age, with some suggesting he is at least eight years older than his 'official' birthday. Born into an Issa nomadic family, he left home when he was 14 and was taken in by the Catholic Mission in Djibouti. He then worked as a street trader, eventually becoming a contractor until the late 1940s when he first went into politics in the Somali and Danakil Youth Club. He soon asserted himself as a leader of the Issa community. He successfully campaigned for more Issa representation in the representative council. He joined the council, which nominated him the representative for French Somaliland to the French senate over 1952-58, where he was a keen Gaullist.

His main opponent at the time was Mahmoud Harbi who was campaigning for total independence from France. At the referendum in September 1958 Gouled countered with a campaign to retain Djibouti's existing status as an overseas territory in the French community. He won and on 24 December 1958 was elected vice-president of the colonial territorial assembly and later, deputy for Djibouti, on a Gaullist ticket, to the French National Assembly, 1959-62. There he campaigned for Djibouti's steady evolution towards local autonomy.

He returned home in November 1963 to fight the local elections under the banner of the Issa Democratic Union (UDI). He won his seat in Djibouti and was was appointed, by Ali Aref, the President of the Council, as Minister for Education (1963-67). But gradually his views became more radical as he confronted the French favouritism towards the minority Afar tribe and its leader Ali Aref. He also distanced himself from the violent demonstrations against De Gaulle when he visited the country in August 1966. But he disagreed with the speed at which France was allowing evolution towards autonomy and so resigned on 20 January 1967. A referendum was called in March 1967. The majority opted for a continuation of the French connection but Gouled was convinced that he should continue to struggle for full independence.

In the French presidential elections of 1969 he deserted the Gaullists for the first time (under Georges Pompidou) in favour of the socialist François Mitterrand. In 1971 he merged his party with the *Ligue Populaire Africaine* (LPA), forming a nationwide national front, and soon became its president. LPA was fully committed to securing independence, by peaceful means, though it was supported by the Somali Coast Liberation Front (FLCS) which used violence. It was a long struggle against Ali Aref supported by the French colonial regime and he suffered many defeats. In 1975 another merger saw the formation of the *Ligue Populaire Africaine pour L'indépendence* (LPAI).

All Somali parties became convinced that full independence was the only way forward and France, having dropped its protégé Ali Aref in July 1976, organised a round table conference in February and a referendum in May 1977. Gouled was returned for Djibouti and his LPA triumphed, securing a 99% vote for independence from 77% of the registered electors. On 16 May he was elected President of the Council of Government and formed an LPA-led coalition.

On 27 June 1977 he led his country to full independence with himself as President of the Republic of Djibouti, the last French colony in Africa. He started by establishing an inter-ethnic cabinet, appointing Ahmed Dini, an Afar, as Prime Minister. He stressed the common 'Arab' identity of both the Issas and the Afars, but ethnic rivalry soon recommenced. Dini resigned by December 1977 and though Gouled deliberately chose another Afar to succeed him, the Afars gradually lost influence.

In March 1979 he announced a new political party, the *Rassemblement Populaire pour le Progres* (RPP) to replace the LPAI. He ensured that he would select the politburo himself. After a change in the law allowing for direct elections for the presidency, he stood as the single candidate and was returned in June 1981 with 84% of the votes cast.

The first legislative elections on a single party list followed in May 1982, in which 65 unopposed RPP candidates were returned. Gouled offered an amnesty to all opponents and some Afars who had taken refuge in Ethiopia returned home. From that time onwards he pursued a policy of continuity with few ministerial changes, little effective opposition, and only minor anti-government violence. In April 1987 Gouled stood again as the sole candidate in the Presidential election and won the endorsement of 90% of the electorate for a further six-year term but it was widely expected that he would stand down before his period of office terminated.

In November he dissolved the government and appointed an enlarged council of ministers comprising 16 members and retaining Barkat Hamadou as his Prime Minister.

His major foreign affairs problem since independence has been to prevent his tiny country from being squeezed by his larger neighbours, Ethiopia and Somalia. In 1979 he concluded agreements with both for closer co-operation in communications and trade. He achieved a major coup in January 1986 by persuading the Heads of State of Ethiopia and Somalia to meet each other and hold peace talks for the first time in Djibouti. Further diplomatic pressure finally secured a peace agreement between the two warring neighbours in April 1988.

He chaired the fifth party congress in March 1991, in which a move towards multi-party democracy was rejected when it was agreed that Djibouti would remain a single party state.

This provoked a major reaction among democrats, the army and the Afar tribe generally, which was still smouldering following the arrest of the veteran Afar politician, Ali Aref Bourhan, after a coup plot in January.

Gouled seemed prepared to ride the storm. He occupied himself by trying to reconcile the parties in neighbouring Somalia, presiding over a successful agreement between six different factions in mid-July 1991.

KAMIL, Mohammed Abdallah
Djibouti politician.

A popular and respected politician who made his mark during the independence period, but being an Afar he found himself unable to survive the ethnic tensions that followed, though he held high office as Prime and Foreign minister for a considerable time. He then became the leader of an underground opposition party, resigning from parliament in 1981.

Born 1936 at Obock. Educated locally and at the Institute of Political Studies, Paris. He began his political career as a member of the Afar Democratic Union, UDA opposing Ali Aref Bourhan from 1965.

He became Secretary-General to the government before independence and on 29 July 1976 was unanimously elected Prime Minister of the

Council of Government which took over from Ali Aref. He concluded negotiations with the French for a referendum on independence which took place in May 1977. He also agreed on the presence of French troops which would guarantee Djibouti's independence.

But the predominantly Issa *Ligue Populaire Africaine pour L'indépendance* (LPAI) won the referendum handsomely and its leader Hassan Aptidon, formed the new government. He made Kamil his Minister of Planning and Development in May 1977. In July he was reshuffled to Minister of Foreign Affairs. He stayed in government longer than most of the other Afars and became chairman of an Afar commission that presented a list of grievances to President Aptidon.

When Ahmed Dini, the Afar Prime Minister resigned in December 1977, Aptidon tried to compensate in February 1978 by appointing Kamil Prime Minister while he retained the Ministry of Foreign Affairs and Defence, and by appointing other Afar ministers to replace those that had resigned. But the Afars were still frustrated because the Prime Minister did not have real powers to counterbalance those of the President. Little progress was made on this and Kamil also criticised Gouled's excessive dependence on France and his pro-Somalia policies. He finally resigned in September.

In June 1979 he announced the formation of an underground opposition party, the *Front democratique pour la liberation de Djibouti,* (FDLD), which grouped two Afar opposition parties that had been banned earlier. He remained in parliament but resigned along with seven other prominent opposition politicians on 7 August 1981. He was arrested and accused of distributing leaflets and undermining national and popular unity but released on 26 October. From then on he found himself in the political wilderness.

EQUATORIAL GUINEA

Population: 356,000 (1990, World Bank)
Independence: 12 October 1968
Head of State: Teodoro Mbasogo Nguema Obiang
Government: The President is Head of State, leader of government and Supreme Commander of the armed forces. He has the power to appoint and dismiss ministers and determine and direct national policy. He is advised by a state council and a house of representatives.
Parties: *The Partido Democrático de Guinea Ecuatorial* (PDGE) is the governmental party. A number of movements in exile seek the restoration of democracy.

OBIANG, Teodoro Nguema Mbasogo (Brigadier-General.)

President of Equatorial Guinea, 11 October 1979 –

Tough, cunning and a survivor. He came to power vowing to restore democracy after the cruel dictatorship of his uncle Macias Nguema, but he had been closely associated with the old regime and had been accused of many crimes. Soon it became clear that he intended to establish an equally authoritarian dictatorship, though he gave it the trappings of constitutional form. His regime soon became unpopular and opposition continued both inside the country, where there were a series of coup attempts, and outside where various opposition parties set themselves up in exile.

Born 1942, an Esangui (Fang) from Acoa Kam, Mongomo district. Nephew of Macias Nguema. He went to secondary school in Bata and did military training at Saragossa military academy in Spain 1963-65. Returned home and joined territorial guards as a second lieutenant. When his uncle Macias Nguema took power in 1968 he was appointed Military Governor of Fernando Po and director of the Playa Negra prison. Promoted Lieutenant-Colonel, commander of the national guard and aide-de-camp of Macias Nguema 1975.

Already unpopular and associated with the regime, he worked for Macias in the systematic elimination of all opponents. He was not paid a salary but lived off the takings from the Hotel Bahia in Santa Isabel.

Early in 1979 one of his brothers, complaining about not being paid for eight months, was executed on Macias' orders and Obiang began to plot a coup. On 3 August 1979 he overthrew Macias with the tacit approval of Spain. He described his uncle as the envoy of the devil, son of Lucifer, president of sorcerers. He proclaimed an amnesty for refugees overseas and released an estimated 5,000 political prisoners. But very few exiles returned as he was too closely identified with the Macias regime. Macias was apprehended, tried and sentenced by a joint civilian-military court and executed by firing squad.

On 11 October 1979 Obiang was sworn in as the second President. He secured immediate economic aid from Spain but he also embarked on the alternative policy of developing deeper relations with France. In June 1980 he attended his first Franco-African conference in Nice. By May 1983 he was advising the population to learn French.

Early in 1981, in order to gain control of Mba Ada's Exigensa company, he claimed that a coup attempt had been organised by Ada. He made himself the principal shareholder. He also ordered the arrest of 150 suspected opponents, said to have been involved in the alleged coup.

A new constitution approved by 95% of the voters provided for a return to civilian government after a seven-year transitional period. But the constitution was heavily criticised for giving him excessive powers as President. Afterwards an amendment was added that made him President for a further seven years from 2 August 1982. A further coup attempt by military personnel close to the President was revealed in May 1983. Two officers involved were executed in July.

Though he boasted, in 1984, that Equatorial Guinea was no longer a country that appeared on the UN list for violating human rights, in 1985 and again in 1986, the UN Human Rights Commission complained of "flagrant and repeated" violations.

In August 1983 he organised the first legislative council election in 19 years. An estimated 50,000 voters returned 41 representatives, all personally nominated by Obiang.

On 19 December 1983 he secured membership for Equatorial Guinea of the hitherto 'Francophone club' of the Customs and Economic Union of Central Africa (UDEAC). It joined the allied Bank of Central African States (BEAC) on 27 August 1984. France granted a budgetary credit of 55 million French francs and it became a member of the Franc Zone on 2 January 1985.

In a major reshuffle in January 1986 he assumed the defence portfolio previously held by his uncle Mba Onana. In July he claimed that his uncle had been involved in a coup attempt while he was away in Paris attending the 14 July national day celebrations. The leader of the plot was executed and 12 co-conspirators received up to 20 years' imprisonment, while his uncle was given two years house arrest and released a year later.

On 12 October 1986 he had himself promoted to Brigadier-General by the commanding officer of the military academy of Saragossa, in Spain. In May 1987 Amnesty International published a damning report on the use of military tribunals often presided over by ministers who are members of the Nguema family, and for the severity of the penalties they imposed.

In August 1987 he ended the ban on formal political activity and announced the establishment of a 'governmental party', the Democratic Party of Equatorial Guinea (PDGE) on the same lines as Macias' former PUNT party.

Legislative elections were held in July 1988, but several opposition politicians were given life sentences for alleged involvement in a plot against Obiang's life, in September.

Early in 1988 press reports began to appear alleging that Equatorial Guinea had forged links with South Africa, that a contract had been signed for the construction of a satellite tracking station and that South Africans had offered to extend the airport at Malabo. This caused consternation in Nigeria, which demanded the expulsion of all South African nationals from Guinea. Obiang bowed to Nigerian pressure and said that five South Africans would be asked to leave, but later he expelled the Nigerian representative from Malabo and protested to the UN that Nigeria was meddling in its internal affairs.

On 25 June 1989 he was returned as the sole candidate for another Presidential term. This was duly confirmed on 2 August 1989 when he took the opportunity to promise his people, "to open up a democratic dialogue with the full participation of all sections of society without discrimination."

He steadfastly refused to respond to opposition calls for multi-party democracy in 1990/91. In January 1991 he launched a wave of arrests of political opponents suspected of discussing democratisation. They were detained without trial and reportedly tortured.

ETHIOPIA

Population: 49.0m (1990, World Bank)
Head of State: Legesse Zenawi (Meles)
Government: An all party conference on 1 July 1991 in Addis
Ababa established an interim government with an 87-member Higher
Council and Meles Zenawi as interim President. He appointed
Tamrat Layne as Prime Minister, pending the organisation of
democratic elections in 1993. A new constitution is being drawn up.
Parties: The majority party in the interim government is the
Ethiopian People's Revolutionary Democratic Front. Other parties
are in the transitional government.

ASFAW, Lagesse
Ethiopian politician. Former head of organisation, Workers Party of
Ethiopia.

*A pro-Soviet hardliner and heavyweight debater who made much of the
running in Council of State debates, his power was on the wane even before
the collapse of Mengistu Haile Mariam's government. A sergeant in the
army at the time of the revolution, he established himself as a leading
ideologue and organisation man in the Dergue and the Workers Party of
Ethiopia which followed. Also a member of the Politburo. Once seen by
the Soviets as a possible candidate to replace Mengistu, he is reported to
have changed some of his pure Marxist beliefs before the change of
government.*

Born into an Amhara family settled in the Harar region. He joined the
army and was assigned to the Third Division, where he became Mengistu
Haile Mariam's personal assistant from the time of the revolution in 1974
until 1976. In 1976 he became a founder member of Abyot Seded
(Revolutionary Flame), the official party of the Provisional Military
Administrative Council or Dergue. He was only commissioned in late
1977 and not promoted to captain before 1979.

In February 1977 he was appointed to the military and political affairs
committee, where he was able to play a key role in the gradual
politicisation of the army. He was also in charge of distributing arms to
various army units, which put him in a strong position with the army
commanders. On the political front he fought for supremacy against the
other embryonic Marxist organisations that were struggling for power.
He purged the Wasleague party in 1978.

Always keen to establish a Soviet-style constitution, he played a major
part in the organisation of the return to civilian rule and democratic
socialism. In 1980, he was switched from supervision of the military
cadres to becomes a member of the executive and standing committees
of the Commission for the Organisation of a Party for the Workers of

Ethiopia (COPWE). At the founding Congress of the Workers Party of Ethiopia (WPE) in September 1984, he was elected to the central committee and the politbureau.

In 1984 he was put in charge of the highly controversial resettlement programme in which over half a million people were moved from the famine-hit regions in the north to the less affected lands in the west and the south, amid widespread allegations of excessive force and insufficient funding, infrastructure or organisation. In the same year he organised the arrangements to establish a civilian constitution by supervising the referendum, elections to the national assembly (Shengo) and the drafting of a new constitution. After the establishment of the new structures in September 1987 he did not win a post in the Council of State (cabinet) or Council of Ministers but remained a member of the politbureau of the Workers Party of Ethiopia.

In June 1988 he was put in charge of the Third Revolutionary Army campaign against the Tigrean rebels and retook some of the garrisons previously overrun, though only temporarily. Following further defeats in February 1989 he ordered the complete abandonment of the whole region.

BERHANU, Bayih (Lt-Col)

Ethiopian soldier and politician. Foreign Minister, 4 November 1986–November 1989, Former Vice-President, State Council.

One of the most sophisticated of members of the Mengistu regime, trained as a lawyer and very widely travelled, not just to the Soviet bloc but to all parts of Africa and the world at a succession of international conferences.

He made his mark on the legal and later the foreign and political affairs committees of the Dergue and followed with a distinguished career as Minister of Labour and Foreign Minister (1986-89) before being appointed Vice-President of the State Council.

An Amhara from Gojjam. He joined the army and did officer training at Harar Military Academy. He also found time to do legal studies. He was a major at the time of the Ethiopian revolution in June 1974 which overthrew Emperor Haile Selassie. He became a member of Provisional Administrative Military Council (PMAC) and chairman of its legal committee in 1975, a post he held until July 1976, when he took over the foreign and political affairs committee after the execution of Major Habte. He resumed the chair of the legal committee in December and switched to a reconstituted foreign affairs committee in February 1977. From July 1976 he was also the chief Ethiopian negotiator in the unsuccessful talks with the Eritrean liberation movements. He became a member of the standing committee of PMAC and head of its foreign affairs department, 1978-83.

When the government began preparations for legitimisation of the regime and the return to civilian rule in 1980, he was elected to the executive and central committee of the Commission for the Organisation of a Party of the Workers of Ethiopia (COPWE). When the Workers Party of Ethiopia (WPE) was finally formed in September 1984 he became a member of its central committee and politbureau.

Mengistu Haile Mariam appointed him Minister of Labour and Social Affairs on 23 April 1983, a post he held until 4 November 1986 when he was made Foreign Minister. His position was enhanced because since 1984 the OAU has held its summit meetings and preparatory meetings of foreign ministers at its permanent headquarters in Addis Ababa. This enabled Berhanu to regularly present the Ethiopian position to his brother Africans. It also allowed him to deflect international criticism over the Eritrean question. He played a major part in signing a peace agreement on 4 April 1988, restoring diplomatic relations with Somalia after more than two decades of hostility and war.

In November 1989 Mengistu relieved him of the Foreign Ministry and made him Vice-President of the State Council, which is the Ethiopian equivalent of the cabinet.

After the Ethiopian People's Revolutionary Democratic Front took power on 28 May he took refuge in the Italian embassy.

DESTA, Fisseha (Lt-Col)
Ethiopian soldier and politician. Former Vice-President.

Former President Mengistu Haile Mariam's deputy, long considered to be one of his chief supporters, a loyalist from the time of the Ethiopian revolution in 1974. His position was enhanced because he was a Tigrean and there was the hope that he could help solve the Tigrean nationality problem. He was also one of the main organisers and administrators of the Dergue and one of Mengistu's main troubleshooters, taking on a range of unusual assignments.

A graduate of the Harar Military Academy and a member of the palace guard unit of the First Division. He was one of the young officers of the Armed Forces Co-ordinating Committee which seized power from Emperor Haile Selassie during 1974. He became Assistant Secretary General of the ruling Provisional Administrative Military Council, (PMAC) or Dergue in March 1977 and chairman of its administrative committee. He was appointed deputy secretary-general of PMAC in mid-1978. As the government felt its way towards civilian rule, he became, in 1980, a member of the executive and central committee of the Commission for the Organisation of a Party of the Workers of Ethiopia, (COPWE). From 1980-83 he was also vice-chairman of the Council of Ministers.

In 1983 he organised the seminar to discuss the imposition of national military service. The Workers Party of Ethiopia was finally formed in 1984 and he was elected to the central committee, the praesidium and the politbureau of the party. In 1985 he also became chairman of the party's Justice, Administration and Defence Commission. In the elections to the first Shengo (parliament) on 14 June 1987, he stood for

Adwa constituency in the troubled Tigre region and won by 6,272 votes against 1,574 for his two opponents. When military rule formally ended with the implementation of a new civilian constitution on 9 September 1987, the PMAC was formally suspended but he was appointed Vice-President of Ethiopia and Vice-President of the State Council. The Shengo then appointed him chairman of its committee for organisation and administration.

He was detained in the ideological college Yekatit 66 after the Ethiopian People's Democratic Front took power in May 1991.

GEBRE–KIDHAN, Tesfaye (Lt-Gen)

Ethiopian soldier and politician. Briefly Acting Head of State 21 – 28 May 1991.

Though Mengistu Haile Mariam, smarting from another defeat at the hands of the Eritrean liberation movements, once criticised him for spending too much time in the Hilton Hotel, he remained one of his closest personal allies. Though a member of the politburo, he made light of ideology and remained a soldier in charge of defence, either as a minister or party supremo.

From an Amhara family settled in the Harar region. He joined the army and went for training to the Holeta Military Academy, where he first met Mengistu Haile Mariam. After graduating he joined the Third division's tank battalion. He was promoted to major in July 1974. After Emperor Haile Selassie was deposed in September 1974, he became a member of the Provisional Military Administrative Council (PMAC) standing committee in charge of defence.

He was promoted Lt-Colonel in December 1974 and Brigadier in December 1978, after distinguished service on the Ogaden front during the victorious war against Somalia, 1977-78. After that he took overall command in the war against the Eritrean guerrillas, spending much of his time in Asmara. In 1980 he became Minister for Defence, touring army units and trying to boost flagging morale. He also travelled extensively abroad particularly in Africa and the Eastern bloc.

When government began to prepare for the legitimisation of the regime and return to civilian rule he was elected to the executive and central committees of the Commission for the Organisation of a Party for the Workers of Ethiopia (COPWE). Despite the failures of successive campaigns by the Ethiopian forces against the guerrillas in Eritrea, he was promoted from Brigadier to Lt-General on 2 March 1982.

On 16 March 1987 before the elections to the National parliament, he lost the ministry of defence to Maj-Gen. Haile Georgis Habte Mariam, but remained member of the new Council of State (Cabinet) under the new constitution in charge of Defence. He was appointed chief administrator of the state of emergency declared in Eritrea after the disastrous defeat in Af Abet in March 1988.

After a failed coup attempt in 1989, he was placed in charge of the court martial of 13 generals implicated in the plot.

Tesfaye is believed to have recommended long prison sentences for the men, but he was over-ruled by Mengistu who personally ordered their execution. Tesfaye then resigned as chairman of the court martial, and received considerable backing from the public for his stand.

When Mengistu fled the country, unannounced on 21 May 1991, with the forces of the Ethiopian People's Democratic Front at the gates of Addis Ababa, he was nominated Acting President by the Council of State. He called for an immediate ceasefire and offered to share power with the rebels. "I shall strive to bring peace and an end to the suffering of the Ethiopian people", he said in an emotional address on 22 May. He freed 187 political prisoners. But the EPRDF rejected the peace call and by 28 May their forces had occupied Addis Ababa. Meanwhile Kidhan had organised peace talks in London, but he was an isolated figure, easily side-lined as his opponents seized power.

He took refuge in the Italian embassy in Addis Ababa.

MENGISTU, Haile Mariam

Former Ethiopian Head of State from February 1977. President, 11 September 1987 – 21 May 1991

The toughest and most single-minded Marxist leader on the African continent. He clung to orthodox Stalinist Marxism until forced to change his stance by the loss of Soviet support. His ruthlessness was demonstrated by the way he survived more than a decade in power. Several times he was involved in ordering the execution of colleagues, reportedly even taking a personal part in extempore shootings. He obstinately refused to face up to the almost total economic failure of his regime nor did he show any inclination to solve the nationality problem. His major achievement was to achieve continuity in government but only at a huge human and ethical cost. He fled the country on 21 May 1991 as rebel troops were at the gates of the capital.

Born 1940, his father was from the Shoan house of the Amhara tribe, the ruling class in Ethiopia at the time of Haile Selassie and earlier. His mother came from a southern tribe. He was educated locally and joined the army as a career soldier. After attending the Holeta Military Academy, he graduated as a second lieutenant in 1966 and rose to the rank of major in the Third Division. He was a little known ordnance officer, in charge of military supplies, when the Ethiopian revolution first started, in February 1974.

He played little part in the early stages of the revolution, until he was sent to Addis Ababa as representative of the Third Division to the Armed Forces Co-ordinating Committee. Many other officers were senior to him and competed for power in the turbulent early years of the revolution.

Though various other senior officers were given the titular position as Head of State in the early years, it soon became clear that real power lay with the Armed Forces Co-ordinating Committee, which after 12

September, when Emperor Haile Selassie was deposed, became the Provisional Armed Forces Co-ordinating Committee (PMAC), or Dergue, where Mengistu was elected vice chairman. He rapidly made his mark, proving to be a charismatic speaker, coining the future slogan of the revolution, 'Ethiopia tikdem', Ethiopia first. He was single-minded, hard-working, dedicated and ruthless and prepared to ensure his own survival at all costs.

On the overthrow of Haile Selassie, the first army officer to hold power was General Aman Andom, a senior officer who held the post of Chairman of the Dergue. He lasted only three months and was killed by forces loyal to Mengistu in November 1974 after disagreements over his role as a figurehead, over Eritrea and over the trials of members of the old regime. Mengistu still held back from assuming the dangerously exposed position as chairman and allowed General Teferi Bante to take over from Andom. Bante held the post for two years before falling prey to Mengistu's growing power. Mengistu organised a putsch against his opponents in the Dergue in February 1977. Teferi was executed and Mengistu finally assumed the highest office in the land.

Mengistu had been on the standing committee of the Dergue since December 1976 and was chairman of Abyot Seded (Revolutionary Flame) when it was founded as the Dergue's own political organisation.

A new challenge came from Vice-President Colonel Atnafu Abate. Mengistu ordered his execution on 11 November 1977 following the publication of a document listing 12 specific charges. His execution left the Dergue with only 60 of its original 120 members.

The Dergue set about establishing a Marxist socialist state in Ethiopia in which the landowners' property was seized and distributed to state farms and co-operatives. Industry was nationalised. Peasant associations were set up carrying out their own land reform programmes. Dissident groups were banned and eliminated, even those adopting a Marxist-Leninist line like the Ethiopian Peoples' Revolutionary Party.

Mengistu's problem was to legitimise and civilianise his regime and yet maintain control. He set up a commission in December 1979 to find the right solution. Called the Commission for the Organisation of a Party of the Workers of Ethiopia (COPWE), its central committee was still more than two-thirds military. The Central Committee of COPWE gradually took over the functions of PMAC , though most of the same loyalists to Mengistu appeared in both bodies. The trade unions and women's associations were restructured and in March 1983 he announced plans to draw up a new constitution to suit a people's democratic socialist republic.

In September 1984, to coincide with the tenth anniversary of the revolution the Workers Party of Ethiopia (WPE) was finally established. Mengistu assumed the role as its secretary general. Real power remained concentrated in his hands and those of the comrades that had survived with him since the revolution. The WPE was modelled on the Soviet CCP, with a single party under a Politbureau and Central Committee with power concentrated in the hands of the leader.

A draft constitution was eventually published in July 1986 and endorsed by 81% of voters in a referendum in February 1987. On 14 June 85% of registered voters participated in the elections of an 835 seat national parliament (Shengo). Mengistu and all the members of the politbureau of the WPE were returned as deputies (Mengistu was returned unopposed in a constituency in Addis Ababa). The Shengo in its inaugural meeting then unanimously elected him as President on 11 September 1987. As President he is also Chief Executive, Commander-in-Chief of the Armed Forces, chairman of the council of ministers and of the state council.

In 1988/89 there was a massive upsurge in activity by the Eritrean and Tigrean liberation movements. Major military gains were made, with the Tigrean People's Liberation Front taking most of Tigre under its control. The armed forces became increasingly demoralised as they took huge losses in the unwinnable war. On 16 May 1989 Mengistu left for a visit to Berlin and this was the signal for a major coup attempt, involving many of the top generals. Maj-Gen Haile Giorgis Habte Mariam, the Minister of Defence, was shot dead when he refused to join them, but troops loyal to Mengistu rallied to him, killing most of the rebel generals within 24 hours. Within two days troops in the second Army at Asmara also rebelled.

Mengistu unhesitatingly returned home and confronted the mutineers. On 19 May he celebrated his victory before half a million flag-waving demonstrators in Addis Ababa's Revolution square. He had survived, but at a cost of losing at least 30 senior officers (14 top generals), with 193 others (24 generals) held for questioning - virtually his entire high command. He quickly reappointed new commanders (pulling some old colleagues from out of retirement) and rebuilt the military establishment.

But his regime remained weaker than ever, with the rebel movements in the ascendant and the economy in a parlous condition. Over the years the economy has been drained by the cost of the secessionist wars to the extent that almost 50% of the Ethiopian budget is allocated to defence and Ethiopa owes the Soviet Union an estimated $3,500 million for military assistance. Other international debt repayments consume 20% of export earnings.

In this situation Mengistu found himself faced with criticism even among members of his own politbureau who had remained loyal throughout the coup attempt. Some wanted economic liberalisation, others wanted a deal with the rebels. Suddenly on 5 June 1989 the Shengo announced that peace talks would be held with the rebels for the first time. Mengistu was clearly behind the initiative but said that any talks would preclude the negotiation of secession of any part of Ethiopia. But eventually he agreed to talks without preconditions which started on 7 September 1989 in Atlanta, Georgia, USA. By mid-1990 no substantive progress had been made but further talks with the Eritreans and Tigreans were scheduled.

Victories by the TPLF and the EPLF in the early 1990s and the gradual withdrawal of Soviet military support led Mengistu to further radical changes. He announced the abandonment of Marxist-Leninism as a guiding ideology and on 5 March 1990, said that the WPE would be dissolved and replaced by a new party to be called the Democratic Unity Party of Ethiopia. He invited all opposition groups to join him under the new party umbrella but no positive response came from any of his opponents.

As the wars against the rebels deteriorated, with rebel forces getting nearer to Addis Ababa, Mengistu made a speech of desperation on 23 June 1990. He admitted that his country was "on the verge of collapse" and in "very grave danger more than ever before". He announced another drive for new recruits (virtually all conscripts) while pleading with his opponents for further peace talks.

Gradually his opponents pressed home their advantage as his demoralised army collapsed and surrendered. By mid-May 1991 Mengistu had accepted that he could not win the war and made plans to escape. He sent his family out of the country to Zimbabwe. On 21 May with the forces of the EPRDF at the gates of Addis Ababa, he left town by helicopter telling even his aides that he was going to inspect his troops. Then he instructed the pilot to take him to Nairobi. Finally he went to Zimbabwe, which gave him political asylum.

TEDLA, Addis (Lt-General)

Ethiopian soldier and politician. Deputy Prime Minister, September 1987, Chief-of-Staff, Armed Forces, June 1989 – 28 May 1991.

An Amhara, he was in at the beginning of the Ethiopian revolution and was always a Mengistu loyalist. He travelled extensively, particularly on military missions to the Soviet Union, in the Eastern bloc and in sympathetic African and Arab states. In the extensive military reorganisation which was needed following the attempted coup of May 1989, he was made Chief-of-Staff of the armed forces, but he was unable to prevent defeat by the EPRDF guerrillas, in May 1991.

An air force major at the time of the revolution in June 1974, he was a member of the Armed Forces Co-ordinating Council from the outset. He became a member of the Provisional Military Administrative Council (PMAC) and was second-in-command of its defence committee until December 1976. He was then elected to the standing committee and became co-chairman with Lt-Col Tesfaye Gebre-Kidhan of the defence committee. He took special responsibility for transport, helping to relieve the port congestion at Assab in 1979. In October 1979 he was appointed deputy chairman responsible for development and planning on the Dergue's standing committee.

When the government began preparations for the legitimisation of the regime and return to civilian rule in 1980, he was elected to the executive and central committees of the Commission for the Organisation of a Party for the Workers of Ethiopia (COPWE). At the founding congress of the Workers Party of Ethiopia in September 1984, he was unanimously elected to its central committee, politbureau and praesidium. In December 1984 he was appointed deputy commissioner of the Central Planning Commission.

In September 1987 he was appointed Deputy Prime Minister and a member of the Council of State which assumed over many of the functions of the PMAC and consisted of most of the same members. It oversees national affairs when the Shengo (parliament) is not in session. He became Chief-of-Staff of the army in June 1989, after the attempted coup of May, in which dozens of senior officers were killed.

WOGDERES, Fikre Selassie (Capt.)

Ethiopian airman and politician. Prime Minister, 20 September 1987 - 10 November 1989.

Unlike many of his colleagues he was a member of the air force, not the army, at the time of the revolution in 1974. A diabetic with a taste for high living, he still played a major role and was established on various military committees before Mengistu Haile Mariam had finally consolidated his power. A Marxist ideologue who was in charge of the COPWE ideological committee in the early 1980s, he was something of a rival to Asfaw Legesse. His relationship with Mengistu fluctuated over the years. He was relieved of his duties as Prime Minister on 7 November 1989, though few believed the official explanation that it was "for health reasons."

An Amhara from Shoa, he joined the Ethiopian air force. He was a captain when he played a part in the coup of 1974 which overturned Emperor Haile Selassie. He went on the first political indoctrination course in the Soviet Union in 1975. He was a member of the Armed Forces Co-ordinating Committee's social affairs committee until July 1976, when he was put in charge of the Zemetcha campaign, when the students were sent to the rural areas to mobilise the peasants. After Mengistu Haile Mariam finally took charge, he became secretary-general of the ruling Provisional Military Administrative Council (PMAC) or Dergue and a member of its standing committee in May 1977.

He joined two of the Marxist parties that were vying for power in the aftermath of the revolution, but when the Wasleague party was purged in 1978 by Lagesse Asfaw, he continued with the government-sponsored Abyot Seded (Revolutionary Flame).

When the government began preparations for the legitimisation and civilianisation of the regime in 1980, he was elected to the executive and central committees of the Commission for the Organisation of a Party for the Workers of Ethiopia (COPWE). He was also made head of COPWE's ideological department until he was appointed deputy chairman of the Council of Ministers on 20 April 1983.

At the founding congress of the Workers Party of Ethiopia (WPE) in

September 1984 he was unanimously elected to its central committee, praesidium and politbureau.

In March 1987 he became deputy Prime Minister under Mengistu Haile Mariam. The elections to the new parliament (Shengo) took place on 14 June and he was elected unopposed to an Addis Ababa constituency. On 20 September Mengistu made him Prime Minister and a member of the Council of State, which has taken over many of the functions of PMAC and is in charge of national affairs when the Shengo is not in session. He remained a member of the Politbureau of the Workers Party of Ethiopia.

In mid-1989 he was put in charge of the committee trying to negotiate an agreement with the Eritrean People's Liberation Front, but he was relieved of his post as Prime Minister on 7 November 1989 for what were officially described as "health reasons". A government statement said that he was "retired at the decision of the Political Bureau and in accordance with the constitutional powers of the President. Although he had been given the necessary medical treatment his illness did not allow him to fully discharge his responsibilities." But diplomats in Addis Ababa found it difficult to believe that he had retired voluntarily.

He was detained in the ideological college Yekatit 66 when the EPRDF took power in May 1991.

ZENAWI, Legesse (Meles)
Head of State, 22 July 1991 –

When he emerged into the international spotlight at the London conference of May 1991, after 17 years in the Tigrean bush, he appeared nervous, cautious and reasonable. But in his early career he was a committed marxist, one of the founders of the Marxist Leninist League of Tigre. His battle for control of leadership of the TPLF was ruthless. His conversion to moderation and his alliance with the Americans was startlingly sudden, but seemed based on pragmatic realism.

Born: 9 May 1955 in Adua, in the north of Ethiopia. His father was a Tigrean and his mother an Eritrean both from feudal families. Meles is his *nom de guerre*, which he took from a student leader Meles Tekele who was coldbloodedly murdered by the Mengistu regime in May 1975.

He was sent to the General Wingate school, which was run on the lines of a British public school. In 1971 he went to Addis Ababa university to do medicine, but he interrupted his studies to take up the struggle before the coup against Emperor Haile Selassie, which began in February 1974. He abandoned his course in the second year, and went to fight in the bush.

At the time he was a dyed-in-the-wool marxist but was soon in opposition to the brutal regime of Mengistu Haile Mariam. He quickly perceived that Mengistu was simply concerned with setting up an authoritarian regime under the cloak of communism, and that he had no interest in democracy.

He was one of the founders of the Marxist Leninist League of Tigre, which curiously claimed the Albanian version of socialism as its model. It provided the ideological base for the Tigre People's Liberation Front (TPLF), which was founded to lead the revolt in Tigre province in February 1975.

At that time the TPLF worked alongside the Tigre Liberation Front (TLF) but Zenawi claimed that the TLF was responsible for the killing of the most able children of political opponents, in the Tigre region. Though the leadership wanted the alliance with the TLF for strategic reasons, Zenawi campaigned tirelessly and at risk to his own life, against this.

His view finally prevailed. The TLF was eliminated and its leadership arrested, imprisoned and later executed. The victorious TPLF began to establish control of those areas where the Mengistu regime's writ was weakest. They drove out the freebooting bandits and gained the confidence of the locals by establishing organised local government. At the same time they began to build an effective guerrilla army.

The TPLF, in alliance with the Eritrean Liberation People's Front, which armed and trained it, was determined to drive other liberation movements out of its Tigrean patch. It eliminated the Ethiopian Democratic Union by early 1978 and later clashed with the Ethiopian People's Revolutionary Party, which it drove out of Tigre. By 1980 it controlled most of the Tigrean countryside. During the famine of 1985 relief aid was distributed strictly according to the recipients part in the national struggle.

Meles led a powerful faction inside the TPLF and in 1985 made a bid for leadership. Two other important leaders had to be defeated and he made a sustained challenge for leadership that was never entirely resolved.

In 1985 relations with the EPLF deteriorated sharply, with recrimination on both sides. But militarily the TPLF prospered, by 1988 it had liberated most of the north of Tigre and by August 1989 its forces were advancing on the Ethiopian capital, Addis Ababa.

By that time Zenawi was gradually asserting political command. One of his problems was to give the TPLF a broader base as a national and not merely Tigrean party. He did this by establishing the Ethiopian People's Revolutionary Democratic Front in February 1989 to incorporate other allied movements. This gave the EPRDF the claim to be representing most revolutionary forces in Ethiopia outside Eritrea. It also advanced his own career.

Zenawi became Chairman of the Supreme Council of the EPRDF. At the first EPRDF Congress in January 1991, he ensured that much of the Marxist ideology was jettisoned in favour of a more pragmatic approach that would win international approval.

By March 1990 his forces were within 160 kilometres of Addis Ababa. After consolidation, the final push to the capital was remarkably swift in May 1991. Mengistu fled the country on 21 May and the EPRDF tanks finally rumbled into Addis Ababa on 28 May.

The US supported the EPRDF in occupying the capital "to restore order" and brokered a peace conference in London where Zenawi emerged nervously, into the media-limelight, claiming to be a man of reason, tolerance and pragmatism. He rapidly agreed to the right to self-determination of Eritrea and to that of any other Ethiopian nationality which desired it.

After further talks on 1 July in Addis Ababa, a new government was formed drawn from all allied movements but with the EPRDF in clear majority. On 22 July he was elected Head of State by the ruling transitional council.

GABON

Population: 1.19m (1990, World Bank)
Head of State: Omar Bongo
Independence: 17 August 1960
Government: A national conference in March 1990 established an interim government prior to elections which started in September. President Bongo resigned as secretary general of the PDG, but remained Head of State. The ruling party established a majority over all opposition parties combined. A Prime Minister was appointed as head of government.
Parties: Majority party, the *Parti Democratique Gabonais* (PDG). Opposition parties include the Gabonese Progressive Party (PGP) and the Morena Bucherons.

BONGO, Ali (Martin)

Gabonese politician. Foreign Minister 22 August 1976 - 7 June 1991

The namesake of President Bongo, he comes from the same Franceville area in the extreme south east of the country. He worked for a long time in the President's own office as a close adviser before being promoted to Foreign Minister in 1976. His close connections with the President persisted and he retained his post despite the many reshuffles in the Gabonese government. He championed the President's cause in the row with France in the early 1980s and in a series of mediation efforts in Chad and Southern Africa.

Born 4 July 1940 at Lekei. Educated locally and at the Ecole Normale of Mitzic. He started his career in education, becoming a school director in Franceville, then inspector for primary schools in the Upper Ogooue region. Shortly after President Bongo took power in November 1967 he became deputy director to the President's Cabinet 1968-69. He was then appointed Commissioner-General for Information, April–December 1969. He returned to the President's entourage as Secretary of State to the presidency for Penitentiary Services, 1969-70, then for National Education, 1970-72, and becoming Omar Bongo's personal representative 1972-73.

After his long spell in the President's office he became Minister of Education and Scientific Research, 1973-75, of National Education 1975-76, and of Foreign Affairs and Co-operation August 1976-81. He became Minister of State for the same ministry in August 1981. He is the most senior minister below the four deputy prime ministers.

He survived the major cabinet reshuffle of 27 April 1990 when Bongo brought in a new team, and retained his post in the first multi-party government appointed by Prime Minister Casimir Oye-Mba. But on 7 June 1991 after five years in the post, he was disqualified from holding office through no fault of his own; under the new constitution ministers had to be 35 years of age and he was only 31.

BONGO, Omar (Albert Bernard)
President of Gabon since 28 November 1967 -

One of Africa's first generation nationalist leaders, who has held power for more than two decades. A clever, hardworking man, whose years of virtually unchallenged rule have made him remarkably vain. He delights in getting foreign visitors to sit through hours of film in which he is depicted as a larger-than-life, Black hero who led his people out of the wilderness to Nirvana. By his own admission his weaknesses are his impatience and impulsiveness. He does not stand on ceremony and believes in performance rather than style. He holds right-wing views, endorsing development by market forces, leaning heavily on French friendship and carrying on open trade with South Africa.

He is essentially a realist with little time for intellectualism. An authoritarian who expects to be obeyed, he believes in strict division of responsibilities and making his ministers realise their dependence by frequent cabinet reshuffles and stressing to Assembly members that they owe their positions to him. In March 1990 he promised to introduce multi-party democracy in response to changes at the international level and the aspirations of the younger generation.

Born 30 December 1935 in the village of Lewai, near Franceville, in a minority tribe in the south-east corner of the country. He soon left his local village for the primary school in Brazzaville and then the technical college where he completed a diploma in commerce. Returning home to his birthplace in 1958 he worked for a year as a civil servant before being conscripted into the air force. Demobilised on 27 October 1960, he joined the Ministry of Foreign Affairs at Libreville. His talents were spotted early and in March 1962, he became deputy director and in October director of Leon M'Ba's presidential office. From February 1963 to April 1964 he was in charge of information though considered to be too young for full ministerial rank.

After the attempted coup of February 1964, M'Ba brought him in as a man he could trust, to take charge of national defence. On 24 September this appointment was confirmed when he became Defence Minister. He remained as the President's aide, and was also a special commissioner in the State Security Court set up to try the 1964 coup plotters. In August 1966 he became Minister for Information. In September M'Ba, then seriously ill in Paris, confirmed him as Vice-President; in November he was put in charge of Co-ordination, Defence, Planning, Information and Tourism.

In the Presidential elections of March 1967 he was confirmed as Vice-President on a joint ticket with M'Ba. By the time M'Ba died on 27

November 1967, he was already firmly in power and took over the next day as President. He also took on the posts as Prime Minister and Defence Minister. He pledged to remain within the major guidelines defined by M'Ba but warned, "I am neither the same age (he was 32, M'Ba had died at 65) nor have the same training, nor the same character as my predecessor." But he maintained the strong alliance with France and a belief that private enterprise was the answer to Gabon's development. He frequently repeated the slogan, "Give me a sound economy and I will give you stable politics."

He announced a new policy of renewal, brought in younger ministers, released a number of political detainees and within a year, on 12 March 1968, announced the formation of the new Gabonese Democratic Party, with himself as secretary-general. On 8 May 1958 he recognised Biafra and remained a maverick during the Nigerian civil war. He frequently reshuffled his ministers, often taking important portfolios himself. In December 1970 he held no less than seven besides the presidency.

He set his heart on three major economic projects. The Kinguele dam was started in 1969 and he was able to open the first two power units in January 1973. Work on the development of Owendo port started in June 1968 and was completed in 1979. But the project closest to his heart, the building of the great Transgabonais railway, started in May 1974. It was one of the largest and most costly projects to be carried out anywhere in Africa, built with French support in the teeth of opposition by the World Bank and most international development strategists.

Twelve years later in December 1986, after expenditure of 650bn CFA francs ($1.6bn), the 962-km line had been built through rain forest and ravine, across mountains and rivers to Bongo's birthplace at Franceville in the extreme south-east of the country. Since then it has begun to prove its worth in evacuating timber from Gabon's huge forest reserves.

In September 1973 Gabon severed diplomatic relations with Israel and in October 1973, during the Arab-Israeli war he announced that he had been converted to Islam and had changed his name from Albert Bernard to Omar. He had been heavily influenced by Colonel Gadaffi who had promised him considerable foreign aid.

He became chairman of the Organisation of African Unity (OAU) in June 1977 when the annual conference was held in Libreville. Expenditure on the conference and prestige projects was so large that it seriously affected an already deteriorating economy and Bongo was obliged to institute a rigorous austerity programme in 1978. Later this became a full-blown structural adjustment programme under IMF supervision in which Bongo enforced retrenchment in the civil service and salary cuts.

Bongo was re-elected President, as the sole Presidential candidate in December 1979. He triumphed easily again in November 1986, by not allowing the opposition candidate to organise an effective campaign. Though Bongo maintained control through the single party, a non-violent opposition group the *Mouvement de Redressment National*

(MORENA) appeared in the early 1980s, with offices in Paris and support among students and the younger generation. Thirty-seven of its members were brought to trial in November 1982 and sentenced to up to 20 years' hard labour, but in the years that followed Bongo gradually pardoned them, the last being released in June 1986. He also called several times on exiles to return and participate in a democratic debate within a single party, but opposition continued despite repeated requests of this nature.

Bongo retained his control by balancing party rivalries. He made Leon Mebiame his Prime Minister and entrusted him with most of his functions as head of government in mid-1981, but after the third PDG Congress in September 1986 he had four deputy prime ministers, 297 central committee members, and 44 members of the party political bureau.

He managed to hold off MORENA's challenge particularly after 1988 when the party became involved in its own leadership dispute. But Bongo remained susceptible to criticism. In 1988 French newspapers were seized after publishing allegations concerning the misuse of French aid. In July 1989 he managed to persuade the president of the outlawed MORENA, Father Paul M'Ba Abessolo, to return home after 12 years of exile.

On 3 October 1989 four men were arrested, including the commander of the presidential guard, following the discovery of a coup plot against President Bongo. In March 1990 he called a national conference in response to considerable rioting and unrest and confirmed the findings of a special commission which had backed democratisation. He said he wanted development towards a multi-party system. This was confirmed on 22 May by a special resolution of the PDG party.

Bongo took the opportunity to carry out a major reshuffle, dropping his long-standing associate Leon Mebiame as Prime Minister and appointing Casimir Oye-Mba in his place. Bongo also introduced a number of opposition members, bringing 18 new ministers into a smaller, streamlined cabinet. Elections were held in September 1990, with the PDG getting an overall majority. With consummate political skill Bongo put himself above the electoral tumult as a neutral President.

ESSIMENGANE, Simon

Gabonese politician. Deputy Prime Minister, January 1987–

His wide experience in administration, government and as President of the Supreme Court have led him to his present position as one of the most senior men in goverment.

Born 16 October 1930, at Nzamelene in Bitam district. Educated at *Ecole des Cadres Superieurs de l'Afrique Equatoriale Francaise* and *Institut des Hautes Etudes d'Outre-Mer,* Paris. Local government 1950-60. Assistant Prefect Lastourville, 1960-61. Further studies in Paris 1961-63. Prefect Ogooue-Ivindo, Deputy Director of Labour,

Director of Information, Inspector of Public Establishments and State Companies at the Presidency 1963-65. Prefect of Upper Ogooue 1966-1970.

He became the Minister Delegated to the Presidency (Information) 1970-72. Minister of Industry and Tourism 1972. Public Health and Population 1972-73. Commerce and Handicrafts 1973-75. Minister of State for Agriculture 1975-78. Delegate to the Presidency February 1978. President of the Supreme Court. Fourth Deputy Prime Minister 6 January 1987. He was redesignated Minister of State in charge of the fourth constitution working group on 27 February 1990.

MEBIAME, Leon

Gabonese politician. Prime Minister, 17 April 1975–29 April 1990.

With a police background and long record of loyalty, Leon Mebiame was deputy to President Bongo from the early 1970s. Despite Bongo's numerous cabinet reshuffles, he remained trusted and firmly established in the number two spot until the major constitutional change of April 1990. His all-round ability which won him rapid promotion in the early years and his long administrative experience groomed him into an efficient head of government. While President Bongo comes from one of the minority tribes, he represented the larger Fang group in government.

Born 1 September 1934 in Libreville. Educated at the *College Moderne*, Libreville and the *Centre de Preparation aux Carrieres Administratives*, Brazzaville and the *Ecole Nationale de Police*, Lyon, France. Started his career as a policeman. Posted to Chad 1957-59. Promoted Superintendent 1960. Advanced training at *Surété Nationale*, Paris 1960-61. Deputy Director *Surété Nationale*, Gabon 1962-63. Director 1963-67. Promoted in Ministry of Interior. Became Minister of State for Labour, Social Affairs. Vice-President January 1968.

With the abolition of the Vice-Presidency in January 1975, he became Prime Minister, thus retaining his number two spot in the state hierarchy. In addition became Minister of Co-ordination April 1975, moving to Housing and Town Planning 1975-78, Land Registry 1976-78, Agriculture February 1978. He took over some of the functions of the Head of State from President Bongo, while retaining his Premiership in August 1981. Took over responsibility for Establishments on 10 March 1982. President Bongo called on him to form a new government on January 6 1987.

He paid a four-day official visit to Tunisia in July 1987 when he met President Bourguiba and Yasser Arafat, the PLO leader, reassuring him that Gabon would not recognise Israel. He was dropped as Prime Minister on 29 April 1990. This followed months of serious social disturbances, culminating in a National Conference which brought major constitutional change. Bongo had been forced to bring in a new team in response to the mounting demand for multi-party democracy.

OYE-MBA, Casimir
Gabon politician. Prime Minister 27 April 1990 -

A super-educated technocrat and banker, typical of the new wave of prime ministers who have been pushed into power in the early 1990s. Unlike the old guard in Gabon, he was not a Bateke, nor a Muslim, and probably not a Freemason, yet he was selected by Omar Bongo who was all of these, as his best qualified successor. He inherited an economy in crisis and a people in ferment over the prospect of elections and multi-party government.

Born 1942, a Fang in the Estuaire region near Libreville. Educated locally, then taking up law and science studies he went to the University of Rennes, France. He went on to study banking at the Centre for Financial and Banking Studies at the *Caisse centrale de cooperation économique (CCCE)*.

He soon got his career underway as Director General, then Governor of the Bank of Central African States (BEAC), becoming an acknowleged expert in finance and economics.

On 27 April 1990 he was hauled out of a meeting with the French Finance minister, called in Libreville to examine the future of the franc zone, to be told that he had been appointed Prime Minister.

His immediate task was to restore an economy in crisis, find the money to pay a new round of pay increases agreed by President Bongo, produce a new budget and prepare the country for multi- party elections. He also had to facilitate Bongo's retirement from party politics to a neutral role as father of the nation.

One of his first acts was to cut the size of the cabinet from 41 to 29 ministries despite resistance from vested interests.

On 19 November, after the PDG won an overall majority in the first multi-party elections, Bongo chose him once again as Prime Minister, so he continued in office.

Oye-Mba appointed a new cabinet of 26 ministers and 10 secretaries of state. Most, but not all of the portfolios, were held by the PDG as it had a majority in parliament. Eight portfolios went to the opposition.

He expressed the hope that the new multi-party government would put an end to social and political agitation so that the economy could be revived.

On 7 June 1991 Bongo surprised the nation by announcing the resignation of Oye-Mba saying there was an urgent need to put an end to the "internecine tensions fostered by politicians". Under the new constitution Oye-Mba had lost his foreign minister Ali Bongo, simply because he was not old enough (31) to hold ministerial rank. The qualifying age was 35.

But Bongo could not find another suitable prime minister and reappointed Oye-Mba to the post on 18 June. Four days later Oye- Mba appointed his third cabinet, again with 26 ministers.

RAWIRI, Georges
Gabonese politician. First Deputy Prime Minister, February 1980– 29 April 1990

Few men could be identified with a more concrete symbol of his work and achievement than Georges Rawiri. He was the minister in charge of the 650bn CFA ($1.6bn) Transgabonais railway at its inception in 1975 and saw it through to completion in December 1986. He always ranked in the top handful of ministers in all cabinets after he first made his mark in information by founding Gabon's radio and television systems. After 1980 he has ranked number three in the Gabonese hierarchy.

Born 10 March 1932 at Lambaréné. Educated at the protestant school Ngomo and the Lycee Jean Baptiste Dumas, Ales. Head, technical centre Garoua Radio Station 1957, Libreville Radio Station and founder of Radio Gabon 1959. Director Radiodiffusion Gabonaise 1960. Radio Television Gabonaise 1963. Counsellor for Foreign Affairs 1963.

His first ministerial appointment came when Pesident Bongo made him Minister for Information, Tourism, Posts and Telecommunications 1963-64, then Minister of State and ambassador to France 1964-71. Minister of State for Foreign Affairs and Co-operation 1971-74. He became the personal representative of the Head of State and Minister of State for Economic Co-ordination 1974-75.

He was placed in charge of the great new Transgabonais rail project as Minister of State for Transport and the Trans Gabon railway office in April 1975. While continuing these responsibilities he became assistant to the Deputy Prime Minister in 1978. First Deputy Prime Minister and Minister of Transport, February 1980. In August 1988 his portfolio was reconstituted. He retained the deputy Premiership and added the ministries of Forests, National Parks and Fisheries. He was redesignated Minister of State in charge of the first Working Group on the Constitution on 27 February 1990.

GAMBIA

Population: 870,000 (1990, World Bank)
Head of State: Sir Dawda Jawara
Independence: 18 February 1965
Government: Parliamentary democracy with an official opposition and other parties allowed to operate. Executive power vested in the President who is Head of State and Commander of the Armed forces.
Parties: People's Progressive Party has held power since independence. Opposition parties have contested all elections but have won only a small proportion of parliamentary seats.

CAMARA, Assan Musa
Gambian Politician. Vice-President October 1972-77

Over six feet tall and a man of great integrity and administrative ability, he has never really fulfilled the promise that seemed to beckon when he was Vice-President. He has had wide experience in government, as Foreign Minister and as a governor to the IMF, but he lost Jawara's confidence and turned to opposition politics where he has made little headway.

Born 1923 in Mansajang village in a Muslim Fullah family. Converted to Christianity in the St Mary Catholic Mission school, Bathurst, and at the Catholic Mission School, Kristu Kunda. He was a teacher from 1948-58, then he took up full-time politics. In 1960 he stood and won a seat as an independent member. He joined the United Party and was offered a ministry by Pierre Saar N'Jie when he became Chief Minister in 1961. He won a big personal majority in the elections of 1962 but the United Party was defeated and afterwards he crossed the carpet to the ruling Progressive People's Party.

He was rewarded in 1963 by being named Minister of Education until 1965 when he took on Works and Communications, returning to Education, Labour and Social Welfare from 1966-68. He was then promoted to Minister of External Affairs (1968-74), Local Government and Lands (1974-77) and Vice President from 9 October 1972 to 1977. It was during this period that he returned to Islam and dropped his Christian names, Andrew David, taking on Assan Musa instead. He was demoted from the Vice-Presidency in the cabinet reshuffle of 9 April 1977 and made Minister for Education, Youth and Sports and then Finance and Trade, June 1977. He became an IMF Governor for The Gambia in September 1977.

Frustrated by his lack of promotion he was one of three ministers in February 1986 who formed the centrist reform party, the Gambia People's Party. On 29 March he was elected the party leader. President

Jawara said that Camara had betrayed him "while he was still Vice President" and had encouraged members of the opposition, but Camara denied this and said that he had done his best to assure the President. The GPP drew some support from the Fullah and Serahuli regions of The Gambia but did its reputation no good when its deputy leader was arrested on fraud charges connected with trying to raise funds from abroad.

In March 1987 Camara and Sherif Dibba both challenged Jawara in the presidential elections, but he secured only 13% of the vote compared with 28% for Dibba and 59% for the President himself. In the legislative elections the GPP lost all three of its former seats and was practically extinguished as a force in Gambian politics.

DIBBA, Sherif Mustapha
Gambian politician. Vice-President May 1970 to September 1972.

Frank, open and friendly, Sherif Mustapha Dibba was once the Vice-President and heir apparent to Sir Dawda Jawara but he fell out and went into opposition politics. A fastidious and tidy man, setting himself high standards of discipline which he also expects from those who work with him. He was blamed, but exonerated, for involvement in the attempted coup of 1982 and has twice stood against Jawara since in Presidential elections, without success.

Born 10 January 1937, the son of a traditional Mandinka chief and farmer at Salikin in the Central region of his country. He was educated at the Armitage school and Methodist boys High School before getting a job as a clerk in the United Africa Company.

He continued working for the largest trading company on the west African coast until he resigned to go into full-time politics. In February 1959 he helped Jawara prepare the constitution of the People's Progressive Party and became its first assistant secretary-general, a post he held until he left the party.

He won a landslide victory in his home constituency of Baddibu in 1960 and repeated the performance in 1962, when the PPP was returned to power. He became Minister of Labour 1964, Local Government 1965, Works 1966, Finance in 1968 and Vice-President in May 1970.

In 1972 he resigned the Vice-Presidency, following an incident in which his half brother was found in a government vehicle, carrying smuggled goods into Senegal. President Jawara accepted the resignation but sent him a letter exonerating him of blame.

But he was soon pardoned and reinstated in official posts. He was appointed Minister Plenipotentiary and Ambassador Extraordinary to the European Economic Community from 1972-74 and returned to become Minister of Economic Planning and Industrial Development over 1974-75. On 31 July 1975 Dibba was dismissed as a minister and later expelled from the ruling party, with Sir Dawda claiming that he had spearheaded a campaign of opposition within the cabinet.

Though the exact nature of the rivalry between the President and his chief lieutenant was not clear, Dibba was trying to mount a challenge as he demonstrated when he announced, in September 1975, that he was forming a new party, the National Convention Party. It was the second opposition party to be formed in The Gambia. The old United Party, which once held power, was still in existence though only a shadow of its former self.

Dibba's NCP shared much of the same ideology as the PPP, which showed that it was mainly a vehicle for disgruntled elements from the former government. In the first electoral challenge of 1977 the NCP ousted the United Party as the main opposition, winning five seats to the UP's one but this was not very significant in proportion to the ruling PPP's 28 seats.

Though Dibba campaigned on behalf of the rural farmers, he was really identifying himself with the same people as President Jawara and he was unable to make much impact on the entrenched rule of the PPP.

A crisis came with the attempted coup by the Marxist-leaning Kukoi Samba Sanyang who tried to seize power and actually kidnapped Jawara's wife and other hostages. Dibba was not involved in the coup but he was arrested and charged with complicity and held in detention before being cleared.

He survived to challenge the government in the elections that followed in 1982 but lost his own Baddibu constituency that he had held since independence to Dr Lamin Saho. At the same time he challenged Jawara in the Presidential elections but Jawara took 72% of the vote and Dibba only just over 25%.

Dibba challenged again in March 1987 when he found himself fighting not only the government but a new party, the Gambia People's Party (GPP) formed by three other dissident ministers including the former Vice-President Assan Musa Camara. Dibba secured 28% of the vote, a fraction more than in 1982, and the NCP party increased its seats from four to five, but Dibba was again defeated in the Central Baddibu constituency.

JAWARA, Dawda Kairaba (Sir)

President of The Gambia since 24 April 1970, formerly Prime Minister.

Alhaji Sir Dawda Jawara is one of the longest serving leaders in Africa. He has been in charge in The Gambia since 1963 when he became Prime Minister. He has followed the constitutional conventions of a multi-party system, abiding by the rule of law, although he has been astute enough as a politician to win successive democratic elections. He is gentle, god fearing, pragmatic and tolerant. His rule has been peaceful and uneventful with the exception of the sudden, bloody coup attempt which rocked his country in July 1981. He was restored to power with the help of Senegalese troops and since then The Gambia has returned to its normal, peaceful ways.

Born May 1924, at Barajallay about 150 miles from the capital, then called Bathurst - now Banjul. He was one of six children of a Muslim Mandingo farmer. He was sent to Bathurst to stay with friends and was educated at the Muslim primary school then the Methodist Boys Grammar School.

He did further studies at Achimota College in Ghana and won a scholarship to Glasgow university in 1948, where he was president of the African Students Union, qualifying as a veterinary surgeon in 1953. In 1954 he returned to The Gambia and practised as a vet from 1954-60. In 1955 he became a Christian, took the name of David and married Augusta Mahoney, the daughter of Sir John Mahoney, Speaker of the House of Assembly. They had five children before their divorce in 1967. In 1965 he reverted to Islam and changed his name from David to Dawda.

He took up serious politics in 1959 and helped form a party that represented the up-country people which became the People's Progressive Party. After the May 1960 elections he served briefly as Minister of Education. But he resigned when the colonial governor appointed the leader of the opposition United Party, Pierre Sarr N'Jie, as Chief Minister.

But this decision was put to the test in 1962 when he won a slender majority over his opponents in the United Party. When self-government was introduced on 4 October 1963, he became The Gambia's first Prime Minister and led his country to full independence on 18 February 1965.

He was a cautious, pragmatic and democratic ruler who laid great emphasis on the practical economic development of his country. The Gambia benefitted from his solid conservative rule and improved its agriculture, while earning most of its revenue through trade and smuggling which flourished with Senegal. Before the drought of 1977, recurring again in the early 1980s, The Gambia was remarkably free of foreign debt.

Jawara brought his country to republican status in 1970 and became the first President on 24 April. His Presidential position was duly confirmed on 28 March 1972 when he was returned after his PPP had won 28 out of the 32 seats, winning 63% of the votes cast. The Gambia was distinguished from a number of neighbouring countries for putting most emphasis on economic development and for running a tight, agriculturally driven economy, helped by tourism and trade with Senegal.

But in July 1981, when Jawara was away in Britain attending the royal wedding of Prince Charles, a group of disaffected rebels with connections with the minority party, the Movement for Justice in Africa (MOJA-G) took many prisoners hostage including Lady Jawara and came within an ace of seizing power. But Jawara invoked the defence agreement that he had earlier signed with Senegal and the Senegalese sent 3,000 troops to restore his government. The rebel leader Kukoi Samba Sanyang fled the country and took refuge in Libya. Though the coup plot was exposed before any damage could be done, the three coup leaders were sentenced to long terms of imprisonment.

As it was Senegalese troops who rescued Jawara in 1981 and remained behind in The Gambia to restore peace, Jawara was in no position to resist Senegalese pressure for closer union between the two countries. After February 1982 the two countries came together in the Senegambia Confederation with a common confederal assembly and a shared stance on military and foreign affairs. But further pressure to push The Gambia into full Federation and economic union was strongly resisted by Jawara, reflecting majority opinion among his countrymen.

Since 1981 The Gambia has returned to its peaceful ways. Jawara held free and fair elections in 1982 and in March 1987. Both times he won huge majorities despite the challenge in 1987 by two new parties, supported by former ministers who put up a determined fight. A third party, the People's Democratic Organisation for Independence and Socialism, which inherited the mantle from the old MOJA-G party, secured only one per cent of the vote and did not win a single seat.

But Jawara's PPP won 31 out of the 36 directly elected seats and secured 58% of the vote. In the Presidential elections he was challenged by two old colleagues, Sherrif Dibba and Assan Camara. He won 59% of the poll compared with 72% in 1972.

At the end of August 1989 President Abdou Diouf of Senegal began to pull his troops out of The Gambia as the situation deteriorated with Mauritania. Diouf also suggested that the Senegambian union between the two countries be 'frozen', a proposal that was gladly accepted by Jawara. The Senegambian confederation was then brought to a formal end.

GHANA

Population: 14.86m (1990, World Bank)
Head of State: Jerry John Rawlings
Independence: 6 March 1957
Government: Military government under the Provisional National Defence Council chaired by Rawlings, but on 10 May 1991 it accepted the principle of multi-party democracy and promised to draw up a new constitution by the end of 1991. No dates were given for elections. It rules through an almost entirely civilian cabinet.
Parties: Political parties have been proscribed since the coup of December 1981, but a number of opposition groups have begun to function.

ABBEY, Joseph Leo Seko (Dr)

Ghanaian civil servant, economist, High Commissioner, Ambassador to USA December 1990 -

Highly educated and extremely able he is one of the most outstanding in a whole generation of prominent Ghanaian economists and civil servants. His educational record at universities in Britain and the USA shines with achievement. Since then he has twice taken command of the Ghana economy, under the Acheampong regime and even more notably when he helped to rescue it from the acute crisis of the early 1980s. He then made an easy transition to the highest diplomatic posts as High Commissioner in Canada and Britain, and Ambassador to the US in December 1990.

Born 15 August 1940. Educated locally, then at London School of Economics, 1961-64, when he gained a BSc in Economics. After a brief period as Assistant Statistical officer in the Central Bureau of Statistics, he went on to Iowa State University 1965-68 to get an MSc statistics in 1967 and a PhD statistics in 1968. He became a lecturer in economics at the Univeristy of Ghana 1968-74, taking leave of absence to be an Associate Research Fellow the University of Western Ontario, Canada 1971-73 to take his MA in Economics.

Bristling with academic qualifications, he took on the job as a research fellow at UNCTAD in New York, 1973-74. He returned home and was drafted by the government of General Acheampong to serve on the Economic Planning Commission a post he held while continuing as a government statistician and economist.

In May 1978 on the retirement of the distinguished Economist Dr Robert Gardiner, he was appointed Economic Commissioner and remained in that post under Jerry Rawlings until the military handover in September 1979. He played no direct part in the Hilla Limann government which followed, but was one of the economists who put together the 1981-82 budget which was rejected by parliament on the grounds that it was unrealistice and did not address the problems of the country. He also became an economic consultant for the UNDP/ECA and the Chairman of the Premier Bank.

In 1982 after Jerry Rawlings "second coming" he brought Abbey back onto the National Economic Review Committee 1982-83. Then in June 1983 he was appointed Executive Secretary of the Policy Monitoring and Implementation Committee and Acting PNDC Secretary for Trade. Ghana had suffered a series of disasters including drought and a fall in food production. Rawlings initial policies of socialist self help and pulling the economy up by its own bootstraps were not working.

Dr Abbey, Kwesi Botchwey and other pragmatists persuaded Rawlings that a fundamental change in economic policy was needed. In this regard he played a major part in the launch of Ghana's Economic Recovery programme, 1983-86 by advocating orthodox financial and fiscal measures to tackle the collapsing economy. He said that at this stage Ghana had been declared a "worst case situation" by the World bank. But the Bank and the IMF were prepared to help in return for serious economic restructuring.

He asked for a diplomatic appointment and on 6 March 1984 he was made High Commissioner to Canada until 30 September 1986 when he was promoted to High Commissioner in Britain. There he won many friends for his country and established excellent diplomatic relations between Ghana and Britain. His appointment as Ambassador to the US in Washington in December 1990 marked a rapid improvement in relations between his country and the US and the Washington institutions like the World Bank and IMF.

AHWOI, Ato Kwamena
Ghanaian politician. Secretary for Fuel and Power.

An accountant, finance officer and financial manager whose special skills have proved invaluable to the Rawlings government. He also had particular experience with the Volta River Authority and wrote a series of books on the way Ghana had been exploited in the development of its power and alumina industries. It was these writings that brought him to Rawlings attention and got him promoted to highest office as a Secretary (Minister) for Trade and later for Fuel and Power.

Born 12 June 1944 at Akroso in the Eastern region. Educated at Prempeh College, Kumasi 1958-64 going on to the University of Ghana, Legon 1964-67 where he obtained a BSc in Economics.

He then joined the Volta River Authority as an assistant accountant, 1967-70 rising to Assistant Finance Officer. He took a three month course in Financial Management from June-September 1972. He continued at Harvard University where he took a Master's degree in public administration, majoring in economic development. He returned to Ghana in 1973 as Finance officer for the Volta River Authority.

In 1974 he left the VRA and joined the Aluminium Industry

Commission as a Finance Officer and rose to become Director of Finance and adviser to the Chief Executive in Financial matters. By the time Jerry Rawlings had taken power on New Year's Eve 1982, Ahwoi had already writen a number of publications including the VRA and Valco (Volta Aluminium Company), expounding his thesis that Ghana had been exploited over the sale of its power to the multi-national corporation. Ahwoi wrote a number of other books on the same subject. Rawlings recognised him as a like-minded radical and appointed Ahwoi to his National Economic Review Committee to monitor the activities of the financial institutions. He took a leading part in the negotiations with Valco when the company needed increased power for two new potlines. He also introduced the 'Akuafo' cheque system, in which cocoa farmers were paid by cheque that they could cash at local banks. This prevented fraud.

He became special assistant to the PNDC Secretary for Finance and Economic Planning and in March 1984 was promoted to Secretary (Minister) for Trade with special responsibility for cocoa affairs. On 20 April 1987 he was reshuffled to become Secretary of Fuel and Power with added responsiblities for the Internal Revenue Secretariat and the Structural Adjustment Programme. This programme backed by the World Bank and the IMF included policies to control public expenditure, reform state owned enterprise, liberalise trade and rehabilitate the cocoa sector. It was an extension of Ghana's already successful Economic Recovery Programme.

ANNAN, Daniel Francis (Justice)
Ghanaian judge and politician

A handsome man with greying hair who has become the father figure of the Rawlings revolution. Now very much part of Rawlings "inner cabinet" and a constant voice in his leader's ear. Before the coup Annan was a distinguished judge and farmer at Kumasi, with wide interests outside his work - In the early 1970s he was Chairman of the Boxing Promotion Council, in the 1980s, Chairman of the Press Freedom Complaints Committee, in 1983, President of the Ghana National Olympic Committee. He remains a moderate, liberal minded influence on the Rawlings regime.

Born 7 November 1928 in Accra. Educated at the Accra Academy, 1939-45. He continued studies at London University gaining an intermediate arts degree in May 1948, before going to Hull University to pass a Bachelor of Laws degree and win the Prizeman in Law award, June 1956. Called to the bar at the Middle Temple in 1958.

He returned home and was appointed Assistant Crown Counsel at the Attorney General's Department, 1958-61. He became State Attorney in 1961, Senior State Attorney 1962-64 and Circuit Court Judge, 1964. In 1966 he was appointed a High Court Judge and in 1971 Appeal Court Judge.

When Jerry Rawlings took power in the coup of 1 January 1982, he was not given a position immediately in the Provisional National Defence Council but he was appointed in July 1984, after three of the original seven man PNDC had resigned or been dismissed. Later in the year he was made Vice Chairman of the PNDC. He was also made Chairman of the National Commission for Democracy, set up in 1987 to work out ways of devolving power to the "grass roots". He frequently represented Ghana at international meetings and conferences.

ASAMOAH, Obed Y. (Dr)

Ghanaian lawyer and politician. Secretary of Foreign Affairs, 21 January 1982 -

A pragmatic, moderate politician formerly associated with right wing parties. But he was an Ewe and trusted by Rawlings who, somewhat surprisingly, appointed him his Secretary for Foreign Affairs in his first cabinet in January 1982. He has held this post ever since through numerous cabinet reshuffles in which other more senior members of the Provisional National Defence Council have fallen from favour. His legal training and natural level headedness has given him consistency and authority as Ghana's spokesman on foreign affairs.

Born 6 February 1936 at Likpe Bala in the Volta region. Educated at Achimota Secondary School in Accra before going to Woolwich polytechnic in London in 1955 to do GCE "A" level. In 1957 he entered King's College, University of London to read law. He got his LLB in 1959, was admitted to the Middle Temple Inn of Court and was called to the bar in 1960. He practised intermittently as solicitor and advocate at the Ghana supreme court, then in 1962, continued legal studies at Columbia University Law School, to gain a masters degree (LLM) in 1965. He also worked for the Carnegie Endowment for International Peace in New York as a research assistant on issues before the UN Assembly with specific assignments on human rights.

He returned home in 1965 to take up a lectureship at the University of Ghana law faculty, 1965-69. He was a member of the Constituent Assembly which drafted the constitution for the second republic in 1969 and the third republic in 1979.

His first real success in pure politics came when he was elected to parliament in 1969 as a member of the National Alliance of Liberals led by Nkrumah's former minister Komla Gbedemah. This party went into opposition to the government of Kofi Busia, but another military government was established when Lt Colonel Ignatius Acheampong seized power in January 1972 and political parties were banned. When Lt Gen Fred Akuffo took over he appointed Asamoah as a member of the constituent assembly to draw up a new constitution. The assembly sat for four months and reported on 28 April 1979.

He then became General Secretary of the United National Convention led by William Ofori Attah. On 26 September 1981 when four opposition groups merged to become the All People's Party he was elected as its General Secretary under the overall leadership of Victor Owusu. But within a few months Jerry Rawlings seized power on New Year's Eve 1982. Somewhat surprisingly, given his connections with old style parties in the past, he was appointed on 21 January as Secretary (equivalent of minister) for Foreign Affairs. Though he came close to resignation after being branded as one of the "enemies of the revolution" by student organisations, his appointment was reconfirmed on 9 May when Rawlings drew up a new cabinet.

He soon showed himself to be a pragmatic Foreign Secretary; when asked about following Zaire's lead in establishing diplomatic relations with Israel like Zaire, he gave a very calculating answer, "Although the Israelis have technological know how which Ghana could use ... it would not make up for the loss of economic aid to Ghana from the Arab countries."

In November 1982 he represented Ghana at the unsuccessful OAU summit in Tripoli. On 1 February 1985 he chaired the meeting of the OAU Liberation Committee in Accra and on 31 March he was in Burkina Faso as head of the Ghana delegation to examine ways and means of integrating the two countries. Throughout his tenure as foreign secretary he has been concerned with relations with neighbouring Togo which has often been sympathetic to Ghanaian dissidents. In September 1963, after suspicion had fallen on Togo for permitting the serious coup attempt of June, Dr Asamoah reactivated the Ghana-Togo demarcation commission. But he was still chiding Togo for other incidents in March 1987. In May 1987 he visited Abidjan and complained to President Houphouet Boigny about Ghana dissident activities in his country.

BOTCHWEY, Kwesi

Ghanaian lawyer and academic. Secretary for Finance and Economic planning, 9 May 1982-

An intelligent, well organised lawyer, economist and academic who turned himself into a miracle-working Secretary for Finance and Economic planning under Jerry Rawlings. He turned the collapsing Ghana economy around and laid the foundations for sustained economic revival in the face of harsh criticism from the ideological purists, who felt he was betraying the socialist principles of the revolution. But his clarity of thought and persistence of action brought international acclaim for the way Ghana had achieved a rare economic miracle.

Born 13 September 1942. Educated locally before going to the University of Ghana, Legon where he gained a Bachelor of Law degree. He went on to Yale, in 1968 to study for his masters, continuing his studies at Michigan University.

He then went to Zambia where he was a lecturer of law at the University of Zambia, 1970-72, moving to the University of Dar es Salaam 1972-74. He returned home and was appointed senior lecturer in law at the Faculty of Law, University of Ghana, 1974-82. There he was a strident critic of the IMF and described himself as a marxist. He wrote several critical papers against devaluation proposed by the government of Dr Hilla Limann.

After the coup of 1 January 1982 Jerry Rawlings persuaded him to drop academic life and become Secretary (equivalent to minister) for Finance and Economic Planning, on 9 May. He took over at a time that Ghana was facing a massive economic crisis with spiralling inflation, a heavy debt burden, industrial stagnation and shortages of even the most basic commodities.

Botchwey suspended the 1981/82 budget, carried over from the previous regime and embarked on a series of short term measures to save the situation. He then convinced Rawlings that orthodox economic strategies were needed to handle the crisis and that this would involve the co-operation of the International Monetary Fund and the World Bank. This may have conflicted both with his own and with Rawlings aspirations towards socialism and self help, but he did not obstruct Botchwey who introduced his first economic recovery programme 1983-86. He restored incentives to production and exports, devalued the cedi, and maintained tight fiscal and monetary control. In return he obtained credits from the IMF, World Bank and the international banking system generally.

Botchwey's strategy worked and he gradually revived the economy, cut inflation, increased production and restored the flow of goods to the shops. This in turn brought further foreign loans and assistance. But the economic gains were often criticised on the grounds that they had been achieved at the expense of betraying the principles of the revolution. Students, trades unionists and the unemployed were particularly critical.

Botchwey stuck to his strategy and Ghana gained the reputation of a miracle economy that had turned itself round. In November 1985 he introduced his second Economic Recovery Programme, 1986-88 in which he reduced balance of payments and budgetary deficits, introduced a measure of privatisation, and reformed major sectors of the economy. A Structural Adjustment Programme followed for 1987-90 to reduce inflation still further and achieve payments surpluses.

ENIN, Aanaa Naanna (Mrs)
Ghana civil servant and politician.

One of the new breed of emancipated, Ghanaian women leaders. Formerly a key member of the Provisional National Defence Council and important because she was the only woman member of that ruling body, but never in the "inner cabinet" of Rawlings government, nor a secretary in charge of a specific portfolio. Rawlings dismissed her from the PNDC in October 1989.

Born 1939 in Accra. Educated locally before going to study microbiology at the University of Frankfurt, West Germany. She returned home to work in the management of the State Fishing Corporation where she took every opportunity to attend conferences on food production and promotion. At a Food and Agriculture Organisation workshop she presented a paper on fish and fish products.

When Jerry Rawlings needed to make up the numbers of the PNDC on 18 August 1982, after two resignations, he appointed Mrs Enin to the ruling body. In March 1983 she was part of the Ghana delegation to the Non Aligned summit conference in New Delhi, India. In May 1983 she led the Ghana delegation to the 6th Economic Community of West African States (ECOWAS) summit in Conakry, Guinea.

On 24 October 1989 Rawlings dismissed her from the PNDC on the grounds of alleged disrespect against members of the public and officials as well as other conduct "incompatible with revolutionary humility". She was immediately appointed Secretary for Mobilisation and Social Welfare.

IDDRISSU, Mahama (Alhaji)
Ghanaian banker and politician.

A banker with wide experience as director of a variety of state corporations, he made particular contributions to the Ghana Commercial Bank, the State Transport Corporation and the National Investment Bank before going into politics. His political career started haltingly when he was in opposition during the regime of Dr Hilla Limann, but he established himself in the Rawlings government and rose to become a full member of the People's National Defence Council.

Born 15 August 1939 in the Upper West Region of Ghana. Educated at Wa Primary School, 1944-48 and Tamale Senior Boys Boarding School where he completed his elementary education in 1950. He went on to Tamale Secondary School in 1951 and completed his Cambridge School certificate in 1955.

He joined the Standard Bank of Ghana 1955-61 before going to the Ghana Commercial Bank as a branch manager, serving in many remote parts of the country. While in his home town Wa, he was appointed to the Urban Council management committee. In 1970 he went to India for a management training course in the Indian State Bank. He returned to the GCB and was appointed auditor. He became Chairman of the State Transport Corporation 1972-73.

He was sent to the London branch of the bank in 1973 and returned home again to become Grade Area Manager in 1975. He served as President of GCB Officers Association, 1977-78. The military government of General Frederick Akuffo noted his growing interest in public affairs and brought him into government for the first time as Commissioner for Local Government in October 1978. He remained in this post when Jerry Rawlings first took power in June 1979.

During the elections which followed he became a member of the

United National Convention party led by William Ofori Atta and he briefly became deputy leader of a five party opposition grouping, the All People's Party. When Rawlings had his "second coming", he appointed Idrissu Secretary (Minister) for Transport and Communications on 21 January 1982, despite protests in some of the local press over his political connections in the previous civilian regime. But Rawlings continued to show confidence in him and he continued to hold his portfolio. On 3 October 1984 he was appointed to the select ruling body, the Provisional National Defence Council.

MENSAH, Joseph Henry
Ghanaian politician. Opposition leader.

A brilliant economist with a distinguished record both at home and internationally. In politics he had a brief period of glory as Finance Minister under Dr Kofi Busia, but since then he has been ploughing the unfertile field of opposition politics. In recent years he has been in exile mostly in London. He founded the Ghana Democratic Movement in 1983 but has found himself politically frustrated and has been harrassed in the American courts following allegations about arms purchases, though nothing has been proved against him.

Born 31 October 1928. Educated at Achimota College, the University College of Ghana, London School of Economics and Stanford University, USA where he got an MSc in Economics.

He started his career in Ghana as an assistant inspector of taxes in 1953 but soon found more scope for his talents as a research fellow of University College, 1953-57 becoming a full lecturer at the University of Ghana, 1957-58.

He then took an appointment at the United Nations in New York, 1958-61. He returned to join the Ghana government under Nkrumah as Chief Economist, Principal Secretary and Executive Secretary of the National Planning Commission. As a first class economist he saw how Nkrumah's policies were gradually bringing Ghana to the brink of bankruptcy. He became increasingly critical of the doctrinaire socialists surrounding the seat of power. In 1965 he left, once again to become a UN economist and Director of the Division of Trade and Economic Cooperation at the Economic Commission for Africa. He held this post until 9 April 1969 when General Afrifa, who had taken over as National Liberation Council Chairman, asked him to become his Commissioner of Finance.

His major problems were the rescheduling of Ghana debts while bringing growth to an almost stagnant economy. He laid early emphasis on agricultural development and imposed a development levy to help bridge the gap between rural and urban incomes. Returned as Progress Party MP for Sunyani in the August 1969 elections, he continued as Dr Busia's Minister of Finance and Economic Planning from September 1969 to January 1971 and Finance Minister until the military coup of 13

January 1972.

In his attempt to encourage Ghanaians to become farmers he became a director of Odumase Farms Ltd in May 1971. In doing this he was alleged to have infringed the constitution by becoming a director of a commercial enterprise. He resigned his directorship and was defended by the Premier in Parliament against opposition attacks.

When Ghana was hit by the 1971 collapse of the cocoa price a struggle ensued between Busia and Mensah over devaluation. Finally Busia forced a devaluation of a truly massive 44% which led to near panic inflation and gave the soldiers an excuse to intervene. He was detained on 13 January 1972 and released on 3 July 1973.

On 8 October 1975 Mensah was brought to trial on charges of sedition. He had published material alleged to have brought Colonel Acheampong's government into public disaffection. He admitted publishing the document, which was not diclosed in public, but denied that it was seditious. In November he was found guilty and sentenced to eight years hard labour.

On 16 June 1978 he won an appeal and was set free. But when Lt.Gen Fred Akuffo came to power he found himself disqualified from holding public office under the Elections and Public Disqualifications Decree of 1 January 1979. This precluded him from taking part in the elections of June 1979 though he was a member of the National Popular Front Party, led by Victor Owusu, which followed in the tradition of his old Progressive Party. He withdrew his candidacy for the presidential election to stand against Dr Hilla Limann in the elections of June 1979 in favour of Owusu.

After Jerry Rawlings seized power for the second time Mensah went into exile abroad and in April 1984 formed the Ghana Democratic Movement, in London, open to all Ghanaians who believed in the restoration of democracy.

In December 1985 he was arrested in Newark, New Jersey and charged with conspiracy to buy missiles, anti-aircraft guns and other weapons for shipment to Ghana. The case dragged on for years but twice the case against him was invalidated on technical reasons though his two co-defendants were convicted. At his second trial in September 1986 the jury deliberated for 17 hours, over three days, but could not reach a verdict.

OBENG, Paul Victor

Ghanaian politician, Chairman of PNDC Secretaries (Ministers) July 1985 -

With the unusual background as a chartered engineer, and holding the job of Co-ordinating Secretary he is the technocrat and organisation man of the Provisional National Defence Council. He frequently heads Ghanaian delegations to overseas countries and to international meetings.

Born 19 August 1947, though a native of Adansi Akrokerri in Ashanti, he was born at Akim Oda in the Eastern region. Educated at the University of Science and Technology, Kumasi where he obtained a BSc in mechanical engineering. He became a chartered engineer, member of the Institute of Marine Engineers (UK) and member of Ghana Institute of Engineers.

He started his career with the Overseas Brewery, Accra, the producers of Club beer. He later joined the motors division of the United Africa Company (UAC) as an engineer management trainee. He rose to assistant workshop manager in the machine shop division. He then joined Mankoadze Fisheries, a Ghanaian firm as a marine workshop engineer where he rose to be technical director.

After Jerry Rawlings assumed power on New Year's eve 1982, he was appointed to the ruling Provisional National Defence Council as Co-ordinating Secretary, the equivalent of Prime Minister in April 1982, but he did not become an official member of the PNDC itself until July 1985, when he took on the additional responsibilties as Chairman of the Committee of PNDC secretaries. One of his major specialisations is to lead high level political and economic delegations to foreign and neighbouring African countries. He has frequently accompanied Jerry Rawlings abroad and attended the summit meetings of the Organisation of African Unity in 1985 and 1986 and the Commonwealth summit in Vancouver, Canada in 1987.

OBIMPEH, Steve G.

Ghanaian naval officer and politician, Secretary for Agriculture 1 June 1986 -

Enthusiastic, friendly and a born organiser, he rose fast to become one of Ghana's most experienced and senior naval commanders. He doubled up by serving and advising on a number of public boards. He made his mark by organising the resettlement of the tens of thousands of Ghana refugees thrown out of Nigeria in 1983. This brought him to the attention of the Rawlings government who appointed him Secretary of Agriculture in June 1986. He then pulled off a second triumph by presiding over a major revival in Ghana agriculture with huge production increases in sorghum and maize.

Born 28 September 1941 at Vakpo in the Volta region. He attended the government Secondary Technical School at Takoradi from 1957-62 after which he joined the Ghana navy. He did his cadet training at the Britannia Naval College, England, April 1962-63 before being attached to royal navy ships as a midshipman.

He returned to Ghana in August 1965 and was appointed a first lieutenant on GNS Komenda. Later he became Captain of GNS Afadzato, September 1966-September 1967.

He returned to Britain in September 1966 and did further training including a course on navigation at HMS Dryad, a junior staff course at

Greenwich and an international tactical course at Woolwich.

On his return to Ghana he became base operations officer at Takoradi naval base and later second in command at the naval base at Tema. He was promoted to Acting Lieutenant Commander. He also had a spell as Captain of GNS Ejura and the senior officer in charge of the training squad. He became the acting officer in charge of Takoradi naval base and was promoted to temporary commander in May 1972.

While pursuing his naval career he served on a number of public boards and corporations including Ghana Railways and Ports Authority, 1972-73, the State Shipping corporation 1975-77 and was chairman of the Ghana Staff College Control Board, 1979-81.

He went to the USA Naval Staff College in July 1973 and passed out with distinction in December 1973. He returned home to resume command of the Takoradi naval base. In October 1975 he was transferred to Accra to take up the directorship of naval personnel and administration at naval headquarters.

He went for the naval command course at the Naval War College, USA in June 1975 and was awarded a masters degree in maritime strategy and management. He returned to Ghana in August 1978 and became chief staff officer at naval headquarers. He was promoted Commodore in April 1979 and became Chief of Naval Staff (Navy Commander) in June.

When tens of thousands of Ghanaians were evicted from Nigeria in 1983 he became the successful co-ordinator of the National Task Force with the responsibility of resettling them. He later became Chairman of the National Mobilisation Committee.

On 1 June 1986 he was appointed Secretary (equivalent of minister) for Agriculture, where he presided over a revival of Ghanian agriculture, achieving huge production increases in sorghum and maize assisted by the Japanese Sasakawa project.

OWUSU, Victor
Ghanaian lawyer and politician

Handsome, balding and growing old gracefully, he comes from one of the renowned Ashanti Royal families. A lawyer by training he soon made his mark in politics as a leading figure of the right. He spent most of his life in opposition trying to rally the Ghanaian establishment against the early socialist experiments. He did have a brief spell in office, holding senior ministries under the military governments of the late 1960s and under Kofi Busia. But he failed in the presidential elections against Limann in June 1978. He then became a formidable opposition leader and still remains the focus of opposition in any future civilian government.

Born 26 December 1923 at Agona-Ashanti. Educated locally and at the University of Nottingham and London. He was called to the bar in Lincoln's Inn in 1952 and returned home the same year to start a legal practice.

In 1956 he stood as a United Party MP in the pre-independence elections for Agona Kwabre. In parliament he and his UP colleagues came under continual harrassment by the Nkrumah regime which was swept to power at independence in March 1957. In 1961 he lost his parliamentary seat and was detained under the Preventive Detention Act. He was released in June 1962, powerless to combat the excesses of the last years of the Nkrumah government.

After the military coup of 24 February 1966, the National Liberation Council government made him Attorney General, 1966-69 a post he held concurrently with Minister of Justice from 1967. He took on Labour and Social Welfare in February 1968.

On 9 April 1969 Brigadier Akwesi Afrifa, who had just assumed power, briefly made him his Commissioner of External Affairs. But saying that it was the wrong job for him and aggrieved over the sacking of a colleague, he resigned and prepared instead for elections prior to the return to civilian rule.

On 6 September 1969 Busia re-appointed him to the prestigious post of Minister of External Affairs, but he hardly had time to address himself to foreign policy issues when he was switched back to become Minister of Justice and Attorney General on 27 January 1971. In March he rebuked the students of the University of Ghana, (where he had just become Chairman of the University Council) for demonstrating against their Vice Chancellor, describing their action as irresponsible. In August he introduced a bill in the National Assembly to forestall the revival of Nkrumah's Convention People's Party. He said the act had been introduced because of the behaviour of Nkrumah supporters "at the lunatic fringe of our society."

After the military coup by Colonel Ignatius Acheampong in January 1972, Owusu found himself in the cold once again. In March 1978 he was arrested with other political leaders for demonstrating against the results of the March referendum on union government. The coup which toppled Acheampong on 5 July 1978 brought his release. Jerry Rawlings seized power but maintained previous plans to return Ghana once again to civilian rule.

The June elections were contested by five parties but were mainly between those who followed in the Nkrumahist tradition and those, like Owusu, who inherited the tradition of the old United and Progress Parties. Owusu first had to be exonerated from the findings of the assets commissions that had earlier barred him from office.

A review tribunal set aside adverse findings that had been made against him. This allowed him to stand as leader of the Popular Front Party which won 42 seats against Dr Hilla Limann's 71. He then stood against Limann in the Presidential election and was again defeated by 1,118,405 votes to his 686,132. He graciously conceded defeat and said he would do nothing "to obstruct or frustrate" Limann's efforts to "carry out the people's mandate".

On 26 September 1981 he was elected as leader of the All People's Party, a coalition of four opposition groups worried about the lack of economic progress made by the Limann government. But within a few months Jerry Rawlings had seized power on New Year's Eve 1982 and Owusu's electoral ambitions were dashed.

Under Rawlings he retired from public life and went into private business. But on 21 August 1986 he was suddenly arrested for "treasonable acts to destabilise the government". All opposition movements concluded that the government had victimised Owusu to distract public opinion from its own economic failures. He was held in detention until February 1967 when he and 12 others had the charges against them suspended. A PNDC statement said, "the time they have spent in custody has at least made them realise the gravity of allowing themselves to be used or misled by those who seek to retard national progress." After his release Owusu went back into private life.

RAWLINGS, Jerry John (Flt.Lt)

Ghanaian politician. Head of State June-September 1979 and 1 January 1982-

Popular, young, handsome and dashing, Rawlings was the people's darling when he swept aside the last of the old order and first assumed power in June 1979. He was the leader of a leftist-populist regime that took harsh reprisals against corrupt officials. But he kept his promise to hand back power to the civilians. His disappointment at recurring corruption and indecisive government brought his "second coming" on New Year's Eve 1982. This allowed him to clear up corruption and introduce a measure of participatory democracy, but he did not fulfil his early marxist promise instead he showed himself a pragmatic, realist bowing to economic necessity and re-establishing good relations with the West while maintaining a leftist rhetoric.

Born 22 June 1947 in Accra, the son of a Ghanaian, Ewe mother and a Scottish father. Educated at Achimota school where he got his general certificate of education at O level in 1966 and at the Ghana Military Academy at Teshie.

He joined the airforce as a flight cadet, in Takoradi in August 1967 and became commissioned as a pilot officer in January 1969, winning the "Speed Bird Trophy" as the best cadet in flying and airmanship. He was promoted Flt Lieutenant in April 1978.

Always highly politically conscious, he became associated with a group of young radicals, mostly young military officers and NCOs, who planned a coup against General Fred Akuffo on 15 May 1979. He was highly critical of the political and economic bankruptcy of the old regime and, when political parties were legalised at the beginning of 1979, emerged as the voice of a new populism that was sweeping the country. He and a small group of officers were arrested and on 28 May faced a court martial for leading a mutiny of junior officers and men. Rawlings courageously took the opportunity in court, to denounce the corruption of previous years.

On 4 June his soldiers sprung him from military custody and took him direct to the radio station where he announced the setting up of the Armed Forces Revolutionary Council, AFRC, with himself as Chairman. He ruled by decree in a populist regime which set about the task of eradicating corruption and setting up a new order, with puritanical zeal. A number of past leaders and three former heads of state were summarily executed and people's courts imposed arbitrary punishment for corruption and other offences.

But Rawlings made it clear that he had no intention to hold onto power and said that the elections for the return to civilian rule would go ahead as planned. The elections were held one week early, Dr Hilla Limann's People's National Party triumphed and he won the presidential elections.

The handover took place on 24 September 1979. But Limann's government was weak and indecisive and Rawlings, though holding no constitutional position, was continually breathing down his neck as the guardian of the "gains made on 4 June (his revolution)". Rawlings made several speeches warning the people about the dangers of misuse of power by the Limann government, which responded by harrassing his closest associates.

On 1 December Rawlings was forced to resign his commission. He heard about his retirement on Radio Ghana after meeting Limann earlier that day, when the matter was not discussed. But ironically this actually strengthened his position by freeing himself from his obligations to the government as a serving officer. On 22 October 1980 he was detained on the grounds that he was planning the training of revolutionaries. He was freed but came under close surveillance as the government became increasingly paranoid about coup plots. Limann's rule became increasingly weak, while Rawlings chafed at its failure to fulfil the promise of his revolution.

On 1 January 1982, his much discussed "second coming" became fact and he seized power in a coup which started at 3 am on New Year's eve. Slight resistance by isolated military units had ended by the time he made his first broadcast at 11 am. He said the armed forces had been forced to intervene again because of the failure of the Limann government to combat corruption and a deteriorating economy. He said he had come to restore democracy in which the needs of the people were heeded by government. He said this was not just a question of abstract liberties, "it involves above all, food, clothing, shelter and the basic necessities of life."

He set up a Provisional National Defence Council, PNDC as the supreme ruling body initially consisting mainly of soldiers. On 21 January 1982 he established a 16-member civilian government, with cabinet ministers called secretaries, who were told to see their appointments merely as "a chance to serve the people sacrificially."

He sought to implement leftist-populist policies and to decentralise power, by setting up People's Defence Committees in an attempt to create mass participation. He also tried to democratise the army. But this replacement of old institutions with new caused conflict and uncertainty. It also unleashed ethnic feelings with Rawlings relying increasingly on his own Ewe people, while PNDC leaders from other ethnic groups were forced out, often accused of plotting. A number of attempted coups were soon being reported.

Rawlings found the Defence Committees often exceeded their powers and was forced to gradually clip their wings. In December 1984 he "restructured" the committees and their power dwindled thereafter. Students who had welcomed the second coming became gradually more estranged in the face of economic hardship and the need for austerity measures.

Rawlings may have wanted to run a marxist economy and to lift it up by its own bootstraps with the help of Eastern bloc countries, but was soon persuaded by his orthodox Finance Minister Kwesi Botchwey, to realign towards the West and to adopt conventional cures. Harsh austerity budgets were passed from 1983 and Ghana accepted tough International Monetary Fund conditions and heavy devaluation of the cedi. Rawlings decided to adjust to economic realities and run the economy on pragmatic lines. He stressed and succeeded in obtaining a rapid expansion of local food production. Goods returned to the shops but only at a price.

In his early years Rawlings forged close relationships with a number of left wing states including Libya and Burkina Faso, where he developed a particularly close relationship with its ruler Thomas Sankara. He visited Burkina many times and there were even tentative plans to create a common currency. Rawlings was devastated by Sankara's assassination in October 1987, although he made a point of maintaining good relations with his successor Blaise Compaore.

In December 1988 he instituted a programme of staggered local elections in the different regions of the country. Voters were asked to vote for individuals (not parties) who could represent them in 18 district assemblies. Turnout was low though this seemed to be a first hesitant step towards a return to democratic civilian rule.

On 10 May 1991, in response to massive international and internal pressure, he announced his acceptance of multi-party government. This volte-face brought a burst of activity. On 17 May a law setting up a National Consultative Assembly to prepare a draft constitution was published. A committee of experts was to draw up the document.

On 20 June conditional amnesty was granted to all political exiles, asking them to return home. At the same time very tough action was taken against political demonstrators in Ghana. Rawlings showed he was determined to relax power only on his own terms.

TSIKATA, Kojo (Captain)
Ghanaian soldier and politician.

*Taciturn and a listener rather than a talker, seldom seen in public. He is
regarded as a shady character because of his low profile stance and his
position as head of National Security. He regards himself as a Trotskyite.
He is the strongman behind the Rawlings regime. Some observers rank
him more powerful than Rawlings himself. He came under suspicion in
previous military regimes and was subjected to strict surveillance and
gained considerable unpopularity for some of his actions as a member of
the Rawlings government. One of the many Ewes in the Rawlings
government, he is married to a black South African.*

Born in Keta in the Volta region. Educated locally and at Achimota
Secondary School, Accra. He joined the army and did his training in
Ghana and Sandhurst Military Academy in England. He was among the
Ghanaian military contingent sent to the Congo by Kwame Nkrumah in
a peace keeping operation but later he was sacked by his master.

When Nkrumah was overthrown in 1966 and went into exile Tsikata
became a strident critic of the new military regime which put a price of
10,000 cedis on his head for anyone who could capture him dead or alive.
He remained in exile until Lt.Colonel Ignatius Acheampong took power.
Acheampong brought him back and made him deputy Managing Director
of the state owned Diamond Marketing Board. But he fell out with his
mentor and was arrested at the end of 1975 and put on trial on 19 May
1976 accused of plotting a coup against the Head of State.

The coup plot became known as "one man, one machete" as this was
said to be the chosen weapon of the coup plotters who planned to
slaughter government ministers with machetes. Tsikata claimed that he
had been beaten on at least five occasions and that a confession had been
forced out of him, but he was sentenced to death. He was awaiting
sentence to be carried out when his luck turned; Acheampong was
himself deposed on 5 July 1978 and he was released.

He again left Ghana for Angola and not much was heard of him until
Jerry Rawlings came to power in June 1979. He returned and took up an
undisclosed position in Rawlings' inner cabinet. But his travails started
again when Rawlings handed over power to Dr Hilla Limann who, saying
that he was a threat to state security, mounted a 24-hour military
surveillance on him. He was followed by heavily armed military
intelligence wherever he went, an operation which simply stimulated
public interest in him. It was clear that he was being victimised as a way
of getting at Rawlings, but the two remained close and Tsikata waited
until the coup of New Year's eve, 1972 which brought Rawlings his
"second coming".

Tsikata resumed his low profile work with the Rawlings government
as special adviser. Then some time later in a TV interview he revealed
that he was also in charge of National Security. He later became a full
member of the ruling Provisional National Defence Council (PNDC),

officially head of national security and the PNDC member in charge of foreign affairs.

In June 1982 three distinguished High Court judges were kidnapped and murdered for standing out for the independence of the judiciary. Army personnel including Tsikata himself were allegedly implicated in this event, which shocked many Ghanaians. A Special Investigations Board under High Court Judge Samuel Azu-Crabbe published its report confirming that he "master-minded" the plot. Two minor figures were found guilty of the murders and executed.

In October 1982 Tsikata became involved in a power struggle with another member of the PNDC Sergeant Alolga Akata-Pore. The regime attempted to cover up the dispute, but Akata-Pore appeared publicly to announce a reconciliation. Then in November another PNDC member Brigadier Nunoo Mensah resigned. Whatever happened in the inner councils of the PNDC, Tsikata had emerged triumphant.

On 27 February 1983 he claimed to have unveiled an attempted coup in which he among most other members of the PNDC, had been selected for assassination. Another coup attempt was foiled in June when an attempted infiltration was made from Togo. The rebels briefly seized the Ghana Broadcasting Station and demanded the arrest of Tsikata for his alleged involvement in the judges case.

During his tenure of office he had a long battle with the CIA whom he accused of being behind his harrassment in past regimes. He claimed that the CIA had presented a dossier on him to all governments after the fall of Nkrumah. He may have found his own CIA files when he took over national security. He took advantage of the CIA scandal when a CIA operative in Ghana passed on CIA secrets to her Ghanaian lover. A major row erupted between the intelligence services of the two countries and Tsikata was behind a dramatic spy-swap, expulsions of individuals suspected of spying on both sides and a threat by the US to withold its aid programme.

In July 1985 he officially relinquished his title as special adviser to the PNDC and was confirmed as being responsible for National Security and Foreign Affairs.

GUINEA

Population: 6.98m (1990, World Bank)
Head of State: Gen. Lansana Conté
Independence: 2 October 1958
Government: Military government by the Military Committee for
National Recovery after the coup of 3 April 1984 replaced by the
Committee for National Recovery (CRN) renamed Transitional
Committee for National Regeneration (CTRN) in January 1991. The
President rules through a part-civilian Council of Ministers.
Parties: President Sekou Touré's *Parti Democratique de Guinée*
(PDG) was dissolved after the coup of 1984 and other parties banned,
but several groups are still organised outside Guinea, mainly in
France.

CONTÉ, Lansana (General)
Guinea President, 3 April 1984.

*A professional soldier who found himself pitchforked into power in the
military coup which followed President Sekou Touré's death in March
1984. He declared himself in favour of democracy and an open society but
has found political rule a difficult process. Naturally reserved and his
own man, he has not been able to maintain the unquestioning loyalty of
his lieutenants though he has won majority approval of his people. He has
become heavily dependent on French advice and assistance and economic
prompting from international institutions. He claims to have set Guinea
on course for the gradual restoration of democratic liberties.*

Born circa 1945 into the Soussou tribe. He joined the army and did his
military training in the Soviet Union unlike the privileged officers of an
earlier generation who had done all their training in France. He rose
rapidly in the army though there were a number of officers senior to him,
including General Lansana Diane who was arrested at the time of the
coup.

After the death of President Sekou Touré when undergoing emergency
heart surgery in the Cleveland Clinic, Ohio on 26 March 1984, the
military carried out a coup to prevent the prolongation of an unpopular
regime. The principal coup leaders were Colonels Conté and Diarra
Traoré. They seized power on 3 April, one week after Sekou Touré's
death. Conté established a Military Committee of Recovery (CMRN) and
became President, with Traoré as his Prime Minister.

Hundreds of political prisoners were released and their places were
taken by the leaders of the former President's *Parti democratique
Guinéen.* Conté said his coup marked "the end of a bloody and ruthless
dictatorship". He set about creating a free and open society based on
private enterprise and closer relations with the West. Foreign investors

soon flocked back, showing particular interest in Guinea's mineral potential and the need to rebuild the infrastructure. Many of Guinea's two million exiles began to return home.

Conté liberalised the economy and devalued the currency in line with IMF proscriptions, while maintaining financial austerity and successfully pursued an open and magnanimous style of government in the first year. But a power and personality conflict soon began between Conté and Traoré. Conté responded by slimming down the cabinet and personally taking on the powers of Prime Minister and Minister of Defence, demoting Traoré to the Education Ministry.

This seemed to entrench Conté in power, but on 4 July 1985 Traoré decided to seize control while Conté was away at a meeting of West African states in Togo. He made a speech from the local radio station, saying that he had taken over. But loyalist troops began to fight back and Traoré and six other ministers were arrested, while Conté, still not sure of the outcome, demonstrated his courage by flying home to what turned out to be a jubliant welcome.

Rid of his main rival, he reshuffled his cabinet in December 1985 and brought in a majority of civilians for the first time since independence. He banished other key ministers to remote rural governorships to keep them out of the way. He also distanced himself from members of his own cabinet and promoted himself to Brigadier-General. In March 1986 the Information Minister resigned, saying that he could no longer bear to belong to a government of profiteers whose members were unable to gain audience with the President. He complained that there had only been three cabinet meetings since December 1985 and that Conté had established one-man rule.

In January 1988 Conté granted amnesty to 67 political prisoners, including Sekou Tour's widow and son. In April district council elections were held as part of a gradual return to a democratic society. But there was considerable opposition to his gradualism and to his plans for cutting the bureaucracy in the civil service.

Demonstrations in Conakry in January 1988 led to another reshuffle of ministers in which his second-in-command, Major Kerfella Camara, was removed as permanent secretary of the CMRN and banished to Kankan in Upper Guinea as local minister.

On 4 April 1990 Conté was promoted to the rank of Division General.

On 16 January 1991 he bowed to international and internal pressure and dissolved the CMRN replacing it with the Transitional Committee for National Regeneration (CTRN) which would rule until pluralism was introduced within five years. The opposition described this period as far too long in the light of present changes in Africa.

GUINEA BISSAU

Population: 1.01m (1990, World Bank)
Head of State: Joao Bernado Vieira
Independence: 23 September 1973
Government: A framework-law was adopted on 8 May 1991 which substituted a constitutional for a revolutionary republic. The ruling party surrendered its monopoly and pluralism was allowed for the first time. Elections are pending the revision of the constitution.
Parties: Former single party - *Partido Africano da Independencia da Guiné e Cabo Verdé* (PAIGC). Four other new parties were in the course of formation in mid-1991.

CABRAL, Luis de Almedia

Guinea Bissau politician. President September 1974 – November 1980

Though he did not have the charisma of his brother Amilcar, he was one of the principal leaders of the PAIGC and played a leading role in the liberation struggle. He survived to become President of his country at independence. But his economic policies were not successful and he failed to carry all his colleagues with him. This exposed him to the coup of November 1980.

Born 1931 in Bissau, Portuguese Guinea though he came from a mestico, Cape Verdean family. He, together with his brother Amilcar Cabral, was one of the founders of the African Party for the Independence of Guinea and Cape Verde (PAIGC), which was founded clandestinely in Bissau on 19 September 1956. He became a member of the politburo and central committee.

After a local education, he became an accountant with the Portuguese company, Companhia Uniao Fabril. When the Portuguese secret police started to investigate the PAIGC, he left temporarily for Guinea Conakry. By 1961 he was back organising the National Union of Guinean Workers (UNTG). He became the union secretary-general in 1961. When the liberation war started later in that year he took to the bush and by 1963 was put in charge of the Quitafine frontier zone.

In 1965 he became a member of the PAIGC war council and in 1970 a member of the executive committee for the war, with responsibility for reconstruction in liberated zones.

His brother was assassinated in Conakry on 20 January 1973, but the war of independence was going well and the Portuguese had already lost large areas of the country by the time of their coup in April 1974. A peace agreement was signed on 10 September 1974 and Cabral became President of the Council of State.

He tried to maintain the democratic and socialist forms of government that the party had established in liberated areas during the long war of independence, but there were massive economic problems, with 150,000 left homeless by the war and agricultural production devastated. Socialist economics made things worse and there were chronic deficits on payments and trade.

There was also considerable tension in the PAIGC between those who wanted closer union with the Cape Verde islands under Cabral's leadership and the more nationalist aspirations of the African majority in Guinea Bissau, who resented the dominance of the Cape Verdian mesticos.

On the night of 14 November 1980 Joao Bernado Vieira seized power. He arrested Luis Cabral, had him expelled from the party and put him under house arrest. He was tried and sentenced to death, but held in house arrest until international pressure secured his release on 30 December 1981. He was allowed to go into exile, first to Cuba and then to the Cape Verde islands.

CABRAL, Vasco (Dr)

Guinea Bissau politician. Second vice-president, council of state, 9 March 1990-

One of the longest-standing freedom fighters of the PAIGC who was imprisoned for nearly six years by the Portuguese. He has served as Minister of Economic Planning both under Luiz Cabral and Joao Vieira. Always considered to be one of the pro-Moscow faction in the party and frequently in conflict with his colleagues. He made something of a come-back with his appointment as second vice-president of the council of state in March 1990.

Born 1924 in Guinea Bissau but of mestico, Cape Verdian descent. Educated locally and at Lisbon University, 1950. Arrested by the Portuguese and held in prison for almost six years, including two years of solitary confinement (1954-59). He returned to Lisbon university, completed his degree in economics and fell under the influence of Amilcar Cabral who was in Lisbon at the time. He also met Agostinho Neto the future Angolan leader. Back in Guinea Bissau he joined the African Party for the Independence of Guinea and Cape Verde (PAIGC) and was elected to its central committee and war council.

In September 1973 at the first meeting of the National Assembly when independence was declared, he was elected to the 15-member council of state with specific responsibility for economy and finance. This position was confirmed when independence was granted by the Portuguese and he became State Commissioner for Economic Development and Planning under President Luis Cabral.

His socialist economic policies were not successful and the failure of the economy contributed to the coup by Joao Vieira in November 1980. He was wounded and temporarily sought refuge in the Swedish embassy, but he survived because of his good international economic contacts, on the secretariat to the National Council and as Minister of Economic

Planning. Then in November 1981 he was elected as Deputy President to Vieira. But he was always regarded as more left wing and pro-Soviet than the new president and was reluctant to change rigid economic policies that had emptied the shops and failed to revive the fledgling industrial sector. He lost his ministerial post in a reshuffle on 14 May 1982 though he was given a senior post in the party, as a member of the council of state. This was confirmed under the new constitution of May 1984. He became second vice-president of the council in March 1990, in charge of six other ministries.

VIEIRA, Joao Bernardo
Guinea Bissau President, 14 November 1980 —

Given the nom de guerre 'Nino' in the guerrilla war against the Portuguese, he was a man of great popularity and ability. Though firmly entrenched as number two to the former President Luis Cabral, he had personal differences and his followers resented rule by a mestico from Cape Verde. This prompted the coup of 1980. Since that time Vieira has himself found it difficult to stave off challenges to his own power. There have been several coup attempts, mainly inspired by his closest colleagues. He has gradually developed his links with the West and has liberalised his economy beneath the screen of socialist rhetoric. This has been a point of contention with the purists of the original revolution. In May 1991 he supported a new law, which was introduced into the National Assembly making Guinea Bissau a pluralist state.

Born 1939 in Bissau. Developed an early interest in politics and joined the *Partido Africano da Independencia da Guine e Cabo Verde* (PAIGC) in 1960. The guerilla war against the Portuguese started at the end of 1961 and the PAIGC soon established a base from which to operate. Vieira, under his *nom de guerre* Nino, was made the political and military chief of the liberated area of Catio (1960-64). During this period he did advanced military training in Nanking, China.

Then followed a decade of gruelling guerrilla war in which the countryside was gradually liberated and held by the PAIGC which set up an alternative administration and tried to revive war damaged agricultural production. He became military chief of the important southern front and member of the political bureau (1964-65); vice-president of the council of war (1965-67); responsible for military operations (1970-71); member of the executive committee of the council of war (1971-73).

A significant advance in his career came when he was made deputy secretary-general of PAIGC 1973. He became President of the People's National Assembly and the State Commander of the armed forces after elections had been held in the liberated areas and a National People's Assembly had unlilaterally proclaimed independence on 23 September 1973. Portugal formally withdrew from Guinea Bissau on 10 September 1974 after the Portuguese revolution had overthrown Salazar. He became one of the four members of the permanent secretariat of the party, the highest decision-making body. He was also made Minister for the Armed Forces in the first independence government.

In 1978, when the Prime Minister Francisco Mendez was killed in a car accident, he took over his post.

On the night of 14 November 1980, he took power in a coup and set up a nine-man National Revolutionary Council. Former President Luis Cabral was put under house arrest and was held for more than a year until December 1981. The coup was mainly a reaction by black mainland Africans being ruled by Mestico leaders from Cape Verde (both Guinea Bissau and Cape Verde were ruled by the PAIGC party). Vieira was also reacting against a new constitution that had been passed only four days before the coup, strengthening Cabral's powers as President against those of Vieira as Prime Minister.

Vieira's new military council was composed entirely of mainland blacks. He reaffirmed his commitment to socialist policies and at a special PAIGC congress rebuked the previous regime for departing from the policies of Amilcar Cabral. His problem was to legitimise the change of power and organised party elections, but most of those chosen in January 1981 were those that had been involved in the coup. In a government reshuffle in May 1982 Vieira took the portfolios of defence and security while keeping his other functions as Head of State and Commander-in-chief of the armed forces.

In July 1983 Vieira announced the discovery of a plot against him and further members of the pre-coup leadership were arrested. In August three ministers were dismissed for embezzlement. The politicking seemed part of a power struggle between Vieira and his Prime Minister, Victor Saude Maria. Maria was sacked on 11 March 1984 and took refuge in the Portuguese embassy, thinking he would be accused of plotting. He had been opposing the President over constitutional changes that would have weakened his post as Prime Minister (a situation analogous to the one which actually provoked Vieira's coup in 1980). Vieira promised that no action would be taken against him and stuck to his word as Maria went into exile.

Vieira then pushed through constitutional changes which strengthened his powers and abolished the post of PM. Another coup attempt was unmasked on 7 November 1985 involving Paulo Correia, the first Vice-President who ranked number two in the party. Correia had opposed Vieira's economic stabilisation programme seemimgly imposed by the IMF. Vieira put Correia and his co-conspirators on trial and after sentence six, including Correia, were executed. Other detainees implicated in earlier coups were released, the cabinet and party were purged.

Vieira pursued his policies of economic liberalisation and reduced state control over trade in an attempt to increase foreign investment. He worked together with the World Bank and IMF and organised a devaluation of the Guinean peso by 41% in May 1987, though he maintained subsidies on essential commodities. This increased inflation and political tension and there were reports of another coup attempt in August 1987.

In foreign affairs he is mainly motivated by the need to increase foreign economic assistance and by the necessity of maintaining good relations with neighbouring Guinea and Senegal.

On 1 June 1989 he was re-elected President by a council of state elected on the same day as a new National Assembly.

Under pressure from external opponents and critics in early 1990, he first promised to democratise the party and then to introduce a multi-party state. A committee was established to see what constitutional changes would be required in April. He said, "We are going to open up the system so that the people can choose the party that works best, but this must not be a tribal party." His greatest fear was the introduction of tribalism into politics.

On 8 May 1991 he supported the introduction of a framework-law into the National Assembly which made Guinea Bissau a constitutional rather than a revolutionary state. It also legalised multi-partyism.

KENYA

Population: 24.78m (1990, World Bank)
Head of State: Daniel arap Moi
Independence: 12 December 1963
Government: Republic within the Commonwealth. Presidential government through a National Assembly and Council of Ministers. Single party system.
Parties: Sole legal party since 1982 - Kenya African National Union (KANU). Unauthorised opposition groups exist within the country and abroad, in exile.

KARANJA, Josephat Njinga

Politician, academic and diplomat. Vice-President March 1988-May 1989.

A brilliant academic and diplomat who went into full-time political life fairly late after he had been high commissioner in Britain and Vice-Chancellor of Nairobi University for long periods. He combines academic excellence with intellectual confidence. His powers of persuasion and gentle diplomacy, plus his evident loyalty, suddenly won him appointment as Kenya's fifth Vice-President, but one year later he was attacked by fellow parliamentarians, jealous of his sudden rise. He was brought down in a vicious campaign in which old scores were settled and President Moi did not intervene to save him.

Born 5 February 1931, a Kikuyu, in Githiga, Githunguri. Educated at Kagumo government School and at the prestige Alliance High School, Kikuyu and at Makerere University, Kampala, where he won a diploma in education, before being expelled for his political activities. He went on to higher studies at the University of New Delhi, Georgia University and Princeton, New Jersey, where he completed a D.Phil. He became a lecturer in African studies at the Fairleigh Dickinson University, NJ, (1961-2), then Lecturer in African and Modern European History at the University of East Africa (1962-63).

He was then spotted by Jomo Kenyatta and given his first non-academic job as high commissioner to Britain 1963-70, where he established wide-ranging contacts with the British establishment. He returned home to the presitigious post of Vice-Chancellor of the University of Nairobi 1970-79.

He resigned from the University of Nairobi in 1979 and decided to go in for politics by running for the Githunguri seat in the Central Province of Kikuyu country. He lost the election narrowly to the Minister of Manpower, Development and Employment, Arthur Magugu. He petitioned the High Court, but the powerful Minster of Constitutional Affairs Charles Njonjo appeared to already know the outcome when he said that nothing would change Magugu's election. Karanja stood for Githunguri in 1983 but was again defeated.

He then decided to switch his seat to the more cosmopolitan constitutency of Mathare in Nairobi in November 1986 after the dissident MP Andrew Ngumba had left the seat vacant and gone into exile. He triumphed and had a big fund-raising rally in Mathare for the KANU party, which was given the seal of approval by President Moi by his attendance. Within a few months he was made Assistant Minister of Research, Science and Technology in a mini-reshuffle in January 1987.

He had been in this post for less than a year when he was appointed Vice-President and Minister of Home Affairs and National Heritage, on 24 March 1988. This move by President arap Moi had been caused by the demotion of Mwai Kibaki who had been his Vice-President and the unofficial representative of the majority Kikuyu tribe since Kenyatta's death in 1978. Moi wanted a break with Kibaki, but he did not want the Kikuyu to feel deprived of a leader. He also wanted a man who would campaign actively to improve Kenya's human rights record. He chose Karanja as a Kikuyu who was relatively politically inexperienced, despite his brilliant diplomatic and academic record.

But Karanja survived in the hot seat of the Vice-Presidency for little more than a year before fellow parliamentarians started a vicious campaign to bring him down. They complained that he had overstepped his authority during President Moi's absence and had treated other members with contempt. Even more extreme charges questioned his loyalty and whether he had ties with the Ugandan government. Karanja denied all charges as "totally unsubstantiated, malicious, tendentious and contemptible, orchestrated by my known political enemies and rivals." He also reaffirmed his loyalty to the President, but Moi was clearly not disposed to do anything to save him and accepted his resignation as a minister and from the party on 1 May 1989. The authorities then confiscated his passport. He was officially expelled from KANU on 15 June 1989.

KIBAKI, Mwai
Kenyan Politician. Vice-President 11 October 1978-24 March 1988.

Laid back, tolerant, fond of his sport and the good things in life, he had an impeccable record from the early days when he helped organise the newly formed Kenya African Union, to his days of maturity as a top minister (Finance, Planning or Home Affairs for more than two decades). He reached the peak of his career serving nearly ten years as a loyal, unambitious Vice-President before being dropped unceremoniously by President Moi. Some say he had become too relaxed and easy-going before his dismissal, others that he was merely a victim of Moi's growing authoritarianism.

Born 15 October 1931 at Othaya, near Nyeri of Kikuyu parents. He went to Othaya primary school, Karima Catholic Mission, Nyeri Boys

School and Mangu High School. He continued at Makerere University (1951-54) where he took a BA and won a special prize for being the best arts student.

After a short period with Shell in Uganda in 1955, he went to London School of Economics to read for a BSc in Economics (1956-59). He returned to lecture in economics at Makerere, but with the elections of February 1961 imminent, he started to organise for the newly formed Kenya African National Union. The party won the elections but he did not stand himself; instead he was elected to the legislative assembly of the East African Common Services Organisation.

In the pre-independence elections of May 1963 he stood for KANU in the Nairobi, Doornholm constituency and won his seat, being appointed Parliamentary Secretary to the Treasury.

When Kenya became a republic in December 1964, he went to the Ministry of Economic Planning and Development as Tom Mboya's assistant minister. Kibaki, with his sound administrative ability, complemented Mboya well and the two formed a powerful economic team.

Over 1966-69 he was Minister for Commerce and Industry. In 1968 he led the East African team in negotiations with the EEC. In the ministry he pressed ahead with Africanisation of the distributive trade and the participation of government in commerce and industry.

After Mboya's tragic death in July 1969 he had the ministry of Planning and Development added to his portfolio. In December 1969 he stood for the Nairobi constituency of Bahati and was returned to be appointed Minister of Finance. Economic Planning was added to his portfolio from 1970-78.

On the death of Jomo Kenyatta, he was appointed Vice-President by Daniel arap Moi on 11 October 1978 while retaining the Ministry of Finance. He was shuffled sideways in February 1982 to become Minister of Home Affairs and at this stage was described as part of a powerful triumvirate dominating the political scene, including President Moi and Charles Njonjo.

But Kibaki's influence gradually began to decline and Njonjo was disgraced as President Moi took more power to himself. In the elections of 21 March 1988, Kibaki was challenged at the polls for the first time in his career but still triumphed, gaining 99.8% of the vote in his Othaya constituency in his homeland Nyeri. But he and President Moi had been moving apart for a considerable period, disagreeing on style, minor issues and personality differences. Kibaki's style was deceptively easy-going and detached and this could have been mistaken for indolence.

On 24 March 1988 Moi dismissed him from the Vice-Presidency and dropped him from his post as Minister of Home Affairs, demoting him to Minister of Health. (Josephat Karanja, who replaced him as Vice-President was himself to last only a brief period.) The move came as a major disappointment to his electorate, friends and the Kikuyu people in general who felt that their leader had been unfairly removed.

LIJOODI, Japeth Livasia
Kenyan politician.

One of the fast rising stars of the Kenya African National Union. Formerly a planner and FAO representative who broke into Kenyan politics on his return from abroad in 1988. He won the Shinyalu parliamentary seat at his first attempt and went on to become an assistant minister and later National Party Treasurer.

Born 1936 in Kakamega district, Western province. Educated at Solyo primary school and later Kamusinga Secondary where he obtained his Cambridge school certificate in 1959. He then went to Indiana State University, USA to read economics, graduating with an MSc in 1967.

He returned to Kenya and joined the civil service as a planning officer. By 1978 he had become chief of development planning at the Ministry of Agriculture. He joined the Food and Agricultural Organisation in 1982 and became its representative in Nigeria until 1988 when he returned home to contest the Shinyalu parliamentary seat, in March, for the Kenya African National Union. Though a political novice in a country of hard boiled politicians, he won the seat at his first attempt and was appointed Assistant Minister for Information and Broadcasting.

He also made rapid progress in the party, being elected organising secretary for Kakamega, replacing the veteran politician Burudi Nabwera. He stood in the mini-party elections of June 1989 after the death of Moses Mudavadi, a powerful provincial baron in the party. He was returned as national party treasurer, a important post in the KANU structure which gave him automatic membership of other top party bodies such as the Executive Committee, National Governing Council and Delegates Conference.

MAGUGU, Arthur Kinyanjui
Kenyan politician. Minister of Commerce, 1 May 1989-

An articulate and fearless man who has figured as a minister in every government since President Moi first came to power in 1978. His value as a 'utility' minister is demonstrated by the five different posts that he has held over the last decade. He has become the most senior cabinet minister for the powerful Kikuyu district of Kiambu and has considerable influence in the Kenya African National Union.

Born 1935 in Githunguri, Kiambu district in a Kikuyu family. Educated locally, then at La Verne University, California, where he took his BA. He proceeded to the University of Stockholm, Sweden where he read for a diploma and later a masters degree in economics. He returned home to become a lands settlement officer in the Ministry of Lands and Settlement.

He made his first political challenge in 1969 when he beat the former Mau Mau detainee, Waira Kamau, in a bitter battle for the Githunguri seat. He has held the seat ever since though challenged in 1974 by

Josephat Karanja, who was himself later to become Vice-President. He beat off the challenge again in 1979 when he survived a petition against the result in the High Court and in 1983, though Karanja was determined to secure a seat for himself in the Kenyan parliament.

When President Daniel arap Moi took over following the death of Jomo Kenyatta in 1978, he held elections and formed a new government on 28 November 1979. Magugu was given his first appointment as Minister of Health in Moi's new team. Moi's first major reshuffle followed in February 1982 when he transferred Magugu to the Ministry of Finance, a post he held for only a brief spell because on 1 October 1983 he was moved to Housing, Works and Physical Planning and on 1 April 1986 to Transport and Communications.

Moi's reshuffles came frequently in the mid-1980s and on 24 March 1988, when Magugu's old rival Dr Karanja was made Vice-President, he was transferred to Manpower, Development and Employment, a new ministry that was formed specifically to handle labour planning and development, employment policy and Kenyanisation. But with the sudden downfall of Karanja in May 1989, Magugu was again reshuffled to the Ministry of Commerce.

MAINA, Charles Gatere
Kenyan civil servant and diplomat.

A thoroughly professional civil servant specialising in education. He made his mark as prinicipal of the Kenya Institute of Administration and then Secretary-General of the East African Community as it was entering its final death throes, in the 1970s. Maina was powerless to arrest the disintegration of the community but was compensated by being appointed Kenya's Permanent Representative to the UN.

Born 1 March 1931, a Kikuyu at Nyeri. Educated at Kianjogu, Tumutumu, Kagumo and Makerere University. He took up teaching (1959-61), becoming a district education officer (1962), provincial education officer (1962-64), assistant chief education officer (1964-66), deputy secretary for education (1966-68). Over 1968-71 he was the principal of the Kenya Institute of Administration.

Next he won the important post of Secretary-General of the troubled East African Community, 1971-74. It was a disheartening job because the Community was beginning to break up under nationalist pressures. Many of them originated in Kenya which was dissatisfied with the running of the common service organisations jointly owned by the three countries Kenya, Uganda and Tanzania. In compensation for his East African disappointments President Kenyatta chose him, in 1974, as Kenya's Permanent Representative to the United Nations.

MOI, arap Daniel

Kenyan politician. President since 10 October 1978 —

Formerly considered to be a pale shadow of Jomo Kenyatta, Moi as President gradually revealed himself as a man with ideas of his own - a stern authoritarian with a tough side to his nature encouraged by his strict Christian upbringing. The attempted coup in August 1982 shortly after he assumed power was damaging to his confidence. He was also suspicious that the dominant Kikuyu tribe were scheming against him. This led him to drop the main Kikuyu leaders like Charles Njonjo, Mwai Kibaki and Josephat Karanja, while politically neutralising most of the rest. He has played an influential role in Africa and the OAU while remaining a staunch friend of Britain and the West.

Born 1924 in the Sacho location of Baringo district in Kenya's Rift Valley Province in Western Kenya. He is a Tugen, a tribe which forms part of the Kalenjin group famous for its long distance runners and its loyal soldiers and policemen.

Educated at African Mission School, Kabartonjo and then at the American Inland Mission School and the Government African School at Kapsabet in the highlands of Western Kenya. After teacher training, in 1945 he became a teacher at Kabarnet, with many of Kenya's present Members of Parliament among his pupils.

He was soon appointed headmaster in Kapsabet, leaving in 1948 to become a teacher in Tambach teacher training school (1948-54), returning as headmaster in Kabarnet (1955-57). He took up politics comparatively late in 1950. In October 1955 he was nominated as a representative to the Legislative Council. He was one of the first eight African MPs to be returned in the direct elections of 1957.

He played a quiet, back-bench role in his early days as an elected member, first emerging as a political heavyweight in 1960, when he split from his Kikuyu and Luo colleagues to become chairman of the Kenya African Democratic Union, an alliance of opposition parties. When KADU was dissolved in 1964 he joined the Kenya African National Union (KANU), the ruling party in Kenya today.

Moi became Minister for Education (1961-62), Minister for Local Government (1962-64) and Home Affairs (1964-67). He was president of KANU for Rift Valley Province (1966-67). He then succeeded the ailing Joseph Murumbi as Vice-President in 1966.

During the whole of his vice-presidency he was under the shadow of Jomo Kenyatta and the all-powerful Kikuyu group which dominated national affairs, but he kept a low profile and bided his time. Though the Kenya constitution laid down that he, as Vice-President, should be the successor in the event of Kenyatta's death, a group of leading Kikuyu campaigned to change the constitution and ensure that the leadership would be kept within the Kikuyu tribe. But Kenyatta was not prepared to upset the constitutional system. He had worked well with Moi who had given him faithful service and Kenyatta did not particularly favour any of the potential Kikuyu aspirants.

In the event, when Kenyatta died on 23 August 1978, Moi succeeded him quite smoothly. He was sworn in as Kenya's second President on October 10 1978. He had the support of two prominent Kikuyu leaders in Mwai Kibaki, who was to become his Vice-President, and the powerful Minister of Constitutional Affairs, Charles Njonjo.

Everyone expected Moi to follow closely in the Kenyatta mould and he indeed coined his own slogan *Nyayo*, meaning footsteps, which refers to following in the footsteps left by Kenyatta. But Moi soon showed that he had ideas of his own and he immediately started to tackle widespread corruption in government and business circles and the dominance of the Kikuyu tribe in the top positions of state.

But he never had the charisma of Kenyatta and was unable to handle the rivalry between his immediate lieutenants, nor do very much for the mass of the population who were suffering from unemployment, high inflation and the inequable distribution of wealth.

This situation led to the attempted coup of August 1982 in which Kenyan airforce officers tried to grab power. The coup was violent and brought heavy loss of life and major economic damage in terms of looted shops and houses. Order was however restored by army loyalists.

President Moi became chairman of the OAU for 1981/82, remaining chairman until June 1983 when he was succeeded by Ethiopia's Colonel Mengistu. It was a time in which the OAU was bitterly divided over the question of the admission of the Saharwi Arab Democratic Republic as a member-state. Moi adopted a peacemaker's role and eventually worked out a compromise formula which allowed for SADR's admission.

But in the 1980s Moi's rule became increasingly repressive, with less regard for human rights than shown by Jomo Kenyatta. After the attempted coup he considerably reduced personal and press freedom, detained dissidents in different walks of life and became overly suspicious about potential opposition movements. By pushing out of office the only main Kikuyu challenger, Charles Njonjo, in 1983, he reinforced his own position, though this was at the cost of general dissatisfaction in the Kikuyu community.

Moi also found considerable dissatisfaction among students and opposition from the churches against his repressive policies. But he was convinced that there was a serious threat to security from a dissident movement known as 'Mwakenya'. Moi launched a massive hunt for those responsible. Few identifiable dissidents were found, but more than 100 people thought to hold anti-government sympathies were arrested by the end of 1987. He clashed with the National Council of Churches which thought that he was using the threat of Mwakenya to crush the opposition. In July 1987 Amnesty International published a report accusing the Kenyan government of trying to silence the opposition by detention without trial and by the use of torture.

In December 1986 parliament increased presidential powers by transferring control of the civil service to the president's office and by giving the president the power to dismiss the attorney-general and auditor-general and in July 1988 to dismiss judges at will. Parliament also instituted a new system of voting in which voters had to queue publicly behind the candidates of their choice. This system produced a KANU-approved list of candidates in February 1988, while Moi himself was returned unopposed for a third term in March.

In an extensive government reshuffle after the election Vice-President Mwai Kibaki was demoted to Minister of Health and replaced by Josephat Karanja another Kikuyu but with less popular following, who in turn, lasted only just over one year in the number two spot.

During 1990/91 Moi was fighting a rearguard action against opponents who wanted the introduction of pluralism and multi-party government. He claimed that any liberalisation would simply introduce tribalism and defended Kenya's single-party system. He did, however, introduce some reforms concerning party membership and allowed open voting after abandoning the system in which voters had to queue behind the candidates of their choice.

In foreign affairs Moi ensured that Kenya played a disproportionately important role in Africa and the OAU and remained a staunch friend of Britain despite some suspicion of Britain's sympathies during the Charles Njonjo affair. He was irked by American and British campaigns against Kenya's human rights record. He remained suspicious of the intentions and instability of the Museveni government in Uganda, while gradually growing closer to socialist Tanzania.

MUHOHO, George Kamau
Kenyan politician, former Catholic priest.

An extraordinary man with an extraordinary background. Well connnected with the blue-blooded Kenyatta and Koinange families, he took the most unusual route into politics. "Father Muhoho" as he is still nicknamed, became a brilliant Catholic priest, theologian and Vatican diplomat. He speaks seven languages fluently - Kikuyu, Swahili, English, French, German, Italian and Spanish. He was instrumental in setting up the UN Environment Programme headquarters in Nairobi and an environment secretariat in the President's office. But he came off badly when a dispute about the diminishing elephant herd erupted during his tenure of office as Minister of Tourism and Wildlife, and he was then reshuffled to Research, Science and Technology.

Born 1938 in Kiambu, a full brother of Mama Ngina Kenyatta, the widow of the late Jomo Kenyatta. Educated in Kiambu, then at Kabaa Secondary School in Machakos where he gained a school certificate in 1956. In 1957 he entered Morogoro Senior Seminary, Tanzania, where he spent three years reading philosophy and another four years studying theology. He graduated in 1963 as a bachelor of theology and became a Catholic priest.

In 1966 he enrolled for a doctorate programme in canon law at the

Pontifical Urbanian University, Rome. He did a doctoral thesis on the development of Kenyan educational policy in 1970, then attended the Pontifical Academy which trains Vatican diplomats. He served as a Vatican diplomat at the European Economic Community headquarters in Brussels (1970-73).

On his return home he was made Catholic chaplain to Nairobi University. He took a leading part in establishing the headquarters for the UN Environmental Programme (UNEP) in Nairobi, by acting as liaison between the Kenyan government and the UN secretariat. In 1974 he founded the National Environment Secretariat in the President's office. In 1975-76 he was the chairman of the inter-governmental preparatory committee for the Habitat conference. At the conference itself, in Vancouver in 1976, he chaired the first committee. He became director of the UNEP information department in Nairobi, 1978-83.

He ceased to be a priest in 1976, obtaining President Kenyatta's help to secure a papal dispensation from Pope Paul IV. In January 1977 he married Jane Njeri Koinange, a law graduate and former company secretary for Lonrho. She was also politically influential, being daughter of former MP John Mbiyu Koinange and niece of Kenyatta's powerful minister, Peter Mbiyu Koinange.

In 1983 he decided to go into politics and contested the Juja parliamentary seat for the Kenya African National Union. He won the elections and remained a back-bencher until October 1984 when President Daniel arap Moi made him assistant minister for water development. Ten months later he became assistant at the ministry of education, science and technology.

On 1 June 1987 he was promoted to full Minister of Tourism and Wildlife. He successfully defended his Juja seat in the March 1988 parliamentary elections. He also became the KANU chairman of the important Kiambu branch, defeating the once powerful leader of the conglomerate tribal organisation the Gikuyu, Embu and Meru Association (GEMA), Njenga Karume.

But hardly had he resumed as minister when a major row erupted over the poaching of Kenyan wildlife. He became involved in a dispute with Dr Richard Leakey, chairman of the Kenyan Wildlife Society over the rapidly diminishing number of elephants remaining in the Kenyan game parks and over a secret document listing prominent officials involved in poaching. Muhoho could not be persuaded to publish the list of those involved. As the debate widened into a general dispute about the future of Kenya's wildlife, he was transferred to become Minister of Research, Science and Technology in May 1989.

MWANGALE, Elijah Wasike
Kenyan politician. Minister of Agriculture, 6 June 1990-

A quiet, pipe-smoking intellectual lecturer from Egerton College who became an able, ambitious and well connected minister under President

Moi, first as minister of Tourism and Wildlife, then as Foreign Minister. Known for his outspoken and fearless statements. Still prominent in the party and cabinet as Minister for Agriculture. He has wide business interests including a share in a casino and a fertiliser company.

Born 1939 in Kimilili, Bungoma district. Educated locally and at Egerton College (1961-63), gaining a diploma in agriculture. He continued his studies in West Virginia University, USA, where he gained a BSc degree in agriculture and a masters in Soil Science (Agronomy).

He returned to Egerton where he lectured in chemistry. In 1969 he stood for Bungoma East and won a seat for the Kenya African National Union, to parliament. In March 1975 he was appointed chairman of the 15-man select committee set up to investigate the disappearance and assassination of the former minister and MP Josiah Kariuki. He stuck by his terms of reference and refused to have his committee report doctored to serve the interests of those involved. He gave copies to the Press before presenting the official report to the President at State House. The report accused the police of a massive cover-up to hide the circumstances of the murder and recommended the suspension of the commander of the para - military General Service Unit, who was the last person to have been seen in Kariuki's company.

When President Moi came to power on the death of his illustrious predecessor Jomo Kenyatta, new elections were called. Then on 28 November 1979 Moi appointed a new cabinet, making Mwangale his Minister for Labour. On 20 June 1980 he was reshuffled to the important revenue-earning Tourism sector. With the growing environmental concerns of the 1980s his ministry was expanded to Tourism and Wildlife in the first major reshuffle of February 1982.

In June 1983 President Moi announced the discovery of a 'traitor' conspiring with an unknown foreign power, but it was Mwangale who identified him in parliament as Charles Njonjo thus launching the long-running 'Njonjo affair'. On 1 October 1983 Mwangale was rewarded and promoted to Foreign Minister replacing the long-serving Robert Ouko. In October 1986 he led the Kenya delegation to the 8th summit of the Non-Aligned Movement in Harare. During 1987 he had increasing problems defending Kenya's human rights record which came under attack abroad. He also became involved in a worsening of relations with neighbouring Uganda. Suddenly on 1 June 1987, President Moi reshuffled him to become Minister of Agriculture. After a short spell as Minister for Livestock Development, he was reappointed Minister of Agriculture on 6 June 1990.

NABWERA, Burudi
Kenyan politician. Minister of State in President's Office, March 1988.

A highly experienced Kakamega politician who has served as Kenya's ambassador to the USA and the UN but had a rather chequered career as an MP, not always able to hold his seat against another popular local

*man. He made his mark when he briefly became secretary-general of
KANU and became an important minister in President Moi's own office.*

Born 1927 in North Nyanza, now Western Province. Educated locally
and at the London School of Economics and Makerere University where
he got a BSc degree and a Diploma in Education. He became a teacher
in Maseno school, Nyanza and African Girl's High School (now Alliance
Girl's High School) Kikuyu, in Kiambu. He joined the colonial civil
service, 1957-58.

He entered politics in 1962, after the Mau Mau rebellion was over and
was elected Kenya African National Union executive officer for
Kakamega district. In 1963 he won the Lurambi North constituency in
the pre-independence Legislative Assembly and in the same year was
appointed Kenyan ambassador to Washington and later to the United
Nations in New York.

On his return home in 1969, he stood for parliament and easily
regained the Lurambi north seat and in 1974 beat four opponents in
winning again. But in 1979, after the electoral commission had split his
seat into two, he suffered a crushing defeat in the newly formed Lugari
constituency, by the virtually unknown Joshua Angatia. President
Daniel arap Moi consoled him by appointing him to the boards of a
number of state-owned companies. He stood again in the elections of
September 1983 and was again defeated by Angatia. After this defeat he
was appointed chairman of Chemelil Sugar Company and chairman of
the Moi University Council in Eldoret.

He then surprised many observers when he was elected secretary-
general of KANU on 2 July 1985, to replace Robert Matano, in the first
national party elections since October 1978. His victory was ensured
when he won the backing of the party's national governing council and
particularly of the powerful party boss Moses Mudavadi.

Meanwhile his old constituency had been subdivided by the
Presidential Boundaries Commission and in the March 1988 elections
he enjoyed an overwhelming victory in the new Lugari constituency.
After the elections on 21 March, President Moi appointed him a minister
in the President's office with responsibilty for supervision of provincial
administration, internal security and immigration.

His fortunes underwent another change when his former sponsor
Mudavadi decided to take on the secretary-generalship of the party
himself, leaving Nabwera as his branch secretary in Kakamega.
Nabwera's fortunes were not fully restored until the unfortunate death
of Mudavadi in February 1989. On 1 May 1989 he was confirmed as
Minister of State in President Moi's office.

NGEI, Paul

Kenya politician and minister.

*A tall, burly, powerful man, one of the youngest and most militant of the
early nationalist leaders, when he was arrested and detained with*

Kenyatta, in 1952. He was in every cabinet since independence. Never one to eschew the hurly burly of electoral politics, he has been in some tough battles and disputes, but he kept his Kamba following and proved an indispensable support to successive Presidents, until he lost his parliamentary seat and ministry in November 1990.

Born 1923 in Machakos, the son of Paramount Chief Masakau. Educated at Alliance High School, Kikuyu, and Makerere University (BSc Economics).

He fought with the British troops in the World War and returned to found and edit the most outspoken of all the licensed African newspapers, *Uhuru wa Mwafrica*. Appointed branch secretary of the Kenya African Union in Machakos in 1945 and rallied his Kamba people to the party. He rose to deputy national general secretary by 1951.

Arrested with Kenyatta and four others on 22 October 1952 and charged with managing Mau Mau. On 8 April 1953 he was convicted and sentenced to seven years imprisonment, but kept under restriction to 1961 when he became president of the Kenya Farmers and Traders Union.

He joined the executive of the Kenya African National Union but quarrelled with a faction led by Tom Mboya, which challenged his leadership, and broke away to form his own African People's Party. He was elected to parliament in May 1963 as an APP member for Machakos North. As a result he was the only senior colleague left out of Kenyatta's independence cabinet.

He was appointed chairman of the Maize Board in 1963 and was returned to government as Minister for Co-operatives and Marketing in 1964. He was made Minister for Housing and Social Services in 1965, but was suspended in February 1966 during a government enquiry into maize shortages. He was reappointed Housing Minister (1966-74), Local Government Minister (1974-75) until he was unseated after a High Court found that he had "blatantly coerced and threatened" another candidate to withdraw his candidature. Pardoned by President Kenyatta under a special bill, he restood the election and was returned as MP for Kagunda. He was appointed Minister for Co-operative Development in March 1976.

On his election as President, Daniel arap Moi made him Minister for Works on 28 November 1979 and switched him to Minister of Livestock and Development in February 1982, Minister of Environment and Natural Resources on 15 August 1984 and Minister for Water Development on 1 April 1986, Livestock Development on 1 June 1987 and Minister of Culture and Social Services on 24 March 1988.

In the elections of March 1988 his opponent, the former army chief of staff, Jackson Mulinge should have been automatically elected after getting more than 70% of the vote under the newly introduced public queuing system, but Ngei complained to President Moi and accused the Attorney-General, Mathew Muli, of intimidating voters and canvassing for Mulinge. A second, secret ballot was held which he won.

On 1 May 1989 in the reshuffle which followed the fall of Vice-

President Josephat Karanja he was switched again to become Minister of Manpower and Development. In the same month he was sentenced to six months imprisonment for contempt of court on refusal to comply with the court ruling over a land deal. But some time after the court ruling no action had been taken.

On 22 November 1990 he was declared bankrupt with debts of more than £400,000. He lost his parliamentary seat and his ministry. He had been Kenya's longest serving Minister. He commented, "I have nothing to do but pack my bags and return to my farm".

NJONJO, Charles
Kenyan lawyer and politician.

A complex character. A hard worker who keeps fit, dresses smartly and takes sauna baths. Respected rather than loved by many contemporaries, he has a charisma that sometimes aroused envy and suspicion. A dominant Attorney-General and later Minister of Home Affairs, he became so powerful that President Moi became suspicious of his intentions and brought about his downfall in 1984. He denies that he was involved in any disloyalty to the man whom he had helped to power; an exhaustive commission of inquiry found otherwise, then Moi appeared to give him the benefit of the doubt by pardoning him. Whatever the final verdict of posterity, the Njonjo affair will go down as the most celebrated power struggle in Kenyan contemporary history.

Born 23 January 1920 at Kibichiku, Kabete in Kiambu, the son of ex-Senior Chief Josiah Njonjo, one of the earliest nationalist leaders of the Kikuyu Central Association, who became one of Kenya's great farmers. Educated at the CMS mission school, Alliance High School, and King's College Budo, Uganda. He continued at Fort Hare University, South Africa, where he completed a BA in 1946.

After a public administration course at Exeter University, he spent three years at the London School of Economics reading social anthropology. Called to the bar at Gray's Inn in 1954, he returned to Kenya to become Assistant Registrar-General in 1955, rising fast in government service to become Acting Senior Crown Counsel in 1961, Deputy Public Prosecutor 1962 and Attorney-General in 1963. In 1964 he became a co-opted, ex-officio member of Parliament where he acquired a reputation as a legal draftsman. He drafted the amendment which abolished Kenya's *majimbo* (regional) constitution and gave the country a basis for national unity.

He gradually built up a position of political power for himself and became a strong supporter of Daniel arap Moi, heading off a challenge by a Kikuyu-led clique designed to prevent Moi from acceding to the Presidency on Kenyatta's death in 1978. After Moi's accession to power, Njonjo consolidated his own position and resigned from his post as Attorney-General, on 18 April 1980, so that he could take on a direct political role.

He decided to enter parliament and persuaded the member who had recently won a seat for the Kikuyu constituency to stand down. He then was nominated unopposed as the new MP on 26 April. President Moi made him Minister of Home and Constitutional Affairs where he established himself, arguably, as the second most powerful person in the Kenyan political heirarchy.

The attempted coup of August 1982 was violent and brought heavy loss of life and economic damage. It severely shook public confidence and Moi began to become suspicious as rumours circulated that Njonjo might make a bid for power. In May 1983 Moi suddenly announced that certain unspecified foreign powers were grooming an unnamed politician to take over as president. A wave of speculation followed and Njonjo's name was mentioned in the National Assembly. Attacks multiplied as his enemies settled old scores and Njonjo resigned his seat in the Assembly in June.

On 29 July Moi announced Njonjo's suspension from the cabinet and the party and the appointment of a judicial inquiry into the affair. Njonjo repeatedly protested his innocence, but the inquiry took its course, starting in January 1984 and continuing until August. Three high court judges presided over 110 days of hearings and listened to 61 witnesses. The Commission then retired to prepare a report while a purge started of Njonjo's associates.

The commission finally published its report on 13 December 1984 and found Njonjo guilty of a number of offences including involvement in the attempted coup of 1982 and of an abortive attempt to overthrow the Seychelles government in November 1981. It also found that he had "collaborated with South Africa" in disregard of Kenya's national interest. It alleged that he had allowed South Africans to enter and import arms illegally into Kenya.

But much of the evidence presented had been inconclusive and contradictory and few felt that Njonjo deserved all the mud that had been thrown at him. Even President Moi did not want to press the matter too far. He granted Njonjo a pardon in a speech marking Kenya's 21st independence anniversary on 12 December 1984. Moi said that Njonjo had served his country faithfully until some time in 1980, "when he started entertaining misguided ambitions."

Though Njonjo was pardoned he was not rehabilitated and retired from public life altogether.

NYAGAH, Jeremiah Joseph Mwaniki

Kenyan politician. Minister since 1963.

A devout Christian and keen educationist, scout leader, school governor and family man. He was never particularly favoured for high office, coming from the Embu people, who are closely allied to the Kikuyu but not near to the centre of power. But his moderation, level-headedness and reliability endeared him both to Kenyatta who gave him the longstanding agriculture ministry for many years, and to arap Moi who kept him on in a succession of senior ministries.

Born 1920, at Kigare in Embu district, educated locally and at the select Alliance High School 1936-40 before going on to Makerere (1940-43) for his teacher's diploma. He became a teacher at the Teacher's Training College at Kahuhia in Fort Hall. He went on to become headmaster 1944-47 and then headmaster of the Government African School, Embu 1952-53 before going to Oxford for a teacher's diploma. In 1956 he became an assistant education officer.

Elected to the Legislative Council for Embu in 1958, he was returned again in February 1961. His moderate views and the respect he engendered in other members led to his appointment as Deputy Speaker in the Legislative Council in 1960. After further electoral victory for Embu south in May 1963, he was chosen as a junior minister in the Ministry of Works, on the formation of the independence cabinet. Junior Ministries in Lands and Settlement and in Home Affairs followed in 1964. Then in 1966 he became Minister of Education. This was followed by Natural Resources (1968), Information and Broadcasting (1969) and Agriculture, a ministry he held for nine years (1970-79), followed by Livestock Development (1979-80) Culture and Social Services (1980-82), Water Development (1982-85) and Environment and Natural Resources (1985-90) Livestock Development (6 June 1990-)

OKONDO, Peter Habenga

Kenyan businessman and politician. Minister for Labour, February 1984 – 22 August 1990.

One of the most widely experienced ministers in Kenya today with political connections going back to the Kenya African Union in the late 1940s, service with the United Nations and the Economic Commission for Africa, and extensive business interests in Kenya. Married to a white wife, urbane, with an English accent, he is an accountant by training, and is today a director of about 20 companies. After a brief period as a minister before independence, President Moi persuaded him to put his private businesses on the back burner and serve as a minister again from February 1984. He resigned in August 1990 following the outcry prompted by his indiscreet remarks over Bishop Alexander Muge.

Born 1 February 1925. Educated at St Mary's College, Yala, in Kenya. St Mary's, Kisubi, Uganda to take his Cambridge school certificate. He went on to Roma College, Lesotho, and the University of Cape Town, South Africa, where he took a Bachelor of Commerce degree.

His interest in politics started early and he joined the Kenya African Union (KAU) the precursor to KANU, and rose to become its auditor-general in 1951 shortly before the party was proscribed. He was arrested during the Mau Mau emergency in 1952, but escaped from detention a year later and fled to Uganda where he worked in the Ugandan Civil Service (1954-59) as an accountant, becoming a deputy secretary in the

Ugandan Treasury in 1957 and auditor for the Shell company in Tanzania in 1960.

In 1961 he returned home and became a member of the Kenya Legislative Council for Bu Samia (now Bunyala) for the Kenya African Democratic Union (KADU) and an Assistant Minister of Finance. He was promoted to Minister of Works in 1963. In the same year he lost his seat to James Osogo who was standing on a Kenya African National Union ticket.

He then joined the Economic Commission for Africa, the United Nations organisation based in Addis Ababa, Ethiopia, and worked as head of African Transport Development Studies (1963-64). He went on to the Economic and Social Council, New York where he became secretary to the Economic Committee (1965-67). He returned home in 1968 to go into private business, first with Habenga Trust in 1968, then Menengai Investments in 1973, Tysons-Habenga (Real Estate Agency) 1976 and Phoenix of East Africa Assurance Company, 1980.

He then switched back to politics, being elected MP for Busia South in June 1980 after James Osogo had been found guilty of electoral malpractices and had lost the seat. In April 1981 his only opponent, William Diffu, was disqualified and Okondo was returned to parliament unopposed.

On 28 February 1984 President arap Moi made him Minister for Co-operative Development. He was reshuffled on 15 August 1984 to Transport and Communications where he engineered a border agreement with Somalia which allowed the peaceful transfer of people and trade across the frontier. President Moi again moved him to become Minister for Commerce and Industry on 7 January 1985, and Minister for Labour on 1 April 1986.

A ferocious war of words developed over human rights issues, during 1990, between church spokesmen and the government. Okondo in the heat of the moment warned Bishop Alexander Muge that if he preached in Busia district he might not return alive. The bishop defied the warning but on his return from the meeting he was killed in a vehicle crash. In the outcry that followed Okondo felt that he had no alternative but to resign.

ONYONKA, Dr Zachary Theodore
Kenyan politician. Minister of Planning, March 1988 -

The youngest minister appointed to any Kenyatta cabinet, earning his promotion by his outstanding academic ability as an economist. He brought a new technocratic approach to his ministerial responsibilities. A tee-totaller and non-smoker, he continued his ministerial career under President Moi. A setback came with the September 1983 elections, but he was returned to the cabinet, as Minister of Foreign Affairs in 1987 and Planning in March 1988.

Born 28 February 1939 in Meru where his father Goderiko Mairura was stationed as a sergeant-major in the army. His home is at Kisii where his grandfather, Chief Mairura, died at an estimated age of over 100, deeply respected by the tribe and a source of knowledge for historians and researchers.

Educated at Mosocho, Nyaburu and St Mary's schools. He won a scholarship to the Inter-American university at Puerto Rico, where he gained his BA in 1963 and won the *Wall Street Journal* award as the best graduate of his class. He entered Syracuse University as assistant to the director of East African studies. He won a Rockefeller Foundation fellowship and took an MA in June 1965, PhD in 1967 and Doctorate in Economics in June 1968. He returned to lecture in the Department of Economics at Nairobi University (1968-69).

He resigned to fight the Kisii West seat in the general election, winning from the former Minister for Local Government, Lawrence Sagini. Kenyatta appointed him Minister for Economic Planning and Development, the youngest member of his cabinet, as part of a policy to bring in new blood in 1969. The ministry was rationalised and added to Mwai Kibaki's Ministry of Finance in October 1970. He then moved to the Ministry of Information. This was followed by the Ministry of Health in 1973, Education in 1974, Housing and Social Services in 1976.

When President Moi came to power on the death of Kenyatta, Onyonka's unbroken ministerial record continued. He was appointed Minister of Economic Planning and Development on 8 November 1979. During the elections of September 1983 he appeared in court in Kisii on 29 September accused of being involved in a shooting incident concerning a supporter of a rival candidate, in the final stages of the election campaign. His ministry was then merged with the Ministry of Finance. He was acquitted on 12 March 1984 of murder, but he was not brought back into the government until 1 June 1987 when he was given the prestigious Ministry of Foreign Affairs.

After winning his seat outright in the March 1988 elections, by securing 78% of the voters who had to queue up behind the candidates of their choice, he was once again restored to the Planning and National Development portfolio on 24 March 1988.

SAITOTI, George (Professor)

Kenyan politician and academic. Vice-President 1 May 1989-

A quiet, self-effacing and modest man, with academic rather than political roots. His PhD Thesis was entitled "Mod 2K - Theory of the Second Iterated Loop on a Sphere and other topics." He was suddenly brought into politics by President Moi, who nominated him for parliament and made him his Minister of Finance in 1963 and then promoted him above more powerful and experienced colleagues to the Vice-Presidency on the resignation of Dr Josephat Karanja. He seemed to have been chosen because he was primarily a technician and loyalist rather than for his political connections.

Born August 1944. There is some mystery over his parentage. Some friends remember him as George Kinuthia, a Kikuyu name. His mother was Kikuyu and his father was probably a Masai, or possibly he adopted the Masai name Saitoti when his family moved to Kajiado in Masailand, in pre-independence days. Educated at Ollolua Primary and the Catholic Primary, both at Ngong near Nairobi, then at Mangu High School, Thika 1959-62, going on to Brandeis University, USA in 1962. He graduated in 1967 with a BA in mathematics. He went on to Sussex University in Britain, where he took a masters in science, and then a PhD at Warwick.

He returned home in 1971, to become a mathematics lecturer at Nairobi University, rising to senior lecturer and head of the mathematics department in 1978. At the university he worked under Vice-Chancellor Dr Josephat Karanja whom he later displaced as Vice-President. Later he went into commerce, becoming chairman of Mumias Sugar Company and a director of Kenya Commercial Bank. He rose to become the bank's executive chairman in 1982.

His career took a dramatic turn after the snap elections of 1983 when President Moi, looking for a professional Minister of Finance, suddenly nominated him to parliament and immediately promoted him minister on 1 October. As Minister of Finance he had to cope with deteriorating terms of trade, a growing balance of payments and budgetary deficit, a sharp decline in foreign exchange reserves and burgeoning government spending. But despite these difficulties he maintained the confidence of the President as a skilled financial manager.

Before the March 1988 elections he campaigned vigorously in the Kajiado north seat. The local Masai invited him to become their official spokesman but he turned down their offer to preserve his parliamentary independence. However he prevailed on the incumbent MP, Philip Odupoy, to stand down and he was returned unopposed. He was also elected chairman of the Kenya African National Union for Kajiado district.

President Moi re-confirmed him as Minister of Finance on 24 March 1988. His fortunes took another dramatic turn on 1 May 1989, when he was suddenly chosen as Vice-President and as vice-president of KANU, after the sudden and complete eclipse of Dr Josephat Karanja who was brought down, following a vicious political struggle with fellow parliamentarians.

WAKO, S. Amos
Attorney General, 13 May 1991 -

A bright young star of the Kenya legal profession with considerable international experience. A moderate, soft spoken, liberal. Only one month before he was surprisingly appointed Attorney General in Kenya, he was elected for a two year term as one of the three vice chairmen of the UN Human rights committee. Clearly President Moi appointed him with the objective of improving Kenya's human rights record, that had gained such bad international publicity. His release of political prisoners immediately after his appointment boded well for the future.

Born: 1945 in Bukhayo location, Busia district. He went to local primary and secondary schools, going on to study law at Dar es Salaam university, where he graduated with a bachelor of law degree. He continued at London Univeristy studying economics and international affairs and getting his masters degree in law.

He returned to Nairobi to take up law and went into partnership in Kaplan and Stratton one of the leading law firms. But he did not confine his activities to bread and butter cases at home. He soon became involved in legal affairs on a wide international plane.

He was honorary secretary general of the Africa Bar Association from 1968. He was Chairman of the Law Society of Kenya (1979- 81). He was also the first secretary general of the Inter African Union of lawyers, formerly the Association of National Associations, founded in 1980. He became a member of the International Commission of Jurists in 1981.

He has had wide experience as an arbitrator in international disputes. His government nominated him as a conciliator under the Vienna Convention of Law Treaties. Between 1982 and 1985 he served as the secretary general of the UN Board of Trustees of the voluntary fund for Victims against Torture.

In September 1990 he was chairman of the 23rd biennial conference of the International Bar Association which was due to hold its meeting in Nairobi, but was moved to New York at the eleventh hour. The Kenya government was not keen that international lawyers should have a platform in Nairobi to raise human rights issues, as its record was very patchy. The IBA's official reason for shifting the meeting was given as the " security situation in Nairobi ". Wako was deeply angered at the sudden switch in view of the elaborate preparations his organising committee had made for the conference. At first he felt like boycotting New York, but thought better of it and attended the meeting where he denounced the IBA's assessment of the security situation in Kenya pointing out that many other parts of the world were far more dangerous, including the USA.

In April 1991 he was appointed for a two year term as one of the three vice chairmen of the UN Human Rights Committee. One month later, on 13 May 1991 he was appointed by President Moi as Attorney General.

It was an open secret that Moi was trying to do something about the abysmal human rights image that Kenya had gained internationally, a record that had been reinforced by the former Attorney General, Matthew Muli who had sanctioned the arrest of a number of political opponents.

Almost immediately after his appointment Wako released all political prisoners except those facing specific charges. One of the first to be released was Gitobu Imanyara, the editor of *Nairobi Law Monthly,* who had been charged with sedition. " We are not going to hinder any individual's right to express his freedom of speech because that is enshrined in the constitution of Kenya," he said. He then neatly side-stepped the issue of government overriding the law," There is no way that the larger interests of government can at any point be brought into conflict with the rule of law. The Kenya government stands for the administration of justice and the rule of law. That indeed makes the task ahead much easier than would be otherwise envisaged."

LESOTHO

Population: 1.73m (1990, World Bank)
Head of State: King Letsie III (Mohato Seeiso)
Independence: 4 October 1966
Government: Constitutional monarchy, with effective power in the hands of Colonel Elias Phitsoane Ramaema, Chairman of the Military Council, following the coup against Maj–Gen. Metsing Lekhanya of 30 April 1991. Elections promised by June 1992.
Parties: Political parties were allowed to organise themselves following the lifting of the ban in May 1991.

KHAKETLA, Bennett Makalo

Lesotho politician. Minister of Justice and Prisons, 27 January 1986- 22 February 1990.

Precise, schoolmasterly and a strong Anglican. He is an hardened veteran of Lesotho politics who started his career with Ntsu Mokhehle's Basutoland Congress Party, then formed his own Basutoland Freedom Party. At one stage he even flirted with the Soviets but later became the champion of King Moshoeshoe II. In the political wilderness during the Leabua Jonathan regime, he was taken straight out of prison to be made Minister of Justice and Prisons after the military coup of January 1986.

Born 1914 of peasant stock at Qacha's Nek. Educated at local mission schools, he became a teacher after getting a primary teacher's certificate in 1932. He then began teaching at various schools in South Africa. He enrolled at the Bantu High School in Heilbron and worked privately towards a bachelor of arts degree in Sesotho and politics at the University of South Africa. Following another spell as a teacher when he rose to become principal of Charterson High School, Nigel, in South Africa, he returned to Maseru in 1953 to teach at Basutoland High School.

It was at this time that he took up politics. In 1955 he became editor of *Mohlabani* (The Warrior) the newspaper of the Basutoland Congress Party (BCP) which had been founded by Ntsu Mokhehle. His political activities caused his dismissal as a teacher.

He was elected deputy leader of the BCP (1959-60) which won the district council elections of January 1960, gaining 73 of the 162 seats. He was then indirectly elected to the Executive Council and was given the portfolio of Health and Education. After quarrels with Mokhehle over the powers of the paramount chief, he resigned from the party on 29 December 1960 and founded his own Basutoland Freedom Party (BFP) in April 1961. A year later he merged the BFP with the Marematlou Freedom Party (MFP) which was then led by Chief S.S. Matete.

He attended the World Peace Congress in Moscow in 1962 and

received financial help from the Soviet Union, returning home to become president of the MFP in 1963.

At the time of the party upheavals in 1969 he became secretary-general of the party. On 30 January 1970 he was arrested and held in detention under a state of emergency called by Chief Leabua Jonathan, who saw the election results running against him.

Khaketla remained in opposition during the Jonathan era. A month before the military coup of 20 January 1986, he and a number of other leaders made an unauthorised visit to meet Pik Botha, South Africa's Foreign Minister, where the future of the Jonathan government was probably discussed. On his return he was detained. When the soldiers supported by South Africa engineered the coup, the poacher turned gamekeeper. Maj-Gen. Justin Lekhanya took him straight out of prison and appointed him Minister of Justice and Prisons on 27 January 1986, a post that he held until 22 February 1990.

LEBOTSA, Mohomane Masimole
Engineer. Minister of Highlands Water Project and Energy, 19 March 1988 – 22 February 1990.

One of Lesotho's first qualified engineers, he now applies his special skills as Minister in charge of the Highlands Water Project which aims to sell Lesotho water to South Africa to earn his poverty-stricken country a large and regular income. More of a technocrat than a politician, he was formerly Minister of Works.

Born 1927 at Hlotse in the northern district of Leribe. Educated at St Saviour's Primary, then Hlotse Government Intermediate School where he passed standard six examination in 1940. He moved to Basutoland High School where he completed his senior certificate in 1945.

After teaching for a year at Morija Training School, went to Fort Hare for his BSc. He returned home and taught at Lesotho High School until September 1952 when he went to Edinburgh University to gain a BSc in engineering (1952-56). Almost immediately he joined Sir William Halcrow, the London consulting engineers (1956-62). He gained an MSc in Engineering at King's College, London in 1962 and became a member of the Institution of Civil Engineers (MICE).

He returned home to join the civil service in 1963 working as a structural engineer, becoming Chief Engineer. He left this position in 1970 to become a teacher, later the principal, of St Agnes High School. He moved to the National University as Director of Works in 1973.

After the military coup of 20 January 1986 his engineering skills were recognised and he was appointed Minister of Works, a post that was reoriented to Highlands Water and Energy on 19 March 1988 so that he could concentrate his attention on the R5 billion, Highlands Water Scheme under which Lesotho is to sell its water to South Africa on a lucrative contract basis. He was relieved of this post at the same time that some of the Military Council were removed in February 1990.

LEKHANYA, Justin Metsing (Major-General)
Lesotho soldier. Chairman of Military Council, 20 January 1986 – 30 April 1991.

A quiet policeman turned soldier, who virtually created the Lesotho paramilitary forces. A good administrator, who cared for the welfare of his men. He became popular and secured a power base with his paramilitary force which often clashed with the Youth Wingers of Chief Leabua Jonathan's party. After the South African blockade at the end of 1985 and consultations in Pretoria, he carried out the successful coup of 20 January 1986. Though he had ample personal motivation and the backing of the King and many Basotho, he was also under considerable South African pressure. He was deposed by disgruntled soldiers in the military coup of 30 April 1991.

Born 7 April 1938, son of a primary school teacher at Ha Koptjoane in Thaba-Tseka district. He attended primary school at St Francis Mission and Paray School in Thaba-Tseka (1952-54), then secondary school at Christ the King High School, Roma (1955-57). He was keen on boxing and soccer.

He left school and went to South Africa to work as a shaft clerk at Springs gold mine (1958-59). He joined the mine's athletic team and continued his education by correspondence course.

He joined the police (then Basutoland Mounted Police) on 1 June 1960 and was soon qualified as an instructor at the Police Training School at Maseru. In 1965 he switched to the newly formed Police Mobile Unit, as the only Mosotho officer. It had been set up by the colonial government to face the growing unrest in the country prior to independence.

He was promoted fast and was selected for further training at the Scotland Police College (1972-73) and at the Police Academy, Washington, DC in 1973. On his return he was appointed deputy commissioner of police at Maseru. He was promoted on 1 April 1974 to police commander, with the rank of Brigadier. He then took a leading role in building up Lesotho's defence forces which evolved from the Police Mobile Unit. He proved a creative administrator who expanded the unit into a self-reliant entity.

He took great interest in the education and welfare of his men. One of his more unusual ideas was to provide a mini-bus service for the police which, under careful management, grew into a regular fleet of buses serving commuters between Maseru and the suburbs. He established a private night school at Maseru barracks which provided training for soldiers before going abroad for advanced studies. He was also behind the formation of an air wing to improve access to the mountainous hinterland. A clinic was opened near the barracks in 1977, which later provided assistance to the public in the locality.

In September 1977 he was promoted major-general, taking command of the PMU and later the Lesotho Paramilitary Force when it was formed in 1980. He was the driving force behind the building of new barracks at

Makoanyane with up-to-date accommodation, training and recreation facilities.

In the mid-1980s the government of Chief Leabua Jonathan was becoming increasingly unpopular. It cancelled the 1985 elections and appointed its candidates to all posts in the Legislature. The economy was in severe difficulties and South Africa was becoming increasingly concerned over Jonathan's establishment of diplomatic relations with communist countries.

In retaliation South Africa established a blockade on Lesotho, which was forced to negotiate. Lekhanya went to Pretoria with a Lesotho delegation on 17 January 1986 and South Africa virtually dictated its terms.

The following day fighting broke out between members of the Paramilitary Force and Jonathan's Youth Leaguers which wanted Jonathan to adopt an even more radical stance. Lekhanya saw that this was politically unrealistic and also saw how unpopular Jonathan's policies had become with the majority of the Basotho. This prompted him to take power in the early hours of 20 January 1986, saying, "For too long the nation has been plunged into a political quagmire, with politicians unable to solve the country's problems."

He banned political activity, repealed the parliament act and issued Lesotho Order No.1 which placed the legislative and executive authority under King Moshoeshoe, advised by a five-man Military Council and an 18 member cabinet. The real power lay with the Military Council, with himself as Chairman and as Head of Government.

On 6 February a general amnesty was offered to all who had been convicted or had gone into exile for offences of a political nature. On 26 March a security pact was signed with South Africa in which both countries agreed "not to allow their territories to be used for the planning and execution of acts of terrorism against the other." This was announced by Lekhanya who was making the first visit by a Lesotho Head of Government to South Africa since independence. In practice it meant that Lesotho withdrew its support of the ANC, while South Africa pledged not to assist the Lesotho Liberation Army in South Africa. Ties with South Africa were strengthened further with the eviction of the communist embassies and the decision to go ahead with the Highlands Water Scheme designed to sell Lesotho's water to its neighbour.

In September 1986 Lekhanya held discussions with the main opposition leaders and restructured his council of ministers, but political activity remained banned and no time-table towards civilian rule was offered.

In October 1986 Lekhanya addressed the 41st session of the United Nations General Assembly in New York and stressed that his was a peace loving country that advocated dialogue in solving international disputes. In March 1988 further talks were held with South Africa on common issues.

In a bizarre incident in December 1988 a student was shot dead at the

Maseru Agricultural College campus. At first, his driver, a Sergeant Mojakhomo, accepted the blame but suspicion later fell on Lehanya himself. The Lesotho military council spent months considering the issue and finally decided to set up a commission of inquiry into the affair. At the inquiry Lekhanya said that he had heard "the screams of a woman in grave danger". She was being attacked by an unknown assailant. He said that he had tried to arrest the man. "My intention was not to kill him at all. My intention was to apprehend him." Lekhanya refused either to step down or resign from the military government over the affair.

The rivalries between his faction and that of the King were aggravated by this affair. They came to a head on 19 February 1990 when he arrested three members of the military council, including the two Letsie brothers, the King's cousins. He then stripped the monarch of all his constitutional powers, leaving him with nothing but his titular authority. He promised that Lethoso would have democratic civilian rule by 1992 and as a first step set up a nationally representative Constituent Assembly, which first met on 28 June 1990.

Though there had been trouble among his soldiers over pay and conditions, and conspiracies in the higher ranks, the coup of 30 April 1991 took Lekhanya entirely by surprise. Early that morning he was suddenly arrested by a group of young officers led by a previously loyal deputy, Colonel Elias Phitsoane Ramaema. At 11 am he was marched to the Lesotho broadcasting station and forced to read a resignation statement over Radio Lesotho. In a trembling voice he said that he was resigning in the interests of the nation in order to satisfy the people's aspirations. He was then driven away and incarcerated in the maximum security prison.

Later he was released and put under house arrest. He was allowed to circulate fairly freely, doing his own shopping in Maseru. Later he was reported to have fled to South Africa.

LETSIE, Joshua Sekhobe
Lesotho Colonel. Member Military Council, 20 January 1986- 20 February 1990.

Formerly one of the strong men of the all powerful Military Council, he was arrested when King Moshoeshoe was stripped of his powers in February 1990. A prime mover of the military coup of January 1986 which removed Chief Jonathan's civilian government. Related to King Moshoeshoe and a close ally, his stock has risen and fallen with those of his monarch. Before his fall from power he was not thought to be in favour of further democratisation or return to civilian rule in Lesotho and had been dismissive of various attempts by church leaders seeking to reconcile government and various factions within the country.

Born 17 November 1947, son of Chief Dinizulu Nako Letsie, at Makhalaneng, Maseru district. Primary and secondary education in Maseru (1962-66). On 1 April 1967 he joined the Police Mobile Unit

(PMU). After three years' training he emerged as a sergeant in 1971, and continued with further specialised training.

In 1976 he was promoted warrant officer and second-in-command of his platoon and joined the PMU Private School where he completed his higher education in 1977. He was appointed adjutant to major-general Metsing Lekhanya (1977-82), promoted Captain in 1978 and major in 1979. He went on further specialised training abroad. In 1982 he was promoted lieutenant-colonel in command of the second battalion. He then became chief instructor with the Lesotho Paramilitary Forces as liason officer to the British Army Advisory and Training Team.

He was one of the prime movers of the military coup of 20 January 1986 which ousted Chief Leabua Jonathan. He was rewarded by being promoted full colonel and by being appointed to the five-man Military Council, set up to rule the country.

He then played a major part in government, being responsible for the overall supervision of the ministries of Education, Health, Disciplined Forces, Interior, Defence, Internal Security, Chieftainship Affairs and Rural Development. This huge range, which included the key areas of defence and internal security, gave him power but made him a threat to General Lekhanya. It was he who had consultations with the exiled opposition leader Ntsu Mokhehle and persuaded him to return home permanently. He also entertained the church leaders pressing for the reconciliation of various political factions, but has given them short shrift, telling them to set their own houses in order first.

On 19 February 1990, after allegations of an attempted coup when King Moshoeshoe was stripped of his powers, he was arrested and dismissed from the Military Council.

LETSIE, Thaabe

Lesotho Colonel. Member Military Council. Foreign Minister 18 March 1988-20 February 1990.

A tough soldier who worked his way up through the ranks. A prime mover of the military coup of January 1986 which removed Chief Leabua Jonathan's civilian government. With one of his hobbies listed as "martial arts", he became one of the strong men of the all-powerful Military Council which rules Lesotho. He was given wide supervisory responsibilities over many other ministries, including Finance, the Palace and Foreign Affairs. He is related to King Moshoeshoe. In March 1988 he doubled up as Minister of Foreign Affairs, with prime responsibility for Lesotho's foreign relations with the black African states and South Africa and for his country's overall image abroad. But his alliance with the King rebounded and led to his arrest when Moshoeshoe was stripped of his powers in February 1990 and he was dismissed from the Military Council.

Born 4 April 1940, son of Chief Sekhobe Letsie, at Qeme, Ha Thaabe, Maseru District. Attended primary and secondary schools at Qeme and Maseru (1946-57). Went to work in the South African mines until 1961.

Returned to join the Lesotho Mounted Police (1961). Transferred to the Police Mobile Unit, in 1964. He attended the Lesotho Paramilitary Force Private School to complete his higher education. Promoted to sergeant in 1961, he rose briskly through the ranks, becoming an officer. He did further specialised training in East Africa, Europe and the Far East, becoming company commander, battalion commander, military protocol officer and Air Wing Commandant. He achieved the rank of lieutenant-colonel in 1978.

He was a prime mover of the military coup of 20 January 1986 and was rewarded with his promotion to full colonel and membership of the Military Council, set up to rule the country. He then played a major part in government, being responsible for the overall supervision of the Palace, Transport and Communications, Finance, Tourism, Sports and Culture. From 18 March 1988 he also became Minister of Foreign Affairs. In March 1988 Lesotho and South Africa concluded friendly and successful negotiations on matters relating to their common border.

After an attempted coup in February 1990 when King Moshoeshoe was stripped of his powers, he was arrested, briefly detained, and dismissed from the Military Council.

MOKHEHLE, Ntsu

Lesotho politician. Opposition leader.

The torchbearer of African nationalism in Lesotho, now ageing, following a period of exile in the South African Homeland of Qwa Qwa. A tough and fiery politician, he once said: " I abhor violence, but because I get excited when I talk and because I am ugly, I seem violent to others." The turning point in his political career came in the elections of January 1970 where victory at the polls was snatched from him by Chief Jonathan. He was forced into exile and his supporters were victimised. This led to the formation of the Lesotho Liberation Army and the turbulent period that followed during the last days of the Jonathan era. He has now returned with most of his men and is politically quiescent.

Born December 1918, son of a sheep farmer at Mamathes, a village in the Berea district. Educated at the village school then sent to St Matthew's College, Grahamstown, South Africa. Entered the University College, Fort Hare in 1940. Expelled for political activity in 1942, then readmitted in 1944 to complete a Master of Science degree in Zoology. He went on to do teacher training, gained an educational diploma and started teaching in South Africa in 1950.

A member of Lethoso's first nationalist movement, the League of the Common Man, in 1942 he took part in the African National Congress Youth League in South Africa. In 1952 he founded the Basutoland Congress Party and became its first president. Three years later at Maseru, where he was principal of the primary school he launched the party newspaper *Mohlabane* (The Warrior).

At the District Council elections in January 1960, he won the

Teyateyaneng seat and his BCP topped the polls with 73 out of the 162 seats. But in the indirect elections to the Executive Council B.M. Khaketla, then deputy party leader, was chosen instead of him. Khaketla broke away to form his own party while Mokhehle struggled to maintain unity in his own group.

In December 1965 he walked out of the the constitutional conference in London, demanding fresh elections before independence. Mokhehle sided with King Moshoeshoe in his struggle with Chief Jonathan. He was arrested on 5 January 1967 and given a suspended sentence of 12 months' imprisonment for incitement to violence. In November he was arrested again on similar charges but released on bail and allowed to take part in the election campaign of January 1970.

Chief Jonathan thought that he might be losing the elections so he declared a state of emergency and arrested Mokhehle. After 17 months he was freed on 7 June 1971. At first he tried to co-operate with the government but when it became clear that his apparent victory in the 1970 elections was not to be recognised, he led his faction of the party into opposition. He tried to form a united front with other opposition groups but this also failed.

In January 1974 five police stations were attacked by armed bands, allegedly followers of Mokhehle. Jonathan cracked down with severity and Mokhehle fled the country to South Africa, leaving 200 of his supporters detained and 14 charged with treason. The government announced that all criminals and fugitives (including Mokhehle) would be permanently banned from Lesotho.

This situation led to the formation of the Lesotho Liberation Army as the military wing of the BCP, based and trained in South Africa which carried out a number of attacks on individuals and installations in Lesotho from 1981. After the military coup of 20 January 1986 Mokhehle, still in exile, demanded the immediate restoration of the 1966 constitution and the integration of the LLA into Lesotho's defence forces and free elections within six months. These demands were rejected by the new military government which signed a security agreement with South Africa under which support was withdrawn from the LLA.

On 20 May 1988 Mokhehle returned home for the first time for 14 years, to hold peace talks with the Lesotho government. He was given guarantees of safety for himself and his followers, but no political concessions. He then returned to his place of exile in the South African Homeland of Qwa Qwa. After a series of talks with the government he returned permanently, on 16 February 1989, with most of his LLA combatants. His security appears to have been guaranteed in return for the disbandment of the LLA. He began a new political chapter by playing a major part in the Constituent Assembly set up in June 1990, to return Lethoso to civilian rule.

He went on record in November 1990, saying when South Africa was totally free it would be "inconvenient" for Lesotho to remain independent. He thought it might become a part of the new South Africa.

MOSHOESHOE II,
Former King of Lesotho, 4 October 1966 – 12 November 1990.

A modern-minded monarch with great political concern for his people. Trained in politics in Oxford and always concerned about political and social development, he clashed bitterly with Chief Jonathan in the early years of independence over his role as a constitutional monarch. This led to house arrest and exile. Bearded, bespectacled and conservative by nature, he accepted his position until the military coup of January 1986, when the executive and legislative powers were restored to him under the advice of the military council. His constitutional limitations allowed him to do a wide range of welfare work for his people, taking a keen interest in educational and social issues, establishing scholarships and trusts. He is Chancellor of the University of Lesotho and has held the chancellorship of the University of Botswana, Lesotho and Swaziland, in rotation with the other Heads of State. He plays tennis, squash and rides horses. He is a keen farmer and is an owner and breeder of race horses. He was deposed by the military regime of General Metsing Lekhanya in November 1990.

Born 2 May 1938 as Constantine Bereng Seeiso, eldest son of Paramount Chief Simeon Seeiso Griffith, head of the Basotho people, at Salang village in the mountain district of Mokhotlong in western Lesotho.

Educated at Mokhotlong Primary School, then Roma College 20 miles from Maseru. In 1954 he was sent to the Roman Catholic Ampleforth College in Yorkshire, England. Then to Corpus Christi College, to read Politics, Philosophy and Economics (PPE). He did another BA degree in Law at the same college. Before completing that degree he was recalled to prepare to be proclaimed Paramount Chief of the Basotho Nation (Motlotlehi) on 12 March 1960.

He took a keen interest, as an observer, in the 1958 and 1964 constitutional conferences in London. In June 1966 he expressed concern at his country being hustled into independence and urged a delay in the hope that a means could be found of lessening South African influence. He refused to sign the conference report on 17 June 1966 because the new constitution denied him responsibility for foreign affairs or defence.

Chief Jonathan challenged him to abdicate in favour of the regency of his wife Queen Mamohato or give up his political activities. He made a counter-proposal for a referendum on his constitutional position. After a temporary truce in August 1966, the dispute led to rioting, with 11 killed and 160 arrested. He was proclaimed King at independence on 4 October 1966, but tensions persisted and on 28 December 1966 Jonathan placed him under house arrest, accusing him of being in league with the Congress Party to create a political upheaval. On 5 January 1967 he signed a document accepting automatic abdication if he went beyond his constitutional role.

The two clashed again when Jonathan suspended the constitution and seized power on 30 January 1970 after the early results showed the elections were going against him. He claimed that the King had virtually abdicated by breaking his 1967 pledge in addressing an election meeting and urging support for the Congress party. The King was put under house arrest at the palace on 2 February 1970.

Chief Jonathan announced on 31 March 1970 that the King was leaving the country indefinitely and appointed Queen Mamohato regent. On 4 April 1970 the King arrived in Holland and installed himself in a first-floor suite at the five-star Wittebrug Hotel at Scheveningen near the Hague. He stayed there until 5 November when, after talks with Chief Jonathan, he agreed to end his exile and return to Maseru on 4 December 1970. He signed an Office of the King document, banning him from taking part in politics.

After the military coup of 20 January 1986 which toppled Chief Jonathan the King had both legislative and executive powers restored to him under the provisions of the 1986 Lesotho order No.1. But in practice he had to act on the advice of a five-man Military Council chaired by Major-General Metsing Lekhanya. The relationship between the King and the Military Council has often been strained, particularly on questions of South African interference in Lesotho affairs.

His struggle for more authority deepened when Lekhanya was brought before a judicial inquiry in 1989, accused of killing a student. Though Lekhanya was subsequently cleared, rivalry between the two factions continued. In February 1990, Lekhanya arrested and detained three members of the Military Council most loyal to the King, including his two cousins. The King then refused to officiate at the swearing in ceremony of the new members chosen as their replacements. Lekhanya then took the opportunity to strip the King of his constitutional powers, leaving him with nothing but his titular authority. He went into 'temporary' exile in London, where he campaigned for constitutional changes.

On 12 November 1990 Lekhanya announced that he had been finally dethroned, with crown prince Mohato Seeiso installed in his place.

He continued to live in exile in London. He took a major part in establishing the International Institute for the Promotion of Human Rights and Democracy in Africa in August 1991.

MOSOEUNYANE, Khethang Aloysius
Lesotho soldier. Member of Military council, January 1986 - February 1990

A man from a humble background who had to work in the South African mines before his formal education was completed, but after joining the Police Mobile Unit, which later became the Paramilitary Force, he used every opportunity to further his education, gradually passing more advanced exams while winning regular promotion. He achieved the rank of colonel in 1980 and was ready for appointment to the Military Council after the coup which toppled Chief Leabua Jonathan in January 1986.

He is a catechist of the Roman Catholic Church and was a member of the police choir for many years. He was dismissed from the Military Council and briefly detained in the struggle between Lekhanya and the King's supporters in February 1990.

Born 13 March 1942 in Berea. He attended primary school at Masoeling (1950-56) and passed standard six examinations at Sion Roman Catholic Mission, 1959. He went to work in the South African mines (1960-64).

He returned to join the Police Mobile Unit as a trooper. He completed his secondary education at the Lesotho Paramilitary Forces Private School, then did courses in management, supervising, storekeeping and accountancy with the Civil Service Training Centre (1972-73). He passed police academy local law examinations and progressed to the University of Botswana, Lesotho and Swaziland in 1973. He attended further advanced courses in security maintenance and intelligence overseas, (1974-82). He was promoted to the rank of colonel in 1980.

After the coup of 20 January 1986 which toppled Chief Leabua Jonathan he was appointed to the all-powerful Military Council which rules the country. He is responsible for the supervision of the ministries of Works, District Co-ordination, Justice, Law, Constitutional and Parliamentary Affairs, and the Food Management Unit. When a struggle for power erupted between General Lekhanya and King Moshoeshoe in February 1990, he and the Letsie brothers were removed from the Military Council and briefly detained, while the King was stripped of his constitutional powers.

RAMAEMA, Elias Phitsoane (Colonel)
Lesotho soldier. Assumed power 30 April 1991 –

A low profile retiring man, apparently loyal deputy to Maj.Gen. Metsing Lekhanya. He was thrust into power after the military coup of 30 April 1991. Earlier as a member of Lekhanya's Military Council, he appeared to endorse all his government policies. He emphasised this view, after taking power when he repeated that there would be no policy changes, in the process of returning the country to civilian rule.

Born 10 November 1933, at Mapoteng in Berea district. He attended primary school in Mapoteng, 1947-52. He continued at Roma college, where he completed higher education in 1956.

He then went to work in the Welkom President Steyn Mine in South Africa, 1957-58. He returned home to join the Mobile Police Unit, which later became the Lesotho Paramilitary Force (LPF). He earned rapid promotion and went for specialised training abroad in 1978 and 1984, finally emerging as a Colonel in the LPF.

After the coup of 20 January 1986, which toppled Chief Leabua Jonathan, he was appointed to the all-powerful Military Council which ruled the country. Gen. Metsing Lekhanya virtually made him his deputy, responsible for the overall supervision of the ministries of

Planning, Public Service, Labour and Manpower Development, Broadcasting and Information, Social Welfare and Pensions.

Trouble was brewing in the army in April 1991. A group of young officers began a general strike in support for a demand for higher wages. Ramaema had been a loyal deputy to Lekhanya since they both carried out the coup against Chief Jonathan in January 1986. Whether he was directly behind the coup which ousted Lekhanya on 30 April 1991, is open to question. But as the senior military officer involved, he emerged as leader.

Lekhanya was deposed and humiliated by being made to confess to his mistakes over Radio Lesotho and was briefly imprisoned, but his treatment thereafter was lenient and he was held under a fairly free regime under house arrest.

Ramaema also continued with Lekhanya's planned programme, saying there would be no change in government policy and that the timetable towards civilian rule and democratisation would not be altered.

Indeed on 13 May he repealed the ban on party politics in order to give people time to prepare for the elections in 1992 and the restoration of democracy. But the public remained tense and serious rioting broke out on 20 May, after an African woman was beaten to death for stealing a T-shirt from a South African owned chain store.

The incident was the signal for serious rioting, which lasted several days, to avenge the girl's death. Ramaema was forced to impose a curfew and to escort some foreigners out of the country to take refuge in South Africa.

On 10 June Ramaema relieved 20 officers of their duties after an attempted coup allegedly to reinstate Lekhanya.

SEKHONYANA, Evaristus Retselisitsoe
Lesotho politician. Minister of Finance January 1986 – 29 April 1991.

Coming from one of the leading Basotho families, his uncle being formerly deputy prime minister, he became a prominent politician in his own right and chairman of the Basutoland National Party, the ruling party under Chief Leabua Jonathan. But despite his political background he is seen more as a financial expert and technocrat, one who held unbroken ministerial responsibility since 1971. When the 1986 coup came his political connections were overlooked and he was reinstated in his old Ministry of Finance where he had served previous governments. He left for South Africa the day before the military coup of April 1991.

Born 22 March 1937 at Mount Moorosi, Quthing district. Primary education at Phamong, Mohale's Hoek district to 1950. Secondary at Roma College (1951-55). He went to Canada to St Francis Xavier University in 1961, transferring to Sir George Williams University, Montreal, completing his BA degree in 1966. He was then awarded a Carnegie Fellowship to study diplomacy at Columbia School of

International Affairs.

He returned home to join the Ministry of Foreign Affairs. A year later, in October 1968, he was posted as counsellor to the Lesotho mission to the United Nations, in New York. He distinguished himself on various committees and returned home in 1970, and was soon appointed Minister of Finance, Commerce and Industry, the youngest member of the cabinet of September 1971. He was elected chairman of the ruling Basotho National Party and held this post until all political activity was banned following the coup in January 1986. He was also Leader of the House in the Interim National Assembly.

He became chairman of the boards of various parastatal companies. In 1975 he led the Lesotho delegation in the negotiations with the EC. In August 1981 he was shuffled to Minister of Planning and Economic Affairs. He was given the additional portfolio of Foreign Affairs from February 1983 to August 1984.

He won the Moyeni constituency for the Basotho National Party in the 1985 elections and was reconfirmed as Leader of the House from October 1985 until the assembly was abolished after the coup of 20 January 1986. Despite the fact that he had been a leading member of the BNP, the new military government had enough respect for his financial expertise to bring him into the first post-coup government with the portfolio with which he started his ministerial career in 1971 - Minister of Finance. In September 1986 he was given the additional supervision of Agricultural Co-operatives and Marketing. He survived the constitutional crisis of February 1990 and remained Minister of Finance.

But the day before the military coup by Colonel Ramaema, on 30 April 1991, Sekhenyanya left for South Africa on "official business". Sekhonyanya said later in an interview with *Radio South Africa* that he knew a coup was coming for some time and that it came as no surprise to him. Hence his departure for South Africa.

TSOTETSI, Michael Nkhahle

Lesotho soldier. Member of Military Council, January 1986 -

A progressive farmer and keen soccer fan who often accompanies the Lesotho team on overseas tours, he shares a similar background with many of his colleagues on the Military Council. After a spell in the South African mines he joined the Police Mobile Unit, which later became the Paramilitary Force. There he won rapid promotion and was ready for appointment to the Military Council after the coup which toppled Chief Leabua Jonathan in January 1986.

Born 12 December 1938 at Thupa-Kubu Ha Thafeng in Berea district. Educated at the Bethany Roman Catholic Mission (1949-56) where he passed his standard six examination. He enrolled at Roma College for his secondary education.

He then went to work as a mine clerk at Randfontein mine in South Africa (1959-60). He returned home the next year and worked as a store manager of the Fraser group. In 1964 he joined the Lesotho Mounted Police as a trainee. He became a detective in Hlotse. He returned to Maseru to join the Protective Security Unit of the Police Mobile Unit in 1966, and the PMU proper in 1969.

Doing additional courses in local law and other relevant subjects, he won rapid promotion becoming a lieutenant-colonel in 1978. He worked as public relations officer for the police.

After the coup of 20 January 1986 which toppled Chief Leabua Jonathan, he was appointed to the six-man Military Council which rules the country. He is responsible for the overall supervision of the ministries of Agriculture, Trade, Industry, Tourism, Water, Energy and Mining and Co-operatives.

LIBERIA

Population: 2.51m (1990, World Bank)
Head of State: Interim President, Amos Sawyer
Independence: 26 July 1847
Government: Interim government under Economic Community of West Africa States (ECOWAS) auspices until such time as internationally monitored, multi-party, democratic elections can be held. Previous constitution had a two chamber assembly, with powers divided on the American model between executive, legislature and judiciary.
Parties: The ban on political parties was lifted in mid-1984 when a number of parties were allowed to contest the 1985 elections. Most of the old parties dating from the Samuel Doe regime were still in existence ready to make a comeback after Doe was ousted.

JOHNSON, Yormie (Prince)
Liberian guerrilla leader.

A bluff and hearty soldier who emerged as leader of a second guerrilla group during the 1990 campaign to oust President Samuel Doe. At first he fought and trained alongside Charles Taylor, but later he broke away to form his own Independent National Patriotic Front and lead his own forces in the attack on Monrovia, the Liberian capital. More sympathetic towards the Americans than Taylor and resentful of Libyan interference in Liberian affairs. He showed an ambivalent attitude towards the interim government set up under Amos Sawyer and resigned from it in August 1991.

Born 1959, a Gio from Nimba county in the north-west of Liberia. He joined the Liberian army in 1971. He did officer training at the officer candidate school in Camp Todee and was commissioned as a Lieutenant in 1974. He took a course in military police tactics at Fort Jackson, South Carolina and returned to become commander of the Liberian military police with the rank of Captain. But in 1977 he was involved in a serious car accident and was not able to continue his career in the army.

Johnson was personally involved in the failed coup attempt by his kinsman General Thomas Quiwonkpa, in November 1985. Quiwonkpa was captured, brutally killed and his dead body was driven around Monrovia in a Landrover, before it was cut to pieces.

This left an indelible mark on Johnson who in 1987, joined Charles Taylor in the National Patriotic Front of Liberia to organise opposition to Samuel Doe. The guerrillas were given assistance and training in Libya. Johnson resented the necessity to depend on Libya, but he reluctantly undertook training there as the most practical means to organise opposition to Doe.

He was part of the small invasion force of guerrillas under Charles Taylor, which on 24 December 1989 crossed from the Côte d'Ivoire into northern Liberia. Doe attempted to put down the invasion using brutal repression against Gio and Mano people who began to identify themselves with the guerrillas and provide them with new recruits.

Early in 1990 personality and ideological differences began to emerge between Taylor and Johnson, who gained the following of a group of kinsmen prepared to give him their loyalty. In February the two groups split. Johnson was said to have had the support of the US State Department which was suspicious of Taylor and his Libyan connections.

Gradually the guerrillas were successful. After taking most of the main provincial towns in the first half of 1990, by June they were on the outskirts of the capital, Monrovia. By this time the real divisions between Johnson and Taylor had emerged. Each was running separate guerrilla forces and there was much bad blood and public recrimination between them. Taylor accused Johnson of having 12 of his own troops executed, Johnson said that they had been found guilty of stealing and desertion.

Johnson named his group the Independent National Patriotic Front. His forces were actually the first into the capital, forcing their way onto the Monrovia peninsula in July, and proved most effective in the advance towards Doe's executive mansion.

At the beginning of August Johnson took 16 foreign hostages in an attempt to force the Americans to intervene. He thought this was the only way to end the bloody conflict. As to his own ambitions, he told reporters "I don't want power. I want a fair election. I will get Doe, he is not going to get away."

As fighting developed between Doe's forces and the guerrillas, and between the guerrillas themselves, Johnson came to the conclusion that the only solution would be intervention by an outside force. Eventually this came when the Economic Community of West African States (ECOWAS) sent a five-nation military team (ECOMOG) to occupy Monrovia on 24 August 1990. Johnson reacted favourably, though he was told that there would be no place for him in an interim administration.

A fortnight later, on 9 September, he invited Doe for a "consultation" at the ECOMOG headquarters in Monrovia. Doe met the ECOMOG commander but then shooting broke out between his forces and Johnson's. Doe was wounded badly in the legs and taken prisoner. Eyewitnesses claimed that he had walked into a trap, deliberately set for him and that the ECOMOG troops had stood by, failing to give him proper protection. He was captured by Johnson's troops, tortured and interrogated and in a grisly scene had his ears cut off in front of the television cameras, while pleading for his life. A day later on 10 September he was put to death without trial.

This was not the only killing at the hands of Johnson's troops. Johnson himself admitted, in a report in his newspaper the *Scorpion*, that he had executed four of his own men at the end of 1990. One man had been found guilty of espionage and the others were convicted for armed robbery and intimidating innocent civilians.

But in other respects Johnson cooperated with ECOMOG and actually lent them his forces in the war that developed against Charles Taylor. As attempts were made to set up an interim government, Johnson was a signatory to the ceasefire of 28 November and pledged his support for the disarmament of the warring factions. But he was inconsistent in the support he gave to the interim government. Later his troops had to be confined to their main bases.

He attended successive peace conferences early in 1991 and the all-Liberia conference of 15 March and was prepared to abide by the agreements reached by ECOWAS, the interim government of Amos Sawyer and local politicians. He condemned the invasion of Sierra Leone by Taylor's allies on 23 March and pledged to help the Sierra Leone government. He promised to send military equipment on a special flight to Freetown. He blamed Taylor for the invasion.

In August 1991 Johnson resigned from the interim government after the legislative assembly had debated his conduct and the allegation of executions carried out in his name. The assembly decided to launch a full investigation before referring the matter to the justice ministry.

SAWYER, Amos
Interim President of Liberia, August 1990 –

A fair and liberal minded academic turned politician who found himself thrust into the crucible of Liberian politics when he was made head of the interim government in August 1990. He has tried to establish peace in Monrovia while bringing more of Liberia under interim government rule. But he was frustrated by the personal ambition of Charles Taylor, who remained in control of most of the country. He stubbornly refused to recognise Sawyer as the universally recognised interim President and remained intransigent despite the best efforts of Sawyer to bring him into the political process.

Born 15 June 1945 in Greenville, Sinoe county to Abel and Sarah Sawyer. He had two sisters and five brothers. He went to school in Greenville but then left for Harper, Maryland county when his father got a job as a revenue collector. He went to Cape Palmas high school. From there he went to the US on the student exchange programme. He returned to attend the University of Liberia, where he majored in political science and graduated summa cum laude.

He did graduate studies at Northwestern University, Evanston, Illinois where he got a masters and later a PhD in political science in 1973. He returned home to lecture at the University of Liberia.

In the early 1970s he threw himself into the move to democratise his country. He was a founder of Susuku, a private, anti-poverty programme and the Movement for Justice in Africa (MOJA) which was originally intended to be a support group for the liberation of southern Africa. It soon became a radical group in the West African region, much feared by local governments. He became the Chairman of the Provisional National Committee of MOJA, but was always on the moderate wing of the group. In 1979 he announced his candidacy for the mayor of Monrovia. He was challenged by the True Whig Party which had been in power in Liberia for over a century. He campaigned as the "new broom" on a populist anti-poverty ticket. Though nominally standing as an independent, he said during the course of the campaign, that his membership of MOJA was no disadvantage to him. Most voters identified him with MOJA. He frightened the government so much that President Tolbert postponed the election until June 1980.

The government of Master Sergeant Samuel Doe took power on 12 April 1980. He appointed Sawyer the chairman of the commisson to draft a new constitution. This constitution was adopted by referendum on 3 July 1984.

But on 20 August 1984 Doe ordered his arrest with four others on charges that he had masterminded a "communist plot" to install a socialist government in Liberia. A week earlier he had announced the formation of the Liberian People's Party, which had been immediately banned by Doe. He had also clashed with Doe over the implementation of the constitution, specifically the guidelines for the registration of political parties.

But the idea that the mild mannered academic, who stood to gain so much from the constitution that he had just drafted, should be involved in subversion, was clearly seen to be highly improbable.

Students at Liberia university demonstrated and refused to attend classes until he was released, whereupon Doe's troops stormed the campus and shot five dead, wounding dozens and raping women students. Doe dismissed the entire staff accusing them of being academic stooges. Leaflets appeared on the streets denying that Sawyer was involved in any coup and saying it was all a plot by Doe to hold onto power himself.

On 7 October, Sawyer and 10 others were released, because Doe did not want to appear to be against the democratic process, but Sawyer who had already declared his intention of standing against Doe in the presidential elections, was banned from politics and forbidden from giving press interviews. The Liberian People's Party which he had helped found in August 1984 was also banned in August 1985 by the interim national assembly for pursuing "ideologies foreign to Liberia".

In 1986 Sawyer went to the US to do a fellowship at the African studies centre of Indiana University. Later he moved to Washington DC where he helped form, in January 1988, the Association for Constitutional Democracy in Liberia (ACDL) a pro-democracy movement. He became its first executive director.

When Charles Taylor launched his invasion of Liberia on Christmas eve 1989, Sawyer's ACDL agreed that such an incursion was inevitable but did not pledge full support for Taylor.

The chaos and the killing in Liberia became such that the Economic Community of West African States (ECOWAS) decided to intervene through its military force ECOMOG on 24 August 1990. It did not prevent the murder of Doe on 10 September 1990, but it was imperative to restore order.

Sawyer was chosen to head an interim government in August, by the ECOWAS Banjul conference where there were representatives of Liberia's political parties, the warring factions and the 13 counties. But he stayed in Sierra Leone for two months afterwards because of the fighting in Monrovia. He flew into the Liberian capital on 21 November 1990 in a Nigerian helicopter, where a guard of honour was waiting for him.

But his problems had just begun because despite an agreed ceasefire fighting continued and ECOMOG only controlled the capital and some of the suburbs, while Charles Taylor remained dominant in most of the rest of the country.

Sawyer tried to prevent further clashes between the forces of Prince Johnson and the remainder of the Doe army. On 4 January 1991 he appointed a cabinet while stressing that he did not want to stay in power for more than a year. He also warned Charles Taylor that the country belonged to all Liberian people and not to any single warring faction. At the all-Liberia conference in Monrovia on 15 March, he pushed for democratic elections by October, but was frustrated by Taylor's intransigence. In March Taylor's forces crossed into Sierra Leone intent on causing trouble there too.

The 27th summit at Abuja of the Organisation of African Unity, in June 1991 showed its support for Sawyer by accepting him as leader of the Liberian delegation and allowing him to take his place at the conference with full honours, while denying the claim of Charles Taylor.

TAYLOR, Charles
Liberian guerrilla leader.

A clever, flexible and ambitious personality who spent his early years in overseas study, business and exile politics. A flashy dresser whose gold chains and medallions gave way to snazzy combat fatigues with Commander-in-chief emblazoned on his chest, when he became a guerrilla commander. He describes himself as a "cold-blooded capitalist" and a worshipper of Reaganomics. After a brief spell in the early 1980s working for Samuel Doe he fell out with him, went into exile and raised the standard of revolt. Much to everyone's surprise his handful of guerrillas that invaded from the Côte d'Ivoire in December 1989 became an invincible force that swept him to power in the greater part of Liberia.

Born 1948 of mixed parentage - Liberian mother and American father. He grew up in Liberia where he had his early education. He went to the US in the 1970s where he attended Bentley College in Waltham, Massachusetts gaining a BA Econ. He worked as a mechanic in a plastics factory and continued with his studies and political activities.

He returned to Liberia from the United States in 1980, at the invitation of former President William Tolbert as part of a delegation of the Union of Liberia Associations in the Americas (ULAA), a movement representing over 30,000 US-based Liberians. Tolbert had invited the ULAA leadership home to show them that efforts were underway to democratise his government.

A few days after his arrival, in an interview with the local radio station, Taylor expressed surprise about the state of the country and said he had been misled as to the true facts while abroad. That night he attended a rally of the main opposition party, the Movement for Justice in Africa (MOJA) and thanked the MOJA leaders for opposing repression and dictatorship in Liberia.

A few weeks later Sergeant Samuel Doe seized power, in April 1980, and named Taylor the managing director of the General Services Agency, the government procurement agency, where his job was to do bulk purchasing for government ministries.

The government alleged that Taylor stole $900,000 from the agency, but at the time he was not charged. He was simply transferred from the GSA to the Ministry of Commerce where he was named an assistant minister, scarcely a demotion! He was also inducted into the army as a major. (At the time Doe insisted that all ministers should take on military rank and be responsive to military discipline.) The government accused Taylor of malpractice only after he had left the country, in 1984.

He found refuge in the United States and was actually under arrest in Boston, awaiting extradition proceedings against him, when he escaped by sawing through the bars of his cell and lowering himself to freedom on knotted bedsheets.

He then returned to Africa, courting support from Libya and Burkina Faso and started his new style career as a guerrilla leader with a mission to liberate his people. Drawing support from his new found friends, he formed the National Patriotic Front of Liberia (NPFL) and established a base in Côte d'Ivoire.

On 24 December 1989 he led 200 rebels over the border into Nimba county where the Gio people were generally antipathetic to Doe's government. There were long memories of Doe's brutal treatment of Taylor's friend, Gen. Thomas Quiwonkpa who was killed in the attempted coup of November 1985. Starting from scratch the revolt caught the local imagination and when Doe tried to repress it with brutal reprisals, thousands fled and those who remained gave the guerrillas their support.

Doe's undisciplined and unpopular forces failed either to defeat the guerrillas or cow the local population. Taylor proved himself an adept and flexible commander who within months had built a force of 2,000 men which was winning victories through central Liberia.

He held a whole succession of press conferences at regional capitals in liberated areas, in which he accused Doe of heinous crimes and threatened terrible vengeance: "If I find him unarmed, I will arrest him. I will put him on trial. If he is armed I am going to shoot the son of a bitch myself. I am not going to miss that opportunity." He also blew his own trumpet: "Doe has never had a man like Charles Taylor to confront him, this is a real fight... Liberians are coming over to us by the thousand simply because of everything this boy has done."

His campaign against Doe's undisciplined and demoralised soldiers was brilliantly successful. By July 1990 his troops were fighting in the suburbs of Monrovia and controlled most of the country.

On 27 July he announced that President Doe's government had been dissolved and replaced by a National Patriotic Assembly of Reconstruction with himself as President. He appointed his close associates and members of his own family as ministers. He promised to start an electoral process which would bring elections within six months allowing all political parties to participate. But already ECOWAS was threatening direct military intervention.

This intervention came when ECOWAS sent a five-nation force (ECOMOG) into Monrovia on 24 August 1990. It rapidly occupied much of the city but Taylor's forces dominated most of the rest of the country, after Doe's killing on 10 September.

Taylor resented the ECOWAS intervention, which barred him from power and the imposition of an interim government under the exiled politician Amos Sawyer. He continually claimed that Liberians could work out their own problems and did not need interference from outside powers. But he had to face the reality of ECOMOG's presence and every pressure was brought to bear on him to sign a peace agreement and then find a formula where democracy and stability could be restored in Liberia.

He was a signatory to the ceasefire of 28 November, in which hostilities were to cease and the troops of all factions were to be confined to their barracks and disarmed. The fighting gradually petered out, but Taylor was not prepared to relinquish power by disarming his troops.

The pattern was then set with the ECOWAS powers trying to persuade him to enter an interim government and prepare for democratic elections and Taylor's refusing to trust his opponents or the democratic processes they proposed. Instead he persisted with his own government.

He prevaricated at successive conferences early in 1991 and refused to attend the all-Liberia conference in Monrovia on 15 March, which gave the broadest representation to all parties in the conflict.

His frustration was reflected in the invasion of neighbouring Sierra Leone starting on 23 March, by troops led by Foday Sankoh, who had been dismissed from the Sierra Leone army when he tried to forment a coup. At first Taylor denied any involvement in the invasion, but later it turned out that his NPFL forces took a major part alongside dissident Sierra Leoneans. After initial successes the invasion was contained by Sierra Leonean government and allied ECOMOG troops.

Taylor found the OAU ranged against him when it barred his delegation from the summit conference at Abuja (Nigeria) in June and allowed his rival Amos Sawyer to take his seat on behalf of Liberia.

A further attempt to co-opt Taylor into the peace process was made by his erstwhile ally, President Houphouet Boigny at Yamoussoukro, on 30 June. Taylor agreed to preserve the peace but remained reluctant to diminish his power by disbanding his forces and continued to block travel by civilians in the areas of the country under his control.

MADAGASCAR

Population: 11.91m (1990, World Bank)
Head of State: Didier Ratsiraka
Independence: 26 June 1960
Government: Presidential rule by a President elected by universal adult suffrage every seven years. Theoretically a multi-party democracy but opposition parties are dependent on presidential licence.
Parties: The *Avant Garde de la Revolution Malagache* (AREMA) party has government backing and enjoys an overwhelming majority in the National Assembly. There are nine other weak and fragmented political parties. Some external opposition parties have joined the umbrella organisation, the *Union des Opposants Malagaches Exterieurs* (UOME).

RATSIRAKA, Didier
Malagasy naval officer. President, January 1976-

He came to power in a flush of revolutionary enthusiasm determined to build a temple of Malagasy socialism as laid down in his Revolutionary Charter or little red book, Bokymen. Social and ethnic tensions, a failing economy and a series of attempted coups turned him into a cautious statesman seeking compromise and consensus, gradually democratising his regime. He was also forced to come to an arrangement with the International Monetary Fund and reverse many of his socialist policies in order to secure international assistance and attempt to revive the economy. He has proved remarkably resilient and a survivor in his diverse and flamboyant country, with its long history of ethnic and class division.

Born 4 November 1936, at Vatomandry near Tananarive. A Betsimiraka, educated at the College St Michel, Tananarive, Lycee Henry IV, Paris, before deciding on naval training at the French Officers Naval School at Lanveuc-Poulmic. Commissioned as an engineer officer of signals, he served with the French navy on corvettes. He then attended the Ecole Superieure de Guerre Navale in Paris and was promoted captain.

As a young officer he was much more concerned with political developments than others in the wardroom. He gained an insight into diplomacy as defence attaché at the Madagascar embassy in Paris, (1970-72). He was appointed Minister of Foreign Affairs in May 1972.

He returned to Paris in January 1973, leading a delegation to renegotiate the agreements made at independence. He began with a unilateral renunciation of all agreements - military and educational. At one tense stage in the talks General Ramanantsoa recalled him for an emergency cabinet meeting. He pursued a hard bargain, clearing French troops from bases at Tananarive and Ivato, as well as having the French Indian Ocean headquarters removed from Madagascar.

In the turmoil that followed the assassination of the new ruler, Colonel Ratsimandrava, in which he played no part, the military directorate voted Lt-Commander Ratsiraka into power on 15 June 1975. This appointment was confirmed by a referendum of December 1975, in which he won 95% of the votes cast by 90% of the registered electorate. He ruled through a Supreme Revolutionary Council (CSR).

He adopted a highly radical policy, nationalising the banks, insurance and shipping companies, the petroleum refinery and mineral resources. He closed the US satellite tracking station, took over the leading French trading company and made a series of broadcasts detailing his policies which were later published as *Bokymen*, the "little red book" or Revolutionary Charter. He promised to use the army to help in development and to carry out agrarian and administrative reforms. But despite its radical stance it was still a military government until in 1976, when the Vanguard of the Malagasy Revolution (AREMA) party was formed. It dominated the local and legislative elections to the National Assembly in June 1977.

With his position consolidated, he set about improving relations with Western countries. He paid a state visit to France in September and met President Giscard d'Estaing to mend relations with France. He travelled widely in other parts of the world too. On 28 February 1980 he announced the discovery of a plot aimed at his assassination and the overthrow of his government. This led to the arrest of the opposition leader Monja Jaona, followed by widespread riots, and demands for reforms in education and action to tackle unemployment. He adopted a policy of reconciliation and released Jaona and persuaded him to bring his party back into the umbrella organisation, the National Front for the Defence of the Revolution (FNDR).

Another attempted plot occurred in January 1982, allegedly, organised by high-ranking officers, aided by a priest and a sorcerer. Ratsiraka's answer was to stand again for another seven-year term as President in November. Jaona stood against him but was defeated by four million votes to one million.

Meanwhile, the economy was deteriorating fast and he was forced to enter into negotiations with the International Monetary Fund which demanded strict reforms in return for credits. But he found many of the conditionalities politically unacceptable and by only partly accepting the package, weakened his own position. Urban and rural violence followed, with rioting in the capital provoked by gangs of youths practising Kung-Fu.

Ratsiraka caused further opposition by trying to cut back the number of students in higher education. This caused a wave of student protests in November 1986 which continued well into 1987. Ratsiraka postponed for a year the legislative elections due to be held in 1988. After further delays, elections were finally held in March 1989. This time three other candidates were allowed to stand and he had his vote cut to 63%, with his major opponent polling 20%. He was sworn in for his third presidential term on 23 March 1989 and said that he "totally and sincerely respected" the choice of those who had not voted for him, "You have exercised your right in accordance with democratic rules...We will listen to your voice and will endeavour to reconcile your demands with the aspirations of the majority."

As the wind of political change reached full force in Africa 1991, Ratsiraka was fully exposed. Serious trouble started in June, when Ratsiraka was abroad, with demonstrators out on the streets protesting over the lack of progress in democratisation and calling for a national conference. Ratsiraka countered by saying that an elected parliament and multi-party system already existed and that there was no need for further change. But the opposition stepped up its demands, this time for a provisional government, to replace the existing regime.

Daily demonstrations took place through July as the political temperature rose. As Ratsiraka made concessions the opposition stepped up its demands. On 22 July he declared a state of emergency. In August hundreds of demonstrators were killed at massive rallies all over the country when Ratsiraka's guards and troops opened fire.

Law and order then disintegrated, with the provinces declaring Federal status, the army saying that it was ready to assume power and the opposition announcing Ratsiraka's deposition. By the end of August his days seemed numbered.

MALAWI

Population: 8.76m (1990, World Bank)
Head of State: Hastings Kamuzu Banda
Independence: 6 July 1964
Government: Presidential government through a single party system. The President is both the Head of State and Government. In practice parliament is a rubber stamp organisation and cabinet ministers only exist at the whim of the President.
Parties: The sole authorised party is the Malawi Congress Party. Three opposition groups exist in exile. Some of their leaders have been assassinated or kidnapped for persistent opposition.

BANDA, Hastings Kamuzu
Malawian doctor of medicine and politician. President, 6 July 1966-

Once hailed as the Little Messiah of his country when he returned to lead his country to independence after living in exile for 40 years, he later became a lonely and isolated figure remote from other African leaders and from friends and colleagues in his own country. Over the years he became an autocratic dictator who systematically crushed all opposition and eliminated all those that dared to challenge him.
Still an extraordinary mixture of explosive African nationalism, Scottish missionary zeal and the innate conservatism of an African chief. He is a man of single minded individualism, choosing his own friends and going his own way. This led him to strange foreign alliances with the Portuguese, South Africans and even the Mozambique National Resistance guerrillas, until recently when he has moved marginally closer to Mozambique and his African neighbours.

Born 14 May 1906, according to Banda, who wants to appear younger than he actually is. His true birth date is about 1898. His parents were poor subsistence farmers. He was called Kamuzu, the Chewa for "little root" which is said to have cured his mother's barren condition. He started school in 1905 and took on the name Hastings from a missionary at the Livingstonia Church of Scotland School.

He continued his schooling at Chilanga Primary School, under instruction from his uncle, and passed his standard three in 1914. Two years later he and his uncle set off on foot for South Africa, stopping to earn money as a hospital orderly at Hartley near Salisbury, where he first resolved to become a doctor. After a spell in the Natal coalmines he eventually reached Johannesburg and became a clerk-interpreter at Rand goldmines. It was at the mines that he heard the Ghanaian educationist J.E.K. Aggrey. He continued his studies, passed his standard eight and became a member of the African Methodist Episcopal Church, which financed his further education in the US.

He began his studies at the AME Wilberforce Institute, Ohio, where he completed his diploma in three years, going on to study political science at Indiana University. He graduated as a bachelor of philosophy at the University of Chicago before going to the Meharry Medical College at Nashville, Tennessee. He qualified as a doctor in 1937 and went to Scotland to complete his medical studies at Glasgow and Edinburgh in 1941. He established practice in Liverpool in the same year, then worked in various British hospitals during the war.

He moved to London in 1945 and set up in Kilburn where he had over 4,000 patients, most of them white. His house became a meeting place for African nationalists such as Nkrumah, Kenyatta and Harry Nkumbula. The Nyasaland African Congress (NAC) was created in the 1950s and he gave it support from London. He became a determined opponent of the creation of the Central African Federation and consistently campaigned against it in Britain. But the Federation was created in 1953 and a disillusioned Banda left to become a doctor in Ghana. Nkrumah offered him a government post but he preferred to practice medicine in Kumasi.

Other NAC leaders such as Henry Chipembere and Kanyama Chiume, who were fighting a losing battle against Federation in Malawi, finally persuaded him to return home. He arrived at Chileka airport on 6 July 1958 to a tumultuous welcome. He spoke to the crowds in English being lost for words in his native Nyanja. He was elected president-general of the NAC on 1 August 1958 and made a series of inflammatory speeches. His campaign against the Federation, though stressing non-violence, was so intense that a state of emergency was declared on 9 March 1959 by the inflexible Protectorate government.

Banda was arrested and sent to prison in Gwelo, Southern Rhodesia, with other Malawi leaders. There they planned the future of their country while Banda wrote his autobiography. The colonial government established a commission of enquiry under Mr Justice Devlin who cleared Banda of blame while saying there had been some incidents of intimidation by the NAC. After 395 days in detention he was freed on 1 April 1960. He set off on a speaking tour of Britain and the US. The new British colonial secretary was prepared to be flexible and called a Lancaster House conference where Banda led the Malawi Congress Party (successor to the NAC).

On 5 August 1960 a new constitution was agreed introducing a ministerial system leading to direct elections of Africans to the Legislative Council. He returned to London in December 1960 to attend a Federal Review Conference alongside Kenneth Kaunda from Northern Rhodesia and Joshua Nkomo from Southern Rhodesia. The conference accomplished nothing directly but the Federation was doomed, though it dragged on until 31 December 1963.

Banda returned home to concentrate on the Malawi elections and after a vigorous campaign the MCP took 99% of the lower roll votes and all 20 of the lower roll seats and two higher roll seats. On 3 September 1961 he became Minister of Natural Resources and Local Government, then Prime Minister on 1 Feburary 1963. Complete independence came on 6 July 1964, six years to the day after his return from exile.

Almost immediately he faced a cabinet crisis. On 7 September 1964 he dismissed three of his colleagues including Orton Chirwa, the Minister of Justice who had helped him to power. Three others resigned. Banda ousted them from the MCP and soon instituted one-man rule. Malawi became a one-party state in mid-1965. He adopted a system of government similar to that of a pre-colonial chieftainship. He revived African traditions, exercised control over morality, even styles of dress.

He was elected President on 6 July 1966, when Malawi became a republic. A weak attempt at an invasion was mounted in October 1967, in which Yatuta Chisisa, the former Minister of Home Affairs, was killed, but afterwards there was little open opposition to Banda. On 6 July 1971 he had himself voted life president and brought his ministers, the parliament and the party totally under his personal control.

In foreign affairs he rejected the socialist, African nationalist line adopted by the Organisation of African Unity and neighbouring countries and pursued close alliances with Portugal and South Africa. In May 1970 he invited the South African premier John Vorster to Malawi and President Fouche in March 1972. In August 1971 he was the first black African Head of State to visit South Africa.

In February 1977, after another alleged coup attempt, Banda felt that he had consolidated his postion sufficiently to allow the release of up to 2,000 detainees, but by then most of his main critics were abroad, joining thousands of exiles already in other countries.

The first general elections for 17 years were held in June 1978. Previously Banda had simply drawn up a list of MPs himself, in 1978 he was prepared to vet the list of candidates then allowing elections to proceed.

The main feature of the 1980s was the way in which Banda removed his main challengers. In January 1980 Aleke Banda, once considered a likely successor, was expelled from the MCP for a gross breach of party discipline. Gwanda Chakuamba was sentenced to 22 years' imprisonment in March 1981. On Christmas Eve 1982, Orton Chirwa and his wife and son were arrested near the Zambian border. Chirwa had been one of Banda's original colleagues and a main opposition hope.

Another opponent, Dr Attati Mpakati, who was beginning to organise an efficient opposition movement, was murdered in Harare in March 1983. In May 1983 other possible successors to Banda - Dick Matenje, the secretary-general of the MCP, and Aaron Gadama, Minister for the Central Region, were killed in a mysterious car crash. Even John Tembo, who appeared to be Banda's choice as a successor, was stripped of his post as Governor of the Central Bank in April 1984, though he was later entrusted with special assignments for his master.

During the mid-1980s Banda drew closer to his African neighbours whom he had earlier spurned. In October 1984 he signed a general co-operation agreement with Mozambique and hesitatingly reversed his earlier policy of supporting the Mozambique National Resistance guerrillas. The Mozambicans were still complaining in July 1986 that Banda was continuing to secretly support the MNR, but by April 1987 Malawi troops had been sent to Mozambique to help protect the Nacala railway against guerrilla attack. In the years that followed the Mozambican refugees in Malawi, who had become a heavy strain on the economy, were gradually sent home.

TEMBO, John Zenas Ungapake
Malawian politician, former minister and Reserve Bank Governor

Always an out and out loyalist with an eye on the main chance - succession to President Banda. A man of power and authority, he was as much valued by his master as disliked and reviled by his opponents. A formidable force both in the Malawi Congress Party and in the highest offices of state, but Banda was reluctant to confirm him as his successor and kept him in reserve for special assignments during his later years.

Born September 1932 at Dedza 50 miles south-east of Lilongwe, son of a Chewa minister. Educated at Senior Primary School Kongwe, Mlanda School, Ncheu, Blantyre Secondary School and Roma College, Basutoland, where he graduated in 1958. Diploma of education Salisbury, Rhodesia, 1959.

Worked for Colonial audit department (1949-55) between school and college. Began teaching after Roma college, at Kongwe secondary school. Assistant Headmaster 1960. As a keen party man he contested the first elections under the self-government constitution and won the seat for Dedza North in 1961. Banda made him Parliamentary Secretary for Finance in 1962.

Became Minister of Finance in the first independence government on 6 July 1964. Though there were many early resignations and dismissals he remained loyal and concurrently took on responsibilites as Minister of Trade, Industry, Development and Planning. Minister of Trade and Finance (1968-70). Appointed governor of the Reserve Bank of Malawi August 1970.

In May 1983 Banda announced his intention of taking a year's sabbatical leave. This set off a power struggle between Tembo and Dick Matenje, a prominent minister and the secretary-general of the Malawi Congress Party. Matenje was then killed in a mysterious car crash in May. It was thought that Tembo was being groomed for succession especially when Chakakala Chaziya, the previous Finance Minister, replaced Tembo as governor of the Reserve Bank on 2 April 1984.

It was assumed that Tembo would be appointed as Secretary General of the MCP, but no appointment was made and on 24 August 1980, Tembo was only appointed an ordinary member of the party executive committee and not to any senior posts. It still seemed most likely that Tembo was the heir apparent, but Banda did not want him, or any other

Malawian politician, to become sufficiently confident to build an alternative power base. Nor did Banda want to be ousted prematurely.

But he was sent by Banda on special missions. In late 1984 Tembo attended a congress of the Romanian Communist party. In July 1985 diplomatic relations were established for the first time with Romania and Albania, the first Eastern bloc countries ever to have relations with Malawi.

Malawi had been frequently accused of giving support to the Mozambique National Resistance (MNR) rebels. It claimed that it was only harbouring bona fide refugees. Tembo was appointed by Banda to tour the other Frontline States to explain the Malawi position. He was made head of the Malawi delegation to the joint defence and security commission with Mozambique in September 1986. In March 1987 Malawi decided to join Tanzania and Zimbabwe in deploying troops against the MNR.

MALI

Population: 8.52m (1990, World Bank)
Head of State: Lt–Col. Amadou Toumany Touré
Independence: 22 September 1960
Government: On taking power, on 26 March 1991, Touré promised that measures would be taken to organise free and democratic elections as soon as possible. A Prime Minister was appointed on 2 April. A national conference was called for 29 July which enshrined multi-party politics. The Transitional Committee for Health of the People (CTSP) was set up to run the country until the military returned to their barracks on 1 January 1992.
Parties: When political parties were legitimised, the first to be formed was the Rally for Democracy and Progress, formed on 19 April 1991, followed by a plethora of other parties.

LY Sekou (General)
Malian soldier and politician.

A close colleague of Moussa Traoré he served as a senior minister from 1978. A strong supporter of law and order, he was much valued by Traoré who used him to settle student and teachers disputes in the early 1980s and two border disputes with neighbouring Burkina. He remained with Traoré longer than most other top officers and ranked high in the Mali hierarchy, but he fell from power with the coup of Amadou Touré in March 1991.

Born 1933 at Segou. Educated locally, finishing at the Officers school, Strasbourg. He returned to become a teacher in Mali from 1951-52. In 1961 he switched to the army becoming a trainee instructor. Promoted lieutenant he continued as an instructor in the Kati Officers School, 1964-68.

After the military coup of 19 November 1968 which brought Moussa Traoré to power, he switched back into civilian life and became Mayor of Nioro, in the Sahel, 1968-70 and then Administrator delegate in Bamako district, 1970-78. He then won a post in the Presidency as Secretary of State in charge of the interior 1977-78. On 28 February 1978 Traoré carried out an extensive purge and promoted Ly as a minister for the first time in charge of the Interior and Urban Development.

He became the chief Malian negotiator in the border dispute which erupted between Mali and its southern neighbour Upper Volta (now Burkina Faso), in November 1979. He helped establish a joint commission to investigate claims to a strip of land along the border not clearly demarcated on French colonial administrative maps. A month later he was involved in stopping a long student strike in which young demonstrators looted shops and burned vehicles. Further trouble followed when school teachers went on strike and academic colleges did not open in 1980.

On 22 August 1980 Traoré, appreciating his role during the student troubles, appointed him Minister of National Education, a position he held for six years until 1986. He started by suspending all schools and colleges in October 1980. It was not until July 1981 that he was able to get them back to work and functioning normally. On 5 June 1986 Traoré relinquished the Defence portfolio, which he had held personally since 1978, and handed it to Ly, who found himself confronted by another outbreak of border trouble between Mali and Burkina Faso. A ceasefire was arranged, prisoners were exchanged and both sides agreed to mediation by neighbouring states. Ly remained Minister of Defence for two years before returning to National Education in June 1988.

As Africa's wind of political change began to blow through Mali, Gen. Ly assumed an even more important role. On 8 January he was made Minister of Interior and Basic Development with the difficult brief of countering the wave of popular agitation for democratisation. On one occasion, in February he spoke for five hours with a number of reformist groups demanding an independent inquiry into the shootings and deaths of demonstrators and the recognition of the people's right to assemble.

When President Traoré was ousted, less than a month later, Sekou Ly fell with him and was dismissed as minister, on 28 March 1991.

TOURE, Amadou Toumany (Lt-Colonel)

Malian soldier and politician. Transitional president, 26 March 1991 –

An avuncular, approachable figure, refreshingly modest and open, known to all his friends as ATT. He started as a history teacher but switched to the military because of better career prospects. This placed him in a moral dilemma because he grew to actively hate the confrontationist policies of President Moussa Traoré. Finally he felt a coup was the only solution, but he promised to hasten the transition to plural government, saying that the army would go back to its barracks by 20 January 1992. He did not take up residence in the presidential palace but remained in a small three roomed house in the military quarters of his parachute regiment.

Born 1943 in Mopti. Educated locally before going to train as a history and geography teacher in Bamako, where he graduated in 1969. He decided to take up a military career and was admitted to the *Ecole Militaire Interarmes (EMIA)* at Kati, on a three year course. He was promoted Lieutenant. He became a parachute instructor, doing courses both at Riazan in the Soviet Union and Pau in France. Promoted to captain in the 33rd parachute battalion in 1978, he served for eight years as commander of the presidential guard, becoming commander of his battalion in 1985. He was made a Lieutenant Colonel in 1986.

He was posted to the *Ecole Superieur de Guerre* in Paris, from April to December 1990. On his return to Mali no job could be found for him until 22 March 1991, when he was put back in command of his battalion. His resentment at this treatment added to years of dissatisfaction with the government of Moussa Traoré were among the prime motivations for the coup of the morning of 26 March. Even more important were months of peaceful protest, countered by repression by the government which turned its guns on the people killing hundreds. The government's heavy handedness had provoked the coup which made Touré, " really ashamed of being an army officer". He commented, "Moussa no longer served the interests of the country. He was opportunist, a total nepotist, a flatterer who made huge mistakes".

Touré began plotting the coup on 22 January, the day before a big protest march in Bamako. He then took the risky course of convincing the other senior officers that a coup was necessary.

"I repeat. All the army did was carry out what the people, the youth, the women and the democratic organisations wanted. We did what remained to be done. We captured Moussa. That act reconciled the army to the people".

He was quick to seek out opposition leaders and pledge his commitment to the democratic process. He promised his troops would return to their barracks on 20 January 1992, after he had organised legislative and presidential elections.

He became acting Head of State in charge of the Transition Committee for the Salvation of the People (CSTP), which would supervise the transitional government.

Shortly after taking power he said, "The army has no claim to exercise power and has learned the lessons of the disastrous policies carried out in its name directly or indirectly. It has also been associated with racketeering, favouritism and repression. It has been used against its own people."

One of his first acts was to dismiss eight senior generals, and the Defence Minister Mamadou Coulibaly.

On the 25 March the day he had assumed power and arrested Moussa Traoré he was the target of an assassination attempt. His car was raked with bullets as he returned to the parachutists barracks. Another assassination attempt was mounted on 14 July, by a minister who wanted to cover up the fact that he had embezzled funds allocated to a reforestation project, but the plot was foiled.

Touré called a national conference on 29 July to work out a draft constitution for a pluralist form of government. He said this would later be submitted to a national referendum.

Apart from the restoration of public confidence, he inherits all Mali's endemic problems - massive poverty aggravated by drought, a huge debt burden and heavy payment deficits.

TRAORÉ MOUSSA (General)
Malian Head of State, 19 November 1968 – 26 March 1991.

Always very much of a soldier who saw it as his duty to hold power and rule his turbulent nation. He lived in modest quarters in the main military camp. In recent years he tried to democratise and civilianise his government but he was always reluctant to install full multi-party democracy. His reluctance to delegate and suspicion of other potential challengers brought him twice to appoint Prime Ministers, only to dismiss them when he found they were not lightening his burden of office. He survived a number of coup attempts and continual unrest and agitation from the comparatively powerful unions, students, womens and professional bodies, until he was finally ousted in the coup of March 1991.

Born 25 September 1936 at Kayes, in the north west of Mali on the fringes of the Sahara desert. He came from a peasant family but was bright enough to win a place at the Kati cadets school. He joined the French army, became an NCO and finally entered Frejus military college in France.

At the age of 24 he returned home and was made a Lieutenant in the Malian army in 1964. He became an instructor at the Kati Inter-Services school just north of the Malian capital, Bamako.

On 19 November 1968 he led a group of 14 young army officers into the capital. He then assembled the Popular Militia and disarmed them before occupying the key positions in the capital and arresting the then President Modibo Keita. He announced over the radio that a Military Committee of National Liberation (CMLN) had been established and that the regime of "Keita and his lackeys" had been overthrown.

Keita had been one of Africa's original socialist leaders, in the same camp as Kwame Nkrumah and Sekou Touré of Guinea, but he had totally mismanaged his impoverished country incurring huge deficits on the budget and balance of payments. He quarrelled with France and was cut off from French aid and assistance. The Malian currency became worthless and the government soon ran out of funds. Keita tried to counter the growing crisis by imposing austerity measures.

This was the situation that allowed Moussa Traoré to carry out his peaceful coup. He allowed existing institutions such as the trades unions and the single party to exist, but imposed the supreme authority of the Military Committee for National Liberation (CMLN), which was virtually a military junta. Gradually the power of Keita's organisations were eroded. He suppressed the national trade union in 1970 and arrested union leaders in 1971. By 1974 a new party the Democratic Union of the Malian People (UPDM) was established and in principle charged with preparing the way for civilian rule.

But Traoré was always reluctant to take the final plunge and relinquish what has become a system of government by decree. In 1974 he organised a referendum on a new constitution which was to bring civilian rule in five years. It was overwhelmingly carried, but there was considerable resistance to the delay among students, trades unionists and civil servants. Sporadic civil strife led him to hold onto power past the 1979 deadline. But Presidential and legislative elections were held in June 1979 on a single party list, provided by the newly formed

Democratic Union of the Malian People (UPDM).

At an extraordinary congress of the UPDM in February 1981, his powers were extended when he was given authority to appoint and dismiss the Prime Minister and other ministers. In 1985 another special congress of the party was called to change the constitution so that he would be eligible for a second term as President.

One of Traoré's major problems was the economy which was weak in consequence of recurrent drought, high oil prices and the paucity of export commodities which consist mainly of low priced cotton and groundnuts. In the 1980s Traoré took up policies of economic liberalisation and privatisation to achieve a more efficient production base, but moves in this direction were resisted by the students and trades unions who are comparatively radical and well organised compared with those in neighbouring countries.

In June 1986 he appeared ready to divest himself of some of the responsibilities of government and appointed a Prime Minister for the first time since Yoro Diakité had fallen from favour in 1971. He also relinquished the Defence portfolio to Gen Sekou Ly. But in June 1988 he had another change of heart, abolished the post of prime minister once again and reassumed charge of the Defence portfolio.

During 1990 Mali was swept up in the wind of political change that was blowing through Africa. Traoré was compelled to hold a series of conferences but he wanted reform to be confined to the ruling UPDM party. But the opposition, that sensed he was weakening, wanted far more extensive democratisation. Its demands took the shape of frequent demonstrations at the end of the year.

By January 1991 the National Union of Malian Workers were out on strike, making pay demands as well as expressing political discontent. Riots took place at the end of January with several deaths, and severe looting, as Traoré desperately sought to try and pacify his opponents.

But the more he tried to be reasonable, the greater the pressure from the forces ranged against him. Students and their teachers went on strike in February as the unemployed demonstrated in the streets.

The day before he fell from power he was asked whether he was ready to install multi-party government. He answered, "It is not up to me to refuse or accept multi-partyism. That is not my problem. My problem is to give a free choice to the people". He did not have the opportunity, at 1 am on the evening of 26 March 1991 he was arrested by soldiers under the command of Lt–Col. Amadou Touré. He was driven under armed guard to the military air base.

MAURITANIA

Population: 2.1m (1990, World Bank)
Head of State: Col. Maawiya Ould Taya
Independence: 28 November 1980
Government: Military rule following the coup of July 1978 which deposed the one-party regime of Mokhtar Ould Daddah. Government since April 1979 by the Military Committee for National Salvation, headed by the President. A new constitution setting up an Islamic Arab Republic was passed on 12 July 1991. It provided for an elected president and parliament and a free press.
Parties: All parties that threaten "national unity" remain banned, but several opposition groups operate in exile, mainly from France.

SALEK, Mustapha Ould Mohammed (Col)

Mauritanian politician. Former Head of State, 10 July 1978 – 6 April 1979.

A soldier and executive who seized power from President Moktar Ould Daddah in the hope that he could bring peace with the Polisario guerrillas who were harassing his country for siding with Morocco against them. Salek wanted neutrality and an end to the war but he found himself up against Morocco, which had troops stationed inside Mauritania and enjoyed the support of France and the USA. Other Mauritanian factions were opposed to his policies. He fell from power after holding office for only nine months. In February 1982 he tried to mount another coup attempt and was sentenced to 10 years' imprisonment, but released early in December 1984.

Born circa 1928. Trained as an army officer at the Saumur Military Academy in France. Returned home to join the army, rising to become Chief of Staff of the armed forces (1968-69). Seconded to become director of the National Import/Export Corporation (SONIMEX), but brought back into the army on 15 July 1977 to take command of the critical northern (third military) region to protect the country against the raids of the Polisario guerrillas from Western Sahara.

In February 1978 he was again appointed Chief of Staff of the armed forces. This was the ideal platform for him to carry out the bloodless military coup of 10 July against the government of President Moktar Ould Daddah who had been in power for 18 years. Salek set up a Military Committee for National Recovery (CMRN) which claimed that the former government had been overthrown for being "corrupt, anti-national and unpopular."

But the main rationale for the coup was the need to take action to halt the war against the Polisario guerrillas. Salek announced, "We are certainly going to set out a calendar of work to start a process which will have to lead us to peace." The same day Polisario declared a ceasefire and within a month peace talks started in Paris in September, then Tripoli in October. But the talks failed.

Unable to extract Mauritania from the Saharan quagmire, the unity of the CMRN came under threat as rival factions jostled for power. Salek's early promises to return the country to civilian rule were broken, bringing increased unpopularity to the regime. On 20 March 1979 Salek assumed absolute power, promising the evacuation of all Moroccan troops and rapid unilateral disengagement from the Saharan conflict. He dissolved the CMRN, replaced it with a Military Committee for National Salvation (CMSN) and made a clean sweep in a new cabinet.

But he offended too many factions. Forty members boycotted his new council and on 5 April he was forced to resign and was stripped of his powers by his colleagues who installed Lt-Col Ahmed Bouciefin his place. He remained titular Head of State for a month, finally resigning on 3 June to be succeeded by Lt-Col Mohammed Old Louly (after Boucief had been killed in an aircraft accident on 27 May).

On 6 February 1982 he was involved in an unsuccessful coup attempt and was arrested along with the former Prime Minister, Sid'Ahmed Ould Bneidjara. He was put on trial, convicted and sentenced to 10 years' imprisonment with his property confiscated. On 21 December 1984 he was amnestied by the new head of state, Lt-Col Maawiya Ould Sid'Ahmed Taya, and released from jail.

TAYA, Maawiya Ould Sid'Ahmed (Colonel)
Mauritanian soldier. Head of State, 12 December 1984-

A small, somewhat self-effacing man, a career soldier with a reputation for integrity and honesty. Coming from a relatively small ethnic group in the Atar region north of Nouakchott, he was never involved in the main political and tribal intrigues. A relatively tolerant and liberal Muslim, he is said to be less politically committed to Islam than his predecessor, Mohammed Haidallah. He enjoyed early support from the left-leaning Mouvement Nationale Democratique. He achieved many reforms in his first years in power, facing his first real test when inter-racial violence broke out between Mauritanians and Senegalese in April 1989.

Born 1943 at Atar. He joined the army and soon entered the limelight by becoming aide de camp to Mauritania's first President, Moktar Ould Daddah. He rose to deputy Chief of operations in 1976 and became a commander in the northern region during the Sahara war against the Polisario guerrillas from Western Sahara. He was promoted to deputy Chief of Staff 1978-79.

On 10 July 1978 Mustapha Ould Salek took power in a bloodless military coup on a peace-with-Polisario platform. Taya emerged as a minister and a member of the Military Committee for National Salvation, CMSN. On 16 January 1979 Ould Salek made him his Minister of Defence in the first major cabinet reshuffle of his regime. He remained in this post only until March as Salek struggled to conclude peace with the Polisario, finally resigning in June. Taya became Chief of Police (1979-80). His relative, the new Head of State, Mohammed Haidallah, appointed him Army Chief of Staff, (1980-81).

He became leader of the military faction in the government and would have liked to assume power as Head of State at that time, but Haidallah finally persuaded him to become Prime Minister and Minister of Defence in April 1981. He picked a small military cabinet to replace the outgoing civilians. Haidallah tried to steer a tenuous course between the Polisario and Morocco and Libya, whom he suspected of trying to destabilise his regime. A coup attempt occurred at the end of February 1984, so Haidallah, wanting more direct personal control, dismissed Taya from the Premiership and took it over himself. Taya was told to resume his post as army chief of staff.

On 12 December 1984 while Haidallah was attending a Franco-African summit meeting in Burundi, Taya assumed power in a bloodless palace coup. The next day he formed a new government containing most members of his old cabinet. He reaffirmed his recognition of the Saharwi Arab Democratic Republic. He amnestied many political prisoners, including the former President Mustafa Ould Salek, and said that he would aim for greater economic and social justice. He also endorsed the mass education policy first announced by the military government in 1982, but not put into effect.

Internally he maintained his power by judiciously shuffling his ministers and lieutenants. Between 1985 and February 1986 he carried out no less than seven cabinet reshuffles of varying importance.

On 13 April 1985 he restored relations with Morocco while continuing to recognise SADR. He also signed on 9 April 1985 a border agreement with Algeria, establishing a common frontier after three years of negotiation. His next move in his "friendship-with-all" policy was to restore diplomatic relations with Libya, after paying an official visit to Tripoli in January 1986.

But he faced an upsurge of black African protest against the increasing Arabicisation of the country. Many black Mauritanians were arrested, provoking a wave of civil disturbances. In October 1987 more black Mauritanians were arrested after a reported coup plot.

Taya introduced some democratisation at local government level, with multi-party elections held in municipalities in December 1986 and at department level in January 1988.

Perhaps the greatest blemish on his record was the violent riots of April/May 1989 between his country and Senegal in which tens of thousands of citizens were forced to flee racial violence. More than 15,000 Senegalese fled Mauritania after Arab Mauritanians had turned on the Senegalese (blacks) in Nouakchott. Taya protested that he had "always sought good relations with his neighbour". He blamed the Sengalese authorities for allowing the looting of Mauritanian shops and the attacks on Mauritanians living in Senegal. But the expulsions from Mauritania spread to blacks in general, not just those of a specifically Senegalese nationality. Senegal television attacked him personally, accusing him of "having contempt for anything black."

During 1991, even relatively isolated Mauritania felt the wind of change blowing through Africa. Taya was under attack for his human rights record, particularly his treatment of the blacks and for his failure to democratise his regime.

The human rights organisation, Africa Watch claimed that at least a thousand blacks were arrested between November 1990 and January 1991. Some Mauritanian sources put the figure at several thousand. They were accused of plotting a coup in November. On 15 April 1991 Taya ordered the immediate release of all black detainees to mark the celebration of Id el Fitr. But repression and torture of black suspects continued.

Taya also announced political reform. He was not prepared to call a national conference, which he dismissed as "ridiculous and undemocratic" but he did order the drawing up of a new constitution to set up an Islamic Arab Republic. This was duly approved by a large majority on 12 July. Theoretically the new constitution guaranteed freedom of association, thought and expression, a two chamber national assembly and a President elected on a six-year term. But even as the referendum was being discussed, two former ministers were put under house arrest for demanding more effective democratisation.

MAURITIUS

Population: 1.03m (1990, World Bank)
Head of State: Queen Elizabeth through the Governor General
Prime Minister: Aneerood Jugnauth
Independence: 12 March 1968
Government: Parliamentary government led by the Prime Minister who comes from the majority party.
Parties: The majority party at the August 1987 elections was the *Mouvement Socialiste Mauricien* with 26 seats, followed by the *Mouvement Militant Mauricien* (21), the Mauritius Labour Party (9), and the *Parti Mauricien Social–Democrate* (4).

BOOLEL, Sir Satcam

Mauritian lawyer and politician. Deputy Prime Minister, September 1987 – 17 August 1990.

A Hindu barrister and one of the father figures of party politics in Mauritius. A colleague of the late Sir Seewoosagur Ramgoolam in the late 1950s and stalwart of the Mauritius Labour Party. Even after the party lost its overall grip on Mauritian politics, he remained an important political force in practically every coalition government and one of the most senior ministers. He was sacked by Prime Minister Anerood Jugnauth when he refused to endorse moves to make Mauritius a republic in August 1990 and became leader of the opposition.

Born 11 September 1920 at New Grove. Educated locally and at London School of Economics and at Lincoln's Inn, London, where he took his LLB. He returned home towards the end of the World War to go into government service (1944-48). Then went into private practice as a barrister (1952-59). At that time the Mauritius Labour Party dominated local politics under the leadership of Seewoosagur Ramgoolam, but Boolel stood and was elected to the Legislative Council in 1953 as an independent. He did not join the Labour Party until 1955 when he became a member of its executive committee. He switched constituencies to Montagne Blanche and won the elections for that seat in 1959 and 1963.

When the ministerial system was introduced, he became one of the first ministers in 1959 as Minister of Agriculture, a post he held until 1967 when Ramgoolam switched him to Education and Cultural Affairs. He represented Mauritius in the constitutional conferences leading to independence on 12 March 1968. As the MLP gradually lost its total dominance of Mauritian politics it formed an alliance with the Muslim CAM in a new Independence Party. Boolel joined the new coalition. Shortly afterwards, in 1969, he became acting Prime Minister, before being switched to Minister of Environment in 1974. Later he had

Agriculture and Natural Resources added to his portfolio.

In 1983, when Sir Seewoosagur Ramgoolam was designated to become Governor-General, Boolel assumed the leadership of the Labour Party and on 27 August was made Minister of Economic Affairs and Development in the coalition government of Prime Minister Aneerood Jugnauth. When the MLP decided to withdraw from the government Boolel was dismissed from the cabinet. But Jugnauth found it difficult to sustain his coalition in the face of various scandals and resignations.

On 24 July 1986 he brought Sir Satcam back into his government as Second Deputy Prime Minister and Minister of Foreign Affairs and Emigration and Attorney-General. Faced with further drug scandals, Jugnauth went to the polls again in August 1987. The government alliance triumphed and in September 1987 Sir Satcam was reinstated as Minister of Foreign Affairs and Justice and as First Deputy Prime Minister.

Sir Satcam refused to go along with government plans to replace the Queen of England as Head of State by a President. Jugnauth made this a question of collective responsibility and as Satcam refused to support the republican bill, he was dismissed on 17 August 1990. He took the Labour Party out of the government coalition and thus became leader of the opposition.

DUVAL, Charles Gaetan (Sir)
Mauritius lawyer and politician.

A brilliant and mercurial lawyer who has played a continuous if interrupted part in Mauritian politics since the late 1950s. "King Creole", the hero of of the Creole minority, his contribution to government has been restricted to co-operation as a minority partner in various coalitions. Passionate and hot-headed, he has great charisma and has often held the balance of power between government and opposition. Accused by his opponents of carrying his beliefs to the point of violence, he has nevertheless had a profound influence on his country's evolution.

Born 9 October 1930 at Rose Hill. Educated at Royal College, Curepipe, going on to study law at Lincoln's Inn, London, and the University of Paris law faculty.

He returned home and went into politics in 1958 and became a member of Curepipe town council and later its chairman, 1960-61 and again 1963-68. In the coalition government of 1964, Sir Seewoosagur Ramgoolam made him Minister of Housing, Lands and Town and Country Planning. He attended the London Constitutional Conference in London in 1965 where, leading his Mauritius Social Democratic Party (PMSD), he opposed independence for fear of discrimination against the Creole minority by the Hindus.

He was dropped from the cabinet in November 1965 but came back in the elections of August 1967, as leader of the Parti Mauricien, campaigning under the slogan "Independence means starvation," to become the first member for Grand River North-west and Port Louis West. The PM took its opposition to independence to extremes and there were violent clashes between Christians and Hindus in January 1968, when British troops had to be brought in to keep order.

Independence came on 12 March 1968 with Duval becoming leader of the opposition in parliament. In November 1969 Ramgoolam decided to strengthen his government against a new radical challenge, by forming a coalition with the PMSD (which had reverted to its original name) and Duval was made Minister of External Affairs, Tourism and Emigration. In the same year he was elected mayor and later Lord Mayor, of the capital of Port Louis, an office he held until 1974.

In December 1973 the coalition between the Labour Party and the PMSD broke up when Duval left the government following disagreements. Duval supported French plans to build a naval base on the island. He was also in dispute over tax issues. But in the December 1976 elections, Duval lost his own seat while Ramgoolam found himself again in a minority to the radical Militant Mauritian Movement (MMM) and was forced to reform a coalition with the PMSD. Duval, smarting from the electoral defeat, turned down the offer of a nominated ministry.

At the next election the MMM finally triumphed and formed a government. It was not until the August 1983 elections that the new Prime Minister, Aneerood Jugnauth, wanting to form another coalition, brought in Duval as his deputy and Foreign Minister. Later he became Minister of Justice and on 1 January 1986, Minister of Tourism and Employment, while retaining his Deputy Premiership.

Mauritian politics became clouded after a number of MPs were found to be involved in drug trafficking. A reformed drug trafficker gave evidence to a commission of inquiry-naming various MPs. Sir Gaetan offered to resign so that he could defend himself at the commission of inquiry and interrogate the witness, but Prime Minister Jugnauth refused to accept his resignation, saying he still had his "complete confidence".

On 12 August 1988 Sir Gaetan left the government after disagreement over the sharing of coalition seats in forthcoming elections and over wages and employment policies. On 23 June 1989 he was arrested and imprisoned after being accused by police of "giving instructions to commit murder" against his political opponent Paul Berenger in 1971. Eighteen years previously Berenger's car had been bombed and shot at and another man had died. Those involved were PMSD supporters and when they were released they told the police that Duval had provided them with guns and ordered the killing. Duval was briefly imprisoned but violence in Curepipe forced his release. Duval then threatened "revolution in the streets if the judiciary is manipulated." He was brought to trial early in 1990, then released but prohibited from leaving the country pending a judicial inquiry into the allegations.

JUGNAUTH, Anerood (Sir)
Mauritian politician. Prime Minister 1982-

A Hindu lawyer who worked his way into opposition politics in the days that the Mauritian Labour Party dominated government. He worked as a civil servant and lawyer until he was brought into government as a minister by the British Governor. After independence he joined the Militant Mauritian Movement which swept the polls in the 1982 elections. He emerged as Prime Minister. Since then he has found that he is not the radical he once was, and has been trying to practise realism and create a government in the stormy seas of Mauritian politics, dominated by caste, class and personality conflicts.

Born 29 March 1930 in a Hindu, family of planters of the Vaishya merchant caste at La Caverne, Vacoas. Educated at Palma Church of England School. Secondary education at Regent College, Quatre Bornes. He became a teacher at New Eton College. He joined the civil service in 1949, and went to London to pursue law studies at Lincoln's Inn. He was called to the bar in 1954 and returned home to practise in Port Louis. His love of unorthodox politics caused him to join the Independence Forward Bloc movement. In 1963 he defeated a sitting minister in the elections and became a member of parliament for the Piton Riviere du Rempart district.

He took a prominent part in the pre-independence negotiations in London in 1965. He was then appointed by the Governor, on the advice of the Prime Minister and leader of the Mauritius Labour Party, Sir Seewoosagur Ramgoolam, as Minister of State for Development in 1965. On 8 August 1967 Sir Seewoosagur reshuffled him to Minister of Labour in the pre-independence alliance.

The Militant Mauritian Movement (MMM) was formed by Paul Berenger in 1970. Jugnauth, then a senior crown counsel and president of the Mauritius Family Planning Association, resigned from the civil service on 1 October 1971 and joined the new movement, soon to become its president.

He went into opposition, serving as the official leader of the opposition in parliament (1976-82). In the elections of 11 June 1982 he led an alliance of the MMM and the Parti Socialiste Mauricien (PSM), a splinter group from the ruling labour party. The alliance won a landslide victory, taking all 60 directly elected seats, ousting Ramgoolam who had held power since before independence in 1968.

But within four months the governing alliance began to break up, leading to the resignation of Jugnauth's deputy, Harish Boodhoo and the founder of the MMM, Paul Berenger. Jugnauth described the defections as tantamount to treason and formed a new cabinet on 28 March 1983, followed by a new political party, the Mauritian Socialist Movement which, he said, would take on the ideology of the old MMM. But as he controlled only 29 seats of the 66 in the legislative assembly, he called general elections for August which he fought in alliance with the Labour

Party and the Mauritian Social Democratic Party (PMSD) under the leadership of Sir Gaetan Duval. The alliance won 41 of the 66 seats. Jugnauth won his own seat at Riviere du Rempart while his opponent Paul Berenger lost at Quatre Bornes.

Personality conflicts continued as Jugnauth dismissed Sir Satcam Boolel, who had just become the leader of the Labour party (on Seewoosagur's appointment as Governor-General), from his cabinet. Jugnauth spent much of 1984 trying to curb "unbecoming press reports" on the rowdy parliamentary affairs and in March 1985 he tightened up on press freedom, prohibiting comment that was damaging or injurious to the government.

In 1985 a drug scandal broke, with four MPs discovered trying to carry heroin through Amsterdam airport. Jugnauth refused to resign as none of his ministers were involved. But a number of ministers did just that, resigning on a "matter of principle", while Harish Boodhoo who had become Jugnauth's main collaborator, was himself implicated.

Jugnauth again put his popularity to the test by calling elections on 30 August 1987 which he fought in alliance with his former allies. His majority was reduced but he was able to form a government. He regained his old seat at Piton Riviere. He made Sir Gaetan Duval his deputy, only for him to resign on 12 August 1988 following disagreements over the sharing of coalition seats and over wages and employment policies. Jugnauth was forced to form a new cabinet, this time heavily dependent on the Labour Party. But to avoid the embarrassment of defeat the alliance did not even attempt to contest the October 1988 municipal elections. On 11 June he was knighted by the Queen of England.

On 6 November 1988 a man dressed as a Hindu priest suddenly drew a gun and fired two shots at him. He escaped unhurt, though a bodyguard was injured in the hand. On 3 March 1989 he escaped a second assassination attempt when a young man ran up to him brandishing a knife at a religious ceremony in Grand Bassin. Sir Aneerood attributed the attempts on his life to his campaign against drugs: "I have felt that my life has been in danger ever since I launched a national crusade against the drugs mafia. I have received death threats both from abroad and from Mauritius." The attack came amid clamour from opposition politicians over the arrest of the former Mauritian high commissioner in London on charges linked to drug trafficking.

Jugnauth was determined to change Mauritius status from a monarchy with the Queen of England as Head of State, to a republic. But moves in this direction were opposed by his coalition partners in the Labour party, including his deputy Sir Satcam Boolel who was dismissed over this issue in August 1990. The Labour Party then joined the opposition.

For a time Jugnauth ran a minority government until he formed a pact with the Militant Mauritian Movement, giving them six ministers in September. Even with his new allies, he did not have sufficient votes to secure the required constitutional change on the republican issue.

MOZAMBIQUE

Population: 16.04m (1990, World Bank)
Head of State: Joaquim Chissano
Independence: 25 June 1975
Government: From 1975 Presidential rule through a single-party Marxist Leninist state, but from July 1989 the communist ideology was officially abandoned. A new constitution was then drafted providing for a range of democratic rights and the election of the President by direct universal suffrage. On 6 February 1991 a new law legitimised the formation of other political parties.
Parties: The former single party was the *Frente de Libertação de Moçambique* (FRELIMO). Democratic opposition parties started to organise in 1991 while a final peace agreement was sought with the *Resistencia Nacional Moçambicana* (RENAMO) also known as the MNR.

CHISSANO, Joaquim Alberto
Mozambican politician. President 4 November 1986-

Though a Marxist by upbringing, he is also an urbane and articulate pragmatist who drew his strength from being a founder member of FRELIMO from 1962 and his country's Foreign Minister from independence to the time he succeeded Samora Machel as President in November 1986. Less spontaneous and charismatic than Machel, he pursues similar policies with systematic thoroughness. His 13 years as foreign minister and fluency in Portuguese, English, French and Swahili, gave him wide-ranging international contacts that stood him in good stead when he became President on Machel's death in November 1986. He has honoured and strengthened the Nkomati accord with South Africa, though he originally opposed it. He also allowed the FRELIMO party to move away from the official ideology of Marxism to a more moderate form of socialism. He has pursued economic liberalisation and the opening to the West though he also has many friends in the Eastern bloc.

Born 22 October 1939 at Chibuto in the Province of Gaza. After an impoverished childhood and lonely school years at a local primary school and Xai-Xai Secondary High School, he emerged as one of the first black children to graduate from the Liceu Salazar in Lorenço Marques (Maputo). In 1960 he went for further studies to Portugal.

After failing anatomy in his first year, he left for France and returned to Mozambique as one of the original founders of FRELIMO in 1962. He became a member of the central and executive committees of the party in 1963 and secretary to the party's first leader, Dr Eduardo Mondlane. He shared responsibility for security and defence with Samora Machel at FRELIMO's training camp in Kongwa, Tanzania and helped coordinate the armed struggle against the Portuguese. He became the chief representative of the exile-wing of FRELIMO in Tanzania. He was away when a parcel bomb killed Mondlane in 1969. In the ensuing struggle for leadership he played a conciliatory role bringing together Samora Machel, Marcelino dos Santos and Uria Simango in a temporary alliance.

While Machel remained in exile, he was appointed Prime Minister in the transitional government, set up in September 1974 that led Mozambique to independence on 25 June 1975. During that period he played a major part in the discussions with the Portuguese government over the arrangements for independence. After independence no provision was made for a Prime Minister in the new People's Republic, but Machel appointed him Foreign Minister, a position he retained for more than 13 years.

At the Third Congress of the party in February 1977 he was re-elected to the Central Committee and appointed to the Standing Committee which later became the Politbureau. He stood in the first general elections of 1977 and was elected to the People's Assembly and the Standing Commission of the Assembly. He was promoted Major-General when ranks were introduced into the armed forces in 1980.

Surprisingly he played no part in the drawing up, or the signing of the Nkomati accord with South Africa, on 16 March 1984 and was probably in disagreement with Samora Machel on the treaty in which Mozambique and South Africa agreed not to support or harbour liberation movements inside their own countries. However he accepted the party discipline once the agreement had been signed.

Samora Machel was killed in a mysterious plane crash just over the South African border near Komatipoort, on 19 October 1986. The FRELIMO Central Committee met on 3 November 1986 and elected the 47-year old Joaquim Chissano as head of the party and President.

As President he has pursued Machel's policies of the opening to the West and the cultivation of a multiplicity of international friends. He has also forced Malawi to abandon its position of supporting the rebels of the Mozambique National Resistance, MNR and encouraged the use of Tanzanian and Zimbabwean troops, on the government side, in the guerrilla war. He offered an amnesty to the MNR guerrillas and achieved limited success with some defections.

Economically he has continued with the liberalisation of the economy and domestic reform involving co-operation with the International Monetary Fund. The lifting of price controls and the introduction of wage flexibility were given his blessing. But the economy still suffered the consequences of the war and recurring drought and floods. Politically, faced with the need to achieve peace and national unity, he endorsed the move at the FRELIMO Congress in Maputo, on 31 July 1989, away from a strictly marxist programme to one of more moderate socialism.

A new constitution was then drafted which came into force on 30 November 1990 establishing a multi-party political system and the right to private ownership. It also enshrined an independent judiciary. Opposition groups soon emerged and began to organise themselves.

Chissano's problem then became that of establishing a lasting peace agreement with the MNR. Peace talks started in mid-1990 and continued throughout 1991, with backtracking, prevarication, delays and changes in conditions on the part of the MNR, though the government was bending over backwards to achieve a durable agreement.

At the beginning of June 1991 a coup plot was revealed involving the former chief of staff Colonel-General Sebastaio Mabote and other military officers. Chissano dismissed it as a plot by South Africans of the extreme right, but most independent commentators thought it was due to the demoralisation of the Mozambican army, trapped in an endless war.

DOS SANTOS, Marcelino (Dr)

Mozambican politician. Former Vice President, June 1970-June 1977.

The elder statesman and grandfather of the revolution, he was long known as the theorist and driving force of the liberation movement. A poet with a neat moustache and carefully trimmed beard, he echoed nationalist aspirations in verse and had them published in French. Though Vice President and technically the most senior member of the party and politburo he was considered to be neither young nor vigorous enough to be chosen for the Presidency on the death of Samora Machel in October 1986.

Born 1931 in Maputo, of mixed race. He was educated in Lisbon, then did post-graduate studies in Paris. Appointed secretary general of the Conference of Nationalist Organisations of the Portuguese Colonies (CONCP) in April 1961, with headquarters at Rabat, Morocco. In July 1961 he became a mediator when Adelino Gwanbe was ordered out of Tanganyika for threatening an invasion of Mozambique.

In June 1962 he was one of the key figures who brought about the merger of three nationalist parties into Frente de Libertacao de Mocambique, FRELIMO. He helped organise the party and launch the armed struggle in September 1964. He became Secretary for External Affairs and represented FRELIMO at the OAU ministerial meeting in Nairobi in December 1965. He became FRELIMO's major fund raiser and travelled the world to build up support for the liberation movement. In February 1969 he was appointed the Vice President of FRELIMO.

On 1 July 1970, he gained recognition from the Pope when he was received at the Vatican along with Amilcar Cabral of Guinea Bissau, and Agostinho Neto of Angola.

On 25 June 1975 he invested Samora Machel as the first president of independent Mozambique and four days later was appointed Vice President and Minister for Development and Economic Planning in the first independence government. In this post he was hampered by the sudden exodus of the Portuguese which left the economy in chaos. This was followed by the war with the MNR guerrillas. In December 1977 the post of Vice President was abolished but he continued as Minister of Planning and Development and Secretary to a new Permanent Commission.

When Joaquim Chissano took power following the death of Samora Machel in a plane crash on 19 October 1986, he was the oldest of the candidates considered for the presidency. He lost out to the former Foreign Minister Joaquim Chissano by unanimous vote of the Central Committee. Chissano did not give him a cabinet appointment, and he was made Secretary of the Permanent Comission of the Popular Assembly. He remained the senior figure in the politburo.

GUEBUZA, Armando Emilio

Mozambican politician. Minister of Transport and Communications, 11 January 1987 –

A senior member of the Frente de Libertacao de Mocambique, FRELIMO. As Minister of the Interior, he was in the running to succeed Samora Machel after his death in an airplane accident in October 1986. His emotional commitment to the cause that leads him to occasional errors of judgment worked against him, but he remained the powerful Minister of the Interior and a senior member of the party. He played a major part in the peace talks with the MNR, 1990-91.

Born 20 October 1943. Educated at primary and secondary levels in Lorenco Marques (Maputo). He was a student activist in NESAM and made early contact with the original members of FRELIMO who founded the party in 1962. He was arrested by the Portuguese secret police, PIDE and imprisoned for six months. On release in 1963 he fled to Tanzania and began to work for FRELIMO on a full time basis.

He did military training, then taught in FRELIMO schools, later being appointed inspector of schools in Tanzania and the liberated areas. At the Second FRELIMO Congress in 1968 he was elected to the Central Committee and later to the Executive and Political-Military Committees. In 1971 he became the National Political Commissar for the party.

After the Lusaka agreement in September, a transitional government was formed by the Portuguese High Commissioner Rear Admiral Vitor Crespo, who made him Minister of Internal Administration on 20 September 1974. During this period he was responsible for organising the "dynamising groups", the popular vigilantes that were largely responsible for the mass exodus of the Portuguese. Over this he clashed with Joaquim Chissano.

After independence on 25 June 1975, Samora Machel appointed him Minister of the Interior. He held this post competently, but made a mistake by introducing an "operation production" campaign in which thousands of people were sent to labour camps on charges of corruption or prostitution. This was the main reason that Machel demoted him on

29 June 1977 to Deputy Minister of Defence and Political Commissar for the Armed and Security Forces.

At the third party congress in February 1977 he was confirmed as a member of the Central Committee and was appointed to the Politbureau of FRELIMO. He was elected to the people's assembly at the first general elections of 1977.

In 1979 he was appointed Minister Resident in Cabo Delgado province, the extreme north east corner of the country. When military ranks were introduced into the Mozambican army in 1980 he was appointed one of three Lieutenant Generals. In December 1981 he was transferred to Sofala province as Minister Resident. In June 1983 he resumed his post as Minister of the Interior.

After President Chissano came to power in November 1987, he needed a strong man to protect the railway system against guerrilla attack. He appointed Guebuza Minister of Transport and Communications on 11 January 1987.

MACHUNGO, Mario Fernandes da Graca

Mozambican politician. Prime Minister 17 July 1986-

A politically astute and pragmatic personality, he comes from a leading assimilado family from the Nampula area in the north. Unlike the other FRELIMO leaders he is the only trained economist in the party and he did not take an active part in the struggle in the bush and was elected relatively late to the Political Bureau. This militated against him in the leadership stakes on the death of Samora Machel, as did a number of mistakes he had earlier made as Minister of Planning, but as a top technocrat he has emerged as First Prime Minister with a heavy responsibility for economic affairs.

Born 1 December 1940 at Chicuque-Maxixe in the province of Inhambane. Educated at Muhana Mission primary school in Lorenco Marques (Maputo) and a technical school where he did a commercial course. In 1960 he left for Portugal to continue his studies and enrolled at the Institute for Higher Learning in Economic and Financial Sciences (ISCEF). He had to do odd jobs to finance his course.

While on holiday in Lourenco Marques in 1962 he made contact with the nationalist groups that were already in existence. He joined the *Frente de Libertação de Moçambique,* FRELIMO and became an "underground militant."

He returned to Portugal and became President of the student's union at ISCEF, but he was expelled for his anti-colonial activities and prohibited from continuing his studies. He was only able to complete his degree in economics in 1969.

FRELIMO ordered him back to Mozambique after completing his studies. He worked as an economist for the National Development Bank while carrying out clandestine missions for the party. In 1974, already considered to be a FRELIMO veteran, he was appointed the Minister of

Economic Cooperation in the Transitional Government set up to lead his country to independence on 25 June 1975. In 1976 Samora Machel made him Minister for Industry and Energy. In October 1978 he was reshuffled to Agriculture and in April 1980 was given the additional portfolio of Planning.

At the Third Congress of FRELIMO in February 1977, he was elected to the Central Committee and the Politbureau of the party. He was re-elected to these posts in the Fourth Congress of 1983. As minister of Planning he produced an economic plan Perspectivo Indicativo, PPI with the co-operation of the East Germans, which turned out to be so impracticable that it had to be shelved. In May 1983 he was placed in charge of Zambezia province in addition to holding his planning portfolio. In April 1986 he returned to Maputo to continue as Minister of Planning.

In July 1986 the Central Committee elected him to become the party secretary for economic policy. On 17 July 1986 President Machel, who wanted to free his hands to concentrate on defending his country against South African insurgency, appointed him the first Prime Minister. He maintained this largely administrative post under President Joaquim Chissano when he took power in November 1986.

VELOSO, Jacinto Soares

Mozambican politician. Minister for International Cooperation, 24 April 1986 –

A white Mozambican who had an unusual route into FRELIMO through the Portuguese airforce. He actually joined the guerrillas by flying his plane from Maputo to Dar es Salaam and deserting the airforce. He was given two tough assignments after independence first as head, later Minister of Security battling against the Mozambique National Resistance and reprisals by the South Africans. Then Samora Machel made him Minister of Economic Affairs to tackle the ailing Mozambican economy.

Born 11 August 1937 in Maputo and educated locally. Continued university studies in Portugal where he entered the military academy and became an officer in the Portuguese airforce.

He returned to Mozambique but deserted the airforce by flying his plane to Dar es Salaam where he joined the Frente de Libertacao de Mocambique, FRELIMO in 1963. He was initially sent to FRELIMO's mission to Algiers, but he was recalled to Dar es Salaam and taught at the FRELIMO Secondary School until 1968. He was then appointed to reorganise the Algiers office.

He played a part in the discussions leading to the Lusaka agreement in September 1974 at which the transition to independence was agreed. He was appointed one of the three members of the Joint Military Commission formed under the agreement. After independence on 25 July 1975, President Machel appointed him Director of the National Security Service, SNASP in October. At the Third Party Congress of FRELIMO in February 1977 he was elected to the Central Committee and Politbureau. He was elected to the People's Assembly in the first general elections of 1977. On 3 April 1980 he was appointed minister to head a new ministry of security. Here his main task was to tackle the guerrillas of the Mozambique National Resistance, MNR and to prevent South African raids and reprisals. He held a conference with his Zimbabwean counterparts in May 1980 concerning the MNR menace.

When military ranks were introduced into the Mozambican army in October 1980 he was given the rank of Major General. After the Fourth party Congress in May 1983 there was a major reorganisation of government. Samora Machel appointed him Minister of Economic Affairs in the Presidency, where he shared responsibility with Mario Machungo for gradually liberalising the stagnant economy and for encouraging foreign investment and growth. On 24 April 1986 President Joaquim Chissano transferred him to a new Ministry of International Cooperation, where he became responsible for further negotiations with South Africa.

NAMIBIA

Population: 1.63m (1990, World Bank)
Independence: 21 March 1990
Head of State: Sam Nujoma
Government: Parliamentary democracy based on the US model, with two chambers, a bill of rights, independence of the judiciary and an executive president putting legislation through a freely elected National Assembly.
Parties: The South West African People's Organisation (SWAPO) is the majority party and forms the government. Main opposition party - Democratic Turnhalle Alliance.

GAROEB, Moses Makue
Namibian politician. SWAPO Administrative Secretary 1969-

Born 14 April 1941. Educated at St Augustineum Training College, Okahandja like many of his political colleagues, before going on to Pennsylvania State University, USA to get a BSc in 1965.

He joined the South West African National Union (SWANU) in 1959, while still only 18 (before the South West African People's Organisation (SWAPO) had been created) and was a petitioner to the United Nations on behalf of the Damara people. SWAPO was founded by Sam Nujoma and Toivo ya Toivo in January 1960, but Garoeb did not join until he had completed his studies. In 1969, while still only 28, he was elected administrative secretary at the 1969 Consultative Congress in Tanga, Tanzania, an important meeting when the party mapped out its future strategy. He was also elected to the Politburo and the Central Committee.

He was one of the top leadership to return home early and help organise SWAPO's election campaign in November 1989. SWAPO emerged as the majority party with Garoeb winning a seat ranked number five on the party list.

GEINGOB, Hage Gottfried
Namibian politician. Prime Minister, 21 March 1990-

Started young with the South West African People's Organisation, SWAPO and became a youthful representative of the party at the UN and in the USA for seven years while still pursuing his studies. He made a particular contribution by popularising and establishing the name Namibia, instead of South West Africa, in the course of writing for international journals. Became the Director of the UN Institute for Namibia in Lusaka which was designed to train Namibians to run their country after independence. Nicknamed "Mr Teacher" by his students, he proved himself an able administrator, chosen to organise the SWAPO election campaign prior to independence. He chaired the successful constitutional drafting committee, before being promoted as the first prime minister of independent Namibia.

Born 3 August 1941 at Otjiwarongo. Educated to standard eight, he was expelled from school for demonstrating against the poor quality of meat served in the school canteen and against the Bantu education system. But he took teacher's training at Augustineum Training College, Okahandja and became a primary school teacher at Tsumeb. He joined SWAPO in 1962 and became assistant SWAPO representative in Botswana, 1963-64. After a brief spell in the Congo (Zaire) he went to the USA in 1964. He studied at Temple University High School to qualify for university entrance and went on to Manhattan College in 1965, then to Fordham University, New York, 1965-70. Took his masters degree at the School for Social Research, New York 1970-72. While still doing his studies he had been appointed SWAPO Organising Secretary and Central Committee member at the Tanga (Tanzania) consultative congress in 1969.

Though his New York university wanted him to continue and do a PhD, SWAPO asked him to take up the key post of political affairs officer in the office of the UN commissioner for Namibia, thus becoming SWAPO representative to the UN and the USA.

He was promoted a Politburo Member and the first Director of the UN Institute for Namibia in Lusaka, Zambia, July 1975. In June 1987 he was one of the leaders of a SWAPO delegation in Lusaka which received a group of white Namibian lawyers eager to discuss the future of Namibia after independence. He returned from exile to Namibia, under the UN agreement on 18 June 1989, as Director of elections to help organise the pre-independence election campaign.

He was unanimously elected by the constituent assembly members to chair the constitutional drafting committee, which drew up a model, democratic constitution for his country. His efforts were rewarded when he was made Prime Minister designate in the pre-independence shadow cabinet on 21 December 1989 and in March 1990 the first prime minister of independent Namibia.

GURIRAB, Theo Ben
Namibian politician. Foreign Minister, 21 March 1990 –

A skilled and experienced negotiator who became the South West African People's Organisation's top diplomat and spokesman as the Secretary of Foreign Affairs in 1986. He is also a member of the politburo and central committee. He returned home in June 1989 under the UN agreement to help organise the pre-independence elections. He was rewarded with one of the most senior posts in the independence cabinet as Foreign Minister.

Born at Usakos. Educated at the Rhenish Mission Primary School, Usakos. Teacher training at Augustineum Training College, Okahandja.

Went to USA to study international relations .

Became SWAPO represenative for North America until being appointed UN Mission Chief in 1972. Addressed the UN Security Council in November 1976, attacking the big powers for refusing to endorse a total arms embargo on South Africa. He described their refusal as "an inimical act which shows how far the imperialist powers are prepared to go to defend their interests in Namibia." He became SWAPO's principal spokesman and in 1978, helped facilitate the initative by the Western Powers to get South Africa to negotiate. He also played a major part during the negotiations leading to the acceptance of UN resolution 435 of August 1978, which laid down the process for returning Namibia to independence.

He was the chief SWAPO spokesman at the UN sponsored conference on Namibia, in Geneva in January 1981 and continued his campaign for sanctions against South Africa. Appointed Secretary of Foreign Affairs for SWAPO in 1986. He was one of the first SWAPO leaders to return home under the UN resolution 435, on 18 June 1989 to help organise the pre-independence elections, in which SWAPO won a comfortable majority. He was appointed Foreign Secretary designate in the pre-independence, shadow cabinet of 21 December 1989 and went on to become Foreign Secretary in March 1990.

One of Gurirab's main challenges after independence, was the relationship with South Africa, particularly over Namibia's demand for the transfer of Walvis Bay to Namibian sovereignty. Many talks with South Africa over the issue during 1990/91, failed to achieve satisfactory results.

HAMUTENYA, Hidipo

Namibian politician. Minister for Information and Broadcasting, 21 March 1990 –

An ambitious and dynamic member of the dominant Kwanyama faction of the Ovambos and a member of the Poliburo and Central Committee of the South West African People's Organisation. He became its Secretary for Information and Publicity in 1981 and has played a key role as party spokesman since. He was one of the first SWAPO leaders to return home under UN resolution 435 to help prepare the pre-independence elections.

Born 1939 in Ovamboland. Educated at St Mary's Mission School, Ovamboland. Teacher training at Augustineum Training College, Okahandja. Went overseas for studies in Romania, then to Lincoln University, Pennsylvania, USA where he got a BA. He took his masters at McGill University, Montreal, Canada.

Joined SWAPO and with the help and encouragement of the party spokesman Hage Geingob, became Secretary for Information and Publicity, 1981. In January 1982 he acknowledged the contribution of the Western Contact group in its efforts to negotiate a settlement for Namibia. In July 1982 he attacked the principle of linkage in which the

Cubans were asked to withdraw from Angola in return for withdrawal of South African troops, before independence for Namibia.

On 18 June 1989 he was one of the first batch of SWAPO leaders to return home under UN resolution 435 to help prepare the pre-independence elections. He then consolidated a dominant position in the party though he clashed with some of his colleagues over the lack of funds for the electoral campaign and the handling of the complaints by returning members of SWAPO who claimed that they had been detained and badly treated by the party when residing overseas. After the November 1989 elections in which SWAPO triumphed he was returned as number 11 on the party list. He was appointed shadow minister for Information and Broadcasting in the pre-independence cabinet of 21 December 1989, and later confirmed as minister, on 21 March 1990.

KALANGULA, Peter Tanyangenge (Rev)
Namibian politician, leader of the Christian Democratic Action for Social Justice (CDA).

A tough and determined minister turned politician. He became a leading light as President of the Democratic Turnhalle Alliance and its only prominent SWAPO supporter. His withdrawal from the Alliance in 1982 reasserted his independence and allowed him to concentrate on the welfare of his Ovambo people through the local administration. He pursued policies of Africanisation and has been highly critical of the conduct of the South African police. This has won him local respect, but everything now depends on how his relationships develop with SWAPO.

Born 3 December 1926 at Omafo in the Kwanyama sub-group of the Ovambo tribe. Educated at St Mary's Anglican Mission School. Matriculated 1943. Qualified as a teacher by correspondence courses. Started theological studies at the Federal Seminary of Southern Africa, Alice, SA and St Bede's Seminary, Umtata. He returned home to teach in Ovambo for two years before becoming a civil servant. He was ordained at the Anglican Mission in Ovambo in 1971, in the same year a dispute in the church led to his founding of the Ovamboland Independent (Anglican) Church.

He was nominated to the Ovambo Legislative Council in 1973 as part of the Ovamboland Independence Party (later the National Democratic Party, NDP) which joined the Democratic Turnhalle Alliance, DTA in 1977. He was appointed Minister of Roads and Works in the cabinet of the Ovambo Legislative Assembly in 1977, with education added to his portfolio in 1978. He was part of the Ovambo delegation to the Turnhalle constitutional conference 1975-77 and worked on the constitutional committee.

In 1977 he took the NDP into the DTA. He fought the 1978 elections under this banner and became a DTA member in the first national assembly, 1979-83. In 1980 he was elected Chairman of the Ovambo Executive Committee and President of the DTA. In 1981 he was also appointed NDP President. He wanted the DTA to merge and form a single party, but failing to persuade his colleagues, he relinquished his National Assembly seat in 1981 and pulled his party out of the DTA itself in February 1982.

In May 1982 he founded the Christian Democratic Action for Social Justice, (CDA) and most of his associates in the NDP followed him into the new party. He managed to retain his party's seats in the National Assembly and in the Ovambo assembly. In Ovambo he proved himself an efficient administrator, introducing English as a medium of instruction in all schools and Africanising the civil service wherever possible. He also tried to protect his people against harassment by the South African security forces.

Like other small parties, his CDA found it difficult to generate enough funds to register for the November 1989 elections.

KATJIUONGUA, Moses Katjikuru
Namibian politician. President SWANU-TG.

A highly educated journalist, active early with Namibia's oldest nationalist movement, the South West African National Union, SWANU, but he was never able to establish the popular following nor the international recognition accorded to his rivals in SWAPO. His party suffered a further setback when he chose to attend the Multi Party Conference in 1983. His party split and his rivals attacked him for being a sell out and taking a ministry in the transitional government.

Born 24 April 1942 to Theophelus Katjiuongua counsellor of Chief Hosea Kutako and friend of Tshekedi Khama. Primary school in Aminuis and college in Bechuanaland. He went to the Swedish Confederation of Labour College 1956-59, to Magdeburg, East Germany to study journalism 1961-62 and then Stockholm University 1978-80 to get a BA in political science and administration. He stayed on to get his MA in International affairs, economics, human geography and theoretical philosophy. He then travelled to Carleton University, Ottawa for further studies.

His political activities continued concurrently with his studies, after he left Namibia in 1959. It was the South West African National Union, SWANU which gave him a scholarship to study in Magdeburg, East Germany from where he went to work in the SWANU office in Cairo.

He attended the All African People's Congress in Moshi, Tanganyika in 1963. Made a trip to China where he met Mao Tse-Tung, then worked in the SWANU office in Dar es Salaam. In 1966 he attended the Tri-Continental Conference in Havana, Cuba before resuming his studies at Stockholm University. He continued to serve on SWANU's External Coucil and edited the *Windhoek Review.*

In 1982 he returned home and was elected SWANU president. He led the SWANU delegation to the Multi Party Conference in September 1983, but his party split on the question of participation in the internal settlement. A congress called by opponents relieved him and his supporters of their posts on the Central Committee in 1984. He called another Congress and reconstituted SWANU, and was elected President of SWANU-Transitional Government, but the dispute continued between the two groups, weakening the party's influence.

He attended the Lusaka talks in September 1984 as party leader while the 'other' SWANU condemned him from Botswana and talked about a possible merger with SWAPO (which never materialised). On 10 May 1985 he was appointed Minister of Manpower, National Health and Welfare in the cabinet of the Transitional Government of National Unity. He fought the November 1989 pre-independence elections under the National Patriotic Front banner and was the only member of the party to win a seat.

MUDGE, Dirk Francis

Namibian politician. Leader Republican party.

A reforming liberal by South African standards, Dirk Mudge dominated Namibian politics in the 1975-83 period in the first attempt to achieve an internal settlement. He was the first white politician to advocate a black majority government under universal suffrage. He also supported Namibianisation and equal pay for equal work but he was obliged to work through a system set up by the Pretoria government and he could never shake the loyalty of the majority of the black people towards their own leaders in SWAPO. Thus in all the coalitions of the late seventies and early eighties he was caught between Pretoria and African Nationalism and fighting to hold the uncertain centre ground. He remains leader of the Republican Party and Chairman of the Democratic Turnhalle Alliance, which won sufficient seats in the November 1989 elections to have a fundamental influence on the drafting of the Namibian constitution.

Born 16 January 1928 at Otjiwarongo. Educated locally. Graduated from Stellenbosch University with a B.Comm in 1947. A farmer, he became a member of the National Party and won a seat for Otjiwarongo in the South West African legislative assembly in 1961.

In 1969 he won the leadership of the NP in the assembly and was Deputy NP Chairman under A.H.du Plessis. As du Plessis was occupied most of the time as a cabinet minister in South Africa, Mudge found himself in charge of the SWA administration from 1965. He was appointed to the advisory council of the South African Prime Minister in 1973. He convened the Turnhalle Constitutional Conference in 1975 and served as its Chairman. In 1977 he challenged du Plessis for the party leadership, but failed and formed a breakaway Republican Party in October.

The groups which had participated in the Turnhalle Conference, composed of a large number of narrowly based ethnic parties, then reformed themselves as the Democratic Turnhalle Alliance and elected Mudge as their Chairman in November 1977. As Chairman of the DTA and RP leader he dominated the Constituent Assembly in 1979 and the first National Assembly 1979-83. In June 1980 the National Assembly elected a ministerial council with limited executive powers under his chairmanship. But increasing frustration and tensions between the DTA and the Pretoria government led to his resignation on 12 January 1983, saying he "no longer wished to be part of this futile exercise." The Council of Ministers resigned with him. In retaliation the Administrator General (appointed by Pretoria) dissolved the National Assembly and the Ministerial Council and assumed direct rule.

Mudge remained Chairman of the DTA and was elected as Chairman of the newly formed Multi-Party Conference in November 1983. But the MPC suffered from much of the obloquy and secessionist tendencies as the DTA. Mudge attended most talks arranged with SWAPO in Geneva in 1979 and 1981 and Lusaka in May 1984, but South Africa was never able to tempt them into any form of internal power sharing. Its answer was to set up a Transitional Government of National Unity. Mudge joined the cabinet as Minister of Finance and Governmental Affairs on 10 May 1985 until the government was disbanded early in 1989 in the run up to the Namibian elections in November 1989.

The DTA gained a respectable 28.6% of the votes in the pre-independence elections and he won a parliamentary seat as number two on the DTA list. He was then able to influence the drafting of the Namibian constitution by insisting on proportional representation and a bi-cameral system which was accepted. But he was not offered a ministerial post in the provisional government.

NUJOMA, Sam Saffishuna

Namibian Politician. President of Namibia, 21 April 1990 —

A big, round roly-poly of a man, bearded and agreeable, he established his leadership because of his popularity rather than any intellectual dominance. He held SWAPO together through two decades of frustration and disappointment in exile and did an excellent public relations job bringing his people's plight to world attention and particularly the United Nations, which recognised SWAPO as the sole legitimate nationalist party in Namibia. At independence on 21 March 1990, he became President of his country.

Born 12 May 1929 eldest of a farm worker's family of ten at the northern village of Etunda, in Ongandjera district, 60 miles from the Angolan border. While helping his father to herd cattle, he had a little schooling at the Okahao Finnish Protestant Mission and then was sent to help his aunt at Walvis Bay in April 1943. He moved in September 1949, to stay with an uncle at Windhoek where he had his first lessons in English at St Barnabas Mission.

He joined the State railways as a sweeper, then a clerk and tea boy. His first political stirrings came when he saw an African worker denied compensation after an accident in the shunting yards.

He left the railways in March 1957 for a clerical job in the Windhoek municipality. Then he took up a job at a wholesale store, spending his spare time studying pamphlets on Africa's liberation struggle. In April 1959 he and Toivo ja Toivo founded SWAPO. From then on, he was a marked man. Police shadowed him to every meeting. Trouble arose when he organised bus boycotts and protests against forced removal, at Katatura in which riots occurred. He was arrested and held for a week in December 1959.

SWAPO decided that he should go abroad and present his people's case to the United Nations, rather than be harassed by the police at home. He left Windhoek on 29 February 1960 dodging border police, military patrols and immigration officials until he arrived in Tanzania. There Julius Nyerere gave him a letter which served instead of a passport to enter Sudan and eventually Ghana. He arrived in New York on 12 June 1960 to appear before the committee on South West Africa.

After six months in New York he set up SWAPO provisional headquarters in Dar es Salaam in March 1961. He decided to challenge the South African claim that anyone was free to move in and out of Namibia. In March 1966 he chartered a plane and arrived back in Windhoek. He was seized by the police and taken straight to prison. Then he was driven back to the airport and forcibly put on a plane back to Zambia.

When the International Court of Justice refused to rule on the legality of South Africa's administration of Namibia, SWAPO decided to take up the armed struggle. He was personally given a start by the Algerians who gave him a machine gun and two pistols. Other arms followed which his guerrillas smuggled across the African continent.

The guerrilla war started officially on 26 August 1966 when SWAPO launched attacks on targets in the north of Namibia. In the first 18 months there were severe setbacks with the arrest and imprisonment of 37 SWAPO members, including Toivo, in February 1968. He regrouped his men, sent more personnel into training and formally launched the People's Liberation Army of Namibia in December 1969.

In October 1971 he made a major impact when he gave evidence to the UN Security Council on the continued South African occupation of his country. SWAPO helped organise the strike of December 1971 against the contract labour situation.

From 1975 South Africa sought an internal settlement with local minority parties, but SWAPO under Nujoma stuck to the UN formula passed on 29 September 1978 which laid down steps for the "early independence of Namibia through free and fair elections under the control and supervision of the UN." In January 1981 Nujoma led the SWAPO delegation to the Geneva conference which collapsed within a week.

In May 1984, after the release of Toivo and another attempt at setting up a durable internal administration, further talks were held in Lusaka under the Chairmanship of Kenneth Kaunda to tempt SWAPO into an internal settlement. Nujoma did not attend personally but insisted that the only solution would be in accordance with the internationally accepted UN plan. The talks failed.

More serious talks were resumed after South Africa's military defeat at Cuito Cunavale in August 1988. This time South Africa was prepared to agree to implement the UN peace plan according to resolution 435. On 13 December an accord was signed in Brazzaville, confirmed later on 22 December in New York. This set the independence process rolling for Namibia.

In April 1989 Sam Nujoma made a fatal mistake by ordering his SWAPO guerrillas to return home bearing their weapons, in defiance of the peace accord. The result was that hundreds of SWAPO guerrillas were killed by the South Africans before being forced to withdraw, but by June the exiles were able to return.

At first Nujoma remained overseas while his chief lieutenants organised SWAPO's pre-independence election campaign. But he returned home on 14 September, in time to assume control and led his party to win 57.3% of the votes in the November 1989 elections. He was returned as number one on the SWAPO list and became President designate. He proved flexible in the drafting of a constitution and was unanimously elected President on 16 February. He brought his country to independence and was sworn in as President, on 21 March 1990.

He rapidly established very good race relations and respect for the rule of law in his country. Two white ministers and some leaders of other parties were included in Nujoma's independence cabinet. He showed himself ready to govern through a system which safeguarded democracy, through a number of constitutional checks and balances. In establishing stability he exposed himself to criticism from radicals who wanted more rapid social change.

SHIPANGA, Andreas Zak

Namibian politician. President of SWAPO-D, 1978 —

A restless soul whose early career reads like the cover of a best selling paper back. But he was an important early nationalist who ended up in SWAPO. The turning point in his career came when he quarrelled with the SWAPO leadership and was imprisoned in 1976, in Zambia and Tanzania for 22 months. This embittered him against the SWAPO leadership and set him on a new tack. He founded a breakaway party, the SWAPO Democrats, returned home and eventually became involved at attempts at an internal settlement. He also became a minister in the Transitional Government. He and his party were heavily defeated in the pre-independence elections of November 1989.

Born 26 October 1931 at Odangwa, in the Ndonga sub-group of the Ovambo tribe. Educated at Ondangwa Primary School, 1939-46, Ongwediva Boys School 1947-50. Teacher training at Oniipa Teacher's Training College.

Became a teacher in Ovambo 1954-55. He tried to stowaway and sail to Europe. Put off ship in Lobito, Angola, he found a job working for a timber company. Adventurous and restless, he tried working as a gold miner but lasted only eight hours underground. Became a machine tool operator in Bulawayo, Rhodesia, then successively a fisherman, clerk, a stringer for the South African Liberal newspaper *Contact* and a commentator in Cape Town.

While in Cape Town he made early contact with Toivo ja Toivo. In 1957, along with Toivo, Fanuel Kozongozi, Emil Appolus and others, he became a founder member of the Ovamboland People's Congress, which was renamed the Ovamboland People's Organisation in 1959 and the South West African People's Organisation, SWAPO in January 1960, with Sam Nujoma as its President. Became Chairman of the Cape Province branch of the party 1959-63. He also helped form the Maoist Yo Chi Chan club in Cape Town with Dr Kenneth Abrahams in 1961.

He returned to Namibia in 1963 as a full time SWAPO organiser, but hearing there was a warrant out for his arrest because of his association with Yo Chi Chan, he fled to Bechuanaland (Botswana). In a bizarre incident he was then kidnapped by the South African police and imprisoned at Gobabis for 20 days until the British authorities had him released and offered him permanent asylum in Bechuanaland. In the same year SWAPO sent him to be its representative in the Congo and then in Cairo 1964-69.

At the 1969 Tanga Congress he was elected SWAPO Secretary for Information. He was based in Dar es Salaam 1970-71, then Lusaka. He became critical of Nujoma's leadership of the party and was first suspended from the party in 1974, then arrested with nine members of the executive committee and up to 2,000 ordinary SWAPO members in 1976 and imprisoned in Zambia on the orders of President Kaunda. When he started Habeas Corpus proceedings he was transferred to Tanzania and held in solitary confinement for 22 months until his release in 1978, after his wife had run an international campaign to draw attention to his plight.

He went to London, then Sweden, where he founded the SWAPO Democrats, SWAPO-D, in 1978. He returned to Namibia in August 1978. SWAPO-D joined the Namibia National Front in 1979 and after that organisation wound up in 1980, took his party into the Multi-Party Conference in October 1983. On 10 December 1985 he was appointed Minister of Nature Conservation, Mining, Commerce and Tourism in the cabinet of the Transitional Government. He and his SWAPO-D party were heavily defeated in the November 1989 elections, not winning a single seat.

TOIVO ja TOIVO, Herman Andimba
Namibian politician. Secretary General SWAPO, 14 August 1984. Minister of Mines and Energy, 21 March 1990 –

The father figure of Namibian nationalism. Involved with most of early nationalist organisations and a co-founder of the South West African People's Organisation, SWAPO with Sam Nujoma. After 17 years imprisonment on Robben island, he joined the other SWAPO leaders in exile in 1984. He returned to Namibia in time to register for the elections in September 1989. A venerable and ageing leader, he still has a major part to play in the future of his country. He was elected shadow minister for Mines and Energy in the pre-independence cabinet of December 1989.

Born 22 August 1924 at Umungundu in the north, son of a catechist at the Finnish mission, Odanga. His name is actually Finnish and means 'Hope and Hope'. Educated at St Mary's Mission School, run by the Anglicans. After teacher training he returned to St Mary's to become a school master and continued his studies under a Finnish missionary. In 1942 he enlisted in the South African army and served until 1945 in South West Africa and South Africa as a guard at military installations. On demobilisation he went to Cape Town where he took a job as a railways policeman, continuing his studies in his spare time. He joined the Modern Youth Society, a multi-racial organisation which supported national liberation movements.

In the late 1950s he smuggled a tape recording describing the iniquities of the migrant labour system in a copy of "Treasure Island" to New York where it was given as evidence to the United Nations. He was a founder member of the Ovamboland People's Congress at the end of 1958, out of which SWAPO eventually evolved, in January 1960. He became the first President of the party but while he was still setting up the organisation he was arrested in April 1959 in Cape Town and deported to northern Ovamboland to live in restriction.

On 9 September 1966 he was arrested again and flown to Pretoria. Interrogated harshly, he was held as accused No.24, until his trial began on 7 August 1967. He was accused of receiving training in guerrilla warfare and of "terrorism with the intent to overthrow the present government." He made a statement in court accusing South Africa of abusing the "sacred trust of the mandate." He continued, "Who would not defend his property and himself against a robber? And we believe that South Africa has robbed us of our country."

He was sentenced with eight others, on 9 February 1968 to 20 years imprisonment. On 1 March 1984, when members of the Multi-Party Conference appealed on his behalf, he was released though four years of his sentence were still to run. Speculation was that the authorities hoped that his release might divide the SWAPO leadership and create a pole of resistance to the external leadership of Sam Nujoma. But Toivo was reluctant even to leave jail as he had come to symbolise the struggle of his people and did not want to be free "until they are free."

He was able to move in and out of Namibia and travelled to Lusaka to have talks with Sam Nujoma who had taken over from him as SWAPO leader on his imprisonment. He was appointed to the SWAPO politburo. He went into permanent exile joining the other SWAPO leaders in 1984.

On 14 August 1984 he was appointed Secretary General of SWAPO by the Central Committee, meeting in Luanda. He returned to Namibia in September 1989 in time to register for the pre-independence elections. Placed number four on the SWAPO electoral list he won a seat in parliament and was made shadow minister for Mines and Energy in the pre-independence cabinet of 21 December 1989.

WITBOOI, Hendrik

Namibian politician. SWAPO Vice-president. Minister for Labour, 21 March 1990 –

Chief Hendrik Witbooi is both a chief and pastor to his people, living in the Gibeon area in southern Namibia. His role as an internal leader of the South West African People's Organisation, SWAPO and his southern following gives him a key role in the future of his country, as most of the rest of the Swapo leadership are Ovambos from the north. A cautious politician, he keept a low profile and concentrated on local politics, until the pre-independence elections in November 1989 when he triumphed as number two on the SWAPO list.

Born 7 January 1934 at Gibeon. Grandson of Chief Hendrik Witbooi who led his Nama tribe from South Africa into Gibeon and settled there in the mid-nineteenth century. Educated at the Rhenish Mission School, Gibeon, Methodist Church School, Mariental and African Methodist Episcopalian School, Gibeon. He did teacher's training at Augustineum Training College, Okahandja. Became a teacher, then a pastor and principal at the AME school.

Active in nationalist politics from the early 1950s, when he was a petitioner to the United Nations together with the Herero Chief Hosea Kutako. He founded the Democratic Party of Namibia in 1975. Took his followers into SWAPO in 1977 after the break up of the Namibia National Convention (SWAPO remained a legal party within Namibia). Elected to the SWAPO politburo, he became Vice President in April 1983. This made him SWAPO's most important "internal leader".

Placed second on the SWAPO electoral list he triumphed in the November elections and on 21 December 1989 was appointed shadow Minister for Labour, Public Service and Manpower Development in the pre-independence cabinet. This appointment was confirmed in the first cabinet after independence, on 21 March 1990.

NIGER

Population: 7.47m (1990, World Bank)
Independence: 3 August 1960
Head of State: Ali Saibou
Government: Democratisation began with the setting up of a preparatory committee, which took the form of a transitional government, in May 1991, to prepare for a national conference which finally opened on 29 July.
Parties: Following the military coup of April 1974 all political parties were banned. A single ruling party, the *Mouvement National pour une Société de Développement* (MNSD) was formed in August 1988. Other parties were permitted in November 1990.

AMADOU, Hama

Niger politician. Minister of Information, 15 July 1988 –

One of President Ali Saibou's "men of action not sophists", part of a new team of younger ministers. He worked his way up from customs officer to Minister of Information and membership of the Executive Bureau of the ruling political party.

Born 1950 at Youri near Niamey. Educated locally, 1957-63. Secondary school, 1963-68. He trained as a customs officer, 1968-71.

He went into the customs service and became a regional inspector of customs at Zinder and Maradi, 1971-74. He took further education at the National Administration School, ENA in Niger for further adminstrative training 1974-78. He returned to local administration as the assistant prefect of Agadez 1978-80 and the Secretary General to the prefecture at Zinder 1980-82.

He then went to the International Institute of Public Administration in Paris for further training in commercial management, returning to become a sub-prefect in Tahoua. An interesting break came in 1984 with his appointment to Director General of Radio and Television. He next won the prestigious post as director of cabinet of the President of the Supreme Military Council, then President Seyni Kountch, in 1985. On 15 July 1988 the new President Ali Saibou appointed him Minister of Information.

On 17 May 1989 he was elected to the Executive Bureau of the ruling National Movement for the Developing Society (MNSD) and became its secretary general.

BAKO, Mahmane Sani

Niger politician. Foreign minister, 19 May 1989 –

A foreign affairs specialist with almost all his experience confined to the Foreign ministry apart from a brief spell as ambassador to the European Community. At the age of only 34 he was first appointed Foreign minister.

Born 25 April 1951 at Tessaoua. Educated locally 1957-63, and at the Lycee National, Niamey 1963-71. He then went to the University of Benin, in Lome, Togo, 1971-74 and at the University of Abidjan, 1974-75, where he studied law and international relations. He did post graduate studies at the Institute of International Relations, Yaoundé, Cameroon.

He joined the United Nations desk in the Foreign ministry in July 1976 and was promoted the Director of International Organisations in the ministry in January 1977. In January 1979 he became the Assistant Secretary General of the Ministry of Foreign Affairs and Co-operation and in October was promoted to Secretary general.

His career took a leap forward in September 1981 when he became Director of the Cabinet of the President of the Supreme Military Council, then the late Seyni Kountché. On 23 September 1985 Kountché appointed him Minister of Foreign affairs and Cooperation, in place of Ide Oumarou who had been elected Secretary General to the OAU. On 2 September 1988 the new President General Ali Saibou sent him to be the ambassador to Belgium and the EEC, but he was brought back on 19 May 1989 to the Foreign Ministry.

OUMAROU, Ide

Niger politician. Secretary-General of OAU, July 1985 – July 1989.

A quiet, retiring, Muslim who neither drinks nor smokes, trained as an economist and journalist, he was a thoroughly professional Secretary General of the Organisation of African Unity, keeping a very low profile and yet getting the job done. He has written several novels, some of which are best sellers in French speaking West Africa. He is a father of ten children.

Born 1937 in Niamey. Educated at the renowned William Ponty School, Dakar and the Institut des Hautes Etudes d'Outre Mer, Paris, where he studied economics and government planning. He began his career as a journalist in the Ministry of Information in 1960. At the age of 24 he was made editor of *Le Niger* 1961-63 and became Director of Information 1963-70, and Commissioner for Information 1970-72. He was then transferred to become Director General of Posts and Telegraphs.

His career took off when Lt Colonel Seyni Kountché assumed power in April 1974 and recruited him as his Chief of Cabinet in May. This made him the President's closest aide for the next five years.

Kountché then promoted him to become Niger's Permanent Representative at the United Nations in New York in 1979, where he presided over the security council meeting in May 1980 and July 1981 and frequently chaired the African group of nations.

On 14 November 1983 he was recalled to become Minister of Foreign Affairs and Cooperation a post he held until July 1985 when he took over from Peter Onu of Nigeria who had been acting Secretary General of the Organisation of African Unity after several deadlocked elections in 1983 and 1984. The electoral struggle continued against Blondin Beye the Mali Foreign Minister until finally Oumarou secured the necessary 34 votes on the seventh round.

In November 1985 he accompanied Abdou Diouf the Chairman of the OAU on what he described as a "productive and fruitful tour" of the frontline states. In February 1986 he announced that three regional offices of the OAU had to be closed in an effort to cut costs (member countries had not being paying their dues to the organisation). This raised considerable criticism but the Council endorsed his cost cutting measures at the summit in July 1986.

He always placed emphasis on the economic salvation of the continent and got the OAU to give priority to economic subjects at successive summits. In 1987 he travelled extensively to try to arrange a settlement to the Chad conflict. In 1988 he defended the OAU against a swingeing attack in the Auditor General's report which alleged misappropriation, improper accounting, irregular disbursement of money and improperly maintained accounts. He dismissed the claims, by a board of external auditors, as "tendentious and subjective."

In July 1988 he was defeated by Tanzania's Deputy Prime Minister Salim Salim when he stood for another term as the OAU Secretary General.

OUMAROU, Mamane

Niger politician. Prime Minister 15 July 1988 – 2 March 1990

With a brilliant record as an administrator in local government he was made Prime Minister when only 38 years old. He continued as the loyal servant of President Seyni Kountché until his friend and chef du cabinet was involved in a coup plot. He was dismissed but returned to the second most senior post in the country when General Ali Saibou restored him to the Premiership. He was again dismissed in March 1990 following unrest and pro-democracy demonstrations.

Born 1945 at Diffa. Educated locally 1952-57 and at the Lycee National, Niamey 1958-63. Diploma from the National Administration School, ENA in Niger, 1964. He then went to Ottawa, Canada and won a diploma in public administration from the Institute of International Cooperation at Ottawa University.

In 1967 he returned home and became a municipal secretary at Zinder, continuing as Assistant Prefect 1974-75. He was then transferred as a sub-prefect to Mirria 1975-76. His career in local government continued when he was made mayor of Maradi 1976-81. His excellent record as an administrator and his interest in Samaria youth organisations earned him his first ministerial appointment as Minister of Youth, Sports and Culture in September 1981. An even more remarkable promotion followed in January 1983 when he was made Prime Minister by President Seyni Kountché.

In a broadcast to the nation on 6 October 1983, he announced that an attempted coup by a group of armed men had been foiled during the absence of Kountché. Unfortunately for Oumarou his own Chef du Cabinet, a personal friend, was implicated in the plot and he was dismissed as Prime Minister on 15 November. But he continued as President of the Council of National Development (a new style constituent assembly) and still ranked number two in the power hierarchy. From 26 October 1987 until 15 July 1988, he was sent back to his old hunting ground as ambassador to Canada but was then recalled to immediately resume his duties as Prime Minister by the new Head of State General Ali Saibou. He was again dismissed on 2 March 1990 following clashes between police and government which resulted in three deaths.

SAIBOU, Ali (General)
Niger President, 10 November 1987 –

A bluff and hearty soldier, with a warm and welcoming personality. Always popular with his troops. A bon viveur and extrovert who does not eschew the good life. His success and steady promotion was due also to his unflinching loyalty to his kinsman, Seyni Kountché during his presidency. He succeeded him without challenge on his death in November 1987. Since assuming power he has proved to be conciliatory and liberal and promising constitutional reform while, in practice, still keeping tight military control.

Born 1940 in Ouallam in a Djerma-Songhai family. Educated locally then at the army school in Kati, Mali and at St Louis, Senegal. He returned home to pursue his army career on 1 August 1961. In September he went for training at the Officers School, Frejus, France completing his training in 1964 as a Second Lieutenant. He then served with different garrisons - company commander at N'Guigmi, 1964-68 and at the Tondibiah Training School, 1969-70. He went to Montpellier for further infantry training and then to the Staff college in Paris. He returned to become commander of the Tondibiah Training School 1973-74.

He was a captain, based in Agadez, a thousand kilometres from Niamey when the army first took power in April 1974. The Chief of Staff, Seyni Kountché ordered him to march on the capital at the head of his mechanised division. He carried out his orders by driving, without stopping for 24 hours, in an open-topped jeep.

This feat of courage and loyalty endeared him to Kountché who brought him into his first cabinet on 17 April 1974 as Minister of Rural Economy and Environment. In June he had Public Assistance added to his portfolio. Then in November he was appointed Chief of Staff of the

Armed Forces and relinquished his ministerial portfolios.

In July 1975, March 1976 and again in October 1983 he scotched coup attempts against Kountché by refusing to join the coup plotters. On the last occasion he was captured and held overnight until loyalist troops regained control.

He was promoted Chief of Staff of the armed forces on 1 April 1976 and the trusted friend of Kountché who failed to persuade him to take on the honorific post of grand chancellor. When Kountché died of a brain tumour in a military hospital in Paris, after prolonged and unsuccessful treatment in France, there was no argument about the succession. Colonel Ali Saibou assumed power on 14 November 1987. He was the automatic choice of the Kountché family which was was keen that the succession should remain in the hands of the Djerma and not pass to the most populous Hausa tribe.

Ali Saibou's first words when he assumed power were that there would be no major change of policy under his leadership. But he promised to lead a fresh onslaught on the problems of development though that would be along the lines already laid down by his former mentor. He was faced with an economy suffering from both budgetary and payments deficits. France had to provide $350m to carry out the development plan of 1987/88.

He also found his drought prone country, on the fringes of the Sahara desert, was facing a deficiency in food production - particularly a shortfall in cereal production of more than 300 million tonnes. One of his first acts was to appeal to international donors for food aid.

He then made a major gesture of reconciliation when he freed almost all the political detainees in the country including the former President Hamani Diori, who had been under house arrest. Other members of the Diori clan returned to Niger following an appeal by Saibou for all exiled Nigeriens to return home. Diori thanked him for his effort at national reconciliation and Djibo Bakari, the leader of the main opposition Sawaba party, also came to thank him and to encourage him in his new liberalisation policies. Saibou said he wanted to respect public liberties and strive for " true national reconciliation" though he would not tolerate "disorder or anarchy."

Saibou went further by setting up a Government think tank to create a constitutional committee in January 1988. The 27 members were drawn from all walks of life and had the task of reviewing the constitution with the minimum of delay. He lifted the ban on political organisations in August and announced the formation of a new ruling party the *Mouvement national pour une société de développement*, MNSD. But he actually increased the strength of the military presence in government, though he continued to promise eventual return to civilian rule. At the MNSD Congress of May 1989 he was elected Chairman and the sole candidate for the December 1989 elections. By then promoted to the rank of General, he triumphed as the only presidential candidate.

After student demonstrations in February 1990 were brutally

suppressed by the police, leaving three dead, he carried out a complete reshuffle of his cabinet and brought in a new Prime Minister, Aliou Mahamidou.

On 15 November 1990, nine months after the student demonstrators were killed, he stated his commitment to the introduction of multi-party democracy. He also allowed the formation of opposition parties and changed the name of the government party to MNSD-Nassara (meaning "triumph" in Hausa). At the party congress in March 1991 all the military withdrew from the party. Some officers were retired, but Saibou himself managed to hold onto both his civilian and military rank.

Saibou then tried to sidetrack the opposition into forming a transitional government, but this move was strongly resisted by the opposition and he finally agreed to the holding of a national conference. The national preparatory committee made the mistake of including only one woman among the 68 representatives and this led to a week of protest marches and sit-ins. Saibou himself wanted more representation for the rural areas. After some delay the conference opened on 29 July.

Saibou, in his opening address, asked participants not to "dig up the dustbins of history". But the conference had a mind of its own and declared its sovereignty on 31 July. The government delegation pulled out, but three days later it was back still complaining about the lack of rural representation.

NIGERIA

Population: 116m (1990, World Bank)
Independence: 1 October 1960
Head of State: General Ibrahim Babangida
Government: Military government pledged to return the country to civilian rule by 1992. After existing parties failed to satisfy the authorities, two state sponsored parties were set up.
Parties: Social Democratic Party and the National Republican Convention. During 1990/91 these were preparing for elections.

ABIOLA, Moshood Kashimawo Olawale

Nigerian businessman. Chairman of Concord Group.

One of Nigeria's leading business tycoons who made his fortune with International Telephone and Telegraph and through his publishing ventures with Concord Press, the most successful publishing group in the Federation. A thrusting businessman, who has always been prepared to take a long-term view, he has used much of his wealth to endow public institutions and help philanthropic causes. He also had political aspirations and rose to become a challenger for the presidency in the mid-1980s, but gave up politics in disgust when his aspirations were frustrated. He was conferred one of the highest traditional titles, the Aare Ona Kakanfo (field marshal) by the Alafin of Oyo in 1987.

Born 24 August 1937 in Abeokuta, Ogun State. Educated at Baptist Boys High School, Abeokuta, 1951-56 and the University of Glasgow, 1961-63 to study accountancy. In 1965 he became deputy chief accountant of the University of Lagos Teaching Hospital and in 1967 financial controller of Pfizer Products Ltd. In 1969 he joined the company where he was to establish his business reputation – International Telephone and Telegraph (Nigeria) – rising to vice-president of ITT for Africa and the Middle East and chairman and chief executive of ITT Nigeria in 1971.

ITT made his fortune and his reputation as a business tycoon while Nigeria was still under military rule. When the ban on politics was lifted in 1978 he threw himself into politics as a member of the National Party of Nigeria (NPN).

He set up the Concord Press of Nigeria, whose newspapers, the *Daily* and *Sunday Concord* and *African Concord* magazine, were to challenge the established press and develop top newspaper readerships.

He hoped the newspapers and magazines that he published and his position as one of the leading Yorubas in the NPN would earn him promotion in the party. He was already Chairman of the NPN in Ogun state and a national vice president of the party. He challenged Chief A.M.A Akinloye for the national chairmanship and the Yoruba leadership of his zone in the party from the early 1980s. During that period he donated millions of naira to the party in the hope of gaining a leadership position.

He tried to challenge President Shehu Shagari as Presidential candidate at a special party convention in June 1982, but was not selected. His hopes of being chosen as Shagari's running mate were also frustrated. He resigned from the party, saying that all he had received in return for his work and effort was "blackmail, ingratitude and insult".

He retired from NPN politics and concentrated on his publishing, a move that turned out to be fortuitous as the Shagari government had hardly been installed when the military coup of 31 December 1983 put paid to all political aspirations. Political parties were banned and their bank accounts investigated. He wanted to make a return to politics in the post-Babangida Third republic but came under the ban imposed on all previous politicians. He challenged this decision in the Lagos High Court but failed to have the disqualification lifted.

ADEDEJI, Adebayo

Nigerian academic, administrator. Executive Secretary Economic Commission for Africa, June 1975 – July 1991.

A man of wide international experience and author of many books, articles and speeches. He was Federal Commissioner for Economic Development under General Gowon where he was in charge of a rapidly expanding economy as the Nigerian oil boom produced a huge upsurge in revenues. But he was waiting for an international challenge which duly materialised in the shape of the prestigious post as Executive Secretary for the Economic Commission for Africa.

He took up this job in June 1975, just before the military coup which ousted Gowon. He held the ECA job for more than 16 years and became renowned for his incisive speeches and reports on the economic state of Africa. In July 1989 he published his renowned "African Alternative Framework to Structural Adjustment Programmes." which was widely received as a viable alternative to orthodox IMF policies. One delegate to the OAU summit which praised the new initiative said, "If he was a white man he would have been nominated for the Nobel Peace price".

Born 21 December 1930. Educated St Saviour's School (1940-43) and Ijebu Ode Grammar School, 1944-49. He went on to the University College of Ibadan, Leicester University, (1955-58) where he took a BSc Economics. He returned home to become an assistant secretary in the Ministry of Economic Planning, going on to Harvard on a year's course, before returning home as principal assistant secretary in the Western Nigerian treasury.

He became deputy director of the Institute of Administration in the University of Ife (1963-67), director in 1967 and a professor in October 1968.

In June 1966 he became chairman of Western Nigeria Radio and Television, a director of the Western Nigeria Development Corporation, and a director of the National Manpower Board, 1967-71.

It was work on these government agencies, his academic record and his international activities that led to his appointment by General Gowon as Federal Commissioner for Economic Development and Reconstruction in October 1971. He held this office until June 1975 when he left the Federal government to become Executive Secretary of the United Nations Economic Commission for Africa (ECA). There he carefully monitored the state of the African economy, writing influential annual reports and addressing international organisations.

In July 1989 he issued his "African Alternative Framework to Structural Adjustment Programmes". It was an alternative to IMF policies which demanded too rapid adjustment from impoverished developing countries. It was based on years of research by more than 100 international economists and was rapidly accepted by the Finance Ministers representing most OAU countries.

In January 1991 he organised a conference on the "People's participation in economic development" at Arusha, in Tanzania.

He finally retired at the end of July 1991 and for the first time ever ECA expressed a special "vote of appreciation and thanks...in honour of this great servant". It was the first time that a UN functionary had been so honoured.

The new conference hall next to Africa Hall in Addis Ababa was named the Adebayo Adedeji Conference Centre in his honour. He retired to private life in Nigeria where he expressed an interest to go into politics.

AKINJIDE, Richard Osuolale Abimbola

Nigerian politician and businessman.

An extremely astute and wily politician, academic and jurist who played a leading part as legal adviser to the National Party of Nigeria. He helped Alhaji Shehu Shagari assume the presidency in October 1979 by helping sort out the legal wrangle that followed. As Minister of Justice, he was one of the most influential members of the government. But he began to get more involved in legal and business activities and was not reappointed in Shagari's short-lived second regime in November 1983. After the military coup he fled to England and stayed there despite attempts to have him return home.

Born 4 November 1931 in Ibadan, Oyo state. Educated at St Peter's School, Aremo, Oduduwa college, Ile Ife and at London University (1952-56). He was called to the bar at the Inner Temple in 1956.

Returned home and went into politics, becoming a member of parliament in 1959. He was appointed Federal Minister of Education by Prime Minister Abubakar Tafawa Balewa in 1965 shortly before the first coup of 15 January 1966. He became president of the Nigerian Bar Association (1970-73) and a member of the governing council of the

University of Ile Ife (1975-76). Next he was appointed Pro-Chancellor and Chairman of the Council at the University of Jos.

In 1978 in the run-up to civilian rule he became a member of the National Party of Nigeria and its legal adviser. He came to public attention when he was involved in the dispute over who had won the presidential elections of 1979. Alhaji Shehu Shagari had won the most votes but under the constitution, he also had to win in at least two-thirds of the states in the Federation. It had been assumed that this meant victory in 13 of the 19 states, but Shagari did not achieve this. He was only saved by Akinjide's interpretation of the constitution as requiring approval in 12 and two-thirds of the states.

This interpretation infuriated the supporters of Chief Awolowo and brought much criticism to Chief Akinjide. He became even more unpopular when the decision was subsequently upheld by the Federal Electoral Commission (FEDECO) and the Supreme Court. Akinjide earned the nickname of "Mr Twelve and two-thirds" as a result of this decision. He was rewarded by Shagari who named him his Minister of Justice in October 1979, though the Senate immediately rejected his candidature along with two others without giving any reasons.

His appointment was finally confirmed on 14 December 1979. He played an influential part in the government of the second republic and helped secure the return of the Nigerian National Party in the elections of October 1983 but he was not reappointed to Shagari's government in November 1983 which gave him the chance to concentrate on legal and business activities.

When the coup came on New Year's Eve 1984 the new military government was baying for revenge against those who had held power and prospered in the civilian regime. Chief Akinjide left the country for England before a corruption decree was passed and tribunals had been set up in April 1984, to try those suspected of using their offices to defraud the state.

ANYAOKU, Eleazar Chukwuemeka 'Emeka'
Commonwealth-Secretary General, 1 July 1990 –

Discreet, urbane, always immaculately dressed, described by West Africa magazine as a "diplomat's diplomat", he has spent almost his entire working life handling the delicate and often explosive issues of the Commonwealth. A tireless worker, who totally immerses himself in the issue of the moment, he has been involved in most Commonwealth and many African crises stretching over more than two decades. At the 1989 Kuala Lumpur conference he became the first African to be elected to the post of Secretary-General and pledged himself to carry on the sacred trust inherited from his friend and predecessor, Shridath Ramphal, whose deputy he was for 12 years.

Born 18 January 1933 in Obosi, Anambra state. Educated at the Merchants of Light School, Oba in Eastern Nigeria and at the University of Ibadan. He also attended courses at Cambridge and the Institute of Public Administration, London and the Cavillam Institute, France. He chose international service early in his career and in 1959 joined the staff of the Commonwealth Development Corporation as a management trainee, serving in London and Nigeria. In 1962 he joined the Nigerian diplomatic service. After a period as Chef de Cabinet of the Permanent Secretary of the Ministry of Foreign Affairs he was posted to the United Nations in New York.

He was seconded to the newly created Commonwealth Secretariat at the request of the first Secretary-General, the Canadian Arnold Smith, first in 1966 as Assistant Director and later, in 1971, Director of International Affairs. He survived the immense pressures exerted on him as an Igbo during the the Nigerian civil war over Biafra and remained at his post.

In 1972 he became vice president of the Royal Commonwealth Society and from 1976-81 chairman of the Africa Centre. He is also a member of the committee of management of London University's Institute of Commonwealth Studies and of the governing council of the Overseas Development Institute.

One of his first assignments in the Commonwealth Secretariat was when he was secretary of the commission to tackle the constitutional crisis in Anguilla in 1969. He visited all the Caribbean countries before successfully accomplishing his mission.

He became the emissary for the Secretary-General of the Secretariat to a number of flash points - to Pakistan in 1972 after the secession of Bangladesh; to Zimbabwe and Namibia on the difficult road to independence; to Mozambique, in 1975, to implement sanctions against white Rhodesia and set up a scheme of assistance for Mozambique. He was the Secretariat's observer at the Geneva talks on Zimbabwe in 1976 and helped organise the Lancaster House Conference that brought independence in 1979.

In 1975 he was appointed Assistant Secretary-General and in 1977 was elected by Commonwealth Governments as Deputy Secretary-General in charge of international affairs and the administration of the secretariat. In 1980 he represented the Secretary-General at the tenth independence anniversary celebrations in Fiji and in 1982 chaired the committee which set up a number of co-operative programmes for Asia and the Pacific.

In 1982 he was honoured by the Shehu Shagari government in Nigeria with the award of the Commander of the Order of the Niger. In October 1983 he decided to change his political horizons and quit the Secretariat to launch himself into Nigerian politics, being appointed Foreign Minister in Shagari's post-election government on 10 November 1983. His appointment had hardly been approved by the Nigerian senate when Murtala Muhammed sprang his military coup.

Anyaoku returned to London and the new military government was quite prepared to nominate him for his old post (still vacant) of Deputy

Secretary-General. He was reappointed with the unanimous support of the Commonwealth governments.

When "Sonny" Ramphal announced his decision to retire after 14 years as Secretary-General of the Secretariat, two candidates emerged for his office. One was Anyaoku, the other the redoubtable Malcolm Fraser, the former Prime Minister of Australia, who had the full weight of his country's diplomatic machine behind him. Fraser campaigned hard and long (for more than a year) but at the end of the day he had gained support of only an estimated quarter of the voters. The Commonwealth, which tries to take all its decisions unanimously, never revealed the real voting, but declared Anyaokou the choice of the 46 leaders present. So the first African ever was set to assume the post of Commonwealth Secretary-General.

Making his first public policy statement on 25 July 1991 he committed himself to strengthening democracy among Commonwealth countries in addition to pressing for the end of apartheid.

BABANGIDA, Ibrahim Badamasi (General)
Nigerian Head of State August 27 1985-

Always comfortable as a soldier surrounded by soldiers, a socialiser fond of sport, the good life and the atmosphere of the army mess. A man with a jaunty walk, a ready smile and a rugged determination. Nicknamed Maradona after the Argentinian footballer, because of his deft footwork. Beneath the bluff and comradely exterior is a shrewd political brain that was involved in at least three coups. In December 1983 he walked alone and unarmed into a radio station to persuade rebellious officers to give up quietly. After he took control in August 1987 he had the complex task of holding his huge, populous and quarrelsome nation together while he prepared it for civilian rule.

Born 17 August 1941. One of two children of Muhammadu and Aishatu Babangida, he was born in Minna in the northern Niger state. There he did his primary education before moving to the government college at Bida, one of Nigeria's top schools and the training ground for many other senior military officers. There he received his high school diploma. He enrolled at the Nigerian Military Training College in 1963 and after passing out moved to India for a spell in the Indian Military Academy. Then in 1966 he went to the Royal Armoured Corps in Britain and then in 1974 to the United States Armoury School.

This broad training, combined with further spells at the Command and Staff College in Nigeria and at the Nigerian Institute for Policy and Strategic Studies, brought him swift promotion in the army.

After his commission in 1963, he was made a lieutenant three years later. By the time of the Nigerian civil war he was a commanding officer. He had a clean war record, commanding the 44th Infantry Battalion called "The Rangers". He became a lieutenant colonel in 1974. In 1975 he became commander of the Armoured Corps which he did a great deal to develop. By 1983 he had risen to Major General and Director of Army Duties and Plans, a position that placed him ideally to play a major but unspecified role in the coup that brought the civilian government to an end in December 1983 and installed Muhammadu Buhari in power. He was appointed Army chief under the new military regime.

But though he was not a politically ambitious man, he soon became very dissatisfied with the lack of action by Muhammadu Buhari. He was also dismayed at the way Buhari was becoming more autocratic, curbing the Press and entrusting more power to his number two, Maj-General Tunde Idiagbon, and the National Security Organisation. On 27 August 1985, when Idiagbon was on a visit to Saudi Arabia and Buhari was back in his home town celebrating the festival of Id el Kabir, he took control with the support of a large group of officers who recognised him as a more charismatic and active leader.

In his first few months of power he liberalised Nigeria and freed the Press and released a large number of detainees from the former civilian regime, on the grounds that charges could not be found against them.

But his main problem remained the parlous state of the Nigerian economy and the huge foreign debt which had been accumulated by previous regimes. Another of his early measures was to declare a state of economic emergency and to assume sweeping interventionist powers over the economy.

On 20 December 1985 a coup plot by disgruntled army officers was easily quashed. Up to 300 officers were arrested, among them Major-General Vatsa, an old school colleague, who was tried, found guilty and executed.

After a great deal of public discussion and democratic argument he finally came to an agreement with the International Monetary Fund and introduced tight economic controls and a foreign exchange auction system. This allowed major debt rescheduling by Western governments and fresh loans from the World Bank. But it also resulted in devaluation of the naira, rapid inflation and a wave of social discontent led by the unions. Babangida responded by dissolving the executive of the National Labour Council. But protests spread to students and the professions. He temporarily closed the universities.

In January 1986 Babangida announced that the armed forces would hand over power to a civilian government in 1990. Later he postponed the date to 1992, allowing more time for a thorough preparation. He decreed that none of the politicians of the old regimes or office holders in military governments would be allowed to stand again in the elections. Political parties would also be banned in the transitional period and only two parties would be allowed when campaigning was finally allowed. A constitutent assembly to draft a new constitution was elected in April 1988 and began sessions in June. Babangida then claimed that the competing political parties had failed to qualify under the strict criteria his government had laid down. Instead he insisted that the government would itself draw up the constitutions and manifestoes of two sponsored parties, the National Republican Convention (NRC) and Social Democratic Party (SDP).

On 6 February 1989 he dissolved the whole of the Armed Forces Ruling Council and the National Council of State and reappointed a smaller, more functional body more able to control the country in the run up to civilian rule. He streamlined the state structure still further, sacking many of his close military colleagues in another major reshuffle on 31 December 1989. The move also emphasised his command of the highest decision making body in the country. He wanted to show that he had firm personal control.

On 22 April 1990 junior officers under Major Gideon Orkar, carried out a coup on behalf of the most important northern Muslim states, which declared that they had "excised themselves" from the Federation. The coup makers seized the radio station and accused Babangida of running a "dictatorial, corrupt, drug-baronish, inhumane, sadistic, deceitful, homosexually centred regime". Though this exaggerated verbiage did not convince the majority of radio-listeners, the coup was serious. It came in the middle of the morning rush hour and Babangida's home in Dodan barracks came under severe shelling and attack by road. But within hours loyalist forces had reasserted control

The coup leaders were brought to trial before a military tribunal. In July, 42 of them including Orkar, were executed with Babangida denying all international appeals for clemency.

Babangida continued with the timetable towards civilian rule almost as if nothing had happened. The NRC and SDP were officially registered in March. In July the party leaders and officials were elected.

In August, Babangida pressed ahead with the "civilianisation" of his regime. He abolished the post of Chief-of-General Staff and appointed Vice Admiral Augustus Aikhomu to the new office of Vice President. He also pruned the size of the Nigerian armed forces. Attention then switched to the civil war in Liberia that threatened to destabilise the region and the lives of Nigerians living there. Babangida's solution was to intervene through the Economic Community of West African States (ECOWAS), hitherto a body which was concerned solely with economic affairs. As rebels began their bloody war in Monrovia, the Liberian capital, Babangida persuaded five nations to intervene by sending in an ECOWAS Ceasefire Monitoring Group (ECOMOG) force of 3,000 men on 24 August 1990. Babangida took the lead and provided most of the logistics for the intervention and showed clearly that he was prepared to intervene in the internal affairs of a neighbouring country in the interests of peace and security. He was also the driving force in setting up the interim government for Liberia of Dr Amos Sawyer.

Successful local elections were carried out by the new parties in December, but in January 1991 Babangida announced that their government subsidy would be withdrawn. He felt that they had established themselves and required no more government support.

Severe religious rioting by Shia Muslim radicals recurred in northern cities in April 1991. Babangida had no hestiation in employing the full weight of the security forces to put them down.

On 18 August 1991 Babangida announced that Nigeria had suspended its membership of the Islamic Conference Organisation (ICO). He admitted that membership had given rise to considerable controversy in the country (specifically the Christians had accused him of trying to "Islamicise" the country). Babangida claimed that Nigeria had "never been represented in anyway in the activities of the conference, since the problem started". Clearly he was making a gesture of conciliation to the vociferous Christian lobby.

BUHARI, Muhammadu (Major-General)
Nigeria's Head of State from 1 January 1984 to 27 August 1985.

Soft spoken, dedicated, clear-headed, self disciplined and an avid reader of serious military histories, he played a minor role in the military coup that ousted Yakubu Gowon in July 1975. Later he took power from the civilian government of Shehu Shagari on New Year's Eve 1984. He never had the full confidence of his colleagues and was faced with appalling economic problems inherited from the former regime. He was not popular and was often overshadowed by more dominant colleagues in his own Supreme Military Council. He was ousted from power, with little resistance, by Ibrahim Babangida in August 1985.

Born 17 December 1942 at Daura in the Katsina area of Kaduna, a state in northern Nigeria. He came from the Fulani tribe, the traditional rulers and overlords in the north of the country.

The Fulani, originally a cattle herding people from Senegal, invaded northern Nigeria in the 15th century and imposed their rule over the majority of Hausa in the north. Later, in colonial times, the Fulani rulers led a long and bitter struggle against the British under Lord Lugard.

Buhari joined the army in 1962 and went to the Nigerian military training college at Kaduna and Mons Officer Cadet School in Britain. He later took a course at India's Defence Service Staff College. He commanded a sector of the front in the war against the rebellious Biafrans during the Nigerian civil war.

He played a minor but essential role in the military coup that ousted General Yakubu Gowon on 29 July 1975 and installed Murtala Muhammad. Muhammad made him state Governor of Maiduguri in 1974. Murtala was assassinated; shot while his car was stuck in a Lagos traffic jam, in February 1976. Buhari was then appointed Commissioner for Petroleum and chairman of the Nigerian National Petroleum Corporation by the new regime. The NNPC, which controlled Nigeria's oil production, was going through an unhappy time with accusations in the media of oil and cash going missing.

He remained chairman of the NNPC until civilian rule in September 1979 when he returned to regular army duties. He went on an overseas course and assumed command of the 4th Division. Later he became GOC of the First Mechanised Division of the Army based in Kaduna. He was not the prime mover in the military coup of New Year's Eve 1984, but he shared the disillusionment that the whole army felt about the growing corruption among self-seeking politicians. He emerged as the senior military officer and was unanimously selected by his fellow soldiers as the new Head of State.

But he soon found himself embroiled in Nigeria's growing economic problems. The oil price was collapsing, the economy had been expanding too fast and foreign debt and payments deficits were growing by leaps and bounds. Buhari's answer was austerity and yet more austerity. His cut backs gravely affected the standard of living of the ordinary people and lasted from the time of his accession to power until he was ousted 20 months later. Buhari spent most of the time trying to cure the economy by forcing unpopular measures on the unwilling public.

His regime was also plagued by political scandals in which the old politicians were shown to have escaped from justice with their ill-gotten millions to safe havens in the West. The case of Umaru Dikko who fled to Britain was perhaps the most sensational of many.

Buhari also clamped down on press freedom (using the notorious Decree 4) and other political liberties. He tried to impose his iron discipline on doctors, trade unionists and other professional bodies that tried to resist his austerity measures. But criticism continued, so in July he banned all political debate. This last despairing measure to crack down on civil liberties opened the way to another coup.

The coup came from a group of fellow colleagues and officers in the army. On 27 August 1985 General Ibrahim Babangida, the Chief of Army Staff, simply took control, claiming that: "A small group of individuals had abused their power and failed to listen to the advice of their colleagues or the public about tackling the country's economic problems."

Buhari was detained in Benin the capital of Bendel state. He was released on 16 December 1988.

CIROMA, Malam Adamu
Nigerian businessman and politician.

A Northerner who made his early reputation as a pioneering editor of the New Nigerian *and later held office as Governor of the Central Bank. He became a leading light as secretary-general of the National Party of Nigeria and was promoted to senior ministries under President Shagari. He has concentrated on private interests since the military coup of January 1984.*

Born 1934 at Potiskum in Northern Nigeria. Educated at Barewa College and the University College of Ibadan. He became an administrative officer in the Northern Nigerian civil service (1961-65) and Senior Assistant Secretary of the Federal Civil service, based in Lagos (1965-66). In 1966 he was appointed to the editorship of the *New Nigerian* a new paper with high standards and clear presentation that rapidly established itself as an impartial voice of the north. He rose to become managing director of *New Nigerian* newspapers over (1969-74).

In 1975 he was appointed governor of the Nigerian Central Bank, a position he held as the fruits of the Nigerian oil boom were flowing through the economy, until 1977. General Obasanjo appointed him to the Constituent Assembly, charged with drawing up the new constitution for the return to civilian rule in August 1979. He joined the National Party of Nigeria and rapidly rose to become its national secretary.

In October 1979 President Shehu Shagari appointed him Minister of Industries, switching him to Minister of Agriculture in February 1982 to tackle the problems of President's promised "green revolution".

On 10 November 1983 he was moved again, this time to become the key Minister of Finance, at a time the economy was running out of control, with firm retrenchment needed. But hardly had he assumed office when the military coup under General Buhari swept him from power, on 1 January 1984. He was then detained briefly along with many other top NPN ministers, but was released on 1 October 1984. Since then he has not held high office.

DIKKO, Umaru Abdurrahman (Dr)
Nigerian politician and businessman.

He rose at a comparatively young age to become a powerful, rich, respected and feared Minister of Transport and head of the Presidential Task Force for the importation of essential commodities. His activities resulted in huge wealth and his influence grew in party and government until he became second only to President Shehu Shagari in the government hierarchy. But after the military coup on New Year's Eve 1984, he became the principal target for the new government's anti-corruption crusade. He became the focus of world attention when a bungled attempt was made to kidnap him from his refuge in Britain. His drugged body was found packed in a crate ready to be flown out of Britain by a Nigerian transport plane. Since then he has been embroiled in litigation. He is trying to secure political asylum while the Nigerian government wants to have him extradited.

Born 31 December 1936 in Kaduna state. Educated at the Barewa College, Zaria (1949-54), the Nigerian College of Arts, Science and Technology (1954-58) and London University, where he took his degree in 1965. He was appointed Commissioner of Finance in North Central State 1967-72, followed by Commissioner for Education, 1972-75.

President Shagari brought him into the federal government as Minister of Transport on 14 December 1979. In the same year he was made the chairman of the Presidential Task Force for the importation of essential commodities like rice. In the space of four years he became a very rich man. He helped the NPN financially in its electoral victory of October 1983 and was reinstalled as Minister of Transport and Aviation in the short-lived Shagari government on 10 November 1983.

Two days after the military coup of New Year's Eve 1984 he escaped over the Benin border and went on to London where he had property. The new military government was crying for revenge against those who had held power and prospered in the civilian regime. A corruption decree was passed and tribunals were set up in April 1984 to to try those suspected of using their offices to defraud the state.

Dikko was accused by the government of large-scale corruption, hoarding of essential commodities and enriching himself. When accused by the government of having stolen one billion Naira, he replied: "Whatever money a politician makes goes back to the people because he wants their votes. The military are only talking about money because they can only think of their own bank accounts."

He was also declared to have been plotting a coup and became a "most wanted man" by the Nigerian government. On 5 July 1984 he was seized at gun point outside his house at number 49 Porchester Terrace, Bayswater and, after being drugged was put in a crate labelled "Diplomatic Baggage". His secretary rang the police who alerted all airports. His unconscious body was found by the customs authorities at Stansted Airport, north of London.

This bungled attempt to kidnap him caused an international furore and grievously damaged Anglo-Nigerian relations. The Nigerian government denied that it was involved in the kidnap attempt, though all the evidence controverted this. Sir Geoffrey Howe, Britain's Foreign Secretary, cancelled a visit to Nigeria. Three Israelis and one Nigerian were later found guilty of attempted kidnapping and given jail sentences of between ten and 14 years.

Dikko applied for political asylum in Britain in December 1984. In January 1985 the Nigerian government formally requested his extradition on the grounds that he had diverted large sums of money into his own bank account when he was a minister. Britain turned down his application for asylum in June, but he was allowed to appeal. Meanwhile Nigeria failed in a bid on 9 February 1989 to get him extradited and appeared reluctant to appeal against the decision of the British court.

EKWUEME, Alex Ifeanyichukwu (Dr)
Nigerian Politician. Vice-President October 1979-December 1983.

Modest, quietly spoken, and studious with an unusual background for a Nigerian politician in architecture, he was the ideal deputy to Alhaji Shehu Shagari during his presidency of Nigeria. A firm supporter of the National Party of Nigeria and a valuable deputy in government, he did not enrich himself illegally during the years of civilian rule and was fully cleared by the special judicial tribunal. After his release from detention in July 1986 he caused something of a sensation when he decided to add to his collection of academic qualifications by going "back to school" to study law.

Born 21 October 1932 in Oko, Anambra state. Educated at Anglican schools in Oko, Ekwulobia, and Aguata (1938-44). He went on to Kings College Lagos (1945-50). Attended the University of Washington studying sociology, architecture and urban planning (1952-57). Took his PhD at the University of Strathclyde, Glasgow. Became president of the Nigerian Institute of Architects (1965-68), attending the Congress of the International Union of Architects in 1963 and 1975.

When politics became possible in 1978, he joined the National Party of Nigeria (NPN) and ran on a joint ticket for the Presidency with Alhaji Shehu Shagari and triumphed in August 1979. As deputy to Shagari he played a rather low-key role, but led a number of official diplomatic missions overseas on behalf of his country. His influence won better electoral support for the NPN in Anambra during the 1983 elections. Though threatened with various challenges at early stages of the presidential elections, he stood again as Vice-President in September 1983 and was sworn in for a second term on 1 October 1983.

But after the military coup on New Year's Eve 1984 he was arrested and detained pending investigations as to whether he had corruptly enriched himself during his term of office. A special judicial panel investigating the cases of the detainees found that Ekwueme "was already a wealthy man before he went into politics and that he came out of politics poorer." He was also cleared of soliciting donations on behalf of the NPN. On 3 July 1986 he was released from detention though his movements continued to be restricted.

In 1988 the highly qualified former Vice-President caused something of a sensation by "going back to school". He enrolled at Imo State University to read law. He matriculated in January 1989 but did not attend the award winning ceremony in person.

GAMBARI Ibrahim Agboola (Professor)
Nigerian politician and diplomat

A young and ambitious, highly-qualified, diplomat-politician, currently Nigeria's ambassador at the United Nations. He was foreign minister under General Buhari where he did his best to carry out the policies of an unpopular government as Foreign Minister. Though he was not directly responsible, during his tenure thousands of West Africans were forcibly deported from Nigeria and a farcical attempt was made to capture the Nigerian exile Umaru Dikko in London. He also had to fight hard to restore relations with Britain which were at an all time low. He has survived as Nigeria's ambassador to the UN where he has been a tireless campaigner for southern African causes and a clever representative of his country.

Born 24 November 1944 in Ilorin, Kwara state. He did primary education locally then went on to do higher school certificate at King's College, Lagos in 1964. At the London School of Economics, he gained a BSc in economics, then went to Columbia University, New York to get an MA in 1970, and Ph.D in 1974 in political science. There he also gained experience as a lecturer. He returned to Nigeria to continue lecturing at Ahmadu Bello University from 1977.

He became the Director General of the Nigerian Institute for International Affairs from October 1983 to January 1984, then External Affairs Minister (January 1984 - August 1985), appointed by the military ruler Maj.General Muhammadu Buhari. During his tenure of office the forced expulsion of thousands of West African immigrants took place, as did the botched attempt to kidnap the Nigerian exiled millionaire, Umaru Dikko in London, and send him back to Nigeria in a packing crate. He strongly denies that he, or the government were involved in the kidnapping, but this is not the generally accepted view. As Foreign Minister relations with Britain were at an all time low and Gambari worked hard with his British counterpart, Sir Geoffrey Howe to improve matters.

After the coup by Maj.Gen Ibrahim Babangida on 27 August 1985, he continued in government, unlike most of the other Buhari ministers.

He presented his letters of credence as Nigeria's ambassador and permanent representative to the United Nations, on 22 January 1990.

GARBA, Joseph Nanven (Major-General)
Nigerian soldier and politician. Ambassador to Namibia 19 March 1990—

An unusual combination of keen and successful soldier and committed politicised, diplomat. He enjoyed a brilliant military career in the Nigerian army, rising fast through the Federal Brigade of Guards to Brigadier but when given his chance by being made External Affairs Commissioner under Murtala Muhammed, in 1975 he showed that he had found his vocation. He was the driving force in defining Nigeria's radical and committed foreign policy of that era. Though he appeared to be returning to a military career he re-emerged as Nigeria's permanent representative to the United Nations. In August 1989 he was elected president of the UN General Assembly following intense pressure by his home country. Then in March 1990 he became Nigeria's ambassador to the newly independent Namibia.

Born 17 July 1943 at Langtang. Educated at the Sacred Heart School, Shendam. He joined the army and did his training at the elite Military School, Zaria and at Mons Officer Cadet School, Aldershot and at Camberley Staff College in Britain.

He returned home to become the youngest ever commissioned officer in the Nigerian army, at the age of 19, in 1962. He became a platoon commander in the 4th battalion in 1963, rising to company commander in 1964 and second-in-command of the Federal Guards 1964-65. He became the general staff officer in the 3 HQ, second brigade in 1965. He broadened his experience by being sent as part of the Nigerian United

Nations observer team to monitor the ceasefire between Pakistan and India (1965-66). He returned to become Commander of the Brigade of Guards (1968-75).

When Brigadier (later General) Murtala Muhammed took power from Gen Yakubu Gowon on 29 July 1975, it was Major Garba who announced the overthrow of the previous regime. He repeated the announcement so often, he said: "I became fed up with listening to my voice over and over on the radio." Garba and his men in the Brigade of Guards had played a major part in the coup. Muhammed appointed Garba to the Supreme Military Council and also made him Commissioner for External Affairs. Under the new government Nigeria pursued a radical, militant, foreign policy much less favourable to Britain and far more supportive of black African causes in general.

Under Garba, Nigeria decided to give unequivocal backing to the MPLA government in Angola for the first time. This trend was emphasised after Britain was accused of being involved in the attempted coup of Colonel Bukar Dimka in February 1976, to bring back General Gowon. Muhammed was assassinated and Garba was on the list of those to be assassinated had the Dimka coup been successful.

When Lt. Gen. Olusegun Obasanjo took power, after the assassination of Muhammed, he confirmed Garba's position as Commissioner for External Affairs on 15 March 1976. In a speech to the International Students' Association at the University of Lagos, he spelt out Nigeria's pro-liberationist stance in Southern Africa and explained why it supported the Marxist government of Angola. He said Nigeria placed primacy on African issues thus seeking to fulfil its historical role and carry out its OAU responsibilites. He became president of the UN's Special Committee for Action Against Apartheid.

During 1977 he put his talent for mediation to good effect in disputes between Zaire and Angola, Chad and Libya and in East Africa. At the OAU meeting in May he emphasised that Nigeria had no right to claim leadership of the continent, but said its role had always been mediatory. In August he played his full part in making Nigeria the host for a World Conference for Action Against Apartheid. In September 1978 he and Joshua Nkomo had at least one secret meeting with the Rhodesian leader Ian Smith in an attempt to secure an agreement.

With the return to civilian government in 1979, all serving officers filling civilian posts, were told they would not be allowed to continue as military personnel while holding civilian office. A choice had to be made and surprisingly, in the light of his brilliant diplomatic record, Garba chose to remain a soldier. He was promoted Major-General and became Commandant of the Nigerian Defence Academy at Kaduna. But later he was appointed Nigeria's ambassador to the United Nations.

In August 1989 he was elected to the hotly contested position as President of the 44th session of the UN Assembly. It is not an executive, but a political post lasting for one year. While doing his stint he remained a fellow of the Institute of Politics at the Kennedy School of Government and the Centre for International Affairs at Harvard University. He wrote two books: *Revolution in Nigeria: Another View* and *Diplomatic Soldiering*. He also retained his role as chairman of the the UN special committee on apartheid. On 19 March 1990 he was rewarded for his wide interests and services by being appointed his country's first ambassador to the newly independent Namibia.

GOWON, Yakubu (General)
Nigerian Head of State August 1966 – 29 July 1975.

Africa's youngest head of state when he came to power at 32. A sincere Christian, non-smoker and teetotaller, with a charming and open-minded personality. He emerged in 1966 to lead a country riven by coups and in danger of disintegration. He fought the war to prevent Biafran secession and brought it to an unvindictive conclusion. His big mistake was to postpone the return to civilian rule which gave rival military commanders the excuse to intervene. Later he was accused of being involved in plotting a counter-coup, but he has always denied it and he has been vindicated by history. Possibly a casualty of being too pro-British in his sympathies and outlook at a time his nation was looking for a nationalistic leader. He concluded a politics degree at Warwick University before returning home.

Born 19 October 1934, in the Lur Pankshin division of the northern plateau- the "Middle belt" of Nigeria. His father, an Aga, was an early Christian convert and a keen evangelist. Educated at St Bartholemew's school, Wasasa, Zaria over 1939-49. He gained his school certificate at the government college, Zaria, in 1953.

Officer training Teshie in Ghana, Eaton Hall, then Sandhurst 1955-56. Young officers' course, Hythe and Warminster, returning to Nigeria as a Second Lieutenant. He served on the Cameroon border, the first Nigerian to be appointed adjutant of his battalion, in November 1960.

Served with Nigeria's peace-keeping mission in the Congo 1961-62. Promoted Lt-Colonel June 1963. He was out of the country during the January 1966 coup and returned to be appointed Chief-of-Staff to the Nigerian army by Gen Aguiyi-Ironsi.

Not involved in the second military coup of 29 July (momentarily taken prisoner by the rebels) he was chosen as leader by the northern officers, being one of the most senior army officers and coming from the Middle Belt which provided most of the rank-and-file of the Nigerian army.

Young and inexperienced, he had a burning desire to preserve Nigerian unity. His first priority was to restore army discipline and allay civilian fears. But almost exactly two months after he took over came the violent massacre of the Ibos in the north in October 1966, causing them to flee home and starting the inexorable movement towards the secession of Biafra.

He met Colonel Odumegwu Ojukwu, the Ibo leader, at Aburi in Ghana on 4 January 1967 and made some concessions towards confederalism, but no final agreement was reached and he spent the next seven months trying to persuade Ojukwu to drop his secessionist ideas. He failed. Biafra declared secession. He immediately declared an emergency and divided the country into 12 states, abolishing the old regions.

This master stroke united the rest of the country, removing fear of northern domination in the West, while giving the eastern minorities the hope of freeing themselves from Ibo rule. But it made war inevitable.

Hostilities did not start before July when Gowon called for a "police action" to end secession. The war was to last for two-and-a-half years. Gowon issued a "code of conduct" to his troops and insisted that Biafran civilians were to be treated as Nigerians who had to be won back to the Federation. Throughout the war he was a moderate, not believing in the quick kill. He turned a blind eye to the illegal night-flying of relief supplies into Biafra for over 15 months.

The Biafran collapse came in the first few days of 1970. He kept his word and prevented a bloodbath. Despite serious clashes with relief organisations over methods, he allowed mercy missions to proceed and starvation and disease were reversed in eastern Nigeria within a year.

On 1 October 1970, Nigeria's tenth independence anniversary, he explained why he thought it necessary to extend military rule to 1976. Meanwhile, he said, there would be new elections, a population census and a new constitution.

He entrusted much of the country's civil reconstruction to a new generation of younger civil servants. He then made a big mistake, in a country that was eagerly awaiting the return to civilian rule. With economic problems multiplying, he announced that he was postponing the process indefinitely.

He turned his attention to international affairs, presiding over the final agreements establishing ECOWAS, the Economic Community of West African States. Then on 27 July 1975 he left Lagos to attend the OAU Heads of State conference in Kampala. On 29 July his government was overthrown by a coup led by Murtala Muhammed. He acknowledged the coup had happened and said "I on my part have accepted the change and pledge my full loyalty to the nation, to my country and to the government." But though he was told that he was free to return home, he did not trust the promises and went to Britain to take a course in political studies at Warwick University. The military junta stripped him of his rank as General.

Later, after the assassination of his successor Muhammed, he was accused of involvement and the Nigerian government tried unsuccessfully to have him extradited from Britain. He said, "I give my word as an officer and a gentleman. I was not a plotter. I have done my nine-year stint."

When President Shagari came to power he exonerated Gowon and gave him the opportunity to return home. Presidential amnesty came on

11 October 1981 when Shagari said he was "free to visit or return to Nigeria should he so wish."

He did not finally return until after the elections for a civilian government in October 1983, but he had only been back home for a matter of weeks before the coup by Major-General Muhammed Buhari sent him back to Britain. In October 1987 his rank as a General in the Nigerian army was restored to him by the Babangida government. He then felt free to return to his country.

IBRAHIM, Waziri (Alhaji)
Nigerian politician and businessman.

A man who combines political ambition with a sense of humour and fun. A brilliant self-publicist, he has never been afraid of attracting attention by publicity stunts and unorthodox activities. Twice he ran for President, in 1979 attracting 1.6 million votes, though he came last of the five candidates. Afterwards he challenged President Shagari's victory in the courts. He built up a considerable following in his heartland of Borno and Gongola states but found that it was both politically and financially costly to sustain his Greater Nigerian People's Party (GNPP) through the vicissitudes of Nigerian politics.

Born 26 February 1926 in Yerwa, Borno state. Educated at Damaturu Elementary School, Maiduguri Middle School and Kaduna College (1944-47). He took up business as a haberdasher. He joined the United Africa Company of Nigeria in 1948, rising to become the Kaduna district manager in 1959. Before independence, in October 1960, he went into politics, won a seat in the Federal House of Representatives and was appointed Federal Minister for Health in 1959. This appointment was confirmed by Prime Minister Alhaji Tafawa Balewa who moved him to become Minister for Economic Development in 1961-66, when the civilian regime was overturned in a military coup.

He then left politics, went back into private business as chairman of the Herwa group of companies and as a contractor. He began to build a large fortune. When the Olusegun Obasanjo regime began to make preparations to hand Nigeria back again to democratic rule, in 1979, he was refreshed and ready to participate.

He formed the Nigerian People's Party, later the Greater Nigeria People's Party, from various liberal, anti-fundamentalist groupings supporting free enterprise and a mixed economy which had operated surreptitiously as private clubs before the ban on politics was lifted. Waziri's flare for publicity attracted many groups on the fringes of the establishment including small businessmen, students and youth from the north. The party split on 17 November 1978 and Waziri immediately launched his GNPP.

In the elections of July and August 1979, Waziri came last of the five Presidential Candidates receiving only 10% of the votes, though he did particularly well in his heartland, winning assembly seats and governorships, particularly in Borno and Gongola states.

In March 1982 he joined a coalition of four opposition parties called the Progressive People's Alliance to campaign against the Nigerian National Party government led by Shehu Shagari. But his own party had been considerably weakened by defections and personality clashes when he decided to contest the Presidential elections of August 1983. This time he came fifth out of the six candidates, winning only 2.5% of the votes cast and losing the governorships of Borno and Gongola. But these results soon proved to be of academic interest only, when the whole civilian regime was swept into oblivion by the military coup of 31 December 1983 by Muhammadu Buhari. All political parties were banned and Waziri went back to his business activities.

The military government banned all former politicians of previous regimes from taking part in politics for a period of ten years. Though Waziri fell into this category he continued to nurture his political ambitions and tried again to organise what he called the Brotherhood Club as a political vehicle. He even tried to recruit members to this club at the trial of Balarabe Musa, who was himself on trial for breaking the ban on politics. He took the government to court in December 1988 for trespassing on his GNPP offices and won his case. He was arrested and interrogated by security police in June 1989 but was released without action being taken against him.

IKIMI, Tom Omoghegbe

Nigerian architect. Chairman of the National Republican Convention, July 1990 -

A bright, young architect-designer who turned himself into a "new breed" politician of the 1990s as Chairman of the National Republican Convention, one of Nigeria's two authorised parties. An ambitious, hardworking, family man who believes in building a political base from the grassroots. He emerged as leader of his party against competition from many other favoured candidates. He believes in economic freedom where government pursues "hands off" policies. But he claims that he understands the plight of ordinary people, "I have worked for myself from scratch. So I know where the shoe pinches", he says.

Born 10 April 1944 at Igueben, in the Agbazilo local government area of Bendel state in mid-west Nigeria, the second child in a family of six. His father moved to set up business in Kumba, Cameroon during his childhood. He started education at St Joseph's College Sasse-Buea. A popular, enthusiastic schoolboy, he soon became a leader amongst his peers and academically successful.

In 1961 after a plebiscite, the northern part of southern Cameroons became Gongola state, a part of Nigeria. So he had already "returned home" before he resumed his studies at the Mid-West Polytechnic at Auchi, in 1961, where he gained a City of Guilds London Diploma in Civil

Engineering in 1967. He continued at Ahmadou Bello University taking a degree in architecture in 1973.

He went on to do a summer course at the Architectural Association School in England, then went to Ibadan in 1973 as a pioneering member of the newly formed National Youth Service Corps. He then became an associate partner at the private firm of architects, Ibru, Vaughan-Richards in Lagos, where he rose to become associate partner. In 1977 he set up his own design company, Tom Ikimi Associates, which soon became involved in major projects, hospitals and office blocks. His business was successful and prospered. He told a reporter, "It is true that I have made what could be called money ... Not much, but I am reasonably comfortable."

His early political idols were elder statesmen like Dr Nnamdi Azikiwe, Chief Obafemi Awolowo and Aminu Kano, but he was of a new breed and a bridge-builder in the non-ethnic politics introduced by President Babangida. In May 1988 he became a member of the Constituent Assembly which fashioned a new constitution for Nigeria's Third Republic.

When the new political parties were allowed to organise themselves he became a founding member of the Liberal Convention, rapidly rising to national vice-president. None of the parties met government criteria and all were disqualified and not allowed to register in October 1989. Instead President Babangida imposed two government appointed parties. Ikimi was quick to appreciate his opportunity and joined the National Republican Convention. It was the party conceived by Babangida as being "a little to the right" though it had to draw its support from all regions and ethnic groups.

He had to win the confidence of a bunch of new politicians who had little previous political experience. His charm, drive and organisational abilities, paid dividends. At the NRC convention at Abuja in July 1990, he polled 1,782 votes, three times more than his nearest challenger and was elected national chairman of the party. In the local elections of December 1990 the NRC was narrowly defeated in the elections for the chairmen and councillors in local councils.

JAKANDE, Lateef Kayode (Alhaji)
Nigerian journalist and politician.

A journalist who rose to the top of his profession. He later turned politician and played a major part in Yoruba politics, first in the Action Group, then in the United Party of Nigeria. Twice arrested and detained for clashing with the Federal establishment but always popular in the capital city, where he became the governor. He earned the nickname "action man" for his hard work and concern for Lagos state.

Born 23 July 1929 in Lagos. Educated at Banham Memorial Methodist School, Port Harcourt, Ilesha Grammar School and King's College, Lagos.

He entered journalism as a reporter for the *Daily Service* (1949-52). He rose to become acting editor, then joined the *Nigerian Tribune* as editor in 1953, becoming managing editor in 1954. His career in journalism and publishing then took off as editor-in-chief of Amalgamated Press of Nigeria and managing director of Allied Newspapers in 1960. Then managing director of Amalgamated Newspapers, chairman of the Lagoon Book and Stationery company and chairman of John West Publications.

He also played a major part in the organisation and growth of the Nigerian press in general, as chairman of the Nigerian Institute of Journalism, president of the International Press Institute, patron of the Nigerian Institute of Journalists in Lagos state and the Nigerian Guild of Editors.

He was also a major force in the Action Group Party. In 1963 he was tried and jailed with Chief Awolowo for treasonable felony after the discovery of a clumsily organised plot against the Federal leadership. His experiences in this crisis gave him first-hand material for his book – *The trial of Obafemi Awolowo*. He was pardoned and released in August 1966. He took up politics again with the return to civilian rule in 1979, as a member of the United Party of Nigeria and triumphed in the elections to the governorship of Lagos state.

He won a sweeping victory, securing 91% of the vote in the cosmopolitan capital city, in the elections of August 1983. This was a tribute to his hard work and popularity in Lagos, but with the military coup on New Year's Eve 1984 he was arrested and detained while the finances of Lagos state were investigated. He was never charged but kept in detention until released by General Babangida after he took power in August 1985.

KINGIBE, Baba Gana

Nigerian diplomat and politician. Chairman Social Democratic Party, July 1990 -

High-flying ambassador and civil servant. A self-made man from a humble background, who emerged as one of the new breed of politicans chairing the Social Democratic Party as Nigeria prepared for civilian rule. A true northener from Borno and from a conservative background, his choice as leader of the SDP was somewhat surprising, but it belied his radical upbringing and naturally progressive outlook. He has tried to fashion the SDP as the people's party, "We have no money, our assets are the people, the poor and the masses," he says.

Born 26 June 1945 in a poor northern family of four. He became an orphan early in life and lived with a guardian, Mallam Baba Birkila, a bricklayer in Maiduguri. Birkila a militant in the Native Authority Works Department was a profound influence on him.

Though he was not particularly keen on having a western education, in 1952 he walked to the nearest school and demanded that he be enrolled. In primary schools in Maiduguri and nearby Bama, his education was an immediate success.

In 1958 he was admitted to Borno Provincial Secondary School and in September 1960 won a Native Authority Scholarship to Bishop Stortford public school in Britain, where he studied history and English. He gained a scholarship to read history at Cambridge, but to the surprise of his teachers decided instead to study international relations at the University of Sussex.

His brilliant academic career continued with a doctorate programme in international studies in Switzerland. There Professor Ishaya Audu, the Vice-Chancellor of Ahmadou Bello University persuaded him to return home and work as a research and planning officer, he also lectured on international relations (1969-71).

He then joined the Broadcasting Corporation of Northern Nigeria as head of features and current affairs, sometimes doubling as a newscaster and writer of commentaries.

Though he grew up in the tradition of the Northern People's Congress, he later became one of the intellectuals behind the National Party of Nigeria when it was in power in the late 1970s.

Meanwhile he took a job in the foreign service in 1972, at the Ministry of External Affairs, Lagos. He was posted to Britain and rose fast to become senior counsellor and head of the political desk at the Nigerian High Commission in London. He returned under President Olusegun Obasanjo and worked on the programme that was to return Nigeria to civilian rule in 1979.

In 1981, under the second republic, he was appointed Nigeria's first ambassador to Greece and High Commissioner for Cyprus. Later he was posted to Pakistan by General Muhammadu Buhari's government.

In 1986 he was recalled and appointed a permanent secretary in President Babangida's office. He was then appointed director- general and secretary of the Constituent Assembly set up in May 1988, to prepare for the return to civilian rule.

When political parties were allowed to campaign again under the dispensation of President Babangida, he became the director of organisation of the People's Front of Nigeria (PFN). But this party, along with all others, failed to meet government requirements and Babangida established two government appointed parties instead.

He showed himself politically flexible and threw himself into the organisation of the new Social Democratic Party, which appealed to his instincts as the more left-wing of the two authorised parties. With the support of his PFN colleagues, he was soon in a position to contest the chairmanship of the party, but he was up against an older and respected challenger in Alhaji Mohammed Arzika and was not expected to overcome his countrymen's natural respect for age. But in the upshot, at the SDP Congress in Abuja, at the end of July 1990, he was to prove the pundits wrong and swept the poll, to become national chairman.

In the elections for the local councils in December 1990, the SDP won most chairmanships and council places, indicating that Kingibe was creating the right image for the party among ordinary Nigerians.

MONGUNO, Shettima Ali (Alhaji)

Nigerian educationist and politician.

A modest and cultivated Muslim teacher, educationist and educational reformer in his native Bornu state. More interested in public service and performance than the intrigues of party politics, but he served as a minister under both civilian and military regimes. He became a regular leader of Nigerian delegations to international conferences, before returning to his educational origins at the highest level as pro-chancellor, first of Calabar University then of the University of Nigeria.

Born 1926 in Monguno province, Bornu state in a poor peasant's family. After Bornu Middle School (1939-44) he trained at Bauchi Teacher Training College (1944-46) and the Higher Teacher's College, Katsina (1949-51). He taught at Bornu Middle and other schools between times, going to Moray House College of Education, Edinburgh (1958-59) to take a certificate in social anthropology.

On his return home he became the first Native Authority Education Secretary in Northern Nigeria where he introduced the English language as a first year subject in primary schools and a co-educational programme in 1961. He also promoted women's education, upgrading local girls schools. In the same year he became councillor for education in the Bornu Native Authority and was given the title "Shettima", meaning learned scholar. He continued in the Authority, holding other portfolios including Works, Rural Development and Social Welfare.

Meanwhile, in 1959, he became a Northern People's Congress member of the Federal Assembly for the Kaga-Marghi constituency, to the Federal Assembly. He was given his first ministry as Minister of State in charge of the Nigerian Air force in April 1965. In the same year he was promoted Minister of Internal Affairs and a full member of the Federal cabinet, until the military coup of January 1966.

He was one of the ministers of the old regime with a clean record but it still came as something of a surprise when he was the only pre-coup cabinet minister to be chosen by General Gowon as commissioner in 1967. He took on Industry in June 1967, with Trade added to his portfolio in September.

During the war he travelled widely to keep trade flowing and signed numerous trade agreements for the government. He was also regularly a member of Nigerian delegations to the UN and other international conferences. He became Commissioner for Trade and Industry in October 1971 and for Mines and Power (1971-75).

In November 1972 he was elected president of the Organisation of Petroleum Exporting Countries (OPEC) and was re-elected in March 1973. After Gen Murtala Muhammed took over from General Gowon in the coup of July 1975, he returned to Bornu Local Authority to become Counsellor for Natural Resources and Co-operatives (1975-76). He was a member of the Constituent Assembly that drew up the new constitution for the return to civilian rule in August 1979. But he did not continue in politics in the new civilian regime; instead he became pro-chancellor of the University of Nigeria in 1980. Earlier he had been pro-chancellor of the University of Calabar (1976-80).

OBASANJO, Olusegun (General)

Nigerian Head of State 13 February 1976 – 1 October 1979.

An extremely talented soldier who rose fast in the army on the solid base provided by the Engineering Corps. He had a distinguished record in the Biafran war and shortly afterwards was appointed Chief of Staff of the army. On the assassination of Murtala Muhammed, he found himself the senior military officer and somewhat reluctantly took over the responsibilities as Head of State of Africa's most populous nation. He followed the policy already established by Muhammed of returning the country to civilian rule by October 1979. He achieved this objective and quietly stepped down, also retiring from the army, though remaining one of his country's most senior statesmen in international fora.

Born 5 May 1937 at Abeokuta, Ogun State, in a Yoruba family. Educated at the Baptist High School, Abeokuta. Joined the army 1958, posted to the 5th Battalion Kaduna. Officer training at Mons, Aldershot. Commissioned April 1959. Promoted lieutenant in 1960 and served with the UN force in the Congo. Later joined the engineering unit of the Nigerian army. Promoted captain April 1963 and became its commander.

He did further training on the young officers course at Shrivenham, where he won a citation as the best Commonwealth student ever. Promoted major in January 1965 and became Commander of the Field Engineering Unit. Did a further course at the Indian Staff College and served an attachment to the Indian Army Engineering School, Kirkee. Promoted lieutenant-colonel 1967. Commander of the Ibadan Garrison October 1967–May 1969. Promoted Colonel. Commander of the 3rd Infantry Division, then the 3rd Marine Commando Division operating on the south-east front of Biafra during the Nigerian civil war. Accepted the surrender of the Biafran forces in January 1970.

After the war he resumed the command of the Engineering Corps. Promoted Brigadier October 1972. Further training at the Royal College of Defence Studies, London (1973-74). Appointed Federal Commissioner for Works by Gen Gowon from January to July 1975. Chief of Staff, Supreme Headquarters, 29 July 1975 to 13 February 1976. Promoted lieutenant-general January 1976.

On 13 February 1976, after the assassination of Murtala Muhammed, he took over, somewhat reluctantly, as Head of State as he was the most senior military officer. He continued the same policies and faced the same problems as Muhammed. His task was to return the country to civilian rule by 1979 and to use the burgeoning oil wealth to the best effect. Obasanjo stuck by the timetable and set up a Constituent Assembly to prepare a draft constitution which duly reported in 1978. He also set about rationalising Nigeria's diffuse trade union system by integrating former trade union federations into a single Nigeria Labour Congress, and reducing the number of individual unions from several hundred to 42.

Obasanjo clashed with the Muslims over the the attempt to extend the scope of the Sharia law under the new constitution. He also suffered a loss of popularity as the politicians became impatient for the return to civilian rule and as the army grumbled about the reduction in the size of the armed forces. Oil prices also declined, leading to unpopular budgetary cuts. But he did lift the state of emergency in September 1978 and allowed politicians to get the electoral bandwagon rolling. Obasanjo formally handed over to the new civilian government under Shehu Shagari on 1 October 1979 after 13 years of military government. Shagari said at a farewell dinner that it was "rare in the history of developing countries for those in power to organise their own retirement from government and welcome, indeed entertain, their successors."

Afterwards he retired from the army, returned to his farm at Abeokuta and took up academic work at the University of Ibadan. He made no attempt to interfere in the Nigerian political system. One of his major roles since relinquishing power was to chair the seven-man Commonwealth Eminent Persons Group in 1986, which attempted to promote a dialogue leading to constitutional reform in South Africa. Though this initiative failed, Obasanjo was afterwards short-listed for a number of top-ranking international positions.

In February 1989 he published a book, *Constitution for National Integration and Development,* in which he called for a one party system of government and a unicameral legislature. He said that he was not advocating a classical one-party system, but a duality of political administration with sufficient checks and balances to prevent the usual abuses of a one-party system. This was a radical departure from the constitutional system he established in 1979. On 1 August 1989 he became a special adviser to the International Institute for Tropical Agriculture, based at Ibadan, Nigeria.

On 23 August 1990 he won the Africa Prize for Leadership for the Sustainable End of Hunger. He was elected for championing African agriculture and also honoured for founding the Africa Leadership Forum in 1988 to help develop future leaders in Africa. In 1990 he launched his magazine *Africa Forum.* This was part of an explicit campaign to challenge for the secretary generalship of the United Nations which was due to become vacant in 1991.

OJUKWU, Chukwuemeka Odumegwu

Nigerian politician and businessmen. Leader of Biafra 30 May 1967 – 12 January 1970.

A man of charisma, charm and determination from a rich family with a liberal education abroad. A good soldier, diplomat and establishment figure, he found himself swept up in the tide of Igbo secessionism that led to the Nigerian civil war. Voluble, didactic and something of an actor, supremely confident of his own intellectual ability, he established himself as a tough leader who brooked no opposition as he fought three years of civil war. Yet within a decade he was pardoned, welcomed back to his country and had established himself in a powerful position politically. Though he was later forced out of politics along with most other leading Nigerian politicians, he had already demonstrated his power to achieve a remarkable political comeback.

Born 4 November 1933 at Zungeru in Northern Nigeria, son of a self-made transport millionaire, Sir Louis Odumegwu Ojukwu. Educated in Lagos, finishing at King's College, Nigeria's "Eton", before going abroad to Epsom College, Surrey and Lincoln, Oxford, to study history.

In 1955 he returned to Eastern Nigeria and became an administrative officer before joining the army in 1957. He did two years of officer training at Eaton Hall, Chester, and returned to join the 5th Battalion in 1958. Promoted to major 1961. Served with the Nigerian police force in the Congo (Zaire) and followed with a course at the Joint Services Staff College in Britain in 1962. Promoted to lieutenant-colonel in January 1963, a few months ahead of General Gowon.

In command of the 5th Battalion in Kano, he led the loyalists in the north in the January 1966 coup and was rewarded by being promoted by General Ironsi to Military Governor of the Eastern Region. In the second coup of 28 July 1966, he managed to keep control of his own region and accepted Gowon's de facto leadership though considering him to be junior in rank.

A violent massacre of the Igbos in the north took place in October, sending the remainder back to their homeland. Ojukwu persuaded Gowon to remove northern soldiers from the East and began training and arming his own men though he was still not a convinced secessionist.

He met Gowon at Aburi in Ghana in a last attempt to prevent secession. He came well prepared and tape recorded all talks and gained some concessions towards confederalism. But later the Federal government had second thoughts and Ojukwu said that they had broken their promises.

Gowon made further concessions, but the Igbo elite was hell-bent on secession and Ojukwu was swept along as leader of the movement. On 29 May 1967 he formally declared secession. A month later the Federal troops invaded. The Biafrans counter-attacked in August, taking the Mid-West and advancing into the West, within 70 miles of Lagos.

The Igbo initiative ran out of steam and by October they were falling back across the Niger bridge with Calabar, Bonny and Enugu, the Biafran capital taken. From that point onwards, Biafra was encircled and gradually squeezed.

Ojukwu, committed to secession and fighting for his life, became increasingly ruthless and autocratic internally. At external peace conferences he played for time, while he raised world sympathy and waited for arms supplies. He made a marathon address to the OAU at Addis Ababa in August 1968.

He remained defiant as hunger mounted and morale slumped in Biafra. Despite a brief Biafran counter-attack in the autumn of 1968, Nigerian superior fire-power began to tell. The Biafran collapse came with startling speed in the first ten days of 1970.

On 8 January Ojukwu held an emergency meeting of his cabinet, told them to face the facts and said he would leave to give them a chance to sue for peace.

At 2am on Sunday 11 January, he scrambled aboard a Super Constellation and was taken to the Ivory Coast where he remained in exile living on Houphouët Boigny's private estate at Yamoussoukro.

President Shagari granted him an official pardon in May 1982 in the much more relaxed atmosphere of civilian government, over ten years after the Biafran episode. Most of his lieutenants had already been pardoned and re-established themselves at home. On 20 June he made a triumphant return home after over 13 years in exile to be greeted by an enthusiastic crowd of compatriots.

In October he joined the ruling National Party of Nigeria in what appeared to be a pre-arranged move to rally the support of the Igbo people. He was elected national vice-chairman of the NPN in January 1983, because as he said, he believed in the "coming together of two formerly antagonistic groups." In the September elections he contested the Onitsha senate seat. It was a close election, bitterly contested at the polls and in the High Court. Ultimately he was declared to have lost.

But hardly had the local sensation died down, when the military intervened in the successful coup of New Year's Eve 1984, establishing the government of Maj-Gen. Muhammadu Buhari. Most of the old political leaders were detained, including Ojukwu. He was held in detention until October 1984. On his release he went into private business.

SHAGARI, Shehu (Alhaji)
Nigerian politician. President October 1979-December 1983.

A Fulani teacher with a gentle manner and diffident smile behind his gold rimmed glases, he was one of the first leaders to come out of Nigeria's north. A founder-member of the Northern People's Congress, he was closely associated with the first Prime Minister, Abubakar Tafawa Balewa. Twice forced out of power by military coups, he quietly went back to his farm. But behind the shy exterior was a consummate politician, a man trusted for his sincerity who made an ideal presidential candidate for the Nigerian National Party. He became President in 1979, at a time of great political tension and economic crisis. He found it difficult to hold together the divisive political forces in the face of a looming economic crisis. Though his regime collapsed in an orgy of recrimination and accusations of corruption, he remained personally untainted and still liked and respected by the majority of his people.

Born May 1925 in Shagari where his father was a village headman. His great-grandfather had founded the village and had taken its name for his family. Educated at Yabo elementary, Sokoto Middle School and Kaduna College 1941-44. After teacher training at Zaria (1944-45), he became a science master in Sokoto Middle School (1945-50), and the headmaster at Argungu School (1951-54). After further teacher training courses in Bauchi and Britain he became senior visiting teacher in Sokoto province.

He and a few others founded a cultural organisation in 1949 which eventually became the Northern People's Congress in 1951. In 1954 he stood in the Sokoto West constituency and was returned unopposed.

In 1958 he was made the Parliamentary Secretary to the Prime Minister, Sir Abubakar Tafawa Balewa, who encouraged him in his political career and made him Minister for Economic Development in 1960 for a brief spell before shuffling him to Federal Minister of Establishments (1961-62). He continued to hold successive ministerial appointments throughout the Balewa cabinet until the military coup of January 1966. By then he was the fourth most senior member of the Balewa cabinet.

He escaped being killed during the coup and was in the cabinet which handed over power to General Ironsi. Then he retired to farm at Shagari. He soon returned to public life as secretary of the Sokoto Province Education Development Fund. He joined the North-Western State, becoming Commissioner for Establishments in August 1968 and Commissioner for Education in 1969.

General Gowon noted his quiet professionalism and brought him back to Lagos as Federal Commissioner for Economic Development, shuffling him to take over the important finance portfolio from Chief Awolowo on 10 October 1971, a post he held until Gowon was overthrown in July 1975. He again retired to his farm.

But he was elected to the Constitutent Assembly, the body that was to draw up the new Nigerian constitution, and he became a founder-member of the most influential nationwide party, the National Party of Nigeria. The NPN nominated him, as a politician of experience and a man with few enemies, to represent them in the 1979 elections. He triumphed in a hard fought, five-man presidential race in which he secured 5.7 million votes to 4.9m for Chief Awolowo, his nearest rival. On 1 October 1979 military rule ended and he was sworn in as executive president of the second republic.

He found himself confronted with a complex American-style

constitutional system with a National Assembly and Senate acting as severe brakes to his executive power. There were also conflicts between the Federal and the 19 state governments and five political parties, with the NPN never in outright majority in the National Assembly, Senate or in many of the states themselves.

He saw his principal task was to preserve democracy by sticking to the letter and the spirit of the law even if the process was cumbersome, slow and painful. On the economic front he pursued a mixed and liberal economy and allowed the Nigerian love of private initiative and enterprise to flourish. He tried to ensure that the state held the commanding heights of the economy, and embarked on a heavy spending programme, but the massive influx of oil revenue and expansion of wealth led to severe mismanagement and corruption. The bubble finally burst in April 1982 with the federal budget over-extended and a slump in world oil prices producing a foreign exchange crisis and financial panic.

The mass of Nigerians were jolted from an era of expansion and hope to one of retraction and hardship. Politics became more vicious. Shagari put the popularity to the test in the elections of August-September 1983. The NPN machine worked superbly and he was returned with a larger majority over Awolowo than in 1979. The NPN also secured on overall majority in the house and 13 out of the 19 state governorships. Shagari was sworn in as President for a second term on 1 October 1983. But the opposition complained bitterly of corruption, ballot-rigging, and over-expenditure on election campaigns. Shagari was also faced with a massive economic crisis. He introduced a new cabinet in November and a budget in December where he attempted to minimise the looming economic crisis.

This situation gave the soldiers the excuse to intervene, which they did on New Year's Eve 1984, returning Nigeria to military rule. Shagari was detained on 31 December 1983, along with many other civilian leaders. He was held under house arrest. But he was never considered to have enriched himself while in office and was never brought to trial by any of the special tribunals that were set up to try corruption. However, he was held throughout the whole of the Muhammadu Buhari regime and under President Babangida until 3 July 1986. He was freed from detention and was banned for life from holding public office or engaging in political activity.

SULE, Yusuf Maitama (Alhaji)
Nigerian diplomat and politician.

A quiet teacher, turned politician and diplomat. He has served his country through most regimes since independence as minister, public complaints commissioner and permanent representative to the United Nations. He was often chosen to lead Nigerian delegations to a number of important international gatherings. But he has been quite content to return to his home in Kano when the wheel of politics has turned against him in Lagos.

Born 1929 in Kano. Educated Shahuri Elementary School, Kano Middle School (1940-42), Kaduna College (1942-46), before doing a special teacher training course at Zaria in 1947.

He taught in secondary schools from 1948-55, when he became a visiting teacher. He left to become chief information officer of Kano Native Authority, 1955-56. His interest in politics started early with the Northern People's Congress. In 1954 he stood for Federal parliament, won a seat and became the NPC chief whip. At the time of independence, he was appointed Federal Minister for Mines and Power (1959-66) under Nigeria's first Prime Minister, Abubakar Tafawa Balewa. He led the Nigerian delegation to the conference of independent African states in Addis Ababa in 1960 and proposed the resolution that was to lead three years later to the formation of the Organisation of African Unity.

When the military coup occurred in 1966 he left the soldiers to rule from Lagos and returned to the tranquillity of Kano as State Commissioner for Local Goverment, Forestry and Community Development, 1967-74. After the coup by Murtala Muhammed in July 1975, he was appointed to the novel post of Chief Public Complaints Commissioner, 1975-78.

In 1981, with Nigeria again under civilian rule, President Shehu Shagari appointed him as Nigeria's Permanent Representative to the United Nations. There he became chairman of the UN Committee on Apartheid in 1981, an appointment that was renewed in 1982. When the NPN won power after the elections of October 1983, President Shagari formed a new cabinet and appointed Sule Minister of National Guidance but almost immediately came the military coup by Muhammadu Buhari of 1 January 1984. Sule was detained briefly along with many top NPN ministers, but was released on 1 October 1984.

SUNMONU, Hassan

Nigerian trades union leader. Secretary General of the Organisation of African Trade Union Unity (OATUU) 26 October 1986 –

A self made man whose enthusiasm for trade unions took him fast to the top of his profession. After barely ten years in active trade unionism he became president of the Nigerian Labour Congress, the coordinating body for all Nigeria's unions. He showed his maturity by endorsing government plans to reduce and rationalise the number of unions and introduce training and professionalism at all levels.

Born 7 January 1941 at Akim Eshiem, in the former Gold Coast (Ghana) into a devout Nigerian Muslim family. He and his brother Hussein went back with their parents to their home town of Oshogbo, Western Nigeria when he was six. There he got his early education, 1948-55. He went to the first college of technology at Yaba, Lagos and graduated in 1967 with a diploma in civil engineering.

While still a student he became secretary of the Yaba Technical Institute branch of the Muslim Students Society. Later he became president of the Yaba College Students Union and vice president of the banned National Union of Nigerian Students.

After a brief interlude with the Ministry of Works he went back to college in 1965, then returned to the ministry where he was elected secretary of the Association of Technical Officers. This brought him into full time trades unionism for the first time with the brief to draw up a memorandum detailing the grievances of all his fellow officers. His report was ignored so he got his union affiliated to the Public Works, Aerodrome, Technical and General Workers Union, the umbrella organisation of most technical unions, led by the veteran unionist Wahab Goodluck. He became Goodluck's assistant and then President of the union in 1967.

By 1976 the military government wanted to restructure the 1,000 plus unions into 42 authorised bodies. The PWATGWU became the Civil Service Technical Workers' Union of Nigeria with Sunmonu as the founding president. A few months later he was elected the founding president of the central labour organisation, the Nigerian Labour Congress.

"We brought respectability to trade unionism in the country. The colonial mentality of people in high places was that trades unionists were a pack of never-do-wells and drop outs, who for lack of anything to do, became agitators".

"The table-banging trade unionism stopped with the new NLC in place. Our first plan was to get the NLC firmly established in all the then 19 states of Nigeria...the military government provided legal recognition and gave us a one million naira take-off subvention. We were able to recruit brilliant university graduates".

Under Sunmonu the unions gained a minimum wage for the first time in the history of Nigeria and an annual holiday to celebrate May day and effective training through seminars.

He resisted attempts by the government of President Shehu Shagari to dismember the NLC and weaken the unions generally. For the first ten years, when his attention was concentrated on building and educating the new union membership, he kept out of politics. But when the system was liberalised under President Babangida he took a leading part in organising a worker's party, but this was refused registration along with all the other parties when the government created two parties of its own.

On 26 October 1986, after a bitterly fought contest, he was elected secretary general of the Organisation of African Trade Union Unity (OATUU) in Addis Ababa, a coordinating body for all Africa's unions.

YAR'ADUA, Shehu Musa (Major General)
Nigerian politician, military officer.

Shehu Yar'adua is a northerner who reached the peak of power following the coup against the Gowon government in July 1975 and after the murder of Murtala Muhammed in February 1976, when he emerged as number two in the regime. A radical northerner, very close to Muhammed, he once surprised his listeners by claiming that Lagos port congestion, during the Nigerian oil boom, was due to a "sinister conspiracy of capitalist saboteurs." He put in a determined challenge to make a political come-back in the run-up to the third republic though he was among the politicians banned from political activity by the Babangida government.

Born 5 March 1943, in Katsina, Kaduna state. Educated at the Government Secondary School, Katsina, and the Nigerian Military Training College, Zaria, before going to Sandhurst and the Command and Staff College in Britain.

He returned to be a platoon commander (1964-65), battalion adjutant (1965-67) and commander of the Second Division (1967). He was given command of the 6th Infantry Brigade in the Second Infantry Division during the Biafran war in 1968 and became commander of the 9th infantry brigade at Warri from 1969-72. He took a leading part in the coup against General Gowon that brought General Murtala Muhammed to power on 29 July 1975 and became a member of the Supreme Military Council and the Commissioner for Transport. After the attempted coup on 13 February 1976 when Muhammed was killed, he became the number two in the government of Olusegun Obasanjo as Chief of Staff at the Supreme Headquarters and Vice-President of the Supreme Military Council, a quasi political role where he was chief government spokesman. He was an intended victim in the attempted coup and took part in the investigations as to its motives, trying publicly to lay some of the blame on General Gowon. He said the government was taking legal and diplomatic steps to repatriate Gowon to face trial in Nigeria.

In August 1976 he introduced new measures to reform local government and in October 1976, the new draft constitution, drawn up by the Constitutional Drafting Committee, that was to set the scene for the return to civilian rule. In December he announced the launch of a Southern Africa Relief Fund to provide welfare and assistance to South African refugees. At the London Commonwealth conference in June 1977 he defended Idi Amin's right to attend the conference.

In October 1979, when the government handed over power to the civilians under Shehu Shagari, he retired and took up private business, but he continued to nurture political ambitions. In the run-up to the Third Republic, at the end of the Ibrahim Babangida regime, he wanted to participate but fell under the ban on former public office holders. But this did not deter him. During 1988 he formed an association and travelled the country promoting it. It gave birth to the People's Front for Nigeria which was officially launched on 6 May 1989.

RWANDA

Population: 7.1m (1990, World Bank)
Independence: 1 July 1962
Head of State: Major-General Juvenal Habyarimana
Government: On 10 June 1991 Rwanda officially became a multi-party country with the promulgation of a new constitution. The powers of the President and a new Prime Minister were divided. Opposition parties were allowed to organise and compete.
Parties: Former single party - *Mouvement Revolutionnaire National pour le Developpement* (MRND). A number of opposition parties emerged in mid-1991.

BIZIMUNGU, Casimir

Rwanda politician. Foreign minister, 15 January 1989 –

Generally known as one of the main leaders of the northern "Ruhengeri clan" in opposition to the group led by the President's wife Agathe Kazinga and most of the top army chiefs. He is however supported by a number of ministerial colleagues and President Habyarimana needed his support as one of the principal northern leaders. Hence his sudden appointment in January 1989 as Minister of Foreign Affairs.

Born 4 March 1951 at Gicuba, Nyamugali Commune, Ruhengeri, Rwanda. Educated locally. Read humanities at the National University until 1974. He then took up medical studies, gaining a doctorate in March 1978. He took a masters degree in public health at the University of Illinois, Chicago in 1981, taking a doctorate in 1984.

His interest in political activity started early when he was a student at Rwanda University. He rose to become President of the students association 1973-74. After completing the first part of his studies he became a Professor of public health at the National Pedagogic Institute, 1978-80 and Director of the University Centre for Public Health at the University of Rwanda, 1984-87. He was also appointed President of the National Population Bureau, February 1985–April 1987.

As the leading national expert on public health, he attended innumerable international conferences throughout the world in the 1980s. Clearly his international activities were appreciated by President Juvenal Habyarimana, who suddenly on 15 January 1989, appointed him to his first ministerial post. He was given the senior position of Minister of Foreign Affairs and International Co-operation in place of the long serving Francois Ngarukiyintwali. Almost immediately he attended the Council of Ministers of the Organisation of African Unity in February 1989.

He played a major part in drawing world attention to the invasion of

Rwanda by the guerrillas of the Rwandan Patriotic Front which started in October 1990.

HABYARIMANA, Juvenal (General)
Rwandan politician. President 5 July 1973 –

A charismatic young officer, who became defence minister at the age of 28 and president at 36. From one of the ruling, landowning families from northern Rwanda, he had his early experience in the tough school of bloody inter-tribal conflict in the 1960s. His seizure of power in a bloodless coup in 1973 was a reflection mainly of disgruntlement among the northern Hutu officers, like himself, who were in conflict with the former President's men from the centre. Since then he has entrenched his position, gradually giving more power to civilians and technocrats, while still maintaining firm personal control. He has introduced a single party and has increased the powers of the president. He leans neither to the left or the right. His main problems have been with the Tutsi ethnic minority, Rwanda's burgeoning population, relations with his neighbours in Burundi, Uganda, Zaire, and economic deterioration. There has been little internal opposition and few coup attempts, revealing his close grip on the system he created.

Born 8 March 1937 at Gaziza, in Karago commune, Gisenyi prefecture. Educated locally. He went on to study humanities and mathematics at the college of St Paul, Bukavu, Zaire, before doing one year at the medical school of Lovanium, Zaire. He then quit to become a soldier, joining the Officer's School at Kigali on 11 December 1960. He also trained as a parachutist. He completed his courses with distinction and became one of the first officers in the National Guard, with the rank of second lieutenant in December 1961.

He became Chief of Staff in the National Guard in January 1963 and commander from July 1963. It was at this stage, while still only a major, that he was spotted by President Gregoire Kayibanda and made Minister for the Armed Forces and the Police (1965-73). He was promoted to Major-General on 1 April 1973.

Tribal tensions, disturbances in various parts of the country and discontent among northern Hutu officers prompted Habyarimana to seize power in a bloodless coup on 5 July 1973. He put Kayibanda under house arrest but said that he remained a person "for whom we have great esteem." He banned all political activity, deposed the government and established a Committee for Peace and National Unity in control of northern officers but ruling through a largely civilian cabinet.

He adopted a policy of national reconciliation between Bahutu and Batutsi. On 5 July 1975, on the occasion of the second anniversary of the creation of the second republic, he announced the formation of the National Revolutionary Movement for Development, MRND in which every Rwandan became an automatic member at birth. The next step towards democratisation took effect with the constituion of 20 December 1978, which confirmed Habyarimana as President. The elections of 28 December 1981 returned the first elected legislature (National Development Council) under the single party system. As the only candidate he was re-elected on 19 December 1983. He remained President of the Council of Ministers and Minister of Defence.

At the fifth party congress in December 1985 he again reorganised the party and announced the creation of a school of ideology and salaries for some officials. He was re-elected President for the third time on 19 December 1988.

The combined effects of population pressure, soil erosion and the collapse of world coffee prices in 1989 caused Habyarimana to introduce an economic austerity programme, which added to popular discontent. He began to respond to pressure for political reform when he established a commission of national synthesis to produce a charter for the introduction of a multi-party system on 21 September 1990.

But bad news was compounded by the invasion of guerrillas from the Rwanda Popular Front in October 1990. They were beaten off with heavy loss of life in a campaign extending over several months. The invasion shook Habyarimana who tried to secure an internationally guaranteed peace agreement while pressing ahead with rapid political reform. The constitutional commission reported in April. Habyarimana, confident in his own electoral popularity, actively encouraged opposition parties, "Let them act with speed," he said, "so that we can have several parties by 2 June".

On 10 June 1991 Rwanda became a pluralist state when Habyarimana promulgated the legislation which provided for a Prime Minister and the division of responsibilities between his office and that of the President. The objective in his strategy was to get the Tutsi exiles (mainly responsible for the invasion) to return and compete in democratic elections instead.

SÃO TOMÉ and PRINCIPE

Population: 125,000 (1990, World Bank)
Independence: 12 July 1975
Head of State: Miguel Trovoada
Government: In the first multi-party elections since independence, on 20 January 1991, the opposition PCD defeated the ruling party (MLSTP-PSD). A new government was then formed by Daniel Lima dos Santos Diao. In the presidential elections in March, Miguel Trovoada then defeated Pinto da Costa. A democratic pluralist government was then established.
Parties: Majority party - *Partido de Convergencia Democratica* (PCD). Main opposition party (former ruling party) *Movimento de Libertação de São Tomé e Principe* (MLSTP).

DA COSTA, Manuel Pinto
Former President, 12 July 1975 – 3 April 1991.

Pragmatic and concilatory and yet the absolute ruler of his country for 16 years from independence in 1975 to 1991. He followed a non-ideological line claiming an undefined type of non-marxist socialism. In recent years he was compelled to move closer to the West and accept the strictures of the IMF in return for increased economic assistance. He was one of the first presidents in Africa to accept democratisation and put his presidency at risk in a general election. After his party was defeated, he stood down and did not contest the March 1991 presidential elections.

Born 1937 in Agua Grande. Educated locally and in East Germany where he studied economics. His political career started when he founded the Movement for the Liberation of São Tomé and Principe, MLSTP in 1972. It was set up in exile in Gabon to fight for Sao Tomé's independence from Portugal. He became the party Secretary General, but remained in Libreville, Gabon in the pre-independence period. After the downfall of Salazar in April 1974, demonstrations on the islands, plus continued pressure internationally finally persuaded the new Portuguese government to negotiate with the MLSTP. Da Costa led his delegation in talks in Libreville in September and to Algiers in November, when the final arrangements for independence were made. A transitional MLSTP government was founded on 21 December 1974.

He returned to São Tomé and was inaugurated as President on 12 July 1975, at a ceremony witnessed by the Portuguese and freedom movements from other countries in Portuguese Africa, but by only one head of an independent African state; President Bongo of Gabon who had given refuge to the MLSTP over the years. Da Costa immediately set up his first cabinet including the co-founder of the MLSTP Miguel Trovoada as his Prime Minister and Dr Carlos da Graca as Health minister.

He inherited a small and vulnerable country with most of the Portuguese cocoa planters having fled before independence. He was gradually forced to adopt more radical policies, but was resisted by Dr da Graca who went into exile in Gabon. In February 1978 da Costa complained to the UN that a mercenary invasion was underway. It never materialised, but troops were sent by Angola and Cuba to defend the islands while the supporters of da Graca were detained.

In August 1978 Da Costa called the first ordinary congress of the party to adopt a party programme and set up the MLSTP as a "revolutionary front of democratic, anti-colonialist and anti-imperialist forces."

As disagreements multiplied with some of his main associates, Da Costa took more power into his own hands. He took over the key ministries and held the posts personally, sometimes for years on end. He took over Agrarian reform 1975-78 and Security and Defence 1975-77, then in April 1979 abolished the post of Prime Minister and took over his responsibilities personally in March 1980. He arrested his long standing colleague Miguel Trovoada on somewhat flimsy evidence and held him in detention for two years.

Wanting to move closer to the West, he expanded his own authority further in February 1985, by taking over the Ministry of Foreign Affairs and the Ministry of Planning. He dismissed the Minister of Defence and National Security for a second time in January 1982 and took over his portfolio.

On 30 September 1985 he was re-elected for a third five year term. He also pardoned his old colleagues Carlos da Graca and made him a minister while Miguel Trovoada was invited to return from exile overseas. In October 1987 he announced that the election of the President and members of the National Assembly would in future, be by universal adult suffrage and that independent candidates would be allowed to stand.

In March 1990 he presented a new draft constitution which limited his own presidential office to two terms and introduced a pluralist system. This was duly approved by referendum in July and opposition parties were allowed to operate in August. He also disbanded the secret police. In the legislative elections of 21 January 1991 the writing was on the wall for Da Costa. The MLSTP was soundly beaten by the *Partido de Convergencia Democratica* (PCD), which had within the space of a few months, built enough strength to win 30 of the 55 assembly seats.

Da Costa then decided to stand down and not compete for the presidential elections scheduled for 3 March. He had ruled the country continuously for 16 years since independence in 1975.

He retained his villa and a number of vehicles he had acquired during his presidency and continued to play a leading role in the MLSTP.

TROVOADA, Miguel
Lawyer and politician. President 3 April 1991 —

A popular politician of long ministerial experience who has seen the wheel of fortune turn the full circle in his favour. He started after independence as his country's Prime Minister, but fell from favour and was imprisoned before being allowed to go into exile. But when pluralism was introduced in 1990 he returned and was soon swept to power by winning the presidential elections after the retirement of Manuel da Costa.

Born 1937. He was a founder member of the *Movimento de Libertação de São Tomé e Principe* (MLSTP) along with Pinto da Costa, he held the Foreign affairs portfolio in the party before independence.

In the first government after independence on 12 July 1975, he was named Prime Minister and Minister of Defence and Foreign Affairs. But da Costa took over the defence portfolio himself later in the year. Trovoada retained the premiership but was switched to Economic Coordination , Cooperation and Tourism.

Relationships between the two leading politicians were never smooth. In December 1978 President da Costa, seeing him as a potential rival, abolished the post of Prime Minister, though he continued as minister of Fishing, Industry and Housing.

In October 1979, he called a cabinet meeting to find himself accused by his colleagues of plotting against the government. In fact he had been made a scapegoat for the unpopular collective cabinet decision that the people should be confined to their homes while a census was carried out. He was able to adjourn the meeting and immediately sought refuge in the Portuguese embassy. He was not allowed entry. Though he was granted temporary stay at the UN mission he could not negotiate permanent asylum.

But eventually he was arrested, blamed for instigating political disturbances and held for 21 months until he was finally allowed to go into exile in France, in 1981.

He stayed abroad for nearly 10 years, returning in May 1990, to an ecstatic reception. He had been held up on his way home and was only just in time to register his name for the presidential elections. In August 1990 opposition parties were allowed to operate openly and the *Partido de Convergencia Democratica* (PCD) announced that it would back him for the presidential elections.

The PCD fought the legislative elections in January 1991 and thoroughly trounced the government, winning 33 of the 55 seats in the assembly. Trovoada continued to campaign for the presidency with a slick electoral machine and "Vota Trovoada" T-shirts and caps handed out to the impoverished voters.

Pinto da Costa withdrew his own candidacy together with two other candidates in the presidential race, leaving Miguel Trovoada to secure 82% of the votes, with a 60% electoral turn-out. He was officially installed as President on 3 April 1991, in the first election for the presidency since independence.

He was able to form a strong ministerial team with two ex- ministers, including the former Defence Minister Daniel Daio who became the new Prime Minister. The two were immediately faced with São Tomé's perennial problems - a falling price of cocoa and a stringent programme of economic reconstruction imposed by the IMF.

SENEGAL

Population: 7.67m (1990, World Bank)
Independence: 20 August 1960
Head of State: Abdou Diouf
Government: Multi-party parliamentary democracy. President and National Assembly elected every five years.
Parties: Majority party - *Parti Socialiste Sénégalais* (PS) which controls 103 seats in the National Assembly, the only other party represented is the *Parti Démocratique Sénégalais* (PDS) with 17 seats, but there are many other smaller parties.

CAMARA, Ousmane

Senegalese politician and diplomat.
Outstanding lawyer who became a key figure in government. Security chief, then minister who proved himself firm in handling the demands of trade unions and later students. Tall, gangling, wearing thick-lensed spectacles, he was later sent abroad as ambassador to various countries including Britain.

Born 1933 at Diourbel. Educated at the Lycee Faidherbe, St Louis, then at Dakar University where he obtained a law degree in 1957. He went on to study in Paris and made a reputation as an executive of the left-wing Federation of Black African Students in France (FEANF).

On his return to Senegal he became Government Prosecutor at Thies, 40 miles east of Dakar. He made his name as prosecutor at the high court in the trial of Mamadou Dia, the former prime minister, in 1963. After a series of appointments as Chef de Cabinet in several ministries he was made Director of National Security at the age of 31.

In 1968 he was appointed to the cabinet as Minister of Labour with the mandate to bring the trade unions into line after they had thrown down a challenge to government in the strike of June 1968. From February 1970 to April 1973 he was Minister of Information and official government spokesman. In the reshuffle of April 1973 he was given the specialised post of Minister of Higher Education, at a time of rising student ferment.

He was elected to the politburo of the ruling Socialist Party (PS) in February 1978. He lost his post as minister in 1980 and was sent abroad becoming Senegal's ambassador to Britain.

DIOUF, Abdou

President of Senegal, 1 January 1981 –

A moderate and pragmatic technocrat who has proved himself a formidable politician since he stepped into the shoes of Leopold Senghor in 1981. While pursuing a policy of continuity, he has liberalised the political system and allowed more opposition parties, believing that it is better to have the opposition in the open rather than plotting behind the scenes. He has always enjoyed the support of the powerful Muslim Marabouts who have ensured support for himself and the PS party through successive elections. He has gradually passed power in government to the younger technocrats and has purged the old party "barons". In foreign and African affairs he generally sides with the more conservative states such as Morocco and Chad against the radicals.

Born 7 September 1935 at Louga, 120 miles north of Dakar. Educated at the Lycée Faidherbe, St Louis then at Dakar University and Sorbonne, Paris where he studied law and political science and took his degree in 1959. He won a diploma in 1960 at the Overseas Civil Service School. Returning home, he was appointed Director of International Technical Co-operation in September 1960, then Assistant Secretary-General to government November 1960 to June 1961 and Secretary-General of the Defence Ministry in December. He also joined the *Union Progressiste Sénégalaise* (UPS) in 1961.

He became Governor of Sine Saloum region from December 1961 to December 1962, then was brought back to central government as Chef de Cabinet at the Foreign Ministry (1962-63). In May 1963 he was appointed Directeur de Cabinet at the presidency when only 27 and Deputy Secretary-General to Government, February 1964, then Secretary-General until 1968. He became Minister of Planning and Industry in March 1968. Despite his youth (only 34) and inexperience, he was promoted above the other stalwarts in the ruling Socialist Party (PS) by being unexpectedly chosen by Leopold Senghor as Prime Minister in March 1970. Senghor wanted someone with economic expertise whom he could trust. He still had unhappy memories of the attempted takeover by the former Prime Minister, Mamadou Dia, in 1962 and turned to Diouf who became a member of the National Assembly for the first time in 1973.

As Prime Minister Diouf had considerable freedom of action in economic affairs and was regarded as a representative of the younger generation of technocrats. Senghor's trust was rewarded because Diouf served him with unswerving loyalty over the next 13 years while Diouf proved his quality as an administrator and emerged as the clear-cut number two in the party hierarchy.

After the elections of February 1978, Diouf was able to choose his own ministers for the first time and promptly dropped the Finance and Foreign Minister, Babacar Ba. Diouf gradually strengthened his position in the PS following the demise of Ba in September 1978.

Meanwhile Senghor, who was 74 at the end of 1980, let it be known that he wanted to retire. He duly stood down and Diouf formally took over as President on 1 January 1981. He reshuffled his cabinet but established a policy of general continuity. He became secretary general of the PS on 14 January 1981. He felt the party was so strong that he actually encouraged the formation of opposition parties. He was vindicated as the opposition divided, and re-divided under rival leaders and presented no challenge to the PS majority.

Standing in the first Presidential elections in February 1983, he swept the poll with 83.5% of the vote compared with only 14% for his nearest rival, Abdoulaye Wade. At the same time the PS trounced the seven divided opposition parties, winning 111 seats to eight for Wade's party, which came second.

Opposition parties in 1985 tried to form an alliance but were promptly banned on the grounds that the constitution did not allow coalitions. Members of Wade's Parti Democratique Senegalaise (PDS) then left the party, with the deputy opposition leader, Fara N'Diaye, resigning, in June 1986.

Diouf met Wade in March 1987 as the opposition sought electoral reform, but he was not prepared to make any concessions. Student demonstrations and an illegal strike by the police followed which led to the suspension from duty of most of the police force and Diouf's dismissal of his minister of interior.

A bitterly contested election was held in February 1988 in which a decisive victory was claimed both for Diouf and the PS but the opposition alleged ballot rigging and electoral fraud. A state of emergency was declared and Wade and other opposition leaders were detained. The official election results showed that Diouf had received 73.2% of the votes cast and the PS 103 out of 120 seats in the National Assembly, a solid but by no means overwhelming victory.

Diouf lifted the state of emergency, had Wade released in May and later met him to discuss ways of easing tensions and establish inter-party commissions to discuss political issues. Talks broke down over electoral wrangling, but they did demonstrate Diouf's sincerity in seeking reconciliation. Though Senegal was already a democracy, it too was caught up in the wind of change blowing through Africa in 1990/91. Diouf decided to re-appoint a Prime Minister, for the first time since 1983, who would now be accountable not to him, but to the National Assembly. This was part of a policy of delegating presidential power. Habib Thiam was re-appointed to the premiership on 7 April 1991 and he, in turn, finally persuaded Wade, the long-standing opposition leader, to join his new government, bringing many of his leading colleagues with him.

In foreign affairs Diouf has maintained Senghor's strongly pro-French policies. He has usually sided with the "conservative" African states against the progressives, supporting Morocco in Western Sahara and Chad against Libya. Diouf became chairman of the OAU in 1985/86 where he concentrated mainly on issues concerning southern Africa. One of the most irresoluble problems has been the furthering of the Senegambia union with The Gambia. Though Diouf has pressed for closer union, since the attempted Gambian coup in July 1981, he found his neighbours reluctant to relinquish their autonomy. The Senegambia experiment was finally abandoned in September 1989.

A long dispute with Mauritania started in April 1989 over grazing rights and escalated into a full scale border row lasting into 1990, with tens of thousands of Senegalese living in Mauritania forced to flee home, in the face of racist attacks.

COLLIN, Jean

Senegalese, white politician and former minister.

One of the few white men in a black African government who remained as a minister after 30 years of independence. Despite being a Senegalese citizen and married into the family of President Senghor he was feared and respected because of his position, often accused of being a French Trojan horse within the government. A hard-working, efficient executive, he always wore the same bleu de travail working clothes as other employees in the ministries. His friends and partners saw him as a symbol of Senegal's multi-racialism and as a token of trust among French residents. His transition from the government of Leopold Senghor to that of Abdou Diouf in 1981 was smooth. On 27 March 1990 he retired at the age of 67.

Born 19 September 1924 in Paris. Educated at Lycée Louis-le-Grand and then at the law faculty of the university. He went on to specialise in languages at the French Overseas School and at the School of Oriental Languages.

Entering the overseas civil service, he became secretary to the High Commissioner in Cameroon in 1946 and was then transferred in 1948 to Senegal to be head of the information service and director of Radio Dakar. Over 1949-50 he was in Paris with the Overseas Ministry and then served in Cameroon (1951-56). In 1957 he went to Senegal and became Chef de Cabinet to the Vice-President Mamadou Dia and President of the Senegalese Territorial Council.

Twice Governor of the Cap Vert region, he was Secretary-General to the government for two years and over 1962-64, Secretary-General at the presidency. After the death of André Peytavin, the Frenchman who was Senegal's first Finance Minister, Collin succeeded to the post and held the portfolio for seven years, where his conservative financial policies were balanced by his probity and square dealing. From 1970 to 1971 he also held the Economic Affairs portfolio, but in November 1971 after a mysterious episode over anonymous tracts, which has never been cleared up, he became Minister of Interior (1971-75) and Minister of State for the Interior in March 1975. After a brief interlude he was reinstated as full minister and held the powerful post throughout Senghor's tenure of office. There he reorganised the police and set up a highly effective intelligence service whose agents he picked personally. His detailed knowledge of police archives meant that he had detailed knowledge of most rivals.

When Abdou Diouf assumed the presidency he appointed Jean Collin, on 2 January 1981 as Secretary-General to the Presidency, with the rank of Minister of State. In this post he became just as indispensable to Diouf as he had been to Senghor. He became Diouf's right-hand man, jealously guarding access to the presidency and generally recognised as the second most powerful figure in the Senegalese hierarchy. His role was particularly important in the struggle between the presidency and the powerful party 'barons' of the Socialist party. After attacks by opponents who inconsistently accused him of being in the pay of both France and the Soviet Union, he chose to retire on 27 March 1990.

NIASSE, Cheikh Moustapha
Senegalese politician and former minister.

A man of quick temper and vast experience and influence in government and the Socialist party. He rose to become the number three in the party hierarchy, a close adviser to the president and the party spokesman on foreign affairs, but his career took a dramatic reversal when he struck another cabinet minister at a politbureau meeting in September 1984. He was dismissed from his post and resigned from the party.

Born 4 November 1939. Educated at Lycée Faidherbe, St Louis and the universities of Dakar and Paris. He then attended the national school of administration in Dakar before going into Senegalese government service, becoming director of information and press affairs (1968-69) and Director of the Cabinet (1970-78).

Abdou Diouf, then Prime Minister, had a major purge of his cabinet on 15 March 1978 following an election victory, giving Niasse his first ministerial post as Minister of Town Planning and Environment. A few months later, on 19 September he was promoted to Foreign Minister, on the dismissal of the incumbent Babacar Ba. Niasse held this position until 1984. In the meantime he doubled as Foreign Minister for the first Confederal Cabinet of Senegambia from November 1982 until 1984. In January 1984, during a major reconstruction of the Socialist Party, he was made national secretary for foreign affairs.

But then came a dramatic event which proved a turning point in his career. At a meeting of the politbureau on 19 September 1984, Niasse struck the Information Minister, Djibo Ka, following an altercation. After some days of reflection President Diouf dismissed him from his post. He then resigned from the Socialist Party. Soon he was to start his own political organisation, the *Union Progressiste Sénégalaise*, a party which did not take off. It failed to contest the February 1988 elections.

SOW, Daouda (Dr)
Senegalese physician and politician.

One of the longest standing Senegalese politicians since he was first elected to the National Assembly in 1963. He has always been close to President Abdou Diouf but was also powerful in his own right, being the leader of an important clan and a member of the Socialist Party (PS) politburo. He has been the long-standing president of the International Association of French Language Parliamentarians keen on moves towards a Francophone Commonwealth and the promotion of the French language and culture. He became speaker of the National Assembly and party secretary responsible for educational and cultural activities in 1983 until December 1988, when he resigned following a clash with the powerful secretary to the President, Jean Collin.

Born 1933 at Wiss Wiss in Linguere district. Trained as a doctor of medicine, specialising in psychiatry. He first became a member of the National Assembly in 1963. Leopold Senghor made him Minister of Health on 28 February 1970 and put him in charge of relations with the National Assembly (1971-80) a post he held concurrently with the Ministry of Information from 1971-73. In January 1974 he announced the nationalisation of the cinema network in which the government would have control and "prevent the importation and distribution of morally degrading films".

He had the Post and Telecommunications ministries added to his portfolio, 1974-80. On 2 January 1981, after Abdou Diouf had been sworn in as the new President, he made Sow his Minister for the Armed Forces and in November 1982, when a cabinet was established for the Senegambian confederation, between Senegal and The Gambia, he became its Minister of Defence.

In March 1983 when Diouf dropped some of the powerful Socialist Party (PS) "barons" and switched power back to the National Assembly, he made Sow vice-president of the parliamentary group with responsibility for "holding together" the PS parliamentarians. He was elected president of the group on 12 April 1984. At the meeting of the eighth conference of the Union of African Parliaments, he was made president for a year, on 22 March 1985. He told delegates that his priorities would be the fight against desertification and the role of youth in the development process.

On 9 December 1988 he resigned suddenly from the presidency of the National Assembly following the passing of a motion of no confidence by party deputies. His move was prompted by a clash with the supporters of the powerful Secretary to the Presidency, Jean Collin. A struggle between the clans supporting the two had continued for several months. Sow was accused by the party of "wanting to control everything". He resigned despite President Diouf's reassurance that he wanted him to continue to hold the posts that made him "the second in command in the state".

THIAM, Habib
Senegalese politician, Prime Minister 7 April 1991 –

A key force in Senegalese politics and twice Prime Minister. Originally chosen as a senior minister by President Senghor and then later Prime Minister to his old university colleague Abdou Diouf. His career was interrupted by political intrigue among fellow parliamentarians, but he emerged to take Senegal into another stage of democratisation.

Born 21 January 1933 in Dakar, where he went to school. In 1956 he enrolled at the law faculty at Paris University where he first met Abdou Diouf. They both went on to the *Ecole Nationale de la France D'Outre Mer (ENFOM)*, the training ground for many high officials in the French colonies.

He was a brilliant sportsman as well as a good student becoming the French 200 metre champion in 1954 and again in 1957. He was also politically active, becoming general secretary of the Federation of Black African Students in France (FEANF).

He returned to Senegal in 1960 and went into the ministry of Foreign Affairs and then the Justice ministry.

President Leopold Senghor noticed his talents in 1963 and made him Secretary of State to the Presidency responsible for planning. He later became full Minister for Planning and Development (1964-67) and of Rural Development (1968-73).

In April 1973, he was suddenly dismissed by Senghor for mysterious and undisclosed reasons. He continued as a deputy in the national assembly and worked hard in the *Parti Socialiste*, becoming head of the parliamentary group of the party in February 1978. He also ran the party newspaper, *l'Unité*.

During this period as national secretary for the party, responsible for international affairs, he travelled extensively and made many contacts overseas. He also met and married a socialist ex-parliamentarian from Scandinavia.

When his friend Abdou Diouf took over from Senghor as President on 1 January 1981, he made Thiam his Prime Minister. He developed an authoritative, abrasive style which brought him many enemies even among his own colleagues. The press which supported Jean Collin, the general secretary to the presidency, began to attack him. Diouf also wanted to break the power of the big political "barons" who were a continual challenge to his power. This brought him to abolish the post of Prime Minister on 3 April 1983.

Ever adaptable, Thiam rapidly had himself elected as President of the National Assembly, an important post responsible for organising elections on the death of the president. The Assembly had became more politically important as most of Diouf's old political colleagues concentrated their energies there, while the cabinet was largely depoliticised.

But Thiam was soon sucked into political intrigues. His adversaries managed to pass a law which reduced the mandate of the president of parliament from five years to one. Thiam immediately resigned from all his posts, refusing to be humiliated. He went back into the private sector becoming President of the Industrial and Commercial Bank of Senegal (BICS) and manager of a dairy company, while maintaining close and friendly relations with President Diouf.

As Africa was caught up in the wind of democratisation in 1990/91, Diouf wanted to reform his own imperfect democracy. He decided to delegate some of his powers to a Prime Minister who would this time be accountable to the National Assembly, not to him personally. He offered the post to his old friend Habib Thiam who accepted on 7 April 1991. Thiam went further in his efforts to achieve national reconciliation and democratisation by finally persuading the inveterate opposition leader Abdoulaye Wade to join his government.

WADE, Abdoulaye

Senegalese politician. Leader of the Senegalese Democratic Party.

Maitre Abdoulaye Wade is a lawyer who, for the better part of two decades, was one of the most militant opposition leaders in Senegal. Though he has a great following among dissidents and urban voters he was never able to breach the monopoly of power held by the ruling Parti Socialiste that has been in office since Senegal's independence in 1960. Nick-named the "great bald one" and renowned for his oratory, he failed in several electoral challenges for the presidency. Eventually Diouf persuaded him to lay aside a decade of confrontationist politics and join his government and act as a force for change from within.

Born 1927 in Kébémer. Educated locally before doing higher education in France. A barrister in Dakar and lecturer in economic science at the university, he was until 1974 a member of the ruling *Parti Socialiste* himself, though he was a young militant on the left wing of the party. But when President Leopold Senghor changed the constitution to allow the legal formation of opposition parties Wade broke away, in July 1974, to form the Senegalese Democratic Party (PDS) which he said would be "a party of contribution" and not a "party of opposition". He declared himself anxious to maintain Senegalese democracy but to show new ways of tackling old problems.

But within a year there were serious clashes between supporters of the PS and of the PDS in which Wade found himself defending 18 of his supporters who had been detained after the incidents.

At the first conference of the PDS in Dakar in August 1975 Wade defined the five principles of the party: restoration of democracy, no over-exploitation of resources, political independence, African unity, and solidarity with other liberation movements. But one of the few areas in which there was actual disagreement with the ruling party was that the PDS wanted the voting age to be lowered to 18. At the conference Wade claimed a membership of 126,000.

The first full congress of the PDS was held in February 1976 and Wade was confirmed as secretary-general. He said that the main difference between his party and that of the government was that he would implement socialism and not simply play lip service to it.

In the first test of electoral strength - the municipal elections of

November 1976 - the PDS won less than a tenth of the poll and only two out of the 81 Rural Councils, and none of the urban councils. Wade however declared himself as the only challenger to Leopold Senghor in 1978. He won only 169,672 votes compared with 800,882 for Senghor and secured 12 out of the 100 seats in the National Assembly.

This defeat was bad for the morale of the PDS and when President Abdou Diouf came to power he added to its problems by allowing a proliferation of political parties. This weakened the opposition and caused a number of PDS members to leave Wade and form their own organisations. Other members of the party were detained for suspected subversion and accepting Libyan money.

Wade stood against Abdou Diouf in his first Presidential elections in February 1983 but was again defeated securing only 14% of the poll compared with Diouf's 83.5%, while winning only eight seats, though the PDS remained the main opposition party.

Wade became particularly critical of the government's supine acceptance of harsh IMF measures to restructure the economy. He called for a government of national unity and for a campaign of prayers every Tuesday in defiance of a government ban. This led to the arrest of some of his supporters. In June 1985 Wade took the PDS into an alliance of opposition parties called the Senegalese Democratic Alliance. In August he and 15 of his members were arrested and charged with holding unauthorised meetings, but the charges were thrown out of court.

A bitterly contested election was held in February 1988 in which Wade claimed extensive ballot rigging and electoral fraud. Official results showed that Wade had won 25.8% of the vote in the Presidential election compared to Diouf's 73.2%. The PDS also increased its representation to 17 seats in the assembly. But Wade claimed that according to his figures he came out top with 50% of the votes compared with Diouf's 40%. The protests were such that a state of emergency was declared and Wade detained. Diouf released him in May and established inter-party commissions to discuss differences, but talks soon broke down over electoral recriminations.

Wade went into exile in Paris and stayed there for seven months, writing two books. Wade alleges that Jean Collin, the Minister of State in the President's Office, met him three times and tried to tempt him back with offers of a ministerial post. Wade refused all blandishments but later returned home to a triumphal welcome from thousands of his supporters in March 1989.

He remained in opposition, resisting all offers by government until the new Prime Minister Habib Thiam finally persuaded him to become a Minister of State on 8 April 1991, ranked number three in the hierarchy. Three other PSD colleagues joined the government at the same time.

SEYCHELLES

Population: 73∅,000 (1990, World Bank)
Independence: 29 June 1976
Head of State: France-Albert René
Government: Presidential rule under a one-party system, through a Council of Ministers and a National Assembly. The President is limited to three five-year terms of office.
Parties: Sole authorised party - Seychelles People's Progressive Front (SPPF). There are a number of exiled opposition parties including the Seychelles Democratic Party (London) and the Seychelles National Movement (Brussels).

RENÉ, France-Albert

Seychelles politician. President 5 June 1977-

A quiet, methodical man of mixed European and Creole parentage, who had a much clearer vision of the realities of politics and more steady purpose than his great rival James Mancham. A shrewd lawyer and cunning businessman despite his socialist leanings, he seized power in June 1977 and introduced a more non-aligned socialist system and later a one-party state. At first opposition was expressed in a number of attempted coups, but gradually, as he has consolidated his power, he has been able to become more relaxed and restore some of the basic freedoms.

Born 16 November 1935, the son of a plantation manager, raised on the island of Farquhar. Educated at St Louis College, Victoria, and St Moritz in Switzerland, where he intended to train for the priesthood until he changed his mind and went to St Mary's College, Southampton and to King's College, London, to study law.

He went home and was called to the bar in 1957, but returned to the London School of Economics for a further two years (1962-64), when he became an active member of the Labour Party. He returned home again, bought himself a piece of property on Mahé island's highest peak and started in politics as the founder and leader of the Seychelles People's United Party (now the Seychelles People's Progressive Front) in 1964. He also organised the first trade union on the islands in the same year. In 1965 he became a member of the Legislative Assembly.

He was close to a number of leaders on mainland Africa and always wanted independence from Britain. His main rival, James Mancham, leading the Democratic Party, at first wanted close association with Britain. Mancham changed his stance in the elections of 1974 and won convincingly but agreed to form a coalition which was put into effect at independence on 29 June 1976. René had become Minister of Works and Land Development in 1975 and became Prime Minister, while Mancham became President after independence.

On the night of 5 June 1977, when Mancham was away attending the Commonwealth Conference in London, the SPUP staged an armed coup d'etat in which several people lost their lives. René denied foreknowledge of the plan, but was sworn in as the President and formed a new government. The constitution was suspended and National Assembly dissolved.

René ruled by decree and laid emphasis on fishing and trading enterprise instead of concentrating on tourism and adopted a more non-aligned foreign policy rather than being totally dependent on the West. He set up a constitutional commission to draw up a new constitution which introduced a one-party state under the SPUP, renamed the SPPF.

After a coup plot in April 1978, allegedly involving foreign mercenaries, the government assumed emergency powers, including detention without trial and press censorship. René claimed to have discovered a further two coup attempts in July and November 1981. The latter involved South African mercenaries who were sentenced to death but pardoned by René as an act of clemency. He then appealed to Tanzania which supplied 400 troops to guard against further coup attempts, but these duly materialised in October 1982 and November 1983, though they were not successful.

In May 1984 he was nominated as the sole candidate to stand for a second five-year term of office. In September 1986 René personally assumed the duties of the Minister of Defence and streamlined other ministries. He amended the constitution in May 1988, consolidating his own power by allowing the nomination of members of the party to take the seats of those who became absent from the assembly. Despite earlier indications that he might retire, he stood as the sole presidential candidate, in June 1989, for a third five-year term and obtained 96% of the votes cast. During 1990/91 there was considerable activity and re-grouping of opposition parties based overseas, but no indication that René was prepared to move in the direction of democracy.

In foreign policy he maintained a non-aligned stance, as a member of the Commonwealth and the OAU. He is also part of the pressure group to make the Indian Ocean a demilitarised peace zone.

SIERRA LEONE

Population: 4.1m (1990, World Bank)
Independence: 27 April 1961
Head of State: Major-General Joseph Saidu Momoh
Government: A National Constitutional Review Commission was set up, under Dr Peter Tucker, in August 1990 which recommended a return to plural democracy in April 1991. After ratification by parliament the bill was approved by referendum in August 1991, with no election date fixed.
Parties: Former single party - All People's Congress (APC), now being challenged by opposition parties including the Sierra Leone Alliance Movement (SLAM) and the Sierra Leone Democratic Party (SLDP) and the National Unity Movement.

BUNDU, Abbas

Sierra Leonean diplomat and politician. Executive Secretary of the Economic Community of West African States, January 1989 –

A brilliant lawyer specialised in international problems. A long-time executive of the Commonwealth Secretariat where he advised countries and organisations on issues concerned with independence and international relations. President Stevens later brought him back to Sierra Leone as a minister and he helped to democratise the parliamentary system after Stevens retired, before taking on the important post as the executive secretary of ECOWAS.

Born June 1944 at Gbinti in Dibia chiefdom, Port Loko district, north west Sierra Leone. The son of an Islamic scholar and trader. He was educated at St Andrews School in Bo, the Methodist Boys' High School and St Edwards School, Freetown. In 1966 he obtained a place to study law at the Australian National University and went to Canberra where he became a Bachelor of Law. He was called to the bar both in Australia and New South Wales. He also worked in the Attorney General's office of the Commonwealth in Australia before going to Churchill College, Cambridge to do a Master's and a D.Phil, specialising in constitutional and international law. He did a thesis on rebellion in international law, focussing on coups in Africa, particularly in his own country.

In 1975 he took a post in the Commonwealth Secretariat in Marlborough House, London, as chief projects officer, then assistant director for international affairs. He became legal adviser to the government of Belize when it was in dispute with Guatemala. He was legal adviser to Zimbabwe's Patriotic Front in the period running up to the Lancaster House conference in 1980 that brought independence.

In 1982 he was asked by President Siaka Stevens to return to Freetown as an MP and Minister of Agriculture and Natural Resources.

In 1985 after a vigorous debate in parliament he was reshuffled to the Ministry of Tourism and Cultural Affairs.

After President Momoh came to power in October 1985 he continued as a backbench MP. A good constituency MP, he was relected in May 1986 and in his own words "remains a parliamentarian in cold storage." In January 1989 he was appointed executive secretary of the Economic Community of West African States (ECOWAS), based in Lagos, Nigeria. This organisation groups together 16 member-states which pledged themselves in 1975 to form an economic community. Bundu was faced with an organisation where his predecessor had been sacked six months previously and members were considerably in arrears on their dues. Though ECOWAS had lofty goals little real progress had been made on trade liberalisation or monetary integration.

Under his leadership ECOWAS took on a political dimension when it was used by its members as a vehicle for intervention in the Liberian conflict. Five of its members sent in troops of the Ecowas Ceasefire Monitoring Committee Group (ECOMOG) in August 1990. Bundu concentrated on his economic responsibilities stating in April 1991 that the Community was still committed to establishing a single monetary zone in West Africa by 1994.

CONTEH, Abdulai Osman (Dr)
Sierra Leonean politician. Former Minister of Foreign Affairs, Attorney-General 3 April 1987 –

Top athlete in the early 1970s, a keen gardener, and ambitious politician. He was the youngest ever Foreign Minister for Sierra Leone when Siaka Stevens appointed him in May 1977. He served as Foreign Minister for seven years and Finance Minister for two years after that but was then sacked by Stevens and had to wait for President Momoh to bring him back as Attorney-General in April 1987.

Born 5 August 1945 at Pepel, Northern province. Educated at Sierra Leone Muslim Association Primary, AME Boys High School, Albert Academy. He went to King's College, London and graduated as a Bachelor of Laws 1969. Postgraduate studies took him to Lincoln's Inn where he became a barrister 1970. Returned home and enrolled in the Sierra Leone Supreme Court as an advocate in 1971. Returned to Britain, King's College, Cambridge, where he obtained a bachelor of law degree and Ph.D. He also represented Cambridge in athletics and later ran for his country in the Commonwealth Games, Jamaica (1966) and the African Games, Nigeria (1972).

Back in Freetown he went into private practice in 1974 and became a law lecturer at Fourah Bay College and secretary general to the Sierra Leone Bar Association (1976-77). Returned unopposed in the May 1977 elections for Kambia West and was immediately appointed Minister of Foreign Affairs - the youngest in Sierra Leonean history. He held the post continuously until 5 September 1984 when Siaka Stevens made him

Finance Minister in an attempt to rescue the economy. Conteh had been a critic of the tough financial measures of the former incumbent, Salia Jusu Sheriff. But then on 27 June 1985, in a major reshuffle, he lost his portfolio just 24 hours before he was due to present his budget. He had fallen out with his leader over economic policy. He was not reappointed in President Momoh's first cabinet in November 1986 but he was brought back quickly as Attorney-General and Minister of Justice on 3 April 1987.

JUSU-SHERIFF, Salia
Sierra Leonean Second Vice-President, 3 April 1987 –

A brilliant and highly articulate chartered accountant - the first to qualify in his country. He achieved fame as a leader of the Sierra Leone People's Party, the opposition party, a post he held against increasing odds until being forced into the APC, under the single party state, in 1978. He was then made Minister of Finance, by Siaka Stevens to rescue the ailing economy. He was only partially successful but he survived to be promoted Vice-President by President Momoh in April 1987, when he came to power.

Born 1 June 1929. Educated at Bunumba Central School and Fourah Bay College before going to King's College, Durham. He graduated as a bachelor of commerce in 1954, did further training as a chartered accountant and then returned home to practise accountancy in private business.

He stood for parliament as a Sierra Leone People's Party candidate, and won a seat in the 1962 general elections and was spotted as a young man of talent by Sir Milton Margai; was made Minister of Natural Resources. He moved to Trade and Industry in 1963, then to Health.

He won the Kenema South in March 1967, but was not allowed to take up his parliamentary seat because of the military coup which followed. Inside the party he challenged Sir Albert Margai's leadership but eventually compromised. He became parliamentary leader, while Sir Albert became overall party leader.

When Siaka Stevens, the All People's Congress leader, was restored to power on 26 April 1968 he formed a coalition government and offered some portfolios to SLPP members. Jusu-Sheriff decided to give the national government a trial and took up his old health portfolio.

But he soon clashed with Stevens in parliament. He was arrested at his Kenema constituency, then released without charges being brought. On 1 July 1968 he resigned his ministry and became the official parliamentary opposition leader. In the May 1973 elections he was declared to have been returned unopposed, but later his nomination was nullified.

There followed a long period in the wilderness when he went into private practice. Wanting to retain his seat as an MP, he was forced to join the APC when Sierra Leone became a one-party state in June 1978, but though Stevens wanted to use his skills to put the ailing economy in order he did not finally persuade him to become Minister of Finance until

May 1982. The expected economic miracle did not materialise and he was demoted to Minister of Planning and Economic Development on 5 September 1984.

When President Momoh took over in November 1986 he offered Jusu-Sheriff the Ministry of Health but he declined this relatively minor ministry and did not return to government until he was made second Vice-President and Minister of Lands and Human Environment on 3 April 1987.

KAMARA, Abu Bakr
Sierra Leonean politician. First Vice-President, 3 April 1987 –

A devout, ambitious Muslim lawyer who has gradually risen to top posts as a Judge and Chairman of the High Court. His political career started late in 1977 when he was returned unopposed in his home area, Port Loko, and then immediately given top ministries by his mentor, Siaka Stevens. He appeared to lose the confidence of Stevens towards the end of his rule, but bounced back under President Momoh as second and finally first Vice-President.

Born 29 July 1929 at Mabanta Bulum, Bureh chiefdom, Port Loko district. Educated at Holy Trinity School, Ebenezer School, Prince of Wales School, and then London University to do law studies. Graduated LLB from Holborn College of Law (1960), LLM (1962), returned home and set up in private practice (1962-71). High Court Judge (1971-72). Appointed pro-chancellor University of Sierra Leone, then Chairman of Court (1973), and chairman of Sierra Leone Airways (1976).

Returned unopposed in elections of May 1977 for Port Loko North. Appointed Minister of Finance by Siaka Stevens in 1977, Attorney-General and Minister of Justice December 1978. Frequently he was made acting Vice-President when Sorie Ibrahim Koroma was indisposed.

A temporary check came to his career on 27 June 1985 when Siaka Stevens suddenly demoted him from Minister of Justice to the Ministry of Health, but this situation was only to last until President Momoh took power. On 29 November 1985 he promoted Kamara to second Vice-President with ministerial responsibility for Lands and Country Planning.

When first Vice President Francis Minah dramatically fell from power, after being accused of plotting a coup on 3 April 1987, Kamara was appointed to the vacant post.

KOROMA, Abdul Karim
Sierra Leonean politician. Foreign Minister, 17 June 1985 –

Highly qualified academically and a college lecturer, he is one of the younger generation of Sierra Leonean leaders who has gradually worked his way up through parliament and the party to become Foreign Minister, a post he has held since Siaka Stevens' time.

Born 1945 at Mabonto, Tonkolili district, Northern Province. Educated at Regent Amalgamated School. Magburaka Boys School, Sierra Leone Grammar School, He went to the University of Durham where he graduated in history, English and international relations. He won a diploma in education from Fourah Bay College (1968), an MA in modern history, University of Sierra Leone (1975) and an MSc in international politics, University of Southampton.

He became a teacher at Magburaka Boys School (1968-71) and then a lecturer at Freetown Teacher's College (1973-75). Wanting to develop a parliamentary career, he stood as an All People's Congress member and was returned unopposed for Tonkolili North in May 1977.

Siaka Stevens made him Minister of Education (13 May 1977), a post he held until May 1982 when he was shifted for party reasons to become Regional Minister for Northern Province in May 1982. His big break came on 17 June 1985, when he was only 40 years of age. He displaced the long-standing Foreign Minister, Dr Sheka Kanu. He maintained that post throughout the remainder of Siaka Stevens regime and was confirmed in the position by President Momoh when he took over in November 1986.

MOMOH, Joseph Saidu (Maj-General)
Sierra Leone President, 28 November 1985 –   Formerly Army Chief.

A bluff and jovial soldier who started his career with ultimate accolades. He was popular with the army, the patron of sports, and yet he was aware enough to keep his political options alive by maintaining membership of the ruling All People's Congress and by accepting Siaka Stevens' nomination to parliament in 1973. It was from this base that he was chosen as a safe successor to Stevens in 1985. Since then he has found the intractable problems of the Sierra Leonean economy and public demoralisation have presented a major challenge.

Born 26 January 1937 at Binkolo, Safroko Limba chiefdom, Bombali district, Northern province. Of a mixed tribal background but mostly Limba like Siaka Stevens. Educated at government rural school, Wilberforce and WAM Collegiate Secondary School. He enlisted as a private in the West African Frontier Force in 1958. Did preliminary officer cadet training at Teshi, near Accra, Ghana. Followed by an officers' cadet course in Kaduna, 1962 and Hythe, England, in 1962, passing out as the most outstanding overseas cadet, winning the baton of honour. He did further training at Mons Officer Cadet School at Aldershot in 1963, where he again won the sword of honour for being the best overseas cadet, then at Zaria, Nigeria, in 1964.

Commissioned as 2nd Lieutenant in the Royal Sierra Leone Military Force in 1963, he rose to lieutenant in 1964, captain 1965, adjutant of the 1st Battalion of the Sierra Leone Regiment and major in March 1967, when he became commander of the Training Depot at Wilberforce

Barracks. Deputy adjutant and quartermaster general in November 1968. Commander of the 1st battalion in March 1969. Promoted lieutenant-colonel in October 1969, colonel 1970, force commander November 1971 and brigadier 1973. He was the first Sierra Leonean to be appointed Major General in 1983.

Appointed member of parliament and minister of state by President Siaka Stevens in October 1973. Reappointed 1977. Besides being an officially appointed MP, Momoh also preserved a political platform by being an active member of the All People's Congress, the ruling party.

As Stevens approached his 80th birthday and neared the end of his seven-year term of office he frequently said that he wanted to retire but over the years he had lost faith in almost all the politicians who had supported him. He felt that they were all either too light-weight or too self-seeking to fulfill the role of President. And they did not carry enough respect of the nation at large. So after a long delay and much speculation, Stevens decided to play safe and persuade the commander of his armed forces Major General Joseph Momoh to succeed him.

Momoh was at first reluctant but was eventually persuaded and agreed to stand. Stevens then canvassed all the other possible contenders and got them to agree to stand down. So on 1 August 1985 the APC unanimously elected Momoh as the single Presidential candidate. Stevens appeared to be rewarding him for his loyalty and for keeping him in power through a succession of political and economic crises over 17 years.

His election as the sole Presidential candidate, on 1 October 1985 was a formality, but at the same time it was a popular occasion, with 2.78 million Sierra Leoneans voting in favour and only 4,096 against. The people had decided that Momoh was a disciplined and honourable man who could get rid of some of the corruption of the old politicians.

At first he was popular but he faced intractable economic problems and was obliged to apply IMF sponsored austerity measures resulting in major price increases. In January 1987 student demonstrations broke out over food allowances and rising prices. In March, Momoh declared that a coup plot had been discovered. More than 60 were arrested and 18 sent for trial. Among them was the First Vice-President Francis Minah, who was charged with treason and after a five-month trial sentenced to death. He and five others appealed but the death sentences were upheld in October 1988.

Momoh struggled to curb corruption in an atmosphere of economic stringency. He forced the resignation of a number of ministers implicated in various financial scandals. A deputy finance minister was given a six-year prison sentence for fraud. In November 1987 he declared a state of economic emergency and announced 59 measures designed to curb hoarding and smuggling.

In August 1990 he announced various reforms that would democratise the party without allowing full-blown multi-party government.

But pressure for constitutional change was already growing and later in the same month, he set up a constitutional review commission under Dr Peter Tucker, to decide whether or not to change to a multi-party system. It soon became clear that the public at large did want political change, but Momoh still wanted to hold general elections before the results of the commission were ready.

In March 1991, rebels supported by Liberia's Charles Taylor, invaded the country, seizing a number of key towns and causing immense damage and loss of life. Nigerian and Guinean troops were called on to support the beleaguered Sierra Leonean forces and gradually the rebels were repulsed. The invasion finally pushed Momoh into espousing pluralism. The Tucker Commission also came down firmly in April in favour of a multi-party system. On 23 May Momoh praised the work of the commission and said that he supported the changes recommended. He also agreed to extend the life of the sitting parliament to give time for the introduction of the new system.

TARAWALLIE, Mohamed Sheku (Maj-General)

Sierra Leonean Force Commander and Minister of State, 29 November 1986 –

A professional soldier with little political ambition who has gradually worked his way up through the ranks to become forces commander immediately under President Momoh.

Born 15 January 1939 at Kabala, Koinadugu district. Educated Kabala school, Magburaka central school, and Bo school. Enlisted as an officer cadet 1961. Military training Nigeria and Mons Officer Cadet School, Aldershot.

Commissioned as a second lieutenant April 1962. Attached to Duke of Wellington's Regiment, Colchester before returning home. Rose rapidly to lieutenant-colonel in 1971 as commander of the 1st Battalion Republic of Sierra Leone Regiment. Posted to a senior military officers course at Latimer, Buckinghamshire 1970-71, then promoted Colonel.

Promoted Sierra Leone Force Commander and Minister of State by President Momoh in his first cabinet, the day after his inauguration on 29 November 1985.

SOMALIA

Population: 6.23m (1990, World Bank)
Independence: 1 July 1960
Interim President: Interim President Ali Mahdi Mohamed
Government: Interim government endorsed by six parties at
Djibouti conference in July 1991. Provisional government to continue
in Mogadishu under the old 1960 democratic constitution pending free
elections within two years. President Mohamed would continue as
interim president. Other major posts shared on an ethnic basis.
Agreement did not cover Somaliland (Northern Somalia) which
declared its independence on 18 May 1991.
Parties: United Somali Congress (USC) forms the backbone of the
interim government supported by six other parties.

ABOKOR, Ali Ismail
Somali politician. Former Vice-President, July 1971 - June 1982.

*A relatively unknown captain at the time of the coup by Siyad Barre in
October 1969, he moved up the ladder of power faster than most of his
contemporaries and was promoted colonel. Handsome, smart and
youthful, he became Siyad's right-hand man and a stack of
responsibilities were thrust upon him. He was promoted to Vice-President
and remained in that post for more than a decade, besides being deputy
secretary-general of the party. Then came his sudden arrest and detention
in June 1982 for being involved in a coup plot. After many years he was
convicted to death by firing squad but President Siyad exercised clemency
and commuted the sentence to house arrest.*

Born 1940 and one of the few Somali officers to be trained at Sandhurst.
In March 1970 he was appointed Secretary of State for Information and
National Guidance. On 29 July 1971 the Supreme Revolutionary Council
(SRC) made him one of the three Vice-Presidents along with Brigadier
Hussein Kulmiye and Brigadier Mohammed Ali Samatar. When the
Somali Revolutionary Socialist Party (SRSP) was formed and the powers
of the SRC were transferred to the party, in July 1976, he was appointed
secretary-general for party affairs until 1979.

Political honours were heaped upon him. He remained third Vice
Chairman and became Chairman of the People's Assembly in 1980-81
and chairman of the Political Committee of the SRC, a post he held in
conjunction with the deputy secretary-generalship of the Somali
Revolutionary Socialist Party.

On 9 June 1982 he and seven other leading politicians were arrested
for what the government described as "collaborating with an unnamed

foreign power to undermine the state." They were expelled from the party, stripped of their parliamentary privileges and detained without trial. After a long delay a summary trial was held. On 7 February 1988 he and the former Foreign Minister, Omer Arteh Ghalib, were found guilty of founding a subversive organisation comprising armed groups opposed to the unity and security of the nation. They were sentenced to be executed by firing squad but President Siyad exercised clemency by commuting the death sentence to house arrest.

AFRAH, Hussein Kulmie (Major-General)

Somali politician. Speaker of Parliament, 15 February 1990 – 27 January 1991.

One of the most loyal and constant lieutenants to President Siyad Barre. He held top ranking positions without a break after the coup of October 1969, holding the post of Vice-President and Deputy Prime Minister over 1973-90. An amicable, tolerant and down to earth figure, he is not considered to be as ideologically committed as some of his colleagues. He was one of the most senior members of government who had good contacts in Italy.

Born 1920 at Margeh. Educated locally and at the Italian Secondary School, Mogadishu and the Italian Officers Academy, Rome. He returned home to become a shopkeeper until 1945 when he joined the police force. He went for a course at the Criminal Investigation Department in Kenya in the same year and returned to become an Instructor and Translator at the Police Training School in Mogadishu. He continued teaching at his old school, the Italian Secondary in Mogadishu (1950-54) and at the Officers Academy (1954-55).

His political career started when he became Aide de Camp to the former President Abdulla Osman in 1960. After the coup of 21 October 1969 which brought President Siyad Barre to power, he discovered that no outside interests were involved and agreed to become a member of the Supreme Revolutionary Council (1970-76). On 23 February 1970 he was appointed Secretary of State for the Interior. He proved himself indispensable to Siyad and was promoted Major-General and appointed Second Vice-President on 9 July 1973.

When the Somali Revolutionary Socialist Party (SRSP) was formed and the powers of the SRC were transferred to the party, he became a member of the Politburo. Siyad also took the opportunity on 9 July 1976 to make him Deputy Head of State. In February 1980 Siyad carried out an extensive reshuffle, abolishing the three Vice-Presidential posts including that of Afrah, but he was appointed instead as Assistant to the President for Presidential Affairs. By 1982 he was restored as Second Vice-President, while continuing to be Siyad's adviser.

On 22 February 1985 he became Minister of National Planning. The new post of Vice Prime Minister was added to his responsibilities on 31 January 1987. On 15 February 1990, following one of the most extensive reshuffles by President Barre and Prime Minister Mohammed Ali Samater, he was appointed speaker of the Somali parliament. He survived in Mogadishu after Barre was ousted on 27 January 1991.

AHMED, Mohamed Ibrahim (Major-General)
Somali soldier and politician.

Nicknamed Liqliqato, he served in a number of prominent positions as ambassador to the Soviet Union and West Germany and Secretary of State for Agriculture and commerce before becoming the Chairman of the Standing Committee of the People's Assembly.

Born 15 August 1921 at Jamana, Kisimaio. Educated locally. Did military training and fought with the Italian Army in 1939-41 when he changed over and joined the British Army for the remainder of the war. He was sent for military training to Britain after the war, returning home in 1948 to join the Somali police force. He continued training at the military academy in Italy (1952-54) and returned home to resume duties with the police becoming the Second Commander of the Somali police force in 1960.

When Somalia built up its post-independence army, he transferred to the military in 1962 and won rapid promotion, being appointed Brigadier in 1968 and Second Commander of the military forces in 1969. After the military coup of October 1969, he was appointed to the key post of ambassador to the Soviet Union (1969-70), at a time when Soviet Somali relations were at their best.

He was switched to ambassador to West Germany (1970-74) returning home to be appointed Secretary of State for Agriculture on 6 December 1964. He was reshuffled to Minister of Commerce on 1 April 1978 until 1981, when he was appointed Chairman of the Standing Committee of the People's Assembly. He maintained this post throughout the 1980s, until Siyad Barre was driven from power on 27 January 1991.

BARRE, Siyad Mohammed
Somali soldier, President 21 October 1969-27 January 1991

A largely self-trained and self-educated policeman and soldier who imposed strong, authoritarian rule over his country after seizing power in 1969. A professed Marxist, with a strong Islamic faith he was faced with the continual factionalism of the Somali clans and power groups. He imposed his will by assuming strong personal control, but only at the expense of basic liberties and effective democratisation of his military regime. Power was concentrated in his hands and that of a small central committee largely formed by military officers. Though badly injured in a serious car crash in May 1986 and a heavy smoker, he appeared to have made a steady recovery. His major success, before his overthrow, was in improving relations with his Ethiopian neighbours.

Born 1919 in a cattle-raising family of the Marehan clan, in the Upper Juba region. The Marehans are part of the Darod confederacy clan group which lives west of the Shebelle river. Educated at the elementary school at Lugh, but his parents died when he was only 10 years old and he had no financial backing to continue a proper education, so he joined the police, when the British took over from the Italians in 1941. By the time the British left in 1950 he had become Chief Inspector, the highest rank ever achieved by a Somali.

The Italians established their trusteeship administration and in 1952 he was chosen to attend military academy in Italy, being promoted second lieutenant shortly after his return home. He continued to educate himself in politics and adminstration and learnt to speak and read Italian, English, Arabic and Swahili fluently.

In April 1960, when the Somali National Army was founded, he became its Vice-Commandant, with the rank of colonel. On 24 July 1965 he was promoted Commandant of the army with the rank of Brigadier-General and in 1966, Major-General.

Like many younger officers he was a dedicated socialist and became dissatisfied with the self-seeking corruption of the early Somali politicians, who had taken over when Somalia became independent in July 1960. This prompted the military coup which he organised on 21 October 1969. He said that he had intervened to combat "tribalism, corruption, nepotism and misrule".

He dissolved the National Assembly and set up a Supreme Revolutionary Council which instituted military rule. His rule was Marxist inspired and authoritarian and this led him to be shunned by the old colonial powers. He turned to the Soviet Union to assist his impoverished, drought-ridden country with its paucity of natural resources.

But though proud of his Marxism, Siyad was also a practising Moslem who frequently invoked God in his speeches. Though he never put Islam before his political beliefs, he worked hard until he had won acceptance of his country as part of the Arab League in February 1974.

In 1976 he tried to give his regime increased authenticity by setting up the Somali Revolutionary Socialist Party (SRSP) on the Soviet model. It provided for a National Assembly with a single list of candidates nominated by the Central Committee. But effective power was still concentrated in his hands. He was unanimously elected as President by the People's Assembly on 26 January 1980 for a seven-year term. His presidency was confirmed in December 1986 for a further seven years.

The Soviet alliance ran into difficulties in the mid-seventies. Over 3,000 Soviets based in Somalia remained aloof from the ordinary people and brought little in the way of economic assistance. Siyad was consistently wooed by the conservative Arab states. But it was the Soviets themselves who brought the final break when they failed to get Ethiopia and Somalia to drop their differences and enter a confederation. The Soviets then quite cynically dropped Somalia to back the larger and more populous neighbouring power.

Siyad tried to take advantage of the chaos created by the aftermath of the Ethiopian revolution in 1974 to seize the disputed Ogaden region. Somali troops invaded in July 1977, but after initial successes the Soviets and their Cuban allies intervened and gave Ethiopia the necessary logistical and military help to turn the war in their favour.

After his defeat Siyad dropped his military ambition and concentrated his energies on trying to prevent the incursions of the Ethiopia-based Somali National Movement.

Siyad was badly injured in a car crash in May 1986 and on recovery he decided to try and seek peace with Ethiopia and reduce the external pressures on his regime. Talks with his former enemies started in January 1986, when Siyad visited Djibouti and there met the Ethiopian leader, Mengistu Haile Mariam for the first time. Further talks followed until a peace agreement was finally achieved in April 1988. This finally cut Ethiopian support from the Somali National Movement which mounted a full scale invasion of northern Somaliland.

Siyad threw everything into the defeat of the SNM and ruthlessly suppressed the north, arresting hundreds of Isaq suspected of being sympathetic to the rebels. Western human rights organisations alleged that government troops were slaughtering the local population.

Gradually he lost control of the north, except for the main towns, as the SNM won more popular support. Though he made promises of constitutional reform, few trusted him. At the end of 1990 a new rebel movement, the United Somali Congress, sprang to life around the capital Mogadishu. Within a few weeks Siyad Barre's corrupt and bankrupt regime had been overthrown. On 27 January 1991 he fled his palace and went into hiding as the rebels seized the capital.

GHALIB, Omar Arteh

Somali politician and diplomat. Prime Minister, 6 September 1991 -

A cultured and educated man who speaks five languages fluently. He spent a lifetime in public service for his country and over six years in the jails of Siyad Barre without trial, accused of supporting the rebel Somali National Movement. But when he emerged from prison, he proved himself a true nationalist patriot and was rewarded by being appointed Prime Minister in the turbulent days at the outset of the new Somalia's interim government.

Born: 1930 in Hargeisa. Educated locally then at St Paul's College, Cheltenham and at Bristol University. He started his career as a teacher (1946-49), then became the headmaster of various elementary schools, (1949-54). He was vice-principal of the Intermediate school at Sheikh (1954-56), principal of the intermediate school at Gabileh (1958). He then went into full time government service, becoming officer in charge of adult education 1959, then assistant district commissioner in Hargeisa, 1960, and district commisoner of Erigavo 1960-61.

He was posted overseas to become first secretary in the Somali embassy in Moscow 1961-62. He then went to the United Nations and was made rapporteur of the special committee on South West Africa (1962-63). He was the counsellor of the permanent mission of Somalia at the UN, 1962-64.

Promotion then came in the form of the ambassadorship to neighbouring Ethiopia, 1965-68. He attended the OAU Council of Ministers and the summit conferences in Cairo, Accra and Addis Ababa (1964-66). In 1969 he was elected to the Somali National Assembly. He was also the leader of a small splinter party among the 86 other parties in the parliament at that time.

He was the only parliamentarian to continue in the new government of Maj. General Siyad Barre when he seized power in a military coup on 21 October 1969. He then became Secretary of State for Foreign Affairs in the Barre government (1969-76).

He claims that he worked for Barre "wholeheartedly with all sincerity...I feel proud that Somalia was a star of Africa at that time and that we hosted the OAU in 1974". He was shuffled to the Ministry of Culture and Higher Education (1976-78) at which time he was a member of the influential political and social committee. He then became a minister in Siyad Barre's office (1978-80), before being made speaker of the People's Assembly (1982).

On 9 June 1982 he was arrested with seven other senior Somali parliamentarians accused of "working with a foreign country to undermine the very existence of the nation". Among his alleged co-conspirators was Vice President Ismail Ali Abokor and a number of other ministers. They were all expelled from the Somali Socialist Revolutionary Party and expelled from parliament. They were never tried, but were accused of conspiring with the rebel Somali National Movement (this was a largely Isaq group and Omar Arteh was an Isaq from the north).

In November 1984 a Somali airlines Boeing 707 was hijacked on a flight to Jeddah in order to secure the seven men's release, just a few days before they were due for execution. The leader of the hijackers said afterwards that they were not terrorists but struggling for justice and true independence for the Somali people. As a result of their action the Somali government promised not to execute their prisoners.

On 2 May 1987 the Inter-parliamentary Union ended its 77th conference with a call for the release of the seven who had been held without charge or trial, and incommunicado since 1982. The IPU expressed alarm at the state of health of Omar Arteh and regret at the way the Mogadishu government ignored many appeals made on the prisoners behalf.

They were not brought to trial before 1988 when the four non-Isaq were acquitted for lack of proof, but Ismail Ali Abokor and Omar Arteh were both sentenced to be executed by firing squad. A chorus of international protest led by Amnesty International claimed that the two were the victims of a gross judicial error and that they should be immediately released. They were joined by the Arab states where Omar Arteh had built many friendships over the years. Siyad Barre then thought better of it and exercised Presidential clemency.

On 14 February they were released from prison, but put under house arrest. They were allowed to go home but told by the President himself "not to go outside". Omar Arteh commented later, " When I came out of jail I still tried to convince the dictator that he could correct the situation in which he had lost the confidence of the people, but he refused my advice. I repeated this up to 24 hours before he was finally ousted, telling him that despite all he had done to me I forgave him, as I did not want to see his family ruffled up or harmed. I advised him to leave the country in honour with his head up as his comrade Mengistu (of Ethiopia) had done. But he rejected me...In my troubles I always refrained from saying too much about him, and the atrocities committed by the clique around him, because I want Somalia to be saved or at least to save what can be salvaged... I don't want to disclose things which might be sickening to outsiders."

Omar Arteh was also particularly grateful to all those who had agitated for his release when he was detained without trial. He said that he had been arrested for "telling the truth," though he was accused of supporting the SNM.

Omar Arteh was appointed the prime minister of the interim government by President Ali Mahdi Mohammed on 29 January 1991, after Siyad Barre's fall from power. He then began to tour Africa, Arabia and the world seeking recognition for his new government and financial assistance.

But in the share-out of jobs at the reconciliation conference in Mogadishu in July 1991, he was not confirmed as Prime Minister. Possibly his Isaq origins counted against him. On 20 August, he tendered his resignation. But Mohammed failed to find any other suitable candidate and on 6 September 1991 he was reappointed Prime Minister for two years and asked to form a new government.

MOHAMMED, Ali Mahdi
Interim President, 29 January 1991 -

A moderate, pragmatic leader with broad political and business experience but little personal following outside Mogadishu. He emerged as a compromise candidate first in the ranks of the United Somali Congress. This was endorsed later by six other guerrilla groups, but significantly it was not he but his main rival General Aideed who emerged as Chairman of the USC, while he became interim president of his country.

Born: 1940 in Mogadishu into the Hawiye clan. He was educated locally and later became a school teacher. He went on to do community health training in Egypt and Italy, 1963-66. On returning home he served as director of the malaria control programme in the Ministry of Health.

He took up politics and was elected as deputy for Jowhar, Benadir region on 26 March 1969. When Gen Siyad Barre seized power on 21 October 1969 he was arrested together with many other politicians and held in prison for a number of years.

After his release with political avenues closed to him, he took up business, making his mark as a hotelier, owning the Makkah el-Mukarram hotel in Mogadishu. He also served as a director for the United Nations Children's Fund (UNICEF) in Mogadishu. He continued covert opposition to the increasingly unpopular Barre regime.

He was one of the 114 private citizens, elders and intellectuals who risked their lives by signing an open letter in mid-May 1990 condemning the policies of the regime. Known as the *Manifesto*, it called for an end to government policies of deliberately killing unarmed civilians, and the destruction of major towns, wells and reservoirs in opposition areas.

When Barre began arresting members of the Manifesto group, he fled the country and began to raise money for the United Somali Congress which had established an overseas office in Rome. He became a member of the USC political wing, returning to Somalia late in 1990 when the rebel movement began to establish a foothold in the suburbs of Mogadishu.

Mohammed was not a guerrilla fighter, but provided funds and supplies to them in their successful push into Mogadishu in January 1991. When Siyad Barre finally fled the capital on 27 January 1991, Mohammed was proposed as interim-president by the USC and approved by 130 elders from different Somali clans.

The violence persisted with fighting between government troops and supporters of Barre who was still esconced in his home region of Garba Harre in the Gedo region, near to the Kenya border. Other incidents occurred between different clans and factions. Even the leadership of the USC was contested with Ali Mahdi's main rival General Aideed finally emerging as Chairman of the USC.

But Mohammed's main problem was that the other freedom fighters who were not in Mogadishu, felt they should have been consulted even on the formation of an interim government. The people of northern Somalia were so aggrieved that they finally persuaded their leaders to declare secession and set up the independent state of Somaliland.

But the different factions in the south were finally reconciled at a meeting in July 1991, between six political groups in Djibouti, when it was agreed that Mohammed should continue as interim president for two years, until free elections could be organised under the original 1960 constitution. He was confirmed in office by being sworn in as president on 18 August 1991 at a meeting attended by representatives of the parties at the Djibouti conference.

SAMATER, Ali Mohammed

Somali politician. First Vice-President 1976 – 9 January 1990.

Perhaps the most loyal and politically mature of all Siyad Barre's deputies. Until the sudden dismissal of the entire cabinet on 9 January 1990, he was Barre's constitutional successor and first Vice-President. He was reinstated in his post as Prime Minister and allowed to select his own cabinet in February but was dismissed again in September. He served faithfully as Barre's number two after the military coup of October 1969. Though trained in the Soviet Union at a number of military institutions, including tank schools beyond the Urals, he was considered to be a quiet pragmatist.

Born 1931 at Chisimaio, in one of the minority clan groups from southern Somalia. Educated at the intermediate school Mogadishu and the Military Academy Rome.

He returned to join the Somali police (before the army was established) rising to become commandant of the police force in 1956, at the age of 25. He was chief at Merca (1956-58) and promoted to Major-Adjutant (1958-65) as Somalia built up its post-independence army. He went for further training to the Military Academy, Moscow (1965-67) and was promoted Brigadier General in the new national army in 1967.

He was the most senior general in the Somali army and played a major part in the military coup which brought Siyad Barre to power on 21 October 1969. Already Commander-in-Chief of the Somali armed forces, Barre made him Vice-President in the Supreme Revolutionary Council and Secretary of State for Defence on 29 July 1971. He was promoted Lieutenant-General in 1973. In 1976, when an attempt was made to civilianise the regime and the SRC theoretically transferred its powers to the Somali Revolutionary Socialist Party, he was appointed vice-president of the party and a member of the politburo.

As Commander-in-Chief of the army and Minister of Defence, he organised the early successes of the Somali army in the Ethiopian war in 1977-78. It took a huge airlift of men and material by the Soviet Union to defeat the Somali forces which had, by that time, overrun the whole of the Ogaden.

On 27 April 1981 Siyad carried out an extensive purge of the top leadership of the SRC and surprisingly Samater lost his job as Chairman of the Defence and Security Committee as Siyad announced that he would rule personally by decree. But this was just a temporary blip in Samatar's career because on 2 March 1982 he was reappointed Minister of Defence while remaining first Vice-President.

When Siyad was badly injured in a car crash in May 1986 he declared a state of emergency and automatically acted as leader under the constitution. On 31 January 1987 he was named as Prime Minister by

Siyad and asked to chose his own government. He took the opportunity to create three Deputy Prime Ministers.

When the Somali National Movement invaded northern Somalia in April 1988 he threw everything into the campaign and the armed forces under him ruthlessly suppressed the north, but he was also the messenger to the world, who carried the news of a general amnesty and the release of all political prisoners in January 1989. He was dismissed along with all other members of the cabinet on 9 January 1990, but after a lengthy power struggle he was reinstated as Prime Minister and was able to select his own cabinet on 15 February. He was able to drop most of his old opponents in the old cabinet and to oust the President's half brother, Abdurahmane Jama Barre, from the Foreign Ministry and the cabinet. For the time being Samater appeared to have strengthened his own position, but in another capricious change of personnel, Siyad dismissed him and the whole cabinet on 3 September 1990.

SILANYO, Ahmed Mohammed

Chairman of the Somali National Movement, 1984 –

The unchallenged leader of the SNM after 1984, he forged the rebel movement into an effective fighting force. A fluent speaker of Somali, English and Arabic, he was also mainly responsible for its wide publicity and support in the world at large.

Born 1936 in Burao, then British Northern Somaliland Protectorate. Educated locally, then at the North West Polytechnic, London and the University of Manchester where he earned a BA in 1963 and an MA in 1965 in Economics.

He returned home and joined the Ministry of Economic Planning and Co-ordination and worked his way up the civil service. In 1969 he was appointed Minister of Planning and Co-ordination and chairman of the National Planning Commission.

After the coup by Siyad Barre in October 1969 he remained in government, being reshuffled to Secretary of State (Minister) for internal trade on 27 March 1973 and in 1978 chairman of the National Economic Board, an inter-ministerial body responsible directly to the President. From 1980-82 he returned to be Minister of Commerce.

During his 17 years as a senior government official, he attended several sessions of the United Nations, the OAU, the Arab League and the Islamic and Non-Aligned Conferences, often leading the Somali delegations.

In 1982, when several senior northern officials were arrested and subjected to long periods of imprisonment without trial, he gave up trying to work within the system and left the country. He arrived in Britain and began to mobilise Somali exiles in Britain into the Somali National Movement. He became the UK chairman of the party.

He travelled extensively to Scandanavia, the Arab Countries and the USA and at the SNM congress in 1984 was elected chairman of the

Somali National Movement, being elected for a further three-year period in 1987 at the second congress in March. He authorised the unsuccessful attack carried out with Ethiopian support in the Togdheer region in February 1987 and the successful capture of Hargeisa prison in May in which the prisoners were released.

In April 1988 Ethiopia and Somalia finalised a peace agreement, thus destroying the SNM's Ethiopian support. So Silanyo authorised the invasion of northern Somalia in May 1988 in which the SNM seized many major towns after bitter fighting with government troops. Though he has remained an active leader of the SNM he has also found time to travel, raise funds and explain the policies of the SNM throughout the world.

SOUTH AFRICA

Population: 35.4m (1990, World Bank)
Head of State: Fredrik Willem de Klerk
Government: Presidential system. In terms of the constitution still in place in 1991, the President, Senate and House of Assembly are elected by whites and only whites may stand for election. Parliament consists of three Houses - white, Coloured and Indian. Negotiations were pending in mid-1991 between the government and other groups over the future of the country and shape of the constitution.
Parties: Parties have been allowed to operate freely since de Klerk lifted the ban on African parties on 2 February 1990. Government party – National Party (NP). Main white opposition parties - Democratic Party, Conservative party of South Africa and Herstigte Nasionale Party. Main African parties - African National Congress (ANC), Inkatha Freedom Party (IFP), Pan Africanist Congress (PAC), Azanian People's Organisation (AZAPO). The ANC has various allies such as the South African Communist Party, the United Democratic Front and the Mass Democratic Movement. Coloureds and Indians also have parties which attract their community support.

BOESAK, Allan (Rev)
South African political leader, former churchman.

Young, forceful and committed, Dr Allan Boesak was a former moderator of the Dutch Reformed Church in Bellville, Cape Town and president of the World Alliance of Churches. He resigned both offices after an extra-marital affair with an Afrikaner TV newscaster. Politically he came to prominence during the 1980s when most politicians and political organisations representing non-whites had already been banned. He was a founder member and later a patron of the United Democratic Front until that too was banned. But during the wave of protest in the mid-1980s, he found himself, like other church leaders, as one of the main voices in the anti-apartheid struggle. Always prepared to risk arrest, detention and personal vilification, he has continued to denounce apartheid and play a political role though limited by the scandal that lost him much moral authority.

Born 1945 in Kakamas, Cape region, into a religious family. He served as a sexton in his local Dutch Reformed Church (DRC) while he was still at high school. He decided to enter the church and went to Bellville Theological Seminary, graduating in 1967. He worked in Sendinkerk (Mission Church) Paarl before going to the Kampen Theological Institute in Holland in 1970, for further doctorate studies.

He gradually became more interested in the political aspects of his ministry and joined the Broederkring, a ginger-group within the Dutch Reformed Church. Elected chairman, he addressed the inaugural conference of the Alliance of Black Reformed Christians in Southern Africa, demanding radical change in the church's attitude towards the apartheid system.

At the Ottawa meeting of the World Alliance of Reformed Churches in August 1982, he was unanimously elected president of the organisation, which represents about 150 reformed churches internationally. He introduced a motion that apartheid be declared a heresy contrary to the gospel and was behind a resolution which suspended two of the South African Calvinist churches from the World Alliance. On his return home in September he was elected Assessor of the Sendinkerk (the branch that ministers mainly to the Coloured community) Church in Cape Town.

When President Botha, at the end of 1982, introduced his proposals for a tricameral constitutional system, with no representation for blacks, Boesak set about uniting the opposition. He was behind the formation of the United Democratic Front (UDF) and gave the principal address at the launch of the party at Cape Town in August 1983 when he was elected a patron.

He then became a prime mover in a number of UDF campaigns to reject the new constitution and stop the elections of non-white candidates to the tricameral parliament.

In June 1984 he was elected senior vice-president of the South African Council of Churches. In November 1984 he visited Australia and encouraged the government not to change its anti-apartheid policies. In May 1985 he met Oliver Tambo and leaders of the ANC in Lusaka, Zambia.

In February 1985 he was suspended as a church minister for admitting that he had a relationship with a white woman who worked for the South African Council of Churches. The affair had been deliberately leaked to the press by the South African security services. Boesak was temporarily suspended from duties, but was reinstated within weeks.

In the course of 1985 he came increasingly into open confrontation with the police. Twice he was arrested. On 27 August he was charged for planning a march of thousands, in defiance of a police ban, to Pollsmoor Prison, Cape Town to demand the release of Nelson Mandela. He was transferred to Pretoria for detention in the face of an international outcry. On 20 September he was freed on bail though his passport was withheld. On appeal, bail restrictions were relaxed by a Cape Town magistrate who found him a man of "high moral principles."

As the tide of protest in the townships grew, he joined Bishop Desmond Tutu and other leaders to discuss the deteriorating situation in Alexandra Township with President Botha in February 1986. He travelled widely in 1986, carrying the anti-apartheid message to the world. He met the Swedish Prime Minister Ingvar Carlsson and later travelled to Thailand, Hong Kong, USA and Switzerland, where he received an honorary degree at Geneva University.

In September 1986 he was elected moderator of the Mission Church of the DRC. In April 1987, when the Commissioner of Police issued new regulations tightening up the emergency regulations, Alan Boesak, Bishop Tutu and other church leaders attacked the new moves in St George's Cathedral, Cape Town. He called on the Dutch Reformed Church to denounce the new regulations.

At the beginning of 1990 he met a glamourous, 33-year-old TV producer, Elena Botha, the niece of the former hardline cabinet minister Stoffel Botha. His affair was discovered when the couple booked into a Cape Town hotel in July 1990 and the scandal broke in the press. A tearful Boesak announced his resignation as a minister and resigned as the head of his church and as head of the World Council of Reformed Churches. He continued his political career.

BOTHA, Roelof Frederik "Pik"

South African politician. Minister of Foreign Affairs, April 1977 —

Deriving his experience almost entirely from his lifetime's service in the field of foreign affairs, he has developed a more enlightened and tolerant world view than many in his own cabinet. Definitely identified with the "verligte" (progressive) wing of the Nationalist party. He is bereft of experience of Nationalist politicking at home and this has left doubts in the party as to whether he can be entrusted as a guardian of the Afrikaner heritage. This was reflected in the elections for the party leadership when PW Botha (no relative) stepped down in January 1989. Pik was fairly easily defeated in the first round of the party elections.

Born 27 April 1932. Educated at Volkskool Potchefstroom and the University of Pretoria. He joined the Department of Foreign Affairs in 1953 and served as a diplomat in Europe from 1956-62. Member of the South African legal team when the case of South West Africa was before the International Court of Justice, the Hague (1963-66). Legal adviser to the department of foreign affairs 1966-68. Under-Secretary and head of the SW Africa and UN sections in the department (1968-70). Nationalist member in the House of Assembly (1970-74).

Ambassador and permanent representative to the UN (1974-77). In October 1974 he made a celebrated speech to the UN, saying that South Africa did not condone discrimination purely on the grounds of race. He also became ambassador to the USA (1975-77). His long experience in the foreign field led to his appointment by Prime Minister B. J. Vorster as Minister of Foreign Affairs in April 1977, a move that was welcomed by some black delegates at the UN. One African ambassador remarked, "If he can influence the South African government along the lines of his private discussions with some of us at the UN, some of South Africa's problems will be solved."

Under Botha South Africa continued with its destabilisation tactics in neighbouring states but in the 1980s it gradually adopted a more conciliatory approach, leading to the Nkomati accord with Mozambique in March 1984 in which South Africa agreed to cease its support for the Mozambique National Resistance (MNR) rebels. Pik also worked towards a ceasefire in Angola and a settlement for Namibia. After a number of false starts and broken promises, Botha took a leading part in securing the agreement by which South African troops were withdrawn from Angola by 1 September 1988 and an agreement was finally signed, in New York, to start the independence process in Namibia on 22 December 1988. Pik Botha made an impassioned speech declaring the peace deal a triumph and appealing for reconciliation between South Africa and black Africa: "We are removing race discrimination," he said. "We want to be accepted by our African brothers"

When President PW Botha suffered a stroke he stood down from Nationalist Party leadership. Pik Botha stood for the leadership elections that were hurriedly organised on 2 February 1989. But in round one of the elections he gained only 16 votes, well behind the other three candidates. The party clearly saw him mainly as a foreign affairs specialist, with spectacular recent successes in that field, but not as one who could be trusted with the dismantling of apartheid.

During 1990 he played an active part in making good the damage South Africa had done, by establishing better relations with Namibia, Angola and other frontline states.

He also confessed on British Television that he was ashamed of the policy of apartheid that whites had inflicted on blacks in his country. On 30 November 1990 he made a visit to see President Moi in Kenya, it was the first time in nearly two decades that there had been high level contact between the two countries.

BOTHA, Pieter Willem
South African Politician. State President 5 September 1984 - 14 August 1989.

Known as the "old crocodile", respected rather than loved, a strong personality, tough and proud and subject to fits of violent temper. His lifelong connection with the National Party and his fourteen years as Minister of Defence (1966-80) made him the strong man of Afrikaner politics when he took over as Prime Minister. He had shown himself to be a clever politician, consummate organiser and someone who worked closely, through the State Security Council, with the military, but at the same time he was expected to introduce change and reform. He started on a reformist ticket, achieved major constitutional change and gave Coloureds and Indians a whiff of power, but in the face of a strong right-wing white backlash, he suddenly changed course and pulled back from further reform. Some say his retreat from reformist promise was inevitable given the loss of seats to the right. Others say he was too old and set in his ways even to introduce power sharing. Surprisingly, he had become unpopular also within his own party and cabinet, which were keen for him to stand down after he had a stroke in January 1989. He eventually resigned after a public quarrel with FW de Klerk in August 1989.

Born 12 January 1916 at Telegraaf farm in the Paul Roux district of Orange Free State. Educated at Paul Roux and the Voortrekker Secondary School at Bethlehem, before going on to study law at the Grey University College, Bloemfontein. He soon became interested in politics, helping the National Party during by-election campaigns.

He entered full time politics at the age of 20. After meeting Prime Minister Malan, he became an organiser for the National Party in Cape Province. In September 1941 he became assistant secretary of the Cape party. He was among those who formed the neo-fascist movement Ossewabrandwag in the Cape in 1939. However when the OB split with the main National Party in August 1941, he resigned.

He stood for parliament in 1943 but lost to the United Party candidate. He continued as an NP organiser and in 1946 was made party Information Officer for all four provinces. He drafted political pamphlets listing the weaknesses of opponents and the points on which they could be attacked. In the 1948 election he stood for George, won the seat and played a major part in organising the election in which the NP came to power. He was rewarded by being promoted chief secretary of the party in Cape Province.

Dr Verwoerd gave him his first government appointment as Deputy Interior Minister in October 1958. Three years later he became Minister of Community Development and Coloured Affairs in August 1961. On 5 April 1966 he was promoted to the important Defence Ministry, a post he held for 14 years. It was a time the Labour government in Britain imposed an arms embargo on South Africa which he condemned as "sheer madness." It forced him to look for alternative supplies and found France prepared to fill the vacuum. He also began, very effectively, to develop South Africa's own arms industry. He established South Africa's first missile testing base in Zululand in 1968.

He was elected leader of the NP in the Cape, and on a national level became a member of the State Security Council, a body set up to advise the government, which came to be dominated by defence and military interests. Botha's emphasis on British obligations to South Africa under the Simonstown agreement of 1955, was rewarded when the Conservatives won power in June 1970 and Britain accepted an order for helicopters. In the meantime, under his ministerial direction, South Africa had become self-sufficient in small arms. He was also responsible for the South African raid on Angola in December 1975 which took the South African forces to within a few miles of Luanda, the Angolan capital, before being forced to retreat.

When B. J. Vorster resigned he entered the race for the premiership and was fortunate because a scandal clouded the chances of his main rival, Dr Connie Mulder. He defeated both Mulder and R.F.Botha and became Prime Minister on 28 September 1978. He still retained the

Defence portfolio and took on National Intelligence.

It was thought that he would introduce reforms and one of his first gestures was to become the first Prime Minister to visit the black township of Soweto. He reorganised government, reducing the number of government departments, cutting the number of cabinet committees to four and upgrading the role of the State Security Council.

He engineered the abolition of the Senate in 1980 and established a President's Council with nominated members. Though under heavy attack from right-wing splinter groups and faced with heavy losses at the 1981 elections, he pressed ahead with his plans for constitutional change. In November 1983 he called a referendum on a new constitution in which he would give some power to the Coloureds and Indians (but none to the Blacks) while at the same time replacing the post of Prime Minister with that of a strong executive President. He was chosen as the first President on 5 September 1984.

He won overwhelming support in the referendum and established a tri-cameral system with white, Coloured and Indian Houses and a cabinet in which he selected one Coloured and one Indian minister.

He then announced that he would set up a National Council to work out a new constitution that would give Blacks a voice in government. His hopes were shattered by black frustration at not being given power in the new constitution. The black townships exploded into revolt and Botha countered by introducing a state of emergency in July 1985. Thousands died and were detained in the months that followed.

Botha's political response was indecisive. It was expected that he would introduce major new changes in his "Rubicon" speech of August 1986, but instead he pulled back and stressed his determination to maintain law and order. He called elections for May 1987 and won a comfortable majority though the right-wing parties again made sizeable gains.

Botha again showed that he had shelved reform by renewing the state of emergency and by imposing yet more stringent curbs on the press and trade unions. But he did begin to take steps to ease the conditions of the ailing Nelson Mandela and responded fast by releasing detainees when they went on hunger strike.

On 18 January 1989 he had a sudden stroke that put him out of circulation for several weeks. He agreed to stand down as leader of the National Party, though he held onto the Presidency. The crisis revealed how much pressure there was within his own party to replace him and hand over to a younger man. After initial resistance, he grudgingly agreed to go. It was expected he would stand down after the elections of September 1989 but he became enraged at a proposed trip by his successor FW de Klerk to visit Kenneth Kaunda, without consulting him. After a public slanging match he suddenly resigned as President on 14 August 1989. He resigned from the National Party in February 1990 in protest at the return from exile of Joe Slovo, the general secretary of the South African Communist Party.

BUTHELEZI, Gatsha Mangosuthu (Chief)
South African politician. Inkatha leader.

A moderate and talented leader who believes in the "politics of the possible" rather than the win-all approach of orthodox African nationalists. His moderation is shown in his desire to see a multi-party system and a mixed economy in an independent South Africa. His weakness has been that he operates from the Zulu-based Inkatha party which has strong support in rural areas but much less in the cities, even in his home area Durban. The need to exploit this tribal support and his rejection by the mainstream nationalists has led to considerable feuding, violence and bloodshed between them and his followers. His stock fell heavily when it was shown in July 1991 that Inkatha had accepted funding from the South African government. But he remains a political and intellectual force to be reckoned with in the future of his country.

Born 27 August 1928 into a prosperous family related to the Zulu royal line through his mother Princess Magogo. Educated at Nongoma, the Kwazulu capital, then sent to Fort Hare where he graduated in 1951 with a BA degree in history and Bantu administration.

Became an interpreter in the government's Bantu department in Durban, 1953 until he was installed chief of the Buthelezi tribe in Mahlabatini district, 1957. Assisted King Cyprian in the administration of the Zulu people. Elected leader of Zululand territorial authority on 9 June 1970, a title subsequently change to Chief Minister. He became involved in repeated clashes with Zulu traditionalists who wanted to curb his power. They installed King Goodwill as their leader on 3 December 1971 but he insisted that henceforward the king's role should be largely ceremonial.

Having rejected South Africa's Bantustan system he eventually decided to work through it, becoming the first black Prime Minister of the new Kwazulu Bantustan in April 1972, while continuing to oppose separate development and rejecting full independence for his fragmented territory. Always a believer in the "politics of the possible", he defended this ambivalent stance by saying that he could use his position as a platform to fight apartheid.

In November 1976 he founded and became leader of a new movement, the Black Unity Front, which was supposed to promote unity and the ultimate federation of the Homelands. At the same time he began to form his Inkatha movement based on a defunct Zulu cultural organisation. The movement grew rapidly, reaching a membership claimed to be over 200,000 and became the ruling party in the Kwazulu Bantustan.

Aware of criticism for fostering a tribally based organisation, he tried to forge a political alliance on 11 January 1978 between black, coloured and Indian groups. He said the objective was "to lay the foundation for a possible future multi-racial convention to map out a non-racial community and a new constitution for South Africa." But while he has always been prepared to co-operate with the ANC, that organisation finally condemned him and his policies. This was the forerunner of considerable conflict, violence and bloodshed during the 1980s, between Inkatha and the more orthodox left-wing parties.

In 1980 he set up a non-racial commission formed of various interest groups which came up in 1982, with the "consociational solution" which would grant Africans representation in the central state, but he flatly rejected the new constitutional dispensation proposed by the Government in January 1983, and the formation of a National Council in January 1986, thus keeping his options open for further constitutional developments.

Violence between Buthelezi's supporters in Inkatha and the ANC began in 1985. Both sides called for peace talks, but no positive action was taken even after Nelson Mandela's release in February 1990. The two men seemed reluctant to meet each other unless they could be sure of committing their followers to a lasting peace.

On 29 January 1991 a meeting was finally arranged. The two men pledged to try and end the violence between their supporters in the townships. But the violence continued well into 1991 despite further talks between the leaders in April and at committee level between the two groups. A peace agreement was finally signed in September 1991.

Buthelezi declared himself ready for constitutional negotiations with the government. His hand was considerably weakened when the *Daily Mail* revealed in July 1991 that the South African government had been financing Inkatha from a secret slush fund. At first Buthelezi denied any knowledge of government funding for his party, but the *Mail* produced documents to show that he had actively sought the assistance of the security police as a means of countering the growing influence of the ANC. Buthelezi's personal assistant M. Z. Khumalo resigned his post, saying that he had kept the source of funding secret from his boss.

CHIKANE, Frank

South African minister and political leader. Secretary-General, South African Council of Churches, July 1987 –

One of the younger church leaders who despite suffering persecution and brutality has helped carry the African struggle throughout the 1980s. Though his own Apostolic Church would not sustain him in his political activities, he found a way through other committed church organisations and through the United Democratic Front. Frequently detained and tortured, he never relinquished his political commitment, but became more determined to carry on the struggle.

Born 3 January 1951, the son of a pastor in the Apostolic Faith Mission. Educated in Soweto, matriculating at Orlando High School in 1971. Continued at University of the North to study science. Became a leader of the Students' Christian Movement, though Christianity was considered to be irrelevant by most black students who actually banned the SCM from operating on the university campus. By 1974 the atmosphere had changed and he emerged as the chairperson of the SCM. He also became involved in black consciousness politics. He broke down during his final examinations due to pressure of political work and was not allowed to re-sit them by the university authorities.

In 1975 he joined the Apostolic Faith Mission and was taken into the ministry in 1976. He worked in a Krugersdorp congregation from 1976-79 and after completing the course was ordained in 1980. But the church was conservative and concentrated on religious matters. It frowned on his political involvement and suspended him for a year. But he continued his ministry and started a number of community and social projects.

His political involvement continued. He became a follower of Steve Biko, attending the Azanian People's Organisation (AZAPO) congress in 1979 and forming the Krugersdorp Residents' Organisation. Again his church objected and suspended him. He became active in the Institute of Contextual Theology. In September 1982 was appointed its full-time co-ordinator and in 1983, its general secretary.

He became further involved in political protest. He was detained in January 1977 and tortured so badly that he was unable to walk after detention. He was detained again in June 1977 and January 1978. While in prison his hair was torn out. On his release he was in such pain that many of the youth in his congregation left to join the guerrilla struggle with the ANC. He was detained again under the Terrorism Act from November 1981 to July 1982.

In August 1983 he was one of the founders of the United Democratic Front, delivering the opening address to the movement at Mitchell's Plain, Cape Town. When other UDF leaders were detained in 1984, he joined the national executive. He also became deputy president of the Soweto Civic Association. In February 1985 he and other Soweto leaders were detained and charged with treason. Released on bail, his trial dragged on until he was acquitted on 6 December 1985.

On 1 July 1987 he was appointed secretary-general of the South African Council of Churches, replacing the activist cleric Christiaan Beyers Naude. The SACC is the umbrella organisation for most of the English-speaking churches that became politically outspoken under the leadership of Archbishop Desmond Tutu in the early 1980s.

In 1989 Chikane collapsed and was admitted to hospital on at least four occasions. On one occasion this occurred in the USA where analysis showed his clothes had been impregnated with poison.

DE KLERK, Frederik Willem

South African politician. President 14 September 1989 –

A worrier and chain smoker who conceals a nervous dispostion behind a bland exterior and perfect manners. Described as the archetype of white South African "middle of the roadism". He is considered to be solid but unimaginative, powerful but cautious, of unquestionable integrity but not inventive. He has developed being non-committal into a fine art. Unlike

PW Botha who was fiery and powerful, he is articulate and even-tempered, always ready to weigh up any situation, then to compromise.

He showed that he accepted the need to get rid of apartheid immediately after his assumption of the presidency in September 1989. He released Mandela and established good relations with him. He abolished the last trappings of apartheid in 1991.

Born 18 March 1936 in a powerful Afrikaner family in Johannesburg. His great grandfather was a senator, his grandfather stood for parliament twice, his aunt married the Prime Minister JG Strydom. His father was general secretary of the Transvaal National party from the watershed year of 1948, when the Nationalists took power, to 1954.

He became politically involved as a youngster, joining the youth section of the National Party while still in his teens. He later served on the executive of the Afrikaanse Studentebond, then the "finishing school" for future leaders of government. He became editor of the campus newspaper at Potchefstroom University where he graduated in law in 1958.

He practised as a small town attorney at Veereniging from 1961-72, while serving as the chairman of the local NP divisional council. He was appointed to a law professorship at Potchefstroom University and entered parliament after the NP's Vereeniging seat became available. He moved quickly through the party structures serving on a range of select committees and commissions, eventually being appointed president of the Senate, a post he held until 1976.

Meanwhile, he held a range of cabinet posts – Posts and Telecommunications (3 April 1978), Sport and Recreation (14 November 1978), Home Affairs, Social Welfare and Pensions, Mines, Environmental Planning, Energy and Education in 1984. As minister of Home Affairs his progress towards scrapping the Group Areas Act and the Immorality Act was painfully slow. He laid great stress on "community controls", whereby residents would decide who should be admitted to live in their home areas.

As Education Minister he came under fire for a bill which proposed harsh controls over political activities on university campuses, with swingeing cuts for university institutions that did not apply them.

The NP split in 1982 and some members defected to the Conservative Party in reaction to the introduction of a three-chamber parliament where coloureds and Indians were given seats for the first time. He did a great deal to heal the divisions within his own party. He then became leader of the NP in the Transvaal. With the advent of the tricameral constitution he became chairman of the ministers of the Council in the House of Assembly, while retaining his national education portfolio.

In 1988 he came out strongly against the head of the South African Rugby Board, Dr Danie Craven, who held talks with the African National Congress in Harare. He said he was shocked that Craven had by-passed the government and "turned to a terrorist organisation." He said that talks with the ANC were absolutely unacceptable as long as it persisted in its present activities.

His hour of triumph came after President PW Botha had a heart attack early in 1989. Hurried elections were called on 2 February 1989 to find a new leader of the NP. There were several fancied candidates including Barend du Plessis, Chris Heunis and Pik Botha, but de Klerk won easily in the first round and then narrowly beat Barend du Plessis in the final round of the elections. He then emerged as the new leader of the National Party.

Relations between himself and President PW Botha became increasingly acrimonious as 1989 progressed. Whenever a quarrel loomed he rallied the party and the cabinet behind him and surprised everyone by confronting the "old crocodile". It was expected that he would succeed after the elections of September, but a furious row blew up over a proposed visit to Kenneth Kaunda in Zambia and Botha resigned in a fit of rage, leaving him to be sworn in as acting President on 15 August.

He was unanimously elected President by Parliament on 14 September 1989, in an atmosphere of hope and goodwill from all races. He affirmed his commitment to radical change but did not explain how this would be effected. He took various measures to end petty apartheid and released seven senior veterans of the ANC including Walter Sisulu, but not, at first, Nelson Mandela. As time passed it became clear that he had abandoned apartheid as an official policy but he was only cautiously edging towards talks with the black African leadership. After Mandela was released in February 1990, he rapidly built a respectful relationship with the nationalist leader and embarked on several rounds of negotiations with him.

In February he also lifted the ban on African parties including the ANC, PAC and the Communist Party. From April ANC members began to return from exile, though de Klerk insisted that they would not be given a blanket amnesty.

On 2 May 1990 he held the first negotiations ever, between the government and the ANC, since the party was first formed in 1912. He promised to lift remaining apartheid legislation while the ANC agreed to end the armed struggle with government. In June the state of emergency was partially lifted except in Kwazulu where violence between the ANC and Inkatha persisted. In September, de Klerk persuaded the National Party to take the radical step of opening its ranks to people of all races.

In October he secured the repeal of the Separate Amenities Act, which for 37 years had been a pillar of apartheid legislation. This was followed, in February 1991, by all the remaining apartheid legislation. In March he tabled proposals for extensive land reform, aimed at immediately establishing a million black homeowners and releasing 1.25m acres of land for purchase by black farmers.

These moves were interspersed with several tours abroad to explain to the world how apartheid was being abolished, while asking for the lifting of sanctions and for new investment.

Negotiations with the ANC were severely set back when the local press revealed in July 1991 that government had been secretly financing Inkatha. De Klerk denied that this funding had been used to encourage Inkatha violence, or that it signified that his government had been pursuing a double agenda. He demoted the two main ministers involved and pledged his determination to get the political negotiations back on track as soon as possible.

Du PLESSIS, Barend Jacobus

South African politician. Minister of Finance, August 1974 –

The modern administrator and technocrat par excellence of the National Party, with a background in computers, training, finance, banking and information technology. When he turned his full attention to politics his rise was fast and unchecked. He became a full minister in November 1983 and held the tricky Education and Finance portfolios, where he came to the attention of PW Botha who brought him into the President's office. He was only narrowly defeated for the election to the leadership of the National Party in February 1989. He continued as Minister of Finance under de Klerk and backed his reformist policies.

Born 19 January 1940 in Johannesburg. Educated at Baanbreker Primary School and Voortrekker High School where he matriculated in 1956. Went on to Potchfestroom University where he took a B.Sc in 1960. He did teacher training, then started to teach mathematics in 1962 at the Hoer Seunskool Helpmekaar, Johannesburg.

He then altered course and joined the South African Broadcasting Corporation as an administrative officer. He trained on computers in the new data processing department before becoming administrative secretary in the office of the director general. In 1968 he joined IBM where he did further training in banking and finance at the IBM graduate school of Banking in Princeton, USA.

His interest in politics was born in his family and he worked on behalf of the National Party before formally joining in 1966. In 1972 he stood for Roodepoort City Council, in 1973 he became deputy mayor, and in 1974, mayor. A few weeks later he stood as the NP candidate for Florida and took the seat from the opposition United Party.

In parliament his computing and administrative skills put him onto the select committee on public accounts (1976-81), the National Party study group on finance (1979-82) and made him information officer for the party (1977-81). He also chaired a committee investigating broadcasting in Southern Africa. During this period he also built a string of directorships in private companies.

His first major ministerial appointment came when he was appointed Deputy Minister of Foreign Affairs and Information in 1982. He travelled with the Foreign Minister Pik Botha to the first discussions with Angola on achieving a peace settlement in Southern Africa.

He was appointed Minister of Education and Training on 23 November 1983 where he immediately found himself confronted by the wave of school boycotts at that time. He met with Bishop Desmond Tutu and school leaders in an attempt to defuse the situation. He tried to make himself directly accessible to students and teachers and announced that in his own department there would be no racial restrictions on promotion.

He was appointed Minister of Finance in August 1984 at a time when the economy was under siege with a massive devaluation of the rand, low prices of gold and other exports and international disinvestment. He had to deal with a foreign debt crisis and secure new international credit lines.

In November 1986 PW Botha brought him into his President's Office. His wide-ranging administrative talent had clearly caught the President's eye. When Botha suffered a stroke and resigned the party leadership in January 1989, Du Plessis was his most favoured successor. Elections were hurriedly organised on 2 February 1989 and he ran FW de Klerk a very close race losing in the final round by 61 votes to de Klerk's 69.

HANI, 'Chris' Martin Thembisile
South African politician. ANC Executive Committee 1974 –

One of the new group of "young lions" in the African National Congress that is aspiring to top leadership. A highly active, intelligent and courageous member of the national executive of the ANC since he was 32. He was deputy commander of the armed wing of the party, Umkhonto we Sizwe from 1982, succeeding Joe Slovo as Chief-of-Staff in October 1987. He is also on the ANC Political and Military Council and a member of the South African Communist Party. He has been widely tipped in the press to rise to the very top of the ANC leadership at a time when the older generation must soon be replaced by the new. He was in dispute with the leadership over the policy of bombing soft, civilian targets in the armed struggle against apartheid before it was abandoned.

Born 28 June 1942 at Cofimvaba, Transkei, in a family of six children. His father, a construction worker and trader, was an active member of the African National Congress, while his uncle was a member of the Communist Party of South Africa. He was educated locally and at Matanzima Secondary School (1954-56) and Lovedale Institute, Alice where he gained his Cape senior certificate in 1958.

As a child he wanted to become a Catholic priest, but in 1957 he turned to politics and joined the ANC Youth League while still at school. He went to Fort Hare University (1959-61), learnt Latin and became fascinated by the politics of early Rome which sharpened his political feelings. He protested against the take-over of the university by the Department of Bantu Education. In 1961 he was suspended for campaigning against the creation of a Republic in accordance with the non-collaboration policy called by the All-in Africa Conference at Pietermaritzburg. He continued his studies at Rhodes University and graduated with a BA in Latin and English. He started his career as an articled clerk in Cape Town but only stayed the course from 1962-63. He gradually became more involved in trade union affairs and worked for the South African Congress of Trade Unions (SACTU).

The ANC was banned but Hani courageously went underground, working for its armed wing *Umkhonto we Sizwe,* and was elected to its Committee of Seven in Western Cape. In 1962 he was arrested at a road block and found to be carrying banned pamphlets. He was detained and charged under the Suppression of Communism Act. But he secured bail and had the nerve to attend an ANC conference at Lobatsi in Botswana.

On his return he was immediately re-arrested and detained in Zeerust and Mafeking before being tried and sentenced to 18 months' imprisonment under the Suppression of Communism Act. He appealed, lost and went into hiding while on bail. The ANC then agreed that he should leave the country and undergo military training.

During the civil war in Rhodesia Umkhonto frequently fought alongside the guerrillas of the Zimbabwe African People's Union. Hani fought in a number of battles against the Rhodesian troops where he came under aerial attack as well as fighting conventional guerrilla warfare.

Eventually Umkhonto was forced to withdraw to Botswana where the government was already under intense pressure from South Africa for allegedly harbouring ANC rebels. Hani was arrested and charged for possessing weapons and sentenced to six years imprisonment. He served two years and then was released and allowed to travel to Zambia.

In 1974, after his election to the National Executive of the ANC, he returned to South Africa to build the ANC organisation in the Cape region. He then moved to Lesotho and stayed there for seven years. In 1981 he narrowly avoided death when explosives were put in his car. In 1982 he went to Zambia where the ANC in exile had its headquarters and was appointed deputy commander of *Umkhonto we Sizwe.* He succeeded Joe Slovo as Chief-of-Staff of Umkhonto in October 1987.

In 1988 Hani became involved in the controversy over the use of violence in the South African struggle. The older leaders of the party under president Oliver Tambo did not want acts of terror to be carried out against soft civilian targets. But Hani, leading a younger group of young lions in the party, disagreed. After a bomb blast at Ellis Park rugby stadium, in Johannesburg, where two people were killed and 30 injured, he gave an interview to the *Weekly Mail* saying, "We are prepared to see a wasteland if that is the price of our freedom... Their (white) life is good. They go to their cinemas, they go to their *braaivleis* (barbecues), they go to their five star hotels. That is why they are supporting the system...The bombs were to tell the whites we can creep and crawl next to you. Be careful, we are developing and will be able to do something big within your areas." After the release of Nelson Mandela in February 1990, Hani returned to South Africa. He attended the first ever talks between the ANC and government on 2 May 1990. He was also prominent at the SA Communist party relaunch on 29 July 1990.

At the 48th National Conference of the ANC in July 1991, Hani received the most votes from the 2,000 delegates, demonstrating his popularity in the party despite his communist connections.

MALAN, Magnus André de Merindol (General)

South African soldier and politician. Minister of Defence, October 1980 – 29 July 1991.

One of the most powerful figures in South Africa with his dual role as a voice for the military and as an experienced National Party minister. President PW Botha relied on him heavily for advice and action on all matters concerning state security, the war in Angola and the position of the powerful State Security Council of which he is an ex-officio member. He is one of the few who understands and has had experience of the whole South African power structure. Though he had a heart by-pass operation in May 1986, he seems fully recovered. His experience and powers of organisation ensure that he will continue to play a key role in the future.

Born 30 January 1930 the son of a professor of chemistry who later became an MP and Speaker of the House of Assembly. Educated at the Hoer Seunskool and at Dr Danie Craven's Physical Education Brigade, Kimberley, where he matriculated. He went on to Stellenbosch University to take a B.Comm. degree and then to Pretoria where he enrolled in the first military degree course for officers, taking his B.Sc.Mil in 1953.

He was first commissioned in the navy and served with the marines on Robben Island before being transferred back into the army as a lieutenant. He rose fast in the army and took a number of advanced military courses, emerging as the commanding officer of the South West Africa command and later the military academy and Western Province command. He was promoted army chief in 1973 and chief of the defence force in 1976.

As chief of the defence force he saw his role as political as well as military. He worked closely with P. W. Botha, first when the latter was Minister of Defence and later when he became President. Malan helped work out a total strategy against external threat and internal insurrection. On 7 October 1980 he was made Minister of Defence. He had come to the conclusion that he had advanced his career as far as he could in the army and was looking for a wider political role. It was only then that he joined the National Party and sought a seat, which he won at Modderfontein.

From 1983 he began to allow the army to assist the police in controlling internal unrest. The troops were used on a number of occasions in the 1980s as protest and defiance grew in the townships. He introduced Joint Management Centres, a euphemism for an early warning system which would apprise the government of unrest in any part of the country. These JMCs were directly answerable to the State Security Council, a body which became highly influential in national policy-making under the presidency of PW Botha.

At one stage it was felt that the SSC and the military generally might resist the attempt to achieve a military settlement with Angola and independence for Namibia, but Malan did go along with Foreign Minister Pik Botha to a number of peace talks with the Angolans and Cubans during 1988 in which it was finally agreed that South African troops be withdrawn from Angola by 1 September 1988. Malan's agreement to this agreement was partly forced by the bad defeat suffered by South African troops when exposed to superior Cuban airpower, at Cuito Cuanavale after invading Angola in August. The peace talks also resulted in an agreement, in December 1988, to bring independence to Namibia.

Malan was demoted to the relatively uninfluential post of Minister of Housing and Works on 29 July 1991, after the "Inkathagate" scandal in which it was proved that a secret government slush fund had been used to finance the Inkatha Freedom Party.

MANDELA, Nelson Rolihlahla

South African ANC President, July 1991 —. Imprisoned 12 June 1964, released 14 February 1990.

A large man with a persuasive voice and a big heart, a former heavyweight boxer and long-distance runner, he is the universally acknowledged leader of the African nationalist movement. He has spent most of his active life under imprisonment. Through 25 years of detention he remained a figurehead and rallying force, not only for the African National Congress, the majority African nationalist party in South Africa but for everyone who wanted an end to apartheid in South Africa. His role is now crucial to the future. Many white South Africans, even members of the white government, recognise that no peace can come to their trouble-torn country without Mandela's participation.

Born 18 July 1918 at Qunu near Umtata in the Transkei, the son of a Tembu (Xhosa) chief, but he renounced the chieftaincy on his father's death. His second name Rolihlahla means "One who stirs up trouble". He was educated at a mission school and Methodist boarding school until he went to Fort Hare University in 1938 to read law. He was expelled in 1940 for being one of the ringleaders in a student strike. He took up politics in 1944, joining the ANC and founding the Youth League.

In December 1952 he and his friend Oliver Tambo, who became Chairman of the ANC, established the first African law firm in Fox Street, Johannesburg. Soon came his first real test of courage when he led a nationwide defiance campaign against the race laws, which resulted in 8,500 people being arrested and imprisoned in protest against apartheid.

He became president of the Transvaal ANC and his continual

opposition led to a series of restrictions and detention orders. On 4 September 1953 he was banned from public meetings for two years . On 5 December 1956 he was charged with high treason and his trial dragged on until he was acquitted on 29 March 1961. Immediately afterwards he organised a massive stay-at-home in protest against the move to turn South Africa into a republic. A state of emergency was declared and he was arrested and detained for several months without charge.

Next he went into hiding, becoming known as the "black pimpernel" as he continued to rally and organise the ANC. He smuggled himself out of the country and on 8 August 1962 addressed a conference of nationalist leaders in Addis Ababa, Ethiopia. Returning home, he was captured at a road block on 5 August 1962 and sentenced to five years' imprisonment.

Then came his greatest test. He was put on trial as leader of *Umkonto we Sizwe* (the spear of the nation) the guerrilla wing of the ANC, and convicted of incitement and illegally leaving the country. On 7 November 1962 he was sentenced to five years imprisonment and refused to appeal.

When most of the top ANC leaders were arrested at a clandestine meeting at Lilliesleaf farm, Rivonia, he was put on trial again on 20 October 1963 with eight other ANC and Communist Party leaders, charged with plotting violent revolution.

On 20 April 1964 he gave the memorable four and a half hour speech in his defence, extracts of which were later issued as a long playing record. He was sentenced to life imprisonment. They were sent to the notorious Robben Island, where South Africa detained its more important political prisoners.

In April 1982 he was transferred to Pollsmoor maximum security prison near Cape Town, where his wife Winnie was occasionally allowed to visit. President Botha several times offered to release Mandela but always on conditions, the main one being that he would have to promise to renounce the use of violence as a political instrument. Mandela turned him down flat saying "Prisoners cannot enter into contracts ... I cannot and will not give any undertaking to renounce violence at a time when the people are not free."

Mandela saw the South African government as being to blame by using violence to ensure its power. The ANC adopted violence as a method only after decades of failure for its passive and non-violent methods.

In January 1986 President Botha again repeated his offer to release Mandela under certain conditions. This time he did not mention the question of violence, but instead suggested that Mandela's release should be linked to the release of the Soviet dissident Anatoli Scharansky and of a South African officer captured in a raid by the Angolan authorities. The Soviets released Scharansky, but Botha later said that his conditions had not been met and that Mandela would not be released.

In August 1988 Mandela was diagnosed as having tuberculosis. He was transferred from prison to Constantiaberg Clinic and then in December into a "suitable, comfortable and properly secured home" at the Victor Verster prison in Paarl. By then Botha and his successor, de Klerk, were looking for a face-saving formula that would allow the release of Mandela, so that real negotiations could be started with the most important African leader.

Mandela was finally released to scenes of great rejoicing and enthusiasm on 11 February 1990, after more than 25 years in detention. There was no bitterness in his heart, all he wanted to do was to negotiate an end to apartheid and democracy for his people as soon as was practicable.

He adopted a pragmatic line at the first talks with government in May and other meetings which followed. He was able to negotiate a partial ending of the state of emergency and the amnesty of political exiles in return for a promise to abandon the armed struggle. He established a good relationship with President de Klerk, but was highly critical of the role of the police in putting down the violence which spread to the townships in August.

In December 1990, at the ANC's first consultative conference to be held on South African soil for 30 years, Mandela complained about the growing violence on the part of Inkatha. He accused the government of pursuing a double agenda, "While de Klerk and his colleagues have had to go along with the ANC initiative for a peaceful solution, there is a simultaneous attempt to destabilise, undermine and if possible crush the ANC and its allies."

He declared 1991 the year of political emancipation and called for an all-party congress to set up a constitutent assembly that could work out the constitutional future. But this was rejected by de Klerk who wanted to keep the political initiative in government hands.

In January, a meeting was finally arranged between Mandela and Chief Buthelezi to try to end the fighting between supporters of Inkatha and the ANC, that was damaging black unity.

In May, Mandela's wife Winnie was sentenced to six months imprisonment on charges of kidnapping and being an accessory to assault on four township youths. She appealed, but the prolonged court proceedings added to the personal pressures on Mandela.

Mandela threatened several times to break off negotiations with government unless it acted to halt township violence.

Relations were further exacerbated with the discovery in July that the security police had been funding Inkatha from a secret slush fund. Mandela was enraged.

Though the disclosures justified his allegations about government pursuing a double agenda, they also embarrassed him because his critics said that he had been putting too much trust in de Klerk's promises.

At the ANC's 48th National Conference at Durban, in July 1991 he was, for the first time, elected unopposed as the ANC President, replacing his ailing friend Oliver Tambo who was given the honorary post of National Chairman.

MANGOPE, Lucas Manyane
South African politician. President Bophuthatswana 1977 –

He came from a conservative background of long-established chiefs and was a firm believer in separate development, but his views changed with experience and he only took the leadership of the Bophuthatswana homeland because he felt it would provide a means for the political and economic advancement of his people. He is a liberal at heart who regards free speech and a free press as essential parts of the democratic system, but the opposition to his government has virtually withered away. Bophuthatswana was heavily affected by the township troubles of South Africa in 1985-86 and he tried to deal with the unrest as humanely as possible. Bophuthatswana is still considered to be the most benign of all the homeland governments.

Born 23 December 1923 at Motswedi, Zeerust, Transvaal into a family of chiefs. Educated locally doing his senior certificate at St Peter's College, Johannesburg and the Diocesan Teacher's Training College near Pietersburg where he was awarded a teaching diploma.

He then joined government service, working from 1947-49 in the Department of Native Affairs before going for higher teacher training at Bethel College, Lichtenburg. He then started teaching at secondary schools in the Transvaal.

On the death of his father in September 1959 he succeeded him as Chief of the Motswedi-Barutshe-Boo-Manyane tribe and served on the Bantu Education Advisory Board. On the formation of the Tswana Territorial Authority in 1961, he became vice-chairman. In 1968 he was appointed chief councillor of the executive council and in June 1972 chief minister of Bophuthatswana.

In 1974 he resigned from the Bophuthatswana National Party and became leader of the new Bophuthatswana Democratic Party (BDP) but he maintained his position as Chief Minister.

When Bophuthatswana became independent on 6 December 1977, he became President and Prime Minister in the BDP government. During the independence celebrations he launched a bitter attack on Pretoria, referring to the "wicked non-consolidation that has dealt a cruel and deadly blow to our independence." He was referring to the fact that Bophuthatswana had been left with a fragmented territory formed of seven separate bits of land.

Though opposition parties were tolerated, the BDP swept the polls in October 1982, winning all 72 seats. On 11 July 1984 he was elected unopposed for a second seven-year term of office.

But considerable opposition sprang up in 1985 among students and the unemployed. After demonstrations against a visit by PW Botha he closed the universities. Later in the year came bus and education boycotts, then a riot, in March 1986, when eleven died as a result of clashes with the police. He set up a commission of inquiry to investigate and managed to curb further confrontations between police and squatters. In November 1990 over 60 supporters of the ANC were arrested on suspicion of fomenting a plot to assassinate Mangope. He said the ANC had incited its supporters to reject their "democratically elected government." In reply, Nelson Mandela described Mangope as a "puppet leader."

MBEKI, Thabo Mvuyelwa
South African politician. ANC National Executive Committee 1975 —

One of the new generation of young leaders that is now emerging in the African National Congress. From a highly educated, cultivated family background - with both his parents politically involved teachers - he has emerged as one of the moderates and diplomats in the party and is particularly well known in Britain and the West as a publicist and exponent for the ANC in his capacity as director of information. He wants to capture the middle ground in Black South African politics by uniting the moderates and uncommitted behind the ANC and by taking advantage of the changing political situation in the country.

Born 18 June 1942 at Idutywa, Transkei. The son of Govan Mbeki, the veteran African National Congress leader. Educated at Butterworth Primary School and Lovedale High School, Alice. He joined the ANC Youth League while still a schoolboy. Lovedale was closed after a strike, so he studied at home and matriculated at St John's High School, Umtata in 1959.

He completed his A-levels in 1961 and took an economics degree as an external student at London University. The ANC was banned in 1960, after the Sharpeville massacre, but Thabo still worked for the party, under the direction of the ANC leader Duma Nokwe who gave him a home in Johannesburg. In 1961 he helped organise youth demonstrations against the introduction of a Republic. He formed the African Students Association in December 1961, but it floundered when many of his colleagues were arrested in the purges of the years that followed.

He was ordered by the ANC to leave South Africa in 1962 and went to Bechuanaland and Rhodesia where he was arrested and held in Bulawayo prison. He might have been deported if the British Labour MP Barbara Castle had not taken up his case in parliament. Ultimately he was allowed to leave via Bechuanaland for Tanzania where he was granted political asylum. Later he left to study economics at Sussex University, graduating in 1966.

He then worked for the ANC in London (1967-70), before doing military training in the Soviet Union and moving to the ANC headquarters in exile in Lusaka, Zambia. He began to represent the party on a quasi-diplomatic level, going to Botswana to open new offices, serving as the official representative of the ANC in Swaziland (1975-76), and Nigeria (1976-78), while spending periods in Lusaka.

He was elected to the national executive committee in 1975 and in 1978 became political secretary in the office of the president. After the Kabwe conference of the party in 1985 he took on the job for which he is best known as the ANC's external director of information. He helped organise the meeting in July 1987 when the ANC met 61 members of the white community (mostly Afrikaners) in Dakar, Senegal, for informal discussions on the future of South Africa. Mbeki led the 17-man ANC team and stressed that both sides had agreed on a "democratic, non-racial South Africa that we want." In November 1987, Thabo's father Govan, the second-in-command to Nelson Mandela, was released after 23 years' imprisonment on Robben Island.

The ANC held its first international conference in Arusha Tanzania in December 1987 in which much discussion was given to the use of violence in the nationalist struggle. Mbeki chose to stress sanctions and boycotts in contrast to the militants who wanted to continue the armed struggle. He returned to South Africa after the release of Nelson Mandela in February 1990. He attended the first ANC meeting with the government in May.

At the 48th National Conference of the ANC in July 1991, he received the second highest vote for the National Executive Committee demonstrating his popularity in the party, but he was not voted to a top ranking position in the leadership.

MODISE, Johannes (Joe)

South African politician. Member of ANC Executive Committee. Commander of *Umkhonto we Sizwe*.

One of the few non-communist members of the African National Congress National Executive Committee. Largely self educated, he emerged after the detention of Nelson Mandela and other leaders, as commander of Umkhonto we Sizwe, the armed wing of the ANC, in 1965. Since then he has been in control of the military wing of the party, a position of great influence and patronage, which did not enhance his popularity with the rank and file. In recent years he has been involved in a long drawn out power struggle with his number two in Umkhonto, Chris Hani.

Born 23 May 1929 in Doornfontein, Johannesburg. Primary school in Kliptown and the Fred Clark Memorial school, Nancefield. He did further private studies up to form five. Worked as a van and lorry driver for various employers in Johannesburg.

His political stirrings started when he joined the African National Congress Youth League, in Newclare, in 1947. He became a part time organiser for the ANC in the early 1950s. He was a leading campaigner against the Sophiatown removals in 1954 and was arrested when trying to prevent the police harassing people.

In 1956 he was one of the 156 ANC members accused of treason, but charges against him and most of the others were later dropped.

When the ANC was banned in April 1960 it formed its armed wing, *Umkhonto we Sizwe* (Spear of the Nation) and Modise was immediately drafted into its High Command. He organised some of its early bombings. He also became involved in the recruiting and transport of Umkhonto volunteers who were being sent abroad for further training. In the early 1960s he began to work underground, full time for Umkhonto.

The South African police captured some Umkhonto members during this period and the hunt was on for Modise. He left for further training abroad. He went to Czechoslovakia in 1963 and the Soviet Union in 1964, before establishing his main base in Tanzania.

Nelson Mandela, the Umkhonto commander, was arrested as were his successors. The National Executive Committee then appointed Modise in 1965, as commander and made him a member of the NEC itself.

Modise was based in Tanzania and Zambia with the task of rebuilding Umkhonto. One of his main objectives was to reorganise the overland routes back into South Africa through neighbouring countries, some of which were frightened to be caught harbouring guerrillas by South Africa.

He then organised his forces to cooperate with Joshua Nkomo's Zimbabwe People's Revolutionary Army (ZIPRA), These large scale, joint operations with the Zimbabwean nationalists in the Wankie area of Rhodesia, became the subject of considerable controversy within the ANC. Modise hoped to open a permanent route for his Umkhonto fighters through the eastern highlands, but largely failed in this objective. Very few ANC fighters reached South Africa.

Modise returned to South Africa in the early 1970s and started to build an underground organisation. The first bombings took place in 1976 directed at first, against government buildings and installations, not people.

Modise was re-elected to the NEC at the ANC Kabwe conference in 1985 where his position was confirmed on the military committee of the ANC and on the military-political council.

While in command abroad, Modise was known as the master of the ANC system of patronage which made the exiles dependent on the ANC for sustenance. He was so adept at this system of control that he earned himself the nickname "Nyawozinodaka" (dirty feet).

When the exiles returned to South Africa under President FW de Klerk's reforms in 1990, Modise returned with them. After initial rivalry between himself and the faction in Umkhonto led by his number two, Chris Hani, he claimed a place in the official ANC delegation in the successful preliminary negotiations with the government in May 1990.

In July a row blew up as to whether the Communist Party through Umkhonto were planning a secret "armed insurrection" against the government. Modise, not being a CP member, was not directly involved, but the Umkhonto line was that the armed struggle had not been abandoned. The organisation was simply preserving its structures in case of any breakdown in talks.

At the 48th National Conference of the ANC in July 1991, he was returned both to the National Executive Committee and the National Working Committee with high votes from fellow delegates, but no promotion to the top rank of leadership.

NKOBI, Thomas

South African politician. Treasurer-General ANC, 1973 –

Involved in ANC politics since the 1940s, now treasurer-general of the party, officially ranking number three. Also one of the vice-chairmen of the powerful political military council, which co-ordinates the armed struggle. Very much a member of the old guard of the party, only a few years younger than Nelson Mandela.

Born 2 October 1922 in Plumtree, Southern Rhodesia. His father went to work in the gold mines in South Africa and later became a trader and taxi fleet owner. The family moved to South Africa in 1933 and Nkobi went to an elementary school in Alexandra township and then to Hlatinkulu School and Adams College, Natal, before returning to matriculate at the Bantu High School, Johannesburg in 1946. He went on to Roma University, Lesotho where he took a BCom degree.

He joined the African National Congress Youth League in the late 1940s, attending the 1949 Bloemfontein Congress. In 1952 he joined the ANC's Defiance Campaign and became a party representative for Alexandra Township.

He was a prime organiser of the Alexandra bus boycott and chairman of the boycott committee in 1957. Next he became involved in the potato boycott (potatoes being grown on farms using forced contract labour where workers suffered inhuman conditions). He was arrested and the police fed him nothing but potatoes for three days, which he refused. Put on trial, he was defended by Nelson Mandela and acquitted.

In 1957 he became national organising secretary of the ANC, travelling extensively from branch to branch. He helped reorganise the ANC under Mandela's direction so that it could operate an underground cell structure. In 1960 he was arrested under the emergency regulations and detained for five months. The ANC was proscribed but he continued to work underground despite frequent banning orders and house arrest.

But he had become a marked man and the ANC asked him to go and work for the party overseas, which he did in April 1963, going first to Botswana then Tanzania and in January 1964 to Zambia, where he became deputy treasurer of the party in 1968.

In 1973 he was promoted to Treasurer-General. He was confirmed in this office at the 48th National Conference of the ANC, on 6 July 1991.

NZO, Alfred

South African politician. Secretary-General ANC, April 1969 – July 1991.

A lifelong member of the ANC and ANC Youth League and secretary-general of the party, officially ranking number two, from 1969–1991. Also one of the vice-chairmen of the powerful political military council, which co-ordinates the armed struggle. Now very much a member of the old guard of the party, almost of the same generation as Nelson Mandela. His position became critically important when Oliver Tambo, the acting president of the party, suffered a reported stroke in August 1989 and had to be rushed to Scandinavia for treatment. He lost the post of secretary-general to Cyril Ramaphosa in July 1991.

Born 19 June 1925 in Benoni, son of a clerical worker in the gold mines. He completed junior certificate in 1942 at the Roman Catholic Missionary School at Mariazell then went on to matriculate at Healdtown Missionary Institute. He then went to Fort Hare to take a BSc degree, but spent much of his time with the African National Congress Youth League and dropped out, in 1946, before he finished his university course.

But he completed a sanitary health inspector's course at Johannesburg Technical College in 1951. He then took up a job as a health inspector in Alexandra township. His work made him increasingly politically aware and committed. He played a leading role in the strikes and defiance campaigns of the early 1950s.

In 1957 he became secretary of the bus boycott committee in Alexandra and in 1958 he was elected to the national executive committee of the ANC. Shortly afterwards he was fired from his job because of his political activities and lost his permanent resident's permit in Alexandra which laid him open to further charges for being in the area illegally. He was also served with a number of banning orders.

In 1961 he was imprisoned for five months at Modder B, the goldmine where his father once worked, which had been converted into a prison. In the same year he was restricted in Mofolo. On 24 June 1963 he was detained under the ninety day detention law and re-arrested at the end of each term. No charges were brought against him, but he ended up spending the better part of a year in detention. He was finally released in February 1964.

Knowing he had become a marked man within South Africa, the ANC asked him to leave the country and work overseas. He left in March 1964 and worked in the ANC office in Cairo until August 1967 when he was appointed chief representative in New Delhi. In April 1969 he was elected secretary-general of the ANC and transferred to the party headquarters at Morogoro, Tanzania.

When Oliver Tambo's health began to fail in 1989, as number two in the party, he assumed a more important role. In August he outlined a detailed peace plan for South Africa on the basis of which the ANC would be prepared to negotiate a settlement with the South African government. He received a high vote for the National Executive Committee on 6 July 1991, but did not get a top ranking post and lost his post as Secretary-General.

SISULU, Walter Max Ulyate
South African politician. Deputy President ANC, July 1991 –

The organising genius behind the African National Congress and for 22 years its Secretary-General. At one stage even more senior in the party than Nelson Mandela. A driving force behind the Defiance Campaign and ANC initiatives of the 1950s and 1960s. His administrative ability allowed him to harness his intellect to specific causes. Released in October 1989, with his health apparently unimpaired, he immediately assumed a leadership role in harmonising African opinion in preparation for talks with the new de Klerk government. He was elected deputy president of the party in July 1991.

Born 18 May 1912 into a poor Xhosa family in the Transkei. His Anglican school mission education was cut short at the age of 15 so that he could earn his keep in a Johannesburg dairy in 1927.

After a variety of jobs in mines, factories and a bakery, he tried to run his own estate agency, but it closed after two years. He joined the African National Congress in 1940 and played an active part in the Youth League, becoming its treasurer, where he took a militant stand. He led a campaign against Africans joining the armed forces during the war.

During the African mineworkers strike in 1946 he tried to bring out other workers in their support. He was elected to the Transvaal provincial executive of the ANC and in December 1949 persuaded the ANC to accept the Youth League's "Programme of Action". He was also elected Secretary-General of the ANC.

In 1950 he became one of the joint secretaries of the co-ordinating committee linking the Communist Party and the Indian Congress. They called a national strike to protest against the race laws in June 1950.

Sisulu, at this time, was reaching the peak of his power because the ANC president, Dr Moroka, was living away from the centre of action in the Free State. The success of the Defiance Campaign in 1952, with Sisulu marshalling 8,500 volunteers to break the race laws, was largely due to his skill as an organiser. Banned in December 1952 under the Suppression of Communism Act from attending public meetings, he became an underground worker.

He was re-elected Secretary-General in 1952 and in 1953 embarked on a five-month tour that took him to China, the Soviet Union, other Eastern bloc countries and the UK. The journey shaped his views about communism. He accepted its economic achievements, but disliked the limitation of political freedom under Stalin. It also broadened his views and confirmed his desire to work with other racial groups, putting him among the moderates and against the Africanists in the ANC who wanted to go it alone.

In December 1956 he was among the 156 political leaders (including Nelson Mandela) arrested and charged with high treason. He cleverly fought a protracted legal battle and was finally acquitted in March 1961. But in the interim he had been detained for several months under the emergency regulations introduced in 1960. The ANC was banned and he was placed under house arrest. He was continually harassed by the police and arrested a number of times for breaking his restrictions.

On 3 March 1963 he was sentenced to six months' imprisonment for incitment to strike and furthering the aims of the ANC. Released on bail pending appeal, he vanished from his home on 20 April 1963 and went underground to join *Umkhonto we Sizwe*, the armed wing of the ANC.

On 11 July 1963 he was arrested at Liliesleaf Farm, which served as the underground headquarters for the ANC, along with Govan Mbeki and other top ANC leaders. He was held in solitary confinement until the trial opened on 29 October. In his defence Sisulu told the court "The African people have the right to revolt against repression." He denied that it was ANC policy to "commit murder either directly or indirectly", but he said that he could not continue to preach non-violence when racial discrimination was so oppressive. On 12 June 1964 he was convicted for planning acts of political sabotage and sentenced to life imprisonment.

He was sent to Robben Island with Mandela and the other leaders. In April 1982 just as he was turning 70, he and Mandela were sent to Groote Schuur Hospital in Cape Town for a medical examination; afterwards they were moved to Pollsmoor prison, Cape Town.

He was finally released on 15 October 1989 to a tumultuous welcome not just from the ANC but from nationalists generally who welcomed him back as one of their leaders. Though grey-haired, and 77 years old he seemed fit and well and had lost none of his political wisdom. Though he was not prepared to call an end to the ANC's armed struggle, together with Mandela he was prepared to adopt a flexible stance in negotiations with the new government of FW de Klerk.

SLOVO, Joe

Former Secretary-General of the South African Communist Party, 1986 - December 1991.

A lifelong campaigner against apartheid who managed to combine the leadership of the South African Communist Party with faithful membership of the African National Congress. Before he was driven into 27 years of exile, he was a famous defence lawyer whose house in Johannesburg was open to friends of all races. He became the leader of Umkhonto we Sizwe (Spear of the nation), the armed wing of the ANC. He returned home in April 1990 to play a major part in the rapidly unfolding history of his nation.

Born 1926, in Lithuania. He moved to South Africa with his parents while still a child. His father was a van driver and as he wanted to study law, he had to work as a dispatch clerk for a chemist while doing his legal studies at Witwatersrand where he took a BA and LLB.

He fought with the South African forces in the World War and afterwards joined the South African Communist Party. Called to the Johannesburg bar, he became a well known defence lawyer, particularly in political cases.

In 1949 he married Ruth First, a well known activist and journalist who was the daughter of the treasurer of the SACP, Julius First. In 1950 the Suppression of Communism Act outlawed the Communist Party. Slovo and his wife were among those to be named under the act, which banned them from giving interviews and restricted other freedoms. The central executive committee voted to disband the party and in 1953, it went underground.

Slovo became a founder member of the newly established Congress of Democrats and joined the Congress Alliance, which co-ordinated the activities of all groups defying the unjust laws being passed by the Nationalist government. He became one of the many communists to join the African National Congress.

In 1954 Slovo was banned from all gatherings under the Suppression of Communism Act, but was not deflected from his political work. In 1955 he helped draft the Freedom Charter. In December 1956 he was accused of treason and further charged with contempt of court for criticising the magistrate's handling of the case. On this he was acquitted and the treason charges against him were dropped in 1958.

Slovo was detained for four months in 1960 under the state of emergency which followed the Sharpeville massacre. He was one of the founders of the military wing of the ANC, *Umkhonto we Sizwe* and became one of its high command.

He went into exile in 1963, just before the police captured virtually the entire ANC leadership in a raid on Liliesleaf Farm, Rivonia. Later he was joined by his wife, who had been detained for four months, and his three daughters.

He rose to become the chief of staff of *Umkhonto we Sizwe* and the most senior and influential white leader in exile. In the late 1970s he was based in Maputo, Mozambique where his wife was killed in 1982 by a parcel bomb. He had to leave Mozambique in 1984, following the signing of the Nkomati accord with South Africa, which obliged Mozambique to reduce the ANC's presence within its borders.

He joined the rest of the ANC leadership in Lusaka, Zambia. At a policy making conference in June 1985, he became the first white member of the ANC executive.

In April 1987, after more than 25 years in the post, he resigned as chief of staff from *Umkhonto we Sizwe*, saying it was difficult to combine his duties with the leadership of the Communist party, but he remained on the ANC executive as one of its most prominent leaders. He also continued to push for the SACP to strengthen its position within the ANC ranks and leadership.

On 27 April 1990, following President de Klerk's reformist initiatives and the unbanning of the ANC and SACP, he returned home. He said, "For those of us who left by the back door and have returned by the front, it is a remarkable feeling." He added that he had returned in a spirit of conciliation. Within weeks in June he organised the first press conference of the SACP inside the country, in 40 years. In July he helped relaunch a new style Communist Party and became its Secretary General.

At the 48th Congress of the ANC in Durban in July 1991, he was returned, with the third highest vote, to the National Executive Committee. He was also ranked number seven on the Working Committee of the party. He took part in all the major negotiations between the ANC and government.

TAMBO, Oliver Reginald
South African politician, National Chairman ANC, July 1991 –

A studious, soft-voiced politician, a man of patience and tolerance, with an unassuming academic air, he has been the ideal leader to hold together the various disparate elements in the ANC, divided between the moderates and the communists and feuding over the use of violence. He became its voice overseas and its chief policy-maker who kept the party on course. Perhaps the greatest tribute to Tambo was from Nelson Mandela, writing a foreword to a new book on him in 1987: "Oliver Tambo is much more than a brother to me", he wrote "he is my greatest friend and comrade for nearly 50 years...There is no difference between his views and mine." But now well over 70, he has suffered a number of strokes and is near to the point of having to give way to a new generation of nationalist leaders. He has been undergoing medical treatment in Sweden.

Born 27 October 1917 in a peasant family in Bizana, Pondoland, about 100 miles south of Durban. Educated at Ludebe, the Methodist Mission School (1924-29) and at the Anglican Holy Cross Mission School (1929-33), then at St Peter's School, Johannesburg.

In 1938 he entered Fort Hare University, graduating with a BSc degree in 1941. Took an education diploma but was sent down for being a ringleader in a student protest one month before his exams. He taught at St Peter's Secondary School (1943-47) where his students included other prominent nationalist leaders. While teaching he took a correspondence course in law. He was so absorbed that he left teaching in 1947 and became an articled clerk in a solicitor's firm. Then in 1952 he registered as an attorney and established the first African legal partnership in South Africa with Nelson Mandela.

He was one of the founders of the ANC Youth League in 1944. In 1945 he was appointed national secretary, then national vice-president of the Youth League and in 1949 he was elected to the ANC executive. In 1954 he was banned, under the Suppression of Communism Act, from attending any public meeting for two years. He became Secretary-General of the ANC (1955-58), and then deputy president-general.

In 1956 he was arrested for high treason but the case was dropped a year later. Under a new party constitution drawn up in 1958 he was appointed to a new office of deputy-president. In 1959 he was served with another order prohibiting him from attending any gatherings for a period of five years. A week after Sharpeville and two days before the declaration of a state of emergency he left the country on 28 March 1960 to carry on the struggle abroad. He made his way via Botswana and Ghana to London.

In 1965 he set up provisional headquarters for the ANC in exile in Morogoro, Tanzania, but spent at least half of his time travelling and doing propaganda work for the organisation. After the death of Chief Luthuli on 21 July 1967, he was the natural successor and became acting president of the ANC.

Since then his task has been to publicise the ANC internationally and interpret its policies in the nationalist struggle. In 1986 he set up a project to establish constitutional guidelines for the ANC in a post-apartheid South Africa.

He held talks with a number of groups of white liberal businessmen and politicians from 1987 onwards. On 8 January 1987 he made the keynote address on the 75th anniversary of the foundation of the ANC, sanctioning the use of bombs against inanimate targets, but not against white civilians. "We must fight this war with clean hands, in a revolutionary way," he said. A project to establish constitutional guidelines for the ANC in a post-apartheid South Africa was published in June 1988, after two years of debate. This clarified such proposals as multi-party democracy, a bill of rights, positive economic discrimination, and the principle of a mixed economy.

On the 9 August 1989 he had a comparatively severe stroke, the third he suffered since 1983, which left him partly incapacitated and meant that he had to considerably lighten his workload. He underwent prolonged treatment in a clinic in Sweden, where Nelson Mandela paid him a visit after his release in February 1990.

He returned to South Africa on 13 December 1990 in time to open the ANC's first conference to be held on South African soil for 30 years. Looking frail and tired, he gave the key-note address.

At the 48th National Conference in Durban, in July 1991 he was given the honorary title of National Chairman while his friend, Nelson Mandela assumed the presidency.

TUTU, Desmond Mpilo (Archbishop)
South African Churchman. Archbishop of Cape Town, 1986 —

A man of courage and charisma whose charming, bubbly personality advanced him fast in the Anglican church hierarchy. He became secretary-general of the South African Council of Churches in 1978, at a time another chapter in the struggle against apartheid was about to start and soon found himself an international spokesman on the major political issues. With most of the major political organisations and politicians banned more and more responsiblity fell on him as a church leader. He stuck strictly to his principles of non-violence, and actually condemned his own people when some of them resorted to burnings and killings during the township uprisings in the mid-1980s, but he pressed for the international adoption of sanctions and courageously undertook peaceful protest though this meant arrest and imprisonment. His contribution to the struggle was recognised by his award in 1984 of the Nobel Peace Prize. He remains politically active and a natural leader of non-violent opinion.

Born 7 October 1931 in Klerksdorp. Educated at local mission schools, and the Johannesburg Bantu High School in Western Native Township (1945-50). Teacher training at the Pretoria Bantu Normal College led to a teaching diploma in 1954.

He became a teacher at Munsieville High School, Krugersdorp (1955-58) when he decided to go into the Anglican ministry, training at St Peter's Theological College. Ordained as a deacon in 1960 and priest in 1961, serving in Benoni.

In 1962 he went to Britain for further studies, obtaining a BA and a Masters in Theology in 1966. He returned to teach theology at Alice in Cape Province and later in Roma University, Lesotho.

He became associate director of the Theological Education Fund of the World Council of Churches in Bromley, Kent in Britain (1972-75), before being appointed Anglican Dean of Johannesburg. He became Bishop of Lesotho in 1976 and secretary-general of the South African Council of Churches in 1978. This gave him the vehicle to fight apartheid internationally and he began to speak out on his various visits abroad. After a visit to Denmark, he was accused by government spokesmen of lack of patriotism and challenged to retract a statement asking for a boycott of South African coal. But the SACC sprang to his defence, saying that a retraction would be a denial of his "prophetic calling". In apparent retaliation the government withdrew his passport in March 1980 just before he was due to travel to Switzerland.

On 27 May 1980 he was arrested along with more than 50 Anglican priests under the Riotous Assemblies Act for marching in protest against the arrest of the former secretary-general of the SACC, Rev John Thorne. He was sentenced to a R50 fine, along with the others.

In January 1981 his passport was restored and he visited the USA, addressing the UN Committee Against Apartheid. He went on to Europe where he met the Pope. On his return to South Africa his passport was again confiscated. In February 1984 the SACC came under strong criticism from a government-appointed judicial commission which accused it of identifying with the "liberation struggle". Tutu responded saying: "Until my dying day I will continue to castigate apartheid as evil and immoral...This commission does not have the theological or moral competence to pass judgement upon us."

In 1984 he was awarded the Nobel Peace Prize which was seen

internationally as a recognition of his endorsement of non-violent means of winning the anti-apartheid struggle. He was the second African to win the prize; Chief Albert Luthuli, the ANC president, won it in 1960. The government did not acknowlege his honour, but allowed him to continue to travel internationally even though his calls for economic sanctions became more persistent.

As the trouble in the townships erupted in 1984-85 he supported the objectives, but condemned violence and threatened in July 1975 to leave South Africa if bomb attacks, burnings and black-on-black violence continued. He appealed to President Botha to let him act as a broker between the government and black leaders. At first Botha refused, but finally agreed to see him and Dr Allan Boesak in February 1986 over the crisis in Alexandra township. He met Botha on two other occasions in June and July 1986. In March 1986 he welcomed the Commonwealth Group of Eminent Persons who had come to South Africa aiming to mediate on the racial crisis.

On 14 April 1986 he was elected Archbishop of Cape Town and thus head of the Anglican church in South Africa. He was the first African to be elected to the post. In April 1987 he went to Zambia to have talks with leaders of the African National Congress. Both sides agreed on the need to establish a non-racial society but not on the means to achieve it. Tutu failed to persuade the ANC to abandon the armed struggle and rely entirely on non-violence.

VILJOEN, Gerrit Van Niekerk (Dr)

South African politician. Minister for Constitutional Development, 14 September 1989 –

Urbane, sophisticated and super-educated at a series of foreign universities which put him in early touch with international opinion and helped to shape his future thinking in South Africa. But he combined these liberal influences with his chairmanship of the Afrikaner Broederbond for six years in the late 1970s. He made his mark later as Minister of Education before being placed by his close colleague, FW de Klerk into the critical post of Minister for Constitutional Development in September 1989.

Born 11 September 1926 in Cape Town, son of a professor of Greek and magazine editor. Educated in Pretoria where he matriculated in 1943. He studied classics and law at Pretoria University, gaining a masters and an LLB. He went to King's College, Cambridge to take an MA, then to the University of Leiden to research the poetry of the Greek poet Pindar, taking a DLit and DPhil in 1955.

Politics was everyday conversation at his home and he took a keen interest in Afrikaner student politics at Pretoria university where he was on the Students Representative Council. He also helped in the formation of the Afrikaner Studentebond (ASB) in 1948, a student group not involved with the various pro-Nazi student movements of the war era.

After his extensive studies overseas he returned to South Africa and became lecturer in classics (1955-57) and then professor (1957-67) at the University of South Africa. He was appointed rector of the newly formed Rand Afrikaans University in Johannesburg in 1967. There he served on a wide variety of academic boards and councils.

He joined the National Party in the late 1960s and became chairman of the Bureau of Racial Affairs. He became chairman of the Johannesburg-West division of the NP and then was elected chairman of the Broederbond, a highly influential and secretive body which formulated Afrikaner policies.

In 1978 he was appointed by Prime Minister P. W. Botha as Administrator-General of Namibia, a job similiar to that of a colonial Governor-General. He organised the transfer of the departments in charge of running the government of Namibia from Pretoria to Windhoek. But in April 1980 he was transferred back to Pretoria as Minister of Education in South Africa. In April 1981 he stood and won the Vanderbijlpark seat for the NP.

As Minister of Education he introduced many reforms which were the product of a lifetime's experience in education. He introduced salary parity for women for the first time. Another achievement was the centralisation of white education under one ministry where national standards could be established.

In September 1984 he became Minister of Co-operation, Development and Education and in September 1985, Minister of Education and Development Aid. In October he introduced new regulations in which student councils were banned from becoming involved in politics or becoming affiliated to outside student bodies.

On 31 January 1985 he said that forced removals of black communities from their homes would be suspended until the government could review its policies. In February he said that the residents of various Cape suburbs would be eligible for leasehold occupation.

President Botha suffered a stroke on 18 January 1989 and the NP held an election for a new leader but though Dr Viljoen was fancied, he did not take part as a candidate in the elections held on 2 February, narrowly won by FW de Klerk. He was rewarded when FW de Klerk finally emerged as President on 14 September and appointed him Minister for Constitutional Development, a key post if de Klerk was to honour his pledge of serious reform.

WORRALL, Denis John
South African diplomat and politician.

A brilliant academic and lawyer with vast international experience who found himself in a highly embarrassing position when attempting to explain the Nationalist government position as ambassador to Britain. Though creating a good personal impression, he finally resigned. Afterwards he established himself as a leader in progressive white politics

– one of the triumvirate of leaders of the Democratic party.

Born 29 May 1935 at Benoni. Educated at the University of Cape Town, the University of South Africa and Cornell University, USA where he studied political science, taking up a lecturing post after completing his degree. He went on to the University of California, Los Angeles and returned to continue lecturing at the University of Natal, the university of South Africa and the Unversity of Witwatersrand.

From 1962-63 he was the Cornell research fellow at the University of Ibadan, Nigeria where he gained first-hand experience of black Africa. He edited the *New Nation* from 1967-74 before becoming the director of the Institute for Social and Economic Research at Rhodes University in 1974. It was that year that he became a senator for the Cape and an advocate at the Supreme Court of South Africa.

He won a seat as the Nationalist MP for Cape Town, Gardens. P. W. Botha made him a member of the President's Council in October 1980.

In 1984 he was appointed ambassador to Britain where he faced a tough time trying to defend his government's policies. He came under intense preessure when President Botha failed to deliver a reform package with his famous Rubicon speech on 15 August 1985. Worrall tried to defend his master in a series of interviews and though he was appreciated for his efforts he clearly found his position difficult to defend. It was frequently rumoured that he might be sent back to South Africa to take on a ministerial post such as information, but these expectations never materialised.

On 30 January 1987 he resigned as ambassador, returned home and announced that he would stand as an independent against the prominent Minister, Chris Heunis, in the 6 May elections. He said that the National Party government "completely underestimates the readiness of white South Africans for fundamental change." After a tough and acrimonious campaign he was defeated in what was formerly a safe NP seat, by only 39 votes. Heunis had done so badly that he seriously jeopardised his chances in the succession stakes. Worrall said that it was "the beginning of something new."

On 17 March 1988 he launched the new Independent party in Somerset West town hall, Western Cape. The party was launched in a new wave of enthusiasm which soon drew a backlash from the clandestine white racists, the "White Wolves" who attempted to sabotage his meetings.

On 4 February 1989 the Independent Party joined forces with two other liberal parties to form the Democratic Party on the principles of universal suffrage and the removal of all racial discrimination. The leadership was to be shared on a triumvirate formed by Worrall, Zach de Beer from the Progressive Federal Party and Wynand Malan, the former National Party MP who had formed the National Democratic Movement.

In the elections of 6 September, all the new party leaders triumphed and the liberal left increased its majority in parliament from 20 seats to 33.

SUDAN

Population: 25m (1990, World Bank)
Independence: 1 January 1956
Head of State: Lt-Gen Omar Hassan al Bashir
Government: Military rule by the Revolutionary Command Council for National Salvation since the Islamic fundamentalist coup of 30 June 1989. The Cabinet is part military, part civilian.
Parties: All political parties were banned following the coup of June 1989, but most of the main civilian parties continue to operate underground. These include the Umma Party, Democratic Unionist Party, Muslim Brotherhood, and National Islamic Front.

ALIER, Abel

Sudanese politician. Vice-President 1971 – 1981.

A lawyer and judge who made his mark when he helped negotiate peace in southern Sudan and then ruled the region during the 1970s, but secessionism in the south and the fall of Nimeiri brought his style of unification to an end. Never over-ambitious, but conscientious and hardworking, he found himself a victim of the vicissitudes of Sudanese politics.

Born 1933, a Protestant Dinka, in Bor district, Upper Nile province. Educated locally and at the University of Khartoum, where he completed a BA in 1959, going on to London University School of Advanced Legal Studies, taking his Masters degree at Yale. He went into the legal profession and rose to become a District Judge in El Obeid, Wad Medani and in Khartoum until 1965, when he resigned to take part in the round table conference on the southern question as an active member of the Southern Front. He was appointed to the constitutional commissions of 1966 and 1968. He stood for parliament in the 1968 elections and was returned as the member for Bor.

After the 25 May 1969 revolution, President Nimeiri appointed him to his first cabinet as Minister for Housing. He was reshuffled to Supply and Internal trade in October 1969. In July 1970 he became Minister for Works. A major promotion came when he was appointed Vice-President and Minister for Southern Affairs in July 1971. He led the Khartoum team of seven to Addis Ababa for negotiations with the Southern Sudanese which resulted in the peace agreement of 27 February 1972.

As a reward he was promoted President of the High Executive Council for the Southern Region (1972-78). Alier and his team of ministers were defeated in the south in the elections of February 1978 and a new government was formed by the former Anyanya, leader Joseph Lagu. Further confusion, with allegations of corruption, followed and in the elections of May 1980 Alier was again returned. Lagu then started his campaign for the division of the south into three regions. In the chaos that followed, Alier was dismissed as President of the HEC, along with his council of ministers, in October 1981 though he remained Vice-President of the republic. While the situation in the south deteriorated, he found himself without a part to play, and occupied himself with the task of trying to revitalise Nimeiri's Sudanese Socialist Union. On 2 May 1984 he was appointed Minister of Construction and Public Works.

With the military coup of 6 April 1985 the old political team was swept aside and Alier retired, at least temporarily, from the centre of the political scene.

AROP, Martin Malwal (Colonel)

Sudanese soldier. Member of the Military Council, 30 June 1989 —

A member of Omar Bashir's paratroop battalion at South Kordofan before the coup which he helped plan on 30 June 1989. Bashir immediately appointed him as a member of the Revolutionary Command Council for National Salvation, where he became the leading defender of the southern cause.

On the second day after the coup he went on record saying he was against the Sharia Islamic law. He also dismissed press speculation that the Military Council was dominated by the Muslim Brothers. He said he would not have participated in the revolution if he had suspected Bashir of Muslim fanaticism. This remark earned him admiration and respect among southerners who were worried that the new military junta might want to adopt the Sharia Islamic law.

BASHIR, Omar Hassan Ahmed el (Lt-General)

Sudanese soldier. Head of State 30 June 1989-

A devout Muslim who says his prayers five times a day and fasts at Ramadan. Though opponents suspect him of having connections with the fundamentalist National Islamic Front, he denies it and claims to be a liberal Muslim from the Khatmiya sect. A young paratroop commander with a considerable following in the army, he was chosen to lead the coup of June 1989, where he put his considerable organisational talents to good use. He assumed power with great enthusiasm, but little political know-how. He immediately took a hawkish stance on many thorny issues and imposed tight military control. A pan-Arabist and pan-Islamicist.

Born 1944 at Hosh Bannaga, from Shendi. He completed secondary school in Khartoum before joining the Sudan Military College to graduate as an officer in 1966. He was trained as a paratrooper before attending staff college in Malaysia.

In 1973 he took part in the Arab-Israeli war, fighting alongside the Egyptian forces on the Suez canal. The Egyptian government gave him a medal for bravery. A paratroop brigadier and senior battlefield commander in the war against the Sudanese People's Liberation Army in the south, he was based in the south Kordofan garrison. He was due to go on a military training course at the Nasser Academy in Egypt when, on 30 June 1989, he took power from Prime Minister Sadiq el Mahdi in an almost bloodless coup.

The coup appeared to have been planned in a hurry though Bashir said that he had considered taking power ever since General Swar el Dahab returned the country to democracy in May 1986. He set up a Revolutionary Command Council for National Salvation as the supreme military body and arrested more than a hundred officers belonging to other factions.

He said his was "a genuine Sudanese revolution, the revolution of the people who rose up against tyranny, corruption, partisanship and sectarianism." He continued, "It's a national revolution, neither leftist nor rightist, not partisan, not Mayist, not racist." By saying the coup was "not Mayist" Bashir was denying any connection with the May revolution of Gafaar Nimeiri and collaboration with him in planning the coup. One of his early gestures was to offer a referendum and secession to the south. But he failed to hold any meaningful talks with John Garang's SPLA and the war continued. As his rule continued its essentially Islamic fundamentalist nature became more apparent.

He abolished the constitution, the national assembly and all political parties and trade unions and closed civilian newspapers. About 30 members of the former government were detained.

After unsucessful attempts to get peace talks going with the SPLA in 1989, negotiations collapsed over the issue of the Islamic law. Hostilities resumed at the end of the year with the rebels making some gains, by taking smaller towns in the south.

Bashir said that he had discovered a coup in April 1990 and ordered the immediate execution of 28 army officers, despite international protests. Another coup attempt in September was also brutally crushed. In October, a former Chief of the Armed Forces and two generals defected to the SPLA.

Bashir's woes continued into 1991 with mounting famine in many parts of the country, discontent in the cabinet and the junta, marked by dismissals and unrest and no progress on the southern situation. He countered by establishing a federal system, in which the northern states (but not the South) came under Islamic law. He released many, but not all, political prisoners in May.

He made further efforts to achieve a peace settlement and persuaded Nigeria's President Ibrahim Babangida to act as a mediator in June 1991. This mediation was accepted by John Garang, but no further progress had been made by the beginning of September.

GARANG de MABIOR, John

Sudanese soldier. Leader of the Sudan People's Liberation Movement, August 1983 —

A tough, intelligent, American trained soldier but also a political thinker of considerable depth. Brought up and educated as a Christian but not a practising church member. He claims to be fighting for the liberation of Sudan as a whole and the introduction of democracy and socialism, but his following has always been confined to the south, and then mostly to the Dinka tribe. Through two military coups in the north he has come close to negotiating peace agreements but has balked at making any final settlement, choosing instead to remain the undisputed leader of his Sudan People's Liberation Army, which draws its support from Ethiopia.

Born June 1945 into a Dinka family in southern Sudan. Educated locally. Went to the USA in the 1960s to take a BA in economics. Always politically conscious, he joined the Anyanya rebel movement, fighting for increased autonomy in the south, in 1970. After the peace agreement on 27 February 1972 with the government of Gafaar Nimeiri, the rebel forces were integrated into the Sudanese army. He rose to become the deputy director of the military research training branch of the army general headquarters in Khartoum. Promoted Lt-Colonel, he was made Commander of the Bor garrison in the south. He went for further studies in the USA in 1979 and earned a doctorate in 1981, being awarded the Gamma Sigma honour award for significant contributions to agricultural science.

On his return home he found Nimeiri planning the radical Islamicisation of the Muslim majority in northern Sudan and the introduction of the Sharia Islamic law. These moves terrified the southerners who already felt that they were being deprived, by the Khartoum government, of recently discovered oil resources. They wanted to fight once more for the gains they had made in the previous civil war.

A number of attacks on Sudanese troops occurred in 1982 and in April 1983 there was a mutiny by southern troops in Bor. Nimeiri then sent Garang to his former command at Bor to negotiate with the rebel troops. Instead Garang defected and in August 1983 formed the Sudan People's Liberation Army from the mutineers and the troops that he had brought with him. The SPLA then proceeded to organise a number of successful attacks in the south, halting the drilling for oil by Chevron and the construction of the Jonglei Canal and taking a number of southern Sudanese towns.

In March 1984 the Sudan People's Liberation Movement was officially formed under Garang's leadership with the objective of overthrowing Nimeiri and installing a people's democratic socialist government. Garang insisted that his aim was to liberate Sudan as a whole, not to win secession in the south. But he did want southern unity, the restoration of the regional government and a share in the resources of timber, grain, water and minerals.

During 1984 a number of foreign workers on projects in the south were captured and held hostage before being freed. Secret negotiations with the Sudanese government were held in September. Nimeiri offered Garang the vice-presidency of Sudan and a position as co-ordinator of economic development in the south, but he turned down the offer, saying that the war's aim was not to make him vice-president and that the settlement had to be on a national basis.

After the military coup led by General Swar el Dahab on 16 April 1985, Garang called a cease-fire. But when the new government decided to hold a referendum in the south on whether to reunite the region, this was rejected by Garang who accused Swar el Dahab of wanting to reunite the south into a super-region under a "mini-military council similar to that in Khartoum." He vowed that the SPLA would intensify its military operations. The war then continued throughout 1985.

Attempts at further peace talks were held in Addis Ababa between the SPLM and the National Alliance for Salvation (NAS), a semi-official alliance of trades unionists and politicans who supported the government. The NAS agreed to abolish Sharia and made other concessions but these were not effected before Sudan returned to civilian rule in April 1986.

The new government under Sadiq el Mahdi offered Garang a place in the Council of Ministers but he said that he would not recognise or take part in the new government. On 20 March 1986 a major conference was called between the SPLM and the National Alliance for National Salvation, an unofficial group of Sudanese politicians, at the Koka dam in Ethiopia. There Garang set out his philosophy in a major speech.

In July 1986 the first direct talks between Garang and Sadiq were held in Addis Ababa but again no agreement was reached. The war resumed, with the SPLA gradually gaining control of a number of southern towns including Rumbek, Kurmuk and Torit in March 1989, while the people starved and relief agencies fought a losing battle to get food through.

Sadiq struggled to keep control of government of the north and could do little but appeal to Garang to respond to peace initiatives. He offered a national conference at which the Sharia issue could be debated. On 1 May 1989 Garang announced a unilateral cease fire for one month in order to discuss the "freezing" of the Sharia law, a constitutional convention and an end to the military pacts with Libya and Egypt.

But while these initiatives were still being implemented, there was the military coup of 30 June 1989. The new regime of General Omar el Bashir suggested further peace talks, but was greeted with considerable suspicion by Garang. He remained silent for a month to assess the new regime. Then he taunted Bashir with the label "junior rebel" and claimed that his regime could not achieve a lasting peace without his support, saying that the SPLA had the power to "lengthen or shorten the days of the junta." He made it clear he would only talk on the basis of a constitutional conference bringing together all the political forces of the country.

Though occasional talks continued through intemediaries such as President Mobutu of Zaire, no direct talks with Omer Bashir took place.

Full scale hostilities were renewed at the end of 1989 and the beginning of 1990. Garang's troops took a number of smaller towns in the south. In October 1990 the former Chief of the Armed Forces and two generals defected to join Garang.

In January 1991 a government in exile was established with Garang as its deputy leader. Another attempt to work out a solution to the conflict was made in June 1991, when Garang agreed that Nigeria's President Ibrahim Babangida should mediate in the conflict. He said that he would honour any agreements reached if talks could be arranged.

KASSIANO, Dominic Gitwawa Bakhit (Brigadier)
Sudanese soldier. Member of the Military Council.

A competent and ruthless soldier who transferred from being an Anyanya rebel to a loyalist government soldier, achieving his military reputation for his campaigns in the south, particularly for wresting the town of Bor from Colonel John Garang's Sudanese People's Liberation Army.

Born in Meridi in Equatoria region in southern Sudan. Early in his career he was recruited to the Anyanya rebels fighting the government of Jaafar Nimeiri. After the peace agreement in of February 1972 he was among the Anyanya integrated into the Sudan army. He went for further training in Canada and gained a Masters degree in military science. He then did an officer's artillery course in India.

He returned home and resumed a full-time military career. When John Garang started the revolt of his Sudan People's Liberation Army (in the tradition of the Anyanya) in September 1982, Kassiano found himself on the opposite side. In command of Sudanese loyalist troops, he achieved an early victory against the southern troops who mutinied at Bor in May 1983 and was honoured with the medal for the "First class order of duty". He continued as commander of the 16th Infantry Brigade in Meridi, Equatoria West, until the time of the coup by Brigadier Omar Bashir on June 30 1989, who appointed him to the Revolutionary Command Council for National Salvation.

LAGU, Joseph Lagu Yanga (Major-General)
Sudanese soldier and politician.

A tough and dominant personality who has played a full part in Sudanese politics from the days when he led the Southern liberation movement as the leader of Anyanya, to today when he is trying to mediate between Joseph Garang and the Khartoum government. Between times he enjoyed a period of rule in the south, as the head of the Southern Sudan Executive Council but he did not find the mechanics of government suited him and only held office for a couple of years. He worked closely with Nimeiri during most of his tenure of office and agreed with him over the division of the south into three regions, but fell out with him over the implementation of the Islamic Sharia law. He has been living in Britain for most of the time since Nimeiri's downfall.

Born 21 November 1931. Son of a schoolmaster in the deep south of Equatoria province, in the Madi village of Moli, near Nimule. Educated at the church mission school of Akot, the intermediate school at Loka and Rumbek Secondary School. He gained admission to the Military College at Omdurman for training as an officer.

He passed out as an officer in May 1960 and was posted to the Northern Command at Shendi. He was next posted to Juba where he first met Nimeiri, then a major at the garrison. Nimeiri was games officer at Juba, teaching the lieutenants to play tennis.

At the time of the launch of the Anyanya (Southern Sudan Liberation Movement) he was on the point of going to Britain to take a course in military law, but instead he deserted the army and joined the liberation movement on 4 June 1963. Four months later, on 19 September 1963, he launched the first Anyanya attack. The rebels were short of weapons but the collapse of the Simba uprising in neighbouring Zaire provided them with a source of arms.

Over the next seven years Lagu launched increasingly ambitious attacks, ambushing convoys and blowing up roads and bridges. Although he claimed to have a liberation army of 7,000 its effective strength was seldom over 2,000. He captured modern Russian equipment from the Sudanese army and continued to harry the Sudanese troops in their fortified encampments.

He remained in the background while the peace agreement was negotiated and emerged from the bush to sign the agreement on 27 March 1972 in Addis Ababa in the presence of Emperor Haile Selassie. He was then appointed a general while his forces were integrated into the Sudanese army. Discontent with the Abel Alier administration in the south and allegations of corruption made Lagu stand in the elections of February 1978.

He defeated Alier and was elected President of the Executive Council for the Southern Region in place of him, but tribal wrangling and manoeuvring continued and disagreements broke out among Lagu's ministers over lack of economic progress. With the National Assembly passing a bill for decentralisation, Nimeiri dissolved both the national and regional assemblies. On 13 February 1980 Lagu resigned his post to "create a fair and suitable atmosphere for the elections". The new assembly elected Abel Alier as his replacement in May.

Lagu then began to campaign for the sub-division of the Southern Region into three, to avoid domination by the centre where the Dinkas had a majority. In June 1982 Nimeiri appointed him as one of the three national Vice-Presidents, in place of Abel Alier, showing that his campaign for re-division had been recognised. In May 1983 the region was divided into three – Equatoria, Upper Nile and Bahr el Ghazal.

This and the introduction of Sharia Islamic law led to the formation of the Sudanese People's Liberation Army in which Lagu did not have a part.

Nimeiri's removal in the coup of 6 April 1985 ended Lagu's vice-presidency. The new transitional government evicted him and his family from the government house where they were living in Khartoum. Feeling that the situation in Juba, where he has a home, was too uncertain, he went into exile in Britain. He eventually became Sadiq el Mahdi's official roving ambassador and remained active trying to mediate between Joseph Garang's SPLA and the Sudanese government. He went to meet Garang in Addis Ababa in 1987, but did not achieve any positive results.

MAHDI, Sadiq el

Sudanese politician. Prime Minister 6 May 1986 – 30 June 1989.

A man of great patience and tact, though often indecisive. When in power his life was a continual struggle to unite his divided country. As the great-grandson of the Abdul Rahman el Mahdi, the man who founded the Mahdists, his background was one of religious as well as political leadership, yet he was personally tolerant, cultivated, and Oxford educated. Throughout his career he was seen as the leader of the Ansars and the Umma party, but his task was to unite the country as a whole behind him to bring peace to the south and establish religious tolerance in the north. Many times he was imprisoned and exiled. He formed different governments as he tried to follow the course of diplomacy and negotiation. It was his failure to bring peace to the south or solve the question of the Islamic Sharia law that led to his downfall in June 1989.

Born 1936. The great-grandson of Imam Abdul Rahman el Mahdi, leader of the Mahdist sect who claimed to receive direct guidance from God. The son of the Imam Sayed Abdel Rahman el Mahdi who re-established the Ansar sect and stood firmly for Sudanese independence rather than union with Egypt.

Educated at Comboni College, Khartoum and St John's College, Oxford. He was the leader and the founder of the Umma Mahdist (now the Umma) party from its foundation in 1945, until its banning by the military regime which seized power in November 1958. He succeeded as Imam in 1959 on his father's death. He played a major role behind the scenes, making it clear that his support, through the revived Umma party, for the military government depended on the army restoring democracy.

He co-operated with the government of Muhammad Mahgoub through an uneasy alliance between the Umma Party and the National Unionist Party. Sadiq was too young to take the leadership at the elections of 1965 and later he was thwarted by the opposition from his uncle, Imam el Hadi, which split the Umma party. But the younger elements in the party chose Sadiq as a more effective leader than Mahgoub and he reluctantly became Prime Minister at the tender age of 30, on 30 July 1966.

He formed a coalition not just of Umma and the NUP but with some Khatmiyya support through the Finance Minister. He began to get the economy under control and tackled the southern problem by planning regional government. However his very success and his decision to stand for the Presidency caused a break-up between his wing of the Umma party and the NUP, whose leader also had presidential ambitions. Thus in May 1967 Sadiq was defeated in the Assembly and Mahgoub was again elected premier. Sadiq remained in opposition and, with strong support from the southerners, defeated the government on several issues. New elections were called in January 1968. Sadiq lost his own seat and his party was heavily defeated by the NUP and his uncle's Umma faction which merged in the Democratic Unionist Party.

However the new Mahgoub government failed to solve the major issues of the economy and the south and gave the pretext for Gafaar Nimeiri to intervene on 25 May 1969. The new government tried to ensure Sadiq's co-operation but he objected to working with the Communists and was arrested on 6 June 1969 for high treason. The government cracked down on the Ansars, confiscated their property and attacked Abba island. Sadiq's uncle Imam el Hadi was killed, but he was allowed to go into exile on 3 April 1970.

He remained in exile until 1972, when he was re-arrested and released in April 1974 to go back into exile. He was accused of attempting to organise various coup attempts against the Nimeiri regime, particularly the one of July 1976, at a time he was living in London. Sadiq accepted responsibility for the coup attempt but denied that foreign mercenaries had been employed.

After long and secret negotiations for a national reconciliation, Nimeiri met Sadiq in Port Sudan in July 1977. He agreed to join the government and Nimeiri's Sudanese Socialist Union but soon disagreements recurred over the Camp David accord. Sadiq resigned both from the SSU and its political bureau. Once again he went overseas. In 1983 he became a visiting fellow at St Anthony's College, Oxford.

Sadiq was allowed to return home but soon fell out with Nimeiri over his plans to introduce the Sharia law and was put in prison for over a year from September 1983 to December 1984. After the deposition of Nimeiri on 6 April 1985, he contested the elections of April 1986 and his Umma party won the largest number of seats (99) in the assembly but not an overall majority. Sadiq became Prime Minister and Minister of Defence on 6 May 1986, just 20 years after his first premiership. He formed a broad-based government, urged the southerners to negotiate an end to the civil war and promised to abolish the Sharia law.

But despite his attempts to launch a new peace initiative at the beginning of 1987, the Southern People's Liberation Movement of Colonel John Garang simply stepped up its offensive and refused to negotiate. It demanded total abolition of the Sharia law as a precondition for any negotiations

Meanwhile in Khartoum, Sadiq found himself hamstrung over the compromise Sharia reforms that he wished to introduce by his lack of an overall majority. He hoped that he could incorporate Sharia into a new law but make it applicable only to Muslims, exempting those of other faiths. He also wanted to institute a government of national unity . To get more support for this he resigned as premier on 16 April 1988 and on 27 April was re-elected for a further two year term, obtaining 196 out of the 222 votes in the national assembly. But he was unable to persuade Garang to negotiate.

His position was dramatically weakened when in December 1988 the Democratic Unionist Party withdrew from the coalition and signed a tentative peace agreement with John Garang. This provoked a constitutional crisis with demonstrations in the streets. Sadiq declared a state of emergency. He was forced into an even closer alliance with the fundamentalists led by Dr Hassan el Turabi, who demanded strict application of Sharia, while the army, which threatened to take control, wanted Sharia set aside, negotiations with the SPLM and the establishment of a broad based "government of national salvation".

Caught between these irreconcilable demands, Sadiq threatened to resign on 27 February 1989 unless the armed forces gave him a free hand to form a new government and work for a peace settlement in the south. He won a temporary reprieve and hesitantly began talks with Garang's SPLA, but he was not moving fast enough to satisfy the already demoralised army.

On 30 June 1989 an army faction led by Omar Hassan el Bashir seized power. Sadiq went into hiding but was captured after a few days and put under arrest.

NIMEIRI, Gaafar Mohammed
Sudanese Politician. President October 1971 – 6 April 1985.

A tough dedicated infantry officer who modelled himself on his hero, Gamal Abdel Nasser, even copying his style and his institutions. At the begining of his regime he systematically destroyed the opposition whether it was Ansar or communist and built national unity. He was also the architect of peace in the south. For most of his regime he appeared a pragmatic, short-sleeved, accessible leader with little time for ideology or ceremonial. A dutiful Muslim but still able to enjoy his whisky. But as his regime became unpopular, and beset by economic and political problems, the master of the political balancing act suddenly lost control in late 1983 and became a born again Islamic fundamentalist. He introduced the Sharia Islamic Law, provoked another civil war in the south, failed to satisfy his people's economic needs and set in train the coup of 6 April 1985.

Born 1 January 1930, the son of a postman at Wad Nubaw'i a suburb of Omdurman. Educated at the Koranic School and El Hijra elementary school, then at Medani Government School and Hantoub Secondary School. One of 12 sixth formers expelled for going on strike against the

Legislative Assembly in 1948, but allowed back after seven days. Entered military college on 25 May 1979 and passed out as a Second Lieutenant on 19 February 1952

After three years with western command he did further training in Egypt. He went to northern command armoured corps at Shendi, fired with enthusiasm for the Nasser revolution. This led to his arrest in 1957 accused of having led his men in support of an abortive coup by Abdel Rahman Kabedia. He was suspended from duty until April 1959 when he was posted to the southern command at Juba. Two years later he was transferred to the unruly infantry command headquarters of the Khartoum garrison.

He was posted out of trouble's way on four courses abroad in Cyprus, Libya, West Germany and Egypt, before returning in time to take an active part in the overthrow of General Ibrahim Abboud in October 1964. Arrested again, he was cleared and posted to western command, Darfur. Two months later he was sent to the American Army Command School at Fort Leavenworth, Kansas where he gained a Masters degree, with distinction, in military science. On his return he was implicated in another abortive coup and was banished to the wilderness at Torit in the south, before being promoted commanding officer of the military school in Khartoum.

It was there, on 25 May 1969, that he carried out the successful military coup against the civilian regime of President Ismail al Azhari and Prime Minister Mohammed Mahgoub. He set up government under the Revolutionary Command Council. At first he leaned heavily on the Communists, giving them three cabinet posts. On 28 October 1969 he took over the premiership. A showdown with the Ansars came in March 1970 when they mustered 30,000 men at Aba Island. Nimeiri sent in his toughest units and up to a thousand people died in the fighting.

This success gave him a brief period of internal stability, but by December 1970 the Communists were challenging for power and Nimeiri had to dismiss the leaders from his Revolutionary Council and to declare himself ready to crush the Communists in the country. The backlash caused the Communist coup of 19 July 1971 in which he was held prisoner in his palace. But two of the coup-makers were hijacked on their BOAC plane and forced to land at Benghazi by Nimeiri's friend, Colonel Gaddafi, who handed them back to Khartoum. This brought the coup to an end within three days and ended the Communist challenge.

Nimeiri was restored to power by loyalist troops and purged the Communists. He called a plebiscite on 30 September 1971 and became the first elected President of the Sudan with a 98.6% vote. He was sworn in on 12 October 1971, stronger than at any time since he seized power in May 1969. He dissolved the Revolutionary Council and established the Sudanese Socialist Union (SSU) as a ruling party and became its secretary general in October 1972.

He then focussed on ending the 17-year civil war in the south and authorised secret contacts with the Southern Sudan Liberation

Movement and with the help of Abel Alier as his chief negotiator eventually reached a peace agreement on 27 February 1972.

In January 1973 he repealed earlier nationalisation measures and passed laws encouraging foreign investment. He also took on key economic ministries personally at critical junctures – Planning (1971-72), Finance (1977-78), Agriculture and Irrigation (1981).

He survived several coup attempts during the 1970s and was determined to achieve a major step to national unity by reconciliation with the Ansar leader Sadiq el Mahdi. Nimeiri met Sadiq at Port Sudan in July 1977 and finally persuaded him to return home and accept office, but soon disagreements recurred over the Camp David Accord between Egypt and Israel and Sadiq went back into exile.

In October 1981 following a series of strikes and demonstrations Nimeiri dissolved the National Assembly, then in November he dismissed his entire council of ministers and declared the leadership of the SSU to be dissolved. But the basic economic problems persisted and further violent demonstrations over sugar price increases occurred in January 1982. Nimeiri called elections, reformed the SSU and spent much time in trying to settle the political infighting in the south.

Suddenly in September 1983 he confounded his friends by introducing the Sharia Islamic Law, which called for the banning of all alcohol and draconian penalties against adultery and theft. After April 1984 he went further with the introduction of martial law. This brought immediate opposition in the south and an intensification of the guerrilla war by the Sudan People's Liberation Army under John Garang. Revelling in his new authoritarianism Nimeiri then arrested his long-time colleague and southern minister, Bona Malwal, and Sadiq el Mahdi, who had earlier returned from exile. The first punishments for theft were carried out in December when two thieves had their hands cut off.

On 29 April 1984, with opposition growing to Sharia and to continuing deterioration in the economy, Nimeiri introduced a state of emergency to clamp down on the enemies of the Islamicisation programme. Public meetings, strikes and demonstrations were banned. In July proposals were put to the assembly to amend the constitution and make Nimeiri an Imam, with a further increase in his powers.

The execution of Mohammed Taha, a respected spiritual leader, for opposing Sharia caused a wave of revulsion even among government supporters. Nimeiri brought further anger on himself by abolishing food subsidies provoking further disturbances. In another abrupt change of policy he then turned on the Muslim Brothers, who had hitherto lent him their support, and put their leaders on trial for sedition. He then lifted the state of emergency and tried to adopt a more conciliatory stance.

A price explosion in basic foodstuffs, following the removal of subsidies, provoked more serious riots but Nimeiri left for the USA to seek further aid for his besieged economy. Almost immediately demonstrators took to the streets.

On 6 April 1985 while he was still in the US, he was deposed in a bloodless military coup led by Lt-Gen Swar el Dahab. Hundreds of Nimerii's officials were arrested and the SSU was dissolved. Nimeiri found exile in Cairo, Egypt, which refused repeated requests to have him extradited. During the last days of Sadiq el Mahdi's regime in June 1989 there were constant reports that Nimeiri was involved in plotting a coup. Sadiq claimed that he had foiled a coup attempt on 18 June, when 14 officers and 48 civilians were arrested. Some protesters went onto the streets calling for his return. But Nimeiri issued a statement denying all involvement.

On 30 June Brigadier Omar Hassan Bashir took power. He revealed no connection with Nimeiri who remained in exile in Egypt.

SALIH, Faisal Ali Abu (Brigadier)
Sudanese soldier. Minister of Interior, 30 June 1989 –

A close colleague of General Omar Bashir who carried out the military coup of 30 June 1989. A liberal-minded Muslim compared with many of his colleagues on the military council who are considered to be Islamic fundamentalists. But he thoroughly endorsed military rule where the soldiers set the limits of democracy. He put it baldly, saying that the "army would never think of handing over power to civilians again."

Born 1944 at Shendi, about 100 kilometres south of Khartoum. He went to the Sudan Military College and graduated as an officer. He studied field engineering on courses in India and Pakistan. He took a Masters degree in military science in Saudi Arabia. Immediately after the coup of 30 June 1989 Bashir appointed him Minister of Interior and a member of the Revolutionary Command Council for National Salvation (NSRCC), the new ruling body.

Shortly after the coup he spelt out some of the policies of the Bashir regime. "The army will never think of handing over power to civilians again... the Revolutionary Command Council will ensure a certain degree of democracy at the right time and in a manner that will achieve unity, strength and security." The RCC was considering the establishment of a "controlled democratic system commensurate with the revolution's tendencies and acceptable to all sectors of society." But despite these early promises military government sympathetic to the Islamic fundamentalists was soon entrenched.

ZUBEIR, Mohamed Salih (Brigadier-General)
Sudanese soldier. Deputy chairman Military Council, 30 June 1989 –

Tall, lean and rangy, from the extreme north of the country. He was a close colleague of General Omar Bashir at the time of the June 1989 coup. He has a gentle and composed manner and the ability to lead men. A devout Muslim and one of the foremost fundamentalists on the military junta.

Born 1944 at el Gadar in dongola in the extreme north of the country. After graduating from the Sudan Military College as an officer, he followed a course on vehicle maintenance in the Soviet Union and a course for commanders in Egypt. Later he went to West Germany to study workshop administration. Immediately after the coup of 30 June 1989 he emerged as deputy chairman of the Revolutionary Command Council for National Salvation, the new ruling body, and Deputy Prime Minister.

SWAZILAND

Population: 778,000 (1990, World Bank)
Independence: 6 September 1968
Head of State: King Mswati III
Government: Government by the King who is Head of State and wields executive authority through a Prime Minister and Cabinet which he appoints. Parliamentary government was abolished and all political activity was suspended in 1973, by the late King Sobhuza. The new constitution of 1978 was based on tribal communities called Tinkhundla and provides for a traditional parliament of advisory capacity only.
Parties: The King's party is the Imbokodvo National Movement; all other parties have been banned since 1973.

DLAMINI, Bhekimpi Alpheus (Prince)

Swaziland politician. Prime Minister March 1983-October 1986.

He rose from relative obscurity to become a tough and determined Prime Minister, considered to be an arch traditionalist and the right man to assure the succession on the death of King Sobhuza. But he became involved in the struggle for power during the interregnum and did not retain the confidence of the new king, Mswati. This led to his trial and conviction for treason and a long term of imprisonment.

Born 26 November 1924 son of Chief Mnisi Dlamini of Hoho district, 22 miles north-east of Mbabane. Educated at Enkaba Primary School, Mbabane Central School and then at Ermelo Secondary School in South Africa.

Over 1941-45 he served in the British 8th Army in the North African and Italian campaigns rising to the rank of sergeant while still only 20 years of age. On demobilisation he took a job at Havelock mines and stayed 12 years. He became a store-keeper.

His political career began when he was appointed *induna* for Enkaba Nkhundula, one of five chiefs. He led the delegation from the Swaziland National Council to London in 1963 for the constitutional conference before independence. He became a member of the Legislative Council in 1964. He spent six months in Britain in 1966 studying public adminstration.

In the 1967 elections he won a seat in the Mlumati constituency and was appointed Assistant Minister of Local Administration. After winning the elections in May 1972 he was transferred as Assistant Minister to the Deputy Prime Minister's Office.

In the confused interregnum that followed the death of King Sobhuza II on 28 August 1982, he was plucked from relative obscurity to become Prime Minister on 23 March 1983. He was considered to be an arch conservative and keen to maintain good relations with South Africa. He was among those who wanted to negotiate a deal with South Africa that would give Swaziland a corridor of land and direct access to the Indian Ocean.

He announced that the 15-year-old prince Makhosetive should succeed his father and at the same time, on behalf of the *Liqoqo* or Supreme Council, he dismissed the Queen Regent on 10 August 1983, and installed Queen Ntombi in her place. This provoked a constitutional crisis and a major power struggle followed. Many leaders were arrested and detained though it appeared at the time that Prince Bhekimpi was simply doing everything in his power to assure the succession of Makhosetive.

But when King Mswati was finally crowned on 25 April 1986 he disbanded the *Liqoqo* in May and on 8 October, without warning dismissed Bhekimpi. On 22 May 1987 Bhekimpi and 12 other leaders were arrested. King Mswati claimed that investigations were going ahead, "into the part they played in the political events in Swaziland in 1983" when Queen Dzeliwe was deposed.

On 27 November 1988 he and ten other prominent Swazis were put on trial for treason before a special tribunal where defendants were not allowed legal representation and there was no appeal. He was found guilty and sentenced to 15 years' imprisonment, though the King later released him. He retired into private life and became an influential chief.

DLAMINI, Barnabas Sibusiso

Swazi politician. Minister of Finance, 30 November 1987 —

A qualified chemist and accountant, one of the new generation of young technocrats brought in by the young King Mswati to replace the old guard that took power during the regency.

Born 1942. Educated locally. Studied chemistry and mathematics for a BSc degree at the University of Wisconsin, then economics and business at the University of South Africa, Pretoria. He continued with an MBA degree in financial management from New York University in 1982. Professionally qualified as an industrial chemist, certified public and chartered accountant. Worked with the Swazi delegation to the UN in New York.

King Mswati III appointed him Minister of Finance when he came to power on 30 November 1987 and confirmed the appointment when most of the rest of the cabinet was sacked on 30 November 1988.

DLAMINI, Mfanasibili (Prince)

Swaziland politician.

Methodical and cautious, he rose from humble origins to become one of the most formidable politicians in his country. He played a major part in the Liqoqo, the Supreme Council, which became the dominant body in the interregnum after the death of King Sobhuza. Though he achieved considerable power, his opponents finally got the better of him and he ended by being tried and convicted of treason and of conspiring to defeat the ends of justice, which brought him seven years of imprisonment.

Born 1939 in the Embekelweni area of the Manzini district where his early years were spent as a herdboy. Educated at the Florence Mission School (1951-56) he left because there was no Standard Five class available.

He became a gatekeeper with Swaziland Canning Company at Malkerns Valley. Went to South Africa where he served six months as an underground loader with the Native Recruiting Corporation. He returned to work in the Havelock mines and then returned to the Florence Mission school to resume his education. He completed his education at Matsapa Swazi National School (1961-63) and then found a job as a weigh-bridge clerk with the Mhlume Sugar Company.

He joined the Swazi National Council in 1963 and became a member of the Imbokodvo National Movement. He won a seat in the first legislative council elections in June 1964 and played an important part in the government committee set up in 1965 to make recommendations for a new self-governing constitution.

As Imbokodvo candidate in the 1967 elections he won a seat at Mphumalanga and was appointed Minister of Local Administration. He held the post until the government reshuffle after the elections of May 1972 when he lost his seat. Instead he was made a nominated member and became Minister of Commerce and Co-operatives on 2 June 1972, a post he held until 1979.

In the confused interregnum that followed the death of King Sobhuza II on 21 August 1982, he became heavily involved in an internal power struggle, as a member of the powerful Supreme Council or *Liqoqo*. The Prime Minister Mbandala Dlamini tried to have him arrested on a sedition charge but he turned the tables on his rival who was dismissed by the Queen Regent, Dzeliwe. Next an attempt was made to dismiss him from the *Liqoqo* by the new Queen Regent, Ntombi, in June 1984. He survived this attempt and remained leader of the conservative faction, but in October 1985 Prime Minister Bhekimpi sacked him and his ally, George Msibi, "in the interests of the nation." Mfanasibili was also relieved of his post as chairman of the civil service board.

In February 1986 he was arrested and charged with "defeating the ends of justice" and of being in possession of firearms and ammunition. He was also accused of trying to ensure the continued detention of Dr Shishayi Nuxmalo and other detainees by influencing witnesses and fabricating evidence. He was convicted and sentenced to seven years imprisonment. Later, after King Mswati assumed power, he was put on trial on 27 November 1987, with Prince Bhekimpi and others for treason (for the part they played in the deposition of Queen Dzeliwe). He was convicted and sentenced to a further 15 years' imprisonment, though the 15-year sentence was later lifted by the King.

Early in 1989 there was an alleged plot reportedly aiming to release him from the Matsapha Central Prison. A Mozambican made his escape by producing a gun, but he failed to free the prince and was recaptured.

DLAMINI, Obed

Swaziland politician. Acting Prime Minister, 12 July 1989 –

A keen farmer, trade unionist and personnel manager who was taken completely by surprise on his appointment as acting Prime Minister by the young King Mswati III.

A pioneer trade unionist, he founded the Swaziland Bank Workers' Union and rose to become secretary-general of the Swaziland Federation of Trade Unions at a time there was considerable labour unrest in the railways, the banking sector and in the breweries. By giving assistance to an ILO expert, Professor A. Ardell, he helped draw up the present Swaziland Industrial Relations act. He remained a consultant to the union movement but joined a commercial bank as an accountant and went on to become personnel manager of Swaziland's largest fruit canning factory, Swazican.

His appointment as acting Prime Minister on 12 July 1989 came as a complete surprise. It came in the traditional way when Obed was called to a meeting at the Royal Cattle Byre. King Mswati III unexpectedly announced that he had made the little known Obed his Prime Minister. Two policemen were then dispatched to take him by the arm and make sure he complied with the King's fiat.

Commentators were divided as to why he had been chosen out of the dozens of eligible Dlamini candidates. It seemed that he had been selected because his experience as a union leader would be needed to deal with a dangerous strike that was brewing in the Financial Institutions and Allied Workers Union, which had already closed the banks. The stratagem clearly worked because, within hours of Obed's appointment, the trades unions called off their action and the banks were able to reopen.

DLAMINI, Sotsha Ernest

Swaziland politician. Prime Minister, 8 October 1986-12 July 1989

An able policeman and security officer, he was plucked from almost total obscurity to become Prime Minister of Swaziland by the young King Mswati III, whom he had once served as his bodyguard. He held his post as PM through successive reshuffles but, just as he appeared firmly established, he was dismissed as suddenly as he had been appointed in July 1989.

Born 1940. Educated locally. Decided to make a career in the police force and joined the Royal Swaziland Police in 1961. Acted for a time as bodyguard to the young Crown Prince Makhosetive (now King Mswati

III). He retired from the police in 1984 with the rank of assistant commissioner in charge of the Criminal Investigations Department. Joined the sugar industry as personnel and security manager at Umbombo Sugar Estate, Big Bend. He was appointed by the King to lead investigations into the political unrest that followed the removal of the former Queen Regent Dzeliwe.

His appointment as Prime Minister came as a complete surprise both to himself and to observers of the Swaziland scene. The King called a 'meeting of the nation' at his kraal on 8 October 1986 where he made a 25-second announcement dismissing the former Prime Minister Prince Bhekimpi and appointing the dazed Sotsha, who was led by the police from his place in the crowd and placed before the King.

In December 1986 he had a personal meeting with PW Botha to protest against a South African raid on the Swazi capital Mbabane, in which six people were kidnapped and two others killed. He later made the first ever public condemnation of South Africa, by a member of the Swazi government by protesting against the "illegal act of aggression."

On 22 May 1987 he gave reasons for the arrest of Prince Bhekimpi and 12 other prominent Swazis. He said an investigation was to be carried out, "into the part they played in the political events of Swaziland in 1983" (in which Queen Dzeliwe was deposed).

On 16 November 1987 the King made a clean sweep of the National Assembly but reappointed Sotsha as a member and reconfirmed him as Prime Minister a week later. He was one of the few ministers of the previous government to retain his portfolio. Then suddenly on 12 July 1989 the King dismissed him, saying in a video recorded statement on Swaziland TV: "The helmsman had decided to do things his own way and chart his own course rather than follow the captain's orders...such an individual is set aside."

MAMBA, George Mbikwakhe

Swaziland politician. Foreign Minister, 30 November 1988 –

Long-standing Swazi High Commissioner to Britain who rose to become the doyen of the diplomatic corps in London. Singled out by the young King Mswati III as his Foreign Minister.

Born 1932. Educated locally then took teacher training but joined the Foreign Ministry in 1972. Became Swaziland's High Commissioner to the UK in 1978. He stayed to become doyen of the diplomatic corps and was awarded the Knight Grand Cross of the Royal Victorian Order (GCVO) by Queen Elizabeth in 1987.

King Mswati appointed him Minister of Foreign Affairs on 30 November 1988, when he carried out his first major reshuffle after the November elections. In this capacity he inherited the problems of Swaziland's relationships with its powerful neighbour, South Africa, which entirely surrounds his tiny country. South Africa was determined to ensure that no haven was given by Swaziland to guerrillas of the

African National Congress and carried out a number of raids on targets in Swaziland to enforce this policy despite Swazi protests.

MSWATI III, Makhosetive
King of Swaziland, 25 April 1986 –

King Mswati III became heir-designate on the death of his illustrious father King Sobhuza II. He was still a minor and had yet to attend school at Sherborne in England. It was a time of great tension with rival factions fighting for power in the kingdom but the clever, handsome schoolboy already had a sense of vocation. He was crowned when he was 19 and had his rule confirmed when he was 21. By then he had already established himself as a man with a mind of his own, determined to be an active monarch, hiring and firing top ministers and dispensing royal clemency to those found guilty of treason. A keen music lover, he is particularly fond of reggae.

Born 19 April 1968, the second youngest of the 69 sons of King Sobhuza II. His mother was Queen Ntombi Latfwala. Before he died on 28 August 1982, King Sobhuza selected him as his successor though he was still only 15 . Prince Makhosetive, as he was then called, qualified according to Swazi tradition in being a left-handed minor without a full brother, but his father must have noted other signs of promise in the young man.

While he was still a minor, Swaziland was ruled by a regent, the Queen Mother Dzeliwe, but in the power struggle that followed the King's death, she was removed from power and Queen Ntombi was installed as regent in her place. Makhosetive was then brought back from Sherborne school in England to be introduced to the Swazi people as their next king. This helped stabilise the internal feuding and he returned to school.

But rivalry between different power factions continued and in January 1986 it was announced that the coronation would take place in April, terminating the regency three years earlier than had been expected. He returned from Sherborne and after a night of closely guarded ritual ceremonies was installed king on the night of 25 April 1986, behind a pallisade of wooden stakes in the royal cattle byre.

The King was still only 19 years old and it was widely assumed that he would still be heavily dependent on his warring courtiers, and that he would have to continue his education under the Swazi elders, with help from staff of the renowned Waterford kaMhala School. But from the outset he declared that authority would remain in his hands and showed his intentions by disbanding the powerful Liqoqo, or Supreme Council, which had arrogated much power to itself during the interregnum.

In October he called a "meeting of the nation" at the Royal Kraal. After the crowds had installed themselves, he arrived and in accordance with custom, sat with the people on the ground, he then got up and made a 25-second announcement in which he dismissed his Prime Minister Prince Bhekimpi and replaced him with a virtually unknown former assistant police commissioner, Sotsha Dlamini.

In May 1987 12 more prominent Swazis (including members of the royal family) were arrested and charged with sedition and treason. He also issued a special decree setting up a special tribunal to preside over cases concerning plotting against the King or the former queen regent. He was authorised to appoint the chief prosecutor and cases could be held in camera without the accused having right to legal representation or appeal. Prince Bhekimpi and the other detainees were eventually convicted of treason, though the King later released them from prison.

King Mswati dissolved parliament in September 1987 in preparation for elections to be held one year early in November 1987. Under the Swazi system the public chooses an electoral college. The college promptly removed all the old MPs. The King was able to nominate ten additional members. He brought back eight former MPs and then virtually selected the cabinet by confirming the appointment of his Prime Minister Sotsha Dlamini and three other cabinet members.

On 19 April 1989 his kingship was confirmed on his 21st birthday and was given special signing powers on instruments of state, which were withheld when he was a minor. In another unexpected move he suddenly removed Prime Minister Sotsha Dlamini on 12 July 1989, justifying himself by telling a parable of a sailor who was not following orders and was taking the ship off course. In his place he appointed the former trades unionist and accountant Obed Dlamini as Prime Minister.

In November 1990 he dismissed his Minister of Justice, probably the most liberal man in the cabinet. This may have been because all the treason trialists suspected of being supporters of the People's United Democratic Organisation (PUDEMO) were acquitted in October.

ZWANE, Ambrose Phesheya (Dr)
Swaziland politician. Leader of the Ngwane National Liberatory Congress

A tall, handsome Catholic, with a fine tenor voice, he was the first Swazi to graduate as a doctor. He became a long suffering Swazi opposition leader who, in the 1960s, tried set up an orthodox radical socialist African political party, the Ngwane National Liberatory Congress. He was heavily influenced by Kwame Nkrumah and the pan-Africanist ideas of that era. He won a wide following among the youth and became leader of the opposition in the democratic assembly, but his success and the fear of radical nationalism alarmed King Sobhuza to such an extent that he abrogated the whole constitution and banned the NNLC. Ngwane was harassed and detained and went into exile, but Sobhuza allowed him back on condition he would drop his political activities. He retired peacefully to doctoring until suddenly he was arrested again on 10 March 1989.

Born 30 April 1924, son of a King's counsellor, at Luhlokohla Ngqulwini in the Manzini district of Swaziland. Educated at Ekuphumuleni Mission School at Bulunga mountain then at St Francis

School, Mbabane, where his uncle was head teacher. He attended St Joseph's Roman Catholic College, in the Manzi district where its head, Father Botha, paid for him to go to South Africa's Inkamana High School in Natal run by the Benedictine monks.

After a first year of medicine at Fort Hare he went on to Witwatersrand University in 1947 and graduated with an MB ChB on 5 December 1951. His first medical post was house surgeon at the Charles Johnson Memorial Hospital in Zululand in 1952. From January 1953 to May 1959 he worked in Mbabane Government Hospital then joined Hlatikulu Hospital in southern Swaziland. He then spent a few years at Ermelo in Transvaal, returning to Swaziland in 1960 to take up politics.

On the formation of the Swaziland Progressive Party in July 1960 he became its general-secretary and represented it in March 1961 at the Third All Africa People's Conference in Cairo. The party split into four factions and he formed the Ngwane National Liberatory Congress on 24 February 1962 at Kwaluseni with the object of working for a "nationalist, democratic, socialist and pan-Africanist state within the fraternity of African States and the British Commonwealth."

He was arrested on 26 June 1963 for fomenting a strike, but was later acquitted. In 1963 his movement tried to broaden its popular base by organising strikes in most of Swaziland's major agro-industries. These strikes were crushed by the colonial authorities and traditional rulers, using British troops. He and all the other executive members of the NNLC were again arrested and charged with public violence. All were acquitted. He then left to attend the OAU conference at Lagos in February 1964 and was offered external offices in Ghana, Egypt and Tanzania.

He fought the 1967 elections, with his party gaining more than 20 per cent of the votes but all the seats went to the Imbokodvo movement - the King's party. After a long tour which took him to China, Kenya, Egypt, Italy, West Germany and Britain he returned home in January 1968 and stayed in Swaziland until the elections in May 1972, nursing his constituencies and resuming his work as a doctor.

In the elections his NNLC won three seats and he became leader of the opposition in the House of Assembly. But such was the fear of the King and the settlers at the victory of a small democratic party that this provoked a constitutional crisis and in April 1973 Sobhuza abruptly abrogated the constitution, banning all political activity and declaring a state of emergency.

On 2 May 1973 he was arrested and imprisoned at Malkerns jail under the 60-day detention without trial legislation. He was frequently imprisoned and harassed in the years which followed. He received three spells of detention in 1978 but when the order came up for renewal the authorities were not ready and released him. He said, "I demanded to leave prison as my children were parked outside waiting for me. I fled the country after their technical blunder." At home a flurry of pamphlets announced the formation of a new liberation movement, but he took up exile in Mozambique. When the government sent a high-powered delegation to President Samora Machel demanding he be sent home, he left for Tanzania.

He returned from exile in June 1979 after 16 months in exile when Sobhuza signed a letter of assurance that he would not be harassed as long as he did not involve himself in public political activity. The letter was countersigned by President Julius Nyerere and the UN High Commissioner for Refugees representative in Tanzania and the Secretary-General of the OAU. He then returned from exile and resumed a quiet non-political life as a doctor in general practice.

His peace was shattered on 10 March 1989 when police suddenly broke into his surgery and arrested him for the illegal possession of subversive pamphlets. Zwane immediately claimed that he had been framed. He said the pamphlets produced by another banned organisation had nothing to do with him, indeed he did not even have the time to read them before the police broke into his surgery and arrested him.

TANZANIA

Population: 26.4m (1990, World Bank)
Independence: 9 December 1961
Head of State: Ali Hassan Mwinyi
Government: Presidential government through a single party with a National Assembly elected on a party list and a Prime Minister and Cabinet selected by the President. The President is chosen by an electoral convention of the party. He has two Vice Presidents one of whom is President of Zanzibar. In March 1991 a presidential commission was established to review one party rule. An opposition group calling itself the Committee for transition towards a multi-party system was established to present an independent view.
Parties: Sole authorised party – *Chama Cha Mapinduzi* (CCM).
Minor, unofficial, opposition parties exist both in Zanzibar and abroad.

BOMANI, Paul Nimage

Tanzanian politician. Minister of State for Special Duties, March – November 1990.

From a well known Tanzanian family he has been in the forefront of national politics since he was the first Tanganyika African National Union MP in the Legislature. A pragmatist, businessman and distinguished ambassador to the USA as well as an expert on co-operatives. He became a minister for all seasons under Julius Nyerere and later Ali Hassan Mwinyi, being moved from one ministry to another according to national requirements. His experience and versatility made him indispensable in successive cabinets, until defeated in the elections of October 1990.

Born 1 January 1925 at Musoma, east of Lake Victoria, the son of a protestant minister. After Ikizu Secondary School he joined Williamson's Diamond Mines as a cashier (1945-47). He took a correspondence course in accountancy and became assistant secretary and later secretary of the Mwanza Co-operative Society. He went on to the Lake Province Cotton Co-operative and did further studies at Loughborough Co-operative College in Britain, (1953-54). He returned home and by 1955 had become general manager of the largest marketing co-operative in Africa, the Victoria Federation of Co-operative Unions.

Active in the Tanganyika African Association from 1952, he joined the Tanganyika African National Union when it was formed by Julius Nyerere in 1954. He became provincial chairman of the party in the Lake Province region. Nominated to the Legislative Council under the colonial government, he was the sole voice of the party. He stood and won his seat in the 1959 elections and was made Minister for Agriculture and Co-operative Development in 1960 and Minister for Finance from

1962-64.

In the 1965 elections he was one of the two senior ministers who lost his seat, but President Nyerere appointed him to one of the official seats as Minister for Economic Affairs and Development Planning (1965-67). At the time of the Arusha Declaration of 1967, which stated that public servants could own only one house, he sold his own for £40,000 to the Japanese ambassador.

He became Minister of Commerce in June 1967, with Industries added to his portfolio in November 1970. In February 1972 when Nyerere brought in a new wave of younger men, he was quietly dropped but re-emerged as ambassador to the USA. On 24 February 1983, he returned to full political life when Nyerere appointed him Minister for Mineral Resources. On 24 April 1984, following the death of Prime Minister Edward Sokoine, his portfolio was extended to include Lands, Natural Resources and Tourism. In this capacity he negotiated a new, permanent border agreement with Burundi in November 1984.

When President Ali Hassan Mwinyi came to power and set up a new government he reshuffled Bomani to Minister of Agriculture and Livestock Development on 6 November 1985. As one of the most versatile and experienced ministers, he was reshuffled again on 23 March 1987, to Labour and Manpower Development. This led him to being appointed chairman of the OAU Labour Commission in April.

On 12 December 1988 he was made Minister of Local Government, Co-operatives and Crop Marketing in a general reshuffle when President Mwinyi eased three left-wing ideologues out of the cabinet. In March 1990, Mwinyi purged his cabinet again in a general drive against corruption and bureaucracy in government and made him Minister of State in the President's Office for "special duties". He was not re-appointed to the cabinet after his defeat in the October 1990 elections.

DIRIA, Ahmed Hassan

Tanzanian diplomat and politician. Minister of Foreign Affairs, 9 November 1990 –

Trained as a political ideologue, he transformed himself over his career into an active and persuasive ambassador who left a strong impression, particularly during his six years in West Germany. One German Minister visiting the then leader of Zanzibar, Ali Hassan Mwinyi, once remarked, "Mr President you are a small island but you have produced a great ambassador." During his six years in West Germany his money-raising efforts achieved a massive increase in West German aid to Tanzania. His financial astuteness caused some jealousy and criticism. Members of Parliament criticised "Tanzania's sultans abroad", but he remained a protege of Mwinyi who brought him home to be Minister of State for Information in his President's Office, and later Minister for Information in September 1989, where he campaigned for better standards in the local press. In November 1990, he achieved a life-long ambition when Mwinyi made him Foreign Minister.

Born 13 July 1937 in Zanzibar. A strong Muslim, he was educated at Gulioni Primary School, Zanzibar. He studied political science at Solianka, USSR (1958-59) and at the Kwame Nkrumah Ideological College at Winneba, Ghana (1960-61) and at Jawharlal Nehru University, India (1970-71). He became a labour inspector (1954-58), a job which led him to become Deputy Secretary General of the Zanzibar and Pemba Federation of Labour (1959-60). He joined the Afro-Shirazi party at its beginnings and became a member of its central committee (1959-63). After the Zanzibar revolution and the coming to power of Sheikh Abeid Karume in January 1964, he became governor of Pemba and Assistant Administrator-General for Zanzibar.

Wanting to broaden his horizons, he took diplomatic training and was appointed by President Julius Nyerere as ambassador to Egypt in 1964, then Ambassador to Zaire in 1969. He returned home to become acting Director of Africa/Middle Eastern Affairs in the Ministry of Foreign Affairs, then assistant secretary to the Ministry of Regional Administration (1969-70). He continued his diplomatic career as High Commissioner to India (1971-77), ambassador to Japan and the Phillipines (1977-83) and ambassador to the Federal Republic of Germany (1983-89). It was here that his reputation became firmly established as a smart operator on behalf of his country.

He went to Germany when its aid had been slashed by the incoming conservative government and Tanzania was struggling to reach an agreement with the IMF. He engaged his talents on what he liked to call "resource diplomacy" and secured dramatic increases in German aid for Tanzania. President Ali Hassan Mwyinyi brought him home and made him his Minister of State in his President's office in March 1989. On 20 September 1989 he was promoted to Minister of Information and Broadcasting. After the elections of October 1990, Mwinyi carried out a major reshuffle. He was promoted to Foreign Minister in place of the long-serving Benjamin Mkapa.

KAWAWA, Rashidi Mfaume

Tanzanian politician. Vice-Chairman of the ruling *Chama Cha Mapinduzi*, 17 August 1990 –

One of the old guard in Tanzanian politics. Standing only 5ft 2ins high, he is a cheerful extrovert with a passionate belief in the socialist values that he and Nyerere pioneered. He worked closely as Nyerere's number two throughout the early years of Tanzanian nationalism. Today as the popular CCM Vice-Chairman he is regarded as the chief torch bearer for the party principles of socialism and self reliance. His power in later years has lain almost entirely within the party. He has become the major ideological critic of the radical reforms that President Mwinyi has introduced since he took power in October 1985.

Born 27 May 1926 at Matepwande in the Songea district. His father was a Ngoni game ranger and his forebears were elephant hunters. Educated at Liwale Primary School and Dar es Salaam Junior Secondary School and the Government Secondary School Tabora.

His parents had insufficient funds to send him to Makerere university so he went into government service as a Public Works Department clerk. In 1951 he joined the Social Welfare Department as a film assistant. He took the lead as a male star in three popular films with himself as producer and scriptwriter.

He joined the Tanganyika African Government Civil Servants Association and became its Assistant General Secretary in 1952 and President in 1954. In 1955 he went into full time trades unionism, forming the Tanganyikan Federation of Labour and becoming its first General Secretary and President, running the movement closely with the national political party, TANU.

In the 1958 elections he was returned to the Legislative Council for Dar es Salaam and was returned again in August 1960 for Southern Province when he was appointed Minister for Local Government and Housing. In April 1961 he started his long association with Julius Nyerere in government as Minister without Portfolio, stepping into the Prime Minister's shoes temporarily in January 1962, when Nyerere decided to withdraw temporarily and devote himself to the reorganisation of the party.

He relinquished this role when he became Vice-President on Tanzania's independence on 9 December 1962. He was the President's principal assistant, helping with executive functions. He was also the leader of the National Assembly. When Tanzania was formed through the union with Zanzibar in April 1964, he became Second Vice President to Abeid Karume and Minister for Defence and National Service. MP for his home district Liwale, since 1965, he played a major part in starting the *ujamaa* villages and in introducing National Service for Youth and the moulding of the Tanzania People's Defence Forces as a training institution for defence and socialism.

In February 1972 he was reinstated as Prime Minister. On 13 February 1977 he lost both his vice-presidency and his premiership to Edward Sokoine and reverted to Minister of Defence. A new chapter in his career started with his election in October 1982 as Secretary General of the ruling CCM party. Always a strong party man, he headed a 10-man committee at the party congress which recommended that party directives should be binding, to reinforce the national policies of socialism and self reliance. On 24 February 1983 he became Minister without Portfolio in Nyerere's office, but there was little promotion from that time onwards in government. His main role was within the party. He was re-elected Secretary General at the third CCM congress by 158 votes to one, in October 1987. He was also elected to the National Executive Committee, the supreme decision making body in the party. In 1990 he became Vice-Chairman of the CCM.

KIMARIO, Muhiddin Mfaume (Major General)

Tanzanian politician. Minister for Home Affairs, November 1985-March 1990.

An exceptional 'soldier of all parts' who helped train the Mozambican freedom fighters, acted as military adviser to the African Liberation Committee and helped liberate Uganda from Idi Amin, besides carrying out the more orthodox military duties. He then transformed himself with equal professionalism into a full-time politician and minister. He held the important Ministry for Home Affairs from November 1985 to March 1990.

Born 28 December 1937 at Bondeni, Moshi district, Kilimanjaro region. Educated at the Muslim Primary School and Majengo District School, Moshi before going on to Marangu Secondary School and Butimba Teachers Training College, Mwanza. He did a spell at Kivukoni ideological college in 1962. He then decided to join the army and went to the Officers Military Training School in Israel in 1963.

In 1964 he was appointed platoon commander of B company in the first battalion and became the first African Adjutant at Lugalo Barracks in the same year. He went for training in the School of Military Intelligence in Britain in 1965 and returned home to become Chief of Military and Security Intelligence at Defence headquarters (1965-67) before being promoted to Company Commander of the 5th Battalion (1967-69).

An interesting posting followed, when he was made commanding officer of the FRELIMO Military Training School, on Farm 17 at Nachingwea, in 1969. This was set up to train the Mozambican freedom fighters then in the final stages of their struggle for independence against the Portuguese. Another unusual assignment was when he became Commanding Officer of the Special Duty Unit and Military Adviser to the Executive Committee of the African Liberation Committee of the OAU, set up to help the freedom movements across the continent, (1971-74).

He was promoted further to commanding officer of Tanzania's Sixth Battalion, (1974-75), Brigade commander in Zanzibar (1978-79) and was then in charge of the Tanzanian 205 brigade sent to topple Idi Amin and liberate Uganda (March-July 1979).

While pursuing his military activities he had become an MP for his home district, Moshi Urban and Mwanza Regional Commissioner and Regional Party Secretary of the *Chama Cha Mapinduzi* (February 1977-November 1978). After his spell in Uganda he went into full-time politics, being appointed Minister of Home Affairs by Julius Nyerere on 26 October 1980 until 1983, when he was reshuffled to Defence and National Service. President Ali Hassan Mwinyi reappointed him to Home Affairs on 6 November 1985. In 1987 he was elected to the National executive committee of the ruling CCM party.

President Mwinyi carried out a general purge against bureaucracy and corruption in government in March 1990. After stern words, he dismissed the whole of his cabinet. Kimairo had been criticised because of the conduct of the Tanzanian police who were responsible to him as Minister of the Interior. He had also been questioned by the CCM National Executive Committee on the performance of his ministry. Mwinyi dropped him from the cabinet, though he may still make a come-back.

MALECELA, John Samuel Cigwiyemisi
Tanzanian politician, Prime Minister, 9 November 1990 –

Though long serving, he is not generally considered to be one of the old guard, in the sense that he lacks any obvious local power base. But as a Tanzanian diplomat, he was once a fiery, militant anti-colonialist and the scourge of Britain's southern African policies in the 1960s and 1970s. Later he became a polished Foreign Minister and High Commissioner to Britain, before being unexpectedly selected by President Mwinyi as his Prime Minister in November 1990.

Born 10 April 1934, at Mvumu, Dodoma in the middle of the country. Educated at a local mission school and at St Andrew's College, Minaki before going to Bombay University, India where he got a Bachelor of Commerce degree in 1959. He did further studies in administration at Cambridge (1961-62).

He was appointed consul to the United States and third secretary to the Tanganyika Mission to the UN, before becoming Tanzania's ambassador to the UN (1964-68). He was elected chairman of the UN committee on decolonisation.

In May 1968 he was transferred to Addis Ababa as ambassador and in January 1969, Minister of Research and Social Services in the East African Community and later Minister for Finance and Administration at the Community headquarters in Arusha.

After the break-up of the Community, President Nyerere relinquished responsibility for foreign affairs and appointed him Foreign Minister in February 1972. He maintained Nyerere's policies of friendship with China and an uneasy relationship with Britain, until he was switched to Agriculture in 1975.

From that time he held successive ministries – Agriculture (1975-80), Mines (1980-82), Communications and Transport (1982-85). But he suffered a shock defeat in the elections of October 1985 in his Dodoma central constituency and was not appointed to President Mwinyi's first cabinet in November. He occupied himself by being appointed as one of the Commonwealth's seven "wise men" who travelled to South Africa, to try and find a way to bring a peaceful end to apartheid. On 12 March 1985 he and his colleagues were able to see the detained South African leader Nelson Mandela at Pollsmoor prison. The Commonwealth team presented its report in June 1986, but it was not accepted by the South African government.

His appointment as Prime Minister came as something of a surprise as Mwinyi had found no way of appointing him to the cabinet after his electoral defeat in 1985 and since then he had not held ministerial rank. But his role as a distinguished minister and high commissioner to Britain had not been forgotten. He was raised to the premiership over the heads of his colleagues on 9 November 1990.

MKAPA, Benjamin William

Tanzanian politician. Minister of Information, 9 November 1990 –

A highly experienced cabinet minister with particular specialisation in Foreign Affairs and Information, having been Minister for Foreign Affairs twice and High Commissioner and Ambassador for his country in key postings to Nigeria, Canada and the USA. He made his mark at the beginning of his career in journalistic management, setting the pattern for the party press and establishing many major publications in the country.

Born 12 November 1938 at Masasi in Matwara region. Educated at Lupaso Primary School (1945-48), Kigonsela Seminary (1951-53), Ndanda Secondary School and St Francis College 1954. He went on to Makerere University College (1957-62) and to Columbia University in the USA (1962-63).

He returned home to become an administrative officer in Dodoma in 1962, rising to district officer and foreign service officer. He returned to Dar es Salaam and became managing editor of the *Nationalist* and *Uhuru* newspapers in 1966 and then the *Daily News*, Tanzania's major national newspaper, in 1972.

Julius Nyerere spotted his talent and made him his press secretary in 1974. He then became Director of the Tanzania News Agency, *Shihata*, in 1976 for a brief period before being promoted to become Tanzania's high commissioner to Nigeria in 1976. On 13 February 1977 a major promotion came with his appointment for the first time to the cabinet as Minister for Foreign Affairs on 13 February 1977. He held the ministry until he was reshuffled to Information and Culture on 26 October 1980 to make room for Salim Ahmed Salim.

In 1982 he was appointed high commissioner to Canada and in 1983 ambassador to the USA. He returned to the Foreign Ministry once again in a general reshuffle on 24 April 1984, following the death of the Prime Minister Edward Sokoine in a road accident. He has been the MP for his home district Masasi since 1985. In 1987 he was elected to the 20-member central committee of the *Chama Cha Mapinduzi* (CCM) in 1987. After six years distinguished service in the Foreign ministry, he exchanged portfolios with Ahmed Diria in November 1990 and returned to the Ministry of Information.

MONGELLA, Gertrude Ibengwe
Tanzanian politician.

A tough and determined career woman who rose fast in both party and government. After carving out a successful career for herself in the administration of teaching she became the only member of the all-powerful Central Committee of the Chama Cha Mapinduzi, in 1982. Generally considered to be an ideologist on the left wing of the party, she opposed many of the conditions imposed by the IMF in the process of economic liberalisation. This led to her being dropped as Minister of Tourism by Ali Hassan Mwinyi in December 1987, though she retained her party position.

Born 13 September 1945 at Ukewere in Mwanza region. Educated locally and at Dar es Salaam University (1967-70). Became a tutor at Changombe Teachers College (1970-75). Curriculum developer, at the Institute of Adult Education (1975-78).

Her interest in politics developed early and she joined the *Chama Cha Mapinduzi* party, becoming a member of the Legislative Council in 1975. By 1982 she had been elected to the 20-member central committee, the supreme organ of the party. She was also appointed head of the CCM Secretariat's Department of Social Welfare.

She became inspector of schools in the Eastern Zone (1981-82). Her first Ministerial appointment came on 5 February 1982, when she was appointed minister of state in the office of the Prime Minister Cleopa Msuya. She was appointed a full minister by the new President, Ali Hassan Mwiniyi. He gave her the Natural Resources and Tourism Portfolio on 6 November 1985–12 December 1987.

At the third Congress of the CCM in October 1987 she was confirmed as a member of the Central Committee, but on 12 December she and two other leading party ideologists lost their jobs. She became a Minister without portfolio. President Mwinyi was quoted as saying that it would give the three more time to concentrate on party matters, but observers felt that the group of three were being pushed out because of their obstruction to the economic liberalisation measures being taken by Mwinyi at the behest of the International Monetary Fund.

MSUYA, Cleopa David
Tanzanian politician. Minister of Industry and Trade, 15 March 1990 –

A calm, urbane, Makerere trained intellectual who has risen through the civil service rather than the party to the highest office. An honest and hard working professional, he was Prime Minister for a brief period between 1980-83 when Edward Sokoine was indisposed. His real challenge came when he became Minister of Finance, for a second term in February 1983, when he had to secure foreign aid for the ailing Tanzanian economy by coming to an agreement with the IMF despite criticism from the ideologues within the party.

Born 4 January 1931 at Usangani in Mwanga district in northern Kilimanjaro region in what he describes as a "very ordinary peasant farmer family." A Christian in a predominantly Muslim district, he went to the Old Moshi Secondary School 1944-49, and the Tabora Government Secondary school 1950-51. He then attended Makerere university in 1952, taking a BA in geography, history and politics in 1955.

He went into government service in the Department of Community Development in 1956, serving as an officer in the field before being posted to Dar es Salaam in 1960 and rising to the head of his department as Commissioner for Community Development in 1961.

As a civil servant he was not at first able to join the Tanganyika African National Union (TANU) but when this rule was relaxed in 1964, he joined the party while pursing his job as a career civil servant as permanent secretary in the ministry of community development 1964-5, Principal secretary in lands and water 1965-67, economic development planning 1967-70, and the Treasury 1970-72.

On 17 February 1972 he was appointed as one of the 10 nominated members as Minister of Finance. His promotion to this senior post was a reflection of his achievements in the civil service and of the long apprenticeship he had in the ministry under the former minister Amir Jamal.

He was shuffled to the Ministry of Industry in November 1975. A major promotion came on 26 October 1980 when he was appointed Prime Minister in replacement of Edward Sokoine who stood down for health reasons. Sokoine was reinstated when his health improved on 24 February 1983 and Msuya was moved back to the "hot seat" as Minister of Finance.

Msuya had an unenviable task, his job was to rescue the ailing economy and reach some accommodation with the International Monetary Fund. This was a necessary course if the country was to get sufficient western assistance, but it was heavily criticised by the party ideologues and sometimes by Julius Nyerere himself, who were reluctant to bow to IMF conditionalities.

Msuya held the post throughout, while he wrestled with the delicate negotiations, which were finally concluded in August 1986, after seven years hard slog. But this achievement was not recognised in the party where he was dropped from the Central Committee at the third congress of the CCM in October 1987.

He remained on the larger National Executive Committee and as Minister of Finance. In March 1990 Mwinyi carried out a thorough-going shake-up, particularly among economic ministries. He switched Msuya from Finance to Trade and Industry.

MWAKAWAGO, Daudi Ngelautwa
Tanzanian politician.

A minister of considerable experience in a variety of portfolios, particularly in Information. He is mainly known for his work in establishing Kivukoni, the ideological college that trains party cadres. His connection with the college has helped give him the reputation as one of the major party ideologues. He was retained as a minister by President Mwinyi, when he succeeded Nyerere, but he remained highly critical of the liberalisation of the economy and the conditions imposed by the IMF. This led to his being dropped by Mwinyi in December 1987, though shortly beforehand his position was confirmed as one of the elected members of the party central committee.

Born September 1939. Educated locally and at Makerere University, Kampala and Manchester University. He started his career in education, becoming a tutor at the ideological college of the party, Kivukoni, in Dar es Salaam (1970-75) rising to vice-principal in 1970 and principal in 1971. He became an MP in 1970 and was appointed a minister for the first time by President Nyerere in 1972. He was given the Information portfolio, a post he held until 13 February 1977, when he was renamed head of Kivukoni college and nominated by Nyerere to the Central Committee of the party, *Chama cha Mapinduzi.*

He was reappointed Minister of Information and Culture on 24 February 1983 and was reshuffled to Minister of Labour and Manpower Development on 24 April 1984 after the death of Prime Minister Edward Sokoine. On 23 March 1987 President Mwinyi appointed him Minister for Industries and Trade. He held this post until 12 December 1987 when Mwinyi appeared to be purging the party ideologues who had been opposing economic liberalisation policies and the structural readjustments demanded by the IMF. His position in the party remained as strong as ever when he was re-elected a member of the Central committee in October 1988 and he was put in charge of propaganda and mass mobilisation in the party.

MWINYI, Ali Hassan
Tanzanian President since 27 October 1985.

A quiet, retiring school teacher and career civil servant. Only five foot tall, he spent most of his life unassumingly in the shadow of Julius Nyerere. After a check in his early career where he courageously resigned as Minister of Home Affairs, he seemed temporarily to be forgotten with few prospects of taking the highest office. But he was the right man in the right place when he became President of Zanzibar in January 1984, where he showed his mettle by bringing calm to the troubled island and a return of prosperity to the economy. This brought him to the attention of Nyerere who overlooked other more senior and colourful candidates when it came to finding a successor. Mwinyi has continued as President of Tanzania in

*the same quiet, workmanlike way as in Zanzibar, restoring the economy
to comparative prosperity by acting as a pragmatic realist rather than a
party ideologue.*

Born 8 May 1925 at Kivure in Kisarwe district,on the mainland though
he was a Zanzibari. His family moved to Zanzibar when he was still a
child. He went to primary school at Mangapwani in Zanzibar from
1933-1936 and Dole Secondary School. Then in 1942 he did a two year
teacher training course going to the Institute of Education at the
University of Durham for further professional training.

He returned to teach at Bumbwini Primary School and Zanzibar
Teacher Training college between 1954-61 when he went back to Britain
to do a two year diploma in education. He became Principal of Zanzibar's
teacher training college in 1963. In 1964 he was appointed principal
secretary to the Ministry of Education in Zanzibar. His political
beginnings were in the Afro-Shirazi Party. He was the deputy treasurer
of the Makadara branch from 1966-70. After the Zanzibar revolution in
1964 he was made assistant General Manager to the Zanzibar State
Trading Corporation until 1970.

From then onwards he came in demand as chairman of numerous
boards and official bodies including the East African Currency Board
(Zanzibar), the Film Censorship Board, the Editorial Board of the
Zanzibar Government Progress Reports, and the National Swahili
Council of Dar es Salaam. He was also a member of the College Council
of the University of East Africa and of the Printing Press Corporation
Board, Zanzibar.

In 1970 Nyerere brought him into his President's office as Minister of
State and in 1972 he was made Minister of Health where he pushed
through a rapid expansion of the health service. In 1975 he closed private
hospitals because they were attracting doctors away from state hospitals.
On 9 November 1975 in appreciation of his efficiency, Nyerere promoted
him to Minister of Home Affairs.

On 23 January 1977 he and another minister resigned when they
accepted, "ultimate political responsibility" for acts of grave misconduct
by junior police and security forces resulting in a number of deaths in
Shinyanga and Mwanza regions. *The Times* (London) said that this
responsible conduct was almost unknown elsewhere in Africa. Nyerere
accepted the resignations, "with a heavy heart." He was then sent to
Egypt as Tanzania's ambassador.

On 5 February 1982 he was back as Minister of Natural Resources
and Tourism. On 24 February 1983 he became Minister of State in the
office of the Vice President and President of Zanzibar, Aboud Jumbe. This
comparatively humble post proved to be Mwinyi's springboard to the top
because, when Aboud Jumbe resigned over secessionist unrest on the
island, Mwinyi was confirmed as interim President. He was officially
confirmed as President of Zanzibar and Interim Chairman of the
Zanzibar Revolutionary Council on 31 January 1984. In February he
began appointing his Zanzibar ministers including Seif Shariff Hamad

as Chief Minister.

On 11 March 1984 the National Executive Committee of the ruling *Chama Cha Mapinduzi* party, obviously guided by Nyerere, nominated Mwinyi as the sole candidate for the Zanzibar Presidential elections which took place on 19 April. He was duly elected and made Vice-President of Tanzania on 24 April.

But this exalted position was still no stopping place in the sudden rise of Ali Hassan Mwinyi. Nyerere confirmed that he would stand down for office at the end of his Presidential term and there was much speculation as to his successor, especially after Edward Sokoine, the Prime Minister, was killed in a car crash. A number of other candidates seemed preferred to Mwinyi, who had in any case only just established himself as President in Zanzibar.

Mwinyi was hard at work to redress the turbulent situation in Zanzibar. He steered Zanzibar politics into a more open phase and improved the life of the people by liberalising trade. But the question of Nyerere's succession became more pressing. When hard choices had to be made at the special congress of the CCM on 15 August 1985, delegates voted 1,731 to 14 for him as the sole candidate for the elections of 27 October when he was duly confirmed as President.

He was faced with an economic crisis caused by lack of foreign exchange and mounting debt and an almost total dearth of consumer goods in the shops. He decided that he had to swallow the bitter pill proscribed by the IMF and ensure assistance even if this was in return for accepting IMF conditionalities. He preceded to liberalise the economy with similar success to that achieved earlier in Zanzibar. He did this with calm authority despite heavy criticism, from the left wing of the party, for abandoning the socialist principles of the CCM.

He also tightened up on the corruption and inefficiency in the government bureaucracy. Nyerere who remained in the powerful post as Chairman of the CCM generously acknowledged that Mwinyi had succeeded in making "the new government look like a government" by tightening up on discipline in the administration.

On 3 November 1990 he was re-elected as President for a second five-year term. He was the sole candidate and won 95.5% of the vote.

In his first post-election cabinet he dropped his Prime Minister, John Warioba, who was a Nyerere appointee and replaced him with his own man, John Malecela, a former minister with great experience and High Commissioner to the UK.

Mwinyi found many voices raised in favour of multi-party government in 1990-91. In March 1991, he set up a presidential commission to seek the views of people all over the country on whether to continue with a single party or to adopt a multi-party system. But all members of the commission had CCM affiliations except the lawyer Mabere Marando who refused to become a commissioner.

The emerging Tanzanian opposition established its own independent committee, under the former minister, Chief Abdullah Fundikira to look into the multi-party question. This was seen as a rejection, by leading democratic dissidents of Mwinyi's own constitutional tinkering. The issue became inflamed by the death, shortly after he was released from detention of another opposition leader Moussa Membar.

NYERERE, Julius Kambarage

Tanzanian President 9 December 1962 – 27 October 1985.

Highly regarded throughout Africa and the world as the father of his nation and as a humane and liberal-minded socialist and Pan-Africanist. He radiates charm and charisma that makes him one of the most beloved leaders in Africa. He is one of the few African leaders to have voluntarily stepped down from office. He was already leader of his country long before independence in 1961. He ruled his country for 25 years and tried to involve all his people in his own homespun brand of socialism. Though his economic policies were not successful, he did create a moral and social climate superior to most of the rest of Africa and he gave his people good educational standards and a strong belief in his philosophies and in themselves.

Born March 1922. The exact date is not known as no records were kept, but as it was raining he was named after the rain spirit. His father, Chief Burito Nyerere, was a none too prosperous petty chief, living at Butiama near the eastern shore of Lake Victoria, with 22 wives and 26 children. Julius was the son of the fourth wife.

His tribe, the Zanaki, is one of the smallest among Tanzania's 113 tribes. At the age of 12, wrapped in an old piece of cloth, he was sent to primary school. He did exceptionally well and entered Tanganyika's only secondary school at Tabora, run on strict English public school lines. He became a practising Catholic.

Over 1943-45 he studied at Makerere College, Kampala. He taught for two years at Tabora and at St Mary's, a White Fathers' school. The fathers encouraged him to go to Edinburgh, the first Tanganyikan to go to a British university.

In August 1954, the Tanganyika African National Union was formed with Nyerere as President. He displayed an unusual talent for organisation and soon had one of the most united nationalist movements behind him.In 1955 he took the anti-colonial case before the Trusteeship Council of the United Nations. In 1957 he served for four months as a nominated member in the Legislative Council and then resigned because the body was making insufficient political progress.

In September 1958 and later in August 1960 the Tanganyika African National Union (TANU) swept the polls. When the country became self-governing in October, Nyerere became Chief Minister and saw his country through to full independence on 9 December 1961.

One month later he surprised everyone by resigning from the Premiership to concentrate on reorganising the party and change it from being a force against colonialism to becoming a positive part of building a new nation. He was soon ready to return to the centre of power as President on 9 December 1962.

In December 1963 Zanzibar, the island off Tanganyika mainland, was given independence. One month later the Afro-Arab government was overthrown. Coup hysteria spread rapidly through East Africa. The army, the Tanganyika Rifles, mutinied and he came near to being toppled. He went into hiding and called in British troops.

In April 1963 when the political leadership in Zanzibar had taken the reins of power from the coup-makers, he announced a union with the Zanzibar Peoples' Republic to create the United Republic of Tanzania, with himself as President. Though there was scarcely any effective opposition, he thought a one-party state was more appropriate and after a Presidential commission made the system official in June 1965.

With the Arusha Declaration of 7 February 1967 he came up with an entirely new approach to the problem of development. He announced the philosophy of *ujamaa* (which means familyhood or sharing on a family basis). This was a philosophy of self-help intended to tap the energies of the people rather than relying on foreign aid or assistance. He followed in 1970 with villagisation, a brand of rural socialism where people came together in *ujamaa* villages to co-operate in production and self-improvement. By the mid-1970s over two thirds of the entire population was living in *ujamaa* villages.

Meanwhile, in the towns he introduced state ownership by nationalisation of financial institutions and greater state participation and control. Then in 1971 he nationalised property.

After further trouble in Zanzibar and the assassination of the Zanzibar President Abeid Karume in 1972, Nyerere took steps to bring the two countries closer together by merging the Zanzibar Afro-Shirazi party and TANU into *Chama Cha Mapinduzi*, the CCM. On 21 January 1977 he was elected its first chairman.

In foreign policy his main concern during the 1970s was the coming to power of Idi Amin in Uganda and ideological disagreements with capitalist-oriented Kenya. The twin strains led to the disintegration of the East African Community by the beginning of 1977. Nyerere gave support to the former Ugandan Premier, Milton Obote, and other Ugandan exiles and helped with the attempted invasion of Uganda in September 1972. Later, following Ugandan provocations, Tanzanian troops successfully invaded Uganda in January 1979. Amin was toppled but Tanzanian troops remained behind to preserve the peace. Some remained until mid-1981.

Nyerere won the presidential elections of October 1980 with a mandate from 93% of the electorate. The 1980s were characterised by economic deterioration and the realisation by many, though not by Nyerere himself, that *ujamaa* and villagisation politics had not worked. The bureaucracy had not been able to provide the basic support needed and Tanzania had been hit by drought and lack of foreign exchange, leading to a shortage of the most basic consumer goods in the shops.

Though Nyerere still had the admiration of the vast bulk of his people, he must have felt disappointed at the lack of practical achievement. In the mid-1980s he began to talk of stepping down from the Presidency at the end of his term of office in 1985. There were worries when his chosen successor, Edward Sokoine, was killed in a car crash and efforts were made in the party to persuade him to stay in office, but on 15 August 1985 he did not stand and Ali Hassan Mwinyi, the Zanzibar President, was selected as the sole candidate for the Tanzanian presidential elections and he was duly sworn in on 27 October 1985.

Nyerere remained in the powerful position as chairman of the CCM and soon became critical of the economic liberalisation that Mwinyi introduced soon after his assumption of the presidency. He complained about the "unplanned retreats from socialism". Though he originally intended to resign from national politics altogether, he became so worried at the economic course the new government was taking that, in October 1987, he was easily persuaded to accept the chairmanship for a further five years where he could counter-balance Mwinyi's economic reforms. He also gave himself more time for international activities such as the chairmanship of the South Commission, which tackles the urgent problems facing the Third World.

He began to express doubts about the efficacy of the one-party system early in 1990, and encouraged the debate on multi-party democracy. He stood down from the chairmanship of the CCM on 17 August 1990, allowing Ali Hassan Mwinyi to take over. In his resignation address he defended the achievements of the party.

SALIM, Ahmed Salim

Tanzanian politician and diplomat. Secretary-General of the OAU, 26 July 1989 –

The brightest, most accomplished and internationally recognised of all the Tanzanian leaders after Julius Nyerere, his brilliant career suffered a severe check when he failed to become the first African UN Secretary-General. He was again disappointed when he became Prime Minister and appeared to be the front runner to succeed Julius Nyerere, but the inner workings of Tanzanian politics denied him the top job, while his Zanzibari nationality prevented him becoming number two. But his international reputation and all round ability finally won him the job as Secretary General of the Organisation of African Unity in July 1989.

Born 23 January 1942 in Pemba (Zanzibar). Educated at Mkoani Primary School, Pemba, then Lumumba college, Zanzibar, taking his masters at Columbia University (School of International Affairs) 1973-74.

His political career started when he became secretary-general of the Zanzibar Youth Movement in 1960. Joined the Umma (masses) party, the breakaway group from the conservative pro-Sultanate Zanzibar National Party in 1963. As its publicity secretary, he edited the newsheet

Sauti ya Umma. Became the executive secretary for the United Front for Opposition Parties. Secretary-general of the all-Zanzibar journalists union.

After the Zanzibar revolution in January 1964 he was sent by the revolutionary government to be Tanzania's ambassador to Egypt (1964-65), then high commissioner to India (1965-68). He returned home to become director of African and Middle East affairs in the Ministry of Foreign Affairs (1968-69).

He resumed his diplomatic activity as ambassador to China from June to December 1969. By then Tanzania's most senior international diplomat, he was posted as permanent representative to the United Nations, where he rose to become President of the UN Assembly. He doubled up as high commissioner to Jamaica and other West Indian islands and Cuba, over 1970-80. One of his major activities during this period was the chairmanship of the UN committee on Decolonisation (1972-79). In 1981 he had the endorsement of the OAU and the backing of about a third of the UN membership to succeed Kurt Waldheim and became Africa's first UN secretary-general. He might have got the job were it not for the veto of the nine Western powers and specifically US opposition.

He returned home to be appointed Minister of Foreign Affairs by Julius Nyerere, on 26 October 1980. He held this influential post with distinction until 24 April 1984, when he was appointed Prime Minister on the death of Edward Sokoine in a motor accident. In 1983 he became the chairman of the Organisation of African Unity Liberation committee for a year.

Further disappointments were on the way because he was one of the favourites to succeed Julius Nyerere when he announced that he was to retire at the end of 1985. Considerable rivalry between himself, Ali Hassan Mwinyi and Rashidi Kawawa ensued at a special *Chama Cha Mapinduzi* congress, but on 15 August 1985 Mwinyi was unanimously selected as the sole presidential candidate.

Mwinyi, like Salim, was a Zanzibari and under the constitution the President and his deputy could not both come from the island, so the very much less well known Joseph Warioba became First Vice-President and Prime Minister while Salim found himself demoted to Deputy Prime Minister and Minister of Defence, posts he accepted with good grace on 6 November 1985.

In May 1989 Mwinyi released him to contest the post of OAU secretary-general. The contest took place in Addis Ababa in July and Salim found himself opposed by the outgoing secretary-general, Ide Oumarou. In the first round Oumarou secured one vote more than Salim, but still not enough to secure the two-thirds majority required. But the third round of voting produced 38 votes for Salim, with nine abstentions and three spoilt papers. He was confirmed as secretary-general on 26 July 1989.

WAKIL, Idris Abdul

Tanzanian politician. President of Zanzibar, 15 October 1985 – 24 October 1990.

His power base was exclusively concentrated in his home island Zanzibar and in his long service in the former Afro-Shirazi party. His ascendancy to the Presidency came fortuitously when Ali Hassan Mwinyi was made President of Tanzania in October 1985. But his election as sole candidate only achieved 61% of the poll and dissension grew within his own cabinet until he claimed, in January 1988, that ministers in his own government were plotting against him. He regained control during the course of 1988, but finally resigned from the presidency at the end of 1990.

Born 10 April 1925 in Zanzibar and educated locally. Went to Makerere university (1944-48) where he received a diploma in education. Took up teaching in Zanzibar schools for ten years. He resigned his headship and stood for election in 1962, becoming a member of the Zanzibar National Assembly. After the revolution in 1964 he became a member of the Revolutionary Council and Minister of Education and National Culture in Zanzibar.

After Tanganyika and Zanzibar united in April 1964, he joined the union cabinet on the mainland in the same month as Minister of Information and Tourism. He went into diplomatic service as Tanzania's ambassador to West Germany (1967), the Hague (1969-73), and the Republic of Guinea (1973-77). He returned home to become director of protocol at the Tanzanian Ministry of Foreign Affairs (1977-79).

He became speaker of the Zanzibar House of Representatives in 1980. He was selected by the CCM central committee as one of the two candidates for the presidential elections on 19 April 1984, following the resignation of Aboud Jumbe, but he withdrew his candidature in favour of Ali Hassan Mwinyi. This was a fortunate move because when Mwinyi was adopted as union President in October 1985, Wakil emerged as the sole candidate for the Zanzibar Presidency. He duly triumphed on 15 October after polling 131,471 or 61% of the votes cast. He then axed six of the cabinet's 12 ministers who had served in the Mwinyi government. On the election of Mwinyi as union President on 6 November 1985, he was appointed Second Vice-President of Tanzania.

Zanzibar has had a long history of dissatisfaction with the union which has resulted in periodic bouts of secessionism and racial rivalry between Africans and Arabs. These recurred in 1988. On 12 January he accused unnamed ministers in his government of plotting against him and declared that a group of dissidents were conspiring to engage mercenaries to overthrow his government. On 23 January he suspended the Supreme Revolutionary Council and assumed control of the armed forces. Chief Minister Seif Shariff Hamad was dismissed, along with five other ministers, mostly from Pemba island, who favoured policies of economic liberalisation. This was widely interpreted as a triumph for the supporters of the former Afro-Shirazi party.

In the run-up to the elections of October 1990, he unexpectedly announced his retirement from the presidency after only five years in office. His successor was Dr Salmin Amour.

WARIOBA, Joseph Sinde

Tanzanian lawyer and politician. Minister of Local Government, 9 November 1990 –

A hard-working lawyer and civil servant who has made his way to the top through his dedication to international activities. A quiet, low-key and unassuming man who has played a major part in drafting the laws of Tanzania. One of the new mould of technocratic leaders who has not risen through the ranks of the party, but as a nominated member was promoted to Justice Minster by Julius Nyerere (who shares a similar Zanaki/Kuliya ethnic background) and then selected by Ali Hassan Mwinyi, on his promotion to the presidency, as his number two. He was demoted from the premiership to Minister of Local Government, in a general reshuffle after the elections of October 1990.

Born 3 September 1940 in Ikizu, Musoma district in the Mara region on the eastern shores of Lake Victoria. A Zanaki/Kuliya. Educated at Sarawe and Ikizu Primary Schools 1948-52, at Musoma Middle School 1953-54, and Bwiru and Tabora Secondary Schools and at Dar es Salaam university (1963-66), where he did legal studies. He joined the profession in 1966, working in the Attorney-General's chambers. Spotted early on for his talents, he was sent as Tanzanzia's delegate to the UN Human Rights Conference in Tehran, Iran. He attended a conference in 1967 on African refugees and two years later helped draft the convention on refugees in Africa. In 1968 he joined Dar es Salaam city council as a solicitor for two years.

He became director of the legal and international organisations division of the Ministry of Foreign Affairs (1971-75). His reputation grew as a representative of his country at international gatherings. In 1971 he headed Tanzania's delegation to the UN Sea Bed Committee, the forerunner of the Law on the Sea conference. In early 1983 he was elected chairman of the Law of the Sea Preparatory Commission (Pepcom). He served until 1987 and helped formulate the Law of the Sea Treaty, persuasively putting the views of of the "Group of 77" developing countries.

He was promoted Assistant Attorney-General (1975-76) and Attorney-General in 1977. It was during this period that he did valuable work redrafting the laws of the country. His first cabinet appointment came on 24 February 1983 when he was made Minister of Justice.A major advance followed on 6 November 1985 when he was unexpectedly appointed Prime Minister and First Vice-President by Ali Hassan Mwinyi. In this appointment he displaced the incumbent Prime Minister

Salim Salim, who could not retain his post under the constitution because both he and the new President were Zanzibaris. In his capacity as Prime Minister, Warioba worked directly as the chief executive of the President. He was also secretary of the powerful Defence and Security Committee. He was dropped suddenly from the premiership in November 1990 in preference for John Malecela. This was taken as evidence that Mwinyi wanted his own man as deputy.

TOGO

Population: 3.34m (1990, World Bank)
Independence: 27 April 1960
Head of State: General Gnassingbé Eyadema
Government: A national conference to establish a pluralist system was called after much prevarication by the government on 8 July 1991. It declared its own sovereignty, suspended the old constitution and elected a transitional prime minister in defiance of the government.
Parties: Former single party – *Rassemblement du Peuple Togolais* (RPT). Other opposition parties were being formed in mid-1991.

EYADEMA, Etienne Gnassingbé
Togo politician. President, 14 April 1967 –

One of longest surviving Heads of State in Africa, yet still comparatively young. He has been in power for more than 20 years and gradually consolidated his own position by his determined, authoritarian rule and the stimulation of the personality cult that developed around him. His search over the years has been for a means to democratise government and conciliate the opposition while still holding real power in his own hands. Under international pressure he has released political prisoners and set up a Human Rights Commission to counter accusations of the use of torture in his prisons. But his past was exposed in a welter of allegations at the National Conference of July 1991, which accused him of serious crimes. His battle for political survival then began.

Born 26 December 1937, a Kabré, at Pya in the Lama Kara region of the north. While still a very young man he crossed with a number of his fellow Kabré into Dahomey (Benin) in 1953 and joined the French army and was sent to Indo-China where he fought for 18 months. In 1956 he was transferred to Algeria, where he served for over four years. Later, in 1961, he was stationed in Dahomey and Niger. After independence in 1960 he ended service with the French army but to his indignation, President Olympio refused to take him into his small National Guard. He then gained acceptance into the military school at Frejus in France but the President still refused to sponsor him.

Instead he became an adjutant in the Togo army, but on the night of 12 January 1963, a group of discontented soldiers, most of them northerners, armed themselves and started to hunt for Olympio. Eyadema emerged as the leader among the disgruntled group.

The actual incident, just before dawn, in which Olympio was shot at the gate of the US embassy, where he was trying to seek asylum, is still obscure, although Eyadema claims that Olympio himself had a gun and was firing. Immediately after he was proud of his role. "I was the justiciar of God," he said at one point. When he later assumed power, however, he was unhappy about references to his part in the assassination and the French newspaper *Le Monde* was once banned for too bald a reference to it.

But the incident was Eyadema's making among the soldiery, if only for the reputation of courage and toughness that it gave him. He was admitted to a new, enlarged Togo army, being promoted captain in May 1963 and major a year later. A conflict between him and Emmanuel Bodjolle, the Chief of Staff of the army, came to a head in May 1965, when President Grunitzky dismissed Bodjolle for "abuse of power" and replaced him with Eyadema who was promoted lieutenant-colonel in October 1965. His remarkable rate of promotion was a reflection of his real power in the army dominated by his Kabré tribe.

In November 1966, when Grunitzky's cabinet had virtually collapsed and there were popular demonstrations in Lomé calling on the army to take power, Eyadema remained loyal, only to overthrow him two months later in January 1967. The apparent contradiction was Eyadema's reluctance to come to power at the head of a popular movement which had been essentially organised by the old Olympio party.

But his coup was chosen to be on the fourth anniversary of Olympio's death, 13 January 1967. At first he said the take-over was temporary and he installed an older officer as Head of Government, but it only took three months before he took power himself on 14 April.

He dissolved all political parties but declared his intention of restoring civilian rule and set up a constitutional committee to draw up a new constitution. But plans for an early return to civilian rule were shelved in response to popular demonstrations.

But his regime still needed legitimacy and in August 1969 he set up a sole political party, the *Rassemblement du Peuple Togolais* (RPT) along the lines of President Mobutu's MPR, stressing the need for a return to authentic African values.

There were at least two coup plots in 1977-78, but when he held a referendum in January 1972 on whether he should remain as President he gained an overwhelming yes vote. On 24 January 1974 he was the only survivor in an air crash in which the pilot and all the other passengers were killed. This was considered to be an attempted reprisal by mining interests for his nationalisation of the phosphate mines. His survival gave an immense boost to the personality cult that was developing around his name.

He further expanded his powers in 1976 when he reduced the size of the RPT political bureau and made all appointments to that body and to the central committee himself. Another attempted coup was discovered in October 1977 and there were demonstrations by students and workers.

But his personal popularity was unchallenged and on 30 December 1979, as sole candidate, he was re-elected President under a new constitution endorsed by referendum. The country settled down to more stable government in the early 1980s as Eyadema continued to foster the personality cult around his name but entrusted government to a new crop of competent administrators.

A period of calm ended in August 1985 with an unprecedented wave of bomb attacks in Lomé, and the distribution of subversive literature. Arrests were made and Amnesty International and visiting French jurists complained of torture being used on political prisoners. A further coup attempt and the discovery of a cache of explosives was revealed in July 1987. In December 1986 Eyadema was re-elected for another seven-year term with more than 99% of the votes cast. In June 1987 he held a series of meetings with leaders of the old political parties, dissolved in the aftermath of the 1967 coup attempt, to discuss ways of achieving national unity. In October he set up a national Human Rights Commission and in January 1987 released almost 300 political prisoners as part of the ceremonies to celebrate his 20 years in power.

While he did not endorse multi-party democracy, he did allow the matter to be discussed publicly on the radio. He also introduced elections in March 1990, in which electors could choose between several candidates none of which were selected by the RPT.

But pressure was already building for a full blown democracy. Though Eyadema organised his supporters in massive demonstrations against multi-partyism in July, the issue would not lie down. Counter-demonstrations in October resulted in widespread violence with four dead and 34 wounded in Lomé. Anti-Eyadema slogans were daubed on walls. Eyadema responded by setting up a commission to draft a new constitution, by the end of December. The commissioners recommended a multi-party system with the division of powers between the President and a Prime Minister. This unleashed another wave of agitation for quicker reform.

After further demonstrations, Eyadema held five hours of discussion with opposition leaders on 18 December and agreed to sweeping democratic reforms, including the calling of a national conference and rapid progress towards multi-party rule. From that point the demand for change gathered momentum while Eyadema prevaricated and delayed.

The conference, attended by 1,000 delegates finally opened on 8 July 1991. Eyadema, in an opening address, defended his record during 24 years of power and appealed to delegates to avoid excesses and the "settling of old accounts." But the conference forced him to agree not to oppose its decisions. Soon delegates were on their feet accusing him of terrible crimes. The conference also suspended the constitution and froze the assets of the ruling party. Two of Eyadema's ministers actually sided with the conference against the government.

Eyadema and the government delegation withdrew from the conference and denied that it had agreed to conference sovereignty. But realising he was being outmanoeuvred, Eyadema ordered the government delegates return after a week's absence. It found the conference in a belligerent mood, having already elected its own transitional Prime Minister. At the end of August 1991 Eyadema had set up a group of wise men to mediate between the government and the conference. His survival was in the balance.

KOFFIGOH, Koku
Lawyer and politician. Prime Minister 26 August 1991 –

A calm, self effacing lawyer who became the first President of the Togolese League of Human Rights. He suddenly emerged into the political limelight at the tempestuous National Conference called to discuss the political future of the country in July 1991. Soon elected as vice-president of the praesidium, the conference chose him as interim Prime Minister, with the task of shepherding his country through to democratic government. In a spirit of reconciliation President Eyadema accepted the conference choice and confirmed him as Prime Minister on 28 August.

Born 1943 in Kpele, near Atakpame into an Ewe family. Early education at the Lycee Gouverneur-Bonne Carrere, now called Lycee Tokoin, where he did his baccalaureat. He went on to do law studies at the University of Abidjan in the Cote d'Ivoire and then Poitiers University, France, where he was called to the Bar in 1976, before returning home a few years afterwards.

After being expelled from Abidjan for leading a students demonstration he steered clear of militant student unions and exiled political parties, though he was sympathetic towards the *Convention Démocratique des peuples Africaines* the most active of all the anti-Eyadema opposition groups. He earned money working as a night watchman and a petrol pump attendant, even singing and playing his guitar in night clubs.

Back at home he established himself as a lawyer, in the Viale chambers where he worked with other prominent lawyers often taking the cases of the poor and the oppressed. Later he set up in his own practice. He rose to become President of the Togolese Bar Association.

His political feelings remained low key, until 20 July 1990 when he launched the Togolese League of Human Rights (LTDH) in the smart Pirogue restaurant. There he made the mistake of inviting a young gendarmerie lieutenant who signed on as a member, who later betrayed the group. But it persisted in its work, revealing the torture and persecution of political activists. It sprang to the defence of the militants who demonstrated in the streets in the riots of October 1990. In revenge the police bombarded its headquarters with tear gas in February 1991. On another occasion he led a delegation to the Presidency to protest against state interference during a trial.

But he did not break onto the political scene until the National Conference called to discuss the democratisation of the country in July 1991. He attended as a member of the LTDH, but was soon elected first vice-president of the praesidium, virtually in charge of organising the conference agenda.

The conference, lasting two months, became a rowdy affair with outspoken attacks on President Eyadema, who finally suspended the conference on 26 August. That same night, with troops trying to get into the building, the delegates elected Koffigoh as interim Prime Minister.

To the surprise of observers, this appointment was confirmed by President Eyadema on 28 August, who was on the point of closing the conference down because of the allegations that were being made against him. Koffigoh closed the conference and paid his first visit to the President, where a tentative reconciliation was established. He then assumed the responsibility of seeing Togo through to full democratic, multi-party government.

UGANDA

Population: 17.35m (1990, World Bank)
Head of State: President Yoweri Museveni
Independence: 9 October 1962
Government: Executive Presidency following the military coup of January 1986. The President is assisted by a cabinet of ministers (mainly civilian) and a National Resistance Council, part elected and part appointed by the President. In February 1989 a commission was appointed to review the constitution within 2 years. The NRC has extended the government's term of office from 1990, when it was due to expire, to 1995.
Parties: Political parties are not proscribed. They include the government party, the National Resistance Movement, also the Democratic Party, the Uganda People's Congress, the Uganda Patriotic Movement and the Conservative Party.

AMIN, Idi Dada

President of Uganda 1971-1979. Living in exile since his downfall.

A huge giant, standing 6ft 3ins tall, but remarkably soft spoken with a polite graciousness and charm. His rumbustious, extrovert manner and immediate friendliness belie the ruthlessness of a man who forced his way to the top and determinedly held onto power. His native cunning and all-consuming suspicion of those around him plunged his country into terror and chaos from which it has never fully recovered.

Speaking from his Saudi Arabian exile in the late 1980s, Amin claimed that he did not understand exactly what was going on under his rule and was powerless to stop the slide into chaos as his military commanders vied for power. In the prevailing atmosphere of terror, survival became the prime motive.

Amin presided over the collapse of Uganda's social and economic structure and passed on a legacy of corruption, cruelty and instability that continues in his unhappy country.

Born 1925 in West Nile, the extreme north-west corner of Uganda. His father was a Kakwa and his mother a Lugbara. Educated at a local primary school, he joined the 4th (Uganda) Battalion of the Kings African Rifles in 1946 and served with the KAR in Kenya during the Mau Mau uprising. A keen sportsman, he was the Uganda heavyweight boxing champion between 1951 and 1960, a formidable rugby player, the only African in the all-white Nile rugby club.

He became one of the first *effendis* - warrant officers, after a course in Kenya in 1959. As the colonial army rushed to Africanise in 1961 before independence, he was promoted full lieutenant - one of the first two Ugandan African officers. The same week he opened his first bank account and ran up an overdraft of about £2,000 after a wild shopping spree down Jinja High Street.

In 1963, after a commanding officer's course at the school of infantry in Wiltshire, he took command of the 1st Battalion with the rank of major. An attempted mutiny had taken place while he was away and President Obote decided to rid himself of British officers; Amin was promoted colonel and deputy commander of the army.

Accusations in the Parliament of gold and ivory smuggling were directed both against Amin and Obote. Amin claimed the large sums passing through his bank account were paid to Congolese rebels. Obote promoted Amin to Army Commander. He became Maj-General in August 1968.

But Obote did not trust Amin fully and started organising the General Service Unit as a second army. Suspicious, he "kicked him upstairs" to a powerless position and promoted new army and airforce commanders in October 1970. He also accused Amin of the disappearance of arms and military funds and left for the Commonwealth Conference in Singapore. Shortly afterwards a soldier came to Amin's house to tell him that Obote had ordered his arrest. Reacting with instinctive sharpness, Amin rallied the majority of the army and at dawn on 26 January 1971 took over.

The coup was popular; he released 55 detainees. The Baganda felt their cause would be promoted; Amin restored the body of their beloved Kabaka who had died in London in exile. But the army was badly divided and inter-tribal fighting broke out at army barracks between February and March, which Amin said he was powerless to control. Archbishop Luwum and two ministers were arrested on suspicion of plotting and executed without trial on 17 February 1972. More killings and murders were exposed and Amin's government rapidly acquired the reputation of being a corrupt and cruel regime.

In foreign affairs relations were strained. President Nyerere of Tanzania gave refuge to Obote. Border skirmishes broke out and led to a major dispute within the East African Community.

Amin started on a friendly basis with Israel, but disappointed by their niggardly policy on arms and aid, turned to Colonel Gadaffi who agreed to support him in return for expelling the Israelis. This he did by 1 April 1972.

Next Amin, on 9 August 1972, gave the Asians 90 days to get out of the country and touched off a diplomatic crisis with Britain. On 7 November 1973 he ordered most British firms and farmers to sell up and leave the country. The economy began its inexorable slide into chaos.

Obote's supporters tried an invasion from Tanzania on 17 September 1972 but Amin still had the support of the majority of the army and stopped the invading forces near the Tanzania frontier.

Internally the killings continued, motivated by the struggle for power, tribal vendettas and the atmosphere of suspicion that prevailed. A small group of Nubian military under the Defence Minister Mustapha Adrisi fought for effective power, sometimes in defiance of Amin himself. The best educated Ugandans were either killed or fled into exile.

Eventually the political opposition from the different groups both inside and outside the country began to coalesce in the Uganda National Liberation Front based in Tanzania. Amin reacted by planning a mini-invasion of Tanzania in October 1978 and attempting to annex the Kagera salient. This gave Tanzania and the Ugandan exiles the cue to mount a full-scale counter-attack in January 1979.

Amin's army was demoralised and riven by internal division and though he obtained the support of about 2,000 Libyan troops he failed to rally his raggle-taggle army, which fled north. Kampala fell on 10 April and Amin deserted his troops and escaped from the country by helicopter. His first refuge was in Tripoli, Libya where his erstwhile ally Colonel Gadaffi gave him temporary refuge. But Amin was an embarassment and held incommunicado and under virtual house arrest until arrangements could be made to give him a refuge in Saudi Arabia.

There he was given a home and placed under strict restriction not to talk to the international press. Occasionally he broke the ban but he survived in Saudi Arabia until January 1989 when he set off on a mysterious mission to visit fellow Muslims in Africa. He arrived in northern Nigeria then Zaire, where he was entertained by President Mobutu. Uganda complained but did not want him to return home. He appeared to be looking for somewhere else in Africa to live, but no African country was prepared to have him and finally he was forced to return to Saudi Arabia.

BATTA, Ronald (Dr)
Ugandan doctor and politician.

A young idealist who threw up his medical career to join Yoweri Museveni's National Resistance Movement, serving as a guerrilla doctor for five years in the bush, before emerging as Minister of State for Defence and later Minister of State for Health. A Madi, with a practical and down to earth attitude towards his job shown by his modest manner and open-necked shirt style of dress.

Born 1 January 1951 in Moyo district, West Nile region. Educated at primary and secondary schools in Moyo, transferring later to St Mary's College, Kisubi near Entebbe. He went to Makerere University in 1973 to study medicine and graduated as a doctor in 1978.

He did his internship in Mulago hospital before being posted to Luwero as the district medical officer. As superintendant of Luwero hospital he witnessed the atrocities of the Obote forces and treated the horrific injuries inflicted on innocent people. Sickened by the worsening situation, he resigned and joined the National Resistance Movement whose main operational area was Luwero. During Yoweri Museveni's five-year campaign he worked as a guerrilla doctor in the bush.

When Museveni finally took power in Kampala in January 1986, he was named Minister of State for Defence and was listed number 32 in the National Resistance Council as a Senior Army Officer, which covers everyone from battalion commander level upwards.

He soon became heavily involved in countering the activities of several different rebel guerrilla groups fighting the Museveni government. In an interview in October 1986 he strongly criticised the British military training of the Ugandan forces. Batta claimed the British instructors had been arrogant, had travelled around Uganda without permission and had failed half the trainees for being sub-standard. Towards the end of his term as a minister he justified the scorched earth policy of the Uganda government, when dealing with rebel infested areas, in which the grain and crops of ordinary people were destroyed.

On 22 February 1988 he was reshuffled to become Minister of State for Health. But on 2 July 1991 when Museveni drastically pruned his cabinet he lost his portfolio.

KATEGAYA, Eriya

Ugandan politician. First Deputy Prime Minister, 22 February 1988.

Possibly the most powerful Ugandan politician after Yoweri Museveni. Carries out many secret missions and visits to foreign countries on behalf of his boss. He was among the first to join Museveni's National Resistance Army guerrillas in the bush in 1981. He was rewarded by being made minister of state in February 1988 and First Deputy Prime Minister in the office of Samson Kisekka.

Born 1945 in Kyamate, Mbarara district. Educated locally and at Mbarara High School (1959-60) and Ntare School (1961-66), in Western Ugandan before going to the University of Dar es Salaam where he graduated in law in 1970.

He became a teacher at the Institute of Public Administration in Kampala, then had a spell as State Attorney, in 1971, before leaving public service to join a private law firm. During the Amin regime he fled to Zambia where he worked as a State Attorney in the Zambian Attorney-General's Chambers (1975-79).

After the deposition of Idi Amin in 1979, he became district commissioner of Bushenyi and Minister of Commerce on 18 May 1980, in the shortlived Uganda National Liberation Front government which ousted President Godfrey Binaisa. When Yoweri Museveni became disillusioned with President Obote and set up his National Resistance Movement and took to the bush in 1981, Kategaya joined him and became secretary for political and diplomatic affairs and a member of the National Resistance Army, High Command.

He held the first press conference given after the capture of Kampala on 26 January 1987 from the forces of General Tito Okello. He claimed that it was a "victory for all peace loving Ugandans and supporters," and appealed to the Okello troops to surrender. On 6 February 1987 he was appointed Minister of State in the office of the Prime Minister, Samson Kisekka. On 22 February 1988 he was promoted to First Deputy Prime

Minister in charge of infrastructural rehabilitation, agricultural and industrial inputs, and supply.

KISEKKA, Samson Babi Mululu
Ugandan politician. Vice-President, 22 January 1991 –

Distinguished as the first African medical doctor. Made a small impact in Kabaka Yekka politics in the early 1960s and then appeared to retire into private medicine and farming. But he emerged as chief spokesman for Museveni's National Resistance Movement when it started its guerrilla campaign in the early 1980s. He was rewarded by becoming Uganda's Prime Minister after Museveni took power. He relinquished this office and assumed the vice-presidency in January 1991.

Born 23 June 1912, a Muganda at Mengo, Kampala. Educated at the renowned King's College Budo, then Makerere University College where he obtained a degree in medicine and surgery in 1954, becoming the first African medical officer in the Ministry of Health. In the same year he launched an English weekly newspaper, *Uganda Pilot*. He attempted to start a political party, but when his hopes did not materialise he joined the Kabaka Yekka (Kabaka only) party and in 1959 won a seat in the Lukiko, the local Buganda parliament. He then went to Riverside Sanitorium and Hospital at Nashville, Tennessee where he obtained a masters degree in medicine, in 1960.

From 1964-66 he served as Minister of Works in the Kabaka's government. But after the Kabaka Yekka alliance split with Milton Obote's government in 1966, he left politics and retired to private medical practice and farming.

During the Idi Amin era (1971-79) he became a leading official in the Seventh Day Adventist Church. He also founded the Kisekka foundation which helps fund Kampala's leading hospital.

In 1981 when President Museveni, disillusioned with the Obote regime, set up his National Resistance Movement, Dr Kisekka joined him. He took up residence in neighbouring Kenya and became the NRM's main spokesman and co-ordinator, trying to gain international standing and support for Museveni's campaign.

In 1985 he joined the prolonged and unsuccessful peace talks between the National Resistance Army and the Military Council of General Tito Okello. When Museveni took power on 29 January 1986 he was rewarded, the next day, by being made Prime Minister. He formed his own cabinet of talented personalities such as the Minister of State, Eriya Kategaya. In August 1987 he appealed to foreign diplomats for international aid to help fund the government amnesty which was extended to the rebels in the north of the country. His plan was to set up ten reception centres to vet the rebels and provide them with relief supplies so that they could become farmers.

In January 1991 he was retired from the onerous post of Prime Minister and was installed in the new post of Vice-President. But he had to assume responsibility as Interior Minister when the incumbent was sacked in May 1991.

MAYANJA, Abubakar Kaakyama

Ugandan politician. Third deputy Prime Minister, 22 February 1988 –

A lawyer turned politician. The great hope of the younger generation in the early 1960s, but caught in the classical Baganda predicament, torn between loyalty to his own people and the desire for national unity. Then sucked into Uganda's turbulent cycle of coups. Brilliant but volatile, he proved a survivor. He became a leading parliamentarian and Muslim spokesman, courageously criticising the excesses of the Obote governments. He was finally restored to ministerial responsibility by President Museveni.

Born 29 August 1929 at Nkokonjeru in a Ugandan peasant's family. Educated at Ngogwe Primary, King's College, Budo (1945-49), and Makerere College (1950-52), where he became a prominent student leader, finally expelled for leading a strike.

On 6 March 1952, he became secretary-general of the Uganda National Congress (UNC), whose constitution he had helped draft. Then he left to study history and law at King's College, Cambridge, finally becoming a barrister in 1959. He returned home, still secretary-general of the UNC, to find the party splitting up.

While away on a course in the USA he was appointed education minister in the Kabaka's (Buganda region) government. Strongly criticised for leaving the UNC and joining a government that was traditionalist and secessionist he said that he wanted to be "a link between Buganda and the rest of the country."

He strove to modernise the Kabaka's government and had the ministry of economic planning added to his portfolio. He resigned his ministry suddenly in May 1964. Instead he stood and was elected as a Kabaka Yekka (Kabaka alone) member in the Uganda national parliament in September 1964.

He became a regular critic of the Obote government and was one of the defence lawyers for the five ministers arrested and detained in 1966. In October 1968 he was detained under the emergency regulations for an article he had written in *Transition* magazine and remained in detention until 1970. After the coup of January 1971, Idi Amin appointed him Minister of Education in his government. Later he was switched to Labour and then retired on 1 December 1972.

When the Democratic Party was narrowly defeated in the elections which brought Milton Obote to power for a second time in December 1980, he led a frustrating time as an opposition MP and saw his Kebaka Yekka party dwindle as Obote consolidated his power.

When President Museveni took power in 1986 he appointed Mayanja to his first government, as an NRA supporter on 8 February 1986. He became Minister of Information and Broadcasting, a post broadened to

Information and Media on 21 November. In order to take some of the weight of office from Prime Minister Samson Kisekka, he was promoted to third Deputy Prime Minister on 22 February 1988. He was given special responsibility for the procurement of essential commodities.

He stood in the first elections since Museveni came to power in February 1989 and won a seat in the National Resistance Council. His ministerial positions were then re-confirmed. He had the Ministry of Justice added to his portfolio in the reshuffle of 2 July 1991.

MAYANJA-NKANGI, Joshua Sibakyalwayo

Ugandan lawyer and politician. Minister of Planning and Economic Development, 10 April 1989 –

A highly civilised and internationally educated lawyer and politician. A committed Protestant Christian from one of Buganda's top families. A strong conservative who became Prime Minister of his king, the late Kabaka of Buganda. His traditionalist views and the experience of his King and people at the hands of Milton Obote made him a lifelong opponent, and he had no desire to be associated with the Amin regime. During the period they were in power he concentrated on his law practice, but later his ministerial abilities were rewarded in the governments that followed.

Born 22 August 1931. Educated at a local primary school (1937-46), Kings College Budo (1947-49) and Makerere University (1950-53) where he studied economics, mathematics and modern history and got a BA. He continued at Keble College, Oxford where he studied monetary economics and public finance (1954-57). He then did law at Lincoln's Inn and qualified as a barrister (1957-59).

He returned home in 1959 and began practising law in Uganda. He helped form a new party in support of the Kabaka, the King of Buganda, by setting up the Kabaka Yekka Youth Wing. In 1962 he was returned to parliament, for the Kebaka Yekka party, as a member for Masaka East. He was immediately appointed Minister without portfolio. In 1963 he became Minister of Commerce and Industry, switching to the Buganda government in November 1964 to become the Katikiro (Prime Minister). It was a difficult time as the Kabaka of Buganda was in continual conflict with the central government of Milton Obote. In May 1966 Obote's troops stormed the Kabaka's palace and sent him fleeing into exile. Nkangi followed him into exile in Britain.

In June 1967 he became a research fellow in the Department of Economics at Lancaster University. He rose to lecturer and Head of the department of monetary economics (1968-71).

When Idi Amin ousted Milton Obote, he returned to Uganda and set up his own legal practice, in 1971. He avoided politics until Amin's downfall when he founded the Conservative Party in 1980. It remained a small, Baganda-dominated group and was totally squeezed out by the two major parties in the elections of December 1980 that brought Obote back to power.

When Obote was toppled by General Tito Okello, Nkangi was brought into government as Minister of Labour in August 1985. But Okello, in his turn, was toppled by Yoweri Museveni who on 6 February 1986 brought Nkangi into his broad-based government, as Minister of Education for the Conservative Party. On 11 April 1989 he was switched to Minister of Planning and Economic Development, where he was confronted with the need to restore Uganda's once prosperous economy.

MUSEVENI, Yoweri Kaguta
Ugandan politician. President 29 January 1986 –

A young and idealistic guerrilla leader who has fought his way to the Presidency of his country. A non-smoking, non-drinking Protestant with a strong work ethic and aspirations to build democracy from the grassroots, he remains burdened with the weight of Uganda's divisive history and the breakdown of law and order which continued from one regime to another after independence. He came to power bearing the hopes and aspirations of all lovers of peace but the path towards stability has been narrow and change has been slow and fragile. He has been criticised for not having a clear policy. His National Resistance Army, which started with the highest of ideals, soon found itself in a life and death conflict with several groups of guerrillas and the methods it adopted to win the guerrilla war were just as vicious and inhumane as those of previous regimes. Museveni found it difficult to discipline his own commanders or find a political solution and peace formula agreed by all Uganda's diverse groups.

Born 1944 at Ntungamo, near Mbarara in south-west Uganda. A Munyankole. Educated at Kyamate Boys school, Mbarara High School and Ntare School before going the Dar es Salaam University to study political science, economics and law (1967-70). While still a student he spent some time doing publicity work for the Mozambican Frelimo movement which had offices in Tanzania during the independence struggle against Portugal. He was invited to visit the Frelimo liberated areas and was given his first insight into guerrilla tactics.

Before he finished his studies in 1970, he became a General Service Officer under Akena Adoko in the new unit set up by the Israelis to counterbalance the existing intelligence service. He worked for President Milton Obote's first government as an assistant secretary for research. But when Idi Amin seized power from Obote in January 1971, he went into exile in Tanzania and took part in several military operations alongside other exiles against the Ugandan dictator. By 1972 his Front for National Salvation of Uganda (FRONASA) had already set up some camps within Uganda. FRONASA was the first to bring explosives and grenades into Kampala during 1972. Museveni encouraged President Nyerere to give his support to the abortive invasion of Uganda in September. He continued to organise FRONASA and by April 1979 had about 9,000 men under his command. He took part in the second great offensive against Amin and this time triumphed.

He was rewarded for his part in the invasion by being made Minister of Defence in the interim government of the late Professor Lule. He was also vice-chairman of the ruling military commission and acted as Head of State when Lule was abroad, but Lule's successor, Godfrey Binaisa, feared that he might be manoeuvering against him and demoted him to Minister for Regional Co-operation. When Binaisa's government was replaced by a Military Commission in 1980 led by Paulo Muwanga, Museveni was appointed vice-chairman.

Milton Obote returned from exile and elections were held in December 1980. Museveni formed the Uganda Patriotic Movement and fought the elections but his party was soundly beaten and he lost his own constituency contest to Sam Kuteesa, in an election marked by serious electoral fraud and ballot rigging.

Museveni blamed Obote for this situation and there were many personality clashes between the two men. He took to the bush in 1981 where he started his own guerrilla movement - the National Resistance Movement. Starting with just a handful of fighters, his disciplined, idealistic approach finally built up a formidable guerrilla force.

When Obote finally fell to the army of General Tito Okello, Museveni wanted to share power, but was offered an insignificant role by the new rulers. He was not satisfied and only signed a peace pact with the Military Council on 17 December 1985, after protracted peace talks held in Nairobi. But the peace agreement proved unworkable from the moment it was signed. The Ugandan army was still harassing and victimising civilians and had totally lost the confidence of the public. So exactly a month after signing the pact Museveni's forces renewed their campaign.

They proved themselves disciplined and tough and yet they treated civilians with respect. They swept through the south of the country and took Kampala on 26 January 1986, after a nine-day offensive. The forces of Tito Okello were put to flight and by the end of March Museveni's National Resistance Army had taken the whole country with very little loss of life. He was sworn into office as President on 29 January 1986.

He announced the establishment of a National Resistance Council with civilian and military representation from all sections of Ugandan politics, proclaiming a policy of national reconciliation. His idea was to build up grassroots democracy based on resistance councils in which the opinions of the people could be reflected. He also flirted briefly with the Baganda who wanted to restore the Kabakaship.

But however well intentioned, he could not suddenly switch on peace in his troubled country. At least three major resistance movements persisted in defying him, particularly in the north of the country. Banditry and lawlessness continued for many years.

Museveni tried to coax the rebels into laying down their arms by declaring repeated amnesties from June 1987 onwards. He had some successes with thousands of rebels dropping armed opposition and many of their leaders joining him in government, but resistance continued into 1989 from isolated factions and his commanders became ever more vicious by adopting a scorched earth policy and terrorising the local population in order to crush the opposition.

Museveni did not carry out an earlier promise of returning Uganda to civilian rule within two years, but in February 1989 he held the first elections to a National Resistance Council with limited powers. The elections gave the voters considerable freedom of choice and they ousted 14 ministers, but without altering the basic power structure that remained in Museveni's hands. In October 1989 he announced that democratic elections and the return to civilian rule would be delayed five years to 1995.

At the OAU summit conference in July 1990, he was elected chairman of the organisation for the year 1990-91. Quizzed about democracy at a press conference shortly after taking office, he said, "Leaders must be elected periodically. They must be accountable. There must be a free press. There must be no restriction on who participates in the democratic process." However, he refused to promote a multi-party system, saying: "There is no reason why a single political party cannot be democratic."

On 8 April 1990 he arrested General Moses Ali, the Minister of Culture, Youth and Sports. As leader of the National Resistance Front, he was the only survivor of the many factions that had joined the government in 1986. He was charged with plotting a coup.

Museveni's challenge in 1990 was to finally bring the guerrilla wars in the north and east to an end. Gradually active operations ended especially after signing a peace pact with the rebels of the Uganda Patriotic Democratic Movement in July. Most other resistance died out in 1990 as Museveni offered successive amnesties, but his army continued to be accused of brutal repression in the north.

At the end of the year Museveni purged many of the Rwandan troops in his army. They immediately joined the Rwandan Patriotic Front and invaded their homeland at the beginning of October. After initial successes they were heavily defeated. Museveni claimed to know nothing of the invasion, though many of his former senior officers were involved and throughout the conflict were armed and supplied from Uganda.

In April 1991 the Foreign Minister and two MPs were arrested and accused of supporting rebel groups in the north. This took place against a further outbreak of guerrilla activity in the region.

NEKYON, Adoko

Ugandan politician. Former Minister.

A seasoned Muslim politician who has survived all the changes of regime of Uganda, holding top ministerial office with Obote's first government and currently with Yoweri Museveni. In his early career he did much to increase his country's prosperity. He was the inspiration behind the Apolo Hotel and Chief Planner of the General Service Unit. Between times he has had long spells in exile in Africa and Europe and has wrestled with the problems of managing Uganda Airlines.

Born 1931 in Apach, a Lango cousin of Milton Obote, he was educated at Ibujje Primary School, Ngora High School, King's College Budo (1949-54) and Kerala University, India (1955-61) where he got an MA in Economics and Political Science.

He returned home and after a period as a clerk-interpreter and trainee sales executive with Shell-BP, he stood for Lango South-East, his home province and won a seat in April 1961 for the Uganda People's Congress. He was appointed Minister of Information, Broadcasting and Tourism in 1962 and Minister of Planning and Community Development in 1964.

He was among those ministers, including Milton Obote, who were accused by Daudi Ocheng in Parliament of being involved in smuggling gold and ivory from the Congo in February 1966. He strongly denied the charges and was glad to see Obote appoint a commission of inquiry into the matter.

After the constitutional crisis that followed, he was, for a few weeks in May 1966, Minister of Agriculture and Co-operatives but then resigned because he disagreed with Obote's plan to amend the constitution and strengthen presidential powers. He spoke out in parliament to this effect.

He remained an active and critical back-bencher and when the military coup occurred on 25 January 1971 he chose to leave rather than remain behind under the Amin government. He went into exile in Dar es Salaam. He did not take part in the invasion of Uganda by the exiles based in Tanzania in September 1972.

He returned home in 1979 and tried to contest the elections for Apach district on a Democratic Party ticket but was blocked by the government, by being detained at a road block on the day that he wanted to present his nomination papers.

Embittered and disillusioned over the triumph of his cousin Milton Obote, he went into exile for a second time in Kenya and Denmark. In 1985 he returned home and the year after became general manager of Uganda Airlines Corporation.

His work in that difficult task, in an airline fraught with problems, brought him to Yoweri Museveni's attention, who made him Minister of Health on 22 February 1988. He was elected as the National Resistance Council member for Maruzi county in the April elections.

On 10 April 1989 he was reshuffled to Minister of Relief and Social Rehabilitation to deal with the growing number of refugees and dispossessed caused by the wars in the north. His ministry was dropped in the reshuffle of 2 July 1991 and he was not given another portfolio.

OKETCHO, Frederick (Brigadier)
Ugandan soldier. Secretary of Defence, November 1989 – 2 July 1991.

An education officer from Tororo who kept his reputation clean by leaving the army during the Idi Amin era, resuming his military career with the Uganda National Liberation Army after Amin fell from power, in 1979. Since then he has earned steady promotion. As a Brigadier, he became Chief of Staff in May 1989 and Secretary for Defence on 26 November 1989. The President took personal responsibility for that ministry in July 1991.

Born circa 1940, the son of a county chief of West Budama in Tororo district. He went to Nyakasura High School until 1957 when he joined Kyambogo Teacher's College. He took up teaching at Kisoko school, Tororo until 1964 when he joined the army as a cadet officer.

He trained at Sandhurst Military Academy in Britain. A lieutenant education officer at the time of the coup by Idi Amin in January 1971 he temporarily left the army and took up business.

He rejoined the army after the overthrow of Idi Amin in May 1979 and was promoted to major and later Lieutenant-Colonel as director of the Jinja school of Infantry, working with the British team of military advisers. He went to the USA for further military training in 1983 and returned home to be promoted full Colonel.

When Basilio and Tito Okello took power in July 1985, he was promoted to Brigadier and helped Brigadier Toko in playing a major part in the unsuccessful peace talks with Yoweri Museveni's National Resistance Army. He was known to be highly sympathetic to the Museveni cause. When Museveni finally assumed power in January 1986, he remained in the army as a Brigadier. He was appointed Chief of Staff in May 1989 on the promotion of Maj-Gen Elly Tumwine and Maj-Gen Fred Rwigyema as Minister and Deputy Minister of State for Defence. When both his superiors were sacked on 26 November 1989, he took over as the new Minister for Defence. But on 2 July 1991, as Museveni drastically pruned the size of his cabinet, he took over the Ministry of Defence from Oketcho.

OTAFIRE, Kahinde (Colonel)
Ugandan soldier and politician.

Tough, determined and abrasive, he was one of the rising stars of the Museveni's National Resistance Army and later of his government. His career continued to climb, until he became Minister of State for Internal Affairs, when he became involved in a number of controversies that caused his dismissal. But he remains an army colonel and influential member of the executive committee of the National Resistance Council and he has youth on his side.

Born 29 December 1950 in Bushenyi, Western Uganda, a Bairu of the Ankole tribe. Educated locally and at Makerere University (1972-75) in the Ministry of Foreign Affairs (1976-80). He was posted to Peking in 1979-80 as an assistant secretary in the Ugandan mission.

When Museveni took to the bush to fight the Obote regime in 1981, Otafire went with him as a recruit trainee. In October 1982 he was appointed a senior officer, member of the High Command and Chief political commissar of the National Resistance Army (NRA). In 1983 he had the responsibilities of the commissioner of internal affairs added to these duties.

After the victory of the NRA over the forces of General Tito Okello on 26 January 1986, Otafire was appointed Deputy Minister of Local Government. In 1988 he was promoted to Minister of State for Internal Affairs. During his period of office he caused controversy by allegedly ordering two buses of the Uganda Transport Company to be impounded by the police. He also ordered a Uganda passport, to be issued to a Rwandan businessman. When the incident was reported to the press he ordered the suspension of the Acting Immigration Commissioner. He was forced to resign following a bizarre incident on 20 October when he was alleged to have drawn a pistol on the wife of the former Justice Minister and Attorney-General, Sam Kuteesa, and sister of President Museveni's wife, Janet.

He continues to work for President Museveni and remains a Colonel in the army, a member of the national executive committee of the National Resistance Council. He is also on the appointments committee.

SALEH, Salim (Major-General)
Ugandan soldier. Army commander May–November 1989.

Educated and hardened in the tough world of guerrilla fighting, this half brother of Yoweri Museveni fought with him throughout the guerrilla campaigns of the early 1980s. After Museveni's accession to power in January 1986 he bore the brunt of the campaigns against the guerrillas in the north and was considered to be the second most powerful figure in government after Museveni himself. Something of an authoritarian, he once recommended that detainees be given more than 30 strokes of the cane rather than being charged in court, where they might be acquitted. He recommended the same treatment for people in rebel areas who failed to turn up for public rallies. He was dismissed as army commander in November 1989.

Born 1957. His real name is disputed. Some know him as Kolebu Akandwanaho, others Suley Rufu. He was born to Mzee Kaguta, a Ugandan and Esther, a Rwandan (who is also the mother of Yoweri Museveni). He acquired the name Salim Saleh when living in exile in Tanzania during the Amin era when he became involved with a Swahili woman and was assimilated into the Swahili culture and Islamic faith.

Saleh, fresh from school, joined the liberation forces that ousted Idi Amin from Uganda in 1979. He teamed up with his half brother, Yoweri Museveni, in his Front for National Salvation (FRONASA), a force of

9,000 men founded in 1979 which took part in the second great offensive which drove Idi Amin out of Kampala. When Museveni was badly beaten in the elections of 1981, he took to the bush once more and began a guerrilla war against the Obote government. Saleh joined Museveni at the birth of the National Resistance Army (NRA) and remained in the bush with him throughout, gradually winning the guerrilla war first against Obote and then against the regime of Basilio Okello.

He emerged from the bush in January 1986 as a hardened guerrilla fighter, a member of the High Command of the NRA (ranking number 24) and a senior commander. When Museveni took control on 26 January 1986, he was promoted Major-General and made Chief of Operations. His main task, in this capacity, was to pursue the war in the north and the east of Uganda against the various guerrilla groups which emerged to contest Museveni's rule. In March 1987 there was a report that he had been fatally injured at Ogur, 15 miles north of Kampala. Though the report turned out to be false, it indicated that he was very much involved in the real fighting.

In May 1989 he was promoted to Army Commander, replacing Major General Elly Tumwine who was appointed Minister of State for Defence. After the massacre at Kumi in July 1989 when over 60 young men were packed into railway wagons and burnt to death, he admitted that an "error" had been committed by his soldiers and apologised to the people of Uganda. At about the same time he addressed the Resistance Council Defence Secretaries in Kampala and suggested that arrested suspects should be given 30-80 strokes of the cane rather than being put on trial where they might be acquitted. He suggested the same treatment for Gulu residents who failed to turn up for the weekly public rallies. He was suddenly dismissed as army commander on 27 November 1989 in a purge of the top army leadership in which the Minister of Defence and the army Chief of Staff were also sacked. Commentators attributed Museveni's move to his dissatisfaction with the growing indiscipline and corruption in the NRA.

SSALI, Jaberi Bidandi

Ugandan politician. Minister of Local Government, 11 April 1989 –

A perennial in Ugandan politics since the downfall of Idi Amin. Being a Muslim, a former Marxist and one of the original supporters of Museveni's Ugandan Patriotic Movement, he has fulfilled a rather unusual role, but his ministerial qualities have placed him in every government in the second half of the 1980s. Whenever Ugandan politics took the wrong turn he diverted his energies to his printing business and sports organisation. He is a major sponsor and former coach of the Ugandan and Kampala city soccer teams.

Born 17 July 1937, a Muslim at Banda near Kampala. Educated at Kibuli primary and Nyakasura Secondary School and the University of India where he took an M.Sc. He returned home to go into business in the Sapoba Publishing Company. In 1962 he joined the Uganda People's Congress, shortly after it had been founded by Milton Obote and became a prominent youth winger. He served as deputy mayor of Kampala city council (1964-66), but he became disillusioned with politics as the struggle between Obote and the Kabaka of Buganda unfolded.

When Idi Amin took power in 1971 he quit politics altogether and concentrated on sports and business, becoming director of Sapoba Bookshop Press, a small printing house. He was also the coach of the Uganda national soccer squad, the Cranes, and the Kampala City Council soccer club.

After the defeat of Idi Amin, when President Godfrey Binaisa came to power he appointed Ssali, on 20 November 1979, to his first ministry in charge of local administration, an appointment confirmed by the military commission on 22 May 1980 when it took power from the President. In the elections of December 1980 he became the secretary-general of the Uganda Patriotic Movement, originally founded by Yoweri Museveni before he quit politics to fight his guerrilla war in the bush. Ssali was briefly detained when Museveni "declared war" against President Obote's government. Released after a month, he returned to his business and sports activities.

Ssali returned to ministerial rank briefly on 28 July 1985, under General Tito Okello, as Minister of Culture and Community Development. When Yoweri Museveni's National Resistance Army finally took Kampala in January 1986, he formed a broad-based cabinet on 6 February and made Ssali his Minister of Labour. He held the post officially under the banner of the Uganda Patriotic Movement. In 1987 he was reshuffled to Minister of Energy and on 11 April 1989 Museveni appointed him Minister of Local Government. The portfolio was renamed Government Affairs on 2 July 1991.

SSEMOGERERE, Paulo Kawanga (Dr)

Ugandan politician. Leader of Democratic Party, 1980. Second Deputy Prime Minister, 22 February 1988 –

A teacher, turned politician, known for his lifelong connection with the Democratic Party, generally considered to be the party of Uganda's Catholics. He has been official leader of the party since 1980. Throughout Uganda's turbulent politics, he has been on the side of constitutional change and the rule of law. Though some would say that he was unfairly defeated by Milton Obote in the Presidential elections of 1980, he accepted defeat and served as leader of the opposition. Eventually his experience and wide support in the Baganda community were recognised with his appointment to Minister of Interior and later Foreign Minister and second deputy Prime Minister.

Born 11 February 1932. Educated at St Mary's College, Kisubi and Makerere University, where he obtained a diploma in education. He went on to Syracuse University, USA for a PhD in Public Administration.

He returned to Uganda to go into teaching in 1950. Always interested in politics, he first became a Member of Parliament in 1961 and secretary to the Democratic Party leader and Chief Minister, Benedicto Kiwanuka, in the elections before independence. He went into exile during the Idi Amin regime. When Amin was toppled from power in April 1979, he became a member of the National Consultative Council that had been set up as an interim parliament under President Yusufu Lule. When Lule was deposed he was appointed Minister of Labour by President Godfrey Binaisa in June, but refused to take office until he had challenged the legality of the change of government in the courts.

On 21 June 1980 he received more than 90% of the votes in the election for the presidency of the Democratic party which approved his candidature to oppose Milton Obote in the presidential elections of September. The elections were bitter and highly controversial, with both sides claiming victory, but finally Obote was declared the winner. Ssemogerere reluctantly accepted the situation and became official leader of the opposition.

When Obote was toppled by the Uganda National Liberation Army in July 1985, he was offered and accepted the post as Minister of Internal Affairs in the new regime in August. He was reappointed to that post in the first government of Yoweri Museveni, established on 6 February 1986. In September he carried out a purge of undisciplined and undesirable police officers and replaced them with new personnel, in an attempt to renew the police force.

On 22 February 1988 he was promoted to Second Deputy Prime Minister and transferred to the Foreign Affairs portfolio. He stood in the first Ugandan elections since Museveni came to power in February 1989 and won a keenly contested seat in the National Resistance Council.

TUMWINE, Elly (Major-General)

Ugandan soldier. Minister of State for Defence May–November 1989.

Nicknamed "Moshe Dayan" by his troops because of the loss of one eye sustained in an attack on Masindi barracks when fighting for the National Resistance Army. He was Museveni's Army commander when the NRA captured Kampala in January 1986. He remained head of the army, despite the tensions between the senior officers of the high command until he was promoted to Minister of State for Defence in May 1989, but he was suddenly sacked in November in a general purge of top army personnel.

Born 12 April 1954 in Rushere, Nyabushozi, Mbarara district; a Munyankole. He took primary education in his home area then went to Henry's College, Kitovu in Masaka district to get his higher school certificate in 1973. He went to Makerere university (1975-77) to take a BA in Fine Arts. He became a teacher in various secondary schools in western Uganda until 1979. After the fall of Idi Amin he joined the Uganda National Liberation Army. He went for further training to

Tanzania's military academy at Munduli, returning home at the end of 1980.

He first came to prominence when he joined the Uganda Freedom Movement led by Dr Andrew Kayiira which was fighting the Obote government in the early 1980s. In 1981 he switched to Yoweri Museveni's National Resistance Army and fought alongside him in the early 1980s. He personally commanded the successful attack on Masindi barracks. He rose to the rank of army commander in the NRA and took part in the final capture of Kampala in January 1986 and was appointed to the ruling National Resistance Council, ranking number 22.

He was strongly opposed to a move by Museveni to re-detain his old UFM colleague, Dr Kayiira, and spoke out against this at a High Command meeting in March 1987. A few days later, on 6 March, Kayiira was found murdered by unidentified gunmen.

He took charge of the war in the north and the east of Uganda against the various guerrilla groups which emerged to contest Museveni's rule. In July 1987 he led a victory over the followers of Alice Lakwena's voodoo battalion near Gulu. In May 1989 he was promoted from army commander to Minister of State for Defence, but six months later, on 27 November 1989, he was suddenly dismissed and sent on a training course in a general purge of the army. Commentators reported that this was an indication of Museveni's dissatisfaction with the growing corruption and indiscipline in the army.

ZAIRE

Population: 35.7m (1990, World Bank)
Independence: 30 June 1960
Head of State: General Sese Seko Mobutu
Government: On 23 April 1990 Mobutu announced the abandonment of the single party system, but opposition groups continued to suffer discrimination. A national conference on democratisation started in August 1991. Government had already been established under a prime minister, responsible for the day to day running of the country. The President was due to become an independent referee, but still in charge of defence and foreign affairs.
Parties: The former ruling party, *Mouvement Populaire de la Révolution* (MPR) faces a challenge from a number of opposition groups both at home and in exile, mostly based in Brussels, including the *Union pour la démocratie et le progrès social* (UDPS), the *Mouvement National du Congo-Lumumba* (MNC-Lumumba) and the *Front Congolais pour le rétablissement de la démocratie* (FCD).

BO-BOLIKO, Lokonga (André)
Zairian politician and trade unionist.

A man of commanding personality, dignified manner and social grace, he is best known as the father of Zairian trade unionism. He engineered the unification of the lay and Catholic unions into the National Union of Congolese Workers, UNTC. He then went on to become president of the National Assembly (Legislative Council) in December 1970. This put him constitutionally second in rank to President Mobutu, though he was not particularly being groomed as his successor. His critics say that this urbane and civilised man lacks driving ambition and competitive spirit, but this is probably why he held high office for so long in his troubled country.

Born 15 August 1934 at Lobamiti in Bandudu region. Educated at Catholic missions and St Raphael Middle School in Kinshasa. In 1955 he went to the Heverlee Louvain Social Studies School in Belgium where he gained a diploma in 1958. He returned to the Congo in January 1969, joined the Confederation of Congo Christian Unions which became the Union of Congolese Workers (UTC) in April 1960 with himself as secretary-general, then in December 1961, as president. He worked on commissions set up to investigate work contracts, collective bargaining and labour legislation generally. Twice, in 1962 and 1963, he was imprisoned for brief periods for his union activities.

He was also a member of the College of Commissioners that replaced parliament in 1960-61. He managed to persuade the three unions to set aside their differences and come together in the National Union of Congolese Workers (UNTC, now UNTZ) and was elected secretary-general. He also became secretary-general and president of the National Council of Congolese Trade Unions.

When President Mobutu restored the National Assembly on 2 December 1970, he needed a new man to control the 420 new members and make them toe the MPR line. Bo-Boliko was chosen for the job. In July 1972 the Assembly was renamed the Legislative Council as part of the authenticity programme. He maintained his position. He was appointed to the political bureau of the MPR in 1968 and has been a member of the permanent committee since 1978 and central committee of the party since 1980.

Mobutu, recognising his services to the Legislative Council and party, made him Prime Minister in March 1979, though he lost this position in August 1980 to Nguza Karl I Bond. In January 1980 he was appointed First State Commissioner. On 27 August 1980 he was made executive secretary to the MPR, ranking number two after Mobutu himself.

BOMBOKO, Lokumba is Elengé (Justin-Marie)
Zairean politician and first Foreign Minister.

Given huge responsibility as Foreign Minister in successive goverments after Congo's independence, he appeared to have retired from politics altogether in the early 1970s, but he was again promoted by Mobutu in the early 1980s only to fade once more from the scene.

Born 22 September 1928 in Boleke, a Momba from Equateur region. Educated locally at Catholic schools, studying administration at Lovanium 1945-51. He worked over 1952-55 in the provincial administration at Coquilhatville. Then went in 1956 to study politics at the Université Libre in Belgium.

He returned home just before independence was suddenly declared on 1 July 1960, plunging his country into chaos. Though he had only just graduated he was made Foreign Minister in Lumumba's first government and later head of the College of Commissioners which ruled the country for one year until parliament was convened in August 1961. He continued as Foreign Minister in successive governments formed by Kasavubu, Mobutu and Joseph Ileo. He did not serve when Moise Tshombe was prime minister (1964-65), but returned to the ministry after Mobutu's second coup on 24 November 1965.

In 1969 he was appointed ambassador to Washington, only to be recalled and arrested during the drive to Zaireanisation in 1971. He then seemed retired from the political scene but was brought back by Mobutu in 1980, again as Foreign Minister where he was promptly dispatched to Brussels to protest at Belgium's harbouring of the then defector Nguza Karl I Bond.

He was then briefly appointed Deputy First State Commissioner (deputy prime minister) and executive secretary of the *Mouvement*

Populaire Africain (MPR). But when Mobutu decided to merge the head of the party with the post of premier Bomboko was dropped.

ILEO, Songoamba (Joseph)
Zaire politician. Prime Minister 1960-61.

He played a major part in the turmoil of the Congo's independence politics, rising to be Prime Minister under Kasavubu and minister under Cyrille Adoula, but he retired from active politics after Mobutu's assumption of power apart from a brief flirtation with the opposition. His son Ileo Itambala is a minister under Mobutu.

Born 15 September 1921 in Leopoldville (Kinshasa). Educated locally, then studied philosophy and sociology in Europe. Returned home to work in the African territories division of the Belgian Governor-General's Office. Became editor-in-chief of the Catholic *Conscience Africaine* newspaper which published, in 1956, the first Congolese demands for political advancement. In 1958 signed the Memorandum of the Sixteen demanding democratic reforms and progress towards self-government. In the same year formed the National Congolese Movement (MNC) with Patrice Lumumba.

He became increasingly dissatisfied with Lumumba's autocratic leadership and after failing to oust him from the party broke away to form the MNC (Kalonji) which advocated a federal as opposed to a unitary system in alliance with Joseph Kasavubu's Abako party. Was a member of the Abako delegation to the Brussels round table conference in January 1960. Elected President of the Senate July - September 1960. Following Lumumba's dismissal on 5 September 1960, Kasavubu nominated him Prime Minister, but his government was neutralised by Mobutu who ruled through a college of commissioners until Ileo was confirmed as Prime Minister on 6 February 1961. However, he was unable to prevent secessionist breakaways and resigned in August of the same year.

When Cyrille Adoula formed his government of reconciliation he appointed Ileo Minister of Information and Cultural Affairs (1961-62), then Minister Without Portfolio in charge of Katanga (1963-64). When Mobutu came to power in November 1965 and formed the *Mouvement Populaire de la Révolution* (MPR) Ileo joined the party and was elected to the Politbureau. He then became president of the *Office National de la recherche et du développement.*

In 1982 he became involved in the formation of the opposition party the Union for Democracy and for Social Progress (UDPS) and entered into talks with the government over recognition for the party but in March he and several other prominent opposition leaders were arrested and held in prison. He was released in 1990 and formed the moderate *Parti démocrate et social chrétien* (PDSC) under his presidency. He joined the "Sacred Union" in the National Conference in August 1991. His son, Ileo Itambala, was a minister under Mobutu from the mid-1980s.

KENGO WA DONDO, Lobitsh Leon

Zairean politician. First State Commissioner November 1982 – October 1986.

Shrewd, tough and unquestionably loyal, he comes from Mobutu's home province of Equateur. He rose fast both in the party and professionally as attorney-general, where he was state prosecutor and made himself many enemies among the dissidents. Though he rose to the number two spot, Mobutu did not feel him a real challenge because of his mixed race descent (son of a Polish father) which barred him constitutionally from presidential succession. The summit of his power came when Mobutu made him First State Commissioner (Prime Minister) in November 1982 to execute a tough IMF austerity programme. He successfully executed the policy, but it brought economic hardship and made him many enemies. Mobutu sacrificed him when he decided to abandon the IMF programme of reform, but then brought him back in December 1988.

Born 24 March 1934 at Libenge in Equateur. His father was Polish, his mother African. Educated locally. He then went to Belgium and studied liberal arts and criminology in the Palace of Justice (1960-61) and then to the Université Libre, Brussels to study law, receiving a doctorate in 1967.

He was a public prosecutor on district and general circuits and then prosecutor-general to the Kinshasa court of appeal. Fast promotion followed from December 1967 when he was made president of the Judicial Council. In January 1968 he became legal and political counsellor at the presidency and attorney-general for the whole country in August 1968. He ruthlessly prosecuted the enemies of the state, including the former Foreign Commissioner, Nguza Karl I Bond, for alleged treason in 1977. Later he prosecuted other dissidents including the 13 Parliamentarians who protested to Mobutu over human rights abuses.

He also won advancement in the *Movement Populaire de Révolution*, (MPR) party, being appointed to the central and permanent committees in the late 1970s. His reputation for toughness and disregard for unpopularity caused Mobutu to make him First State Commissioner (Prime Minister) on 5 November 1982, with the task of cleaning up corruption and introducing International Monetary Fund structural readjustment and austerity. He had considerable success, but only at the expense of internal recession, which brought him considerable unpopularity and led to his dismissal when Mobutu decided to drop the IMF reforms.

In October 1986 Mobutu temporarily abolished the post of First State Commissioner and took over Kengo's economic responsibilities, while demoting him to Foreign Minister. His slide continued and on 22 January 1987 he lost the Foreign Ministry too, and was made head of the Audit Office (Cour des Comptes). He remained executive secretary of the MPR.

Mobutu experimented with various other Prime Ministers in 1987-88 but brought Kengo back on 27 November 1988. His appointment was confirmed in a general reshuffle in May 1989.

MOBUTU, Sese Seko
President of Zaire since 24 November 1965.

He has survived more than two decades of violence, political chaos, armed rebellion and provincial secession in his vast, impenetrable country. A vain, courageous, acquisitive and absolute leader who has always identified himself with the state. He has acted effectively, fast and ruthlessly in successive crises. A prodigious worker, voracious reader and great traveller, he extended his power from army to government, from government to party to become an absolute ruler. His antipathy for communism has made him a natural partner for the West yet he has never been at ease with Belgium, the old colonial power. He failed to create a disciplined and productive economy, or to democratise the political system until forced to do so, and his human rights record is under continual challenge.

Born 14 October 1930 at Lisala in Equateur province, near Oubangui, then called Banzyville from which he later took the journalistic pseudonym "Jose de Banzy". After primary and secondary education at Mbandaka he was expelled for throwing ink at a Belgian schoolmaster and conscripted into the Force Publique.

He trained as an accounts clerk at Luluabourg and stayed there most of his six years of service, reaching the rank of sergeant. He dabbled in journalism and left, in 1956, for a full-time career in the capital Kinshasa, with *L'Avenir* and *Actualités Africaines* rising to editor.

In 1958 he did a course in social studies and journalism and worked for Inforcongo in Brussels. Already a member of Patrice Lumumba's *Mouvement National Congolais*, he frequently put up the new nationalist leader on his trips to Belgium. He organised the MNC office in Brussels and was the MNC delegate, approved by Lumumba to the round table conference in January, April and May 1960, leading to independence. During this period he returned to Kinshasa as Lumumba's senior private secretary.

In July 1960, at the time of independence, Lumumba had him appointed Chief of Staff, second-in-command of the army. Army mutinies erupted a week after independence and he travelled round the country by plane trying to restore morale and discipline. He built his power in the army as the country disintegrated, Katanga declared secession, and President Joseph Kasavubu and Lumumba struggled for power. Early in September Kasavubu dismissed the army commander and announced that he was arresting Lumumba. Mobutu weighed his personal loyalty to Lumumba against doubts about his growing instability and decided to intervene, suspending both him and Kasavubu in the military coup of 13 September 1960. Mobutu set up a College of Commissioners, 15 young university graduates, to run the machinery of government, but he retained effective leadership through control of the army. He concentrated on rebuilding the army and displayed personal courage in dealing with mutinous troops. Katanga secession was terminated by January 1963, largely through the efforts of the UN which withdrew in mid-1964, but immediately Mobutu was faced with widespread rebellions in Kwilu, Kivu and Stanleyville.

Mobutu was promoted lieutenant-general on 11 November 1964 while Kasavubu struggled on with a minority government and more trouble in Katanga. This unstable situation prompted Mobutu and a group of officers to seize power on the night of 23 November 1965. He found himself in charge of a country riven with violence, political chaos, armed rebellion and provincial secession. He started by centralising government, reducing parliament to a rubber stamp and extending his own personal power to all important decision-making bodies.

He introduced a new constitution and started his own party, the *Mouvement Populaire de la Révolution* (MPR) which became the single authorised party in the state. In October 1971 he came up with his policy of "authenticity", whose objective was to decolonise his people's minds and make them proud of their African origins. He started by renaming the Congo as Zaire and getting all citizens to drop their missionary-given Christian names and take on authentic (traditional) African names.

Authenticity gave the people a major psychological boost, but Mobutu's headlong rush for Africanisation, nationalisation of industry and estates, soon brought economic chaos. Bribery and corruption became rampant, government expenditure soared and Zaire ran up huge debts as it became Africa's first major debt-crisis nation.

To rescue himself from this situation Mobutu turned to the International Monetary Fund which tried, over the years, to bring financial discipline to Zaire's economic affairs. But failure to face up to the pain of adjustment caused a major break with the organisation in November 1986. In foreign policy he turned to the USA which saw him as a tough ruler, the only man who could maintain stability in his vast and impenetrable country. Mobutu was seen by the Americans as a bulwark against Communism and a counter-poise to the leftist regimes.

Inside Africa Mobutu has wanted to project the position of Zaire as one of the most important and influential African countries, equalling Nigeria or Kenya. He is convinced that the long-term economic potential of Zaire is in fact greater than either of them, because Zaire has a population of only a quarter of Nigeria's and far greater untapped economic resources.

Mobutu has always been a faithful member of the Organisation of African Unity. Indeed, Zaire has played an active part in almost all OAU operations where it has been necessary to deploy troops rather than pass pious resolutions. On two occasions Zairean peace-keeping forces have been sent to Chad under OAU auspices.

Mobutu also bowed to majority African wishes when he broke diplomatic relations with the Israelis who had provided him with extensive military and technical assistance. In October 1973 he said he had to chose between a friend and a brother. Israel had been a friendly country but Egypt was a brother African country, so he broke diplomatic contact with Israel. But Mobutu missed Israeli assistance and after the Camp David agreements between Egypt and Israel, he found himself able to reopen diplomatic relations once again on 16 May 1982.

Opposition parties began to multiply by the mid-1970s and Mobutu was challenged by the rump of old secessionist movements in the Katanga uprisings of March 1977 and May 1978, which were only crushed with the assistance of French and Belgian paratroops. Other opposition groups persisted in the extreme east near Lake Tanganyika.

In April 1981 Nguza Karl I Bond, Mobutu's Prime Minister and most likely heir, went to Belgium and resigned and began to attack the corruption in the country. It was not until June 1985 after lengthy negotiations that the wounds were healed and Nguza returned home soon to be brought back into government.

Meanwhile, more persistent political opposition was growing in the shape of the Union for Democracy and Social Progress (UPDS) operating from Belgium and internally. A group of UPDS MPs actually dared to criticise Mobutu in the National Assembly in March 1982. Mobutu detained them and only released them after major criticism overseas of his human rights record. In January 1988 UPDS leader Etienne Tshisekedi was arrested, released, rearrested in April and finally tamed by Mobutu who tempted him with various promises concerning the legitimisation of the UPDS. By 1989 Mobutu had succeeded in his main aim of driving a wedge between the UPDS in Zaire and those based externally in Belgium.

Mobutu's love-hate relationship with the former colonial power exploded into the most vocal row with Belgium at the beginning of 1989. It started when Mobutu scornfully declined a Belgian offer of some debt remission. The quarrel blew into a major storm in which the Belgian press exposed the huge amounts of money that he took for his own use from the bank of Zaire and the extent of his personal properties in Belgium and Europe.

With the wind of democratic change blowing through Africa in 1990, Mobutu came under intense pressure. The economy was plunging into chaos, with inflation soaring. An international outcry erupted following the massacre of more than 100 demonstrating students by troops at Lubumbashi University in May. In order to defuse the mounting tide of opposition, Mobutu decided to introduce a multi-party system and announced his resignation as chairman of the MPR so that he could "rise above" party politics. He set up a special commission to draft a new constitution by April 1991 and allowed political parties to operate freely.

These moves unleashed a wave of hitherto suppressed political activity. Opposition parties proliferated and personal attacks on Mobutu became ever more daring. Calls came for him to resign. Mobutu set up a transitional government and desperately reshuffled his ministers as arguments developed over the constitutional conference. He failed in his attempt to co-opt Etienne Tshisekedi, one of the most prominent opposition leaders, as his prime minister in the run up to the conference.

After several delays the conference finally started on 7 August 1991, attended by over 200 political parties. The atmosphere was electric with Tshisekedi threatening that Mobutu would be imprisoned if he lost power.

NGUZA, Karl I Bond
Zairean politician.

A tough, pugnacious Lunda who has enjoyed the most extraordinary love-hate relationship with President Mobutu. Four times in his chequered career he has been appointed Foreign Minister. He has also spent four years in exile as the most vociferous critic of the Zaire government. He returned to do another spell as Foreign Minister before breaking again with his master and forming his own opposition party.

Born 4 August 1938 in Musamba, West Shaba region, in a Lunda family. Primary education with the Xavier Brothers at Likasi. Secondary education under the Benedictine Fathers at Lubumbashi. Studied international relations at Lovanium University. Graduated July 1965.

He returned to the Congo and became an announcer on radio Lubumbashi (1957-60). He then joined Moise Tshombe's private cabinet in Katanga in 1964, before joining the Congolese diplomatic service, serving in the embassy in Brussels (1964-66). He was made the government commissioner to the Belgian mining company Union Miniere (1965-66), counsellor, then deputy to the permanent representative of the Congolese delegation to the United Nations (1966-68).

This international experience was his stepping stone to the Foreign Ministry, becoming minister from 24 February 1972 until 8 March 1974, then again on 4 February 1976. In an extraordinary sequence of events, he was suddenly arrested on 13 August 1977 and accused of having prior knowledge of the first invasion of Shaba. He was tried and sentenced to death for treason, but Mobutu commuted the sentence to life imprisonment. Then within a year he was freed and reappointed Foreign Minister on 6 March 1979.

But he quarrelled once again with Mobutu and in April 1981 resigned, and took advantage of a trip to Belgium to go into exile. He then began to attack the Head of State in the international media for corruption and dictatorial methods. He wrote a book telling of his own arrest, torture and detention in 1979 and gave evidence before a sub-committee of the US House of Representatives. He organised and co-ordinated the external opposition to the government to the extent that the Belgian authorities tried to curb his activities for fear of damaging relations with Zaire.

Then in another dramatic change of course, while a second Shaba invasion was underway, he suddenly took advantage of an amnesty and returned home on 27 June 1985 and joined in the celebrations marking the 25th anniversary of independence. His erstwhile colleagues in the Lumumba-MNC attacked him for his "dishonest, turncoat path", but Mobutu appeared ready to forgive and forget, making him ambassador to the USA in September 1986 and Foreign Minister, for the fourth time on 7 March 1988.

In June 1989 he visited South Africa and had talks with President PW Botha. He called on the Organisation of African Unity to review its strategy of isolating South Africa, saying that the policy had proved to be a disaster. He told reporters that he had visited South Africa to help resolve southern African problems.

In September 1989 after yet another quarrel with Mobutu he went to live abroad. When Mobutu lifted restrictions on opposition parties, Nguza returned home in November 1990 to lead the Federal Union of Independent Republicans (UFERI). He took a leading part in the National Conference of August 1991.

NYEMBO, Shabani

Zairian economist and politician.

A quiet and self-effacing university professor who was plucked out of the University of Zaire by President Mobutu to become Minister of National Economy. Over the next 12 years he was reshuffled through almost every economics ministry in the country. He became a veritable multi-purpose player, struggling with Zaire's overwhelming economic problems and being moved around at the whim of his master until he was abruptly dismissed on 26 November 1988. His economic expertise and wide experience of government make him ideally placed for a come-back.

Born 5 August 1937 at Kayanza. Educated at the Institut Saint Boniface, Elizabethville (Lubumbashi) and the Catholic University of Louvain, Belgium, where he read economics.

He returned home and joined the Bureau of Economic Co-operation attached to the Prime Minister's Office, 1964-65. He then returned to Louvain University to do further economic research (1967-76) and take his doctorate in economics. In October 1976 he was appointed Professor of the economics faculty in the National University of Zaire.

His big break in politics came in February 1977, when President Mobutu pulled him out of academic obscurity and made him State Commissioner (Minister) for National Economy. On 19 August 1977 he was reshuffled to be Commissioner in charge of State Portfolio (investments). In a major reshuffle on 1 January 1980, he was appointed Commissioner for Agriculture and Rural Development, before returning to Economy, Industry and Foreign Trade on 6 November 1982.

He was asked to concentrate on Foreign Trade alone on 1 February 1985, but within a couple of months on 12 April he was sent in as "visiting fireman" to the state copper mining company, Gecamines. On 31 October

1986 Mobutu recalled him as Minister of National Economy and Industry. This was followed by a major promotion to Finance on 22 January 1987. He had the budget portfolio added to his financial duties in February, before reassuming Economy and Industry on 29 July 1987. But on 26 November 1988, he was suddenly dismissed from the cabinet in another of Mobutu's wide-ranging reshuffles of his demoralised economics ministers.

SAMBWA, Pida Nbagui
Zairean banker, politician and minister.

A close relative of President Mobutu, coming from Mbandaka, capital of Equatoria region and the same Bengala tribe. He was a critical and outspoken Governor of the Banque of Zaire in the 1970s and held a variety of economic ministries, culminating in the Premiership in the 1980s, but fell foul of Mobutu's ever-changing relationship with the IMF.

Born 12 November 1940 at Mbandaka where he received his primary and secondary education. He went to the Université Libre in Brussels and took a degree in economics and finance.

He started work as an economic councillor in the Presidency in October 1967 and in 1968 was made administrator of the Economat du Peuple, a state-owned store designed to cut out foreign traders and middlemen. He returned to the Presidency as an assistant director from May 1969 to September 1970. In September he became councillor at the National Bank and administrator of SOCOFIDE, the state investment company.

He was appointed Governor of the Bank of Zaire on 15 September 1970, a post he held throughout the 1970s. As Zaire's economic problems became more critical, President Mobutu wanted him to play a more central role in the economy, appointing him Minister of Economy and Industry on 12 April 1985, then Minister of Planning on 5 July 1985. He held this post until Mobutu had a major row with the IMF in October 1986 over debt repayment and structural readjustment. He carried out a major reshuffle in economic ministries but retained Sambwa as the Minister of Planning, finally deciding to promote him First Commissioner (Prime Minister) in charge of five other economic ministries on 29 July 1987. But on 26 November 1988 he dismissed Sambwa and brought back Kengo wa Dondo who had pioneered the IMF austerity programme of the mid-1980s.

SINGA Boyembe Mosambay (General)
Zairean soldier and politician. Commissioner for Territorial Security and War Veterans 12 May 1989 –

One of the most loyal and trusted of Mobutu's lieutenants. He helped Mobutu to power and saved the day during the Shaba invasions in 1977 and 1978. He has long been Army Chief of Staff. Mobutu's ultimate accolade was when he handed over to Singa the responsibilities for all intelligence services under the strangely named ministry of Territorial Security and War Veterans in May 1989.

Born 10 October 1932 in Ibembo, Haut Zaire. Educated in Haut Zaire and Kasai. Military training at the *Ecole Royale de Gendarmerie Belge* in Belgium, doing further training in the USA and Israel.

He was one of the organisers of the coup that brought Mobutu to power in September 1960 when he began his military career in the gendarmerie. He has held the most senior military and political posts since then. He was Zaire's ambassador to Uganda in 1972 and was brought back into the army to take charge during the two Shaba invasions of 1977 and 1978. After the invasions had been suppressed he was made governor of the Shaba region.

He was promoted to Army Chief of Staff on 1 January 1980 and was elected to the central committee of the *Mouvement Populaire de la Révolution* (MPR) in September 1980. On 8 December 1988 Mobutu divested himself of the portfolio of Minister of Defence and National Security that he had held personally since his accession to power on 24 November 1965, and passed on the responsibility to General Singa.

Mobutu reclaimed this command in May 1989 when he consolidated all his various intelligence services under the Ministry of Territorial Security and War Veterans and put Singa in charge. The plan was that all security services should report to Singa rather than Mobutu as in the past. Some commentators thought that this was an indication that Mobutu was grooming Singa as his successor.

UMBA DI LUTETE, Jean Theodore
Zairean politician.

Dynamic and able and of mixed parentage from the Bas Congo, he experienced rapid promotion while still a young man, enjoying much influence in Mobutu's Presidential office. Later he held a number of ministries and was particularly well known as Foreign Minister and Zaire's representative at the United Nations. But he was dropped in February 1985 when Mobutu sacked eight ministers after disagreements over economic policy. Still youthful in political terms, he is expected to make a come-back.

Born 30 June 1939, at Seke Konde in Bas Congo region. Educated locally, he studied law at Lovanium University and then at the Université Libre in Brussels where he took degrees in maritime and aerial law. He did further training at the Agency for International Development in the USA.

He returned home to become legal adviser to the provincial assembly in the Central Congo until its suppression. He then became Director-General in the Presidency and on 5 October 1967, Vice-Minister for

Foreign Affairs, followed by another spell as Minister at the Presidency. He became the intermediary through whom everyone had to pass in order to see the President. Demoted to Minister of Power in 1970 and Mines on 2 July 1971, he became Commissioner of State (Minister) for Foreign Affairs (1974-75), for Politics (1975-76) and Permanent Representative for Zaire to the United Nations (1976-77).

Then he was moved back to Foreign Affairs and International Co-operation in (1977-79 and 1984-85). He was one of eight ministers sacked by Mobutu on 1 February 1985 when Mobutu broke with the International Monetary Fund over its structural readjustment programme which had brought austerity and high inflation.

ZAMBIA

Population: 7.9m (1990, World Bank)
Independence: 24 October 1964
Head of State: Frederick J. Chiluba
Government: Democratic, multi-party elections of October 1991 unseated Kenneth Kaunda and put Frederick Chiluba, leader of the Movement for Multi-Party Democracy (MMD) in power.
Parties: Opposition parties allowed to organise since December 1990. Former single party – United National Independence Party (UNIP). Majority party – Movement for Multi-Party Democracy (MMD).

CHILUBA, Frederick J
Zambian trade unionist. President of Zambia, 2 November 1991 —

Standing only just over five foot tall, he acquired his reputation as a tough union organiser and negotiator before bursting onto the political scene as one of the leaders of the Movement for Multi-Party Democracy (MMD) in the second half of 1990. Well known as an uncompromising democrat, with a blunt tongue, his position as President of the party was confirmed after fiercely contested elections in March 1991. His party swept to victory in the elections of October 1991 and he became President.

Born 1943 the son of a Bemba copper miner, working on the Zambian copperbelt. Under parental inspiration he took up unionism and emerged in 1975 as Chairman of the Zambia Congress of Trades Unions, the co-ordinating body for most major Zambian unions including the powerful copper miners.

The unions were one of the few organised voices of opposition against the single party system and Chiluba, as the most prominent union leader, became involved in several major conflicts with government over wages, inflation and food subsidies. He remained an outspoken critic known for his blunt speaking.

As the wind of democratic change gathered force in Africa in 1990, he soon found himself among the lobbyists for democratic pluralism. He began to take a leading role in the major opposition party, the Movement for Multi-party Democracy (MMD). In the second half of 1990 it attracted huge crowds to its rallies, particularly on the Zambian copperbelt where Chiluba had a large following. In October he was briefly arrested for holding an unauthorised meeting, because the party was still illegal.

In September the ruling party unexpectedly endorsed proposals to allow the formation of other parties. Chiluba continued to organise and campaign on behalf of the MMD. In February 1991 it published a draft manifesto, but the leadership of the party still had to be resolved and there were many other influential contenders. Chiluba took them on in a vigorous, open presidential contest. He won 63% of the votes beating the veteran politicans Arthur Wina and Humphrey Mulemba into second and third places. He became President of the MMD on 1 March 1991. He was cautious and diplomatic in his acceptance speech saying that he would continue to fight for democracy and that he would liberalise the economy and encourage initiative and enterprise.

His election was widely welcomed in the country as a whole though some groups had reservations because of his Bemba origins and the business community was worried about his long standing union connections. Yet business had funded the MMD campaign with at least $10m.

Chiluba's first task was to contest the form of the new constitution that President Kaunda was trying to impose. He objected strongly because it would strengthen presidential powers at a time when the need was for more parliamentary accountability. His threat to boycott further political discussions brought Kaunda to meet him for the first time and agree to revisions to the constitution that would be acceptable to both sides. The government also agreed to give financial grants to all parties to permit them to contest the elections on an equal footing.

The MMD scored an overwhelming victory in the elections of October 1991, unexpectedly winning over 75 per cent of the votes cast. Chiluba was duly installed as President of Zambia on 2 November 1991.

CHONA, Mathias Mainza
Zambian politician. Former Vice-President and Prime Minister.

As one of the founders of the United National Independence Party (UNIP), one of the first generation of Zambian politicians. Indispensable to President Kaunda in the first two decades of independence, supervising party and constitutional affairs and representing his country at international conferences. He held many top positions in the country before he stood down as party secretary-general in February 1981.

Born 21 January 1930. Educated at Chona school, Chinkuni Catholic Mission School and Munali Secondary school. A clerk-interpreter at the High Court in Livingstone over 1951-55. Published a novel in 1952, *Kabuka Uleta Tunji*, which won the Margaret Wong Medal in 1956. Studied law at Grays Inn, London (1955-58). Admitted to the bar in June 1958. Unable to get a job in a law firm on his return to Zambia, he turned to politics.

During Kaunda's imprisonment in March 1959 Chona challenged Harry Nkumbula in the Zambia African Congress and walked out with his supporters to organise the United National Independence Party (UNIP). He became party president in October, keeping the seat warm so that Kaunda could take over the presidency on 30 January 1960, on his release from prison.

Went into exile in Britain because a warrant for his arrest had been issued during his absence at a conference in Tunis. He ran UNIP's external affairs from London and teamed up with Kaunda at the constitutional conference in London in December 1960. Returned to Lusaka in February 1961 and became secretary-general of UNIP, a post he held until 1969. Entered parliament as an MP for Livingstone in 1964 and became the first Minister of Justice at independence. Home Affairs (1964-66). Minister of Presidential Affairs, 1 January 1967. Minister without portfolio November 1968.

As Presidential trouble-shooter he was transferred in September 1969 to be Minister of Central Province and Minister of Provincial and Local Government. Ambassador to the USA (1969-70). Took over as Vice-President in October 1970, on the resignation of Simon Kapwepwe. He became Minister of National Guidance 1971, Information 1973. During this period his most important task was heading a commission leading to constitutional amendments in December 1972.

At the seventh general party conference on 25 August 1973 he was appointed to the new post of Prime Minister, ranking third in the party hierarchy. Kaunda later explained that he was reluctant to take on this responsibility. He resigned in mysterious circumstances two years later, on 27 May 1973, but remained as Minister of Legal Affairs. Attorney-General (1975-77). Returned as PM on the dismissal of Elijah Mudenda, 20 July 1977.

Stood down as PM and became secretary general of the party on 15 June 1978. Became a super-minister over the Minister of National Guidance on 2 January 1979. When austerity measures were taken during 1981 economic crisis he said that the party would be "ruthless with people trying to undermine it." On 18 February 1981 he stood down (for Humphrey Mulemba) as secretary-general to become an ambassador.

GOMA, Lameck Kazembe Haza

Zambian zoologist and politician. Minister of Higher Education, Science and Technology, 4 April 1986 – October 1991

An academic who became pro-Vice-Chancellor of the University of Zambia before going into politics, as a nominated MP without a proper political power base. He spent much of his ministerial career in ministries connected with education. The exception was a spell (1982-86) as Foreign Minister, where he rapidly adopted the socialist rhetoric of his president.

Born 8 April 1930 at Lundazi, Eastern Province. Educated at Lubwa mission, Munali School, Fort Hare University (South Africa), Cambridge where he gained his MA, and London University where he took a PhD.

He became a lecturer at University College, Ghana before becoming a resident fellow to the Virus Research Institute at Entebbe, Uganda, then as a resident fellow to Makerere University College, Kampala. He returned home to become a Professor in Zoology at the University of Zambia, then pro-Vice-Chancellor of the university.

On 4 May 1975 his politicial career started when President Kaunda made him Minister of Education and a nominated member of parliament. When Kaunda reorganised government structures to give more power to the United National Independence Party, Goma's ministry was put under the chairmanship of Elijah Mudenda's Social and Cultural Committee of the Central Committee.

In 1982 he was promoted Foreign Minister. In this capacity he signed Zambia's first cultural agreement with Cuba on 24 December 1982. He frequently urged the US to use its influence in securing an agreement in Southern Africa.

He said that the US was the "first colonised country to rise up against the colonising power and the first to gain its independence" and "should not allow itself to go down in history as the country that is now indefinitely blocking the last colonised country in Africa (Namibia) from gaining its independence."

On 4 April 1986 President Kaunda moved the former Finance Minister, Luke Mwananshiku, into Foreign Affairs and shifted Professor Goma to Higher Education. On 2 November 1988 his ministry was redesignated Higher Education, Science and Technology.

KAMANA, Dunstan Weston

Zambian diplomat, journalist and newspaper editor.

*As a bright young journalist/civil servant/diplomat, well liked for his tactful handling of sensitive issues, he was soon spotted by Kaunda and taken into the President's office. He became an influential press officer and adviser. Later he wanted more scope and independence and became the editor of the **Times of Zambia**. He has alternated journalism with spells as a distinguished diplomat. A highlight to his career was his service as Zambia's permanent representative to the United Nations.*

Born 19 April 1937 at Mangunza. Educated at St Mark's college Mapanza, then at Munali secondary school, Lusaka, (1953-58). Joined Northern Rhodesian government service 1959. Information officer and later first press secretary at Zambian High Commission, London 1964. Recalled by Kaunda to be presidential press secretary September 1965 to July 1966 when he became Director of Information for two years (1966-68). Director of Zambian Information Services and editor in chief of the *Times of Zambia* (1968-72).

His criticism of MPs in parliament resulted in his removal to become general manager of the Dairy Produce Board. But shortly afterwards, also in 1972, he was appointed as ambassador to the USSR (1972-74), high commissioner to Canada (1974-75) and Zambia's permanent representative to the United Nations (1975-77).

KAUNDA, Kenneth David (Dr)
Former President of Zambia, October 1964 – October 1991.

He was one of Africa's longest surviving Heads of State. For more than 27 years he wrestled with the problems of a small landlocked country heavily dependent on a single important export commodity - copper. He attempted to introduce humanism and African socialism as his guiding philosophies but found resistance among many of the middle class who wanted a more open, capitalist system. His problems became greater as the years passed and Zambia's economic problems multiplied. His early attempts to escape from dependence on copper and its by-products failed and agriculture did not respond to his rhetorical encouragement until the economy reached a serious crisis in the late 1980s, which forced late changes.

Politically he was known for his philosophy of humanism, giving priority to people and their needs. He was also conditioned by his Christian upbringing and faith which remained important to him. An emotional man who often wept in public, he was also an immediate charmer.

A tough political manipulator, for all his professed idealism, he survived by continually reshuffling his top party stalwarts and ministers. Unable to cope with the criticism of a minority of dissidents, he detained a number of his political opponents and became very sensitive to the possibility of coups.

No rival of sufficient calibre or leadership quality was allowed to challenge him and he won his first six Presidential elections without opposition. Excellent as a political strategist and tactician but less happy with economic realities. He neither smokes nor drinks and works long hours. At the same time he knows how to relax, playing tennis, golf, or singing hymns and folk songs. He was finally defeated by Frederick Chiluba in the elections of October 1991. He gracefully stepped down from office and later retired from politics.

Born 28 April 1924, at Lubwa in the north. Son of the first African minister sent to Lubwa by the Presbyterian Mission. The eighth child of a couple married 20 years, he was called "*Buchizya*", the unexpected one. Educated at Lubwa mission school, and Munali secondary school, Lusaka (1941).

After teachers' training he returned to Lubwa to teach in 1943. He became headmaster 1947. Also in 1947 he became secretary of the Young Men's Farming Association, the nursery of the Northern Rhodesia African National Congress. He became the founder secretary-general of the ANC Lubwa in 1948 and secretary-general of the whole ANC in 1950.

In 1955 he was jailed by the colonial administration for possessing banned literature. He became second-in-command to Harry Nkumbula in the campaign against the Central African Federation under which Northern Rhodesia was integrated with Southern Rhodesia and Nyasaland.

He split with Nkumbula in October 1958 and quit the ANC along with other radicals. On 24 October 1958 he launched the Zambia African

National Congress with himself as President. Rearrested on 12 March 1959, he was imprisoned until 9 January 1960. ZANC was banned, so he formed the United National Independence Party on 31 January 1960.

In the first African administration of 30 October 1962, Kaunda became Minister of Local Government and Social Welfare. With a new constitution bringing self-government, he became the youngest Prime Minister in the Commonwealth on 22 January 1964. When Rhodesia made its Unilateral Declaration of Independence on 11 November 1965, he declared an emergency in Zambia and failed to persuade the British government to crush the Rhodesian secession.

On 4 February 1971 he banned the United Progressive Party of his former colleague Simon Kapwepwe, who he had arrested, and kept in detention until the end of the year. He made Zambia a one-party state on 13 December 1972 and persuaded his old mentor, Harry Nkumbula to join UNIP in June 1973.

The fall in the price of copper and closure of the Benguela railway through Angola and the railway through Rhodesia brought the first of a series of economic crises. Kaunda declared a nation-wide emergency in January 1976, put more power in the hands of the party and took over the *Times of Zambia*.

Kapwepwe, released from detention, rejoined the party and brought Kaunda support from his Bemba people, but he died in January 1980.

Economic problems multiplied as Zambia failed to reduce its dependence on copper and the people fought to maintain their living standards. Kaunda took refuge in blaming external causes and particularly South African interference. But many Zambians felt the economy was being mismanaged. In October 1980 an attempted coup brought the arrest of many prominent leaders and former colleagues. But Kaunda maintained his personal popularity with the people in successive Presidential elections in 1973, 1978, 1983 and 1988, always getting more than 90% of the votes cast.

Further protest against economic deterioration came from the universities, students and trade unionists, particularly in the copper mines. In May 1986 attempts to introduce austerity measures to cure economic ills brought resistance from all the above groups and the lifting of subsidies on staple foods caused violent rioting. Kaunda blamed South African interference and accused his political opponents of conspiracy to cause economic destabilisation.

One of Kaunda's major weaknesses was his failure to face up to economic realities. Though he professed a nominal socialism, he experimented with state ownership, mixed ownership, and foreign ownership, varying his policies without a coherent sense of direction. Kaunda tried, but failed to introduce the austerity measures proscribed by the IMF stick; debt was growing and attempts to devalue the kwacha failed. Finally he broke with the organisation in May 1987, thereby causing a halt of much international assistance. He then tried to cure Zambia's economic ills internally, but this style of readjustment was equally painful.

Kaunda played a leading part in the OAU and among the Frontline States and this did bring reprisals and various attempts at destabilisation by South Africa. Kaunda for many years tried dialogue, but he became disillusioned and irritated by the criticism of other African states. However his seniority and popularity in Africa was rewarded with his appointment as the Chairman of the OAU for 1987.

When he attempted to eliminate food subsidies at the end of June 1990 three days of rioting and huge commercial damage followed resulting in more than 29 deaths. Then came an attempted coup, easily suppressed, in which the people seemed to take delight in the news that Kaunda had been toppled.

Opposition then began to organise itself spontaneously, pressing for a multi-party system. Kaunda was reluctant to give way, but first UNIP and then the National Assembly declared themselves in favour of change. A serious opposition group – the Movement for Multi-party Democracy (MMD) held massive rallies in different parts of the country, towards the end of the year.

Kaunda set up a constitutional commission and on 7 December 1990, signed the bill to transform the nation into a multi-party democracy. The Mvunga constitutional commission presented its findings in June 1991. It proposed that the President's powers should be strengthened and that the post of Prime Minister should be abolished. The opposition saw this as a strategem by Kaunda to concentrate more power in his own hands, while allowing token democratisation lower down. It refused to attend talks on a new constitution and threatened to boycott the elections. Kaunda then compromised, talked to the opposition leaders for the first time, and both sides agreed on a mutually acceptable constitution.

Meanwhile inside UNIP, Enoch Kavindele, Kaunda's first challenger for the presidency of the party stood down, allowing Kaunda to win unopposed. The battle lines were then drawn for the national and presidential elections in October 1991. UNIP was heavily defeated and Kaunda gracefully acknowledged the people's decision. After 27 years in power, he stepped down and retired from politics shortly after.

KAUNDA, Wezi Chizuma Burukutu (Major)

Zambian politician. Former soldier. Minister of State for Home Affairs 2 November 1988 – October 1991.

President Kaunda's third son, with his foot already on the political ladder as a junior minister of Home Affairs. A delightfully frank and open personality who has inherited much of his father's warmth and friendliness. In his own right he has had long experience in the army and wide academic training and an LLB degree. He has travelled extensively, besides being for a time, a first division soccer player. Some observers have suggested that he is being groomed for leadership of his country but he is prepared to take his political career one step at a time.

Born 24 December 1951 in Shambalake farm, Chinsali district, Northern province, the third son of Kenneth and Betty Kaunda. In 1958 he was sent to Chilenje lower primary school, in 1959 to Kasisi primary and in 1963 to Burma Road primary. He went on to St Francis College (1964-67) then to St Canisius College, Chisekesie where he rose to become a prefect and a lieutenant in the school cadets. He also played as a striker in the school soccer team.

In 1971 he was sent to Kohima barracks military school at Kabwe. He graduated to the rank of 2nd lieutenant and was subsequently posted to Mufulira, No 1 Engineering Squadron for a year before asking for a transfer to the infantry where he had the possibility of promotion. He was sent to the 1st Battalion Zambia Regiment in Ndola. Over 1973-77 his military career flourished. He rose to full lieutenant and platoon leader and then captain, commanding a company of more than 100 men. His passion for soccer continued as a player in the Green Buffaloes army team, a first division club.

In 1976 he attended a junior command course at the Military Headquarters in Indore, Madya Pradesh state in India. After seven years military service he retired and enrolled in the Law School of the University of Zambia at Lusaka.

In 1981, with his father calling for general mobilisation to meet the Rhodesian crisis, he re-enlisted and was promoted to major, commanding a battalion of reserves at Kitwe. He then returned to his legal studies and graduated with an LLB in 1982. He joined the management training stream in the Cabinet Office, 1982-83. He continued his studies at York University, England, doing a masters course in southern African studies, writing a dissertation on "Zambia and the Southern African Development Co-ordination Council – What is to be gained." In 1985 he started a PhD on "Informatics trans-border data flows."

Deciding to throw his hat into the political ring, he temporarily left York in October 1988 and stood as a candidate in Malambo province, winning a landslide victory for the ruling United National Independence Party. He became the first of Kaunda's sons to take a seat in parliament. On 2 November Kaunda appointed him Minister of State for Home Affairs, under the full minister, Gen Malimba Masheke and later Gen Kingsley Chunkuli. He appreciated his experience under these establishment military figures. At the beginning of 1990 he returned to York in order to complete his PhD studies.

MUDENDA, Elijah Haatukali Kaiba

Zambian politician. Prime Minister 1975-77.

Cambridge trained, a former plant breeder and one of the most civilised of Zambia's older generation politicians. He rose to the peak of his power in the mid-1970s when he became Prime Minister and President Kaunda put him in charge of all the economic ministries in an attempt to stimulate growth in the non-mining sectors of the economy. But he was dropped from office in 1977, though he remains a key member of the powerful central committee of the United National Independence Party.

Born 6 June 1927 at Macha near Choma in the south, son of Chief Macha. Educated locally then at Munali Secondary School (1943-47). He studied at Makerere University College and went on to Fort Hare, South Africa, where he graduated with an MA in 1951. He did further studies at Cambridge (1952-55) where he obtained a BSc in Agriculture.

He joined government service as an agricultural research officer in 1955 specialising in plant breeding. In 1962 he resigned to take up full-time politics and became a member of the Legislative Assembly. In October 1962 he was appointed Parliamentary Secretary to the Ministry of Agriculture. At independence in 1964 he became Minister of Agriculture.

In 1967 he was promoted to Minister of Finance, holding the portfolio for two years at a time when Zambia's financial problems were rapidly growing. He was reshuffled to become Foreign Minister in 1969, becoming an active member of the OAU conciliation committees amongst nationalist organisations in Angola and Zimbabwe. He was elected chairman of a ministerial meeting of non-aligned countries at the UN in New York, on 1 October 1972.

He also became a member of the central committee of the United National Independence Party (UNIP) and in 1973 chairman of the political sub-committee.

On 27 May 1975 he jumped ahead, being appointed Prime Minister by President Kaunda on the resignation of Mainza Chona from that post. In April 1977, Kaunda carried out a major reorganisation of government and extended Mudenda's powers by setting up a National Development Commission under him and giving him the overall supervision of the ministries of Rural Development and Development Planning. But within four months, in a startling reversal of this policy, Kaunda removed Mudenda from office on 20 July 1977 and replaced him with Mainza Chona, the man from whom he had taken over in 1975.

Mudenda continued as a powerful figure in the party, becoming chairman of the rural development sub-committee in 1978, the social and cultural sub-committee in 1979 and the economic sub-committee in February 1981. In 1985 he took on the appointments and disciplinary sub-committee but he did not return to ministerial rank in the 1980s.

MUKANDO, Justin Jeremiah
Zambian agriculturalist and politician. Minister of Agriculture, November 1988 – October 1991.

A technocrat who has spent a lifetime serving his country in his chosen field of agriculture. He was a specialist agriculturalist who gradually worked his way up through government service in agriculture till he became minister of state and finally Minister of Agriculture in November 1988.

Born 13 September 1936 at Mukando village, Serenje, Central Province. Educated at Chitambo Mission School, Mine School Kabwe, Mabonde School, Katondo School and Lunzuwa College.

He worked in the Ministry of Agriculture June 1958 - November 1961, then as a tobacco officer November 1961 - October 1962, project officer at the Ministry of Rural Development November 1970 - January 1971, rising to senior scheme manager of the Tobacco Board of Zambia, (1973-74).

He joined the United National Independence Party in 1960 and became a member of parliament in January 1974. He was appointed Minister of State for Agriculture and Water Development. On 13 February 1983, when Dr Kaunda created a new Ministry of Co-operatives, he asked Mukando to take over as the first minister. This led to considerable rivalry and confusion concerning overlapping responsibilities with the Ministry of Agriculture. The two bodies were fused into one ministry on 2 November 1988 and Mukando was appointed Minister of Agriculture and Co-operatives.

MULEMBA, Humphrey

Zambian politician. UNIP secretary-general 1981-85.

A self-made man who started as a miner, trades unionist and political organiser and worked his way up as MP, minister and secretary-general of the party. Considered to be one of the old guard in the Zambian power structure, he withdrew from a central political role. In 1990 he became active in the opposition Movement for Multi-party Democracy (MMD).

Born September 1932 at Lusaka. Educated at St Canisius College, Chunkuli. He began working as a miner at the big copper mine at Nchanga and later became an assistant personnel officer at the mines. He then went into trades unions, becoming full time secretary of the General Workers' Union. His political activities often landed him in trouble and in 1959 he was rounded up with other political activists as a detainee. In 1960 he was released and resumed work with the United National Independence Party, becoming secretary for the north west province.

He entered parliament in 1964 as MP for Lukusuzi and later that year was appointed deputy speaker, serving for three years alongside Wesley Nyirenda, the speaker. In 1967 he became Minister of State for Cabinet Affairs and Public Service. The following year he was sent as a minister to Luapula province and then in September 1969 to Barotse province.

He was elected MP for Chipata East in 1969 and became Minister of Trade, subsequently having Industry added to his portfolio. He then became Minister of Mines and Mining Development (1970-73). At the Mulungushi conference of UNIP in August 1973, President Kaunda thoroughly reorganised government and the party and made Mulemba the chairman of the sub-committee on the economy and finance while retaining his mines portfolio. He switched to the appointments and discipline sub-committee (1978-81). On 18 February 1981, in a major shake-up of the party, a major promotion came with his appointment to become secretary-general of UNIP in place of Mainza Chona. He held this office until 24 April 1985 when he surrendered his post to Grey Zulu.

MUSOKOTWANE, Kebby
Zambian politician. Prime Minister April 1985-March 1989.

Youthful both in reality and in appearance, he was one of Kaunda's youngest ever ministers when first appointed in 1977. A young technocrat of the post-independence generation he rose fast to become the youngest ever Zambian Prime Minister in 1985, at a time Zambia's financial crisis was at its worst, with major problems in securing an agreement with the IMF. Musokotwane helped secure an agreement but shared the responsibility for escalating prices and rising budgetary deficits. Kaunda still made him Prime Minister in 1985, a post he held until March 1989.

Born 5 May 1946. Educated at Monze Secondary School, David Livingstone Teacher's Training College and at the University of Zambia. He went into teaching in 1965 becoming a demonstration teacher and a headmaster 1968-70 and lecturer 1972-73.

He went into politics and became an MP in 1973. Kaunda spotted him and on 25 April 1977 appointed him, at 30 years of age, to become the new Minister of Water and Natural Resources. On 2 January 1979 he was shuffled to Youth and Sports and on 24 December of the same year, to the senior post of Minister of Finance and Technical Co-operation. But with the economy in a critical position Kaunda needed a senior man with more experience and asked the Prime Minister Nalumino Mundia to take over as Finance Minister. Musokotwane was moved back to the Youth and Sport Portfolio, and then onto General Education and Culture in 1983.

But Kaunda reversed his earlier decision when he promoted him Prime Minister on 24 April 1985 in place of Mundia, at a time when Zambia was involved in extensive discussion with the International Monetary Fund over its suspended stand-by programme. During 1986 Musokotwane actually took over the Finance portfolio, while still holding the premiership, at a time government revenues and expenditures were rising fast in the wake of agreement with the IMF and the introduction of the foreign exchange auction system. But in May 1987 Kaunda broke off negotiations with the IMF and decided to introduce his own economic reforms. Musokotwane had the Finance portfolio taken from him yet again on 13 May 1987.

On 15 March 1989 he was dismissed as Prime Minister. Kaunda described his work as "outstanding" but said that changes at senior post level were "necessary to expose as many leaders as possible to the people." He demoted Musokotwane to Minister of General Education and two days later removed him from that post too.

Musokotwane took his demotion calmly likening politics to a game of football where a manager has to change his team from time to time, but it may have been because he had ignored the Zambian "leadership code" which says that leaders should have only one residence and had built himself a house in the up-market Kabulonga area, which he allegedly intended to let to others. Musokotwane who had served for nearly four years had been in the post longer than most of the other five prime ministers since independence.

MWAANGA, Vernon

Zambian politician and businessman. Foreign Minister, 7 November 1991 –

A political prodigy as a young man. He was Zambia's youngest ever ambassador abroad and youngest Foreign Minister, but he fell out with President Kaunda after he was detained in 1985. Since then he has been in private business. He emerged in 1990 as an active leader of the Movement for Multi-party Democracy (MMD).

Born 25 June 1944, son of a teacher at Choma in Southern Province. Educated at Shunguu school,and Livingstone Trades Institute where he became a card carrying member of the Zambia African National Congress led by Kenneth Kaunda. Later he went to the Technical Secondary School, Lusaka. He completed his academic career in England at the Institute of Commonwealth Studies, Oxford studying political science and international relations.

In preparation for a diplomatic career he was attached to the British embassy in Rome in 1963. After independence in October 1964 he was appointed Deputy High Commissioner to Britain and the youngest ever Zambian ambassador abroad at the age of 21, when he was appointed to the Soviet Union in December 1965. Kaunda recalled him to be his permanent secretary in September 1966, where he handled all the major issues which faced the President over the confrontation with Rhodesia. Next he was appointed Zambia's ambassador the the UN in March 1968. He was elected to represent Zambia on the security council for two years from 1 January 1969 to 31 December 1970 during which period he was also chairman of the Fourth Decolonisation Committee.

He returned home to become Editor in Chief of the *Times of Zambia* and the *Sunday Times* in January 1972. While still only 28 he became Zambia's youngest ever, Minister of Foreign Affairs in December 1973 and a member of the Central Committee of the ruling United National Independence Party in June 1975.

From that point he went into private business as Chairman of Curray Limited from May 1977, Chairman of Fleetfoot Advertising in April 1978, Chairman of the Bank of Credit and Commerce Zambia in June 1980 and Chairman of Zambia Industrial and Commercial Association September 1981. But even during this period as a businessman he was frequently invited for working breakfasts, lunches and dinners with President

Kaunda at state house.

His meteoric rise to power was checked suddenly on 30 August 1985 when he was detained without trial and held inside until 4 April 1986. He claims in his book the *Other Society - a detainee's diary* that the first that he knew about being in trouble was when the police raided his home and presented him with a search warrant for "dealings in foreign currency and smuggled goods." A few days later he was arrested and detained for seven months.

He was never brought to trial. In his book he clinically picks holes in all the accusations against him, but he does not use the book as an opportunity to clear his name.

He says that money allegedly banked in London was declared to the authorities, expatriated legally under the correct documentation and that the amount was for business carried out, in the rand monetary area, over a considerable period of time. He also denied knowledge of many of the business associates that he was said to have contacted. He was finally released without any explanation as to why charges had not been brought.

In 1990 he became one of the leaders of the opposition party, the Movement for Multi-party Democracy (MMD). His party swept to power in the elections of October 1991. On 7 November, President Chiluba appointed him Minister for Foreign Affairs, the same ministry where he had launched his political career as a young man.

SHAPI, Alex Kaunda

Zambian politician. Secretary of State for Defence and Security, 24 April 1985 – October 1991.

A party stalwart and longstanding member of the central committee. He became Secretary of State for Defence and Security in April 1985 where he had to devise policies to counteract destabilisation by South Africa. He claimed that the food riots of December 1986 were part of a "well calculated attack by Zambia's enemies who are out to sabotage the country."

Born 25 October 1932 in Samfya. Educated at St Joseph's Upper Primary School and Lubwe Mission School. He went to Oxford University to do a course in public administration in 1963. Emerged as a political force as a divisional president of the United National Independence Party from 1963-64. Minister of State 1964. Kaunda made him a full cabinet Minister 1969.

At the seventh Mulungushi extraordinary conference in August 1973, when the constitution was amended making the UNIP Central Committee senior to the cabinet, he was appointed to the committee for the first time. On 24 April 1985 he became Secretary of State for Defence and Security and has held that post through a number of cabinet reshuffles.

ZULU, Alexander Grey

Zambian politician. Secretary General of the United National Independence Party (UNIP) from 1985.

A party stalwart, in the top rank of UNIP seniority since 1973. As a close friend of Kaunda and super-loyalist, he has always been a power behind the scenes. He pioneered the co-operative movement and has held a number of top ministerial portfolios including defence. He was in charge of the surveillance of the activities of the different southern liberation movements based in Zambia. He made his mark as Minister of Defence at a time when relations between Zambia and Zimbabwe deteriorated to the point of closure of the frontier in January 1973. He became a super-minister and party representative in charge of the Secretariat for Defence and Security in January 1979. He has twice been party secretary-general 1973-79 and since 1985 when he has ranked number two in the hierarchy.

Born 3 February 1924 at Chipata in Eastern Province. Educated at Mufutu Primary School and Munali Secondary School. Joined government as a water development assistant (1950-53). Bookkeeper in the Kabwe Co-operative Marketing Union. Promoted as first African manager of the co-operative.

An early nationalist he was arrested along with Kaunda, Simon Kapwepwe and others in March 1959. Joined UNIP on his release. Entered government in 1963 as a parliamentary secretary. Kaunda made him Minister of Commerce and Industry and Minister of Transport and Works (1964) in the independence cabinet. He was then reshuffled to Minister of Mines and Co-operative (1965-67). Minister of Home Affairs, August 1967. Minister of Defence (1970-73). He introduced a code of conduct for soldiers in July 1972 . He was responsible for preventing incursions by Rhodesian security forces and for policing the border after its closure in January 1973.

He became a member of UNIP central committee and secretary-general of the party at the seventh general congress in August 1973 at Mulungushi, when the constitution was changed. It was declared that the Central Committee would have superior powers to the Cabinet, thus Zulu found himself ranking number two in the power hierarchy. He became a super-minister in charge of the Secretariat for Defence and Security on 2 January 1979. Zulu remained in this post despite frequent cabinet reshuffles by Kaunda over the years. He returned to be the secretary-general of the party on 24 April 1985, in place of Humphrey Mulemba.

ZIMBABWE

Population: 9.83m (1990, World Bank)
Independence: 18 April 1980
Head of State: President Robert Mugabe
Government: Parliamentary system. One party state officially abandoned at the end of 1990 following an adverse vote in the politbureau. Mugabe has totally changed his thinking on the one party idea, but he retains the presidential system and Zimbabwe remains virtually a de facto one party state until a credible opposition emerges.
Parties: Official party - Zimbabwe African National Union - Patriotic Front (ZANU-PF). Main opposition parties Zimbabwe Unity Movement, Zimbabwe African National Union - Sithole (ZANU-S). (Joshua Nkomo's Zimbabwe African People's Union (ZAPU) was merged with ZANU-PF in April 1988).

CHIDZERO, Bernard Thomas Gibson

Zimbabwe politician. Minister of Finance, Economic Planning and Development, March 1980 –

Arguably the most highly educated and qualified of all the Zimbabwe ministers, he has a strong academic and international background. He is essentially the economic technocrat of the Zimbabwe government, with acquired political experience. Affable and self-assured and a pragmatist in the face of Zimbabwe's economic realities, he has held the economics and finance portfolio since independence. He became a super-minister in charge of all the economic ministries in the reshuffle of January 1988.

Born 1 July 1927 at Salisbury and brought up speaking Shona, his mother's tongue, and Nyanja, the language of his father who came from Malawi. Educated at Salisbury elementary school (1939-45), going to South Africa to St Francis College, Marianhill for secondary studies. He did a bachelor of arts degree in psychology at the University of Botswana, Lesotho and Swaziland (1950-52), staying on for a year to lecture in social psychology and Latin.

Then he studied at Ottawa University in Canada getting an MA in political science (1953-55) before moving to McGill University, Montreal to complete a PhD in 1958, followed by post-graduate research at Nuffield College, Oxford on British policy in Central Africa.

His only direct political commitment was in April 1960 when he joined a National Democratic Party delegation to London protesting against white Rhodesian attempts to amend the constitution.

In 1960 he joined the Economic Commission for Africa in Addis Ababa as economic affairs officer. In 1963 he was appointed representative of the UN Technical Assistance Board and director of the special fund programme. In 1966 he was appointed resident representative of the UN programme in Kenya. In 1968 he moved to Geneva as Director of the commodities division of the UN Commission on Trade and Development. He became deputy secretary-general of UNCTAD.

When Robert Mugabe formed his pre-independence government on 11 March 1980 he was short of economic expertise and asked the UN secretary-general to release Chidzero so that he could become his Economic Affairs and Finance minister. He added Trade and Commerce briefly to his portfolio on 10 March 1981, before reverting to Minister of Finance, Economic Planning and Development. In this capacity he was the architect of Zimbabwe's impressive growth in the first years of independence, followed by recession when commodity prices fell and drought hit agriculture in the mid-1980s. Through good economic management in difficult conditions, he restrained the economy to curb the decline in foreign exchange and the deterioration in balance of payments to keep firm control of a well balanced economy.

On 2 January 1988 Mugabe radically reorganised government to mark the merger of ZANU and ZAPU. He created three Senior Ministers attached to his own office and made Chidzero one of them, in charge of Finance, Economic Planning and Development. In 1990 Chidzero was actively sponsored by his government as a candidate for the post of UN Secretary General.

MANGWENDE, Witness Pasichigare Magunda (Dr)

Zimbabwean politician. Minister of Agriculture and Lands 9 April 1990-

One of the keenest young members of the Zimbabwe African National Union, he was kicked out of the University of Rhodesia for political militancy, but became leader of the ZANU students in Britain during his stay there in the 1970s. He returned home to start a political career, being made a deputy minister by Prime Minister Robert Mugabe and then Minister of Foreign Affairs. In that office he earned himself the nickname of "Mr Resolution 435" because of his assiduous projection of the cause of Namibian independence. In 1988 he swopped posts with Nathan Shamuyarira to become Minister of Information and then became Minister of Agriculture in April 1990.

Born 15 October 1946 in Charter. He spent his childhood years in Buhera and was educated at Zimuto Mission, Goromonzi Government School and the School of Social Work. In 1970 he went to the University of Rhodesia but soon took up politics and became President of the Students Union. He was expelled for his militant politicking in 1973.

He then went to the University of Southampton, England, and graduated in international relations. He went on to the London School of Economics and completed a PhD in the same field. In Britain he continued as a Zimbabwe African National Union activist and was elected president of the Zimbabwe Students Union in Britain and general-secretary of the London branch of ZANU.

In 1979 he was appointed ZANU's chief representative in Mozambique. He returned home to stand in the pre-independence elections of February 1980 elections as a ZANU-PF candidate. He won his seat and was appointed Deputy Defence Minister by Robert Mugabe. In January 1981 he was elected sessional chairman of the OAU committee for Namibia and in the same month, during the general reshuffle which followed the dismissal of Edgar Tekere, he was elevated to Minister of Foreign Affairs.

During his time as Foreign Minister he became heavily involved in the Namibian issue, earning the nickname "Mr Resolution 435"- the resolution that laid down the procedures for Namibian independence. He continued to bring up the Namibian question in all possible international fora.

Following the merger of ZAPU and ZANU and the installation of Robert Mugabe as Executive President, he exchanged portfolios with Nathan Shamuyarira, becoming Minister of Information, Posts and Telecommunications on 2 January 1988. He said he liked a press that informs, educates and entertains, but not one that misleads the people. He said newspapers should avoid unnecessary sensationalism, witch-hunting and character assassination.

MUGABE, Robert Gabriel
Zimbabwe President, 31 December 1987 –

A bespectacled intellectual who seemed more at home with his books and academic pursuits than a man of action. Largely self-educated, through a series of correspondence courses, he soon proved himself to be a man of dedication and principle, a leader of total determination and an excellent guerrilla organiser. He emerged over the years as by far the most effective nationalist leader who made his bid for power with consummate timing. Once in charge he soon showed himself to be more of a pragmatist than a Marxist, wanting to maintain national and racial harmony. He also revealed his ruthless determination to achieve unity and suppress Matabele secessionism and discontent. Gradually he has built his own power, while maintaining a comparatively democratic society and preserving a good economy.

Born 21 February 1924 at Kutama mission in north-west Mashonaland, the son of Gabriel the mission carpenter. Educated at local mission schools. He completed his secondary education and early university studies through correspondence courses, qualifying as a primary school teacher in 1941. He taught in Mpanzure, Dadaya and Empandeni mission schools (1942-45), before going to Fort Hare University, South Africa, graduating with a BA in English and history in 1951.

He returned home in 1952 to resume teaching at Driefontein Mission. He went on to Mbizi government school at Highfield, Harare then Mambo school at Gwelo. In 1954 he obtained a B.Ed by correspondence course and in 1955 moved to Northern Rhodesia to teach at Chalimbana Teacher Training College. He continued his correspondence courses and won a BSc from London University.

In the autumn of 1957 he went to Ghana, then on the threshold of independence, and taught at St Mary's College. It was an exciting time as he witnessed the first African country to gain independence from Britain and it was there that he met his future wife, Sally Hayfron. The example of Kwame Nkrumah and the Zambian leaders, Harry Nkumbula and Kenneth Kaunda, whom he had met earlier, spurred his interest in politics and swung him from the purely academic life that he seemed to have chosen for himself until then.

He stayed in Ghana until May 1960, when he returned to Salisbury to plunge into politics as publicity secretary and youth wing organiser of the National Democratic Party. He opposed the constitutional proposals put up by the British for African representation in parliament. The Africans were offered only 15 of the 65 seats. He mustered enough other critics to undermine the deal. The NDP was banned on 9 December 1961 and he became deputy secretary-general of the Zimbabwe African People's Union (ZAPU). In 1962 ZAPU was also banned and he was arrested and kept in restriction for three months.

He was arrested again after addressing a meeting of Northern Rhodesia's United National Independence Party in March 1963. He and his wife jumped bail and went to Dar es Salaam. There he broadcast regularly on Radio Tanzania's programmes beamed to Zimbabwe.

ZAPU split in 1963 and Mugabe joined the faction led by Ndabaningi Sithole which formed the Zimbabwe African National Union (ZANU). He became the party's secretary-general. On his return to Salisbury in August 1963 he was arrested for a broadcast that he had made in Dar es Salaam. Released on bail, he was rearrested in August 1964 for making a "subversive speech" and again served with restriction orders.

He was to remain under detention for the next decade. He put his time to the best possible use obtaining an LL.B and B.Admin from London University by correspondence courses. While he was still in detention he was elected by the ZANU executive committee to replace Sithole as leader of the party.

International pressure forced Ian Smith to release the nationalist leaders in December 1974. He was set free along with Sithole, Joshua Nkomo and others but no settlement was reached and the guerrilla war continued. Smith tried to arrange an internal settlement led by Bishop Abel Muzorewa, but Mugabe remained opposed. The assassination of Herbert Chitepo in March 1975 caused considerable disruption in the ZANU party, so Mugabe decided to go into exile and take command of the guerrilla war from Mozambique. But international pressure for a settlement continued and Mugabe led a ZANU delegation to a Geneva peace conference in October 1976. In order to present a common front for the negotiations, Joshua Nkomo's ZAPU and Mugabe's ZANU formed an alliance under the Patriotic Front. After many weeks the talks broke down.

Mugabe was elected ZANU president and the commander-in-chief of the Zimbabwe African National Liberation Army, ZANLA at a ZANU congress in Chimoio in 1977. For the next three years he concentrated on the armed struggle, building international support and securing arms and training for his men in Mozambique. Meanwhile, Smith and Muzorewa tried to achieve an internal settlement. But the guerrilla war was going Mugabe's way. He proved himself the best nationalist leader and organiser and began seriously to sap the strength of the Rhodesian forces.

International pressure also intensfied for a permanent solution accommodating all parties. Mugabe thought the time was right and led the ZANU delegation to the Lancaster House conference in September 1979. The talks dragged on for three months, but they were successful and on 27 January 1980 he returned to Zimbabwe to organise the pre-independence elections. The scale of his victory surprised observers. He took 63% of the votes and 57 seats, while Nkomo gained only 24% of the votes and 20 seats. Muzorewa was totally routed, gaining only three seats.

He was appointed Prime Minister of Zimbabwe on 4 March 1980 and took office on 18 April. At first he formed a broad-based government with Joshua Nkomo as Minister of Home Affairs, but the two rivals soon fell out. Mugabe first demoted, then sacked Nkomo, on 17 February 1982 after caches of illegal arms had been discovered on his properties. Mugabe claimed that Nkomo was behind the terrorist groups that still operated in Matabeleland and arrested many of Nkomo's top lieutenants.

This situation sowed the seeds of trouble in Matabeleland and caused Nkomo's flight into exile in London. Mugabe crushed the Matabele discontent with unexpected ruthlessness and raised a storm of international criticism. He also curbed the excesses of the more radical of his own lieutenants and detained Bishop Muzorewa for suspected links with South Africa, in November 1983.

On 8 August 1984 ZANU-PF held its first congress for 20 years and adopted a new constitution which strengthened Mugabe's position and endorsed the aim of establishing a one-party state. An election was called for June 1985. Mugabe triumphed again, increasing its share of seats from 57 to 63 and reducing ZAPU's from 20 to 15. Nkomo returned from exile in August 1983 and Mugabe gradually developed dialogue with him to help restore peace in Matabeleland and to achieve political unity.

Progress was slow and subject to many reverses. In April 1987 Mugabe himself seemed to have lost heart and said that unity talks had been abandoned. Violence flared again in Matabeleland. But talks were on again by the end of the year and by April 1988 agreement was signed to form ZANU-PF.

In October 1987, in another major constitutional change, separate white seats in parliament were abolished and the post of prime minister was to be absorbed into a new executive presidency. On 31 December 1987 Mugabe became the first Executive President.

A major corruption scandal involving some of his top ministers occurred at the end of 1988, over the acquisition of vehicles from the Willowvale assembly plant. Mugabe appointed a judicial inquiry and sacked some ministers, but pardoned others and incurred vocal protest by students and trade unionists. This also stimulated the creation of Edgar Tekere's Zimbabwe Unity Movement at a time Mugabe was trying to finalise the creation of a one-party state by merging ZAPU and ZANU. This was formalised at the ZANU-PF congress in December 1989, but only in the face of considerable opposition outside the ruling party.

Mugabe put the corruption issue to the electoral test in the elections of March 1990. Though there were allegations of intimidation and ballot rigging, he triumphed in the presidential elections by 2.03 million votes to 413,840 for his rival, Tekere, while ZANU won 116 out of 120 seats for parliament. This margin of victory underlined his dominance and allowed him to continue resisting the tide of multi-party democracy and pluralism prevalent in other parts of Africa.

But opposition to a one party state was growing, even in the ranks of his own party. On 22 August 1990 the politburo voted against formalising the single party system. Mugabe then let it be known that he was prepared to bow to majority opinion.

He went further in January 1991, saying that he had accepted the wishes of the majority and that he now applauded those African governments that were embracing pluralism.

On 22 June 1991 ZANU decided to abandon its ideology of Marxism, Leninism and scientific socialism. Mugabe said that radical leftism was being cast aside all over the world so there was "no reason to continue to stick to it."

MUNANGAGWA, Emmerson Dambudzo

Zimbabwean politician. Minister of Justice, Parliamentary and Legal Affairs, 2 January 1988 –

One of the young radicals with total loyalty to Robert Mugabe, he was given responsiblity in the party, even before independence, for security affairs. This position was confirmed when Mugabe made him Minister of State in his office, a post where he soon became known as Minister of Security. There he was plunged into the birth pains of his new country being largely responsible for ending the guerrilla dissidence in Matabeleland.

Born 1946 at Zvishavane. Educated at Lundi School, Mumbwa Boys' School and Kafue School, Zambia. While still a youngster he was a member both of the Zambian United National Independence Party and the Zimbabwe African People's Union, ZAPU.

When the Zimbabwe African National Union (ZANU) was formed by the leaders who broke from ZAPU in August 1973, he joined the new party. He was soon sent to China for military training. He led the first Chinese trained guerrillas back into Rhodesia in 1963. By August his group had already blown up a train at Masvingo. He was arrested in June 1965, charged and convicted of sabotage. Because he was still under age, he escaped the death penalty and was sentenced instead to ten years at Khami Maximum Security Prison. He was released at the time of the general amnesty for Zimbabwe leaders at the end of 1974 and went to Zambia, where he completed his law studies. He was called to the Zambian bar in 1976.

ZANU, which had helped him with his legal studies, called him to Mozambique in 1977 where he was elected to the Central Committee of the party. While still in the bush he became a personal adviser to Robert Mugabe, concentrating mainly on security. This position was confirmed in the pre-independence cabinet of 11 March 1980 when he was made Minister of State in the Prime Minister's office in charge of the Special Branch, then largely a white manned organisation set up by the Rhodesians. He soon found himself busy, with the Mozambique government asking for security assistance to counter the threat from the RENAMO guerrillas. He helped forge the defence and security agreement with Mozambique signed on 10 January 1981. On 19 June 1980 he claimed to have exposed a plot to kill leaders and visiting presidents at the independence celebrations. By the end of the year, as director of intelligence services and chairman of the Joint High Command, he was already involved in action against guerrillas sympathetic to Joshua Nkomo.

In 1981 he was mainly responsible for the tricky operation of integrating the Zimbabwe People's Revolutionary Army (ZIPRA) with those of the Zimbabwe African National Liberation Army (ZANLA) in a national force. His men were responsible for finding the arms caches alleged to be on property owned by Joshua Nkomo in February 1982. In a major reshuffle on 2 January 1988 he was promoted Minister of Justice, Legal and Parliamentary affairs.

MUTASA, Didymus

Zimbabwean politican, senior minister in the President's Office (Political Affairs), 9 April 1990 –

A man of high ideals and itegrity, involved with many welfare projects at the outset of his political career. Banished to Britain for his solid defence of the Tangwena people, he emerged after independence as the speaker of the national assembly, where his idealism and impartiality were put to the test. President Mugabe, wanting to benefit from his maturity and experience, made him what was virtually the post of deputy prime minister for political affairs in April 1990.

Born 1935 at St Faith's mission, Rusape, where he was educated over 1943-50. He continued at Goromonzi government school, completing his secondary education in 1956.

He became an activist in the Makoni Students' Association and was elected as its delegate to the inaugural congress of the African National Congress in 1957. He joined the co-operative community at St Faith's, started by Guy Clutton Brock, until it closed in 1959.

In the same year he established the Nyafaro Development Company at Nyanga and later joined the Ministry of Agriculture as an administrative officer. He also founded a black civil servants' union with the aim of raising black pay rates up to white levels.

After being a delegate to the Victoria Falls Conference which brought the dissolution of the Rhodesian Federation, he went to London in 1963 to present the case for black civil servants who were being made redundant from government service. He used the compensation money to establish the Cold Comfort Society, again with Clutton Brock. This led him to take up the cause of the Tangwena people. His defiance led to his arrest in November 1970 and his detention in solitary confinement at Sinoia and Salisbury remand prisons.

He was released in 1972 on condition that he went into exile. He went to Britain and studied social sciences at the University of Birmingham. In 1975 he became the Zimbabwe African National Union (UK) district chairman. In 1977 he was sent by the party to work full time in Maputo, Mozambique. In 1978 he was appointed to the Central Committee as Deputy Secretary for Finance.

He returned home in 1980 to stand in the pre-independence elections in February. He won his seat and was elected Speaker of the House of Assembly. At the ZANU-PF's first Congress in August 1984, he was also elected to the Politbureau of the party with responsibility for Transport and Welfare.

As Speaker he had to deal with tricky issues such as the abolition of the senate and the disciplining of Ian Smith, the former Rhodesian premier for remarks that parliament considered contemptuous when he criticised sanctions against South Africa.

This matter brought Zimbabwe to the brink of a constitutional crisis when Smith appealed and five judges of the Supreme Court issued a statement in November 1989, attacking Mutasa "for the contempt in which the Speaker holds the Supreme Court and the rule of law."

This referred to Mutasa's statement saying that he would "not pay a cent" of the Supreme Court award of £1,500, to Ian Smith, who had been illegally suspended without pay from the House of Assembly in April 1987. In the event President Mugabe intervened and upheld the compensation to Ian Smith.

After the elections of March 1990, Mugabe wanting to benefit by Mutasa's maturity and experience, reshuffled his cabinet on 9 April and made Mutasa the senior minister for political affairs in his own office. This made him one of the two deputy prime ministers, the other being Bernard Chidzero.

MUTUMBUKA, Dzingai Barnabas

Zimbabwean politician and former minister.

One of the younger generation of ministers in Robert Mugabe's government who held office as Minister of Education throughout the 1980s until he was brought down in the Willowgate scandal.

Born 1945 at Shurugwi. Educated at St Joseph's Mission, Chirumhanzu and other local schools. He attended the University College of Rhodesia and won a BSc in Chemistry and Geology. He went into teaching before going to Sussex University to obtain a Doctorate in Chemistry, gaining admission to the Royal Institute of Chemists. He lectured at the University College of Dublin in 1974.

When most of the active Zimbabwe leaders went to the bush to join the guerrilla war against the Rhodesian government he joined them as a member of the Zimbabwe African National Union. He was elected to the Central Committee in 1977 and became Secretary for Education and Culture. At the pre-independence conferences he was a member of the ZANU delegation to Geneva and Lancaster House.

He stood in the pre-independence election of January 1980 and won the seat of Masvingo North. Robert Mugabe appointed him Minister for Education and Culture in his first cabinet of 11 March 1980. He held that office continuously through the 1980s. In March 1989 he gave evidence before the Commission of Inquiry into Willowvale Motor Industries in which some ministers were found to have obtained new vehicles (in addition to the one they were allowed for personal use) and then to have resold them at a profit in breach of regulations. Mutumbuka told the Commission that he was "unaware" of the price control regulations, but he tendered his resignation to the President and was allowed to depart.

MUZENDA, Simon Vengai

Zimbabwe politician. Vice President, 2 January 1988 –

A veteran party stalwart, from a staunch Catholic background. One of the few Zimbabwe ministers without a university degree, he compensates through his years of political experience and solid service to the nationalist movement. He ranks second to Mugabe as Vice President both of government and of the party.

Born 1922 at Gutu, Masvingo Province in the south east. Educated at Gokomere mission, Domboshawa and Marianhill college, South Africa gaining a diploma in carpentry. He returned home to in 1950 setting up his own furniture workshop in Barbourfields, Bulawayo. There he channelled his early political energies into organising the Barbourfields Tenants Association.

In 1960 he helped form the National Democratic Party, the organisation that was formed after the banning of the African National Congress, the first nationalist party. He became the NDP organising secretary for the Midlands Province. The NDP was also banned and he became administrative secretary of the Zimbabwe African People's Union in December 1961. ZAPU was banned in September 1962 and he was arrested for making a seditious speech and sentenced to 12 years in prison.

He was released after two years, in time for the Zimbabwe African National Union congress of 1964 in which he was elected Secretary General. ZANU was proscribed and most nationalist leaders, including Muzenda, were placed under restriction from 1964-71. He was released in 1971 and started to campaign against the Anglo-Rhodesian settlement proposals, then being tested by the Pearce Commission, in early 1972. He went into exile in Zambia and after Robert Mugabe was released from detention in December 1974 he joined him in Mozambique and helped organise the armed struggle.

In the pre-independence elections of January 1980 he won the seat for Gweru. Already Second Secretary of the ZANU-PF Politbureau, Mugabe made him Deputy Prime Minister and Minister for Foreign Affairs in his first cabinet of 11 March 1980. He relinquished his Foreign Affairs portfolio and moved to Mugabe's office with special responsibility for Defence, on 10 January 1981. His portfolio was again reorganised on 3 January 1984 when he took on responsibilty for Energy and Water resources in addition to his Deputy Premiership. Mugabe became the first Executive President on 31 December 1987, and appointed Muzenda Vice President and second in rank within the cabinet on 2 January 1988.

In October 1988 he vigorously defended the "shoot to kill" anti-poaching policy; "We will not sit back and watch gangs of bandits plunder our wildlife heritage," he said.

MUZOREWA, Abel Tendekayi (Bishop)
Zimbabwean Bishop. Former politician and Prime Minister.

A non-political figure who overnight became the focus of African nationalism when most of the other top African leaders were detained. The first African Bishop to head the United Methodist church in Rhodesia. A remarkable orator who became a cunning politician and briefly the Prime Minister of Zimbabwe-Rhodesia, he was dedicated to non violence - "I cannot even kill a chicken" - he once said. But he could not persuade his brother Africans to back the internal settlement, which entrenched considerable white power. Eventually it was the guerrilla armies who triumphed and carried the day in the pre-independence elections, forcing him out of power.

Born April 14 1925 at Umtali (now Mutare), eldest of a lay preacher's eight children. Educated at the United Methodist school, Old Umtali. He became a schoolteacher (1943-47) and full time lay preacher in Mtoka district (1947-49). He studied theology at the Old Umtali Biblical College (1949-52) and was ordained a minister of the United Methodist Church in 1953. He was a pastor at Chiduku, near Rusape from 1955-58.

He went to the USA on a scholarship to study theology at the Missouri

School of Religion, Columbia, then the Methodist College Fayette, Missouri where he graduated with an MA in religion and philosophy in 1962. He pursued his studies at Scarritt College, Nashville earning an MA in Christian Education in June 1963.

He returned home to become a pastor in Old Umtali and a year later was appointed National Director of the Christian Youth Movement in 1966, then Secretary of the Christian Movement. On 28 August 1968 he was consecrated Bishop of the United Methodist Church of Rhodesia.

He travelled widely in Africa but was banned on 4 September 1970 for trying to work in Rhodesia's tribal trust lands where most of his adherents lived. In April 1971 he was stopped at the Mozambique border on his way to a church conference, declared a prohibited immigrant and forced to return to Salisbury in a cattle train.

He joined the ANC, visited Britain in February 1972 and attracted a 10,000 crowd to Trafalgar Square, London. Still a newcomer to politics, he was approached by a joint ZANU-ZAPU delegation to lead the campaign against the Anglo-Rhodesian settlement proposals, being tested by the Pearce Commission early in 1972.

After most of the main leaders were released in December 1974 conflict broke out in the nationalist movement. Robert Mugabe, Joshua Nkomo and others opted for armed conflict outside the country. Muzorewa at first claimed he was still leader of the ANC and therefore of the external forces but when he was rejected, the ANC was replaced by his own faction, the United ANC and he moved instead towards an internal settlement.

He held abortive talks with Ian Smith in August 1975, these broke down, but in 1977 Ian Smith had firmed his proposals for an internal settlement. These appealed to Muzorewa who lacked substantial guerrilla support but thought he could get majority backing from blacks within the country. On 3 March 1978 he signed an agreement with Ian Smith for a new constitution and transitional government until the end of the year.

Though described by Lord Chitnis, the Liberal peer as a "gigantic confidence trick", elections were held in April 1979 and were won by the UANC. Ian Smith stood down and Muzorewa was sworn in as Prime Minister of the new Zimbabwe-Rhodesia on 1 June 1979. But the guerilla war, against his former colleagues, intensified and it became clear that no permanent solution could be achieved without winning the agreement of the external leaders. The internal settlement was not accepted by the international community or the Commonwealth.

Finally external pressure brought the Lancaster House conference in September 1979. Talks dragged on for three months but were finally successful and on 27 January 1980 pre-independence elections were held. Robert Mugabe swept the polls and Muzorewa was totally routed, gaining only three seats. He stayed in parliament for four years but was arrested in November 1983, accused of having "links with South Africa". Muzorewa denied the charges by Mugabe that he had 5,000 men being trained in South Africa to attack Zimbabwe. He was released from detention on 4 September 1984 and vowed to continue the struggle before going to live in the USA. He returned to fight the elections of June 1975 but was annihilated, losing all three UANC seats including his own. He then decided to leave politics and concentrate on his ministry.

NKOMO, Joshua Mqabuko Nyongolo

Zimbabwean politician. Vice-President, 9 April 1990 –

A father figure of African nationalism. A large, lumbering man a generation older than Robert Mugabe, he built up a strong reputation internationally as a negotiator and pragmatist who was always prepared to seek a solution to the Rhodesian problem. But this goodwill was often denied by his own militants. It required the ordeal of arrest and restriction for the better part of a decade to make him into a tough nationalist leader. But while he was in restriction younger men were emerging. Robert Mugabe proved a better organiser of the guerrilla struggle and better able to capitalise on his larger ethnic base. Nkomo was defeated more heavily than expected in the independence elections of 1980, when the electorate voted almost entirely on tribal lines. This led to the disenchantment of the Matabele both with the government and with Nkomo's leadership. But in an act of statesmanship he reluctantly accepted the need to merge his party with the victors in the interests of national unity. He was promoted to Vice-President in April 1990.

Born 19 June 1917 son of a cattle-owning teacher and lay preacher in Semokwe, Matabeleland. Educated at Tsholotsho School, going on to South Africa in 1941 to Adams College, Natal, and the Jan Hofmeyer School of Social Science in Johannesburg.

On his return home in 1945, he worked as a welfare officer with Rhodesian railways. Most Sundays he was a lay preacher. At nights he studied social science, gaining a BA externally from the University of South Africa in 1951. He was appointed general-secretary of the Rhodesian Railways African Employees Association in 1951, building it into an influential union. It was a stepping stone to politics.

He stood for Matabeleland in the first federal elections in 1953, but lost to M. M. Hove. He consoled himself by building up his party and was elected President of the local African National Congress in 1954. The ANC was reconstituted in September 1957 and again he was elected President. While he was away attending overseas meetings, Premier Sir Edgar Whitehead banned the ANC on 12 September 1959. Rather than go home and face imprisonment, he established a London office for the party at Golders Green. In his absence he was elected president of the National Democratic Party, the successor to the ANC, in October 1960.

He led the NDP delegations to the Federal Review Conference and the Southern Rhodesia Constitutional Conference in Salisbury which ended on 17 February 1961. He accepted a settlement giving the Africans 15 out of the 65 seats in parliament. But when his party angrily rejected the deal he abandoned it.

The NDP was then banned on 9 December 1961. It was succeeded by the Zimbabwe African People's Union and Nkomo was again elected leader. He raised the question of independence at the United Nations and had the Rhodesian problem recognised as an international issue on 18 June 1962. The Whitehead government banned ZAPU on 19 September 1962. Nkomo was in Zambia. On his return he was restricted for three months to Kezi, near Bulawayo.

Released briefly, he campaigned vigorously against the coming of the Rhodesian Front and more extremist white policies. But ZAPU split with Mugabe and others forming ZANU. On 16 April 1964 he was banished to Gonakudzingwa. Though he appealed against the restriction orders and won, fresh papers were delivered. Restriction continued, but he was allowed to meet British ministers on a number of occasions for further constitutional discussions. He was not released until the detente of December 1974.

A battle for the leadership of the nationalist parties then resumed, though in December 1974 under external pressure they signed the Lusaka Declaration of Unity that temporarily united most groups under a reborn ANC. He led a splinter group of the ANC in further abortive talks with the government.

International pressure for a settlement continued. In 1976 the Patriotic Front was formed, with Nkomo as a co-leader with Robert Mugabe, in order to present a common front for the Geneva peace conference in October, followed by the two Malta conferences with the British and the Americans.

All peace efforts failed and he set up an office in Lusaka to organise the armed struggle for his ZAPU party and its armed wing, the Zimbabwe People's Revolutionary Army (ZIPRA). But pressure mounted for a permanent solution accommodating all parties and he was co-opted for the Lancaster House conference which started in September 1979. The talks dragged on for three months, but they were successful and he returned home in January to organise the pre-independence elections on behalf of ZAPU-PF. The elections were tribally motivated and Nkomo was badly defeated, winning only 20 seats, almost all in Matabeleland, compared with Mugabe's 57 seats in other parts of the country (mostly Shona areas).

Nkomo was appointed Minister of Home Affairs in Mugabe's first cabinet. Still smarting from his electoral defeat, he became the butt for Mugabe's militants. Supporters of the two men clashed. Nkomo was given little power and was demoted to Minister without portfolio on 10 January 1981. Trouble continued and Nkomo was sacked on 17 February 1982 after caches of illegal arms had been discovered on his properties. Though Nkomo denied it, Mugabe claimed that Nkomo was behind the terrorist groups that still operated in Matabeleland. Reprisals followed, with many Nkomo supporters arrested and the armed occupation of Matabeleland.

On 8 March 1983 Nkomo fled from his Bulawayo home, took refuge in Botswana and went into exile in Britain. He did not return until August 1983 by which time he was prepared to help restore peace and, reluctantly, to discuss the possibility of party merger in the interests of unity. Progress was slow and subject to many reverses. Nkomo was reluctant to be swallowed up in a party dominated by his erstwhile rivals. But ZANU won the June 1985 elections even more emphatically than those of 1980, taking 57 seats to Nkomo's 15. Nkomo embarked on a series of unity talks and by April 1988 agreement was signed to merge the parties in ZANU-PF. Nkomo was rewarded, on 2 January 1988, by being appointed a senior minister without portfolio, one of the three ministers, in the President's Office who were to form a 'super-cabinet' to oversee policy and review ministerial performance.

Nkomo took this position with good grace and played a major part in getting most of the remaining dissident guerrillas to lay down their arms by the end of May 1988.

His qualities and efforts were belatedly recognised on 9 April 1990, when Mugabe promoted him as one of two Vice-Presidents alongside Simon Muzenda. He was sworn in on 6 August 1990.

SHAMUYARIRA, Nathan (Dr)

Zimbabwe politician. Minister of Foreign Affairs, 21 January 1988 –

A senior and highly articulate member of the Zimbabwe African National Union since it was first founded in 1963. His experience as a journalist took him early into information and publicity in the party. This natural specialisation was confirmed when he became Zimbabwe's first Information Minister, a post he held for eight years. In 1988 he was promoted to Foreign Minister.

Born 1930. Educated at Waddilove Institute near Marondera, qualifying as a teacher. He started teaching, but later switched to journalism. In 1959 he became editor-in-chief of *African Newspapers* but resigned in 1962 after political differences with the proprietors.

His political career started with the Zimbabwe African People's Union (ZAPU) but he was among those disillusioned with Joshua Nkomo's indecisive leadership. When a number of leaders broke away to form the Zimbabwe African National Union he was among them and became a founder member of the party on 8 August 1963. In 1964 he went for further studies to Princeton university, USA, to take a degree in Political Science. He then studied for a doctorate at Nuffield College, Oxford, and then went to Dar es Salaam as a politics lecturer. In 1968 he was appointed ZANU secretary for external affairs.

He advocated unity between ZANU and ZAPU as the best way of furthering the nationalist cause but found himself in a minority. In 1971 he joined with James Chikerema, Nelson Nyandoro and others to found the Front for the Liberation of Zimbabwe (FROLIZI), becoming its treasurer. But the party never got off the ground and failed in its objective to unite the warring established parties, so in June 1973 he led most of his FROLIZI colleagues back into ZANU.

In 1977, as the armed struggle stepped up a gear, he went to Mozambique as the party's administrative secretary. He was already on the politbureau of the party as secretary for publicity and information and a member of the supreme council.

He won a seat in Makonde West in the pre-independence elections of January 1980. On 11 March 1980 Robert Mugabe appointed him Minister for Information and Tourism. In this capacity he had the difficult task of explaining the government viewpoint when under attack in the international press for its repressive policies in Matabeleland. He travelled to Britain several times to counter the accusations of Joshua Nkomo in 1983. After the first ZANU-PF Congress in 20 years, his position was confirmed as a member of Mugabe's new 14-member, hand-picked politbureau, on 12 August 1984.

He was one of the leading supporters of the Pan African News Agency (PANA) when it struggled into existence and was instrumental in offering a Zimbabwe chairman for the organisation in April 1985. On 29 August 1985 he opened a Zimbabwe Broadcasting Corporation transmitter in Beitbridge designed to counter South African propaganda. His good work as Minister of Information for eight years was rewarded with promotion to Minister of Foreign Affairs on 2 January 1988.

TEKERE, Edgar Ziganai
Zimbabwean politician.

A tough, outspoken, courageous nationalist, imprisoned during the independence struggle, who rose to the number three spot as secretary-general of the Zimbabwe African National Union - Patriotic Front. A close colleague of Mugabe who organised the military struggle from Mozambique, he was appointed a minister in Robert Mugabe's first independence cabinet. Accused of murder of a white farmer shortly after independence, he was acquitted, but this was quickly followed by his political downfall. Dismissed from the Cabinet, then from the secretary-generalship, he was finally kicked out of the party. He remained a forthright critic of government and finally formed his own opposition party, the Zimbabwe Unity Movement.

Born April 1937, near Rusape, the son of a Manyika teacher, who later became an Anglican priest. As he was the second son he was given the nickname "two-boy". He went to secondary school at St Augustine's. It was a progressive and libertarian mission school near Umtali, where he joined the City Youth League run by James Chikerema and George Nyandoro. Later he joined the African National Youth League. In 1959 he was detained for political activism. He became a founder-member of the National Democratic Party, joining the Zimbabwe African People's Union in December 1961 after the NDP was banned. When ZAPU split in 1963, Tekere along with Robert Mugabe, joined the faction led by Ndabaningi Sithole and was one of the founders of the Zimbabwe African National Union in 1963. He was elected deputy secretary for youth and culture at the Gwelo Congress in 1964.

He was arrested in August 1964 together with most of the other prominent African leaders and sent into restriction. The specific charge against him was recruiting others to go for military training overseas. He remained in detention for the next ten years.

In March 1974, while still a detainee in Salisbury prison, he and six other leaders sent a letter protesting against Bishop Abel Muzorewa's negotiations with the Rhodesian Premier, Ian Smith. International pressure forced Smith to release the nationalist leaders in December 1974. Tekere was set free along with Mugabe, Sithole, Joshua Nkomo and others. He threw himself straight into the political fray. He set off for the centre of the country where he was to take charge, without even finding time to locate and greet his parents.

Each of the ZANU leaders was given an area of the country; Tekere was given the Midlands and Southern Province. His main task was to explain that the Lusaka agreement was meaningless and the war had to continue. He was also recruiting the youth for training in Mozambique. As the Rhodesian government began to clamp down and re-arrest nationalist leaders, Mugabe decided in April 1975 to go into exile and take command of the guerrilla war from secret bases in Mozambique. Tekere went with him. By 1977 he had risen to secretary-general of ZANU.

He attended the Lancaster House conference in September 1979. The talks dragged on for three months, but they were successful and in January 1980 he returned home to help organise the pre-independence elections. ZANU swept to power and on 11 March 1980, Mugabe appointed him Minister of Manpower and Planning in the first independent government, where he quickly established a reputation as the most outstanding radical and critic of Joshua Nkomo and his ZAPU followers.

On 6 August 1980 he and seven of his bodyguards were charged with murder after the death of a white farm manager. He was arrested and held in custody until released on a Z$50,000 bail. Tekere's lawyers secured a postponement of the trial by objecting to a white dominated jury and white judge presiding over a case involving the murder of a white farmer. On 8 December all the accused were found not guilty as they had been acting for the suppression of terrorism. The presiding judge, John Pittman, was outvoted by his two assessors - an African and a coloured. He said that he disagreed with the verdict and that if his decision had prevailed one of Tekere's bodyguards would have been guilty of murder.

On 10 January 1981 Mugabe dropped Tekere from the cabinet though he told a news conference that it had nothing to do with his trial, "I felt he needed a bit of a rest and I have decided to give him a rest, so that he can recover from the strains he has had and be fit for reinforcing us at a later stage," he said.

Tekere briefly stayed as secretary-general of ZANU-PF, but strains between himself and Mugabe came into the open with mutual recriminations in July 1981. On 6 August he was dismissed from the secretary-generalship, by the central committee after a showdown between moderates and radicals. Tekere had told the meeting that the revolution in Zimbabwe was decaying, and that government officials had lost touch with the black majority.

Tekere remained chairman of the Manicaland party but became increasingly isolated and a strong critic of government. Eventually, on 21 October 1988 he was expelled from the party for an alleged breach of party discipline. He remained defiant, accusing party leaders of taking the country into repression and dictatorship. Outside the party he became even more outspoken following the Willowgate corruption scandal, in which ministers had been buying cars in excess of their entitlements, from the local assembly plant at subsidised prices.

On 30 April 1989 he launched a new opposition party, the Zimbabwe Unity Movement, designed to attract support from all racial and ethnic groups and specifically opposed to Mugabe's plans for a one-party state. In a July by-election in a Harare suburb the ZUM candidate was narrowly defeated. Tekere protested over the banning of meetings and the detention of some of his party members. ZUM gradually emerged as the focus of radical opposition to government, particularly among students and other groups concerned about the plans for a one-party state.

In the Presidential elections of March 1990 he stood against Mugabe for the Presidency, but was beaten, securing only 413,840 votes against Mugabe's 2.03 million. He vowed to continue his struggle for multi-party democracy.

He fell out with members of his own party in June 1991, when the National Executive Council said that he had been "retired" from leadership. He had rejected a new constitution and leadership structure adopted by the Executive.

USHEWOKUNZE, Herbert (Dr)
Zimbabwean politician. Minister of Energy Resources 9 April 1990 –

Fiery and outspoken, always considered one of the radical leaders in the Zimbabwe African National Union. He fell from grace early on and was dismissed as a minister when he criticised Robert Mugabe publicly, but he was brought back as the powerful Minister of Home Affairs when tough action was needed to handle the Matabele crisis and the dissidence which followed. After the crisis passed and gentle conciliation was required, Mugabe again demoted him first to Minister of Transport and then to Minister of State without portfolio, before being brought back into the Cabinet as Minister of Energy Resources in April 1990.

Born 1934, in Marondera. Educated at Madzima school, Marshall Hartley School and the Waddilove Institute before going to the University of Natal, South Africa, to train and qualify as a doctor. His early interest in politics led him to join the Pan African Congress of South Africa, joining the ZANU party on his return home. When the leading nationalists took to the bush in Mozambique in the late 1970s to take up the armed struggle against the Rhodesian regime, he joined them. ZANU sent him as a delegate to the Geneva Conference in 1976. In the same year he was appointed the ZANU secretary for health.

In the pre-independence elections of December 1980 he won his seat for Chinamora. He was elected to the national executive and central committee of ZANU as secretary for health, ranking number seven in the party. Mugabe made him Minister of Health in his first cabinet of 11 March 1980. He became one of the more militant members of the party and clashed early with Robert Mugabe who dismissed him as minister in October 1981, for campaigning against the Public Service Commission, chaired by Mugabe, which decides who gets executive posts in the civil service.

But four months later he bounced back with his appointment as Minister of Home Affairs in charge of the police, on 17 February 1982. He soon became involved in suppressing the dissidents in Matabeleland and in the detention of whites accused of subversion. He also gave his support to the repeated extension of emergency powers, saying that the need for them was "more urgent now than ever before." In March 1983 he broke the news of Joshua Nkomo's flight into exile disguised as a "fat old woman". He then threatened legal action against that the government was coercing his supporters to change sides.

On 3 January 1984 he was reshuffled from the Ministry of Home Affairs where he had been widely criticised for his arbitrary use of emergency powers. Mugabe said of him "whatever his shortcomings he had a brilliant brain". He was demoted to Minister of Transport and Road Traffic. On 11 August he was re-elected to the politbureau in charge of the commissariat of culture.

But his star slipped when Robert Mugabe became Executive President on 31 December 1987. He demoted Ushewokunze to a Minister of State without portfolio, charged with handling party affairs and the preparation for a one-party state. He bounced back when he organised the ZANU campaign against the electoral challenge of Edgar Tekere's Zimbabwe Unity Movement. He was seen singing, dancing and chanting to rouse support on behalf of ZANU at the pre-election rallies. He launched strong personal attacks against his old colleague and pulled off a narrow by-election victory. He accused Tekere of being "devoured by the capitalists" but unfortunately for him this was just before a story broke in the local press showing that he had not paid his workers at Togarepi Property Investments (his farm) for many months and his wife had failed to pay her labourers on another farm. Mugabe brought him back into the cabinet as Minister of Energy Resources on 9 April 1990.

ZVOBGO, Eddison Jonas
Zimbabwean politician and minister.

*A founder member of the main African nationalist parties in the 1970s
and one of the senior representatives of the most populous Karanga clan
in the dominant Shona group. He nevertheless found time, during the
struggle, to further his legal studies and gain the highest possible
academic distinction at American Universities. He played a major part
in early Mugabe governments as Minister of Local Government in charge
of the district commissioners and then as Minister of Justice and
Parliamentary Affairs. His star slipped a little in the late 1980s but he
remained a Minister of State for Public Service in the President's Office.*

Born 1935. Educated at Dutch Reformed Church mission schools,
Waddilove Institute and Tegwani Secondary School, where he
matriculated. He went to Lesotho to the Pius XII University College to
study politics, history and Shona.

His early interest in politics led him to become a founder member of
the National Democratic Party which was set up by Robert Mugabe and
others on 1 January 1960 after the African National Congress had been
banned. He was appointed the chief NDP representative at the United
Nations, New York, and took the opportunity for further studies at Tufts
University, Massachussetts.

He returned in 1963 and on the banning of the NDP became a founder
member and deputy secretary-general of the Zimbabwe African People's
Union (ZAPU). He was restricted and then detained along with other
prominent leaders and held until 1971. He studied law by
correspondence courses, winning an London LLB degree in 1972 and
being called to the bar. In 1972 he campaigned against the
Anglo-Rhodesian settlement proposals being investigated by the Pearce
Commission and then left for advanced studies in the USA. He won an
MA, MA LD and PhD at Fletcher School of Law and an LLM degree from
Harvard Law school. He then taught law as an associate professor at
Lewis University College of Law, Illinois.

ZANU called him to give legal advice at the pre-independence
constitutional conferences. He joined the armed struggle in Mozambique
in the late 1970s and was then sent to the pre-independence Lancaster
House Conference in 1979 as leading ZANU spokesman and legal
adviser.

He played a major role in the pre-independence elections of January
1980 as chairman of the party election directorate. ZANU-PF had a
sensational triumph, winning 57 of the 80 African seats. He won his own
seat at Midlands. Mugabe made him Minister for Local Government and
Housing in his first cabinet on 11 March 1980. He was switched to
Minister for Legal and Parliamentary Affairs on 17 February 1982. In
this capacity he had to ensure that the government had sufficient support
in parliament over controversial issues such as the extension of the
emergency, detention of whites suspected of sabotage and the clearing

of prostitutes from the streets of Harare.

On 3 January 1984 he had the Ministry of Justice added to his portfolio. At the first party congress of August 1984, he failed to get elected to the politbureau, though he was elected to the legal and constitutional committee charged with bringing about a one-party state in Zimbabwe. When Mugabe was elected to executive Presidency on 31 December 1988 he demoted Zvobgo to Minister of State charged with handling party affairs and the integration of ZANU and ZAPU into one party.

Index

Alphabetical index giving name, country and page number